D0429893

JOHANN SEBASTIAN BACH

JOHANN SEBASTIAN

BACH

LIFE AND WORK

MARTIN GECK

Translated from the German
by John Hargraves

HARCOURT, INC.   *Orlando   Austin   New York   San Diego   Toronto   London*

www.HarcourtBooks.com

This is a translation of *Bach: Leben und Werk.*

Music notation illustrations created by Ms. Shoko Komiyama.

Library of Congress Cataloging-in-Publication Data
Geck, Martin.
[Bach. English]
Johann Sebastian Bach: his life and work/by Martin Geck; translated from the German by John Hargraves.—1st U.S. ed.
p. cm.
Includes bibliographical references and index.
1. Bach, Johann Sebastian, 1685–1750—Criticism and interpretation.
I. Hargraves, John.   II. Title.
ML410.B1G36713   2006
780.92—dc22 [B]   2006012390
ISBN-13: 978-0-15-100648-9   ISBN-10: 0-15-100648-2

Text set in Adobe Caslon
Designed by April Ward

Printed in the United States of America
First U.S. edition

K J I H G F E D C B A

CONTENTS

For Beethoven, Johann Sebastian Bach was the "father of all harmony," for Max Reger, he was the "beginning and the end" of all music, and for Claude Debussy he was simply "the Good Lord of music." Many composers, writers, and philosophers of every cultural provenance have eulogized Bach in this manner—they testify to the deep admiration as well as to the respect and humility that one feels when gazing upon the sheerly incomprehensible creativity and greatness that radiates from the work of the cantor of Leipzig's Thomaskirche. To be sure, glorification of this type runs the risk of moving Bach to an inaccessible, remote plane and transforming him into a static monument—but his art is, nonetheless, omnipresent in the music life of today, accessible to everyone. This is the accomplishment not just of vocal and instrumental soloists and musical groups all over the world, but, importantly, also of the recording industry, radio, and television, and, not in the least, the music publishing industry.

Every era creates its own particular image of Bach. Here the prominent German musicologist Martin Geck, one of that country's leading Bach scholars, presents his version, new and up-to-the-minute. I am extremely pleased that his comprehensive seminal work, *Johann Sebastian Bach: Life and Work,* is now appearing in America. I know the author as a significant force in the field of musicology, and I am impressed by his work's accuracy and literary quality, which has elicited admiring reviews from numerous notable personalities in the Bach world. This book was deservedly honored with an important German literary prize that is awarded to the best and most well-written cultural and historical presentation of the eighteenth century.

Martin Geck has given us a biography that is remarkable as much for its skillful use of language as for its sensitivity—a work that is comprehensible and valuable to both the professional and the amateur. In Bach he sees "a man who was so overloaded with duties that one can only shake one's head in wonderment at the greatness of his accomplishments." I myself remain particularly fascinated by the great mass of intellectual concentration to be found in the Bach oeuvre. Bach bridges, like Beethoven after him, a huge expanse connecting order and structure with pure tonal expressivity. On the one hand, no single element overpowers the others, for in Bach's compositions every tone is allotted the place appropriate to it. On the other, though, every sound and every phrase of his music speaks of a love for the smallest detail.

A crucial musical experience of my childhood, by the way, was directly connected with Bach. I was twelve years old when I first heard one of the master's greatest works, the *Art of Fugue,* played on the famous Engler organ in St. Nicholas's Church in my hometown of Brieg in Silesia by the organist Max Drischner and my first piano teacher, Katharina Hartmann. The experience was simply overwhelming. This piano teacher transmitted to me one of the guiding principles of my later conducting career: In interpreting a work of music, one must work with humility and uncompromising respect for the work itself.

Bach intervened, so to speak, a second time in my life, at the end of the last year of World War II, when I had fled from home to the town of Oschersleben in the Harz Mountains, and the cantor there asked me to sing in a performance of the *Christmas Oratorio.* I did and I also worked with him to prepare for my music studies, which I began in 1946 at the Leipzig Musikhochschule, in the city where Bach spent twenty-seven years as cantor of the Thomaskirche and *Director musices.* I spent an equal length of time as conductor of the Leipzig Gewandhaus, an orchestra that performed the cantatas each week in the Thomaskirche and presented the passions and oratorios together with the church choir on the high church holidays. For reasons of personal history, I myself always felt most closely associated with the *B Minor Mass* and the *St. Matthew Passion* in particular, which I performed many times in my career, along with the instrumental concertos, orchestral suites, and the Brandenburg Concertos.

One of the most notable features of Martin Geck's thoroughly enjoyable biography is that he adds, after the classic dichotomy of chapters devoted respectively to life and work, an informative and captivating epilogue, entitled "Horizons." Here Geck gives us quite personal reflections on Bach's art, delving into questions concerning the mystical, rhetorical, and symbolic elements in his music and according them the modest attention they deserve. For in the past, issues such as figural theory and numerological symbolism have been much overemphasized. The significance of Bach's religious convictions is also put into proper perspective, an aspect once memorably characterized by a slogan of his earlier biographer Philip Spitta, who styled the cantor of St. Thomas's as "the fifth evangelist."

Modestly, the author sees his book as part of the aesthetic "history of discourse" on the composer, a history that he himself tries to trace for us; however, he does not wish his readers to disregard the elements of "happiness and dismay" in the reception of Bach's works. His own fascination with the field and his wide perspective on the larger-scale relationships within it result in convincing, penetrating analyses or at least the beginnings of such, which are of use to performer, scholar, and music lover alike. I cannot recommend this book strongly enough to anyone who is interested in Bach's music!

—KURT MASUR

APPROACHING BACH

WHAT DO WE KNOW ABOUT BACH?

"A man in his sixty-seventh year, Herr Johann Sebastian Bach, kapell-meister and cantor of the Schools of St. Thomas, at the Thomas School, *st. ♂* four minor children, hearse gratis."[1] Thus the head burial scribe Andreas Gottlieb Bienengräber records Bach's death on 30 July 1750 in the Leipzig City Council death registry—a sober notation, yet an inaccurate one, for Bach actually died in his sixty-sixth year. The family member, friend, or associate who reported his death to the authorities apparently did not know his exact age.

The inaccuracy by no means implies a lack of esteem: Bach dies a respected man, occupying an important position, and is accorded an official funeral, commensurate with his standing in the community. The fact that his wife, Anna Magdalena, is designated an "alms-woman" signifies not that she is plunged into penury but rather that she henceforth enjoys the status of municipal widow, entitled to a modest stipend.

The incorrect age given for Bach is symptomatic. In this period people attach little importance to personal circumstances, even when the man in question is the distinguished cantor of St. Thomas. It is thus no surprise that relatively little documentation of Bach's life has survived. What we have in Bach's own hand, together with commentary, amounts to a volume of 288 pages, while accounts by others, both handwritten and printed, take up approximately twice that number of pages. It would be impossible, from the 814 *Bach Documents* published by the Bach Archives in Leipzig, to compose a biography that would satisfy our modern expectations, for although these materials, most of them from official sources, tell us a good deal about Bach's professional and artistic career, they provide little insight into his private life. Would anyone really want to fill in the many gaps in the record with trivial archival finds like number 299 in the *Bach Documents,* an excerpt from the Leizpig municipal account books that reveals that on 17 November 1731, in conjunction with the renovation of the St. Thomas School, the executioner Hartmann Hieronymus Heinze "cleaned out" the privy belonging to the cantor's living quarters, for which service he received six pfennigs![2]

We must count ourselves fortunate to have a letter Bach sent in 1730 to Georg Erdmann, a childhood friend now serving as a diplomat in Danzig, in which Bach complains eloquently about his professional circumstances. We also have drafts of a few letters written by Johann Elias Bach, who lived in his cousin's house as a tutor and secretary between 1737 and 1742. From these letters we learn, for instance, that the cantor has a taste for hard cider and "yeast brandy."[3]

Later Bach invites this same cousin to the marriage of his "daughter Liesgen to the new organist in Naumburg, Herr Altnickol," and at the same time confirms the arrival of a "splendid keg of sparkling cider," of which no more than six beakers have survived the journey, presumably because of "the shaking in transport." But since the delivery man and the inspector must receive two groschen each, and six groschen are assessed in local and general excise taxes, the whole thing becomes "all too dear a gift," as Bach notes at once humorously and thriftily in a postscript.[4] In 1950, Paul Hindemith was grateful to have this fragment of the mosaic of Bach's personality when he was composing his speech in commemoration of the two hundredth anniversary of Bach's death—because we possess hardly any other such details.[5]

Bach's first wife, Maria Barbara, bears him seven children. His second wife, Anna Magdalena, is pregnant almost every year between 1723 and 1737, and brings thirteen children into the world. Ten children from the two marriages die soon after birth or at a young age. Four sons become famous, or at least widely known, composers. Johann Gottfried Bernhard, whom Bach describes as having "turned out badly, alas," does not manage to hold on to the organist's posts his father helps him obtain; he dies young. Another son, Gottfried Heinrich, is mentally slow but also musical. In Bach scholarship, the names of the daughters receive only marginal attention: the Liesgen just mentioned marries a pupil of her father's who will play a significant role with respect to the Bach legacy. In 1800 the Leipzig *Allgemeine Musikalische Zeitung* issues a call for donations to support the youngest and last surviving of Bach's daughters, Regina Susanna, a call that evokes an emotional response even in Beethoven, living far away in Vienna.

The Bachs' probable thoughts and feelings emerge most clearly from a musical source, the notebooks Bach put together for his eldest son and his second wife, and possibly for all his sons, for purposes of study and family music making. These notebooks show us a Protestant family who, in the spirit of Martin Luther, read the Bible, sing, pray, study, and play music together, all at the father's direction.

Like the great reformer, Bach seems to have been not only the solicitous head of a large family but also a distinctive personality. At least this is how he appears in the pertinent official documents, each of which will be discussed further in its appropriate context: self-confident, strong-willed, and defiantly assertive of his rights. We sense a streak of obstinacy, suspect a choleric disposition. At any rate, we find none of the obsequiousness that his second-youngest son, the "Bückeburg Bach," will one day display, for instance in 1761, when the younger Bach petitions his lord for more tallow candles:

The great mercy shown hitherto by Your Most High Imperial Lordship the Count to his humble servant and ever received with most humble gratitude allows me to remain so confident that my plea will be heard, that I make so bold, which I beg that Your Lordship not take amiss, as to add that since Your Most High Imperial Lordship has graciously granted me, amongst other benefits, free light, yet since I receive weekly only four lights, which barely suffice for three days; may Your Lordship most graciously deign to command that the Noble Kitchens supply me with the necessary light, at least one per diem. In hopes of being vouchsafed a hearing, with most profound awe and respect...[6]

Even well-documented anecdotes about Johann Sebastian Bach, which might take the place of original source materials, raise as many questions as they answer. For instance, no Bach biography omits an account of Bach's meeting with Louis Marchand: when the two piano virtuosi happen to be in Dresden at the same time, they are summoned "at the instigation and command of several leading figures at court" to participate in a musical contest.[7] But the famous Frenchman ducks out at the crack of dawn with the special mail coach, fleeing the scene of a possible shameful defeat. Magister Johann Abraham Birnbaum recounts this story, without naming a date, in a polemic on Bach's art written in 1739. In 1754, when Carl Philipp Emanuel Bach, together with his pupil Johann Friedrich Agricola, "cobbles together" his father's obituary (to use his own term),[8] he assigns the incident to the year 1717 and adds some flourishes of his own: after Marchand's retreat Bach performs brilliantly at court as the sole "master of the battleground," but is cheated out of the royal prize of five hundred talers—more than a year's income—by a perfidious servant.[9]

The anecdote seems well documented, yet apparently it derives from a single source: Bach's own account.[10] Did he always tell the story the same way, or did he embroider it at will? What details did others invent? We do not know, nor can we reconstruct, for instance, the impression Bach made when he called on Frederick the Great at Sans Souci in 1747, even though Bach's two eldest sons left their versions, gratefully seized upon by all Bach biographers, and a contemporary report appeared in the press as well, one that is often quoted. Yet this description is so flattering, so obviously sympathetic to Bach, that a patron of Bach's seems the most likely author—or perhaps even Bach's son Carl Philipp Emanuel, who had certainly arranged his father's trip to Potsdam. It is also impossible to determine the source of the "royal theme" that Frederick the Great "was so gracious as to play for Bach."[11] In the form in which it has come down to us, this music appears too distinctive to have popped into the Prussian king's head on the spur of the moment when he gave "old Bach" an air on which to improvise. Likewise we do not know what motivated Bach to choose the title *Musical Offering* when he composed his response to the assignment; this title surrounds the work with a kind of halo, but was it what Bach intended at the time?

Whichever way we turn in hopes of discovering more intimate, "personal" information about Bach, we encounter obstacles, because few opportunities existed for expressing the private life of a kapellmeister and cantor in the first half of the eighteenth century. Letters filled with worries and latent jealousy, such as Mozart would write half a century later to Constanze, are not only not preserved—we can be sure they were never penned. Over forty conversation notebooks provide bizarre yet extensive insight into the deaf Beethoven's last decade, but no such source for Bach's life exists. And diaries such as Cosima Wagner's, which record every utterance by the Bayreuth maestro that went beyond the most everyday concerns, are unthinkable for Bach's era.

What matters in any case, when it comes to a great creative spirit, is not the life but the work. If a large quantity of material on a composer's life is available, one is always tempted to explain the work from the biography, or at least to illuminate the work from the life. There is nothing wrong with such an approach; for when the life is worth telling, it imperceptibly merges with the work, which always has something to tell, to form a comprehensive myth. Nowadays such a myth seems more accessible, easier to grasp, more human, than a self-referential oeuvre. In this sense, nineteenth-century music, such as that of Beethoven or Wagner, is already the music of "our" era—demanding, or at least facilitating, identification.

In the case of Bach, we are denied the possibility of such identification. Bach no more composed for us than he lived for us. His music comes from far away; it speaks a language that we understand yet in which we hear echoes of another language, outside our expressive range. The question "What do we know about Bach?" thus quickly gives rise to another: "What do we know about the artist and his work?"

— A circular question!
25 December 2006

THE GRAND OLD MEN OF BACH BIOGRAPHY:
FORKEL, SPITTA, SCHWEITZER

Johann Nikolaus Forkel publishes the first book on Johann Sebastian Bach in 1802, an eighty-two-page work entitled *On Johann Sebastian Bach's Life, Art, and Work: For Patriotic Admirers of True Musical Art.* The author was born in 1749, while Bach was still alive, in a village near Coburg, and in 1779 became Göttingen University's director of music. For years he maintained lively contact with Bach's sons and benefited from their direct, though far from complete, knowledge of their father. On one occasion, Forkel sends Carl Philipp Emanuel Bach, presumably his most generous informant, several *mettwursts* to show his gratitude for notes the younger Bach turned over to him.[1] Yet his sketch of Bach's life is supplemented with all sorts of anecdotal material. Although Forkel made a name for himself with a *General History of Music,* he seems less interested in determining Bach's place in music history than in paying tribute to him as a national hero.

Forkel writes his book at a time when the Germans are resisting the ideas of the French Enlightenment and Napoleon's push for political hegemony, striving instead to establish the concept of a German nation. They find a guiding principle in the notion of cultural unity—Germany as the nation of poets and thinkers. They assert that what distinguishes the Germans from other peoples is their penchant for thoroughness, profundity of thought, moral earnestness, and passion for ideals. Thus Bach is the right man to become a musical national hero in this period. und?

When Forkel characterizes his hero as "the greatest master of musical expressiveness who ever existed," as a composer whose works are "full of character and feeling" in spite of all their complexity and intricacy, he is drawing on his understanding of music as a rhetorical art form, yet at the same time he is introducing the possibility of viewing Bach from other perspectives: not exclusively as the great organ virtuoso, teacher, and master of the fugue, the splendid contrapuntalist and powerful harmonist but also as an artist whose "musical poetic spirit" never lacked for "adequate expressive means for portraying his emotions."[2]

According to Forkel, Bach's genius and originality tower over the artistic spirit of the present. Because of its exemplary nature, Forkel calls the music of "the first classic composer" a "priceless national heritage, the equal of which no other people can claim." Bach's works are intended not merely to delight for the moment; they are directed toward all that is "great and noble" and constitute, "one and all, true ideals and immortal exemplars of art." The "incomparable wealth of ideas gathered therein" will allow future generations to continue discovering something new, even after thousands of encounters.[3] Forkel does not confine himself to general observations, however; he also provides concrete information. He reports respectfully on six generations of musical Bachs; sketches Johann Sebastian's life and character, primarily on the basis of the 1754 obituary, supplemented with information provided by the sons; and offers an assessment of him as an astounding pianist, organist, and teacher. He goes on to formulate thoughts on Bach's compositional style and his tendency to continue altering and improving his compositions throughout his life, thoughts still worth reading today. While Forkel's survey of Bach's oeuvre is cursory and devotes too much space to the keyboard works, it displays an admirable desire for accuracy.

Although it may seem somewhat unfair to call Forkel's small book "more a manifesto than a biography," as does the Bach scholar Friedrich Blume,[4] the work certainly appears rudimentary when compared with the two-volume biography published in 1865 by Carl Heinrich Bitter, a Prussian government official and later minister of finance. For its use of sources and the breadth of its evaluation of Bach's music this book is a significant scholarly achievement. Yet, for all its inadequacies, the work of this "dilettante," who was nonetheless well versed in music history, did not receive the recognition it merited. It was overshadowed by another biography, almost two thousand pages in length, that followed on its heels: the Spitta, as it is still respectfully called today. This work, published in two volumes in 1873 and 1880 by Breitkopf and Härtel, is one of a number of great musical biographies in multiple volumes that appeared in the nineteenth and early twentieth centuries—one thinks of Friedrich Chrysander's *Handel*, Ferdinand Pohl's *Haydn*, Otto Jahn's *Mozart*, Carl Friedrich Glasenapp's *Wagner*, Max Kalbeck's *Brahms*, and Alexander Wheelock Thayer and Hermann Deiter's *Beethoven*. Within this company, Philipp Spitta sets a new standard for the biography of an artist—with respect not to length but to thoroughness. He aims to be as comprehensive as possible; in the era of the *Monumenta Germaniae historica,* he sees it as a matter of honor to document and analyze Bach's life and works exhaustively, in the spirit of modern scholarship; to capture them for posterity; and, wherever possible, to reconstruct them, as components of a "grand" German history. If Spitta shows less interest in satisfying his contemporaries' desire to know something about Bach than in doing justice to Bach, whom he wants to rescue once and for all from oblivion, he nonetheless speaks in the spirit of his age and to his age when it comes to aesthetics. Here he takes the same approach as Forkel, viewing Bach's art as the epitome of what art should be.

Born in 1841 in Hoya, in the marches of the Weser, as the son of a poetry-writing pastor known for his collection of hymns *Psalter and Harp,* Spitta began his career in Reval, where he taught Greek and Latin at a gymnasium. He had written his doctoral dissertation on sentence structure in Tacitus, but from early on music was his real love. As a student in Göttingen he had made the acquaintance of Johannes Brahms, eight years his senior. It was the beginning of a friendship that endured over many years. Despite "some disappointment" with certain works by Brahms and certain features of his compositions, Spitta embraced Brahms's ideal of music, in which north German reserve mingled with features of classicism and Romanticism.[5] Brahms, himself an ardent admirer of the older German tradition represented by Heinrich Schütz, Dietrich Buxtehude, and Johann Sebastian Bach, in later years informed his learned correspondent half playfully, half seriously, that he would love to undertake musical research himself, if only he were as clever as Spitta and capable of more than composing.[6]

In Sondershausen, where Spitta lives after leaving Reval, he completes the first volume of his *Bach*. In 1875, after a brief interval at a gymnasium in Leipzig, he becomes an adjunct professor of music history and secretary to the Royal Academy of the Arts in Berlin. Now he has the leisure not only to undertake the research for the second volume of his Bach biography but also to edit the complete works of Schütz and a selection from the compositions of Frederick the Great. Together with Friedrich Chrysander and Guido Adler, he edits the *Vierteljahrsschrift für Musikwissenschaft* (Musicological Quarterly), and he publishes articles on music history.

When it comes to philological analysis, Spitta has a more difficult time of it with Bach than his colleagues have writing on Handel, Mozart, or Beethoven. The biographical material is sparse, and the surviving works provide little evidence of the original dimensions of Bach's oeuvre. Thus Spitta can feel triumphant when, with the help of a friend from Reval, he manages to track down the famous Erdmann letter of 1730, the most significant document of Bach's private life, in the state archives in Moscow. He undertakes an intensive correspondence to obtain necessary source materials from pastors, cantors, archivists, music researchers, Bach lovers, and others. His posthumous papers include 296 letters from informants who between 1867 and 1873 provided him with material for the first volume of his biography.[7]

At least Spitta has access to the beginnings of serious research on Bach sources. In the anniversary year of 1850, the Leipzig Bach Society is established and launches an edition of Bach's collected works, produced according to scholarly editorial standards. Spitta is able to make use of the first volumes of the series, which will continue to appear until 1900. He can also draw on the extensive corpus of Bach manuscripts under the care of the music librarians in Berlin. Even with these advantages, he deserves credit for his essentially pioneering achievements.

Spitta's *Bach* is not a sweeping historiographic achievement of the sort produced by Leopold von Ranke or Jakob Burkhardt; if nothing else, the meticulous work of reconstruction he was forced to undertake stood in the way. Yet for succeeding generations of music scholars, Spitta set the standard, focusing on Bach's compositions from four principal points of view: philological, historical, aesthetic, and theological-intellectual. To one trained as a classicist, subjecting the texts and the sources to critical analysis came naturally. Among other things, he succeeded through a detailed examination of Bach's paper and handwriting in identifying the periods in Bach's life and career to which the largely undated manuscripts should be assigned. It would take three more generations before scholars could progress substantially beyond this point.

As a music historian Spitta sees the importance of placing Bach's music in the context of its time. In particular, his excursuses on the history of various genres of sacred music in the seventeenth and early eighteenth centuries allow him to portray Bach's oeuvre against the background of northern and central German music and to show what Bach contributed. Spitta's primary intention here is to trace the roots of the composer's inspiration. He concludes that Bach cannot be viewed as a product of his age but only as a genius towering above it. In response to the "raw power" of Bach's sacred music, he comments that it is "as if the genius of two millennia were roaring overhead": "It is almost uncanny to see how unique the B-Minor Mass remains in history."[8]

Spitta never loses sight of the aesthetic qualities of the music, despite his almost obsessive preoccupation with the documentary sources and his exploration of innumerable biographical, typological, regional, social, theological, and liturgical details. He devotes a good deal of attention to Bach as a master of form, but also repeatedly feels compelled to engage in poetic interpretation of his works. Thus, for instance, in discussing the first movement of the Second Brandenburg Concerto, he praises the work for the way it combines "exemplary clarity and simplicity" of structure with "an indescribable wealth of motivic invention and subtle combinations," while at the same time seeing in this music a living example "of everything that constitutes German Romanticism": "This first movement! It gallops along like a squad of youthful horsemen, eyes flashing and plumes billowing atop their helmets! One horseman sends his song of rejoicing swirling into the treetops, then a second, and a third, and the chorus of their companions chimes in mightily; now the singing dies away in the distance...."9

This sort of poetic evocation of instrumental works belongs to a tradition we associate with Goethe, who, upon hearing Mendelssohn perform Bach's orchestral overture in D major on the piano, BWV 1068, is said to have remarked that "in the beginning it moves along with such pomp and dignity that one can almost see a column of elegantly attired ladies and gentlemen descending a grand staircase."10 These interpretations also resemble the thought processes of Wilhelm Dilthey, who detected in the second movement of the Second Brandenburg Concerto "the infinite sweetness of a mood saturated with emotion."11 At all events, Spitta's poetic readings show that instead of consigning Bach to a long-gone "baroque" period, whose sensibility, despite a certain piquant charm, was remote and alien, he wants to bring Bach closer to his own era.

Even with Bach's vocal music Spitta repeatedly makes use of poetic description, although the words Bach set to music could speak for themselves. In response to the final movement of the *Actus tragicus,* "Gottes Zeit ist die allerbeste Zeit," BWV 106, much admired by connoisseurs since the beginning of the nineteenth century as a masterful piece of musical poetry, Spitta writes of "torrents of emotion" that Bach blends from many sources "to convey the mood that filled his imagination." And he raves over the passage in which

> the deeper voices murmuring their dying curse at last softly move upward in three-part harmony, against the countermotion of the gambas, and dissolve like mists into thin air, while the soprano hovers alone above the bass voices, like a moth fluttering over an abyss, as they pulsate more and more softly, and then, at last, when everything has become as still as death, utters the name "Jesus" with her dying breath.[12]

Spitta greatly admired Robert Schumann. In a "Sketch of His Life," published in 1882, he lauds the "magical" style in which this musical writer speaks of music as poetry expressed in notes. The "charming, dramatic vivacity" with which Schumann's fictional brotherhood, the Davidsbündler (the David League), discusses music strikes Spitta as a meaningful way to remind people "of olden times and the works produced in those days."[13] On the other hand, while Spitta considers "dissecting a musical work into its smallest components" unavoidable if one wishes to understand the work "in its historical setting," he recognizes that this process will be of interest only to "a small circle of 'initiates.'" The challenge for the future is to "combine penetrating analysis, which reveals all the elements of a work of art and its various relationships, with poetic synthesis that parades the work before one's inner eye in all its vitality."[14]

Spitta allows himself to use the language of imagery for describing Bach's music only to the extent that such language can be understood as a bridge, in Schumann's sense, between the music and the audience, thus serving as a form of interpretation. In no way does he want to create the impression that the composer intended to paint or portray concrete things. Accordingly, Spitta responds to the question of whether Bach's chaconne-like symphonic introduction to the Weimar cantata "Gleich wie der Regen und Schnee vom Himmel fällt," BWV 18, "is meant to express something specific, perhaps to represent musically the mighty effects that issue from the word of

God": "This I do not believe, since in all his instrumental introductions Bach simply establishes the mood and never pursues descriptive purposes....He wanted only to create a movement to complement the serious character of the cantata."[15]

Here Spitta is arguing within the context of "absolute music," a concept whose purity he, as a Brahms lover, defends on all fronts against Wagner and the New Germans in the battle over musical aesthetics. In his view, Bach, as "the embodiment of the German people's musical genius," has no need of coy, painterly effects to retain the influence he exerts over the present day with his "almost incomprehensibly magnificent sacred works of art" and to contribute through music to a general religious renewal.

Yet Bach's works also resist being forced "into the narrow confines of a churchly ideal." In the spirit of the cultural Protestantism that asserted itself powerfully after the founding of the German Reich in 1871, Spitta sees an artist who articulates "general religious sentiment" while also satisfying the need for "more binding religious forms," to which the current era has once more begun to aspire after a period of excessive secularism.[16] That behind such concepts lurks an even more elaborate image of the ideal German artist becomes clear from the words of the historian Wilhelm von Giesebrecht that Spitta includes in an 1873 letter to Brahms. He intends the quotation to apply to Brahms, and it certainly corresponds to Brahms's view of himself, but it also distinctly reveals the conception Spitta has of Bach:

> It is the duty of the German people to absorb the entire tradition of earlier times, to breathe with its spirit new life into withered forms, to transform rigid regulations, by using its innate individualizing power, into a law of liberty, a law right for all conditions, every place, every nationality.[17]

Art should serve the whole of society, not just the individual; it should husband its inherent possibilities, not squander them on externals; it should be original, yet never kick over the traces. Such ideas, which Spitta projects onto Bach with a gaze as self-confident as it is one-dimensional, amount ultimately, like all pronouncements on art, to a political position. Unfortunately such a position usually remains latent; it may take many generations before the ideological component is recognized in a portrayal of an artist that appears on the surface to be objective.

Spitta sees Bach as the "quintessential Protestant cantor," devoted to the Bible, the chorale, and counterpoint, his feet planted firmly in the tradition of northern and central Germany, a man at home on the organ bench who conducts church choirs and penetrates ever deeper into the heart of things, not only in works like *The Art of Fugue* and the *Musical Offering* but also, for instance, in his chorale cantatas, which Spitta still believes to have been written late in Bach's career. Spitta treats the life of the mature composer with corresponding indifference. When discussing the biographical and artistic circumstances of the young Bach, he is thorough but pays little attention to such details in the later compositions. Entirely consistent in this respect with the nineteenth century's idealist orientation, the biographer views his hero like a tree, rooted in a particular soil but increasingly growing away from it and finally existing as an entity unto itself.

Although Spitta confronts the reader with many details that do not quite fit the image of the "quintessential cantor," his Bach biography became an important starting point for a particular view of the composer; thus it offers a good example of how a scholarly work can contribute to the formation of a myth—when it appears on the scene at the right moment. The myth of the "quintessential cantor" matches only too well the assumptions current in the era of German cultural Protestantism.

In 1962, Friedrich Blume's lecture "Sketching a New Image of Bach" marked the beginning of his attempt to dislodge this myth. At first this undertaking was hailed enthusiastically. In the end, Blume failed, partly because he promised more than he could deliver in his attempt to portray Bach as a worldly man, "immersed in the present" and "wide open to promising trends"; he took too polemical a stance on the subject of the cantor Bach.[18] The more fundamental explanation for his failure is that one can argue against but not circumvent the Bach myth. There is little reason to bemoan this state of affairs: Bach's ability to survive beyond his era derives precisely from his power to generate myth. To take this power from him may multiply the perspectives from which his music can be viewed but at the same time it deprives his art of its historical force. While "enlightened" scholarship must accept the risk of diminishing the object of its study, it need not overdo this tendency out of the desire to call attention to itself.

Patriotism, Prussianism, Protestantism—these are the overarching concepts to which Forkel's, Bitter's, and Spitta's images of Bach adhere, with each scholar placing the emphasis differently. For Albert Schweitzer, born into a family of pastors in 1875 in the upper Alsatian town of Kaysersberg, the sole category is Protestantism. Yet no matter how greatly Protestantism influenced the thinking and beliefs of this future theologian and physician, when he published his book on Bach in 1905 with Breitkopf and Härtel, first in French and three years later in German, the original subtitle revealed which Bach Schweitzer really had in mind: *J. S. Bach, le musicien poète.*[19]

Schweitzer gains his first intensive acquaintance with Bach's vocal music in the mid-1890s, when as a student he serves as organ accompanist to the church choir of St. William's in Strasbourg, famed for its Bach performances. In a lecture he delivers a decade later in Düsseldorf, he recalls how in particular the sinfonia in the *Christmas Oratorio* revealed to him "the full power of the images in Bach's music."[20] When he is studying in Paris in 1899, Schweitzer takes organ lessons from Charles-Marie Widor, practicing, among other works, the *Orgelbüchlein.* The two of them find common ground in discussions of the pictorial richness and symbolism of this music, discussions presumably inspired by *L'orgue de J.S. Bach* (1895), written by the organist and later music historian André Pirro, himself a pupil of Widor's for a time and soon to make further important contributions to the creation of a "French school" of Bach aesthetics. Widor encourages Schweitzer to undertake a study, addressed to organists, of the poetic content of Bach's organ chorales. Schweitzer follows this suggestion and in 1901 submits the idea to the publishing house of Breitkopf and Härtel.

Although no publication results from this proposal, Schweitzer begins to record his thoughts on the relationship between words and music in Bach's cantatas and finally comes back to the publisher with the suggestion that he write a comprehensive book on Bach. He intends to write it in French: instead of competing with Spitta's monumental work, he will appeal to a French-speaking audience. He will produce "not a historical but an aesthetic and practical study"[21] and therefore does not hesitate to rely largely on Spitta for biographical, philological, and historical details. In the book he describes Bach's life and work from a remarkable variety of perspectives yet without lengthy excursuses on music history or references to scholarly sources. One senses the energy with which this man of barely thirty masters his subject and avoids distractions. The author wants to demonstrate that Bach's music has earned a solid position in contemporary musical life: he offers a picture of its richness in genre, style, and compositional method; he illuminates the central aesthetic features of the individual works; and he suggests ways of performing Bach in accord with the current spirit.

While working on this book between 1902 and 1904, Schweitzer serves as an instructor in the department of Protestant theology at the university and as vicar of a parish in Strasbourg; for a time he also directs a research foundation. He performs in concerts and writes a large number of articles on theological subjects. Against this background, his accomplishment in completing the book is impressive, indeed worthy of Bach himself.

Schweitzer writes the first few pages of the German version of the Bach book, which is considerably more detailed than the French version, in the summer of 1906. He is sitting in an inn in Bayreuth, the Black Horse Arms, "after a wonderful performance of *Tristan*." "For weeks I had tried to get down to work. In the exalted mood in which I returned from the festival hall, I finally succeeded."[22] The connection between Bach and Richard Wagner that he forges here is not superficial; since the age of sixteen, when he was overwhelmed by a performance of *Tannhäuser*, Schweitzer has been under the spell of Wagner, the composer but also the philosopher and essayist. In contrast to Schweitzer, Spitta, who on the whole considered Wagner a "brilliant man," characterized *Tristan and Isolde* as "a pigsty" in which he did not like to set foot. In 1881 Spitta commented, in a mixture of amusement and indignation, that a *Tristan* production had filled the stage with "delirium": "For they are all insane, and the composer who could write something like this is doubly insane."[23]

In a 1902 draft for the French version of his Bach book, Schweitzer makes the following programmatic statement:

> *Bach was a poet! This his contemporaries never suspected. Far from appreciating the musical poetry of his works, they saw in him merely the keyboard and organ virtuoso and the grand mathematician of counterpoint. Today we judge the master's abilities more accurately. Thanks to the development music has undergone over the past century and a half, we have achieved sufficient distance to see Bach in all his greatness. The oeuvre of Wagner plays a major role in this reassessment of Bach. In emphasizing the interrelationship between literature and music, and thereby setting the course of modern art, the Bayreuth master has pointed our understanding of art in a new direction, one that allows us to grasp instinctively the unity of poetry and music in every musical work.*[24]

This concept of the reciprocal relationships among the arts, which Schweitzer has already explored in his 1899 dissertation on Kant, provides him with two diametrically opposed approaches to musical aesthetics: Wagner's language of music and words "is intended to allow the emotional content of the text to speak through sound," while Bach attempts "to capture the visual, plastic, characteristic qualities in the text and to express these qualities in music to whatever extent possible, so as to portray the text" and thereby speak to "the listener's imagination."[25]

Sometimes Schweitzer speaks of Bach in terms similar to those

Wagner used in reference to Beethoven: "The German Bach strains to break the bonds of Italian cliché-ridden decadent art," struggles like a giant for his freedom—and loses it time and again. He cites as an example the opening chorus of the cantata "Es erhub sich ein Streit," BWV 19, where Bach portrays in a "brilliantly seized image" the defeat of Satan, but then "out of force of habit" prescribes a "da capo that mindlessly contradicts the music and the text":

> *The entire tragic fate of Bach's art can be seen in this one dal segno. There must be something inherent in any painterly conception of music that explains why its two greatest exponents, the St. Thomas cantor and Berlioz, are oblivious to certain elements that a thoroughly mediocre talent would recognize.*[26]

In Spitta, Schweitzer sees an advocate of absolute music whose hostility toward Wagner blinded him to Bach, whom he then "hitched to the cart of pure music," essentially calling out, "Be still! You are a classic. A classic is one whose tonal line stays at home and does not go roving about seeking adventure and trying to express things that cannot be expressed with such specificity in music." He remarks that "honest, straightforward musicians needed to come along who would listen to Bach's cantatas without preconceived theories and notice that they were not pure music but poetic and painterly music."[27]

Schweitzer certainly does his predecessor an injustice when he charges him with having no eye for the poetic and painterly Bach. Yet having undergone his own formation as an artist under the banner of traditional French musical aesthetics, he sees clearly how embarrassing the "German school" would find any undue emphasis on poetic or painterly qualities. That discomfort begins with the struggle against eighteenth-century French mimetic aesthetics and ends with the academic condemnation of Wagner: in contrast to the "sensualism" of the English and the "materialism" of the French, Wilhelm Langhans declares programmatically in his 1887 *History of Music*, "German idealism finds the essential conditions for the perception of all truth in the human spirit itself."[28]

That perception is especially true of a composer whose music, according to Spitta, is spiritual to the core and therefore furthers a spiritual renewal of the church. It is characteristic of the Protestant tradition to combine piety with emotional asceticism and hostility toward visual images. The artist has a special duty to "serve," and an artist who "speaks" and "paints" too much thrusts his own subjective sensibilities into the foreground. The label "church composer" actually has something of the aura of "state composer" about it, for with their work both must promote order and tranquillity.

We may assume that the polemical lecture attacking "pure music" that Schweitzer delivers in 1928 in Düsseldorf uses such formulations, because at this time the German singing and Bach movements are at their height. Schweitzer is not attempting here to defend Bach's work, in Spitta's sense, as a classic nonsectarian cultural treasure, against various extreme interpretations. Yet his ideal of a "music for the community" prevents him from seeing Bach as a blazingly imaginative, subjective artist. Against such a backdrop, *The Art of Fugue* must be considered more important than the *Orgelbüchlein*.

The Bach scholarship that followed Spitta and Schweitzer has situated the pictorial and poetic qualities of Bach's music within the context of baroque musical theory, an important achievement. According to this theory, musical rhetoric belonged to the skills every composer should master. The insight coupled with this idea, that the "painter" and "sound poet" Bach stood in a firmly established tradition—that of Protestant church music—makes it unnecessary to split his universal music into such dichotomies as "order versus expressiveness," "absolute versus illustrative," "objective versus subjective." It was Schweitzer's justified desire to snatch the discussion of the "correct" understanding of Bach from the hands of the professional musicologists as well as from the youth-oriented Bach singing groups of the time, to make it become the responsibility of all Bach lovers. That international experience and versatile scholarly and artistic inclinations helped Schweitzer in his undertaking should constitute a warning against any form of provincialism in Bach scholarship.

TRANSMISSION OF THE WORKS

Few of Bach's works appeared in print during his lifetime. Among them, the *Clavier-Übung*, published between 1726 and 1742 in four parts, is the longest and most significant work, a demanding corpus of keyboard and organ music in a variety of genres and styles. Most of Bach's works for keyboard and organ circulated among his pupils and admirers in handwritten form; for example, *The Well-Tempered Clavier* existed in dozens of copies even in the eighteenth century. Of the six sonatas and partitas for solo violin and the six cello suites, we have copies that are in the hand of Anna Magdalena Bach and that may have been intended for sale.

Most of the surviving orchestral and vocal compositions were probably known to only a few in Bach's lifetime, even in handwritten form. A good many works existed only in the scores Bach wrote out himself and in the performance materials produced or authorized by him. Presumably he lent out individual works for special occasions; thus in his early Leipzig years he sent vocal parts settings of the Sanctus in the later B-Minor Mass to Count Franz Anton von Sporck in Bohemia, and in 1729 he would gladly have shared a "Passions Musique" with his pupil Christian Gottlob Wecker, working in Schweidnitz in Silesia, had he not needed it himself. In the mid-1730s he gave Carl Philipp Emanuel material for a performance of Easter music while his son was studying in Frankfurt on the Oder and apparently contributing to musical productions at the university.

Although there must have been similar cases of which no record exists, we have reason to assume that Bach's more richly orchestrated instrumental works—his passions, masses, and cantatas—were little disseminated while he was alive. Performance of such music was subject to special conditions, which varied from court to court, city to city, and church to church. Therefore a composer of such pieces created them primarily for his own use—or he succeeded in establishing generally accepted norms and standards. This may have been Telemann's concern, but it was not Bach's; with the exception of the trial balloon represented by the *Clavier-Übung*, Bach did not compose for the marketplace but rather, on the one hand, to supply his daily needs and those of a fairly large circle of pupils, and on the other, to satisfy his constant preoccupation with self-imposed tasks.

This situation naturally had consequences for the transmission of the works. At the time of Bach's death, the only ones in print were, in addition to the *Clavier-Übung*, the cantata "Gott ist mein König," BWV 71, the Schübler Chorales for the organ, the *Musical Offering*, the Canonic Variations on the hymn "Vom Himmel hoch," the canon BWV 1076, and the songs in the collection published by Georg Christian Schemelli. *The Art of Fugue* was in press. As mentioned above, the unpublished works for keyboard and organ existed in numerous handwritten versions owned by collectors and performers. But when it came to the other genres, posterity had to make do with the manuscripts found among Bach's own papers or—as in the case of the *Brandenburg Concertos* and the two first movements of the B-Minor Mass—in the possession of individuals to whom they had been dedicated by the composer.

Did Bach at least keep copies of everything he composed in the course of his life? A general answer to this question is not possible, although individual aspects of each category can be illuminated. We know of situations in which Bach put manuscripts of works of the same type together and so clearly viewed them as complete series or cycles. Examples are the *Orgelbüchlein;* the organ sonatas BWV

525–30; the so-called Eighteen Great Chorales for the Organ, BWV 651–68, the two-part Inventions and three-part Sinfonias; both parts of *The Well-Tempered Clavier;* the works for solo violin BWV 1001–06; the six sonatas for violin and keyboard BWV 1014–19; and the seven keyboard concertos BWV 1052–58. We may assume that Bach as a rule carefully saved and did not lightly part with such collections, including the dedication copy of the *Brandenburg Concertos,* most likely given by him to the Margrave of Brandenburg.

The same is true of the scores of the great oratorios, such as the B-Minor Mass, the Magnificat, the *Christmas Oratorio,* the *St. John Passion,* and the *St. Matthew Passion.* The polished form in which these have come down to us is evidence of Bach's intention to preserve at least his "great" compositions for posterity. It was presumably on the occasion of a repeat performance of the *St. Matthew Passion* in 1736 that he wrote out a new score, not only to represent the most recent version but also to allow the work to appear polished: he used red ink when he incorporated the melody of the chorale "O Lamm Gottes unschuldig" into the opening chorus as well as when he wrote out the text of the Gospels sung by the Evangelist and the soloists. When the first thirteen pages were damaged several years before his death, he carefully repaired them by gluing lengthwise strips to the margins, which had apparently become illegible, and rewriting the missing notes.

We thus gain the impression that Bach himself may have already viewed the *St. Matthew Passion* as a work that would outlast the centuries—likewise the "great Catholic" B-Minor Mass, which he was determined to complete and capture in a score during the last years of his life, a task that cost him great effort. He also took pains to preserve the sacred cantatas for the Sundays and feast days of the ecclesiastical year, which he arranged in annual cycles. If today the existence of only three complete cycles can be proved, although the obituary mentions five, the explanation may involve more than just the natural process by which things disappear; Bach scholars have given serious thought, though without resolving the matter, to the possibility that Bach actually left only four cycles.

Whether Bach wrote considerably more secular cantatas than we can reconstruct today is a question that must be approached with caution. As occasional compositions based on texts that could hardly be used again in other situations, such works had limited usefulness. The many works in this category that have disappeared do not necessarily represent a comparable loss in terms of musical material. Bach often reused large portions of his secular cantatas in other contexts or rewrote them in several stages, so most of these compositions were probably preserved in at least one form. The example of the *Christmas Oratorio* shows how much it mattered to him that this secular music survive beyond the day and the occasion of its first performance: he worked into this six-part series of cantatas for the Sundays and feast days during the Christmas season the music of three "drammi per musica" composed for the ruling house of Saxony: *Hercules at the Crossroads*, BWV 213; "Tönet, ihr Pauken! Erschallet, Trompeten!" BWV 214; and "Preise dein Glücke, gesegnetes Sachsen," BWV 215. He confidently labeled the entire opus an oratorio, a term not commonly in use at the time. The solemnity of this appellation indicated that the work belonged in the same category as the passions and the great mass.

It is difficult to determine how many of the chamber music and orchestral manuscripts left among Bach's papers at his death have been lost. It is striking, at any rate, that the surviving works in these genres are not numerous. Although Bach had ample opportunities and occasions during his years as kapellmeister in Cöthen and as the director of a collegium musicum in his middle period in Leipzig to compose such works, we have several indications that he did not compose that much in these categories. When one surveys the extant orchestral compositions in particular, it seems likely that Bach was preoccupied with these works over long periods; they exist either in several different versions and/or in forms through which one can recognize older versions.

One may conclude that Bach viewed the composition of orchestral music not as a routine task but as an opportunity to give shape to and develop particular conceptions and models through a limited number of exemplars and to present them in a new context as needed. If we accept this premise, it would be unlikely that such a model would not have "survived" in at least one version. The survival of the *Brandenburg Concertos* supports this hypothesis: even if the handwritten dedication copy had been lost, other sources and versions would provide access to five of the six works. We may assume that at his death Bach left behind an extensive but not complete collection of his compositions; he was not a perfectionist when it came to preserving and cataloguing his oeuvre. As he got older, it seems to have been more important to him that a series of paradigmatic works would continue to be performed and discussed after his death. Not until Haydn and Mozart did the idea take hold that a composer should keep track of his oeuvre as consistently and completely as possible with the help of lists—not least of all for purposes of asserting ownership, a consideration that had not yet acquired much importance in Bach's day. For Beethoven it would be a question of prestige to have each of his works receive an opus number and be printed as soon as possible.

Bach's scores are not listed in the inventory made of his possessions upon his death. They seem to have been divided among his heirs ahead of time. Two theories can be formulated as to how the works were distributed. It is conceivable that the two eldest sons from Bach's first marriage, Wilhelm Friedemann and Carl Philipp Emanuel, took the lion's share, consistent with their strong position in the family; what speaks for this theory is that the manuscripts we have today come mostly from the collections of these two. But it is also possible that the musical materials were divided equally among all those entitled to inherit, as were the household items listed in the inventory. The two sons from the second marriage, Johann Christoph Friedrich and Johann Christian; the widow Anna Magdalena; the daughter Liesgen, married to Johann Christoph Altnickol; as well as the two unmarried daughters would have then inherited substantial amounts of musical material. If this second theory is true, many original manuscripts must have been lost, for the surviving manuscripts include only a few from the holdings of these heirs.

Whatever the case, the inheritance of Carl Philipp Emanuel is the best preserved. Supplemented over time through the gift or purchase of the works inherited by his siblings, so that eventually it included all the surviving significant oratorical works, this collection was carefully preserved and small portions of it even put to practical use. As director of sacred music in Hamburg, Carl Philipp Emanuel performed in 1770, 1776, and 1781 the Michaelmas cantata "Es erhub sich ein Streit," BWV 19, for which he replaced the two arias with new ones of his own composition—presumably because of the old-fashioned style of the originals. For one of his Easter cantatas, probably performed in 1778, he used the opening chorus of the *Christmas Oratorio*, "Jauchzet, frohlocket," as the opening movement.

In 1768 Carl Philipp Emanuel included in the program of a public concert the Credo from the B-Minor Mass, to which he had added a brief instrumental introduction. Also performed in this concert were two popular movements from Handel's *Messiah*, and his own *Heilig*, to be performed by a double choir.[1] This concert, which received much acclaim from the Hamburg audience, is significant in the history of music. It marks the moment when Johann Sebastian Bach's vocal works were first used outside the standard choral repertory for church services; at the same time characteristic excerpts of these works were ennobled as indestructible classics of sacred music. Furthermore, this concert shows that in Protestant Germany a "holy musical art" is being established, an art that has outgrown its liturgical function and is being cultivated to arouse reverence at special concerts and, increasingly, in singing societies organized specifically for this purpose.

After the death of Carl Philipp Emanuel Bach, most of the priceless collection of his father's manuscripts that he had amassed passed to his pupil and successor, Christian Friedrich Gottlieb Schwencke, a respected composer and Bach interpreter on the organ and keyboard. Partly by way of Schwencke, partly directly from the estate, Georg Poelchau—the most important among all the private Bach collectors—acquired significant portions of Carl Philipp Emanuel's collection. This private scholar, born in 1773 near Riga, residing in Hamburg from 1799 till 1813 and from then on in Berlin, had the means—not least through recourse to his wife's fortune—to collect printed and handwritten musical works in large numbers, with the intention of establishing an "archive of musical art."[2]

Thanks to Abraham Mendelssohn, Felix Mendelssohn-Bartholdy's father, who served as an intermediary, a substantial portion of Poelchau's Bach manuscripts found their way to the library of the Berlin Singakademie, with which Poelchau was involved from 1814 on as an active member and later also as its librarian. The most significant works from Carl Philipp Emanuel's estate finally landed in Berlin's Königliche Bibliothek, survived the evacuations necessitated by the Second World War, and in the meantime have been reunited in the Staatsbibliothek's building at number 8 Unter den Linden. Today about 80 percent of the surviving Bach autographs are archived there, including many once owned by Wilhelm Friedemann Bach.

This son's treatment of his paternal heritage was by no means as irresponsible as the older Bach literature would make it seem. After Bach's death, Wilhelm Friedemann was probably the only one to perform the vocal works to any great extent: as the organist and musical director of the Frauenkirche in Halle, he needed a large supply of church pieces, and therefore liked to draw for his Sunday and feast day performances on works by his father, carefully revising the parts. He had a particular fondness for the large, elaborate choral movements—such as the chorale "Ein feste Burg ist unser Gott" from the cantata BWV 80.

Finding himself in financial difficulties, Wilhelm Friedemann was forced to sell some of his father's scores around 1760, but he seems to have done his best to make sure they landed in good hands, for instance those of the cantor in Oelsnitz, Johann Georg Nacke, from whom they made their way, by various detours, to the significant collection of the Bach lover, singer, and friend of Mendelssohn

Franz Hauser. According to more recent scholarship, Wilhelm Friedemann kept not insignificant portions of his holdings together until his death.[3]

Wilhelm Friedemann has been criticized for having presented one of his father's works, the organ concerto BWV 596, after Vivaldi, as his own on the handwritten title page and for later passing off some of his own vocal compositions as his father's. It has meanwhile come to light that the father and his sons composed all sorts of works jointly, and that the actual composer in that group occasionally attributed pieces to someone else. Since we have no way of knowing whether Wilhelm Friedemann naively hoped to profit from his "forgeries" and, if so, how, it is better to leave the whole question in the semidarkness that surrounds the last years of Bach's life.

It appears likely that when Bach's widow, Anna Magdalena, also found herself in financial straits, she turned over to the St. Thomas School most of the manuscripts she had inherited. Thus the citizens of Leipzig occasionally had the pleasure of hearing a cantata by Johann Sebastian Bach performed during a church service under the direction of one of his successors as cantor. More frequent were performances of the motets, which had early become showpieces for the St. Thomas Choir.[4] In 1789, no less a visitor to Leipzig than Wolfgang Amadeus Mozart enjoyed one of these performances. If Bach's unmarried daughters inherited any of the manuscripts, it is possible that they sold portions of their holdings to the publisher and music dealer Johann Gottlob Immanuel Breitkopf, who in his catalogue, first issued in the 1760s, listed all sorts of Bach manuscripts for sale.

The collection of Bach items that Johann Philipp Kirnberger began assembling around 1758 for his sovereign and pupil, Princess Anna Amalia of Prussia, consisted in part of copies offered for sale by Breitkopf's publishing house. Kirnberger, one of Bach's pupils, was especially interested in pieces that revealed Bach as a master of counterpoint and "strict style," as a father of German classical music. Today this portion of what came to be called the Amalia Library belongs to the Staatsbibliothek in Berlin. Recently another strand of the Berlin Bach tradition has come to be associated with the name of the musician Johann Friedrich Hering, whose collection grew out of Hering's contact with the composer's two eldest sons. This collection passed into the possession of the counts of Voss-Buch and today can be found in Berlin, along with the holdings of Joseph Fischhof, a representative of the important Viennese Bach tradition.

In his memoirs, Adolf Bernhard Marx, the music scholar from whom we have learned of the rediscovery, by Felix Mendelssohn, of Bach's *St. Matthew Passion*, recounts an anecdote according to which Mendelssohn's teacher, Carl Friedrich Zelter, "obtained the score of that immortal work from a cheese shop, where it was being used as wrapping paper."[5] In the preface to volume 6 of the old Bach edition, one can read that gardeners in the service of Count Sporck used old music manuscripts, perhaps including works by Bach, "to wrap tree trunks."[6]

The "recollection" about the *St. Matthew Passion* can easily be unmasked as Marx's self-aggrandizement. Yet even recently various oddities have been documented. For instance, the original flute part for the cantata BWV 9, "Es ist das Heil uns kommen her," was found in 1971 at a construction site near New York's Water Street. A music lover who happened to be passing by noticed a piece of sheet music sticking out of a pile of construction debris and received laconic permission from the nearest workman to take not only the score but the rubble with it![7]

Such amusing details should not be allowed to distort the larger picture: although Bach's handwritten compositions may not have been kept together after his death, they were certainly not scattered in all directions; a considerable number of them were gathered with great respect, then preserved and handed on. The archival preservation of Bach's manuscripts provides evidence of greater recognition of the composer's stature than the zeitgeist of various periods might suggest. True, here and there a lovely piece may be irretrievably lost, even a sequence of compositions or two may have disappeared without a trace. But the losses are probably not so significant as to distort fundamentally our picture of Bach the composer.

Now that we can no longer reasonably expect new sources to surface, we need to find a sensible solution for an urgent problem: the Berlin manuscripts are threatened by creeping deterioration. As early as the 1930s, important manuscripts in the Staatsbibliothek were covered with transparent sheets of silk chiffon. The musicologist Hans Joachim Moser, noted in his time but given sometimes to rushing into print, viewed the manuscript of the *St. Matthew Passion* in 1959 and made the reverent observation that for this work Bach had apparently "bought the most expensive paper available in Athens-on-the-Pleisse, to emphasize the solemnity of what he was leaving for posterity"![8] Efforts are currently under way to prevent the ink from devouring the paper, and it is even planned to split the individual pages and insert a layer of acid-free paper between the front and back.

PART ONE

THE STATIONS OF BACH'S LIFE

FROM MATINS SINGER TO HOFKAPELLMEISTER

At the end of 1735, Johann Sebastian Bach compiles a genealogy of the "musical Bach family." It begins in the sixteenth century with the patriarch Veit Bach and ends with a reference to Johann Christian Bach, the composer's youngest son, just born. The fifty-year-old chronicler, not yet advanced in years but long conscious of family tradition, offers a rather extensive account of the family's earliest known ancestors, a briefer one of the fifty-three other members of this clan. His narrative includes slightly more detail when he gets around to speaking of himself and his brother Johann Jakob, three years his senior. Might this be the "fratello dilettissimo" upon whose departure from the world he composed the piano capriccio BWV 992, a sort of elaborate musical joke, and whose date of death he cannot recall when the moment comes to outline the man's life?

Of his great-great-grandfather Veit, Johann Sebastian reports vaguely, yet not without some basis in historical fact, that he lived in the sixteenth century and worked as a white-bread baker in Hungary. Into the age of Luther, the German word for bake was *bachen*,[1] so the name might well be connected with his profession, provided Veit had German-speaking ancestors. At any rate, according to Bach, Veit fled to Germany "for the sake of the Lutheran religion," which means to escape the persecution to which Protestants were being subjected. He resumed his trade in the vicinity of Gotha, and while the millstone was turning grain into flour, he would pluck the zither, a popular instrument. "It must have made a right pretty sound! For he let the rhythm be impressed upon him [that is, learned from the rhythm of the mill]," Bach comments with a barely contained grin, and promptly concludes, "And this may be counted the beginning of music amongst his progeny."[2]

This account sounds waggish when one considers that five years before he penned it, Johann Sebastian demanded that the city fathers provide better working conditions for him, arguing that

> the current status musices is entirely different from what it was before, the art having increased greatly, the gusto having changed wondrously, for which reason the sort of Music heard hitherto is no longer pleasing to our ears.[3]

Commingled here with respect for his ancestor is the self-confidence of a fifth-generation Bach who has achieved the status of court kapellmeister and cantor of the Thomaskirche. His distant ancestor was a lay musician; his great-grandfather, Hans, continued his father's trade but also took on the role of a traveling "minstrel"; his grandfather, Christoph, was employed as town musician in Erfurt and later in Arnstadt; and his father was appointed director of Eisenach's town orchestra.

Over many generations, the family tree displays numerous musicians, nothing but musicians, many more than have been named here. One can see the pointlessness of asking whether "musicality" is innate or learned. Does it result from a particular genetic predisposition, or is it the music-saturated air that causes little Johann Sebastian to feel from the first moment that in this world he will thrive only as a musician? He did thrive, even if the circumstances were by no means easy.

In 1668, Bach's father, Johann Ambrosius, at twenty-three a violinist with the Erfurt town musicians, marries Elisabeth Lämmerhirt, the daughter of a respected furrier, who bears him six sons and two daughters. Active in Eisenach since 1671, he achieves considerable prominence. Johann Sebastian, the youngest of his children, is born on March 21, 1685 and baptized two days later at St. George's in Eisenach. The two godfathers are the musician Sebastian Nagel of Gotha and the forester Johann Georg Koch of Eisenach. The Bach House on the Frauenplan, today a much-visited historic site, can no longer be considered the house where he was born; possibly the birthplace was located on Fleischergasse, more precisely on the spot now occupied by number 35 Luthergasse.

The life of the Bach children can be reconstructed only partially. Johann Christoph, the eldest of the surviving brothers, will play an important role in Bach's youth; we shall return to him later. We have already mentioned Johann Jakob, the brother closest to Johann Sebastian in age. He is apprenticed to his father's successor and trains as a Stadtpfeifer (town musician). Later he enters the military service of Sweden as a musician and sees duty on European battlefields as far east as Turkey. Eventually he settles for good in Stockholm as a court musician. The sister Marie Salome marries and moves to Erfurt. Johann Rudolf, Johann Balthasar, Johann Jonas, and Johanna Juditha die young.

EISENACH

In retrospect it seems fortunate that Bach was born in Eisenach, a town with a population of six thousand at the time, and spent the first eleven years of his life there. The town offered in a microcosm, down to the smallest detail, the elements that would become the content of Bach's life as an adult. His parents' house serves as the home of the town musicians' corps. Thronged with apprentices and journeymen, it is filled with music every day, and at a very young age Bach becomes familiar with all kinds of wind and string instruments and learns early what qualities are required of a municipal music director. The town council of Eisenach expressly recognizes his father's abilities, attesting that he has "proven himself so qualified in his profession that, so far as we can recollect, we have not seen his like in these parts."[4] Of course, as leader of the town music corps, he remains an active town musician himself—the master over the apprentices and journeymen. It will be left to his son to rise to the position of music director, overseeing the musicians but not performing.

At the main church, St. George's, Johann Sebastian gains first-hand knowledge of the organ, the figural choir, and *Currende* (music students who would sing in the streets for money). And from the town hall he can hear the brass players sounding their horns from the tower. Little Johann Sebastian surely also accompanies his father now and then when his father presents himself at the Wartburg, the residence of the reigning Duke of Saxony-Eisenach. There the distant sound of courtly suites, concerti, sonatas, and cantatas, probably of high quality, reaches his ear. From 1709 on, the family friend Georg Philipp Telemann will serve as director of music at the court, where French taste prevails; in this period, Bach is "merely" court organist in the neighboring state of Weimar.

Throughout his life, Bach will remain faithful to the musical world of his childhood, as he will to the region of Thuringia and Saxony. His travels will never take him farther than to Lübeck and Berlin in the north, to Carlsbad in the south, and to Kassel in the west.

Eisenach not only provides his musical world but also is the site of his upbringing and education: it is the town of Martin Luther, who learned the *elementaria* two hundred years earlier at the same Latin school to which Bach is now admitted. In the sixth form, the pupils are supposed "to have learned the *Catechismus Lutheri* and in reading, both in Latin and in German, to have made such progress that they have a good beginning at accomplished reading and have also been introduced to writing."[5] The catechism, as well as a canon of ten particular psalms, must be recited word for word to pupils not yet perfectly secure in reading and writing; after that they are expected to read the text and copy it out. Instruction is based on the *Latinitas vestibulum sive primi ad Latinam aditus* by Johann Amos Comenius, which provides simultaneous training in German and Latin, with the texts arranged in parallel columns.[6] The primary objective is to employ traditional texts, songs, and pictures to transmit, from generation to generation and with a minimum of reflection, basic knowledge and truths regarded as theologically and socially essential.

In 1693 Bach enters the fifth form, which means he must have been enrolled previously in another school, since schooling was mandatory from the age of five years on. Perhaps his parents sent him to the master turner and schoolmaster Franz Hering, who lived on nearby Fleischgasse.[7] Since the pupils at this German school did a great deal of their learning from the hymnal, little Bach must have had ample opportunity to dwell on the emblematic depictions of the life of Christ and his disciples in the Eisenach hymnal of 1763. Their graphic and symbolic vividness later found specific equivalents in his compositions: exposure to these early images no doubt influenced the way he would join music and theology throughout his life.

The hymnal, the catechism, Latin texts—these elements dominated the early education of young Bach. We may wonder whether they appealed to him as much as music. Bach scholars, who pore over every available biographical detail, tell us that in the three years at the Latin school he is marked absent 96, 59, and 103 times, respectively.[8] Is he taking refuge in sickness from the constant pressure, or—the more likely explanation—is he helping his father with musical performances? At any rate, life in Eisenach is not easy for this five- to ten-year-old. There is no childhood as we understand it today; this applies to other children as well, but they do not yet have all the music he has in his heart—and on his back! "I had to be industrious; he who is industrious goes far," the adult Bach replies when asked "how he undertook to become such a master in his art."[9] His answer must be understood not as false modesty but as an expression of his involuntary striving to attribute a higher purpose to the harsh challenges he experienced in childhood.

OHRDRUF

At first the challenges multiply, and there is no meaning in sight: in May 1694, Bach's mother is buried, and in February of the next year his father follows her, barely twelve weeks after remarrying. The orphan, not yet ten years old, moves into the house of his eldest brother, Johann Christoph, in nearby Ohrdruf. As organist at St. Michael's, Johann Christoph receives so little income that in 1699 he is forced to become a schoolteacher, against all his natural inclinations.

He also has too little room in his house. Thus the other young brother, Johann Jakob, who has come along to Ohrdruf, soon leaves for an apprenticeship in Arnstadt. Johann Sebastian, three years younger than he, stays—he has no choice. He is sent to the lyceum, a respected six-year Latin school whose pupils usually go on to the university, unless they have dropped Latin and Greek before finishing their secondary education. Bach receives a scholarship, which carries with it duties as a singer of figural and *Currende* music. In the summer of 1695 the school records already note that he is the fourth best pupil, and by the following year he has become the top student in the third form. In March 1700 he graduates and leaves for Lüneburg. His school years have brought crucial educational and musical experiences.

Here we are concerned with the latter. While still in Eisenach, Bach may have received casual instruction on the violin from his father and his first insight into the art of composing from his uncle Johann Christoph, himself a not entirely insignificant composer. But most likely it was not until Johann Sebastian came to Ohrdruf that he began systematic lessons on the keyboard and organ—after all, his brother Johann Christoph, who now assumed the role of father, was a student of Pachelbel's and a competent organist. We do not know whether this brother also composed, but we owe to him the compilation of two very important collections of keyboard and organ music, which include early works by Johann Sebastian Bach: the *Andreas Bach Book* and the *Möller Manuscript.* Johann Christoph did not begin putting together these volumes until after Johann Sebastian's time in Ohrdruf, so it is possible that some of the works in them were given to Johann Christoph by Johann Sebastian, who had encountered them in Lüneburg.

When we seek to establish what young Bach learned from his older brother, we can draw on the famous passage in the obituary:

> *Johann Sebastian Bach was not yet ten years of age when he found himself robbed of his parents by death. He betook himself to Ohrdruff to his eldest brother, Johann Christoph, organist in that town, and under his instruction laid the foundation for playing*

the clavier. Already at this tender age, little Johann Sebastian displayed an uncommon love for music. In a short time he had of his own free will mastered all the pieces that his brother had given him to learn. Yet a book full of clavier pieces by the most famed masters of those times, Froberger, Kerle, and Pachelbel, which his brother possessed, was refused to him, despite all his pleas, for who knows what reason. His eagerness ever to improve his playing inspired him to commit the following innocent deceit. The book lay in a cupboard whose doors consisted merely of gratings. Accordingly, he pried it out of the cupboard at night, when all had gone to bed, for he could reach through the grating with his little hands and roll up the book, which was bound only in paper, and he copied it by the light of the moon, for he did not even possess a light. After six months' time this musical booty was safely in his hands. He was attempting to make use of it, secretly and with extraordinary devotion, when, to his great sorrow, his brother became aware of it, and mercilessly took from him the copy he had made with so much effort. If we imagine how a miser would feel if a ship sank on its way to Peru with a hundred thousand talers belonging to him, we can picture how downcast our little Johann Sebastian Bach felt at this loss.[10]

If this anecdote contains any truth, the older brother was determined that his younger brother should not know the works of Johann Pachelbel and two other composers whose works Johann Christoph liked to hold up to his pupils as exemplary, Johann Jakob Froberger and Johann Caspar Kerll. Recent scholarship indeed ascribes to Pachelbel a smaller influence on the young Bach than became customary after Spitta's biography.[11] Attention has shifted to the influence of the organ chorales composed by Bach's uncle in Eisenach, also Johann Christoph, and by Bach's brother in Gehren, Johann Michael.

The eminent Bach expert Jean-Claude Zehnder considers it quite possible that Bach began composing while still in Ohrdruf; he points in particular to the genre of the choral ricercare. If an organ chorale like "Vom Himmel hoch, da komm ich her," BWV 700, actually goes back to this early period, it would give evidence of extraordinary technical skill, the fruit of thorough instruction, though also without a single note suggestive of the later flowering of genius.

At barely fifteen Bach is recommended—presumably by the new cantor, Elias Herda, previously a bass singer in Lüneburg—to St. Michael's Cloister in that town, where there are not only openings for "matins singers" but also positions offering free room and board. The move to Lüneburg, 350 kilometers away, is not undertaken without reason. Have Johann Christoph's living quarters become more cramped with the arrival of offspring, or has the number of places in Ohrdruf offering free dining privileges shrunk? Perhaps Bach's voice has begun to change, which may have led to the loss of his scholarship.[12] But then the fifteen-year-old would have been recruited as a bass and not "because of his uncommonly beautiful soprano," which, according to the obituary, he did not lose until he was in Lüneburg.[13] At all events, he sets out on foot in March 1700 for Lüneburg, to arrive there before Easter. His classmate at the Ohrdruf lyceum, Georg Erdmann, released from the school several weeks earlier, may have accompanied him.

LÜNEBURG

St. Michael's Cloister should be pictured not as a monastery in the usual sense but rather as a handsome complex consisting of a church, a boarding school for the youth of the nobility known as the Knights' Academy, a Latin school for the burgher class, and the Collegium Academicum, similar to a university. According to its bylaws, the cloister has about a dozen scholarships for members of the "matins choir." "The poor singing scholars," as they were called earlier, not only do "daily duty" at matins and vespers but also participate in the "chorus symphoniacus," whose twenty-odd members are responsible for performing the elaborate figural music. On the list of recipients of matins money for May 1700, Bach appears in ninth place with a sum of twelve groschen; three singers on the list receive a taler, and two others sixteen groschen. Altogether twelve names are listed, as well as two unnamed "expectants."[14]

We do not need to engage in complicated calculations to see how meagerly these singers are paid. It is no coincidence that the scholarship recipients live in the same building as the young noblemen at the Knights' Academy; by performing small services, they can earn some pocket money. Nonetheless, the move to Lüneburg has great significance for Bach: now he need not sign up for a musical apprenticeship but can "study" instead and thereby acquire the qualifications of an academically educated cantor, qualifications that will later become indispensable when he applies for the cantor's position at Leipzig's Thomaskirche.

In Lüneburg's musical history, the name most associated with Bach's time is that of the master organist Georg Böhm. Specialists are perhaps even more interested in the impressive music collection belonging to St. Michael's, which consisted of well over one thousand scores, unfortunately now known to us only from inventories. Bach had daily access to the manuscripts themselves, and therefore to the sixteenth- and seventeenth-century tradition of sacred vocal music. The collection included works by the great Heinrich Schütz, the kapellmeisters Johann Rosenmüller of Wolfenbüttel and Wolfgang Carl Briegel of Darmstadt, the cantors Joachim Gerstenbüttel of Hamburg and Sebastian Knüpfer of Leipzig, and many others, not to forget both older and more recent Italian composers of sacred music, whose settings of Latin texts enjoyed considerable favor in Protestant worship services. Of particular interest to Bach may have been the passions by Christian Flor and Friedrich Funke, considered modern for their time and thus typical primarily of northern Germany.

We do not know which of the many works calling for small, large, or very large ensembles were actually performed and which were merely collected. And we can only speculate as to whether a fifteen-year-old matins singer was allowed—and wanted—to sit in the library, rummage around among the scores, and perhaps take Schütz's *Kleine geistliche Konzerte* up to his room. It is enough to assume that as a singer, copyist, listener, or eager student Bach had contact with at least a small portion of the cloister's holdings and that that contact shaped his understanding of sacred vocal music just as decisively as the later years he spent as organist in Arnstadt and Mühlhausen.

There is recent conclusive proof that Bach studied with Georg Böhm as early as 1700. Two handwritten copies of organ music by Dietrich Buxtehude and Johann Adam Reinken, which had been written out by Bach when he was somewhere between the ages of thirteen and fifteen, were discovered in the Duchess Anna-Amalia Library in August 2006. The Reinken copy seems to have been a sort of apprentice work under Böhm's tutelage. Bach's early familiarity with Reinken's music is confirmed by the obituary, which states: "From Lüneburg he traveled occasionally to Hamburg to hear Johann Adam Reinken, famous at the time as the organist at St. Catherine's."[15]

A certain Simeon Metaphrastes, whose real name was Friedrich Wilhelm Marpurg, describes in his *Legends of Several Musical Saints* (1786) a small miracle that Bach experienced on the way back to Lüneburg from Hamburg. Hungry yet too poor to take proper lodgings at an inn, he grabbed a couple of herring heads that had been tossed from a window onto the street, and lo and behold, he found "a Danish ducat hidden within each."[16]

We do not know who or what induced this generally sober man, who knew and greatly admired Bach's work and had authored a learned "Essay on the Fugue," to surround the young Bach's head with this little halo. Therefore we shall leave this early instance of the cult of genius—"the Lord does not abandon his own"—to examine the reason for Bach's trip to Hamburg. Despite the date given in the obituary, this trip cannot have taken place earlier than the spring of 1702, when Bach finished his schooling in Lüneburg with a university-entry certificate but had not yet found employment.[17]

Bach's purpose in making this study trip was most likely to experience the distinguished organist Reinken and thus gain "direct access to the main repertory of north German organ music,"[18] but no doubt also to expose himself to a master of the pure, indeed strict, style of composing, as Reinken revealed himself in his *Hortus musicus* for three string instruments and figured bass. The obituary does report that Bach learned the art of composing "largely through observation of the works of the famed and skilled composers of the time and through earnest reflection of his own."[19]

If he took the occasion of a longish visit to Hamburg to attend the opera at Gänsemarkt, Bach was able to gain insight early in his career into the dramatic style as it was beginning to take shape in Germany. The obituary provides explicit information on encounters with modern orchestral music:

> From here [Lüneburg] he also had an opportunity to listen frequently to an orchestra maintained by the Duke of Celle and consisting in the majority of French musicians; from this he could establish his mastery of the French style, which in those lands was something entirely new at the time.[20]

Bach need not travel to Celle to encounter the French style of overture, with which he will be preoccupied from his Weimar period on. The "French" occasionally perform at Lüneburg's municipal palace,[21] and one of them lives under the same roof with Bach—Thomas de la Selle, violinist and dancing master at the Knights' Academy, which, in consideration of its noble clientele, places less importance on the humanist educational tradition than on skill in French conversation and "penning charming letters," and of course in dancing, riding, and fencing.[22]

What matters to Bach, however, is the cloister's humanistic and theological educational offerings. The curriculum for the first form, geared to the standards of the university, covers the following subjects: Latin, which includes grammar instruction and reading of Cicero's orations against Catiline and Vergil's *Aeneid;* Greek, with translation of the New Testament; theology, taught from Leonhard Hutter's strictly orthodox *Compendium locorum theologicorum,* whose questions and answers are to be learned by heart; logic, for which the text is Andreas Reyher's *Systema logicum;* and rhetoric from a compendium by Heinrich Tolles. Furthermore, there are introductions to philosophy and the art of poetry, as well as offerings in projection theory, arithmetic, and mathematics.[23]

We do not know the extent to which Bach immersed himself in these subjects, on top of his musical obligations and interests. Yet there is no doubt that the Latin schools in Ohrdruf and Lüneburg helped him develop the framework for a humanistic and theological worldview that would enable the older Bach to become a *musicus doctus*, educated in and committed to traditional values, even without the corresponding university studies.

When Johann Nikolaus Forkel was conducting the research for his book on Bach and submitted a list of questions to Carl Philipp Emanuel, the latter responded succinctly in January 1775 to question 3: "*nescio* [I do not know] in what way he got from Lüneburg to Weimar."[24] Today we are no wiser. If Bach left St. Michael's in the spring of 1702, having met the matriculation requirements for the university, he may have gone to Hamburg for a while and then returned to the region of his youth. In later years he provided a hint as to his whereabouts at the time: in November 1736 he intercedes for his son Johann Gottfried Bernhard with a city councilor from Sangerhausen in Sachsen-Weissenfels, remarking that "almost thirty years ago" he himself was elected unanimously as organist at St. Jacob's but not appointed because the local prince objected. The organist's position in Sangerhausen was in fact available in July 1702, and nothing would argue against Bach's having explored the possibility of working there.

According to what we know today, Bach is seventeen when he applies for his first position. In this connection, a brief look at his contemporaries' careers seems in order. What are Bach's later competitors for the cantor's position at Leipzig's Thomaskirche doing at this age? Georg Philipp Telemann enters the University of Leipzig at twenty and three years later becomes the organist and music director at the New Church in Leipzig. Christoph Graupner attends school and the university in Leipzig for several years before taking a position at the German Opera in Hamburg at the age of twenty-three. Johann Friedrich Fasch also begins his studies at nineteen at Leipzig, directing a collegium musicum there at the same time.

This brief overview may help us understand why the Leipzig city council will later elect Bach cantor of the Thomaskirche only after the three other prominent applicants have withdrawn from the competition: he does not come from Leipzig and, unlike the others, has no university training. What matters here is Bach's own plan for his life: although he chooses advanced schooling and an education over an apprenticeship, thereby keeping important doors open, he is, to a much greater degree than the three other kapellmeisters, a self-made man, one who set his sights high early on and is willing to work hard to achieve his goal. This ethos grows out of the craftsman's approach and will inform that of the educated artist.

With Franz Mund, we may see the years before Bach's Arnstadt period as conforming to the traditional guild system: upon his departure from his brother's house in Ohrdruf, Bach's apprenticeship comes to an end. It is followed by two journeyman years in Lüneburg. The brief employment at the court in Weimar, of which more will be said soon, might be interpreted as a half year's "ripening time," a waiting period before certification as a master.[25] Yet Bach's career soon shoots beyond this craftsman's concept, which he may have inherited from his family: he early comes to see himself as an artist or, to put it more concretely, as a keyboard virtuoso and master organist.

ARNSTADT

Against this background, the respect young Bach enjoys in these years is astonishing and unusual, as are the liberties he takes in awareness of this respect. From March to September 1703 he is paid as "Lackey Baach" from the private treasury of the coregent of Weimar, Duke Johann Ernst, and employed as a musician; probably this is no more than an assistant's position. Yet during this period, in July of the same year, he is allowed to "try out the new organ in

Arnstadt and strike it for the first time," and is paid eight gulden and thirteen groschen, an amount worthy of a "court organist"—the Arnstadt authorities assign him this title to distract attention from his youthful age: where would one normally find an eighteen-year-old organ expert? The precise configuration of the Johann Friedrich Wender organ he examined is not known, but we may assume that there were few deviations from the design laid out by the Mühlhausen organ builder:[26]

Great	Swell	Pedal
Principal 8′	Principal 4′	Principal Bass 8
Viol' Di Gamb 8′	Stillgedakt 8′	Sub Bass 16′
Quinta dena 16′	Spielpfeiffe 4′	Posaunen Bass 16′
Grobgedackt 8′	Quinte 3′	Cornet Bass 2′
Quinta 6′	Sesquialtera 2fach	
Octava 4′	Nachthorn 4′	
Mixtur 4fach	Mixtur 3fach	
Gemshorn 8′		
Cymbal 2fach		
Trompet 8′		

On 9 August, Bach is installed as organist at the same church whose organ he has just evaluated. It is the New Church, which occupies third and last place in the Arnstadt hierarchy. It is possible that his Arnstadt relatives, some of whom were themselves highly respected musicians, exercised some influence on the filling of this position. They may also have made sure that he was paid decently: a stipend for room and board comes from the budget of St. George's Hospital, overseen by a relative of Bach's; a little later this relative was removed from office "on account of many inaccuracies and embezzlements." The salary comes from the collection box, as well as from the brewery tax fund, into which the so-called beer fees are paid. After receiving 27 gulden and 9 groschen as a lackey at the court of Weimar, Bach now earns 84 gulden and 6 groschen per

annum; by contrast, his successor in this post, his cousin Johann Ernst, will have to make do with 40 gulden and 1½ pecks of grain.[27]

All in all, an impressive start. The Bach monument that Bernd Göbel created in 1985 for the Arnstadt marketplace is appropriate: it shows the young artist looking relaxed, legs crossed in a self-confident pose. One need only think of Bach's behavior toward Superintendent Johann Gottfried Olearius before the consistory, the local church governing body, which had summoned him to face various complaints. Here are some excerpts from the dossier "Re: Joh. Sebastian Bach, Organist at the New Church, concerning lengthy travels and Neglect of Figural music" (a few Latin terms are translated and abbreviations interpreted):

Actum the 21st of *Febr.* 1706

The *organist* of the New Church Bach is interrogated as to where he has been so long of late and from whom he received permission therefor.

Ille [he]: He has been in Lübeck to understand various things in his art, but requested permission beforehand of the Superintend[ent].

The Superint.[d] He requested such for only four weeks, but probably stayed away for four times as long.

Ille: He trusts the organ-playing has in the meantime been attended to by the person he recruited for this purpose in such a way that no complaint can be raised.

Nos [we]: Respond that up to now he has introduced many strange *variationes* into the chorale, admixed many strange tones, such that the congregation has been *confundiret* [confused] thereby. In future when he wishes to bring in a *tonum peregrinum* [presumably: modulate into a distant key], he should stay with it and not fall into another too quickly, or, as has been his wont hitherto, even play a *Tonum contrarium* [presumably a dissonant accompanying chord]. In addition to that, it is most troubling that up to now no music-making has taken place at his instigation, seeing as how he does not wish to comportir with the pupils, for which reason he should explain whether he is willing to play both figural as well as choral works with the pupils. For it is not possible for us to provide him with a Kapellmeister. If he does not wish to do it, he should simply say so categorice, so that other arrangements may be made and someone who will do this may be hired.

Ille: If they would only provide for him a proper Director he would certainly play.

Res. [resolution]: To be pronounced within a week.

Eod. [on the same matter]: Pupil Rambach appears and is likewise reprimanded for the Disordres that have previously occurred in the New Church between the pupils and the Organist.

Ille: The Organist Bach has up to now played somewhat too long, but after the Herr Superintendent called his attention thereto, he has fallen promptly into the other extremum, and made it too short.[28]

This document is as interesting as it is astonishing for what it reveals of the historical period and Bach's life: the twenty-year-old organist expresses himself very freely and self-confidently to a church authority who occupies a position far above him. Apparently it does not trouble Bach in the slightest when it is suggested that he seek his fortune elsewhere in light of the criticisms brought forward against him. He seems to know where he can find a new position, or at least that one exists. Did he undertake the long trip to Lübeck with the intention not only of "listening to" the famous Buxtehude, as the obituary states,[29] but perhaps also of inheriting his position at some later date? Word may have reached him that Johann Mattheson, four years his senior, was offered such a position-in-waiting some time earlier, whereupon he went to Lübeck, accompanied by his devoted admirer George Frideric Handel, to feel out the situation. But according to Mattheson's later autobiographical account, he had not "the slightest desire" to enter into a "marital obligation." While Mattheson and Handel travel by coach and during the journey "make many double fugues" to pass the time,[30] Bach undertakes the long trip "on foot"—at least according to the obituary,[31] which in this case does not seem entirely trustworthy.

Even if Bach was merely intent on understanding "various things in his art," it seems rather audacious for a beginner to exceed a paid furlough by two or possibly three months—the documents allow both interpretations. Bach's reply, that there were no complaints about the substitute he engaged, does not make the situation any better; rather, it reveals, all too clearly, that in his eyes anyone is good enough for the people of Arnstadt, whereas he himself aspires to loftier things. Those who find fault with his organ playing do not deserve him!

On this point, the arguments of the superintendent, a man experienced at organizing sacred music, by no means betray pettiness. Although his formulations are a little ambiguous, they show expertise when he explains that Bach accompanies the church choir in too showy a manner. If one listens to Bach's harmonization of the hymn "Herr Jesu Christ, dich zu uns wend" in the organ chorale BWV 726, composed around this time, one can understand the objections raised by his superiors: Bach is playing with the chromatic possibilities of a four-part setting—like a Max Reger before his time—in a way that distracts one from the cantus firmus more than it emphasizes it.

The young hothead has his own understanding of the old saying *Non hominibus sed Deo* (not for men but for God), which Master Buxtehude used as the motto for one of his learned canons: he practices his profession not to serve an apathetic congregation or superiors stuck in the mud of convention but to realize the highest potential of his art. This attitude emerges distinctly from the dry bureaucratic transcript, which furthermore reveals flashes of defiance in Bach. The student and choir prefect Johann Andreas Rambach, four years Bach's senior, has tattled on him, saying that Bach intentionally played too briefly after being reprimanded for playing the organ too long. But Rambach then must answer charges himself, because "on Sunday last he went to the wine cellar during the sermon." He is warned not to create any problems himself, and is punished with four times two hours in jail.

As can be seen from other official minutes, this is neither the first nor the last reprimand Bach will receive for not playing *figuraliter* in his church, or, in other words, for not performing vocal music. To be sure, the employment contract issued on 9 August in the name of the reigning imperial count, Anton Günther von Schwarzburg und Hohnstein, Lord of Arnstadt, etc., mentions only that Bach is supposed to "ply the organ suitably,"[32] yet that does not exclude the performance of small liturgical concertos and cantatas with an ensemble made up primarily of soloists. This type of musical performance in conjunction with the worship service is felt to be modern, and at least in northern Germany it tends to compete with performances by the student choir that the cantor conducts. The musicians perform in the organ loft, while the student choir generally sings in the choir stalls or in a separate loft. In central Germany the modern practice in young Bach's day seems not to have been widespread; the Eisenach rector Christian Juncker considers it a novelty in 1708 when the new ducal music ensemble performs on the first day of Christmas "in the organ loft, with only instruments and a tenor solo."[33]

Since the early cantatas by Bach, written during his time in Arnstadt or Mühlhausen, in part represent such organ music, it is hard to grasp at first why he refuses so obstinately to expand his field of activity in Arnstadt in this way. Initially he indicates that he would gladly participate in making vocal music, "if only a *Director musices* were there"—in other words, a conductor. Although the superintendent has already stated clearly that they cannot provide "a kapellmeister," Bach also demands a "proper *Director*" the second time he is taken to task. The third time around Bach merely intends to "express it in writing," since the reproaches are becoming more threatening: "If he considers it no shame to be with the church and to accept payment, he should likewise not be ashamed to make music with the pupils as ordered and until otherwise indicated. For the intention is that the latter should practice, so as to be more useful for music making in the future."[34]

On closer examination, Bach's behavior is more understandable. The organist has "the reputation of not having good relations with the pupils." According to the testimony of the pupil Johann Heinrich Geyersbach, Bach called him a "rapscallion of a bassoonist." On another occasion, when Bach is crossing the street "with his tobacco pipe in his mouth," this same student, who is three years older than he, confronts him—and Bach draws his sword. Bach for his part testifies that "rather late at night" Geyersbach with six other students as backup "followed him over the market square and attacked him with a cudgel" so that he was forced to defend himself with his sword— probably a relic from his days in Lüneburg.[35]

Whether the incriminating term "rapscallion of a bassoonist" (*zippel Fagottist*) is meant to suggest that when the person in question plays the bassoon, it sounds like someone breaking wind after he has eaten green onions, we cannot be certain. But clearly the conflict grows out of Bach's professional concerns: he has trouble with the students, is dissatisfied with their musical ability, and is not willing to make the effort needed to raise standards in a position that he views as merely a springboard. He does organize performances of vocal music in Arnstadt now and then—although not with the students assigned to him. Among the many criticisms voiced by the Arnstadt consistory is the charge that "not long since he brought a strange damsel into the choir and let her make music."[36] We do not know whether the young woman was his relative and later wife Maria Barbara Bach; but that the cantata "Nach dir, Herr, verlanget mich," BWV 150, may have been performed with a splendid soprano and an inadequate bassoonist is a matter to which we return in a later chapter. At any rate, the record of the consistory meeting tells us that Bach occasionally looked outside the student body for performers.

But back to the organ playing. Bach's duties in this area are not demanding. The organist is expected to appear for the main worship services on Sundays and holidays, for the prayer service on Mondays, for vespers on Wednesdays, and for the early service on Thursdays. He must provide, as the occasion requires, a prelude and postlude and a choral introduction and accompaniment. He must also improvise or accompany the choir during Communion. Such a schedule leaves ample time for his own studies. "Already in his youth, simple reflection enabled him to become a pure and strong master of the fugue," Carl Philipp Emanuel Bach comments, writing to Forkel in 1775, in a variation on his formulation in the obituary. In this context he names Bach's "favorites," who were all "strong masters of the fugue": Froberger, Kerll, Pachelbel, Frescobaldi, Fischer, Strungk, "several excellent old French" organists, and, last but not least, the north German masters Buxtehude, Reinken, Bruhns, and Böhm.[37] Bruhns is already dead, and as far as we can tell, Bach already benefited from hearing Böhm and Reinken during his early time in Lüneburg. That leaves Buxtehude, who possesses the additional advantage of being not only a great master of the organ but also a significant composer of vocal music and the initiator of the famed Lübeck evening concerts, at which the almost seventy-year-old offers a wealth of musical delights, from solo cantatas somewhat influenced by early Pietism to vocal performances with a large ensemble, and multipart oratorios.

Since these performances always take place in November and December, it is hardly a coincidence that after two years in Arnstadt Bach finds himself drawn to Lübeck in late fall. He does not want to return to Arnstadt before experiencing two "extraordinaire" evening concerts on 2 and 3 December 1705, featuring works Buxtehude has composed in modern madrigal form with choruses, recitatives, and arias in the spirit of an oratorio with allegorical figures. One is a grand funeral piece for Kaiser Leopold I, the other a festive coronation piece for his successor, Joseph I. Music "by all the choruses and organs," several choirs, twenty-five violins playing in unison, muted and unmuted trumpets and trombones, drums, French horns, and oboes—such a mass of performers may well have been a new sound to Bach. And there seems to be a slightly ironic undertone in his explanation to the consistory in Arnstadt that he came to understand "various things about his art" in Lübeck.

For Bach it is worthwhile to undertake the long journey and to look for lodgings and possibly some source of financial support in a strange city, a remarkable display of initiative—of the kind encouraged by the superintendent. To be sure, the decision to go to Lübeck did not come out of the blue: in 1703 a relative, Johann Christoph Bach, is living in Lübeck. He is the son of that organist in Eisenach, Johann Christoph Bach, whose acquaintance we made in the context of Bach's early training. The father has died, and the eldest brother, Johann Nicolaus, who is the organist in Jena, is trying from there to persuade the authorities in Eisenach to engage young Johann Christoph, seven years his junior, as the father's successor; the latter is on his way there now for a possible audition.

Because the town council instead wants to make the intermediary himself the new organist,[38] Johann Christoph may have decided to stay in Lübeck, which would put him in the position two years later to take in a relative named Johann Sebastian. If, on the other hand, he is back home by 1705, he can at least serve as a good source of familial advice, perhaps even making the crucial point that Lübeck is always worth the trip. It is well documented that the Bachs had festive family gatherings; the wedding medley (Quodlibet), BWV 524, that young Bach wrote, probably in collaboration with another family member, gives musical expression to the jollity and imaginativeness characteristic of such reunions.

But for now Bach is still in Arnstadt, processing impressions from his visit to Lübeck. He cannot yet apply what he heard and learned there to his vocal music, but to his organ music yes. Here we can literally put our hands on the influence of Buxtehude. This biographical chapter, however, is not the place for a discussion, general or specific, of Bach's compositions for the organ during his time in Arnstadt and Mühlhausen. Although we have few documents dating from this period about his life, the ones we do have must be mentioned here.

The earliest autograph score still extant was in all likelihood composed no later than 1705 and bears the watermark of an Arnstadt paper mill. It is the organ chorale "Wie schön leuchtet der Morgenstern," BWV 739. The script looks juvenile but already has some of the handsome flourishes that will be so impressive in the manuscripts of the violin solos: it is remarkable that an intellectual composer like Bach should have the most beautiful, flowing hand in the history of music. Even Richard Wagner, with his likewise wonderful, almost calligraphic scores, must take a back seat to Bach.

The preservation of this autograph is a stroke of luck, for aside from the *Orgelbüchlein,* hardly any manuscript with keyboard or organ music in his hand has survived from the Arnstadt, Mühlhausen, and Weimar periods. To be sure, many important works have been preserved in copies made by music lovers and pupils of Bach. Indispensable though they are, they hardly help us when it comes to dating the original works. They also raise questions as to the authenticity of a given piece or the reliability of the copy. A good example is the Toccata in D Minor, BWV 565, perhaps Bach's most famous piece for the organ—if indeed it is by Bach.

In recent times, the authenticity of this piece, generally considered an early work, has been challenged because of its many unison parts, excessive use of harmony, and paucity of contrapuntal effects.[39] The transmission of this work is in fact questionable: the copyist of the most important version is Johannes Ringk, generally a reliable and knowledgeable source, but an entire generation after Bach and therefore not a contemporary witness. A number of features in this showy piece seem inconsistent. But would we consider Bach the composer of the capriccio BWV 992—of which more later—if the evidence were weaker? Instead of simply expressing doubts, we would do better to consider the origins of the work: could BWV 565 have developed out of a violin composition[40] or, perhaps more plausibly, from a toccata for the keyboard?

To bridge the gap between the missing originals of individual works and later copies, we have three important manuscript collections. Although their precise dating cannot be established, it can be narrowed sufficiently to allow us to designate the works they contain as "early" or written at the latest during the first period in Weimar.

The *Möller Manuscript* and the *Andreas Bach Book,* both named for temporary owners but put together by Bach's brother Johann Christoph, have been mentioned.[41] The third in this group is the *Plauen Organ Book,* largely written just before and around 1710 and extant today only as a photocopy.

Such collections served practical purposes; thus the *Plauen Organ Book* contains chorale preludes by Johann Pachelbel, Friedrich Wilhelm Zachow, Johann Michael Bach, Johann Sebastian Bach (BWV 720, 735a, and 739), and others.

The compilations by Johann Christoph have additionally, and primarily, the character of private collections. Utterly unsystematic, they contain, often in no particular order, whatever the compiler considered important and entertaining in the genre of contemporary keyboard music. The scores can be copies made from printed or handwritten versions, but there are also personal notes by composers and even tabular lists of ornaments.

When it comes to Johann Sebastian, these collections allow us to glimpse the context in which his early compositions appeared and were experienced by him. It speaks for itself that he is the only member of the Bach family to be extensively represented in both volumes. In the *Möller Manuscript,* the name Bach is even inscribed symbolically: the fragment of a composition, which another source allows us to identify as a "capriccio on BACH by Joh. Andreas Bach,"[42] unmistakably displays these tonal letters at the end of the composition and thus constitutes the first evidence of a conscious musical allusion to the name:

In both the *Möller Manuscript* and the *Andreas Bach Book,* north German keyboard music of the Buxtehude generation predominates, in the form of suites, toccatas, preludes, and fugues. Bach, who entered compositions in both volumes around 1705 or 1706, thus helping shape the collections, would have found there, among other things, biblical sonatas by Johann Kuhnau, a chaconne by Jean Baptiste Lully, and keyboard suites by Nicolas Antoine Le Bègue and Louis Marchand—later his rival at the Dresden cembalo competition.

The *Möller Manuscript* contains a copy of the previously mentioned choral fantasy "Wie schön leuchtet der Morgenstern," BWV 739; the preludes and fugues BWV 531, 549a, and 896; the canzona BWV 588; the toccata BWV 912a; the sonata BWV 967; the suite movements BWV 832; and the prelude and partita BWV 833. The only work preserved in Bach's own hand deserves particular mention: the Prelude and Fugue in G Minor, BWV 535a. The end is missing, but a copy with additions in Bach's own hand exists, presumably made only a few years later, in 1710 or 1711, and an early example of his habit of continuing to work over a piece—probably in the context of his teaching. The revision, BWV 535, shows a clear tendency toward making the movement more consistent and the counterpoint more disciplined: whenever fanciful and bizarre effects cannot be integrated into a meaningful inner structure, they are banished from the piece. In retrospect, both versions are valid—as stations on the way to early mastery.

Against this biographical backdrop, one of the Bach works in the *Möller Manuscript* seems worth lingering over: the *Capriccio on the Departure of the Beloved Brother*, BWV 992. Although we have not been able to establish what necessitates this farewell to a much-loved brother, this brilliant little piece was certainly written before 1707, providing evidence of a composer around twenty who was as sure of himself as he was spirited.

The *Andreas Bach Book*, whose contents show it to be just a few years younger than the *Möller Manuscript*, contains the only work Johann Sebastian transcribed in north German organ tablature: the Fantasia in C Minor, BWV 1121 (extended numeration). It has been identified recently as his work and provides striking evidence of his familiarity with the system of alphabetic notation used often in northern Germany but far less frequently in his native region for transcribing entire works. It would be good to know what occasioned this particular choice of transcription; perhaps Bach wanted to tell his older brother: What I learned in northern Germany should not be left out of your keyboard book! The composition itself clearly shows the great influence on Bach exercised by the organ works of Buxtehude, Bruhns, and Böhm.

The *Andreas Bach Book* also offers us an early version of the famous Passacaglia in C Minor, BWV 582, as well as the organ fugues BWV 574b and 578; the *Organ Fantasia,* BWV 563; the organ chorale "Gott, durch deine Güte," BWV 724; and such keyboard works as the overture BWV 820; the toccatas BWV 910, 911, and 916; the prelude BWV 921, with the final measures in Bach's hand; the Fantasia and Fugue, BWV 944; the fugue BWV 949; and the *Aria variata* (Variations on a Twelve-Measure Aria), BWV 989.

The distinction between organ and keyboard works made in the Bach-Werke-Verzeichnis is not entirely unproblematic, since in the seventeenth and early eighteenth centuries composers often assumed a shared literature for the two types of instruments. In recent years, the "clavier" toccatas in particular have been energetically claimed for the organ,[43] then equally energetically for the piano, with the argument that the figuration in the toccatas was clearly intended for the evanescent notes of the harpsichord and not for the sustained notes of the organ.[44]

In conjunction with the keyboard and organ books that provide such significant information on Bach's early compositions for these instruments, one must mention a source that has only recently come to light and represents a parallel to the *Plauen Organ Book* with its more than 280 organ chorales: the *Neumeister Collection,* which contains 82 arrangements of chorales.[45] Although it was compiled after 1790, its repertory essentially mirrors the organ chorale as it was practiced around 1700 in central Germany. Johann Christoph, Johann Michael, and Johann Sebastian turn up with particular frequency, the last with the thirty *Unica,* BWV 1090–95 and 1097–1120, among other works. Although we do not know what originals the transcriber, Johann Gottfried Neumeister, had at his disposal, it may be assumed that the collection is based chiefly on a repertory circulating in the Bach family. A notation in Ernst Ludwig Gerber's 1812 encyclopedia of composers reveals that the genre of the chorale prelude ranked very high with the Bachs: "I have in my possession a folio amounting to 246 pages from the papers of this famous family of Thuringian organists; it contains 201 handsomely and precisely written figured and figural chorales for the organ." Among the composers, Gerber names Johann Bernhard, Johann Christoph, Johann Michael, and Johann Sebastian Bach, along with Georg Böhm, Dietrich Buxtehude, Johann Caspar Ferdinand Fischer, Johann Kuhnau, Johann Pachelbel, Nicolaus Vetter, Johann Gottfried Walther, and Friedrich Wilhelm Zachow.[46]

The organ chorales by Johann Sebastian Bach preserved by Neumeister certainly belong in the orbit of these masters; written presumably before 1710, they show us a Bach well on his way to the *Orgelbüchlein,* BWV 599–644.

Although the sources for our knowledge of Bach as a young keyboard and organ virtuoso may be sparse, they are telling. To be sure, they do not allow us to reach any conclusions as to how large the actual body of work from that period may have been. They also offer few clues that might allow us to reconstruct in any detail Bach's early career as a composer. Did that career already begin in Ohrdruf, under the watchful eye of Bach's older brother, a student of Pachelbel's? Did the choirboy compose during his Lüneburg period under the influence of Böhm? Which of his works belong to the early years when he was an organist in Arnstadt, which to the period after that significant journey to Buxtehude's Lübeck? What was composed during the months in Mühlhausen, between Bach's move to Weimar and the composition of the *Orgelbüchlein*?

Increasingly sophisticated methods of source critique and analysis are allowing scholars to come up with answers to such questions.[47] While we can benefit from their acuity, we should bear in mind that their hypotheses necessarily rest on the assumption that a composer's oeuvre develops in a straight line toward higher quality, at least within a given genre. This concept of evolution cannot be rejected out of hand, yet we must ask whether it is legitimate to view Bach as a Beethoven type, purposefully setting out to advance a step from one work to the next.

Undoubtedly there are technical standards below which no composer wants to fall once he has attained them. But for one thing, Bach composed far more works for particular occasions than later composers: often he may have had to satisfy the demands of specific patrons or conditions of performance, and we do not know to what extent he experienced such requirements as limitations, or when and where he made compromises or even incorporated thematically his willingness to compromise into his compositional strategy. For another thing, he evidently had his own conception of how his art would mature: he often allowed early ideas to live on in later works and older notions to inform newer ones. No matter how we may speculate about Bach's "development" as a composer, we should not overlook the tension between his desire to find new solutions and his desire to preserve the achievements of the past.

Once we recognize that the available material does not permit definitive answers to all these questions, we are free to enjoy the image that emerges from the existing sources. It is clear that Bach delves relatively early into all the genres of organ and keyboard music. He devotes a great deal of effort to arranging choral works from both the central and northern German traditions; he composes toccatas that have the hallmarks of virtuoso pieces yet are also strict fugues; he takes up the genres of the canzona, the French overture, the suite, song variations in the Italian style, and the program sonata.

As the repertory in the keyboard and organ books indicates, Bach is not composing in isolation but in regular contact with other members of the family active as composers and with full knowledge of an extensive repertory of significant works of the most varied character. The Neumeister collection documents for the organ chorale what is probably true for the other genres: Johann Sebastian is rooted in his family but soon absorbs with avidity an astonishingly broad repertory of the music of his era; at a relatively young age he has an impressive familiarity with German and European styles. On this

foundation he develops his own art, which more and more transcends the work of his contemporaries in quality, originality, and intellectual consistency, and soon gains recognition as outstanding.

Although Bach's epoch is not one that is waiting for a genius, the
knowledgeable observers in his familial and regional surroundings
sense that a person of greatness is developing in their midst. There
is no other way to explain the professional respect he receives, the
presence of his works in collections, and the growing number of
pupils sent to him. The philosopher Hans-Georg Gadamer suggests
as much at the beginning of his early lecture "Bach and Weimar":

> *Johann Sebastian Bach is a child of Thuringia, not the mysteri-*
> *ous product of a destiny that so often allows a genius to appear*
> *unexpectedly and inexplicably in the midst of an indifferent*
> *world and among an indifferent clan. Johann Sebastian Bach*
> *grew up in a music-loving and pious region as the son of a fam-*
> *ily in which a solid legacy of musical gifts had been accumulating*
> *for generations, and his own sons still displayed a goodly portion*
> *of this family heritage.*[48]

MÜHLHAUSEN

If the musician serving as organist at the New Church in Arnstadt
between 1703 and 1707 had been called not Johann Sebastian but
Wilhelm Friedemann Bach, a biographer would have noted conflict
with the authorities, unwillingness to adapt, disobedience—things
would not work out for this man Bach! Wilhelm Friedemann, invited in 1746 to become the organist in Halle, must fulfill the requirement in his contract—handed down from one generation to the
next, and imposed on his father as well—that he accompany the
congregation's singing "slowly and without particular coloration."[49]
As "director musices" he may perform figural music in any setting or
with whatever coloration he pleases, yet he is reprimanded for lending out drums without authorization, for exceeding the leave he was
granted for his father's funeral, etc., etc. In 1764, when he asks to be

relieved of his duties, although he has no other position lined up, an inventory is promptly scheduled, which establishes that a violin bow, a flute, a cornet, a trombone, and several strings are missing, whereas the number of trumpets has miraculously increased—an occasion for recriminations that will hang over him during the last two decades of his life, which he must endure without any guarantees of security.

How different things were for young Johann Sebastian! The wrangling in Arnstadt seems to have had no lasting ill effects, or at least not to reach the ears of people in Mühlhausen, a good sixty kilometers away, for on 15 June 1707 he is installed there as the organist of St. Blasius's. The newly created position is different from the one at Arnstadt's New Church. Although Mühlhausen's stature as a free imperial city has declined with the passage of time, the town still has its self-respect. At its head, after the joint mayors, comes a "senate" with all sorts of subdivisions; and the councilmen who belong to it have a keen sense of their own worth and how it should be celebrated. Thus, for instance, the music performed in church for the annual inauguration of the new council is printed not only as a text but also as a score, an expensive procedure and therefore unusual during this period.

When the librettist writes the words to the cantata "Gott ist mein König," BWV 71, for which Bach is to compose the music, he goes beyond the usual practice: not only alluding to the actual occasion but also masterfully combining the "paternal protection"—already suggested in the printed title—exercised by the old and the new town "regime" and the "deserving Lord Burgomasters" with concepts of honor, dovelike innocence, strength, good fortune, and victory. The texts to Bach's cantatas for the Leipzig council elections will be more modest: in them it is possible to express a direct request, as in the cantata "Ihr Tore zu Zion," BWV 193, where the text reads, "Let them flourish and be just / who hold for you the laws in trust / and not forget the poor among us."

Bach inherits a not inconsiderable legacy as the successor to Johann Georg Ahle, chiefly known as a composer of songs but also active as a music theoretician. The organist at St. Blasius also has some say when it comes to the composition and performance of figural music, as can be seen from his right to compose the annual cantata for the council elections, the so-called council piece, usually scored for a large ensemble. Yet at his installation, when Bach is inaugurated "by means of a handshake,"[50] mention is made only of his obligation to play the organ at St. Blasius on Sundays, holidays, and other feast days. There is no special reference to his taking turns as the organist at the church of the Augustinian nuns, for which he is to receive separate remuneration.

It is not possible to reconstruct exactly how Bach secured the organist's position in Mühlhausen. When he appears for an audition on 24 April 1701, Easter Sunday, Johann Gottfried Walther, a distant relative and a good friend in later years, is already out of the running. In expectation of an invitation, Walther sent in two "church pieces" for the Sexagesimae Sunday services occurring eight weeks earlier in the liturgical year, but he withdrew his application after learning that his chances were slim.

But why would someone submit two complete vocal compositions when he is hoping to become the organist, not the cantor? Can Walther's memory be playing tricks on him when he recalls the incident thirty-two years later?[51] Did he perhaps compose the two pieces independently? And what did Bach submit? Scholars believe it may have been "Christ lag in Todesbanden," BWV 4, which is plausible but remains a hypothesis. It would be more interesting to know what Bach played on the organ, but no evidence exists; the records show only his installation.

Once the town council has promised the position to Bach on 24 May, he appears on 14 June for a discussion of the contract. Such a procedure is not standard practice, for young candidates had little room for negotiation. But Bach presents himself self-confidently: he demands a salary to match the one he received in Arnstadt, which is about twenty gulden more than his honored predecessor's. Additionally he asks the council for the same in-kind benefits his predecessor received: twenty-four bushels of grain, two cords of firewood, six bundles of kindling—this last "delivered to the door instead of to the field," as he stipulates.[52] All these terms having been approved, on 29 June 1707 Bach is able to return to the Arnstadt council the keys to the organ and take up his new position at once.

In Mühlhausen Bach's new organ, like the one in Arnstadt, has only two manuals. That may be one of the key factors behind the proposal for an extensive rebuilding of the organ that Bach presents on 21 February 1708. Jakob Adlung, one of the fathers of organ research, provides a description of the completed project in his standard work, *Musica Mechanica Organoedi,* published posthumously in 1768.[53] From it we can glean what Bach considered a well-equipped organ at the time:

Hauptwerk	Brustwerk	Rückpositiv	Pedal
Principal 8′	Principal 2′	Gedackt 8′	Untersatz 32′
Oktave 4′	Mixtur 3fach	Salicional 4′	Principal 16′
Oktave 2′	Shalmei 8′	Spitzflöte 2′	Subbass 16′
Cymbal 2fach	Quinte 1½′	Sesquialtera	Oktave 8′
Mixtur 4fach	Terz 1⅗′	Principal 4′	Oktave 4′
Violdigamba 8′	Flöte 4′	Quintaton 8′	Mixtur 4fach
Gedackt 4′	Stillgedackt 8′	Quinteflöte	Posaune 16′
Quinte 3′		Oktave 2′	Trumpet 8′
Fagott 16′		Cymbal 3fach	Cornetbass 2′
Quintatön 16′			Rohrflötenbass 1′
Sesquialtera 2fach			

The most costly item on Bach's wish list is a new *Brustwerk,* which will give the organ a third manual. Additionally he makes many suggestions for small changes: the sound of the bass register should have "better solemnity" (*bessere gravitaet*); a new *Fagott* 16′ will "serve for all sorts of new *inventionibus*" and "resonate very *delicat* with the Music." The new viola da gamba 8′ in the *Oberwerk* will "concord admirably" with the *Salicional* 4′ in the *Rückpositiv;* the *Stillgedacht* 8′ in the new *Brustwerk* should be made of wood rather than metal, and as such will "accord perfectly with the Music."

These explanations are probably intended to reinforce the funders' impression of their organist's competence and underline the necessity of the project. They also convey a sense of the pleasure Bach must feel at the thought of the rebuilt organ; a young virtuoso is obviously not satisfied with an instrument that is simply in good repair and well balanced; he needs a powerful bass and interesting combinations of sounds such as one could admire in the Lübeck organs. The "music" to which certain registers would be particularly suited should be interpreted as vocal organ music, which Bach is apparently ready and eager to perform.

This is not to say that during the one year he spent in Mühlhausen he performed a good deal of such music and went beyond his official duties to compose the inaugural music for the new town council. Only the cantata "Aus der Tiefen rufe ich, Herr, zu dir," BWV 131, can be unambiguously recognized as organ music, in particular by the double indication on the original score that it had been performed by the organist Bach "at the wish" of the Mühlhausen pastor Georg Christian Eilmar. That the text expresses penitential impulses does not prove that it was written in response to the devastating fire that took place on 30 May 1707, before Bach's installation, and destroyed 360 houses in the lower town. It is unlikely that an individual pastor would have commissioned a piece of music for an official penitential service. Of course, the cantata could have been performed for an ordinary service during Communion; at least in northern Germany it was not unusual for organists to accommodate requests for special Communion music.

The music for the town council's swearing in, "Gott ist mein König," BWV 71, performed on 4 February 1708, for which Bach receives four gulden and twelve groschen, is his first composition to bear a distant resemblance to the splendor of the evening concerts in Lübeck. The rich instrumentation includes a "choir" of trumpets, with drums, recorders, violoncello, oboes, and strings, reinforced by the concertizing voice of the organ. The vocal choir is limited to four voices, which, however, can be differentiated at will into solo and tutti.

A Mühlhausen chronicle provides a detailed account of the traditional ceremonies that accompanied the swearing in of the new council until they were discontinued in 1758:

> *This grand ceremony was conducted as follows. On the previous day the Council Lane was strewn with sand, up to the steps of the church. On the day after Candlemas the new councilors were elected, and the following day the Council accession took place thus. In the morning between 7 and 8 o'clock the large bell was sounded all by itself; then the Council moved in procession from the town hall into the church. The detachment of riflemen and the young citizenry had to form an aisle of honor. The retiring Council led the procession, followed by the new one, and the end was brought up by the Council pages. The gentlemen of the third Council did not march in the procession, while 2 music ensembles on the Brotlaube and the Kämmerei played against one another with drums and trumpets. The worship service commenced with a hymn, "Praise be to God, &c.," followed by "O Lord, thy name we praise, &c.," whereupon the regent homily was delivered, and after the homily came music in which the new Council was wished good fortune vocaliter and instrumentaliter, which lasted an entire hour and was simply called the Small Council Piece. This work was always repeated on the following Sunday, in the afternoon, at St. Blasius's. After the benediction, the hymn "Lord God, thou art eternal, &c." was performed. Thereupon the newly elected Council stepped forward and lined up in order of rank in the church portal, whereupon they had to swear their oath out of doors, which was read to them by the Syndicus, standing in the doorway. The procession thereupon recessed as it had come, except that the new Council took the lead. Afterward, a great celebration was held at the town hall, to which the baker's guild had to contribute a cake known as the Mahlblatz, the Mühlhausen version of Möhlplatz.*[54]

"Jesu Juva" is the motto inscribed on Bach's first precisely dated autograph score. It is followed, in ornamental script, by the title of the work, "Gott ist mein König," then the instrumentalization, preceded by the general instruction "ab 18. è 22." At the bottom we find in Italian the date and the designation of authorship: "Del anno 1708./da Gio: Bast: Bach. Org: Molhusino." Here there is no need for dedications to the town government and its representatives to take up four-fifths of the title page, as will soon be the case in the printed version; here the young organist is free to enjoy without restraint his first major and publicly appreciated opus, and the title "Gott ist mein König" may carry considerable symbolic significance for him, a man who all his life will have difficulties with earthly authorities.

Although handwritten title pages of the time often display the indication "18. è 22." in this or a similar form, the presence of these instructions as to the orchestral and voice setting of the work gives one pause. In general they indicate that a four-part choir will be used, in addition to fourteen instruments: the tutti sections are to be sung by eight voices, the solo sections by four. But what does "voice" mean—is it identical with "part," or perhaps "voice with written notes," or with "singer"? To this day, the directive "4 è 8" is usually interpreted to mean that there is a choir, and in this choir are four singers for the solo sections. Yet despite its long tradition, this interpretation is by no means unassailable; might the indications refer instead to the actual number of performers?

That would mean that a choir normally consisted of soloists and was doubled in size—from four to eight singers—only when the score had specifically distinguished tutti and solo sections. In the latter part of the seventeenth century, this practice in fact seems to have been fairly common, at least when we look at the new concert-style church music, which was "musicked," usually in addition to the traditional choral polyphony or homophony performed by the school choir, under the direction of the cantor.

Around 1662, the church composer Augustin Pfleger, active in northern Germany, received instructions from Duke Gustav Adolf of Mecklenburg-Güstrow to calculate what it would cost to put together a small court music ensemble; he based his estimate on having two boys to sing the soprano parts, as well as one male alto, one tenor, and one bass. When the duke then expressed his wish to have the pupils of the "chorus musicus" included in the church music, Pfleger responded entirely in the spirit of the distinction between the old and new church music: the students could perhaps be used for a "complete *Choro*," but "to allow the same to perform in *Concerti* would, in my opinion, produce a poor *contento*."[55]

For some years now Joshua Rifkin has maintained that even Bach's choir was made up of soloists.[56] The numerous recordings by his Bach Ensemble allow one to form a clear picture of how this would have worked in practice. This topic will be dealt with in detail later, but for now a warning flag should go up whenever Bach's "choir" is mentioned: for the most part, the vocal works performed in the pre-Leipzig years probably involved only soloists. Such an arrangement seems obvious in any case for the Arnstadt and Mühlhausen organ works; but in Weimar and Cöthen, too, Bach may have operated not with a choir of students but with a small group of court singers.

Bach uses the year in Mühlhausen to enter the married state. Described in the church register as "most honorable gentleman" and "single fellow and Organist at St. Blasius in Mühlhausen," he marries on 17 October 1707 Maria Barbara Bach, his cousin twice removed and half a year older than he was. After the death of her mother, she and her sisters were taken in by the mayor of Arnstadt, Martin Feldhaus, who was related to the family. She appears in the register as "the youngest maiden daughter of the late honorable Herr Johann Michael Bach, organist in Gehren and famed for his art." In his genealogy, Bach will later call his father-in-law an "able composer,"[57] and indeed at the beginning of the nineteenth century the lexicographer Ernst Ludwig Gerber was acquainted with "72 different fugal and figured choral preludes" composed by him, of which twenty-four can be found in the Neumeister collection of organ chorales, which will be discussed below.[58]

On 29 December 1708, when Johann Sebastian and Maria Barbara Bach celebrate the baptism of their first child, Catharina

Dorothea, the family is already in Weimar, Bach having requested release from his employment in Mühlhausen on 25 June of that year. Although only a year has passed since he assumed the position, the city council can hardly stand in his way, for according to the prevailing custom, a summons to the court of a ruling prince takes precedence. The resignation is accepted, however, only "with great regret,"[59] if later oral reports are to be believed, and on the condition that Bach see to it that the reconstruction of the organ is completed. In the end, everything seems to have been resolved amicably, otherwise he would hardly have been commissioned the following year to compose another cantata for the swearing in of the new council, a piece of which today no trace exists. Bach's request for dismissal contains the following passage:

> *Now, God has brought it to pass that an unexpected change should offer itself to me, in which I see the possibility of a more adequate living and the achievement of my goal of a well-regulated church music without further vexation, since I have received the gracious admission of His Serene Highness of Saxe-Weimar into his Court Capelle and Chamber Music.*[60]

Since the author of this request has earlier indicated that because of his increased household expenses he is able to "live but poorly," it is understandable that a position at court and better remuneration should prove tempting. At first sight, his assertion that he will be able to pursue his goal of "a well-regulated church music" more successfully as a court organist than as an organist in the service of a town makes less sense. But the passage immediately preceding the one quoted above provides a further explanation:

> *Although I should always have gladly fulfilled the goal of performing a well-regulated church music, to the Glory of God and in conformity with your will, and would, according to my modest ability, have furthered as much as possible the church music flourishing in almost every township, and often better than the harmony fashioned in this place, and therefore have amassed*

from far and wide, not without cost, a goodly store of the choicest church pieces, as I have conscientiously delivered the project for remedying the faults of the organ and should gladly have performed every other obligation of my office: yet it has not been possible to accomplish all this without obstacles, and there is, at present, little appearance that in future this may change (although it would give great pleasure to the souls belonging to this Church).[61]

The tone reminds us of the bold one Bach occasionally struck in Arnstadt: in many of the surrounding villages the level of figural music is higher than in the free Reich city of Mühlhausen; since no remedy is in sight, the faithful of St. Blasius will probably have to make do without the appropriate "pleasure" for some time, in other words, accept sacrifices in the spiritual and aesthetic sense. Yet Bach himself has done everything to serve his ultimate goal, even establishing a collection of exemplary pieces of church music. If this acquisition, as has recently been speculated,[62] consisted merely of the "old Bach family archive," it would not do much to strengthen his argument. For this collection, which he probably acquired from family members and added to himself, must be pictured as traditional in character rather than as a mirror of modern tendencies in sacred music.

Whatever the case, Bach expresses the greatest dissatisfaction with the state of vocal church music in Mühlhausen. Should this posture be construed as a tactical offensive, intended to preempt objections to his request for dismissal? Or do concrete facts justify his dissatisfaction? The council is very pleased with Bach's achievements in the realm of figural music. He is asked to compose the cantata for the council swearing in not only in the year of his departure, 1708, but also for 1709 and even 1710 from his post in Weimar. We may thus suppose that Bach is annoyed at not being given sufficient scope: in Arnstadt he was supposed to make music but refused because of inadequate conditions; in Mühlhausen he wants to become more involved but is not allowed to!

In this context, his reference to the "goal" of a "well-regulated" church music loses the nimbus it has acquired in the Bach literature. He is not referring in a general sense to his intention of dedicating his life to church music; if that were the case, how could he in good conscience have gone to Cöthen to take up a position with duties related only marginally to church music, and been contented there? Rather he is speaking of a specific goal with regard to sacred music. Figural music must be regulated and composed; there must be an organizational structure in which the various areas of responsibility are clearly delineated and adequate resources are provided, to do justice to the "current state of music."

This last formulation occurs in the "Short but Most Necessary Draft for a Well-Appointed Church Music, with Certain Modest Reflections on the Decline of the Same" that the cantor of St. Thomas will address twenty-two years later to the Leipzig town council.[63] In both cases, Bach's desire to work under "regulated" conditions takes precedence; his refusal to make music in Arnstadt stemmed from this same objection—he was prepared to play the organ but not to direct all the church music under inadequate conditions.

Here, as before, Bach shows himself to be a self-confident and logical artist who makes it clear in every situation that good music requires excellent organizational and material conditions. Much later, in 1730, he will comment in a letter to his old schoolmate Georg Erdmann that in Cöthen he had "a gracious prince, who both cherished and understood Music," and he accordingly expected to spend the rest of his life there.[64] These words express pleasure at finding in Cöthen well-ordered circumstances—at least initially.

In Mühlhausen Bach finds no such circumstances. It is taken for granted that he will serve not only as the organist at St. Blasius's but also as the de facto director of church music for the entire town, even though his contract makes no mention of such an expectation. Since the members of the town council seem to be on his side, he was likely carrying out their wishes when he attempted to put Mühlhausen's church music on an orderly footing. It is easy to imagine the difficulties he encountered in this endeavor.

As mentioned above, the organist of St. Blasius's has occupied an influential position for many generations. It speaks for itself that when Bach composes the "Council Piece" and directs its performance by an obviously distinguished ensemble, he is producing the most notable composition of the year. The instrumentalists on whose services he calls are the council musicians, who shortly before his arrival sought confirmation of their privileged position, from which we can deduce that there are other musical groups in the town eager to perform similar services for pay.[65] Two teachers at the secondary school also function as cantors: Johann Bernhard Stier at the Divi Blasii, and Johann Heinrich Melchior Scheiner at the other of the two principal churches, Beatae Mariae Virginis. Contemporary documents indicate that the two cantors lead a "chorus musicus" or a "chorus symphoniacus."[66]

Bach may have hoped to introduce in Mühlhausen the model he just saw in operation in Lübeck. There, although it was not explicitly prescribed, the organist at St. Mary's, Buxtehude, was in charge of all activities related to sacred music. That such a model could be incorporated into a contract was something Bach would experience in 1713, when he applied for the organist's position at the Frauenkirche in Halle. Article 2 in the document drawn up for him there stipulates that he will

> ordinarily—on high holy and other feast days, as well as on every third Sunday—present, along with the Cantor and the Choir Students, as well as with the Town Musicians and other instrumentalists, a moving and fine-sounding work of sacred music; and on extraordinary occasions—on second and third feast days—perform short figural pieces with the Cantor and the Students, and also at times with various violins and other instruments; and conduct all this in such a way that the members of the Congregation shall be the more inspired and refreshed in worship and in their love of hearkening to the Word of God.[67]

This is an astonishingly clear directive for modern church music: the organist of the principal church in the town "conducts," that is, bears responsibility for, all the vocal music for church services in a dual function: he both provides the traditional "cantoral music" in collaboration with the cantor and bears full responsibility for the modern "organ music," in which mostly shorter solo performances occur, though they may be accompanied by highly skilled instrumentalists.

We can detect the influence exerted in Halle by the Pietist theologian and pastor August Hermann Francke from the explicit references in this document to the meaning and purpose of sacred music. That such music is intended to glorify God is remarkably not stressed; the ad hominem function of church music occupies the foreground; "moving" music, or music that stirs the soul, is intended to inspire and refresh the congregation in its worship and its love for the word of God. It is no accident that this formulation comes about in cooperation with or even on the recommendation of Pietist circles. On the one hand the approach is modern, in that it shifts responsibility for figural music from the office of the cantor, whose pedagogical function has been increasingly attenuated over the centuries, to the position of the organist, who has greater musical expertise and awareness of current musical taste. On the other hand, this arrangement nicely accommodates Pietism, because so long as it is practiced in a spirit of faith and without vanity, the more modern music, with its emphasis on emotional effects, can move the hearts of Christians more effectively than cantorial music based on traditional forms.

In 1713 Bach decides to return the contract to Halle unsigned. He prefers to be promoted to concertmaster in Weimar. He would have been happy in Mühlhausen if the position had been created for him. But apparently such a thing is not to be. Cantors, council musicians, pastors, or the town council itself—either as a group or as individuals—may have expressed reservations, concerned about salary, privileges, spheres of influence, and so forth. All we know for certain is that Bach does not succeed in organizing the circumstances to suit him, which is hardly expected in the short space of a year. Now he will work to achieve his objective in another locale; even if he occupies a lesser position as court organist, a court offers the possibility of rising to the rank of kapellmeister and in that capacity having a free hand to organize things.

A prolonged and unproductive dispute between Superintendent Johann Adolph Frohne and Pastor Eilmar, thirteen years his junior, may also have played a role in Bach's departure from Mühlhausen. Although this theory, formulated and presented at length by Spitta, still enjoys currency in Bach scholarship,[68] there is not a shred of evidence to suggest that Bach was driven away by the "pastors' fruitless wrangling over Pietism and orthodoxy."[69] At issue in the continuing quarrel between the two theologians, neither of whom can be considered a real Pietist, is disagreement not over doctrinal matters, as Spitta posits, but over specific questions, such as whether sectarians should be coaxed back to the church through patient persuasion or castigated without mercy.[70] Although the learned disputes, which were conducted mainly in Latin, may have gone largely unnoticed by the townspeople, the two parties' public struggle for power certainly made itself felt. Yet even this conflict hardly tormented Bach enough to make him to give up his position before a year had elapsed.

Could Superintendent Frohne have been one of those who had no interest in Bach's ideas for organizing Mühlhausen's church music—perhaps because his nemesis Eilmar was on good terms with Bach, at least to the extent that he would later become godfather to Bach's first child? Perhaps the score of the cantata "Aus der Tiefen rufe ich, Herr, zu Dir," BWV 131, contains a reference to Eilmar's "longing" for the simple reason that Bach was waiting in vain for such "longings" on the part of the more highly placed superintendent, who was primarily responsible for St. Blasius's. But in that case, Eilmar's protection would have deserved explicit mention.

WEIMAR

The court in Weimar casts its eye on Bach as a successor to the court organist, Johann Effler, forced by illness to retire, and Bach is eager to go. Although the position offered to him ranks low in the court hierarchy, there are opportunities for advancement, and the salary is substantially higher than that in Mühlhausen, equal to that of Vice Kapellmeister Drese, with the exception of the benefits in kind. The order to the treasury issued by Duke Wilhelm Ernst on 20 June 1708 provides "our chamber musician and court organist" "with an annual salary and allowances" of "one hundred and fifty florins, in cash, eighteen bushels of grain, twelve bushels of barley, four cords of firewood, and thirty buckets of beer."[71] In 1711 the salary will be increased by fifty florins, and in 1713 by another fifteen or thirteen florins. Appointment as concertmaster in March 1714 guarantees Bach a salary of 250 florins.[72] Smaller sums of money came to him from the St. William's Fund, in payment for clavier lessons and instrument repairs commissioned by the duke, and so forth.

Did Bach wear livery as a member of the court ensemble? We cannot be sure, but an obituary for his ducal employer from the year 1730 includes the comment, "His hearing was on occasion delighted by 16 well-trained musicians clad in Haiduks' garb."[73]

When Bach arrives in Weimar on 14 July 1708, he receives an advance of ten gulden "for the conveyance hither of his furniture." His household includes his pregnant wife and her unmarried sister. His Mühlhausen pupil Johann Martin Schubart has also come along; after Bach's move to Cöthen, Schubart will assume the position of court organist in Weimar. He will not be Bach's only pupil, for Bach's reputation as a clavier and organ virtuoso has preceded him. According to the obituary, Bach "played for" Duke Wilhelm Ernst but did not have to submit to a formal audition.

The duke is in his forty-sixth year and has ruled Weimar for twenty-five. Since his early separation from his wife, he has lived alone and is considered a harsh ruler. His motto is "All with God." As a boy of seven, he mounted the pulpit of the court chapel on Ash Wednesday and delivered a sermon, prepared under the supervision of the court chaplain, on Apostles 16.31, soon to appear in print under the title "His Serene Highness the Preacher."[74] By now the church in the entire state of Weimar, and in particular the church consistory, has been enjoined to take its cue only from him. The duke has ordered the reintroduction of confirmation, convoked synods, and made personal inspections. Two years before his death he will establish a seminary for preachers and teachers.

As a religious leader, Wilhelm Ernst follows a middle course between orthodoxy and Pietism. Not at all hostile to the latter, he regularly conducts prayer services in the court chapel and has instituted daily Bible readings. The members of his entourage are strongly encouraged to go to confession and take Communion together; each of them must expect to be questioned by the duke on the content of the most recent sermon. Yet these practices do not stifle cultural and courtly life. In the previously mentioned obituary for the duke, we read, "He took earthly pleasure in lovely flowers and fruits, in good music, in a choice collection of Saxon coins, & an excell. Library."[75]

In the years before Bach's installation, comedies and operas were sometimes performed at court—among them one with the revealing title *Fidelity and Innocence Redeemed*. For the year 1700, the court lists include as many as three female and six male singers—falsettos, altos, tenors, and basses.[76] In 1706 Wilhelm Ernst builds Ettersburg, the summer residence where later Schiller will finish writing his play *Maria Stuart* and Goethe will play the role of Orestes in his own play *Iphigenia*.

The duke's abiding passion is music, and thus he favors the court ensemble, which suffers no significant losses during his reign. In 1714, the year Bach is appointed concertmaster, the ensemble has fourteen regular members: the kapellmeister and his deputy, the concertmaster, four violinists, a bassoonist, and six vocalists. The eight trumpeters and drummers on the list probably play only occasionally for church and chamber music performances. As concertmaster and even later as kapellmeister in Cöthen, Bach probably often sat at the cembalo, but also picked up a stringed instrument when needed. Carl Philipp Emanuel Bach writes around 1774 to Forkel:

> As the most knowledgeable expert and judge of harmony, he liked best to play the viola, with fitting loudness and softness. In his youth, and until the approach of old age, he played the violin with a pure, piercing tone, and thus kept the orchestra under

better control than he could have done with the harpsichord. He understood to perfection the possibilities of all stringed instruments. This is evidenced by his solos for the violin and for the violoncello without bass.[77]

Wilhelm Ernst, the elder of two brothers, ascends the ducal throne upon the death of his father in 1683. At first his coregent is Johann Ernst, later, from 1709 on, Johann Ernst's son Ernst August. The uncle and nephew do not get along and are constantly fighting; one time the older man has the younger man's advisers summarily arrested. Obviously the court musicians cannot remain untouched by these quarrels; although they are supposed to serve both dukes equally, Wilhelm Ernst wants to prohibit them from doing anything for his nephew. The nephew threatens reprisals if they comply with such orders.

Ernst August is a true connoisseur of music. He is adept at the trumpet and violin and takes an interest in dance entertainments. He also has a passion for the chase and "delights in military games."[78] The duke plays an active role in expanding the inventory of instruments and scores. He organizes organ concerts in the court chapel and finances the reconstruction of the organ by Heinrich Nicolaus Trebs in 1713–14.[79] In defiance of his uncle's disapproval, he has the court musicians perform in the Red Palace, his residence as coregent—for instance on the occasion of a birthday party for his younger half brother Johann Ernst.[80]

From the private treasury of the younger coregent come the smaller salary increases that Bach receives in the years 1716 and 1717. Altogether, Ernst August is one of the three rulers who, according to Bach's son Carl Philipp Emanuel, "loved him particularly and were also especially generous to him." The other two are Leopold of Anhalt-Cöthen and Christian von Weissenfels.[81]

More must be said here about Prince Johann Ernst. The birthday celebration just mentioned takes place at the end of 1713. At this time, the seventeen-year-old prince has completed his studies at Utrecht, visited Amsterdam, and brought home a quantity of musical scores. Now he is studying composition with his former keyboard teacher, Johann Gottfried Walther, organist at the Weimar town church, and is composing concertos, which have been partially preserved in Bach's arrangements for a keyboard instrument, BWV 592, 595, 982, 984, and 987. In July 1714 the young prince, seriously ill, leaves Weimar; a year later he dies in Frankfurt am Main.

In retrospect it is difficult to determine which specific suggestions from his "lordships" Bach followed; yet patterns can be detected. The stern Wilhelm Ernst creates a climate that favors the concentrated striving that seems to manifest itself in Bach's Weimar period. The duke's religiosity ensures that sacred music will be taken seriously. We can be certain that Wilhelm Ernst paid close attention to the texts of the cantatas Bach composed; presumably he showed equal interest in what Bach did with them musically. When Bach performed his music for religious services at court, he could count on an alert and knowledgeable audience — rather than narrow-minded, frivolous aristocrats interested only in hunting.

The half brothers Ernst August and Johann Ernst probably devoted their primary efforts to instrumental music and did their part to make the increasing cultivation of the modern Italian concerto style possible at the court of Weimar. That the organ works Bach composed during this period show signs of being influenced by this style no doubt has something to do with this receptive climate.

Of course the court does not exist in isolation; there is also the town of Weimar, the ducal seat. Bach lives, until 1713 and possibly longer, in the house of the falsetto singer and pagemaster Adam Immanuel Weldig at 16 Market Square, across from the Red Palace. There Bach's daughter Catharina Dorothea is born at the end of 1708, and two years later his eldest son, Wilhelm Friedemann. In February 1713 Maria Barbara delivers twins, who die soon after birth. In March 1714 and May 1715 the sons Carl Philipp Emanuel and Johann Gottfried Bernhard come into the world. The former's godfather is Georg Philipp Telemann, with whom Bach is "often together in his younger years," as the godson later recalls. In the year 1783 Bach calls Johann Gottfried an "alas misbegotten son,"[82] he having just left his position as organist in Sangerhausen without notice; nothing is known about the circumstances in which Johann Gottfried dies a year later.

In his Weimar living quarters Bach gives lessons to a gradually increasing number of pupils, who, in addition to the already mentioned Schubart, include Johann Bernhard Bach, Johann Lorenz Bach, Johann Christoph Baumgarten, Cornelius Heinrich Dretzel, Samuel Gmelin, Philipp David Kräuter, Johann Tobias Krebs, Johann Caspar Vogler, and Johann Gotthilf Ziegler. Among them Vogler will come to be considered the greatest master of the organ trained by Bach.[83]

Johann Tobias Krebs busied himself with copying works by Bach. It is to Manuscripts P801–03 in the Berlin Staatsbibliothek, which are principally in his hand, that we owe several pieces from the *Orgelbüchlein*, early versions of the so-called Eighteen Chorales, not definitively put together into a collection until Bach's time in Leipzig, and the choral partitas "O Gott, du frommer Gott," BWV 767, and "Sei gegrüsset, Jesu gütig," BWV 768. In the volumes compiled by Krebs we also find the script of Johann Gottfried Walther, Krebs's second teacher in Weimar.

Walther contributed not only choral fantasias by Buxtehude and Reinken but also the choral partita "Ach, was soll ich Sünder machen," BWV 770, and individual organ chorales by Bach. Even if the manuscripts that have come down to us through Krebs cannot all be dated precisely, they unquestionably constitute the most significant sources by far, outside of the *Orgelbüchlein*, for Bach's activity as organist in Weimar. We would be happy if Bach's free organ works from the Weimar period were as well represented in the Krebs-Walther manuscripts as the organ chorales. They are not, but at least we find there the famous Fugue in G Minor on a "Netherlandish" theme, BWV 542 (lacking a prelude in this version); the Prelude and Fugue in A Minor, BWV 569; the *Pièce d'Orgue* in G Major, BWV 572; the Prelude and Fugue in A Minor, BWV 894; the B-minor fugue on a theme by Tomaso Albinoni, BWV 951; and several works also known from older sources.

We find some details on Kräuter's experiences as Bach's pupil in the files of the Augsburg Scholarchat academy: Kräuter is sent to Weimar with a scholarship, and in an application for an extension that he sends to Augsburg, he explains that he has just begun to make the acquaintance of new Italian and French music—that is, after Prince Johann Ernst's return from Holland. His report on his studies with Bach, dated 30 April 1712, is revealing:

> *...he is a most excellent and withal very loyal man, both in composition and clavier, as well as in other instruments, and gives me without fail 6 hours a day of instruction, which are most needful to me, especially in composition and the clavier, and also at times for practicing other instruments; the rest of the time I spend by myself practicing and copying, for the aforementioned conveys to me all musical pieces I request, and I have likewise the freedom to look through all his pieces.*[84]

Did the pupil from Augsburg also look at the score of Reinhard Keiser's *St. Mark Passion*, which Bach and a helper copied around 1710 or 1712? And does Bach already enjoy enough prestige by this time to perform this work, highly modern for its genre, in Weimar?

Kräuter's hand can be recognized in a major portion of the score of the motet "Ich lasse dich nicht, du segnest mich denn," BWV Anh. 159, whose first forty-two measures were written by Bach himself. Although a number of Bach scholars attribute the entire work to him, it is more likely that Bach provided Kräuter with a beginning, which the pupil was to carry forward.

It is not obvious but also not surprising that Johann Mattheson in his work *Das beschützte Orchestre* reports as early as 1711—in the earliest printed discussion of Bach—"From the famed organist in Weimar / Herr Joh. Sebastian Bach / I have seen things / both for the church as well as for the hand [i.e., for keyboard instruments] that are certainly so constituted / that one must greatly esteem the man."[85]

As an organist, Bach has his chief place of work in the Heavenly Castle, as the castle chapel is called, an allusion to both its tall, narrow structure and the ceiling fresco that simulates an opening into heaven. The organ loft, located in the highest of the building's four levels, houses an organ built by Ludwig Compenius and renovated just before Bach's arrival. In 1714 it is renovated again by the organ builder Nicolaus Trebs, this time certainly to suit Bach's wishes. The configuration can be approximately determined.[86] We can see that the two-manual instrument on which Bach played during decisive years in his career as an organist was not exactly a major one, inviting the performer to engage in virtuoso feats in the north German tradition, but certainly one that accommodated his preference for multiple part settings:

Hauptwerk	Unterwerk	Pedal
Quintadena 16′	Principal 8′	Grossuntersatz 32′
Prinzipal 8′	Viola da gamba 8′	Subbass 16′
Gemshorn 8′	Gedackt 8′	Violonbass 16′
Gedacht 8′	Kleingedackt 4′	Principal 8′
Quintadena 4′	Oktave 4′	Cornettbass 4′
Oktave 4′	Waldflöte 2′	Posaune 16′
Mixtur 6fach	Sequialtera 4fach	Trumpet 8′
Cymbal 3fach	Trumpet 8′	Glockenspiel

In spite of the stern atmosphere at the court, Bach has opportunities to travel, and the more so the longer he stays in Weimar. He is quite often invited to inspect organs—in Taubach in 1710, in Erfurt and Halle in 1716, in Leipzig in 1717, by which time he is already in Cöthen. On such occasions Bach, who enjoyed traveling, not only saw something of the world but also enjoyed the pleasures of the table. The account books afford us a glimpse of how the collegium of the Frauenkirche in Halle dined when the organ was dedicated on 3 May 1716, certainly in the presence of the evaluator:[87]

> For the dining of the esteemed Collegium of the Church...upon
> the installation of the new Organ:
> 1 piece of boeffalamode   boiled turnips
> marinated pike with anchovie   frosted crullers

1 smoked ham	pickled lemon peel
1 ashiette with peas	Cherry preserves
1 ashiette with patates	warm asparagus salade
2 ashiettes with spinache & chicory	head lettuce salade
1 roasted mouton quarter	radishes
roast of veal	fresh butter
Altogether 11 talers 12 groschen	

Bach also travels from Weimar to neighboring courts. For the performance of the *Hunt Cantata*, BWV 208, a birthday tribute to Duke Christian, he may well have gone to Weissenfels in 1712 or 1713. In 1717 he spends time at the court of the Duke of Gotha, Friedrich II, filling in for the mortally ill court kapellmeister, Christian Friedrich Witt. On this occasion he may have performed a passion. Since he receives only twelve talers for his services, hardly more than what the tenor is paid for the same performance, we cannot assume that Bach was remunerated both as conductor and as composer, or that the work performed was identical with the so-called Weimar Passion (D 1 in the numbering of the *Bach Compendium*). Presumably he drew on several sections of this otherwise vanished major work for the second version of the *St. John Passion*.

One important event is his application, already alluded to, for the organist's post at the Marienkirche in Halle in the year 1713. He spends "14 days to three weeks" in that city, lodging at the church's expense at the Golden Ring Inn, the best in town, where he runs up some charges for "beer," "brandy wine," and "dabak." Apparently there is strong interest in his candidacy. After a successful audition, which includes the performance of a cantata, he is elected on 13 December to succeed the respected composer and organist Friedrich Wilhelm Zachow.

He accepts, immediately following the election,[88] for this position seems tailor-made for him: it will allow him to play the organ and at the same time serve as a kind of city musical director, in charge of polyphonic music; never has he come closer to his goal of being put in charge of a well-regulated church music! So why does he postpone giving a final answer and eventually withdraw his candidacy? Is the base salary, smaller than that in Weimar, really the deciding factor? After all, he can expect substantial "accidentia." Among other things, he is to be paid separately for composing cantatas for catechism services and playing the organ for weddings.[89]

In any case, the church collegium in Halle declares itself "astonished" when Bach turns down the position, in February 1714, on grounds of inadequate compensation. The collegium charges that he has merely used the offer to improve his chances of being named concertmaster in Weimar. He defends himself indignantly: "That the Most Honored Church Board should be astonished at my declining the proferred post of organist to which, as they think, I aspired, astonishes me not at all, inasmuch as I see that they have given the matter so very little thought."[90]

This is the Bach we know from letters and recorded statements: instead of relaxing once he has in fact been appointed concertmaster and favoring the well-disposed church leaders in Halle with a few friendly lines, he lets fly a number of barbs, softened only by a cursory expression of regret. And once again, his aggressive response does him no harm: a good two years later, the same gentlemen invite him to an organ evaluation and a hearty meal. In regard to the position, Bach takes care to point out that in the short time at his disposal it was impossible for him to calculate the value of the incidentals that would have come his way and therefore the total income he could expect.

We may take him at his word but at the same time raise the possibility that the duke of Weimar refused to accept his resignation, swearing Bach to silence about the matter, as was his custom, then rewarding him by promoting him to a position created especially for him. Whatever the case, Bach rejects a post that will be assumed thirty-two years later by his son Wilhelm Friedemann—with an identically worded contract. Bach has come one step closer in Weimar to his goal: the notice of his appointment as concertmaster, dated 2 March 1714, mentions his obligation "to perform new works monthly," which indicates that he is to rehearse with the palace musicians church cantatas of his composition and perform them at services.[91] This stipulation does not mean, however, that he will direct all the polyphonic music in the kapellmeister's place; rather he is to add to the kapellmeister's efforts in this area.

This interpretation is supported by the fact that the new position created here for Bach, that of concertmaster, was not considered necessary within the hierarchy of music ensembles at central German courts. The assignment does not say that he is now promoted to the position of orchestra director; rather it pertains to his new activity in the realm of vocal music. A similar development occurred in 1666 at the court in Dresden, when Constantin Christian Dedekind was named *Concertmeister* as part of a special arrangement made just for him. The purpose was to recognize that he functioned as the director of the "little German Musick"—polyphonic music performed for less important occasions—and substituted in this capacity for the kapellmeister and vice kapellmeister.[92]

That a similar provision may have been adopted in Weimar can be deduced from the fact that from 1714 on Bach devotes his energy to the strict style in masses and motets; apparently church services at the Weimar court include a segment in which elaborate kyries are performed. The opportunity to assign them to the new concertmaster is welcome, for not every Protestant court kapellmeister considers them part of his duties. Bach copies out kyries by Marco Giuseppe Peranda, vice kapellmeister in Dresden under Heinrich Schütz; by Johann Marianus Baal, a Benedictine monk active at the Franconian cathedral of Schwarzach; and by Johann Christoph Pez, kapellmeister in Stuttgart.[93] A cello part that Bach composed for the unnamed mass BWV Anh. 29 demonstrates that he must have studied even the old mensural notation system.

Possibly it was already in this period that Bach composed the vocal chorale "Vom Himmel hoch," later performed in Leipzig as part of the Christmas Magnificat, BWV 243a. But it seems unlikely that the splendid chorale "O Mensch, bewein dein Sünde gross," which many scholars claim for the aforementioned Weimar or Gotha Passion, can be ascribed to this period.

With Bach's installation as court organist and chamber musician, his field of activity is clearly delineated. As the organist he works primarily in the church, playing for services but also providing the continuo for performances of polyphonic music, so long as he is not conducting, which his appointment as concertmaster makes his official duty. As for chamber music, he participates in performances by the court kapelle, playing cembalo but also violin or viola as needed. Here, too, he may well have leading roles. He probably conducted performances of his own concertos or secular cantatas.

In our review of this period, we have no way of determining whether he suffered continued resistance by his two superiors or enjoyed their favor. Presumably even before his appointment as concertmaster, the organist Bach, approaching his fourth decade and by now highly respected, had already taken over work from both the kapellmeister, Johann Samuel Drese, and his son Johann Wilhelm, listed as vice kapellmeister, whenever Bach's involvement seemed beneficial to the development of music at court. Perhaps we must relinquish the notion that Bach's Weimar cantatas can be assigned places in a kind of schedule, with Bach composing new pieces on a monthly basis. In its scholarly methodology, the "calendar" of compositions worked out by Alfred Dürr still seems helpful; yet distinctions and corrections of the sort Dürr contemplated from the beginning are also meaningful and necessary.[94]

For one thing, it now seems clear, though we do not yet have archival evidence, that even before being named concertmaster Bach composed cantatas for the religious services at the Weimar court. Possibly he was asked to compose cantatas earlier, if only for special occasions. Thus even with works that fit neatly into Dürr's calendar, we should ask whether they represent or draw on earlier works that Bach wrote. New scholarly discoveries may allow us to determine more precisely how he arrived at the "modern" church cantata.

Furthermore, closer attention should be paid to the question of whether the cantatas Bach composed at that time were also performed outside the church services at the Weimar court. If so, it would help explain the rich variations in his repertoire but also the fact that, instead of confining himself to libretti by the court poet Salomon Franck, he also used texts by Erdmann Neumeister, Georg Christian Lehms, and others. The vocal parts of several Weimar cantatas contain indications that performances occurred at different pitches, which may point to different locations, such as the town church, where during this period Johann Gottfried Walther presided over the music.

The cantata "Ich hatte viel Bekümmernis," BWV 21, offers a fruitful subject for the study of such basic questions and has been analyzed at length in the recent Bach literature. On the basis of a notation on the handwritten score, this cantata is assigned to 17 June 1714 in Dürr's calendar; yet the sources indicate that it must be viewed as a revision of an earlier composition. For what occasion could Bach have written the older version? As early as 1858, the Handel scholar Friedrich Chrysander suggested, perhaps on the basis of information now lost to us, that the work might be connected with Bach's visit to Halle during Advent in 1713, on the occasion of his organ audition.[95]

The church board in Halle decided in July 1713 to commission Johann Michael Heineccius to write a libretto to be given to all the candidates as their text. Since the candidates could not all present themselves on the same day, the head pastor of St. Mary's may have put together a text appropriate for several Sundays. It is therefore not out of the question that parts of the libretto of Bach's cantata BWV 21, also suitable for a number of occasions, go back to Heineccius.[96] Certainly this text shows no clear resemblance to the style of the cantata texts by the librettists Bach preferred in Weimar.

By contrast, the hypothetical early version that Christoph Wolff has reconstructed allows us to recognize that the original text—certainly fitting for the "Pietist" climate in Halle—may have been conceived as a dialogue between Jesus and the soul.[97] In 1714, when Bach undertakes a revision under changed circumstances, the dialogue character is eliminated while the work is "enriched" with a splendid and powerful final chorus, perhaps composed years earlier and quite disproportionate to the rest of the cantata. In this new version, the cantata was performed again in Weimar or Cöthen, also during the summer of 1723 in Leipzig. In 1725, Mattheson presents it to the public in a small printed edition.

This example serves to suggest that in this and comparable cases it does not make sense to measure Bach's music against a paradigm of the work derived from Viennese classicism and the concept of absolute music. Even a formulation such as "Bach wrote the cantata BWV 21 for 17 June 1714" is misleading, for it suggests a unique act of creation, ignoring the likelihood that a date of performance represents merely a way station in a longer history—a history not so much of a work as of a discourse. The analytic process must not focus only on the works themselves, comparing individual versions; rather we should seek to reconstruct the situation in which a version might have been required and how it would have been received by the audience. In Bach's day it made a difference whether one was presenting an audition piece for the town of Halle, a cantata for a religious service at the Weimar court, or a piece of sacred music for St. Thomas's in Leipzig.

Today's listeners have two choices for enjoying Bach's music: they can ignore the context and take in a work "straight" in one of its existing versions. Or they may wish to keep in mind the history and context while listening to the work. The example of the cantata "Ich hatte viel Bekümmernis," BWV 21, shows how the latter approach can deepen the experience. The familiar version from the year 1714 is astonishing for the variety that marks its sections; yet the final movement, "Das Lamm, das erwürget ist," seems completely anomalous. But if one considers the probable existence of an earlier, more consistent version, one need no longer close one's ears to formal inconsistencies but can instead imagine oneself participating in one phase of Bach's "march through the institutions."

It is impossible to know today how carefully Bach kept the commitment he made in 1714 to provide a new piece every month. The calendar that can be drawn up to reflect this commitment has gaps, but the missing works may have disappeared, with the surviving libretti by Salomon Franck providing the only evidence of their titles,[98] or they may never have been composed. We also have cantatas that do not fit into this calendar, such as the Christmas cantata

"Christen ätzet diesen Tag," BWV 63, which make us wonder whether Bach composed works above and beyond his quota for the most important feast days, or whether a particularly choice-sounding work like this was intended primarily for the duke's birthday, which coincided with Christmas.

We can nevertheless detect a trend in Bach's Weimar cantatas that is typical for his entire creative oeuvre: the new concertmaster begins with a great burst of energy; gradually the instrumentation of the cantatas he presents becomes less lavish; and toward the end of his Weimar period his cantata production almost completely dries up.

In terms of text and music, the three first works, performed between March and May 1714, show great consistency; these are "Himmelskönig, sei willkommen," BWV 182; "Weinen, Klagen, Sorgen, Zagen," BWV 12; and "Erschallet, ihr Lieder," BWV 172. In two cases the works include a lengthy "sonata" or "sinfonia," and all three cantatas follow the pattern of a major opening chorus, followed by a recitative based on a passage from Scripture, then three arias and a chorus in the form of a chorale. In two cases a final chorus or the repetition of the opening chorus follows.

After this opening three-part drum roll, Bach seems to have slowed down somewhat, at least so far as we can determine from the existing records. He directs performances of works already composed earlier (which is presumably the case with BWV 21, 199, and 18) and concentrates on solo cantatas, the first among them being "Widerstehe doch der Sünde," BWV 54, and "O heiliges Geist- und Wasserbad," BWV 165. BWV 54 is composed as a solo cantata for alto in pure madrigal style; BWV 165 displays the form that will come to predominate in his Weimar work and then often turns up after his third year in Leipzig: the solo cantata in madrigal style with a four-part final chorus, the latter portion presumably a concession by the librettists to the pious congregation, a concession Bach surely supports. That during this period he also performs solo cantatas by Italian composers we may deduce from a copy in his hand, perhaps from the beginning of 1716, of the cantata "Languet anima mea" by the Viennese court theorbo player and composer Francesco Bartolomeo Conti.

In the meantime Bach composes further cantatas with interesting choral parts: "Der Himmel lacht! Die Erde jubilieret," BWV 31; "Komm, du süsse Todesstunde," BWV 161; "Wachet! Betet!," BWV 70a; and "Ärgre dich, o Seele, nicht," BWV 186a. It is difficult to determine why the number of compositions declines; perhaps Bach was having problems with the court singers available to him as a chorus, or perhaps he was accommodating a preference at court for solo performances. It is also possible that he was indulging his own liking for the solo cantata; we must remember that he is an organist and thus accustomed to making music with soloists. In this genre he achieves a quality that cannot be surpassed. In choral composition, however, he will show in Leipzig that he is still capable of learning.

Bach's Weimar cantata repertoire was not limited to his own compositions. We have evidence that he not only copied the cantata by Conti mentioned above but also one by the court kapellmeister of Dresden, Johann Christoph Schmidt, with the text "Auf Gott hoffe ich." Perhaps copies of church cantatas by his colleague the kapellmeister of Dresden, Johann David Heinichen, could also be found in his Weimar collection of scores.[99]

Bach must have received considerable artistic stimulation from his friendship with Walther, who asked Bach to be godfather to his son, Johann Gottfried, Jr., in 1712. Both men are organ experts; and especially when it comes to the practice of strict counterpoint, Bach can learn from this distant relative, who in 1708 wrote the *Praecepta der musicalischen Composition,* dedicated to Prince Johann Ernst, and later earned wide recognition as a music theoretician and lexicographer. Bach dedicated to Walther the first preserved puzzle canon, BWV 1073, dated 2 August 1713.

Walther copies the fugue on a theme by Giovanni Legrenzi, BWV 574b, as well as the fugue for violin and basso continuo BWV 1026, and Bach and Walther share the task of copying the previously mentioned mass by Johann Baal; we may thus imagine the two of them studying together Girolamo Frescobaldi's *Fiori Musicali* of 1635, famous particularly for three organ masses, using the handwritten version that Bach copied onto 104 folio pages in 1714, according to his own notation. At this time the *Fiori Musicali* are still considered exemplary of strict style, particularly with respect to the ricercare they include. As music for keyboard instruments they occupy a position similar to that occupied in vocal music by the masses of Palestrina, with which Bach is not unfamiliar, at least in later years.

Bach's study of Frescobaldi is not the first attention to older masters of the organ for which we have evidence from his Weimar period. Some time between 1709 and 1712 he copies out Nicolas de Grigny's *Premier livre d'orgue.* Around the same time he must have undertaken his transformation of Johann Adam Reinken's sonatas and sonata movements from his *Hortus musicus,* parts of them in strict style, into the works for the keyboard BWV 954, 965, and 966. These works, too, chiefly preserved in scores in Walther's hand, document Bach's determination to master the art of part writing—initially, to be sure, to apply it to compositions for keyboard instruments.

This is also the period during which Bach begins work on a major project for the organ, the *Orgelbüchlein.* The title, which he added later in Cöthen, is the first in a series of explicit titles with whose help Bach elucidates the systematic and didactic import of the organ or keyboard work in question; the *Orgelbüchlein* will be followed by the two-part Inventions, the three-part Sinfonias, and *The Well-Tempered Clavier.* The title page reads as follows:

Little Organ Book
In which a beginning organist receives given instruction as to performing a chorale in a multitude of ways while achieving mastery in the study of the pedal, since in the chorales contained herein the pedal is treated entirely obligato.
In honor of our Lord alone
That my fellow man his skill may hone.
Autore Joanne Sebast. Bach
P[leno] t[itulo] Capellae Magistro
S[erenissimi] P[rinceps] R[egnantis]
Anhaltini Cotheniensis

At the top of the blank pages in the volume Bach writes the first lines of the text of 164 chorales in the sequence of the liturgical year and the hymnal. Yet over the years he completes only a little over a quarter of the project; the last entries are made in Leipzig. Bach's pattern of tackling large projects but then running out of steam may in this case be explained by compositional difficulties inherent in the undertaking: the collection is pitched at such a high level and laid out with such variety that after forty-six parts are completed, everything has been said that can be said. The project has inadvertently developed from a practical book for organists, perhaps even intended for publication, into a collection of exemplary compositions for experts.

Parallel to the *Orgelbüchlein*, Bach probably composed the partita "Sei gegrüsset, Jesu gütig," BWV 768. Many of the individual organ chorales, composed on a larger scale and preserved in single copies, also belong to the Weimar period. As mentioned before, Bach revised some of them in his Leipzig years and compiled them into the manuscript of the Eighteen Chorales, BWV 651–68.

Since Weimar represented the high point in Bach's composing for the organ, it is regrettable that in this biographical chapter we cannot even begin to suggest a chronology for the individual organ works from this period; specific dating is lacking, and I have already noted the difficulties that arise when one tries to date works solely on the basis of their stylistic features. One general observation can be made here: in the free organ works of the Weimar period Bach can clearly draw on a wealth of experience and inspiration. This becomes evident from a brilliant work such as the Toccata and Fugue in F Major, BWV 540.

In the period before Weimar, Bach received lasting impressions from the imaginative element in the north German organ style. Now he absorbs the principle of concertizing, intuitively grasping its structural significance and dynamic potential and applying these features productively to his composing for the organ. Thus the Toccata in C Major, BWV 564, is clearly shaped by the basic layout of a concerto: the opening movement follows the tutti-solo principle, the following adagio corresponds to the slow movement in an instrumental concerto, and the final movement presents itself as a fugue *concertante*. The Toccata and Fugue in D Minor, BWV 538 (the so-called Doric Fugue), and the Prelude and Fugue in G Major, BWV 541, signal Bach's preoccupation in Weimar—if indeed they were composed there—with the concerto style.

Is this preoccupation a result of the "Vivaldi fever" that reaches epidemic proportions in the first two decades of the eighteenth century in Europe? Bach must certainly have sensed early on how important the Vivaldi-style concerto would become for the development of a "grand" European style: for the first time in the history of music, instrumental music is being organized on a large scale, yet at the same time in gradations—as an autonomous yet transparent form. But Bach is neither an Italian composer nor a composer mindlessly imitating the Italians. Succinctness and sensuality of form are not everything; the search for a *prima causa* of music cannot be suspended any more than the theological-philosophical goal of deriving multiplicity from unity and unity from multiplicity. For this reason he evidently has much room in Weimar to explore strict style. This is the period during which he dwells intensely on the question of how the free and the strict style can be brought together coherently in the bipolar forms of the prelude and fugue—a problem that seems far less urgent to his contemporaries.

Perhaps Bach never did experience the infamous "Vivaldi shock" referred to time and again in the Bach literature, but instead consistently observed and studied the Italian concerto style, bringing ever new questions to bear. Perhaps too much significance has been attributed to the fact that between 1713 and 1714 he did five organ and sixteen cembalo arrangements of instrumental concerti by composers as varied as Antonio Vivaldi, Giuseppe Torelli, Benedetto Marcello the Elder and Younger, Georg Philipp Telemann, and Prince Johann Ernst of Weimar (BWV 592a–96, 972–87). These works may have been written at the behest of the prince, who obviously valued this music and wanted to hear it in his own lessons or in specially organized concerts; we need not see this undertaking as the spark that ignited Bach's own interest in the instrumental concerto as a genre.

We have only fragmentary indications of this interest—first of all in the copies of work by other masters that Bach made during his Weimar years, some of which have been identified only recently as copies, for instance that of a concerto in G major for two violins by Telemann. Bach apparently prepared the copy as a gift for the later concertmaster of the Dresden court kapelle, Johann Georg Pisendel, when this colleague spent some time in Weimar in 1709: at any rate, when the manuscript, which displays the hand of a still fairly young Bach, was discovered among the holdings of the old Dresden kapelle, it was thought to have found its way there through Pisendel.[100] Around the same time or several years later Bach is known to have been studying Tomaso Albinoni's *Concerti a cinque,* opus 2, published in 1700.

We do not know when Bach began to compose concerti of his own. It seems likely that even in his early Weimar years he was not only copying concerti but increasingly composing them. Bach scholarship today leans toward the view that even some of the *Brandenburg Concertos* already existed in early versions during the Weimar period. As of now these are merely hypotheses; they will be discussed further in the chapter on Bach's orchestral works. Here two details should be mentioned that belong in a biographical context: the early version of the first *Brandenburg Concerto,* BWV 1046a, would in some respects make an ideal first movement for the *Hunt Cantata,* BWV 208, whose handwritten score begins immediately with a recitative, omitting an overture; the concerto may thus have been played as early as 1713, or on the occasion of the presumed repeat performance of the work in 1716. According to the more recent view, which is not universally accepted, the fifth *Brandenburg Concerto* was composed in conjunction with Bach's trip to Dresden—for the planned competition with Louis Marchand.[101]

If this event actually occurred in the fall of 1717, Bach would be traveling to Dresden at a precarious transitional moment in his life, when he has accepted a position in Cöthen but has not yet been released from his duties in Weimar. There are several indications that he feels driven to leave Weimar: in 1716 his production of cantatas began to slow, and we now know that by 1717 it has practically come to a standstill. Then there is his previously mentioned engagement at the court of Gotha in April 1717. On 1 December 1716 the old Weimar kapellmeister Drese died, and Bach knows with certainty that Drese's son, as vice kapellmeister, is his designated successor. On the occasion of Bach's installation as concertmaster it was expressly stipulated that he would remain subordinate to the vice kapellmeister.

One year later, when Bach was already in Cöthen, Drese junior did in fact become the kapellmeister. The appointment was made primarily on the basis of the seniority principle, which a ruler intent on keeping his servants loyal had to observe. It cannot be confirmed whether the duke nonetheless negotiated with Georg Philipp Telemann, as Telemann later more hinted than asserted in an autobiographical account.[102]

Bach may have been annoyed at being passed over in this predictable fashion, or he may have simply decided that he would not stay in Weimar with Drese junior as kapellmeister. At any rate, he does not wait for the decision to be made but rather fixes his sights on Gotha and even more on Cöthen. The latter choice seems relatively easy, since the Weimar coregent Ernst August has been married to Eleonore Wilhelmine, the sister of young Prince Leopold von Anhalt-Cöthen, since the beginning of 1716. Perhaps Ernst August relishes the prospect of snatching the great artist away from his despised uncle Wilhelm Ernst, who has forbidden Ernst August to enlist Bach for his private music making.

If these are merely speculations, we do know for certain the date of Bach's formal installation as kapellmeister in Cöthen: 5 August 1717. Prince Leopold prizes his new kapellmeister so greatly that "upon the *Capitulation* [accepting the contract]" Bach is to receive 50 talers and soon thereafter his salary, although the moment when he will take up his appointment had not yet been fixed.[103] On the contrary: a notation from December 1717 by the Weimar court secretary, Theodor Benedikt Bormann, makes it clear that in the preceding months Bach has applied persistently yet futilely for his dismissal:

On 6 November [1717], the quondam concertmaster and court or-
ganist Bach was arrested and held at the County Magistrate's
house of detention for obstinate behavior and forcing the question
of his dismissal, and finally on 2 December was informed by the
Court Secr. of his unfavorable discharge and simultaneously freed
from arrest.[104]

In view of the harsh conditions prevailing in Weimar, Bach probably did not serve the barely four-week sentence merely pro forma; each time the waldhorn player Adam Andreas Reichardt requested his discharge, as happened more than once during the reign of Ernst August, he was sentenced to a hundred blows and imprisonment. When he finally fled, he was declared an outlaw and was hanged "in effigie."[105]

Bach, who can consider himself a protégé of the prince of Cöthen, fares relatively well by comparison; that the prince promptly grants him a new position runs contrary to the custom of the time and points to a special relationship between the two. While imprisoned in Weimar, Bach apparently has access to paper and quill, for "according to a certain tradition," which Ernst Ludwig Gerber passes on in his *Historisch-biographisches Lexikon der Tonkünstler*, Bach writes *The Well-Tempered Clavier* in "a place where dismay, boredom, and the lack of any sort of musical instrument made this way of passing time essential."[106] Since the encyclopedist had in his father a noted Bach pupil as his informant, this report may well be rooted in fact: early versions of *The Well-Tempered Clavier* were indeed written in Weimar.

CÖTHEN

"With an unfavorable discharge"—that is how the thirty-two-year-old Bach must take leave of his Thuringian homeland, accompanied by his wife, his sister-in-law, and four children: Catharina Dorothea, who has just turned nine; seven-year-old Wilhelm Friedemann;

three-year-old Carl Philipp Emanuel; and two-year-old Johann Gottfried Bernhard.

Nonetheless, Bach has no call to accuse his native land of ingratitude. On the contrary. To the extent possible in his day, he has been recognized as an exceptional figure: the people of Arnstadt, who summoned him as an organ expert at a very young age, tolerated his willful behavior with remarkable patience; the people of Mühlhausen continue to commission him to write council pieces, despite his having left their town for Weimar after only one year. Even the bickering over his resignation from his post in Weimar does not imply that the reigning duke fails to value Bach as an artist, an the same time as he shows him no indulgence as a subject.

By now Bach also enjoys a reputation outside Thuringia. Students travel great distances to seek him out. In Halle the church overseers appoint him to evaluate their organ, overlooking what they see as his scornful rejection of the organist's position recently offered him. And a mere two weeks after his release from prison, he turns up in Leipzig, where he evaluates the organ at the Paulinerkirche, but presumably also looks around elsewhere; might he have a chance to succeed the chronically ailing cantor at St. Thomas's, Johann Kunau? Bach may not dance a jig like Telemann, but he is neither timid nor unworldly. And that remains true when he gets to Cöthen. In 1719 he spends time in Berlin, picking out a harpsichord to buy; in 1720 he is invited to Hamburg as an organ virtuoso; in 1721 he goes to the court in Schleiz as a guest performer. In the summer of 1722 he may have visited the court of Anhalt-Zerbst, where the position of kapellmeister is vacant. Ten talers are paid to "Kapellmeister Back of Cöthen for a *Composition* upon our Most gracious Duke's day of birth."[107]

But for the time being Bach is in Cöthen—a considerable improvement in status over Weimar, and a first summit reached on his ambitious climb upward. As kapellmeister, he occupies a position of authority in the court hierarchy. At four hundred talers per annum he is paid no less than the second-highest official, Majordomo Gottlob von Nostitz.

It is not possible to identify with certainty a Bach house in Cöthen; he may have lived at 11 Stiftstrasse or 12 Holzmarkt.[108] There his son Leopold Augustus was born in November 1718, only to die in September of the following year. It was there, too, that death snatched away Maria Barbara; her burial is recorded for 7 July 1720. According to the obituary, Bach was at the baths in Carlsbad with his prince when she died. It is an appealing thought but impossible to document that Bach composed the *Chromatic Fantasy*, BWV 903, in memory of his first wife; an early version possibly goes back to the Weimar period.[109] The significance of the work is by no means limited to its presumed commemorative purpose: preserved in thirty-three handwritten copies from the eighteenth and early nineteenth centuries, the composition established the genre of the free piano fantasia in its modern form.

Neither the cause of Maria Barbara's death nor Bach's reaction is known to us. The surviving documents indicate only that social obligations did not cease for the widower, never one to shirk the demands of the world around him. After accepting the role of godfather to the daughter of his kapelle colleague Christian Ferdinand Abel in January 1720, he does the same in January 1721 for the son of the Cöthen goldsmith Christian Heinrich Bähr, and in September of that year for the son of the ducal cellarer, Christian Hahn. In the second case, the baptismal registry records the name of a godmother, of particular interest here: "Demoiselle Magdalena Wilckens, ducal singer in this town."

Considering Bach's good connections with the court in Weissenfels, it is conceivable that the young singer who appears for the first time in the Cöthen records as a supper guest in June 1721 was hired by Bach himself.[110] At any rate, on 3 December 1721, the thirty-six-year-old widower Bach leads the twenty-year-old daughter of the Weissenfels court trumpeter, Johann Caspar Wilcke, to the altar. Whether the wedding festivities in the Bach house were subdued — as was not uncommon with second marriages — or whether the wine flowed is neither here nor there. Wine bills amounting to the astonishing sum of twenty-seven talers from this period can give those interested in biographical details room to speculate if Bach already had his eye on his future wife when she was hired.

With this marriage, Bach brought into his house not only a second mother for Catharina Dorothea (13), Wilhelm Friedemann (11), Carl Philipp Emanuel (7), and Johann Gottfried Bernhard (6) but also a professional musician. More will be said of her in conjunction with Bach's Leipzig period.

Since the wedding is celebrated in the palace church, Bach owes the Lutheran church a dispensation fee, which, however, he refuses to pay—probably on the grounds that the wedding took place "on orders from the prince."[111] During his time in Cöthen, however, he remains loyal to the Lutheran church of St. Agnes: he pays rent for a pew and takes Communion one to three times a year. He may have been less pleased with the pastor, a somewhat shady figure.

One thing should not be forgotten: when Bach receives his call to the reformed court in Cöthen, he knows that his duties will lie in the secular rather than the sacred realm. It is another matter entirely that he has a tendency to grow restless in any post and to apply for other positions. An appointment to a Lutheran church might have been very welcome. November 1720 finds him in Lutheran Hamburg: the records of St. Jacob's reveal that he applied for the vacant position of church organist. But he cannot stay for an audition; he must "travel to join his prince."[112] That clears the way for an applicant who—in the good old Hanseatic tradition of buying official positions—pays four thousand marks into the church coffers as an installation fee.

Several years later Johann Mattheson recalls in his work *Der musikalische Patriot* the unsuccessful application "of a certain great virtuoso," and quotes smugly from the Christmas sermon delivered at the time by Hamburg's head pastor, the cantata librettist Erdmann Neumeister:

> *[The pastor] believed with certainty that if one of the angels of Bethlehem should come from Heaven and play divinely, wishing to become the organist at St. J., but having no money, he would simply have to fly back whence he had come.*[113]

It is doubtful that Bach seriously considered the vacant position. He would hardly have left his native central Germany to move to the Hanseatic city as the successor to the organist and church secretary, Heinrich Friese. Perhaps he received encouragement on the spur of the moment to apply, but actually had his eye on the position of city cantor and "director musices," the prestige of which was approximately equal to that of the cantor at St. Thomas's in Leipzig. The current city cantor, Joachim Gerstenbüttel, successor to the famous Schütz pupil Christoph Bernhard, was considered an "almost constant *valetudinarius*," or chronically ailing, and was already in his seventy-first year.[114] Indeed he died a few months later. By then Bach was back in Cöthen, and the position was offered not to him but to a more affable genius, Telemann, who accepted it.

Bach seems to have enjoyed great acclaim in Hamburg as an organ virtuoso. An episode recounted in his obituary can easily be brought into connection with his stay in that city, despite a slight discrepancy in the date:

> *During this time, about the year 1722, he made a journey to Hamburg and played for more than two hours on the fine organ of St. Catherine's before the Magistrate and many other distinguished persons of the city, to their general admiration. The aged organist of this church, Johann Adam Reinken, who at that time was nearly one hundred years old, listened to him with particular pleasure. When Bach, at the request of those present, performed extempore the chorale* By the Waters of Babylon *at great length (for almost half an hour) and in different ways, just as the best organists of Hamburg in the past had been wont to do at Saturday vespers, Reinken paid Bach the following compliment: "I thought this art was dead, but I see that in you it lives on."*

But back to Cöthen. There Bach directs a large kapelle; furthermore, as he will write retrospectively in the Erdmann letter, he has "a gracious Prince, who both loved and knew music."[115] At the time of Bach's arrival, the prince is twenty-three and still unmarried. As early as November 1718 he and two of his siblings serve as godparents to Bach's little son Leopold August, his namesake, who will not live long. There is little to suggest that during the five and a half years that Bach spent in Cöthen anything arose to cloud the good relationship; after his departure, he will continue to be titled the "house kapellmeister." He returns several times to the court from Leipzig and performs his works—the last being the *Trauerkantate*, BWV 244a, upon the death of the prince.

In Leopold, Bach finds a ruler who wants to transform Cöthen into a court of the Muses. He has an extraordinary appreciation, formed at a young age, for the arts: after two years at the Knights' Academy in Berlin, the prince sets out on the grand tour, almost completely documented in ledgers and travel journals. During four winter months in The Hague in 1710–11, he attends the opera twelve times; later he acquires, for the steep price of fifty-five talers, "rare works by M. Lully, the printed music"—neither the first nor last purchase of scores on his journey.[116] For evening *musicales* that he himself organizes, he engages up to twelve musicians. On these occasions he plays the harpsichord and the violin.

In London and Venice Leopold also goes to the opera, and in Rome he hires a violin master. Perhaps it was Johann David Heinichen, who at the time was still in Rome on a scholarship. Only a few years later the Saxon prince elector will meet him on his own grand tour and make him kapellmeister at the court in Dresden.

Here are a few highlights of the final stages of Leopold's grand tour: in Vienna he acquires Francesco Mancini's "Book with Twelve Cantatas," sits for the famous portrait painter Johann Kupezky, and buys a violin from the dealer Faschinger. Continuing on to Dresden, he goes to the court opera to hear the famous virtuoso Francesco Borosini sing. On the way back to Cöthen, where he arrives in April 1713, he stops in Leipzig to take in the musical offerings at Zimmermann's Coffeehouse.

The prince spends more than 55,000 talers on the tour, and the resulting costs will prove even higher. While the prince can take a little more time to build and expand an art gallery, whose eventual dimensions and rich holdings will be impressive, and to construct a good-sized orangerie, Leopold turns his mind immediately upon his return to reconstituting a kapelle whose quality is intended to exceed that of the typical central German small court, and he will actually fulfill this ambition.[117]

Leopold sets about hiring members of the Berlin court kapelle, which the puritanical Prussian Soldier King, Friedrich Wilhelm I, has dissolved upon his accession; with them comes the former kapellmeister, Reinhard Augustin Stricker. He is appointed interim kapellmeister to the ensemble as it is taking shape, and in gratitude dedicates six Italian cantatas to the prince in 1715. Stricker has to step aside once Bach is appointed. By the time Bach assumes his post, the ensemble is largely complete. The surviving sources allow us to name seventeen musicians who belong to the kapelle during Bach's years in Cöthen, most of them permanently:[118]

Joseph Spiess	Premier Cammer Musicus (concertmaster)	
Christian Bernhard Linigke	Cammer Musicus, cellist	183 talers
Johann Ludwig Rose	Cammer Musicus, oboist	150 talers
Christian Ferdinand Abel	Cammer Musicus, gambist	150 talers
Karl Friedrich Vetter	Cammer Musicus	137 talers
Martin Friedrich Marcus	Cammer Musicus, violinist	130 talers
Johann Christoph Torlé	Cammer Musicus, bassoonist	130 talers
Johann Valentin Fischer	Cammer Musicus	125 talers
Johann Heinrich Freitag	Violinist, flautist	120 talers
Johann Christian Krahle	Court trumpeter	108 talers
Johann Ludwig Schreiber	Court trumpeter	108 talers
Johann Gottlob Würdig	Town piper, Cammer Musicus, flautist	74 talers
Anton Unger	Court timpanist	72 talers
Wilhelm Andreas Harbordt	Court Musicus, ripienist	52 talers
Adam Ludwig Weber	Town piper	40 talers
Johann Freitag	Ripienist	32 talers
Emanuel Heinrich Gottl. Freitag	Cammer Musicus, violinist	20 talers

The number of ripienists may have been increased by the addition of the score copyist and a page or two who had musical training. As notations in ledgers or other records suggest, cantors, organists, and city pipers from Cöthen also participated in performances at court, ex officio or on an ad hoc basis. The documents also show that musicians from elsewhere were engaged and occasionally, to judge by the size of their honoraria, remained in Cöthen for some time.[119] Although most of the outsiders performed as soloists—the records note guest appearances by violinists, lutenists, and players of the waldhorn and pantaleon—they also joined the ensemble when a particular need arose. All in all, Bach has at his disposal an ensemble superior in both quality and size. Although during his time in office it suffers three deaths and two departures, it does not have to contend with budgetary reductions.

Those who set the tone are the well-paid chamber musicians, some of whom receive substantial increases during Bach's time in office and who without doubt are one and all excellent soloists. It makes sense that Leopold hires Christian Ferdinand Abel, an outstanding virtuoso on the cello and viola da gamba, for the prince plays the gamba himself. But the concertmaster Spiess and the flautist Freitag also stand out in the ensemble—as composers; a significant flute sonata by the latter has recently come to light.[120] Leopold must have viewed the kapelle as the jewel in his crown;[121] he not only took some of the soloists along on his regular trips to Carlsbad but perhaps also showed them off at the court in Dresden, for instance when he attended wedding festivities there in September 1719.

We have somewhat more detailed information about the journey to Carlsbad in the year 1718: in addition to Bach, the prince has with him six members of the kapelle; furthermore, "the princely clavicembalo is shipped to CarlsBad" after them, presumably because they do not find any good instrument there. This step offers a clear indication that the prince cares a great deal about having fine music available.[122] Another instance of Leopold's desire to have excellent keyboard instruments at his court is Bach's trip to Berlin in March

1719; he goes for the purpose of examining and bringing home a new two-manual harpsichord built by Michael Mietke.

The chamber ledgers note reimbursements for rehearsals by the collegium musicum held at Bach's house—another source tells us these are weekly events.[123] It is likely that these rehearsals involve not always the entire kapelle but sometimes the smaller ensemble of chamber musicians. These musicians would have the right to rehearse on their own and without further supervision than the direction of Bach, whose appointment specifically designates him as "Kapellmeister and Director of our chamber music."[124]

It is intriguing to imagine the members of this ensemble performing some of Bach's sonatas, which are by no means easy to play, and also performing the solo parts in concerts, for which at least two or even three vocalists are available in Cöthen.[125] There could be, in appropriate circumstances, performances of the second and fourth *Brandenburg Concertos*, a solo-tutti contrast almost rivaling the richness of Italian orchestration.

Whereas it is difficult in every instance to form a precise picture of the quality achieved in Bach's Leipzig performances, we may be quite certain that in Cöthen the ensemble pieces were always meticulously rehearsed and brilliantly performed. Bach no doubt placed particular emphasis on a differentiated articulation of the vocal solo parts. That conclusion can be drawn directly from the surviving sources (of which, to be sure, there are few) and indirectly from Bach's later practice in Leipzig: there he made notations on the scores with detailed reminders for future performances, perhaps so as to avoid lengthy rehearsals. In Cöthen such rehearsals unquestionably took place.

In discussing the instrumentalists, we should not neglect the vocalists. As the chamber ledgers reveal, most of the vocalists during Bach's first years in Cöthen were guest performers; from 1720 on, the daughters of Monjou, the supervisor of pages, and from December 1721 on, Bach's new wife, Anna Magdalena, held regular positions.

Liturgical and secular festival music is to be provided for the prince's birthday on 10 December and to present congratulations and best wishes to the reigning family of Anhalt-Cöthen on New Year's Day. As far as we are informed, the libretti are penned by Christian Friedrich Hunold, known as Menantes, a poet noted particularly for his opera and passion texts, who was active in Halle but also worked for the court in Cöthen until his death in 1721. In Menantes Bach has a distinguished poet, secular in orientation and an adherent of the "gallant" school of literature. Bach will call upon him during his Leipzig period when he is composing the cantata "Ich bin in mir vergnügt," BWV 204.

Of the congratulatory pieces written in the Cöthen period we know only a few, those later transformed by Bach into religious cantatas: "Der Himmel dacht auf Anhalts Ruhm und Glück," BWV 66a; "Die Zeit, die Tag und Jahre macht," BWV 134a; and "Durchlauchtster Leopold," BWV 173a. Traces of other compositions can be found elsewhere; the *Bach Compendium* follows these traces under numbers B30 and G4–11.

Because so little from this group of works has been preserved, there is a tendency to undervalue Bach's efforts in this area. Yet in all likelihood he planned for these special events with great care. One well-documented example is the prince's birthday in 1718: at least four guest artists are invited to help perform the cantatas "Lobet den Herrn, alle seine Herrscharen," BWV Anh. I 5, and the previously mentioned secular cantata BWV 66a—the discantist Prese and the bass Johann Gottfried Riemenschneider, as well as the violinists Linigke from Merseburg and Johann Gottfried Vogler from Leipzig.

We know little enough about the cantatas Bach composed in Cöthen, but we are really groping in the dark when it comes to his orchestral and chamber works. Cöthen's Court of the Muses certainly has a kapelle whose soloists and ensemble players would be hard to match anywhere. The court is headed by a prince whose musical expertise equals his enthusiasm. There is apparently a splendid collection of scores. Finally, there is a highly motivated kapellmeister, no doubt selected with great care for the position and therefore assured of his prince's full respect. But what works can be definitely ascribed to this period in Bach's life?

First and foremost we must mention the *Brandenburg Concertos*. Bach certainly composed the entire score in Cöthen, dedicating it on 24 March 1721 to Margrave Christian Ludwig of Brandenburg. The handwritten dedication in French reads:

> **Six Concerts**
> *Avec plusieurs Instruments.*
> *Dediées*
> *A Son Altesse Royalle*
> *CRETIEN LOUIS*
> *par*
> *Son très-humble & très obéissant Serviteur*
> *Jean Sebastien Bach*
> *Maitre de Chapelle de S. A. S: le*
> *Prince regnant d'Anhalt-Coethen*

The dedicatory essay, written in less than perfect French, begins:

> *Monseigneur, whereas I had a few years ago the pleasure of play-ing before Your Royal Highness, at Your Highness's command, and whereas I noted on that occasion that the modest talent for music that Heaven has bestowed upon me found favor in Your eyes, and whereas in departing Your Royal Highness deigned to honor me with the charge to send Your Highness some composi-tions of mine, therefore I have, in accordance with Your High-ness's most gracious charge, taken the liberty of fulfilling my most humble duty to Your Royal Highness with the present concertos, which I have scored for several instruments . . .*[126]

We do not know when Bach's encounter with the margrave oc-curred; perhaps it took place during one of Prince Leopold's many trips to the baths or during Bach's journey in 1719 to Berlin to buy the harpsichord. Bach scholars are unanimous in the assumption that when Bach chose the six concertos, he took into account the skills of the Brandenburg kapelle, but that he also delved into a sup-ply of works already on hand from his time in Weimar or Cöthen. Perhaps he felt drawn away from his current place of employment, as was so often the case with him; the dedication would then have constituted a subtle application for a position. Such considerations, however, are of less importance than the recognition that in the form of the *Brandenburg Concertos* Bach was presenting a unique form, at once concentrated and rich in variation, of the ensemble concerto.

Until a few years ago it was taken for granted that most of Bach's orchestral compositions originated in the Cöthen period, when the presentation of such works was included among his official duties. The number of surviving original compositions for orchestra is small: besides the *Brandenburg Concertos* we have only the two violin concertos BWV 1041 and 1042, the double concerto for two violins BWV 1043, and the four orchestra overtures BWV 1066–69. Then, on the basis of new examination and analysis of the existing source material, Christoph Wolff put forth the comprehensive thesis that all Bach's orchestral works for which no handwritten versions from Weimar or Cöthen exist must have been composed in Leipzig.[127] He argued that the collegium musicum in Leipzig, under Bach's direction from 1729 on, provided ample occasions for such compositions.

This thesis has been modified in the light of further considerations. The existing handwritten copies of the violin concerto in E major BWV 1042 and the overture BWV 1069 were prepared only after Bach's death and thus provide no basis for dating these compositions. The overture in C major BWV 1066 may have been copied from an original that can be dated more plausibly from the Cöthen period than from Leipzig. The other works under discussion exist only in the form of scores for the separate parts, prepared for a specific performance and therefore offering no clue as to the date of composition. In particular, new research has shown that the existing versions of the violin concerto in A minor and the overtures in B minor BWV 1067 and D major BWV 1068 belong to a period that can hardly represent their earliest incarnations.[128] Thus although these works cannot be unambiguously reassigned to Cöthen, neither can they be clearly claimed for the Leipzig period.

Cöthen's status as the "town of provenance" is threatened not only from the direction of Leipzig but also from that of Weimar. The six *Brandenburg Concertos* were doubtless first compiled as a collection in Cöthen, although not without a rather long period of gestation. For most of the concertos, older versions existed, in some cases perhaps going back to the Weimar period.[129] While the dating of particular works will continue to be a topic of discussion, it is undeniably true that Bach scholarship faces uncharted territory when it comes to his kapellmeister music in Cöthen—that is, when it tries to locate the kind of concertos and overtures that the director of a large and highly skilled court kapelle would have been contractually required to provide.

We are of course not dealing with dozens, let alone hundreds, of works, such as Bach's contemporaries Telemann, Graupner, Stölzel, or Fasch composed in similar positions. Bach was not a prolific composer; rather, he tended to concentrate on just a few projects and models over a period of time. Yet we wish we could form a picture of him as an orchestral composer as distinct as that of the composer of works for keyboard and organ or of cantatas. The fact that we cannot raises questions. It seems certain that not all the orchestral compositions from Cöthen have survived, but it would be an anomaly in the history of Bach's works if the number of lost orchestral compositions was very large.

For the time being at least, we must thus conjecture that in Cöthen Bach composed relatively few orchestral works—for reasons unknown. Contrary to some speculation, we have no evidence that during Bach's tenure the prince turned his back on the kapelle. It seems far more likely that he really was a man "who both loved and knew" music and therefore remained "gracious" toward his kapellmeister, even though the latter, in his capacity as leader of the orchestra, increasingly performed the works of other composers to give himself time to pursue his own explorations of new territory—the somewhat more sparsely furnished repertories of chamber and keyboard music.

In this realm at least we can form a more distinct picture of Bach in Cöthen, for we have some clearly established dates. The fair copy of *Sei Solo senza Basso accompagnato,* the three sonatas and three partitas for solo violin BWV 1001–06, dates from the year 1720. It is on 22 January that Bach begins the *Klavierbüchlein* for his eldest son, Wilhelm Friedemann. In 1721 he writes the title pages of the first *Notenbüchlein* for Anna Magdalena Bach and the first part of *The Well-Tempered Clavier.* In 1723, at the end of his time in Cöthen, comes the title page of the *Inventions and Sinfonias.*

We should place the solo works for cello BWV 1007–12 next to those for the violin, since they have come down to us in a manuscript written in Anna Magdalena's hand from around 1720. Several sonatas for a melody instrument with harpsichord obligato, which exist only in later handwritten copies, can be assigned to the Cöthen chamber music repertory, but only hypothetically: the six violin sonatas BWV 1014–19a, the sonatas for viola da gamba BWV 1027–29, as well as the flute sonatas BWV 1030a, 1034, and 1035.

Of the first *Notenbüchlein* for Anna Magdalena only a torso has survived. It does, however, contain early versions of five of the six *French Suites,* BWV 812–17, thereby making it clear that this series belongs chiefly to the Cöthen period, to which the works that Forkel rather arbitrarily calls the *English Suites,* BWV 806, should perhaps also be assigned—contrary to the widespread scholarly view that they were composed in Weimar.[130] The practice of family music making, of which we catch a glimpse in the fragments of the first *Notenbüchlein* for Bach's wife, emerges clearly from the second collection of keyboard works dedicated to her: the repertory consists chiefly of movements from suites, smallish dance pieces, religious and secular songs, and elaborated recitatives and arias.

We must jump ahead to the *Notenbüchlein,* not begun until 1725, when Bach was already in Leipzig, in order to highlight the difference between this work and the *Klavierbüchlein* that he put together exactly two months after the ninth birthday of his eldest son. Despite the interruptions in his work on this latter collection, its fundamental character is clearly didactic, with emphasis not only on mastering the keyboard but also on achieving excellence in compositional technique. To be sure, parts of the first section are intended for basic instruction in music and keyboard playing: the little book offers examples of notation, fingering, and flourishes, as well as easy versions of two no doubt carefully selected chorales, "Wer nur den lieben Gott lässt walten" and "Jesu, meine Freude." It also contains the nine little preludes BWV 924–32 and a few dance movements, to whose composition Wilhelm Friedemann may have contributed himself. Telemann and Gottfried Heinrich Stölzel are represented with one suite each. But the volume's real substance consists of early versions, copied only partially by Wilhelm Friedemann, of preludes from the *Well-Tempered Clavier 1,* in the sequence of keys C major, C minor, D minor, D major, E minor, E major, F major, C-sharp major, C-sharp minor, E-flat minor, F minor; also from the two-part inventions known as the Praeambulum, in the key sequence of C major, D minor, E minor, F major, G major, A minor, B minor, B-flat major, A major, G minor, F minor, E major, E-flat major, D major, and C minor; and finally with the three-part sinfonias in the key sequence of C major, D minor, E minor, F major, G major, A minor, B minor, B-flat major, A major, G minor, F minor, E major, E-flat major, and D major.

This listing of the keys may seem tedious, but it provides a telling glimpse into the genesis of the keyboard cycles that were to play such a significant part in music history. Their final form was by no means established at the outset; for instance, Bach may have expected to write only one two- and one three-part invention for each step on the diatonic scale. The repertory of the *Klavierbüchlein* indirectly reveals that he reached two decisions crucial for the final form of *The Well-Tempered Clavier* only at a very late stage: to link preludes and fugues and to include all major and minor keys in the order of the rising chromatic scale.

How important he considered the last-named collections can be seen from their detailed titles; they could have been intended as the basis for a printed version, or at least to make clear to the prince of Cöthen how significant these works should be considered, falling as they did outside the ordinary purview of Bach's kapellmeister's duties.

The Well-Tempered Clavier

or

Preludes, and

Fugues through all the Tones and *Semitones,*

Both in regard to the *tertia major* or *Ut Re Mi*

And in regard to the tertia minor or Re

Mi Fa. For the

Use and profit of musical youth

Desirous of learning, as well as for

The pastime of those already skilled

In these studies, composed and

completed by Johann Sebastian Bach

p.t. Kapellmeister to His Serene Highness,

the Prince of Anhalt-Cöthen, and

Director of his Chamber Music.

Anno

1722

The Inventions and Sinfonias bear the title:

Proper Instruction

Wherein to lovers of the *Clavier,*

And especially those desirous of learning, is shown

A clear way (1) to learn to play cleanly not merely in two

Parts, but also, after further progress, (2) to proceed properly

And well with three *obligato* parts and furthermore, at the

Same time, not merely to have good *inventions* but

To execute the same well, but above all, to achieve *cantabile*

Style in playing and furthermore acquire a strong

Foretaste of *composition.*

Produced

By

Joh. Seb. Bach

Kapellmeister to his Serene Highness

The Prince of Anhalt-Cöthen

Anno Christi 1723

In both cases, Bach signs himself as the kapellmeister of Cöthen, despite the fact that both works were not actually produced as part of his duties in this position but constitute a first major attempt at developing the core of a universal theory of music, using the example of keyboard music as a starting point. The idea is to demonstrate this theory not with a random assortment of models but with a coherent series of significant works. The combination of elementary and sophisticated works, of strict and free style, of order and expressiveness, of systematic planning and lively multiplicity, of spirituality and sensual sound, represents the first potent expression of a complex idea that we will discuss in greater detail later.

The concept of "multiplicity in unity" that finds realization in these works offers a framework into which one can also effortlessly fit the *Brandenburg Concertos* and the violin solos; the former embody the relevant possibilities within the genre of the concerto, in compositions with a colorful ensemble of instruments; the latter restrict themselves, this time in the realm of the sonata and the suite, to a single voice. Although our limited sources prevent us from ascertaining whether Bach composed only the works mentioned or others as well to document his universalist thinking, what has been preserved of his oeuvre speaks for itself: Cöthen offers an important example of how he not only responded to the circumstances in which he found himself at a given time but also pursued step by step his philosophy of musical order. Against this intellectual horizon, we can make an educated guess at the significance of the later years in Cöthen: as conscientiously as Bach fulfilled his duties as kapellmeister, he also gave his creative impulses free rein.

Can this behavior also be interpreted as a sort of "inner emigration" in response to adverse conditions in Anhalt-Cöthen? More recent Bach scholarship has pointed out that during his reign Prince Leopold is trying to repel attacks on two fronts: on the one hand, he finds himself in conflict with his younger brother, August Ludwig, a conflict that forces Leopold to renounce his secundogeniture rule over Anhalt-Cöthen-Warmsdorf and the revenue from that province. After fierce struggles, a settlement is reached in August 1722.[131] On the other hand, Leopold is assailed by the efforts of his mother, Gisela Agnes, to strengthen the position of the Lutheran creed in the principality. Officially the principality is committed to the reformed faith, in conformity with the principle "cuius regio, eius religio," enshrined in the Peace of Augsburg of 1555, for in 1596 Prince Johann Georg forcibly established Calvinism in the town of Cöthen and almost all the villages around. Lutheranism nonetheless retains its loyal adherents for over a century, who now benefit from the fact that Gisela Agnes is herself a Lutheran and energetically pursues the construction of a Lutheran church and the establishment of a Lutheran school in Cöthen. Political confrontations erupt[132] and weaken Leopold's power not inconsiderably.

Whether Bach was affected by these conflicts to the point that he grew weary of his position seems doubtful. In any discussion of his reasons for leaving Cöthen, one should give the most credence to those he cites in his letter to Erdmann. He explains that after the prince married at the end of 1721, his interest in music became "somewhat lukewarm"—perhaps because of his young wife, who seemed "to be an *amusa*."[133] Bach adds that Leipzig offers better educational opportunities for his sons.

We have little evidence that would allow us to comment reliably on the first reason Bach mentions so cautiously. Of course it is conceivable that the nineteen-year-old princess, Friederica Henrietta of Anhalt-Bernburg, had less appreciation for Bach's music than her husband did. In general, though, she seems to have been anything but hostile to music and the other arts. The inventory of her papers includes "A notebook wherein are several small Pieces of music bound in Turkish paper," "a ditto in French binding, with gilt lettering, in a case," "a book bound in brown leather, wherein several Arias are written," "two written books of notes, in Turkish paper," as well as "An aria, with blue gilt-edged paper."[134] The presence of musical scores allows us to infer that she engaged in some music making, and the collection is rather extensive for this young noblewoman, who at the time of her marriage would have only another sixteen months to live.

Bach's reference to the better educational opportunities in Leipzig seems plausible; for the younger boys, the Latin School in Cöthen may have been perfectly adequate, but this was perhaps Bach's last chance to move to a university town!

At any rate, Bach's critical remarks in retrospect about the last years in Cöthen may reflect accurately his mood that it is time for a change. But hasn't this been true at least since 1720, when he set out on his trip to Hamburg, or 1721, when he dedicated the *Brandenburg Concertos* to Margrave Ludwig Christian? In the course of his life, he often feels impatient to leave a place, and at such moments criticism of his current circumstances comes easily. Yet he would surely not have left Cöthen if Leipzig had not exerted the greatest imaginable professional attraction.

On his path from matins singer to court kapellmeister Bach never fails to find recognition—on the contrary, he enjoys a steady, almost steep rise in prestige, such as only a few of his contemporaries are granted. We should take note of his unobtrusive yet remarkably frequent changes in employment—a sign of the searching, seething element in his artistic existence up to this point. Even Cöthen does not signal that he has arrived. In the effort he invests in *The Well-Tempered Clavier* and the *Inventions and Sinfonias* in particular, he proves to be a composer committed not to art dictated by courtly taste but to a kind of music that sets its own standard, a music he wants to explore and express in his own way. In terms of his philosophy of music, the years in Cöthen are a period of seeking and finding. They also represent a high point for Bach with respect to the way his musical life is organized. From the beginning of his career, he has hated having to work with mediocre or inadequate resources. In Cöthen he has everything he needs. In Leipzig he will again have to fight for a "well-regulated church music"—meaning music with enough skilled performers—and will eventually be forced to capitulate.

CANTOR AT ST. THOMAS AND CITY MUSIC DIRECTOR IN LEIPZIG

THE POSITION AND ITS NEW INCUMBENT

Once appointed to the position of cantor at St. Thomas's, Bach changes, almost overnight, a feature of his notational style: the form of the C clef. Does this detail portend the many changes, large and small, that await the thirty-eight-year-old? One thing is certain: he will be working under public scrutiny far more than in any previous post. The Hamburg press alone will devote fourteen reports to the appointment of the new cantor. Perhaps the emphasis reflects the Hamburgers' pique at "their" Telemann's being passed over, but at the same time it suggests the visibility of this particular office even outside the immediate region.

Indeed, for centuries following the Reformation important musicians and composers have been appointed to the cantor's position at St. Thomas's, among them Wolfgang Figulus, Valentin Otto, Sethus Calvisius, Johann Hermann Schein, Sebastian Knüpfer, Johann Schelle, and Johann Kuhnau. The incumbent is always a teacher with academic training. He occupies a position in the hierarchy of the collegium just below the principal (known as the rector) and vice principal, with a teaching load of seven music lessons and five Latin classes per week.[1] He is also responsible for directing the student choir when it performs for church services; but this particular duty reveals the awkwardness inherent in the position, an awkwardness that will affect Bach's work in Leipzig as it did that of his more recent predecessors.

So long as the artistically prepossessing vocal music accompanying the services consisted primarily of variations on the motet form, such as an Introitus motet, a kyrie, a Gloria, and a motet based on a passage from Scripture, the cantor was the ideal director; he could practice the appropriate works with the students during their instructional time, and then they would perform the works without further ado in church. The pieces did not need to be his own compositions. But this type of performance, well suited to the abilities of a student choir, reached its limit in the course of the seventeenth century, when a new concept of sacred music began to make inroads: now progressively minded musicians were no longer content to contribute small choral flourishes to the individual elements of the liturgy; it became their ambition to offer pieces capable of standing on their own—first spiritual concertos, later cantatas in several movements.

Thus Christoph Bernhard, a student of Heinrich Schütz, proclaims the "*stylus compositionis* of performing a concerto over a basso continuo" the new style of the seventeenth century. As a *stylus luxurians* it supplants the old *stylus gravis,* the use of which persists unchanged only in the papal kapelle.

The paradigm shift Bernhard describes has three aspects. First, the manner of composing changes: the motet style, which emphasizes "not so much the text as the harmony," is replaced by the concertizing style, which consists of "fairly rapid notes in part, peculiar leaps, calculated to stir the emotions, more types of dissonance... and good arias that suit well the texts..." A special variant of this style is the "theatrical."[2]

Second, along with the style of composition, the type of performance also changes: the choir tends to be replaced by an instrumental ensemble with vocal soloists that takes its cue from the basso continuo. And third, a new understanding of sacred music makes itself felt: beauty and harmony no longer serve merely to objectify and enhance a given liturgical text; they are now a vehicle for self-representation on the part of the faithful, who raise their voices to God—addressing Him passionately and directly.

Heinrich Schütz, a master of the new style of composing, recognizes the difficulties that the new *stylus luxurians* presents for musicians. Of his *Weihnachts-Historie* he prudently allows only the Evangelist's part with the continuo accompaniment to be printed. The rest of the parts are available exclusively as copies; because it is to be feared "that aside from well-staffed princely Kapelles, such *inventiones* would hardly be able to achieve their intended effect elsewhere,"[3] they must not fall into the wrong hands.

In Bach's day, the new music is referred to as *Figuralmusik*. This term, according to a definition perhaps derived from Christoph Bernhard, in Johann Gottfried Walther's *Musikalisches Lexikon* of 1732, means a kind of music "whose notes are of varying type and significance; and whose tempo varies between fast and slow"—an explanation that sounds simplistic but nonetheless makes it clear that this music is flexible and richly nuanced, reflecting the varied movements of the human emotions. In 1725, when Bach chooses the apparently uncommon term *musica formalis* for this same phenomenon,[4] he is emphasizing a different yet equally crucial component: this music has a "form" deserving of the name; it is not conceived as a mere accompaniment to the text but has its own inherent musical character.

When figural music is presented in the form of a lengthy cantata, it is not merely one piece of music among others included in the service but the "principal music"—that is, the main musical event of the service—Bach addresses it as such in a note he wrote to himself on the structure of church services in Leipzig, using the margin of the cantata "Nun komm der Heiden Heiland," BWV 61. As the opposite of "principal music," Bach mentions "ordinary music," which "can certainly be directed by *vicarios* and *praefectos*."[5]

One can equate the "recital" of the cantata, so often mentioned in the sources, to the sermon, which is always new for the occasion, while the performance of the motet music is equivalent to the reading from Scripture or the singing of hymns: the former is an individual creative accomplishment, the latter the presentation of something already in existence—of central importance as an expression of faith but marginal as an expression of artistic ability.

In the absence of fresh new compositions, the old compendia are used as sources of traditional motet-style pieces. Occasionally these books are "fairly tattered" or even "chewed through and through by mice," as Bach's predecessor in office, Kuhnau, discovers when he undertakes an inventory in 1702.[6] One particular compilation of the traditional repertory published in 1603 turns out to be so useful that it is reprinted time and again: the *Florilegium Portense* of Erhard Bodenschatz, a collection of four- to eight-part motets, most of them in Latin, of which Bach orders new copies several times starting in 1729.

But the *Florilegium Portense* offers no modern concerted music or cantatas. Since such music must adapt to rapidly changing tastes and also be calibrated to the local resources available for performances, it is not always practicable to get it printed; only the director of modern church music in a specific location knows what talent he will have at his disposal and what degree of modernity his superiors will tolerate; he must be flexible, composing his own music in the best case and always aware that it may become the subject of controversy.

Who is the director of local modern music, as it is generally called, without further specification? At courts it is the kapellmeister, in some towns the organist—for instance, in Lübeck or Halle. In the course of the seventeenth century, a division of labor develops: the cantor is academically trained, with strong school ties, the director of the student choir and guardian of musical tradition; while the organist's activity includes composing, performing, directing an ensemble that he himself must recruit from among the available musicians and introducing new ideas in music.

In other towns that have both a Latin school and a cantor's position, there is an attempt to bridge this gap. For one thing, much leeway is given to both modern organ music and cantorial music; for another, the cantor is put in charge of modern music but not excused from his traditional duties.

Leipzig is one city that adopts this compromise. The town has a splendid tradition of vocal organ music. When Adam Krieger is elected organist of St. Nicholas's in 1655, this musician who describes himself as "devoted to the liberal arts" considers it self-evident that he, like his distinguished predecessor, Johann Rosenmüller, will be performing sacred vocal music as well, assisted by the student "collegium musicum." Within a year the treasury of St. Nicholas's grants him one hundred gulden for training two discantists and paying a bass singer, "because the music performed heretofore by the aforesaid Krüger [Krieger] has been pleasing to many and has brought particular fame and distinction to the entire town and notably to the church."[7]

This remarkably enthusiastic articulation of the reasons for an appropriation of funds—not a single statement like this appears in reference to Bach in the Leipzig official documents—reveals the fascination this new music must have engendered, with its emotional, songlike character, but also the motivation for promoting such music: it strengthens Leipzig's reputation as a city of the arts. Of course these comments can also be read as an allusion to the inadequacies of the aged and feeble cantor of St. Thomas's, Tobias Michael. Indeed, a later cantor at St. Thomas's will have to put up with indirect criticism of his musical taste: in 1702, when Kuhnau has just been appointed, a dynamic young mayor, Franz Conrad Romanus, will commission a twenty-two-year-old student to compose sacred music for St. Thomas's in alternation with the cantor. The student is Telemann, recently installed as musical director of the opera and of a student collegium musicum.

The Elector of Saxony has installed Romanus for the express purpose of transforming Leipzig into a modern city—possibly in the face of opposition from conservative circles. A few weeks after Romanus takes office, a decree reaches the Leipzig city council from Dresden, in the handwriting of the bold burgomaster, that without mincing words urges the councilmen to adopt a series of innovations; among those listed are gutters to allow street cleaning and outdoor lanterns on all the houses, practice drills in bird hunting and musket firing, and police checks on coffeehouses. Furthermore, "particularly during the fair, when foreigners come to Leipzig from afar, the music in the churches should be raised to a high standard."[8]

This directive shows that excellent church music is as vital to Leipzig's reputation as the splendid baroque residential and commercial palaces built at the beginning of the eighteenth century, not least of all on the initiative of the young burgomaster. Romanus promotes organ music vigorously, having Telemann appointed organist and music director of the New Church, whose building has fallen into disrepair over the centuries but since 1699 has been used again for services, at the wish of Leipzig's business community.

Romanus also wants to see Telemann appointed to succeed the ailing Kuhnau, which would place a worldly personality in charge of Leipzig's church music. Yet events take a different course: in January 1705, this burgomaster who has achieved distinction at such a young age is arrested for actual or alleged malfeasance in office and dragged off to the Königstein Fortress, where he spends the remaining fourteen years of his life. Telemann, deprived of his great patron, departs that same year for the court at Sorau.

Under Telemann's successors Melchior Hoffmann, Johann Gottfried Vogler, and Balthasar Schott the New Church remains a hub of the new music, inspired by Italian orchestral and operatic style. In 1717, the first passion oratorio is performed in Leipzig: Telemann's score to a text by the poet Barthold Heinrich Brockes. Some find it comical, others a feast for the ears. In 1721, the Leipzig theology student Gottfried Ephraim Scheibel remarks, "I recall that in a certain place on Good Friday before and after the sermon a passion was supposed to be performed. The people would surely not have arrived at church so early and in such numbers for the sake of the preacher."[9] Presumably it is Telemann's passion to which he is referring; at any rate, he describes the situation vividly. It is in this same context that the cantor of St. Thomas's, Kuhnau, complains that he cannot find suitable musicians for performances at his church, for the student musicians have all fallen prey to "the wild opera craze," which also prevails at the New Church: the young gentlemen prefer the "merry music in the Opera, and the coffeehouses, to our chorus," and have no sense of proper church style and devout liturgical music, "for which a specialized and long course of study is essential."[10]

Thus well into the Bach period, Leipzig encourages a vocal organ music that epitomizes the most modern practice, calculated to attract academically trained young people. Yet the city is not ready to accept a division of schoolmastering and composing into two offices. The idea was rejected as early as 1657, when Krieger's application to succeed Tobias Michael was turned down, in spite of the great esteem in which his accomplishments were held. He had stipulated that he should not have to "both labor in the school and act as cantor, like the previous director," for the following reason: "not out of any ambition to cast aspersions on the school position, but because this effort, along with the *Studio Compositionis*, would be too burdensome, considering that one who works himself to the bone in the school subsequently has little desire to put together a musical concert, and if he lacks desire for composing, it tends to turn out poorly." He added that the previous incumbents of the position had "because of the school duties become stiff with indignation and ill humor and suffered poor health."[11]

The council was not willing to compromise. To be sure, with Sebastian Knüpfer it selected a distinguished composer who was also willing to "inform"—that is, to teach—and thus became the first cantor of St. Thomas's to subscribe unhesitatingly to the new concertizing style. The rich instrumentalization in Knüpfer's works reveals plainly that the official Leipzig church music required not only well-trained vocal soloists but also a competent instrumental ensemble. The cantor had to recruit the members of his ensemble from among the eight council musicians—four town pipers, three violinists, somewhat inferior to the former in reputation and salary, and a journeyman musician. In some cases the council musicians may have had apprentices and additional journeymen associated with them. The cantor could also count on funds for student assistants; but these funds flowed sparsely and not with the desired regularity.

Bach's activity in Leipzig can be understood only against the background of the special circumstances prevailing there. As the cantor of St. Thomas's and director of music, Bach faces a structural problem and one not merely organizational but also theological and ideological. This problem, too, must be described in some detail.

Over the centuries, there was probably no Leipzig council member who did not want his city to be important and at least reasonably cosmopolitan. In particular, the enthusiasm for music displayed by the leading officials was far greater than that of most comparable politicians in our day; where would one find today a city council the majority of whose members would argue that for every Sunday and holiday service a concertizing piece as long and difficult as a Bach cantata should be performed?

That the Leipzig city council as a body supports the cultivation of this kind of music shows the desire of an ambitious middle class to gain access to music on which the aristocracy has had a monopoly: music should no longer be heard only in a liturgical or aristocratic context, it should also be experienced as an autonomous aesthetic phenomenon and a source of sensual pleasure. True, the middle class does not yet have at its disposal the institutional and financial resources of a court, nor does its ethos countenance pure pleasure of the sort in which the aristocracy indulges.

It is therefore a matter of both necessity and virtue that the reorientation of middle-class music occurs in a church setting. But on this point opinions diverge—as they would today. The question is how much "modern" church music a normal church service can accommodate without losing sight of its purpose—namely, edification. Skepticism toward innovation, extending well back into the seventeenth century, takes three different aspects. First, the new music represents artistic excellence or even virtuosity, thus appealing more to the churchgoers' ears and lust for novelty than to their desire for devotion. Second, for the faithful who lack any particular musical sensibility or interest, this music is difficult to understand and therefore not particularly conducive to religious edification. Third, it is the sermon, using the spoken and thus unambiguous word, that is chiefly intended to move the hearts of the faithful; what is pronounced from the pulpit should not be overshadowed by liturgical music that goes on too long and assumes too much importance of its own.

It is in this spirit that Duke Ernst the Pious follows up a general visitation in 1645 with the directive that in his province of Saxony-Gotha-Altenburg everyone should "bring his breviary to church and read therein during the figural singing and organ playing."[12] In the subsequent period, important Lutheran reformist theologians inveigh quite frequently against church music that takes the place of "the old, silent devotions," music in which the organists, cantors, pipers, and musicians, "oft unspiritual persons, lead the performances in city churches and play, sing, fiddle, and diddle to their hearts' content": "You hear much roaring and booming, and soaring tones, but know not what it is, whether you should gird yourself for battle or depart from that place; one chases the other in concertizing, and several strive against one another to see who can do it most artfully and echo the nightingale most subtly..." Thus the Rostock theologian Theophil Grossgebauer laments and mocks the goings-on in churches in his 1661 "Watchman's Voice from the Devastated Zion." In 1687, his attentive reader Philipp Jacob Spener, father of the more moderate form of Pietism, expresses a more amiable-sounding but no less disapproving view in a theological assessment: he suggests that extensive figural music be restricted either to the end of the service or to specially arranged performances.[13]

The same spirit informs the comments in the official *Leipzig Church Bulletin: Item, Clear Instructions for the Conduct of Church Services in Leipzig* from the year 1710: there one finds suggestions as to how "one can spend the time during which the organist is improvising a prelude or playing at length (even though some [members of the congregation] have but slight regard for figural or often operatic music) more profitably than in idle chatter." The authors recommend "prayer when the organ is playing or a Latin motet is being sung" (page 5).

The Pietists are not the only ones who worry that artistic church music may take on a significance independent of the service; the concern is shared by many representatives of Lutheran orthodoxy, who need not be hostile to art and music to oppose separating the positions of cantor and city music director. They believe that an academically trained and, if possible, theologically knowledgeable cantor will be best equipped to serve as a municipal music director who prevents the gulf between tradition and modernity from becoming unbridgeable. While a music director without ties to the church would presumably ignore the St. Thomas's *chorus musicus,* a St. Thomas's cantor would include it in his arrangements as a valuable artistic "instrument" and thereby signal the intention to preserve traditional values.

The Leipzig city council does not have political parties in the modern sense but rather conducts its business by consensus. The advocates of opposing positions must therefore eventually reach agreement. This modus operandi has its advantages but also its disadvantages: problems are seldom resolved definitively. This indefiniteness will beset the search for a successor to Johann Kuhnau.[14] In the end, Bach will be hired under the terms of a compromise that he will "strive to honor" on the highest artistic level but never fully accept professionally.

Abraham Christoph Plaz, a sixty-eight-year-old appeals judge; Adrian Steger, about sixty-one; and Gottfried Lange, fifty: in 1722 those are the three Leipzig burgomasters who set the tone in the Leipzig city council. All are well educated, highly respected, and by no means narrow-minded men, and Plaz and Lange have traveled extensively. Plaz was halfway through his studies toward a degree in theology, and had even studied Hebrew, before he decided to make law his profession. In Leipzig he performs various legal functions; he also chairs the governing body of St. Nicholas's and has close ties to the Spener branch of Pietism.

Lange, also a lawyer, already has behind him a career at the court in Dresden. There he rose to the position of manager of the Privy Cabinet, the highest post open to a non-noble. Wanting to see him as "his man in Leipzig," the Elector recommends him for a position on the council. When the council resists, a secret directive arrives from Dresden in 1717, mandating that Lange be elected to the next burgomaster's position to become available, which is done in 1719. As the site of the famous fair, Leipzig is the most important city in Saxony after Dresden, which explains the Elector's desire to make his influence felt there at all times.[15] Lange's wife is a daughter of Joachim Feller, a professor of poetics who serves several terms as rector of the university in Leipzig, sympathizes with Pietism, but also loves music; on the side, he heads the governing body of St. Thomas's and belongs to the consistory.

Steger, from an old, established Leipzig family, is another lawyer, with the title of Hofrat, or privy councilor. His father, a learned man in his own right, served as burgomaster before Steger was elected to the council in 1689. Steger heads the governing board of St. Peter's, which receives from among the singers trained at St. Thomas's, in Bach's words, only "the leavings," namely "those who do not understand Music, but can only just manage to sing a Chorale."[16]

Among the members of the council, Plaz and Steger represent the traditionalists. They cannot disagree in public with the axiom that because of its reputation as a cosmopolitan and commercial city Leipzig needs a music director with an outstanding reputation. But in their hearts they are far more interested in finding a cantor for St. Thomas's. Therefore every mishap in a performance by a candidate from the ranks of music directors gives them a pretext for uttering their formula: "*Ceterum censeo, Cantorem esse eligendum.*"*

The governing burgomaster in the year of the election is Lange, whose general profile is somewhat reminiscent of Romanus, also recommended for the Leipzig position by the court at Dresden. Lange would prefer to see the offices of cantor and music director separated. He places his entire emphasis on hiring a music director and thereby bringing a vibrant modern musical life to Leipzig. Having been appointed head of the St. Thomas's governing board in

---

*"Once again, I submit, a cantor must be elected." This is something of a joke, referring to Cato the Elder's habit of introducing the phrase "Carthago delenda est" ("Carthage must be destroyed") into every speech he made, no matter what the topic was.

1720, he probably used his position to ensure that there, and not only at the New Church, figural passions could be performed, as Kuhnau in fact did for the first time in 1721. That a passion was performed at St. Thomas's in 1723, while the cantor's position was vacant, can probably be attributed to Lange's personal influence.

After Kuhnau's death, the council seems to have gone straight to Telemann, serving at the time as cantor and music director of the four principal churches in Hamburg. Telemann enjoys a fine reputation in Leipzig and an even better one in the rest of Germany and all of Europe. There are other applicants, among them the Magdeburg cantor, Friedrich Rolle; the kapellmeister Johann Friedrich Fasch, serving at the court of Bohemia; and the organist of the New Church in Leipzig, Georg Balthasar Schott. But in the summer of 1722 only Telemann receives an invitation to audition.

Given the candidate's uncontested fame, the conservatives content themselves with demanding that Telemann specifically describe his plans for teaching at the St. Thomas School, a task that the progressives would like to relieve him of entirely. Despite this disagreement, the favorite is elected unanimously on 11 August 1722. Well aware of the situation in Leipzig, Telemann soon takes steps to make sure that he will also be in charge of music at the university church— that is, the church of the Paulines—already overseen by the cantor of St. Thomas's under Schelle and Kuhnau. The council and the university seem prepared to grant the request in this case, whereas a short time later the nonacademic Bach cannot even voice such a request, because the position has already been filled without consultation. Then Telemann withdraws his candidacy; Hamburg has offered him a substantially raised salary of 400 talers.

It is revealing to look at the reasons the "famous virtuoso," as the press celebrates him,[17] names when asking to be discharged from his duties in Hamburg: he mentions not only the higher income he can expect in Leipzig but also difficulties he is having with the caucus of "elders," who demanded that the Hamburg senate forbid the cantor "under pain of severe punishment" to "perform his music for money in a tavern..."[18] One can easily imagine that the progressive wing of the Leipzig council may have made representations to Telemann that in Leipzig he would be welcome to undertake such initiatives without any restrictions.

When the search for a cantor has to be reopened, seven candidates emerge at first. The favorite is now Fasch, who has meanwhile accepted an appointment at the court at Zerbst. He declines the Leipzig position—citing, among other reasons, the fact that he "cannot instruct." At the cantor's auditions held on the first Sunday of Advent, the candidates participating are Georg Balthasar Schott, the Merseburg court organist and music director Georg Friedrich Kauffmann, and the Braunschweig cantor Christoph Duve.

Is Bach already a figure on the horizon? A conversation about questions of remuneration with the rector of the University of Leipzig, Ulrich Junius, which Bach speaks of in 1725, must have taken place during the summer term of 1722.[19] There are also the previously mentioned notes on the order of the service at St. Thomas's that Bach jotted down on the score of the cantata BWV 61. These may go back to the 1722 Advent season and serve as evidence of feelers put out by the Leipzig council; in the Erdmann letter Bach writes that he "delayed my decision for a quarter of a year." Has Bach had his eye on Leipzig for some time, and is he merely waiting for the right moment to apply? Whatever the case, the council minutes for 21 December 1722 record that "several others had presented themselves, such as Kapellmeister Graupner in Darmstadt and Bach in Cöthen."[20]

Of these two, the one who initially makes the stronger impression is the court kapellmeister Christoph Graupner, an alumnus of the St. Thomas School and, like Telemann, a graduate of the Leipzig university. He is apparently eager to move to Leipzig in view of the catastrophic financial situation of the kapelle in Darmstadt. Yet doubtful that his prince will grant him a discharge, the council arranges for two further auditions: for Schott, who thus has a second chance, replacing a candidate who has withdrawn on short notice, and for Bach. Graupner auditions on 17 January, Schott on 2 February, Bach a week later.

"On the Sunday just past, in the morning, the Hon. Kapellmeister to his Serene Highness the Prince of Cöthen, Monsieur Bach, had his audition here at the Church of St. Thomas," the *Hamburger Relationscourier* reports on 15 February 1723. Once it has become apparent that Graupner will not be released by his prince but instead will be tied more closely to the court through the promise of a salary increase, the three semifinalists, according to Burgomaster Lange on 9 April 1723, are Bach, Kauffmann, and Schott, "but all three would be unable to give instruction at the same time, and in Telemann's case the question of a division [of the duties] had already been considered."[21]

Plaz finds the most recent talk of separating the duties "troublesome for significant reasons"and continues, "since the best could not be obtained, mediocre ones would have to be accepted; many good things had previously been said about a man in Pirna."

This vote is occasionally interpreted in the Bach literature as indicating a lack of enthusiasm for Bach, but it actually points in another direction: instead of separating the two offices, so as to spare "the best" the trouble of teaching, it would be better to take a solid schoolmaster. The "man in Pirna" is probably Christian Heckel, who has indeed gained prominence as a historian and expert in ancient languages. Plaz's opinion is not shared by the majority of the councilors, who vote to appoint Bach, with certain stipulations. Unfortunately the council minutes pertaining to this very important juncture in Bach's life are incomplete: "The rest of the minutes were kept by the Hon. Syndicus Job," it says just where things might become exciting.[22]

Although the minutes break off here, the search process continues. On 19 April Bach signs a pledge that commits him, among other things, to provide a certificate of dismissal in the event of his election; to fulfill conscientiously his work as a teacher at the St. Thomas School; to provide individual singing instruction without remuneration, as needed; and to demand no additional funds from the council for a possible substitute Latin teacher.[23]

Prince Leopold grants Bach his dismissal on 13 April 1723 with a laudatory statement. Not yet notified of this step, the council proceeds to a vote on 22 April. The comments of the three mayors, recorded in two parallel sets of council minutes, mirror faithfully the discussion that preceded them. Lange's remarks are summarized as follows: "Bach was Kapellmeister in Cöthen and excelled on the clavier. Besides music he had teaching responsibilities, and [as] Cantor [he] was required to provide instruction in the *Colloquia Corderi* [a textbook of piety, letters, and behavior] and in grammar, which he was willing to do. He had agreed to give not only public but also private instruction. If Bach were chosen, one could forget Telemann, in view of his *conduite*" (likely a reference to the poor manners Telemann displayed in turning down the appointment).[24]

Plaz thereupon shows himself favorably disposed: "Bach must be in good *renommé*, and his person was winning, most especially because he had declared himself willing to instruct the boys not only in Music but also regularly in the school; it would remain to be seen how he would accomplish this last."[25]

Steger articulates the concerns of the conservative camp: Bach "had declared himself ready to prove his loyalty not only as Cantor but also as colleague in the St. Thomas School," and "he should make such compositions as were not theatrical."[26] Steger is the one who evidently has the least interest in artistic church music; in this sense he previously made the slightly irritated comment in connection with Graupner's candidacy that "He was no Musicus" and refrained from voting yea or nay.[27]

After all those eligible have voted for Bach, Lange summarizes the proceedings in his capacity as governing burgomaster; the minutes characterize his comments thus: "It was necessary to select a man of renown, so that the [university] students might be inspired."[28]

Bach is entitled to view his election as a real honor; he does not have university training, a fact that could have given the conservatives ample grounds for objecting; unlike Telemann, Fasch, and Graupner, however, he does not compose operas, a genre that might have appealed to the progressive faction of the council. Yet he is a virtuoso of the keyboard, in no way inferior to Telemann, and will show the Leipzig students what modern music is—all important considerations for Burgomaster Lange, who apparently assumes the role of Bach's protector and, on 27 February 1724, will become godfather to Bach's son Heinrich, who bears Lange's name.

Thus the progressive faction prevails, after seeking the best musician and attending the various auditions and listening knowledgeably. We should not take this election lightly, for Bach is by no means merely a pleasing composer. There may have been some premonition that he would prove to be a difficult artist for Leipzig. When the correspondent for the *Hamburger Relationscourier* notes, in the report mentioned earlier, that the music Bach performed at the audition was "much praised on that occasion by all who can appreciate such things," this simple yet nuanced formulation seems to encapsulate Bach's situation in Leipzig—at the time of his election and later on as well.[29]

The conservatives exact a high price for their willingness to compromise. They essentially dictate into the minutes the stipulation that as cantor of St. Thomas the new man will be firmly attached to the school system and as an artist must practice moderation when it comes to modern church music. These conditions have profound implications for the next twenty-seven years, during which Bach will work and compose in Leipzig. As an instructor, he can hardly count on consideration or support from his rector; as a composer, he will in many cases have to be satisfied with the admiration of a small number of connoisseurs. But above all he is destined to be chronically overworked, a man whose productivity we register only with disbelief and amazement.

Bach displays great skill in the composition of his audition pieces and his performance of them at St. Thomas's. The available sources lend credence to the supposition that on Quinquagesima Sunday he was allowed to present two cantatas, like other candidates. Although it is not possible to determine whether the council imposed specific guidelines for the choice of text and the compositional style, it is clear that Bach handles the situation cleverly: before the sermon he offers "Jesus nahm zu sich," BWV 22, a kind of conventional Sunday cantata that begins with a quotation from Scripture, ends with a choral movement with instrumental ornamentation of the sort that is traditional in central Germany, and altogether does not confront the Leipzig congregation with anything too new or disturbing; we can picture the conservative councilors nodding approvingly.

After the sermon he offers the cantata "Du wahrer Mensch und Davids Sohn," an exquisite piece of liturgical chamber music full of bold effects in the structure of the movements and the harmonies— showcasing himself as the highly accomplished Cöthen kapellmeister. The "chorale" element is more implicit than explicit in the purely instrumental recitative that occupies the middle portion of the originally three-movement work. But since at St. Thomas's a cantata without a concluding chorale is perhaps still considered an abomination, Bach may have been advised to add one to his cantata; the text he was given called for one. From the sources it seems likely that he delved into his supply of finished works and added the artful polyphonic choral version of "Christe, du Lamm Gottes" as a final movement, which, to be sure, appreciably distorts the original proportions of the piece.

> *On 5 May Bach is invited into the council chamber, and after he had taken his place behind the chairs,* Dominus Consul Regens D. Lange stated that although a number of candidates had presented themselves for service as Cantor of the St. Thomas School, but since he had been deemed the most capable for the post, he had been elected unanimously, and he should be presented by the Superintendent here, and should receive the same [salary] as the deceased Herr Kuhnau.
>
> Ille [he, i.e., Bach] expressed his most humble gratitude for being thought of, and promised his complete loyalty and industry.[30]

Bach signs a compact that primarily details his duties as cantor of the St. Thomas School and further commits him not to leave town without the burgomaster's permission; to "so far as possible walk with and among the boys in funeral processions"; and, a tricky provision, not to take on any post at the university without authorization. Point 7 contains the instruction that "in order to preserve good order in the churches," Bach should "so arrange the music that it not last too long, and be of such a nature as not to appear operatic, but rather to inspire the listeners to devotion."[31]

The next hurdle is for Bach to present himself before the consistory and the professor of theology Johann Schmid to undergo the mandatory examination, perhaps not pro forma for a candidate who has neither theological nor any other university training. The previous year, Bach's colleague Conrad Küffner failed such an examination when he was a candidate for the cantorship at St. Katherine's in Zwickau. Schmid had asked Küffner how many chapters the Gospels and the Epistles of St. Paul have, how often Christ's genealogy appears in the Bible, where the statement "That is life eternal" can be found, and what characteristics God the Father possesses as the primary member of the Trinity.[32]

The record confirms that Bach answered the questions put to him (we do not know what they were) in such a way that the examiner considers him eligible for appointment as cantor. All that now remains for Bach is to take an oath and swear his fealty to the Lutheran creed in its strictest form, which includes the articles of visitation of 1593, with their condemnation "of the Calvinist denials and antidoctrine."[33]

For 29 May the Hamburg *Stats- und Gelehrte Zeitung* reports:

> *This past Saturday at noon, four wagons loaded with household items arrived here from Cöthen; they belonged to the former Princely Kapellmeister there, now summoned to Leipzig as* Cantor Figuralis. *At 2 o'clock he himself arrived with his family in 2 carriages and moved into the freshly renovated quarters in the St. Thomas School.*

The Hamburg *Relationscourier* reports further that the newly installed cantor performed his inaugural music at St. Nicholas's on the first Sunday after Trinity—"to generous applause," as the annual chronicle of the Leipzig University notes.[34]

At Bach's installation at the St. Thomas School, which takes place on 1 June 1723 in the presence of representatives of the city and the church, Bach is publicly introduced and given his instructions by way of a text read by the head town clerk, whereupon Christian Weise, Sr., pastor of St. Thomas's, likewise issues instructions in his capacity as spiritual overseer of the school and on behalf of the consistory and the superintendent. This intervention, however, arouses the displeasure of the school's director, Johann Christian Lehmann, who speaks for the council to the effect that the church has no right to issue instructions. An outright confrontation in the presence of the entire faculty and student body is averted in time for the cantor to express his gratitude, after which the student choir performs, bringing the ceremony to a close.[35]

In the official minutes of the installation, Weise notes, among other things, the new cantor's intention of turning over his teaching assignment—five hours per week of Latin with grammar, Luther's catechism, as well as Maturinus Corderius's *Colloquia scholastica*—to the "Tertius" in the collegium for an annual salary of 50 talers. The possibility of hiring a substitute was expressly conceded to Bach, but it had the potential for causing serious problems. If complaints were to arise about the performance of the substitute—as happened, for example, in 1730—Bach would be held accountable.[36]

Buying his way out of teaching the academic subjects does not free the cantor of his responsibility for teaching music classes, giving individual lessons, or meeting his many other pedagogical obligations at this school with fifty-five boarding students. It is no accident that the apartment provided by the school is located right next to that of the rector. As the school's new charter, drafted and adopted in 1723, outlined, the institution is a "*Schola pauperum,* endowed to serve the best interests of the poor." That means that the teachers must act in loco parentis to the scholarship students living at the school "and show each of them paternal affection, love, and solicitude, and be forebearing toward their mistakes and weaknesses while nonetheless expecting self-discipline, order, and obedience."[37]

The emphasis in the charter on treating the boys as pupils, not as serfs, must not have come out of the blue, and the younger ones no doubt suffered at the hands of the older ones. In the year 1701 a complaint against the older students asserts that they burned mice over a candle and deposited them on the teacher's chair; that they dressed and undressed at the wrong times, spilled water on the floor and the tables, smashed windows, and swore at teachers.[38] In 1717, the teaching assistant Carl Friedrich complains about encountering rats and mice on the stairs in broad daylight. In 1733, Christoph Nichelmann, about sixteen years old, runs away from the boarding school; later he will become a highly respected composer and harpsichordist. Given the "gentle and peace-loving nature" that his colleague Wilhelm Friedrich Marpurg ascribes to him in an obituary, we must conclude that the St. Thomas School was too rough for him.[39]

It would be interesting to know how often Bach had to supervise the boys at mealtimes, making sure that "something useful was read clearly and slowly...alternately from Holy Scripture or a *Historico*"—preferably a Latin text, such as Erasmus's *Apophthegmata*, for this was the wish of Rector Johann Matthias Gesner, in office since 1730.[40] We would hope that for this duty Bach found a substitute fairly often, and also for the many major and minor performances by the St. Thomas choir that took place in addition to its principal appearances, for instance the presentation of motets, chorales, and altar music during services on Sundays and holidays, as well as during the numerous supplementary services.

Even if Bach took advantage of the many official as well as unofficial opportunities to hire a substitute, we should not underestimate the daily drudgery with which he had to contend. Thus Carl Gotthilf Kerner reports that he was appointed in 1741 to provide a kind of officiator's services, among them singing the litany in alternation with the choir or the congregation.[41] Even though we may assume that Bach examined the vocal abilities of every pupil at St. Thomas himself and then made the appropriate assignments, this archival detail, discovered more or less by chance, provides insight into the extent of such duties.

Since the St. Thomas School's mission commits it to accept only students from impecunious families, most of its income comes from musical services provided by the boarders. It is therefore not surprising that all fees and the key to their distribution among teachers and pupils are minutely recorded in the new charter of 1723. Along with other members of the collegium, Bach protests against these stipulations, since the new key reduces his income. Was he later able to recoup what was owed him in the form of larger and smaller incidentals from his share in the proceeds for funerals, collections on New Year's, St. Gregory's and St. Martin's, from the *Currende* and the money collected for music between Michaelmas and Easter?

For singing a motet outside a house where someone has died "with a large half of the school, which includes the *chorus musicus*," Bach receives the tidy sum of one taler; yet the school's charter forbids him to perform two or three motets and "have each one paid for separately." If a funeral procession is accompanied only by a "quarter school" without the *chorus musicus*, he receives only 6 pfennigs, whereas the rector receives at least 1 grosch and 6 pfennigs.

That the rector, who is usually also a professor at the university, must likewise rely on such paltry sums indicates the frugality that the officials of the city of Leipzig feel obligated to observe. These conditions differ from those found at many courts, where money flows freely when it is a matter of satisfying the prince's tastes. This does not mean that Bach's financial situation is worse than in Cöthen: in his 1730 letter to Erdmann he estimates his annual income, together with all incidental sources, at about 700 talers, whereas he started in Cöthen with 400 talers. But with this income—if he did not overstate it in the letter for tactical reasons—the number of onerous daily chores and petty calculations also increased.[42]

What makes this situation particularly burdensome for Bach is the dual set of obligations. Unlike his colleagues at the school, he cannot enjoy his leisure when his teaching duties are fulfilled, for then his other life begins, that of a municipal music director who must see to it that the public music is in good shape and that Leipzig maintains its reputation as a city of fine music.

To accomplish this mission, Bach needs a first-rate ensemble of singers and instrumentalists. A city administrator like Burgomaster Steger, not acquainted with such matters in detail, may have assumed when Bach was hired that such an ensemble was already in place: there is the school choir, there are four town pipers and three violinists, along with a journeyman and perhaps an apprentice or two, and there are always musically inclined students on hand. The previous cantor of St. Thomas's managed perfectly well with these resources; why should it be any different for the new one?

Yet Bach's arrival in Leipzig marks a shift in the view of musical art that has been coming for some time but is brought to a head by his understanding of the art, according to which the composer no longer builds on prearranged understandings but operates within the complicated dialectical relation between socially agreed-upon standards and artistic autonomy.

A pragmatist in the post of St. Thomas cantor would reason as follows: I have the school's pupils, the council musicians, and a few students at my disposal; I will adapt my music to those resources. Bach's reasoning goes this way: I have the school's pupils, the council musicians, and a few students at my disposal, and the *St. Matthew Passion* in my head; therefore I need better conditions. The "Short but Most Necessary Draft for a Well-Appointed Church Music," in which he accuses the Leipzig city council in the year 1730 of providing inadequate staffing, contains a passage that captures the spirit of this shift. Bach comments that his predecessors could expect with a good degree of confidence that the council would reward a number of students with scholarships for their participation in church performances. The statement continues:

> *Since, however, the* status musices *is quite differently constituted from what it was previously, for our artistry has greatly increased, and the* gusto *has changed wondrously, and therefore the former style of music no longer resonates to our ears, considerable*

assistance is thus needed all the more, so that such musicians may be chosen and hired as will accommodate the present musical taste, master the new types of music, and thereby be ready to do justice to the composer and his work. Now the few beneficia, *which should have been increased rather than reduced, have even been withdrawn from the* chorus musicus.

It is, in any case, curious that German musicians are expected to be capable of performing at once and ex tempore *all kinds of music, whether it come from Italy or France, England or Poland, just like those virtuosi, for instance, for whom the music is written and who have studied it long beforehand, indeed almost know it by heart and who, besides,* nota bene, *receive generous salaries, and whose efforts and industry are thus richly rewarded; whereas these factors are not taken into consideration, but they [German musicians] are left to their own cares, such that many a one, out of concern for the bread on his table, cannot give thought to improving, let alone distinguishing, himself. To illustrate this statement with one example, one need only go to Dresden and see how the musicians are remunerated by His Royal Majesty. It cannot fail, for the musicians are relieved of all concern for their nourishment, freed of* chagrin, *and each person expected to master but a single instrument; it must be something splendid and most excellent to hear. The conclusion is accordingly easy to draw: that with the cessation of the* beneficia *I am robbed of the power to put music into a better state.*[43]

Bach takes it for granted that the people of Leipzig want modern church music. The traditional sacred music no longer pleases ears that have become accustomed to a higher standard and considerable changes in taste. If Leipzigers want to hear brilliant music equivalent to Italian, French, English, or Polish styles, the musicians must be capable of performing it, must be specialists who can play one instrument superbly.

Senior Mayor Steger must have shaken his head as he read Bach's memorandum, wondering whether the real issue was a well-appointed church music or one artist's ambition. Bach actually wants both: he is a church musician and an artist through and through; he loves the old music and is eager for the new. We would not understand his argument if we did not have his works; they create in the realm of the ideal the synthesis that he does not achieve in his everyday circumstances.

If we examine these everyday circumstances, we must admire Bach's art all the more. At least during the early period in Leipzig, he is ceaselessly caught up in keeping the St. Thomas *chorus musicus* in fine form and drawing the best he can out of the council musicians in his capacity as their official supervisor. But at the same time he is measuring his efforts against the much higher musical standards of the court at Dresden, inviting virtuosi to his house and clearly doing everything to maintain the level of professionalism invoked in his memorandum.

At times he may find himself longing for the calmer days in Cöthen; there he had a bevy of virtuoso musicians at his disposal and ample time for rehearsals. Among the musicians of the Leipzig council ensemble, only the senior member, Gottfried Reiche, stands out as a recognized performer on the horn and trumpet. Time is at a premium for Bach: he must compose a new cantata for almost every Sunday and write out the different parts himself, or—less frequently—prepare an already existing work for a new performance. The work must then be rehearsed and presented—twice for high holidays. For each of the highest feast days, he must supply three cantatas, so that one year calls for sixty cantatas altogether. His energy commands respect, particularly during the early Leipzig years, when he produces a magnificat for orchestra and two passions—to mention only the larger pieces of church music.

Leipzig, City of Churches—that is the title of a 1710 guide to the city's church services, which celebrates the inhabitants' good fortune in having twenty-two services with sermons to choose among every week, and even more prayer services. It is indeed a city of churches and schools into which Bach has moved, and this new environment has its dark side as well: the air around St. Thomas and the school is gloomy; the students wear black, and not only for funerals. We cannot fully understand Bach's time in Leipzig, which despite some great successes and important honors may sometimes have appeared to him like the way of the Cross, if we do not keep in mind the basic constellation: a passionate man and artist confronting a dual establishment of secular and religious power that has perfected methods over the centuries for asserting and reproducing itself.

Arnstadt, Mühlhausen, and Weimar were way stations where a solitary hothead had a fighting chance—if only to extract an ungracious release from his duties. Bureaucratic Leipzig is like an octopus: if one wriggles free of one arm, one is promptly seized by another. To judge by the surviving documents, Bach hardly ever emerged victorious from a conflict with officialdom. The facts that will now be summarized briefly may be few in number, but they represent the kind of tribulations he confronted frequently.

As early as 1724 Bach has to endure a severe reprimand from the superintendent because without permission he has scheduled the *St. John Passion* for St. Thomas's rather than St. Nicholas's, presumably because of technical factors bearing on the performance. In the following years he is on the losing side in a conflict over the "new worship service" at the university. In 1728 he locks horns with the vice deacon at St. Nicholas's, Gottlieb Gaudlitz, over the right to choose hymns for the services; he seems not to have prevailed.

Two years later Bach is chastised by the council for dereliction of duty. He responds at length in the above-mentioned "Short but Most Necessary Draft," trying to persuade the city council of the need for structural changes to the arrangements for public music, although the futility of his attempt must have been painfully obvious to him. Profound bitterness pervades his documents on the "prefect controversy" of 1736–38, in which he asserts his right to select and appoint prefects, even against the will of the rector.

In 1739 he is forbidden to perform a passion because he has not cleared his plans with the authorities. In the year before his death, when the council begins to look around for a successor, the charge is bruited about that the St. Thomas School does not have a single discantist.[44] Accordingly, the minutes of a council meeting held a few days after his death note that "Bach had no doubt been a great musician, but no schoolmaster…"[45]

But to return to the year 1723: Bach has landed not only in a city of churches: Leipzig, along with Hamburg, Lübeck, Frankfurt am Main, and Nuremberg, is one of the great Protestant cities known for their membership in the Hanseatic League and for their commercial fairs. With about 15,700 inhabitants around the turn of the eighteenth century, the city has surpassed Nuremberg and Frankfurt in its importance as a center of trade. Between 1693 and 1720 Leipzig has an opera intended to entertain visitors to the fair three times a year while irritating devout Christians as little as possible; as was mentioned, Telemann became its musical director for a brief period in 1702. Since it would not be possible to pay a permanent ensemble of professional musicians, students at the university carry most of the performances; in other respects, too, they leave their mark on the town's musical life.

Bach is also coming to Athens on the Pleisse, or Little Paris, nicknames for the new, cosmopolitan Leipzig. Despite the ordinances adopted in 1716 and other years against "the frivolous carrying on in coffee houses" and against the "suspect views and new ways of speaking and writing" prevalent at the university,[46] and despite the draconian censorship of books and theatrical performances, Leipzig is a city of enlightened culture.

The writer Johann Christoph Gottsched, who is appointed to a position in Leipzig a year after Bach, publishes the moral weekly *Biedermann* in 1727 and his work on poetics, *Versuch einer critischen Dichtkunst vor die Deutschen* (Essay on a Critical Poetics for the Germans), in 1730. In 1732 he founds the first major German literary periodical, his *Beyträge zur critischen Historie der deutschen Sprache, Poesie und Beredsamkeit* (Contributions to a Critical History of the German Language, Poetry, and Rhetoric)—all in an attempt to break the power of the "prevailing Scythian and Gothic taste" and "Lohensteinian…bombast" and to establish a natural and rational style in literature.[47] In 1748 Gotthold Ephraim Lessing has his first play, *Der junge Gelehrte,* performed in Leipzig. By the time Goethe arrives in Leipzig in 1765 to take up his university studies, the city is considered the intellectual metropolis of Germany.

As we shall see, Bach had several encounters with Gottsched. He worked more closely with Christian Friedrich Henrici, born in 1700, a poet who never made a lasting name for himself in German literature but who has the reputation of having had a revitalizing influence on the literary scene in Leipzig of the time.

Leipzig has less to offer in the fine arts. In Bach's last years, when he needs an official portrait of himself, he has so few choices that he automatically thinks of Elias Gottlob Haussmann, whose local reputation exceeds his talent. To be sure, Dresden is not far away and soon comes to represent for the cantor of St. Thomas the essence of a finer world.

THE EARLY YEARS IN LEIPZIG

How fascinating it would be to accompany Bach on his rounds during his first weeks in Leipzig! What tone does he adopt toward the pupils at the St. Thomas School and the council musicians entrusted to him? What does he discuss with his superiors in the church and the town? How does he wend his way through the tangle of regulations and obligations that must make the court at Cöthen seem positively idyllic?

He probably expends most of his energy on staking out his own sphere of activity as quickly as possible, that is, establishing a "well-regulated church music." Above all, the "principal music" must be organized—for weekly performances that alternate between St. Thomas's and St. Nicholas's on Sundays and holidays. The liturgical focus is the "early service," the so-called office, which begins at 7:00 in the morning and occasionally continues until 11:00. On numerous holidays the music is repeated for the "Vesper sermon," which begins at 1:15 P.M. in a church that has not had a musical performance at the morning service.

From the original printing of the *Christmas Oratorio* we can see how its distribution of performances looks during the 1734–35 Christmas season:

Part 1 was performed on Christmas day, in the morning at St. Nicholas's and at noon at St. Thomas's.

Part 2 is performed on the day after Christmas, in the morning at St. Thomas's and at noon at St. Nicholas's.

Part 3 is performed on the third day, in the morning at St. Nicholas's.

Part 4 is performed on New Year's Day, in the morning at St. Thomas's and at noon at St. Nicholas's.

Part 5 is performed on the Sunday after New Year's, in the morning at St. Nicholas's.

Part 6 is peformed on Epiphany, in the morning at St. Thomas's and at noon at St. Nicholas's.

On Christmas day, Bach also has to provide figural music for the service at the university church.

On high holidays like Christmas day, within the framework of the "principal music," he must also supply compositions based on sections of the Latin liturgy, especially Sanctus movements; in this way Leipzig's fondness for tradition is satisfied. Yet his primary obligation is and remains the presentation, on Sundays and holidays, of a cantata based on the Gospels or the Epistles. He must therefore make sure that for his first year in office, which extends from the first Sunday after Trinity to Trinity Sunday of the following year, he has a complete supply of cantatas and one that is as consistent as possible. Also due in this year is the annual council piece, which must be ready for the celebration of St. Bartholomew's Day on the Monday after 24 August. Each year he receives an official directive from the council to present the piece.

At the beginning of his time in office, Bach must ascertain above all what he can expect of his St. Thomas pupils as soloists or chorists, and of the town pipers and council musicians as instrumentalists, and how many students can be recruited and paid to fill in. He must determine whether the necessary instruments are available and in good repair. He also needs hard-working copyists—over the years, he will employ at least five dozen copyists either full-time or part-time. We have no concrete evidence that upon first surveying the territory he gains the impression that his organizational efforts will give the "satisfaction" for which he later explicitly wishes.

We know equally little about the sources of the texts for Bach's cantatas. His predecessor, Johann Kuhnau, had established the practice of printing the texts of the church music in advance, particularly for performances on high holidays, "so that each can procure a copy to read for himself after the service."[48] Several printed texts that turned up in 1971 in a Leningrad library show that Bach continued this practice. They offer documentation of the cantatas performed in 1724 during the months between the first Sunday after Epiphany and Misericordias Domini, and in 1725 during the weeks between the third and sixth Sunday after Trinity.

The text booklets were produced carefully by the Leipzig publisher and printer Immanuel Tietze, who commissioned copper engravings for the title pages. Even those attending the services who did not feel inspired by the music could take away something from the texts, which were also intended for private devotions at home. A number of pious Christians collected them and had them bound.

Undoubtedly Bach had to have the texts approved by the superintendent—but probably not "each time at the beginning of the week," as Friedrich Rochlitz, a later pupil at St. Thomas, not born until 1769, reports.[49] In that case, he would not have been able to collect a half dozen and get them printed in advance. Yet we should not reject completely Rochlitz's comment that Bach always submitted "several," "customarily three," texts so that the superintendent could select the one that would best complement his sermon. Behind such anecdotal formulations may lie the hard fact that the superintendent now and then refused to approve a text.

If Bach had already composed the music for such a text, he would need to compose a new cantata, which would put him in a tight spot. That may explain why for some Sundays and holidays, particularly in the first year, two cantatas are documented. It seems more likely that, with a few exceptions, two cantatas were actually performed on these days. Perhaps he occasionally had to supply two Leipzig churches with different cantatas, for reasons we cannot discover today. It is probable that now and then he performed two cantatas during one and the same service.

One would have come before the sermon, the other after the sermon, or, to be more precise, during Communion. According to the Leipzig "Order of the Divine Service," which Bach jotted down on the score of the Advent cantatas BWV 61 and 62, there was room for a well-developed piece of music, which on occasion meant a cantata.[50]

It is difficult to reconcile this thesis with the fact that the surviving brochures with texts from the cantata performances never include more than one for each Sunday and holiday.[51] The absence of a second cantata text might be explained by the reduced importance given to a cantata performed during Communion. At least in northern Germany, vocal music during this part of the service was primarily the responsibility of the organist, who would perform special selections chosen to honor prominent guests or representatives of the church. Sometimes a wealthy family might even commission music to accompany its taking of Communion.[52]

That Bach's colleague Gottfried Heinrich Stölzel began his service in Gotha in 1720–21 with a double annual cycle has emboldened Christoph Wolff to venture the hypothesis that Bach, too, might have provided the Leipzigers with a double annual cycle during his first year in office, that is, a two-part cantata or two cantatas every Sunday and holiday.[53] If this theory is correct, Wolff has at the same time found an elegant solution to the puzzle of why the obituary speaks of five annual cantata cycles, while in Bach's life, to the extent we can reconstruct it at present, there was actually room for only four.

Yet it would be surprising if Bach—who, in view of the four double annual cycles and eight single cycles produced by Stölzel, can hardly be described as prolific—had gone to the trouble of composing a double annual cycle during his very first year in Leipzig. The calendar of known performances shows another picture altogether:

in the first annual cycle, two-part cantatas predominate; later on in the year, one-part cantatas predominate, but most have a chorale in the middle, revealing a tendency toward separation into two parts. It seems pointless to speculate whether these works were also broken up, with one part performed before and one after the sermon. Nor can we establish that the very few cantata pairs identified today belonged originally to a complete double cycle; if Bach had planned such an annual cycle, he would probably have provided two cantatas for each Sunday and feast day precisely in the beginning; not until later would he have had recourse to "mere" two-part cantatas, to save himself work. In reality the two-part cantatas date from the beginning of the year, which suggests that a cycle of two-part cantatas may have been planned, but no annual cycle with double cantatas. It can hardly be contested, however, that for some reason he occasionally performed two cantatas at one service.[54]

In the beginning, Bach must have entrusted the writing of his libretti to persons familiar with cultural expectations in Leipzig. Most likely the texts for the 1724–25 annual cantata cycles were the work of a member of the Leipzig clergy or an academic, especially since cycles of song sermons were a local tradition. In spite of all the pressure he was under, Bach apparently spent a good deal of time searching for suitable libretti. The texts of the first two annual cycles reveal familiarity with the Bible and a well-developed theological perspective.[55] Their character reflects his own intentions, as well as the circumstance that in the City of Churches cantata texts were anything but a trivial matter—on the contrary: to a good number of the theologians and pious Christians the texts were probably of greater moment than the music.

Ultimately, our knowledge of the external circumstances under which Bach begins his work is limited. All the more impressive is what he accomplishes: within a period of about four years he creates a mighty corpus of compositions that express his understanding of Lutheran church music. Here a forty-year-old sets out with great energy and full concentration to accomplish his "ultimate goal" of creating "a well-regulated church music to the glory of God." This goal was formulated in simple, pragmatic terms when he made his request for dismissal from his post in Mühlhausen, but its full implications become clear once he is in Leipzig: in the most prominent position Lutheran Germany has to offer a church musician, Bach commits all his skill and passion to fulfilling what he feels he owes to this special position.

In his 1962 lecture "Outline of a New Picture of Bach," Friedrich Blume vigorously disputes such an interpretation. He asserts that Bach was a reluctant cantor of St. Thomas. Upon taking the position, he "delivered a couple of impressive religious works" in the form of the *St. John Passion* and the Magnificat, then composed three annual cantata cycles "as if in a state of creative intoxication," but after that viewed the composition of church music, up to and including the *St. Matthew Passion,* as an "*onus,*" that is as "voluntary–reluctant contributions": "The archcantor Bach, the creative servant of the Word, the steadfastly committed Lutheran, is a myth."[56]

This distinguished musicologist is right, of course, when he maintains that in different phases of his life and in different situations Bach emphasized different things, and even as cantor of St. Thomas he increasingly turned away from composing church music. Yet Blume seriously underestimates Bach's commitment to Lutheran church music; there can be no doubt that this music forms a crucial component of his work as a composer, and the early period in Leipzig is the midpoint of his creative life. Even the epithet "archcantor," despite its somewhat pejorative connotations, is appropriate: for which composer, with the exception of Heinrich Schütz, succeeded better in expressing the idea implied by "Lutheran church music"? That four years are sufficient for laying the foundation of this idea does not contradict the notion of an archcantor; it speaks, rather, for Bach's universality. In other periods of his life he devoted himself with similar intensity to other tasks.

Starting with the first Sunday after Trinity in the year 1723, the assignment is to write Lutheran church music. We can sense the passion with which Bach sets about creating a rich supply of church pieces that he can present to the people of Leipzig as his specific contribution. The aesthetic properties of these works will form the topic of a later chapter; here it is a matter of describing the external events. If he does not have a suitable cantata on hand to revise for performance in Leipzig, he composes a new one for every Sunday and feast day in the liturgical year; at the outset, they are mostly splendid two-part compositions. The new works usually begin with a setting of a biblical passage and always close with a simple four-part chorale. In between are recitatives and arias, with original texts by contemporary poets.

For Christmas in 1723 Bach composes the Sanctus, BWV 238, and the Magnificat, BWV 243a. Interestingly, he inserts into this early version of the Magnificat four so-called lauds referring to Christmas, thereby taking up a local tradition related to the custom of "child cradling." It would be nice to know whom he consulted on this matter and what he found so attractive in these popular musical interludes, which form a clear contrast to the refined tone of his setting of the Magnificat. Perhaps he had these short movements—"Vom Himmel hoch, da komm ich her," "Freut euch und jubiliert," "Gloria in excelsis deo," and "Virga Jesse floruit"—accompanied only by the basso continuo, sung from a special choir loft such as the so-called Swallow's Nest.

Bach's choice is all the more remarkable because the city council in 1702 explicitly rejected the singing of certain Latin responses—antiphones, psalms, hymns, collects—but also the Christmas lauds—a clear criticism of the Saxon Elector's politically motivated conversion to Catholicism. From now on, everything that smacked of old "Catholic" ceremonies was to have no place in Leipzig church services.[57] But apparently no actual ordinances to that effect were adopted.

At the Christmas holidays, three cantatas were of course called for, in addition to the concerted Latin church music. For Christmas Day, Bach used the cantata "Christen ätzet diesen Tag," BWV 63, composed in Weimar, and for the second and third day of Christmas he composed two new cantatas, "Darzu ist erschienen der Sohn Gottes," BWV 40, and "Sehet, welch eine Liebe hat uns der Vater erzeiget," BWV 64. A six-week *tempus clausum,* which meant six passion Sundays in February and March 1724 without figural music, gave him the opportunity to move along and complete work on the first of his passions that have survived, the *St. John Passion.*

Hearing a modern passion is not an unprecedented experience for the people of Leipzig. As previously mentioned, Telemann's passion with a text by Brockes was performed in 1717 at the New Church and in 1721 at St. Thomas's, and presumably in 1723 a passion by Bach's predecessor, Kuhnau, as well. But Bach's accomplishment is of another magnitude. The first performance of the *St. John Passion* takes place during the Good Friday vesper service, on 7 April 1724, and the performance is preceded and followed by controversy. In defiance of the standing agreement that passions in Leipzig should be performed alternately at St. Thomas's and St. Nicholas's, Bach has passed over St. Nicholas's in favor of St. Thomas's, more favorable to his plans given its two thousand–odd seats and a good deal of standing room. He has already sent around text brochures announcing the site.

Four days before the performance he is called before the city council, where he responds to the council's chiding by saying that he would be glad to shift the location, but only if more room could be created at St. Nicholas's and the harpsichord repaired. The council responds sympathetically and agrees to pay for a flyer announcing the change of venue. This flyer, which Bach sends to the printer without further consultation, reads:

> *Since, after completed printing of the Passion texts, it has pleased a Noble and Wise Council that their performance on Friday next should, God willing, take place at St. Nicholas's Church and should, as usual, also alternate with the musics for feast days and Sundays, notice of this is herewith given to the hon. Messrs.* Auditoribus.[58]

It would be hard to miss the decidedly snippish tone of this flyer. Apparently the superintendent has the same impression when the flyer accidentally comes to his attention, long after the passion has been performed. He summons Bach on 23 May and forces him to confess that he did not submit the text of the notice to the council. According to the minutes of the meeting, Bach admits

> *that he had erred, hoped, however, that he would be pardoned as a stranger, unacquainted with local practices. In future he would take heed and communicate on such matters with me, his Superintendent, which had also been impressed upon him most earnestly.*[59]

Considering that this incident occurs in the year after his installation, it is a harsh rebuke. One might pass over this particular conflict, however, were it not that it reveals fundamental positions. The sources do not tell us whether Bach realized that the passion was supposed to be performed at St. Nicholas's. St. Thomas's seemed more appropriate to him, for practical, performance-related reasons but perhaps also because his protector, Lange, headed the board and Christian Weise was the pastor. (That Bach chose the latter as his confessor is somewhat surprising; in 1693 Weise had displayed sympathy for Pietism by becoming the forty-sixth member of the Philobiblicum, founded seven years earlier by August Hermann Francke.[60]) At St. Nicholas's Bach must deal with Abraham Christoph Plaz as head of the board and Salomon Deyling as the pastor and also superintendent.

In his own mind, Bach may have seen it as his right to choose the place where his work would be performed. Perhaps he viewed the performance itself as the result of personal initiative, following the Hamburg example. That he was apparently not reimbursed for printing the text booklets, which presumably contained only the rhymed passages, not the text of the biblical passion, might confirm this interpretation.

Presumably Bach assumed the cost himself, hoping that such a service would be rewarded with special honoraria from wealthy Leipzig music lovers. He must have also paid for the printing of the text booklets for the regular Sunday and feast-day cantata performances and marketed them himself. In Hamburg, this kind of income was taken for granted as "pars salarii" of the cantor and music director.[61] The first performance of the *St. John Passion* took on the character of a concert, even though it occurred within the framework of a church service with a sermon, and it was in this spirit that Bach addressed the change-of-venue notice to the *Auditoribus*—the audience, not the congregation of Christians.

In this connection, it is important to understand that the main churches of Leipzig were not simple gathering places and that the buildings' design meant that visitors did not form a united congregation brought together for a religious service. The interiors actually resembled theaters with boxes.[62] Better-heeled citizens were required to rent a pew, and there was a spatial hierarchy, with gradations extending from standing room to benches and simple pews to the boxes, known as chapels and located in the balconies, which were often accessible from the outside. On one balcony, opposite the pulpit, was the royal box.

The luxurious fittings of the boxes and their good view of the music, which was also performed on balconies, made it natural for their occupants to experience the performance of the passion as a musical entertainment and a social event as well. We find this idea in Zedler's *Universal-Lexikon,* where the entry for "Oratorio" reads:

> *...a spiritual opera or musical presentation of a religious story in the chapels or chambers of great men, consisting of conversations,* Solo, Duo, *and* Trio, Ritornelles, *mighty choruses, &c. The musical composition must be rich in all that this art can furnish of what is meaningful and choice. In Rome, most especially during Lent, there is nothing more common than such* Oratori. *They are especially suited to Bridal Masses, Passions, and other such spiritual or churchly musics.*[63]

Is this what many music-loving Leipzigers want and what Bach is prepared to supply, without—as will be shown—departing from his conception of Lutheran church music? And is it also the very thing the conservatives feared when they made Bach promise, like Kuhnau before him, not to construct his sacred music along theatrical or operatic lines? Unfortunately no reactions to the passion have come down to us, but the splendor, refinement, and profundity of the work must have struck Leipzig like a bolt of lightning—in both the good sense and the bad.

For Bach the daily routine continues. He completes the first annual cantata cycle and on the first Sunday after Trinity in 1724 plunges without a break into the next annual cycle, one of choral cantatas, probably the most ambitious cyclic undertaking in his entire oeuvre. Perhaps this is also the year in which he intends to complete a passion based primarily on hymns. We may speculate further that because he does not have it ready in time for Good Friday in the year 1725, he repeats the *St. John Passion*, replacing several sections that do not perfectly fit the traditional conception of a passion: the introductory chorus "Herr, unser Herrscher," the aria "Ach, mein Sinn," the arioso "Betrachte meine Seel," and the aria "Erwäge." The work now opens with the splendid chorale "O Mensch, bewein dein Sünde gross," which, however, will not remain in that position; after Bach returns for the most part to the first version for a third performance of the passion in 1728 or, more likely, in 1732, "O Mensch, bewein dein Sünde gross" finds its place in the definitive version of the *St. Matthew Passion*.

In 1725, Bach interrupts his work on the annual cantata cycle around Easter, although he needs only a few more pieces to complete it. Later he will fill some of the gaps with the new cantatas BWV 9, 14, 112, 129, and 140. For cantatas to be performed on Easter Monday as well as on the Quasimodogeniti and Misericordias Domini Sundays (first and second Sundays, respectively, after Easter), he secures the short-term services of a librettist who may be one of the librettists he used for the first Leipzig annual cycle; after that the Leipzig resident Marinne von Ziegler takes over for the period between Jubilate and Trinity. It would be interesting to know whether her patron, Gottsched, recommends her to Bach because he is himself unwilling to write religious libretti for Bach. This still-young woman, twice widowed, is the daughter of the burgomaster Romanus, now languishing in the fortress of Königstein. She stands at the very beginning of her career. In 1730 she will be the first woman admitted to Gottsched's German Society, and three years later the humanities faculty of the University of Wittenberg will crown her as the imperial poet. She lives in the Romanus house, a splendid structure erected at the beginning of the century for her father, and turns it into a gathering place for lovers of literature and music in Leipzig society. Christian Gabriel Fischer, a contemporary, gives the following account of her in this period:

> She is as yet a young widow, who, however, on account of a multitude of circumstances, will hardly marry again. Among other things, her Conduite is almost excessively womanly, and her spirit far too lively and alert for her to submit to common male expectations. Her outward aspect is not ugly, but she has rather large bones, a squat figure, a flattish face, a smooth brow, lovely eyes, and she is healthy and rather brown in coloration.[64]

Her collaboration with Bach proves rather short in duration, yet intense. Frau von Ziegler complies with the composer's specific wishes and works into her libretto for the Whitsun cantata "Also hat Gott die Welt geliebt," BWV 68, two arias from the *Hunt Cantata*, BWV 208, with new words. Altogether she provides the texts for nine cantatas. If we compare the wording that Bach uses with the versions the poet publishes in her 1728 *Attempts in Fixed Forms*, we find a number of variations in style and content. He seems to have altered her texts to suit his own purposes, while she restored the texts to their original form for the printed volume.

Although the collaboration between Bach and Marinne von Ziegler does not last long, it should not be dismissed as a mere episode, for it could offer a first example of Bach's turning his back on librettists who belong to Leipzig's clergy, and instead seeking out professional poets of both sexes. In 1725 he is in touch not only with Ziegler but also, as will be discussed later, Gottsched. And 1727 at the latest marks the beginning of his collaboration with Picander, who in that year provides him with the libretti for the *St. Matthew Passion* and the *Satisfied Æolus*, BWV 205.

This Picander, described as "small and frail of body,"[65] is by no means the kind of person who is considered important in Leipzig, even though he has worked his way up, under his real name, Christian Friedrich Henrici, from commissioner of postal operations to collector of district land taxes and city beverage taxes. As a student he is determined to gain a foothold in poetry, and achieves his first successes in Leipzig with wedding poems that do not shun erotic allusions; in all he is supposed to have written 436 such "carmina," "often in the dark of night…, when not the slightest poetic star shone upon me":

> Go forth and play in thy wee bed
> A sweet duet that whirls the head.
> Sustain the chord with all thy might,
> And when thou'st done so through the night,
> Just wait a brief three-quarter's year,
> Thou'lt find thou hast a trio here![66]

But Picander soon develops into an author of comedies, portraying portions of Leipzig society so unmistakably in works like *The Academic Dolce Far Niente, The Arch-Drunkard,* and *The Good Wives' Trial* that one day the city council issues a ban. The ban also applies to certain works by Gottsched—one of those who despised Picander.

Earlier Bach scholars in general gave Picander's frivolities a wide berth, never considering why Bach was on such familiar terms with this ne'er-do-well. But Bach must find it important, after a period of settling in, to emancipate himself from the confining religious circles and open the door to literary Leipzig. It is no doubt for this reason that he specifically commissions Picander to write the libretto for the *St. Matthew Passion*—a work whose conceptional and aesthetic horizon transcends that of utilitarian church music once and for all.

Bach displays Picander's name prominently on the title page of the authoritative handwritten version of the passion; he knows what sort of resource he has in him, and may think that "his" Picander is in no way inferior to the famous Barthold Heinrich Brockes, whose passion libretto "The Martyred Jesus Dying for the Sins of the World" was thoroughly cannibalized for the *St. John Passion,* perhaps with Picander's help. Certainly Picander functions more effectively than Gottsched as Bach's intermediary to Leipzig literary circles. In 1737 Picander's wife serves as godmother at the baptism of Bach's daughter Johanna Carolina, an indication that the families, too, are on friendly terms.

To return to the second annual cantata cycle: although the cantatas composed between Easter and Trinity of 1725 do not belong to the cycle of choral cantatas, that does not mean they lack a home. Bach uses them as the core of another annual cycle, which, however, he gives himself several years to develop. He now draws on older texts by such authors as Erdmann Neumeister, Georg Christian Lehms, and Salomon Franck, apparently unable at first to find a permanent replacement for the librettist on whom he relied for the first two annual cycles. Neumeister and Lehms at least are "old" Leipzigers. Neumeister received his doctorate in 1695 with a dissertation on poetics, and was the first scholar to lecture on German literature at the university. In 1715 Lehms published the anthology *The Gallante Lady Poets of Germany* in Leipzig, where he spent his youth.

In the course of the third year, Bach falls back on some of his own pieces, already on hand, and eighteen cantatas composed by his cousin Johann Ludwig Bach, who was court kapellmeister in Meiningen. The texts were probably written by Duke Ernst Ludwig of Meiningen. The recently found Leningrad text booklets suggest that Bach also performed cantatas by Telemann after Easter in 1725.[67]

Bach seems to have got off track somewhat when it came to the regular composing of choral cantatas. What made him stop composing them so abruptly? The librettist may have left him in the lurch, perhaps also the pastor who combined music with his sermons. Maybe Bach was so worn out from ceaselessly inventing and rehearsing complicated chorales that he wanted time to focus on cantatas based on biblical quotations and set for solo voices. Or perhaps the change should be seen in the context of a recently experienced insult, which would not be unusual for Bach.

The year 1725 was when Bach clashed with the university over the right to perform modern music in the university church, the Pauline church. On 3 March, the minutes of the university council note that Bach is demanding "a Salarium" for "the new worship service in the Pauline church."[68] The music director of this new service, which has taken place every Sunday and feast day since 1710 and is open to all, is Johann Gottlieb Görner, who also functions as the organist at St. Nicholas's. The university hired him shortly before Bach's appointment to the cantor's position. Bach must have been greatly angered by this move from the outset, for during the term in office of his predecessors Schelle and Kuhnau, music at the university was in the hands of the cantor of St. Thomas's, and the same arrangement had been offered to Telemann.

As for the "old worship service," Bach still has the responsibility for singing motets with the choir from the St. Thomas School at the Quarterly Orations, and four times a year he also must present figural music: at Christmas, Easter, Whitsun, and Reformation Sunday. Görner is responsible for the concerted music of the "new worship service." While Bach has up to now worked for the university without extra remuneration, Görner receives the entire amount appropriated for the university music program.

In a complaint addressed to the Elector and dated 14 September 1725, Bach emphasizes that in the last analysis he is concerned not with the *Directorium* of the new—that is, additional—worship service but with the "withdrawal of the salary."[69] Although the university decides a few days later to divide the budget between Bach and Görner, the cantor of St. Thomas's is not mollified. He views it as a failure on the part of the university to provide for its employees' welfare when monies "appropriated and assigned for the proper remuneration of a servant of the Church" are siphoned off.[70] He is not willing under any circumstances to relinquish the significant supplementary income promised when he was recruited.

Apparently Bach enlists legal assistance in formulating his petition to the court at Dresden, from which he expects more just treatment than from Leipzig. The third and longest petition amounts to six dense pages in the *Bach Documents;* appended to it are affidavits from the widows of Bach's two predecessors, supporting Bach's claim. But all these efforts prove in vain; after a lively exchange of letters among the various governmental agencies, early in the year 1726 the decision is handed down that Bach has no right to participate in the "new worship service." Although his contributions to the "old service" are regularly paid for, he seems to have increasingly withdrawn from this responsibility after receiving the decision against him.

It is hard to tell whether Bach fought so hard as a matter of principle or out of actual financial need. His basic annual salary amounts to only one hundred talers, and every reduction in supplemental earnings makes itself felt. Besides, his family is growing: in 1726, the four young children Anna Magdalena has borne him are at home, while Wilhelm Friedemann and Carl Philipp Emanuel are pupils at the St. Thomas School.

In 1726, Bach slows his pace somewhat. On Good Friday he performs the previously mentioned cantatas by his cousin in Meiningen, along with Reinhard Keiser's *St. Mark Passion.* Whether he is angry or merely tired, this is the lull before a great event: on Good Friday of the following year he will present his *St. Matthew Passion,* a work whose importance will extend far beyond the era of its creation, as Bach must sense when he later produces an elegant handwritten version of the score. As we can recognize today, with the premiere of the work on 11 April 1727, the great period in which Bach concentrated on composing Lutheran church music comes to an end.

Since the rediscovery of the *St. Matthew Passion* by Felix Mendelssohn in 1829, it has been generally assumed that the work was first heard exactly one hundred years earlier, in 1729. Carl Friedrich Zelter found this date in "an old church text" but left open the question of whether this really was the first performance.[71] Perhaps Zelter based his dating on the *Serio-Comical and Satyrical Poems* of

Picander, who includes his libretto of the *St. Matthew Passion* in that text, published in 1729, without mentioning a date of performance. As evidence for a 1729 performance, some cite Bach's letter to his student Christoph Wecker of 20 March 1729, in which he writes that he cannot provide him with "the requested *Passion Musique*," since he needs the score himself.[72] It is doubtful, however, that Wecker has the resources in Schwednitz to perform such a difficult work, requiring a double chorus. Perhaps a different passion is meant? Or perhaps Bach needs the score not for a performance but for the composing of the Cöthen funeral music, BWV 244a, some of which is drawn from the passion, as will be discussed later.

The date of 1727 for *St. Matthew Passion* rests primarily on the observation that the viola part of the Sanctus, written around this time and later integrated into the B-Minor Mass, contains some phrases from "Mache dich, mein Herze rein"—an aria that occurs in the passion.[73] But how do we know that this viola part was copied in 1726 or 1727—and by Bach's nephew Johann Heinrich? The question of chronology brings us to an interesting subfield in Bach scholarship, one to which insiders devote entire conferences and which merits at least a brief digression for the benefit of nonspecialists. As was touched on previously, Bach's vocal works, like the rest of his oeuvre, exist almost without exception in undated manuscripts. In the course of almost one hundred years of research, which began with the publication of the second volume of Spitta's Bach biography in 1880 and found its high point in Alfred Dürr's epoch-making 1957 work "Zur Chronologie der Leipziger Vokalwerke J. S. Bachs" (Chronology of the Leipzig Vocal Works of J. S. Bach), yet continues to bring new results to light, scholars have managed to organize the surviving manuscripts so successfully that the dates on which most of the cantatas were first performed can now be pinpointed and entered into a calendar.

Spitta was the first to order systematically the scattered cantata manuscripts into annual cycles and to date them. He began with the idea that manuscripts on paper bearing the same watermark must have originated in the same period. If further indications made it possible to date one of these manuscripts, that suggested a date for the entire cycle. This trained classicist's approach broke new ground and among his successes was the dating of the vocal works from the Weimar and early Leipzig periods, but Spitta's work also resulted in fundamental errors, many of which were not corrected until 1957. For instance, Spitta assigned many cantatas to the period between 1735 and 1744, whereas today we have irrefutable evidence that they belonged to the 1724–25 annual cycle.

To look at just one example, the year 1744 gained prominence in Spitta's dating scheme in a rather curious way: he thought the choral cantata "Du Friedefürst, Herr Jesu Christ," BWV 116, could not have been written before 1744, because the text of recitative 5 alludes to the Prussian soldiers' march through Saxony during the Second Silesian War: "Oh, may by the blows that strike our head / not too much precious blood be shed..." According to Spitta, because the librettist had generally structured his text as a stanza-by-stanza paraphrase of the original church hymn, this recitative clearly represented a free invention inspired by the political situation. Yet a stanza in the hymn to which the "blows" recitative can be traced did exist; he had overlooked it because the hymnal he consulted happened to have the verses arranged in a different order![74]

In individual cases, false datings based on this kind of guesswork, of which Arnold Schering perpetrated quite a few more in the twentieth century, were no disaster. Cumulatively, however, they created the impression that Bach composed many of his church cantatas for specific occasions, and as isolated works. That impression hindered the recognition that he thought in terms of annual cycles, particularly during the first Leipzig period, so decisive for his production of cantatas. These cycles, once identified, lend themselves well to study of his compositional strategies and the relations among the individual works. Another problem with Spitta's assigning the bulk of the cantatas to the period starting in 1735 is that it launched the myth of the "late" choral cantatas, composed by a retrospectively oriented cantor of St. Thomas's. It took generations for this myth to be recognized as such—in the face of fierce resistance from many, including Friedrich Smend, a respected scholar deeply involved in the examination of original sources.

While attempts to date Bach's works by reference to contemporary events were undertaken less and less frequently, increasing attention was devoted to examination of the documents themselves, and the copyists in particular came in for closer scrutiny. On the one hand, changes in Bach's handwriting could be established, providing the basis for a relative chronology. On the other hand, the copyists Bach employed had to be recognized and identified as far as possible: Anna Magdalena, Bach's sons as they grew up, his son-in-law, and especially the students at the St. Thomas School, among them the "chief copyists"—Christian Gottlob Meissner, Johann Andreas Kuhnau, Johann Heinrich Bach, Johann Gottlob Haupt, Johann Ludwig Dietel, Rudolph Straube, and Samuel Gottlieb Heder. For instance, if one could establish when Meissner and Kuhnau, whose writing can be recognized in Bach's audition piece, "Jesus nahm zu sich die Zwölfe," BWV 22, left the school, one would have a *terminus ad quem* for the composition of the pieces they copied.

I myself was introduced by my mentor, Friedrich Blume, into the haphazard "old" chronology of the cantatas, and toward the end of my university studies and later followed with great suspense the process by which a new basis was established for the performance calendar of Bach's Leipzig cantatas. To this day, an international community of scholars is working on achieving greater precision. If we owe the first great breakthrough to Alfred Dürr, the project of establishing a comprehensive chronology of Bach's oeuvre has occupied many scholars, located primarily in Germany and the United States—but with Yoshitake Kobayashi, one of the world's preeminent experts on Bach's handwriting, even Japan has entered the picture.

Let us return to the year of the *St. Matthew Passion*, in which Bach composes another major vocal work, the ode of mourning on the death of the reigning elector's mother, Christiane Eberhardine of Saxony, which begins with the words "Lass, Fürstin, lass noch einen Strahl aus Salems Sterngewölben schiessen" (O Princess, let just one last ray stream from Salem's starry firmament), BWV 198. The occasion of its performance is a memorial service scheduled for the university church on 17 October 1727. Gottsched provides the text and Bach the music.

The service has a political dimension, because the elector's mother has been greatly respected in Saxony; unlike her late husband and currently governing son, she had not yet converted to Catholicism and had to spend many years separated from her husband, who lost interest in her. In another sense, too, the service has political import for Bach, because the initiator of and chief orator at the service, a university student of only twenty-three, Hans Carl von Kirchbach, commissions Bach rather than the university music director, Görner, to compose and perform the ode of mourning.

Görner promptly protests, but allows himself to be placated with a payoff of twelve talers from Kirchbach and reaffirmation by the university of his general rights. The university auditor, however, fails twice in his attempt to obtain Bach's signature on a corresponding statement of understanding.[75] The score of the ode is not completed until 15 October—according to a notation in Bach's own hand— leaving only two days for copying of the individual parts and rehearsals. The service itself begins with a pealing of the bells and a solemn procession from St. Nicholas's to the university church. The Hamburg *Stats und gelehrte Zeitung* reports, "Princely personages, respected ministers, cavaliers, and other foreigners who had been in attendance at the Leipzig fair, found their way to the service, along with a great number of noble ladies, as well as the entire honorable university and the distinguished city council in a body."[76] In an account by the Leipzig historian Christoph Ernst Sicul, published under the title "Leipzig Weeps," the performance is described thus:

> *When, then, all had taken their places, and the organist had played a prelude, the Ode of Mourning written by Magister Johann Christoph Gottsched, member of the* Collegium mari- anum, *was distributed amongst those present by the Beadles, and shortly thereafter was heard the Music of Mourning, which this*

time Herr Kapellmeister Johann Sebastian Bach had composed in the Italian style, with Clave di Cembalo *[harpsichord], which Herr Bach himself played, organ, violas di gamba, lutes, violins, recorders, fleutes douces and fleute traverses, &c., half being heard preceding and half following the oration of praise and mourning.*

Sicul's comment, that Bach composed his "excellent music," as the university chronicler, Johann Jacob Vogel, calls it,[77] "in the Italian style," makes it clear that Bach set Gottsched's ode not according to its stanzaic structure but like a cantata libretto: as a series of choruses, recitatives, ariosos, and arias. Gottsched may be less than edified by seeing his poem's structure flouted in this fashion, but for Bach such freedom is the prerequisite for composing a work on such a grand scale and with such a varied texture. He captures the courtly elegiac tone in masterful fashion. The refined musical language finds its counterpart in the unusually rich instrumentalization: in addition to the traditional string ensemble, the score requires two transverse flutes, two oboes d'amore, two violas di gamba, and two lutes.

If the work did not have a text so molded to a specific occasion that modern performances are rare, its stature would certainly be uncontested, even among Bach lovers. Under the circumstances, it provides evidence of the importance Bach ascribed to the genre of occasional music. To be sure, quite a bit is at stake; for one thing, by collaborating with Gottsched, already highly regarded as a representative of rational literature, Bach can make it clear that he belongs not only to the Leipzig church community but also to the "living and flourishing Leipzig of today"—to quote the city guide mentioned earlier. For another thing, this event gives him an opportunity to present his music before members of the court at Dresden, whose favor becomes all the more important the more the burdens of cantorship weigh on him.

Any account of Bach's early Leipzig years that failed to do justice to his ambitions in the realm of secular music, in all its facets, would be woefully one-sided. The ode of mourning is not the only piece of secular music Bach composes and performs in Leipzig, not even the first written in collaboration with Gottsched; two years earlier the two men worked together for a significant social occasion: the marriage of the Leipzig burgher Peter Hohmann, Noble Standardbearer of Hohenthal, to Christine Sibylle Mencke, daughter of Johann Burchard Mencke, a noted scholar and interim rector of the university. The wedding takes place on 27 November 1725 in the Hohmann house on the market square, described by the art historian Georg Dehio as the finest example of Leipzig baroque architecture.[78]

For this occasion Gottsched composes a "Serenata" that begins "Auf, süss entzuckende Gewalt" (Arise, o sweet enchanting power) and Bach composes a cantata in thirteen parts, unfortunately lost to us (BWV Anh. I 196). An aria that can be reconstructed from various parodic versions, "Entfernet euch, ihr kalten Herzen" (Get ye away, ye ice-cold hearts), gives us a glimpse of how well Bach has already mastered the gallant tone in his early Leipzig period, even if he combines it with other tones, as is his wont. Other cantatas from this period intended for weddings are "Vergnügte Pleissenstadt," BWV 216, with a libretto by Picander; the first version of "O holder Tag, erwünschte Zeit," BWV 210; as well as possibly "Weichet nur, betrübte Schatten," BWV 202, a work that may also go back to Bach's time in Cöthen.

If these works just mentioned belong to the genre of the chamber cantata, the three *drammi per musica* that have survived from the first years in Leipzig are, according to Gottsched, "little operas or operettas," which, however, "seldom find their way to the stage." These pieces, rich in gesture and tone-painterly effects, are all scored for trumpets and timpani; the singers embody mythological or allegorical figures.

Æolus Propitiated, which begins "Zerreisset, zersprenget, zertrümmert die Gruft," BWV 205, was composed for the name day of the philosophy professor August Friedrich Müller in August 1725 and probably performed outdoors at his house on Katharinenstrasse. The *dramma per musica* "Vereinigte Zwietracht der wechselnden Saiten,"

BWV 207, was written to celebrate the installation of Gottlieb Kortte as professor of law in December 1726. In both cases it is likely that wealthy students who loved music both commissioned and helped perform the works. A third work by Bach that was probably performed in the fall of 1729 has not yet been associated with any specific occasion: *Der Streit zwischen Phöbus und Pan* (The Contest between Phoebus and Pan), BWV 201, with a libretto by Picander.

Unfortunately we have only the text booklet for a birthday cantata Bach wrote in honor of the Saxon Elector Friedrich August I, a piece that begins with the words "Entfernet euch, ihr heitern Sterne" and is designated as "evening music" (BWV Anh. I 9). The cantata is performed on 12 May 1727 in the evening "on the market square"— outdoors. We know that there is a festive torchlight procession, accompanied by trumpets and drums.

A later report, however, speaks of a celebration held outside the city with more than forty musicians and over three hundred students present.[79] According to more recent scholarship, Bach used the initial chorus again for the B-Minor Mass around 1748 or 1749, with a new text, "Et resurrexit," an indication of the value he himself placed on the composition.[80]

We know very little about a *dramma per musica* whose libretto begins "Ihr Häuser des Himmels," BWV 193a. It was composed for Friedrich August I's name day, 3 August 1727. Perhaps the music goes back to another original work from the Cöthen period.

The corpus of secular cantatas and *drammi per musica* from Bach's early period in Leipzig may be smaller in volume than the body of church cantatas, but it is in no way inferior in quality or social impact. The works that have come down to us reveal a composer in full command of the vocal chamber and theatrical styles who, unlike in the sacred music genre, can compose without regard for established tradition, that is, largely autonomously. To be sure, his autonomy is sui generis; instead of being merely "pleasing" and "natural," it shows a tendency toward a curiously mixed style and a multitude of perspectives.

In a third realm, too, Bach distinguishes himself during this period: keyboard and instrumental chamber music. In spite of all his public duties, he does not allow the field of composition for keyboard instruments to lie fallow. In 1725 he places the clavier Partitas in A Minor, BWV 827, and E Minor, BWV 830, at the beginning of the second *Notenbüchlein* for Anna Magdalena Bach. They will later be included in his *Clavier-Übung*, which is discussed in the next chapter.

Bach publishes and markets not only his *Clavier-Übung* but also, in the course of the years, keyboard works by Wilhelm Friedemann and the Hamburg composer Conrad Friedrich Hurlebusch, the music lexicon by his relative Johann Gottfried Walther, and the *Generalbasslehre* by the Dresden kapellmeister Johann David Heinichen. In addition, with the particular help of his wife—in most cases certainly for pay—he produces copies or even transcriptions of his chamber music. The very careful copies of the solos for violin, BWV 1001–06, and for cello, BWV 1007–12, which the Staatsbibliothek in Berlin has catalogued under Mus. ms. Bach P268 and P269, were most likely produced for sale. We have been able to determine who commissioned the copies: the Wolfenbüttel court musician Georg Heinrich Ludwig Schwanberger, who was living in Leipzig in 1727–28, apparently in order to study with Bach.[81] He turns up as a substitute godfather at the emergency baptism of Bach's daughter Regina Johanna on 10 October 1728, which suggests that he was actually staying at Bach's house.[82]

Bach also lends out musical instruments and provides technical advice on the development of new instruments such as the viola pomposa and the fortepiano, thereby showing that he by no means exclusively floats in the higher regions of art but is the type of person who also tries to find positive aspects in the everyday life of a musician. Carl Philipp Emanuel offers a vivid description of his childhood home and his father that helps us picture this life:

> *With all his many activities, he hardly found time for the necessary correspondence, and accordingly could not wait for lengthy exchanges in writing. All the more did he have occasion to con-*

verse with decent folks in person, for his house perfectly resembled a dovecote in its liveliness. Everyone found dealing with him pleasant, and frequently edifying.[83]

Bach remains in close touch with the musical life of his day, not least of all through the students who flock to him. Indirectly they also keep him involved in a continuing dialogue with his own works from earlier periods—keyboard works like the *Inventions and Sinfonias, The Well-Tempered Clavier,* or the *Chromatic Fantasy* are standard fare for his students; but Bach probably also gives organ lessons more or less regularly. Schwanberger praises him in a letter to his father-in-law on 12 November 1727 as follows: "I would dearly wish that you might hear Herr Bach on the organ...I have never heard anything to equal this, and I must change my style of playing entirely."[84]

From the year 1728 we have two testimonials to Bach's growing reputation. Gottsched ranks him with Telemann and Handel, and Johann Mattheson, in his magazine *Der musikalische Patriot,* names Bach, Handel, Heinichen, Keiser, Stölzel, and Telemann as composers of whom Germany may "boast"—although Bach comes first merely for the sake of alphabetical order.[85]

Of course 1728 is also the year in which Bach fights with the assistant deacon of St. Thomas's, Gottlieb Gaudlitz, over the right to choose the hymns for the vesper service. The theologian takes the matter to his consistory, which thereupon instructs the superintendent to inform Bach "that when the ministers who are preaching announce particular hymns to be sung before or after the sermon, he shall be governed accordingly and have the same sung."[86]

Bach thereupon argues in a protest addressed to the city council on 20 September 1728 that it has always been the cantor's right to select the appropriate hymns to precede and follow the sermon, taking his cue from the scriptural references and the Dresden hymnal. Furthermore, Gaudlitz has "sought, in place of the hymns chosen in accordance with the established usage, to introduce others."[87] We do not know what other hymns Gaudlitz wants to use, or how the conflict is resolved, but we can imagine that Bach must feel increasingly subjected to slights in his position as cantor. The following years will bring an intensification of such incidents, and at the same time successes and honors in other realms.

THE MIDDLE LEIPZIG PERIOD: "COURT COMPOSER"

The trend established during the early years in Leipzig continues after 1729: while Bach finds himself increasingly in conflict with the image of a dutiful cantor, he widens the range of his artistic activities to an astonishing degree.

In February 1729 he spends several days in Weissenfels to conduct what seems to be an elaborate performance of a birthday cantata for Duke Christian. It is probably on this occasion that his patron makes him titular kapellmeister of Weissenfels—an important replacement for the corresponding title in Cöthen, which probably expired upon the death of Prince Leopold.

A month later Bach travels to Cöthen with Anna Magdalena and his son Wilhelm Friedemann, who has just enrolled at the University of Leipzig to study law. Bach has been asked to contribute to the music at the final obsequies for Prince Leopold, who died several months earlier. At the burial on 23 March and at the funeral sermon on 24 March, he probably conducts the music played by the Cöthen kapelle, augmented by musicians from Zerbst, Dessau, and Güsten. His own offering is a magnificent four-part work, of which, however, only a small portion is new: the mourning music "Klagt, Kinder, klagt es aller Welt," BWV 244a. The opening and final choruses are borrowed from the mourning ode "Lass, Fürstin," BWV 198, and ten further sections come from the *St. Matthew Passion.* For this occasion Bach composes all the recitatives, as well as the setting of the psalm "Wir haben einen Gott, der da hilft," which also provides the text for the memorial sermon.

The old and new librettist Picander works with such professionalism that occasionally it is impossible to distinguish what is the original and what is an adaptation. Precisely this circumstance has given rise to serious doubts as to the originality of the *St. Matthew Passion*, if one accepts the premise that it was first performed in 1729. Was the Cöthen funeral music perhaps the original version, and large portions of the passion merely the result of a skilled parodic adaptation? On the basis of the new chronology, this question has been decided in favor of the passion; in a later chapter we will look into the issue of why Bach would carve pieces out of such a lofty work for other purposes.

Within about a month the former court kapellmeister of Cöthen, now kapellmeister of Weissenfels, can thus be found at two royal seats, performing his music. Such honors might make the Leipzigers proud of their *director musices*, yet those council members who are intent on having a dutiful cantor note his frequent absences with bitterness. In a letter Bach writes to his student Wecker on 20 March 1719, he admits himself that he has been away from Leipzig for three entire weeks—and this just before the pending trip to Cöthen.

It does not help that for the Easter service he plays the organ and receives high praise from the music expert Martin Heinrich Fuhrmann in a treatise on the appropriateness of artistic church music, to which he gives the charming title "The Kapelle of Satan Built onto the Church of GOD":

> *Recently at Leipzig at the Easter Mass [I had the good fortune] to hear the world-renowned Herr Bach. I had thought that the Italian Frescobaldi had gobbled up all the possible art of the keyboard, and that Carissimi was a most precious and delightful organist; yet if one were to place the two Italians together with their artistry on a scale opposite the German Bach, this latter would greatly outweigh the other two, and would send them forthwith shooting into the air.*[88]

What good does it do for Bach to assume the directorship of the collegium musicum and use its resources on the second day of Whitsun to perform the cantata "Ich liebe den Höchsten von ganzem Gemüte," BWV 174, at St. Thomas's—a piece of music with the utmost tonal splendor? Or, when his school's rector, Johann Heinrich Ernesti, dies in October 1729, to have the double-chorus motet "Der Geist hilft unser Schwachheit auf," BWV 226, performed over his coffin? A storm is gathering above Bach's head.

As early as May 1729, when Bach is examining an applicant for a place as a boarding student at the school, dissension may have arisen between him and the rector over the right to decide on admissions. The council has to intervene. There is the sense that something is amiss with the cantorship. On 8 June 1730 the election of a new rector takes place, and Councilman Johann August Hölzel votes for Johann Matthias Gesner with a sideswipe at Bach, saying he "hoped things would go better than with the Cantor."[89]

The council minutes of 2 August 1730 make it clear how deep the dissatisfaction with Bach's conduct in his position must go: the subject on the table is the physical condition of the Church of St. Thomas, but soon the discussion turns to questions of staffing:

> *In this connection it should be recalled that when the Cantor came hither he received a dispensation from instruction; Magister Pezold fulfilled the assignment rather poorly; the third and fourth classes were the seedbed for the entire school, and consequently a capable person had to be placed in charge of them; the Cantor might teach one of the lower classes; he was not conducting himself as he ought (without the foreknowledge of the governing burgomaster he sent a choir student to the country; left town without obtaining authorization, for which he must be reprimanded and admonished). For the present it should be considered whether the above-mentioned classes ought not to be provided with a different instructor; Magister Kriegel was said to be a good man, and a resolution would have to be reached.[90]*

Burgomaster Steger declared:

> *Not only was the Cantor doing nothing; he was not even willing to explain himself; he was not giving the singing lessons, and there were other complaints as well; a change would be necessary,*

*for matters would come a head sooner or later, and he would have
to accept other arrangements.*

The formulation "matters would come to a head sooner or later"
should be taken seriously. Hölzel proposes that "the Cantor's salary
be shrunk," and all the other council members vote in favor, with Johann Job citing as his reason that "the Cantor was *incorrigible.*"[91]

The only one who speaks up in Bach's favor is Burgomaster
Lange, suggesting Magister Abraham Kriegel as Bach's new substitute for the Latin classes. Yet the majority of the council does not
concur. In the following weeks Burgomaster Jacob Born negotiates
with Bach, intending to force him to teach—although without success; on 28 August he reports to the council that he has "spoken with
Cantor Bach, who however shows little desire to work."[92] The decision was then made to appoint Kriegel as Bach's substitute, but at
Bach's expense.

The council actually does take steps to "shrink" Bach's income.
On 6 November money received during the vacancy in the rector's
position is divided among the teachers at the St. Thomas School,
while Bach is left empty-handed, contrary to the recommendation of
the head of the school's governing board. That this situation is no
isolated case can be deduced from a formulation Bach uses in July
1733, when he petitions for the title of composer to the Saxon court,
a subject to which we will return. In this document the cantor of St.
Thomas complains—this in itself is unusual for such a petition—of
insults and reductions in his supplemental income, "which slights,
however, would vanish altogether" if a royal title were conferred on
him. From the year 1739 we also have an audit from the council's
treasury of Bach's income; it, too, seems to have been prepared as the
basis for financial sanctions against him.[93]

Altogether, we receive the impression that Bach's conflict with
the council goes far beyond ordinary tiffs, and that the longer it continues, the more it takes on the character of an actual breakdown in
the relationship. It is against this background that we should see
such things as Bach's report on the condition of church music in

Leipzig under the title "A Short but Most Necessary Draft for a Well-Appointed Church Music, with Certain Modest Reflections on the Decline of Same." On ten handwritten pages, dated 23 August 1730—thus constituting a response to the charges raised against him—he lists what resources are needed and which are available to him for performing church music. The subtext is clear: anyone who rightfully or wrongfully charges the St. Thomas cantor with dereliction of duty should be aware that the *director musices* has every reason to accuse the city council in turn with inadequate attention to his needs.

Bach gives a painstaking inventory, complete with numbers. For "music making" at St. Thomas's, St. Nicholas's, and the New Church, he needs three choruses with twelve singers each, of whom four must be "concertists" and eight "ripienists." Two choruses with sixteen singers each would be preferable, but he counts on only twelve per choir and thus comes out with a total of thirty-six musicians needed for performances of figural music at the three churches; he explains that another chorus with twelve singers should be held in reserve for St. Peter's. Yet in actuality he has only three prefects and fourteen "usable" singers at his disposal. He also enumerates twenty "motet singers, who must first improve themselves in order to be used eventually for *Figural Music*," and seventeen completely "unfit" students. He mentions all fifty-four by name, to make it clear that he is not talking off the top of his head.

He counters the possible objection that he himself is responsible for the lack of capable students by pointing out, "too many poorly equipped boys, and boys not at all talented for music" were admitted; gifted beginners were worn down by being assigned to church services immediately instead of being properly trained over the course of a year for their duties. Whereas Bach's predecessors were able to recruit university students to alleviate the chronic shortage of singers, because these students received scholarships and remuneration from the council, such "beneficia" had been recently withdrawn from the *chorus musicus*. As will be shown later, this support is available only for music performed at the New Church.

Bach is no better supplied for instrumental music; he needs a minimum of eighteen musicians, for he wants at least two players each for the first and second violin, the first and second viola, and the cello, and would prefer three for the violin positions. In addition, he needs a *violone* player, two or preferably three oboists, one or preferably two bassoonists, three trumpeters, and a timpanist. If two recorders or transverse flutes are called for, "as very often happens for variety's sake," a total of twenty instrumentalists is required, not counting the preferred three players for the violins and oboes. But who is actually available: "four town pipers, three professional fiddlers, and one apprentice." Before naming the musicians, Bach remarks grimly, "Modesty forbids me to speak truthfully of their qualities and musical knowledge. Nonetheless, it must be considered that they are partly emeriti and partly also not practicing as regularly as they should be."

To sum up, he says he lacks—"partly to reinforce certain parts, and partly to supply indispensable parts"—two first and two second violinists, violists, and cellists, one violone and two flute players.[94] Individual positions can sometimes be filled with pupils from the school, but then they are missing from the choir.

Bach can hardly have expected that his memorandum would result in meaningful changes; there is no indication that it was even discussed in the council. It seems more likely that he intended the memorandum to serve as an unadorned record of his difficult working conditions. He also makes his demands at an unfavorable moment; after taking over the collegium musicum, he performs several well-staffed cantatas at St. Thomas's and St. Nicholas's, thereby showing that he can improve things without help from the council.

There is no document in this case showing that Bach receives any support from Burgomaster Lange, who is so well disposed toward him. It is striking that starting in 1730 all the funds for university students performing church music are appropriated to the New Church. Has the council concluded that the truly modern music is performed there, and that it is up to Bach to see to it that his music, which is as complicated as it is ambitious and which no one commissioned in this form, be performed according to his standards? Bach may have understood this to be the situation and drawn his own conclusions; for now, his more large-scale works would be heard primarily outside the churches, which means in secular settings.

Bach's "Short but Necessary Draft" gives us insight into his ideas about appropriate scoring, which in turn raises questions about the size of his choir: what actual staffing does he have in mind when he speaks of a "chorus" consisting of twelve students? Since Arnold Schering's book on Bach's church music appeared in 1936, most scholars have accepted, largely without comment, his assumption that Bach's choir "normally" consisted of twelve singers, three each of sopranos, altos, tenors, and basses.[95] But in his memorandum Bach argues for three of each on the grounds that he needs one concertist, one ripienist, and one substitute. He explains further that a choir must have twelve singers so that even when some are absent an eight-part motet can be performed—which means only one singer for each part.

In some of the parts written for the various voices Bach makes clear how the differentiation between concertists and ripienists can look. The cantata "Unser Mund sei voll Lachens," BWV 110, performed on the first day of Christmas in 1725, provides a good example: there is the usual part-setting for four voices, but beyond this there are three voice parts with the headings "Soprano in Ripieno," "Alto in Ripieno," and "Tenore in Ripieno"; the part for the bass has been lost. The additional voices were apparently added for a later performance of the work, sometime between 1728 and 1731, and include only choral sections of the opening movement that Bach now wanted to reinforce so as to achieve a contrast between the tutti and the solo parts, as well as the final chorus.

Why did Bach write out new parts instead of simply adding the appropriate instructions to the existing scores for the original voices? Was the choir particularly well staffed for the new performance, for instance with two concertists and two ripienists for each vocal part? The answer is that four or six singers would have found it difficult to sing from a single score.

It is conceivable that in the period when Bach takes over the collegium musicum and also works elsewhere with more-ambitiously scored works, he actually has a larger number of vocalists at his disposal. Yet it is hard to ignore the wording of his memorandum, which is written about the same time; the calculations presented there suggest that lean staffing may be the rule rather than the exception. The question may therefore be asked, Was it normal for only one person to sing from each score? In that case, at least two scores would have been required for one concertist and one ripienist. If this was true, then Schering's assumption that Bach was constantly switching between solo and tutti in the great choral movements of his cantatas—"A signal from the conductor was sufficient to have the ripienists fall in again at the desired place"—would be incorrect;[96] instead Bach would have made use of the solo-tutti contrast only in certain compositions.

To every Bach expert and Bach lover it is strange indeed to imagine that the composer had only soloists to perform his Leipzig church cantatas; a number of Bach scholars view Joshua Rifkin's speculations along these lines as veritable sacrilege; for if Bach actually performed the great choruses of the Leipzig cantata, the passions, and the B-Minor Mass with nothing but soloists, it would mean that the worldwide practice of performing these works with large choirs has no basis in historical reality, merely perpetuating a myth that first manifested itself with Mendelssohn's rediscovery of the *St. Matthew Passion:* when he performed the work at the Berlin Singakademie in 1829, the choir had no fewer than 158 members!

This debate has not been resolved; a welter of contradictory factors remains to be considered, including the conditions known to exist at other churches. We should note that Gottfried Ephraim Scheibel, mentioned above in connection with his "Scattered Thoughts on Church Music" (1721), remarks of the music at Leipzig's New Church, which he experienced several years earlier as a student, "It should be deemed a waste when a choir has more members than required...If every part or voice is carried by one or at most two *Subjectis,* who perform what is asked of them, the choir is well staffed."[97]

That is apparently less merely a "wish dream, which at least in Leipzig did not correspond to reality,"[98] than experience from performances that Scheibel himself attended. From this point of view, we should reexamine the question of whether Bach's aesthetic sensibility would necessarily have opposed a choir made up entirely of soloists—a practice that he, in his capacity as director of all Leipzig's church music, tolerated at the New Church. At the Dresden court, also, to which Bach increasingly looked the longer he stayed in Leipzig, much of the vocal music was performed primarily by soloists.

Perhaps there is no such thing as *the* Bach choir; perhaps he conducted performances with choirs of varying sizes. One thing is certain: Rifkin, with his provocative theses, is no longer an outsider in Bach scholarship; rather, the proponents of the traditional view must now defend their position with new arguments. Such arguments are few in the latest works on Bach, by Hans-Joachim Schulze and Ton Koopman, both of which appeared in 1999.[99]

Bach's memorandum has a self-confident ring; we hear a *director musices* who understands both the big picture and the fine detail of his métier and has major artistic accomplishments to his credit, precisely in the realm of sacred music. The text shows not a trace of defiance or resignation, at most a touch of impatience in the face of unacceptable conditions. A very different tone characterizes Bach's long letter to his former schoolmate and current patron Georg Erdmann, who is serving as a diplomatic representative of Russia in Danzig. Bach recites a long list of complaints about his current position:

> *(1) I find that the position is by no means so lucrative as it was described to me; (2) many of the supplemental fees that go with this position have escaped me; (3) this place is very dear; and (4) the authorities are peculiar and but little committed to music, such that I must suffer almost constant vexation, envy, and persecution; I shall thus be compelled, with the help of the Lord Almighty, to seek my fortune elsewhere.*[100]

Does Bach have his eye on Danzig? He suggests to Erdmann that he could manage better on four hundred talers in Thuringia than in Leipzig, because the latter city is so expensive. The only position he might consider, that of music director at St. Mary's, will open up in April 1731 with the death of the incumbent, Maximilian Dietrich Freisslich. Perhaps Bach has heard that the fifty-seven-year-old is ailing; but perhaps he also knows that Freisslich has by no means enjoyed a financial bed of roses, has even applied to "be allowed to direct brewing operations" as a sideline, so as to have a chance to increase his income.[101]

More likely Bach's request that Erdmann keep an eye out for possible positions is a shot in the dark. The seven-hundred-taler income mentioned is quite high; if he were to change jobs, it would be only to improve conditions. His descriptions of the authorities as "peculiar and little committed to music," and of the "constant vexation, envy, and persecution" he must suffer as a result, have become almost proverbial in Bach scholarship. Here we have a classic example of the conflict that arises for an artist in public office: he is expected to be both a genius and an obedient subject. Telemann, Carl Philipp Emanuel Bach, and Joseph Haydn were fortunate to find relatively comfortable arrangements. Bach stands too much on principle to be able to accept compromises and forget the grief to which he is subjected. Just as his composer's brain never loses track of a thought once it has occurred to him, his conscience seems to keep a tally throughout his life of his rights and the injustices he has suffered.

In Bach's eyes, it is an injustice that the authorities want to wear him down with teaching—a view that the head of the St. Thomas School's governing board obviously does not share. Once more it is the selection of a new rector for the school that gives the board's head, as a representative of the city council, an opportunity to complain about Bach. Thus on 2 November 1734 Christian Ludwig von Stieglitz notes for the record "that his post...was rendered most difficult by the Cantor, inasmuch as the latter did not do at the School what was incumbent upon him."[102]

It is impossible to discover to what extent Bach was fulfilling or neglecting his duties at the school; he seems to have been conscientious about his church obligations, even if he was now presenting fewer of his own compositions. On Good Friday in the year 1730 he performed the *St. Luke Passion,* BWV 246, once attributed to him but now designated as anonymous; the following year he conducted a performance of his *St. Mark Passion,* BWV 247, with a libretto by Picander.

The composition itself has disappeared, but some movements can be reconstructed, since Bach borrowed generously from himself. The music for the opening chorus, "Geh, Jesu, geh zu deiner Pein," as well as for the final chorus, "Bei deinem Grab und Leichenstein," had previously been used for the mourning ode "Lass, Fürstin, lass noch einen Strahl," BWV 198, as well as in the funeral music "Klagt, Kinder, klagt es aller Welt," BWV 244a. In addition, the music for three arias was taken from BWV 198, and two further arias are thought to have been derived from the cantatas "Widerstehe doch der Sünde," BWV 54, and "Christ unser Herr zum Jordan kam," BWV 7.

Although only small traces remain of Bach's rendering of the passion according to St. Mark, Diethard Hellmann and Gustav Adolph Theill in 1964 and 1980 respectively published reconstructions of this work intended for performance, drawing on other works by Bach. No matter how useful such attempts can be for providing a sense of largely unknown compositions, they are limited by both the "Bach myth" and the vox populi, which demand authentic works, even fragments, as the case may be, but reject reconstructions, however well-intentioned.

On Good Friday in most of the following years Bach offered the Leipzigers further passion performances—alternating between St. Thomas's and St. Nicholas's. In 1732 it must have been the *St. John Passion*—largely in its original form. In 1736 a passion is performed at St. Thomas's "with both organs,"[103] which points to the *St. Matthew Passion.* So in these years, too, he does not avoid works that call for a large ensemble—on the contrary: the surviving sheet music suggests that he tends to increase the number of performers rather than the opposite.

In 1739, during Lent, more unpleasantness arises. The council chastises Bach for failing to seek authorization for his performance of a passion. He responds to Bienengräber, the assistant vital statistics clerk who delivers the message, that such performances have long been traditional; but if it is a question of the text, the one he used "had already been performed several times." Another remark reported by the clerk sounds quite defiant: "He did not care, for he in any case derived no advantage from it, and it was only a burdensome obligation; he would notify the Superintendent that it had been forbidden."[104]

If it really was a matter of the text, the one in question may well have been the original text of the *St. John Passion.* As noted above, even the commanding gestural quality of the opening chorus runs counter to traditional understandings of what a passion should be like. At any rate, Bach probably undertook a revision of the *St. John Passion* in 1739 but left it unfinished; what has been preserved is the fragmentary score P28. Instead he chose to perform Telemann's *Seliges Erwägen.* Around 1742 and perhaps again between 1743 and 1746, he returned to the *St. Matthew Passion,* and in that same period the *St. Luke Passion* was heard as well; in the course of reworking it, he added his version of the song "Aus den Tiefen rufe ich," the score of which turned up in Japan only a few decades ago.

Bach's collection of scores reveals that in his last years he presented a passion pastiche by Handel and Keiser and presumably also one by Carl Heinrich Graun. On Good Friday in 1749 he conducted the *St. John Passion* for the last time—with textual changes in two arias and an arioso. In accordance with the general shift in taste, the drastic imagery is moderated, but the extent to which he actively participated in these changes or simply tolerated them cannot be determined. Here is a comparison of two versions of the same passage:

Original	Revision
Consider how his blood-stained frame	My Jesus, oh, thy painful bitter suff'ring
so wracked with pain	sweet joy doth bring;
forthwith to Heav'n will fly.	purging sin's harsh sting.
Think how, when once	'Tis true, I see with great dismay
the pounding waves	thy limbs with blood arrayed;
of our sins' tide are dry,	yet must this sight awaken gladness.
a rainbow fair lights up the sky	From death and hell it makes me free
in our Lord's name.	and from all sadness.

(All translations, except where otherwise noted, are by Z. Philip Ambrose.)

For the sake of continuity, let us look at the rest of Bach's passion performances, up to the end of his time in Leipzig. We must go back to the middle period. As we have seen, Bach worked energetically at the first two annual cantata cycles during the years 1723–24 and 1724–25. In the 1725–27 period a third cycle evolved more slowly. It too can be reconstructed fairly completely on the basis of existing sources.

But we cannot yet identify two other annual cycles that he must have composed, if the information in the obituary is to be believed. The surviving cantatas can quite plausibly be attributed to three cycles, but the lack of a critical mass of material makes it futile to attempt further reconstruction.

Bach scholars have reacted in different ways to this problem. One thesis that has been put forward asserts that, contrary to the indications in the obituary, which in other respects does not always prove reliable, Bach composed only four or perhaps even only three annual cycles. Other scholars have warned against deducing from the lack of sources that certain works never existed; it is entirely possible, they argue, that these cycles were complete at one time but lost.

There is some evidence of a fourth cycle: in 1728 Picander publishes a cycle of libretti for cantata, with the explicit wish "that perhaps the lack of poetic grace might be compensated for by the lovely work of the incomparable Kapellmeister Bach."[105] We cannot resolve what was wish and what reality; yet in fact Bach cantatas have been preserved whose libretti may have been taken from one edition of Picander's volume: BWV 197a, 171, 156, 84, 159, Anh. 1, 190, 145, 174, 149, 188.

Only the first performance of the cantata "Ich liebe den Höchsten von ganzem Gemüte," BWV 174, can be dated precisely: the score, partly in Bach's hand, bears the date 6 July 1729. The other cantatas exist for the most part in fragmentary form or in later copies; it thus seems quite possible that Bach did not set Picander's texts systematically[106] but rather picked one text or another over the course of years.

The traces that suggest a fifth cycle are extremely scarce, since only a few cantatas have survived from the period after 1730.[107] Except for those five composed and added retroactively to the second Leipzig cycle—BWV 9, 14, 112, 129, and 140, and "Jauchzet Gott in allen Landen," BWV 51—the cantatas are choral texts: "Sei Lob und Ehr dem höchsten Gut," BWV 117; "Nun danket alle Gott," BWV 192; "Der Herr ist mein getreuer Hirt," BWV 112; "Ich ruf zu dir, Herr Jesu Christ," BWV 177; "In allen meinen Taten," BWV 97; and "Was Gott tut, das ist wohlgetan," BWV 100. Only BWV 112 and BWV 177 allow themselves to be assigned places in the liturgical year. The question is: What does Bach have in mind when composing these works whose dating goes to 1735? Are we on the trail of a larger project, with which he wants to demonstrate that ultimately the best choral cantata is a setting of a "straight" text from the Bible rather than one freely based on written texts? Or is he primarily intent, after the inspiration of the first years in Leipzig has subsided, on building up a small but versatile supply of pieces?

It has been shown that after completing or breaking off the annual cycles, Bach performed his cantatas repeatedly, and apparently did not expose the people of Leipzig to music of other composers to any great extent until the forties—when he introduced compositions written by, for instance, his son Wilhelm Friedemann, his son-in-law Johann Christoph Altnickol, and his pupil Johann Gottlieb Goldberg.

We must not forget that we are speaking here of a period in which Bach turns his attention to the Latin mass and the Magnificat, two genres traditionally based on liturgical texts; so there, too, we see a tendency to return "ad fontes." That his involvement with these genres begins in 1733 also has pragmatic reasons: on 1 February the Saxon elector, Friedrich August I, dies in Warsaw, whereupon a period of state mourning commences. Figural music falls silent, and in particular the Good Friday passion music is canceled. Bach thus has both an incentive and opportunity to pursue an ambition that must have been in his mind for quite a while: acquiring the title of a Saxon court composer.

He already has connections with the court at Dresden: he has composed funeral or tribute music for members of the royal family; in 1725 and 1731 he played the organ at the church of St. Sophia, at that time the finest organ in the capital. During his visit in September 1731, important musicians like Johann Adolph Hasse, his wife Faustina, and Johann Joachim Quantz compared Bach's organ playing with Handel's and concluded that Bach had "brought playing of the organ to its greatest heights."[108] An anonymous panegyric appeared in the newsapers, playing on the German meaning of Bach (brook):

> A pleasant brook delights the ear, 'tis true,
> When rushing past the reeds and past high hills,
> Yet higher must I praise this Brook to you
> Whose hand displays such wondrous skills.
> They say when Orpheus played upon his lute
> All animals in the forest thronged to him;
> That our Brook does e'en more, none shall dispute;
> Whene'er he plays, our cup fills to the rim.

In June 1733, when Wilhelm Friedemann is unanimously chosen to be the organist in the very church where his father had such a successful guest appearance, the name Bach again comes to public attention in Dresden. In the meantime, Johann Sebastian has been working on his Magnificat, BWV 243; perhaps the performance marked a festive fresh beginning for Leipzig's church music on the feast of the Annunciation, on 2 July, after the end of the country-wide mourning period.[109] The watermark on the new score is the same as that for the various parts of the Missa BWV 232[1]. Thus at least an external link exists to that other work with a Latin text, on which Bach is presumably working at the same time, a work he will dedicate to the Saxon Elector as a sonorous expression of fealty.

The parts for the different voices are written out in some haste but with great care. They are designed in such a way that a performance can take place in Dresden without Bach's participation. In addition to Bach himself, Wilhelm Friedemann, Carl Philipp Emanuel, Anna Magdalena, and an unknown scribe are involved in the copying; no students at the St. Thomas School seem to have served as copyists. Evidently Bach is thinking not of his obligations in Leipzig but of his hopes for Dresden. Such hopes find concrete expression in his application for an appointment:

Most Serene Elector, Most Gracious Lord!

To Your Royal Highness I convey in deepest devotion the present modest work of that knowledge which I have acquired in musique, with the most humble request that Your Highness look upon it not regarding its poor composition but with most gracious eyes, according to Your Highness's world-renowned clemency; and thereby deign to take me under Your Most Mighty Protection. For some years and until the present, I have held the Directorium *of the music at the two principal churches in Leipzig, but have blamelessly had to suffer one indignity or another, and on occasion also a reduction of the fees associated with this position; but these injuries would vanish altogether if Your Royal Highness were to be so gracious as to confer upon me the title of Your Highness's Court Kapelle, and would let Your High Command for the issuance of such a decree go forth to the proper place. This most gracious fulfillment of my most humble request will bind me to Your Majesty in unending reverence, and I pledge with the most indebted obedience to show at all times, at Your Royal Highness's most gracious wish, my tireless zeal in the composition of* musique *for the church as well as for the orchestra, and to devote all my forces to Your Highness's service, remaining in constant fidelity.*

Your Royal Highness's most humble and most obedient servant,
Dresden, 27 July 1733   *Johann Sebastian Bach*[110]

Bach travels to Dresden himself to deliver this petition along with the score for the Missa. Since at first no sign of success can be detected, he continues to remind the Elector of his existence, paying tribute to him by composing and performing further grand celebratory cantatas. At the end of 1736 the longed-for decree finally arrives; dated 19 November, it declares that Bach "because of his ability" is most graciously granted "the title of Compositeur to the Royal Court Orchestra."[111] On 1 December Bach is in Dresden to express his gratitude with a concert on the new Silbermann Organ at the Church of Our Lady. Presumably it is on this occasion that the Russian ambassador, Hermann Carl, Imperial Count von Keyserlingk, confers the patent on him in the name of the Elector.

No matter how probable it is that Bach composed the Missa expressly for Dresden, this undertaking would have been a shot in the dark had he not reached an agreement in advance with Jan Dismas Zelenka, who was serving at the Dresden court as the substitute for the kapellmeister and composer of sacred music. On the one hand it shows tact on Bach's part that he dedicates to the Catholic prince not a cantata but a short mass, consisting of a Kyrie and a Gloria. But is there a place for this work in the court worship service, where as a rule full-length masses are performed and since in the Gloria Christ is addressed as "Altissimus," which corresponds to Leipzig custom but not to Catholic practice?

Should we consider Protestant city churches in Dresden possible sites for a performance, and should we also keep in mind the possibility of a performance in Leipzig, even though the preserved parts of the score seem to have been written out with Dresden in mind? In any case, on 21 April 1733 the new elector, Friedrich August II, participates in a service at St. Nicholas's in Leipzig, to receive the homage of that city; a coronation mass would certainly have been appropriate to the occasion!

We have no information suggesting that the work was performed in Dresden. The scores for individual parts found there have been examined for signs of use, and many arguments have been made for and against such a performance, yet no definitive conclusion has been reached. It seems sensible to make a virtue of necessity and see the Missa not only as a musical expression of fealty to the Elector but also as an indication of Bach's growing interest in the genre of the Latin mass. We do know that in 1738–39 Bach wrote two short masses, BWV 234 in A major and BWV 236 in G major; since the sister works BWV 233 in F major and BWV 235 in G minor have a similar structure, there seems to be justification for assigning them to the same period.

Bach's son-in-law Altnickol prepared a copy of all four masses around 1747–48, an indication that Bach saw them as constituting a coherent body of work. The Kyrie and Gloria, BWV 232^1, do not belong to this complex; with them, Bach has a higher purpose in mind during the last years of his life...

The Sanctus compositions BWV 237 and 238, written between 1736 and 1742, and the Christmas music "Gloria in excelsis deo," BWV 191, composed sometime between 1743 and 1746, also belong to the genre of Latin church music—a genre with which Bach was becoming increasingly engaged, not only in his own creative work but also in his assiduous copying and adapting of others' works. We can point to a whole series, no doubt part of a larger collection, of copies made for the most part in the thirties and early forties, most or all in Bach's hand: short masses by Francesco Durante, BWV Anh. 26; by Johann Heinrich von Wilderer, Antonio Lotti, Johann Ludwig Bach, BWV Anh. 166, as well as by an anonymous author, BWV Anh. 25; six complete masses by Giovanni Battista Bassani, two anonymous Sanctus movements, BWV 239 and 240; a Magnificat by Antonio Caldara, BWV 1082. The latest of these copies can be attributed to Bach's last creative period; that is certainly true of the copy of Palestrina's *Missa sine nomine*, done in 1742, and the adaptation of the

Sanctus from Johann Caspar Kerll's *Missa superba*, which can be dated to that same year.

The works just mentioned do not merge seamlessly with Bach's own to form a corpus of Latin church music that could be seen as the counterpart to his second annual cycle of Leipzig cantatas. Yet it is unmistakable that in the course of the 1730s Bach withdraws from the routine of providing cantatas based on pericopes, that is, scriptural excerpts. Weary of the constant search for librettists and the requirement of having the libretti approved, he resorts more and more to using work already on hand; at the same time, he is demonstrating to the Leipzigers that he is not willing to keep chasing after libretti that are acceptable to theologians and connoisseurs of poetry alike.

Cantatas with choral texts of a more general nature offer an alternative for a while. But in view of the unsatisfactory working conditions in Leipzig, Bach probably finds it more interesting to take advantage of his position as Dresden court composer to intensify his exploration of Latin church music—a genre suitable for both Leipzig and Dresden.[112]

Against this background, the fact that the music in the four short masses BWV 233–36 seems to have been borrowed almost without exception from existing church cantatas appears in a specific light: perhaps Bach no longer wants to see his church cantatas with their libretti become obsolete and unusable. Does he want to rescue not only his secular cantatas but also parts of his sacred ones? His major rescue, that of the *drammi per musica*, took place several years earlier: between 25 December 1734 and 6 January 1735 he introduces his *Christmas Oratorio* to the Leipzigers at six worship services. The opening choruses and arias consist to a considerable extent of quotations, especially from the cantatas *Hercules at the Crossroads*, BWV 213, and "Tönet, ihr Pauken! Erschallet, Trompeten," BWV 214.

The aesthetic value of these self-quotations will be discussed in detail later, in the context of a comprehensive assessment of the *Christmas Oratorio*. For the present, suffice it to say that, with the possible exception of its sixth and final part, this work is anything but a secondhand composition; it is a creation of great artistic power. During his Leipzig period Bach managed to produce four great original works in oratorio style that soar above their time: the *St. John Passion*, the *St. Matthew Passion*, the *Christmas Oratorio*, and the B-Minor Mass. Chronologically, the *Christmas Oratorio*, composed around the halfway point of the period, can be seen as a light and readily accessible bridge between the mighty columns of the passion and the mass.

Let us return to everyday life in Leipzig in the year 1736. For the Easter Fair, Georg Christian Schemelli brings out a collection of religious songs, among them many numbers that, according to Bach's preface, are "in part newly composed, in part...improved in the bass continuo." Whether and to what extent the works catalogued as BWV 439–507 are actually Bach's compositions has not been demonstrated conclusively. But if the *Schemelli Hymnal* strikes a contemplative, gently Pietistic note, the "prefect dispute" that breaks out at the St. Thomas School during the summer of that same year is conducted with extraordinary bitterness. The affair is set in motion by the improper behavior of the first choir prefect, Gottfried Theodor Krause, who treats the pupils under his supervision with excessive harshness and is therefore himself condemned by the rector to a shameful flogging in front of the entire school. Bach intervenes with the observation that it was he who recommended to Krause that he treat the pupils sternly. But when the rector does not relent, Krause leaves the school. His successor is a second prefect named Krause, but Johann Gottlob. Bach's and Rector Ernesti's contradictory accounts make it impossible to tell whether this initially interim appointment constitutes a breach of Bach's guaranteed right to appoint the prefects, as Bach claims.

At all events, Bach is not satisfied with Krause 2, and replaces him a few weeks later with Samuel Kittler. Krause 2 complains to the rector, who more or less openly takes his side and, after further back and forth, forbids the pupils on pain of "hard punishment" to sing under Kittler's direction. In a petition to the city council Ernesti reports on Bach's further behavior:

As soon as the First Prefect reported this to the Cantor on my orders, the latter promptly runs to the Superintendent, bringing the same unfounded charges against me that he first brought against Your Magnificence and You, Most Noble Sirs, after he had failed to obtain the desired resolution from the Superintendent; and declares at the same time that on the following Wednesday (i.e., the day before yesterday) he will submit the matter to the Consistory. Now, although the Superintendent gave him no resolution, other than to say that he would inquire of me how the affair was constituted, and that the affair itself could not be decided either by him or by the Consistory without communication in advance with the Lord Patrons and the Director—yet, on the pretext of having received an order from the Superintendent, he compelled the Second Prefect, Küttler, to leave St. Nicholas's and to go with him to the First Choir at St. Thomas's, from which he with great commotion expelled Prefect Krause, already singing there. I went from the Church to the Superintendent to inquire whether he had given any such order, but learned that he had said nothing other than what I have already reported. I then recounted the entire matter to him, as I have told it here to Your Magnificence and you, Most Noble Sirs; whereupon he fully approved my conduct in the matter, and agreed that the current disposition should remain in effect, as I had arranged on orders from the Director, until the latter might return and settle the matter, as it was more fitting that the Cantor submit ad interim *to the Director and Rector than vice versa. I informed the Cantor of this decision, but received this answer: that he would not comply in this matter, no matter what the cost. Now, since after lunch each of the two Prefects had returned to the place to which I had assigned him, Bach again chased Krause from the choir with great shouting and racket, and ordered the student Clause to sing in the Prefect's stead; this he did, apologizing to me after church for having done so. How, then, can the Cantor contend that it was not a student of the School but a university student who sang? The Second Prefect, Küttler, he banished from the table, that evening, for having obeyed me.*[113]

In Bach's version of the conflict, addressed first to the city council, then to the Leipzig consistory, and finally to the Saxon elector, we of course find no reference to Bach's outbursts, which Ernesti reports with perhaps some exaggeration, but no doubt also generally in line with what actually took place. Bach chooses to emphasize the incompetence of Krause 2, who according to him mistakes 4/4 time for 3/4 time. And from letter to letter Bach focuses more sharply on underlying principles: he insists on his right to appoint the prefect as he sees fit; for the prefect is his representative in directing the *chorus musicus*.

The conflict drags on. The council, which does not officially take note of the dispute until 6 February 1737 and then does so "with dismay,"[114] acts cautiously, apparently waiting for Krause 2 and Kittler to finish their schooling at St. Thomas and go on their way; then the cards will have to be reshuffled. For as annoyed they must have been with Bach, they surely had no desire to see him fly off the handle in response to a decision that displeased him and subject the St. Thomas School to mockery in the city. Besides, certain members of the council may have agreed with Bach's position, while condemning his lack of self-discipline. A provisional but nonbinding resolution by the consistory, dated 5 February 1738, is the last extant document bearing on this matter.

A handwritten history of the school, compiled in 1776 by Johann Friedrich Köhler, relies chiefly on the reminiscences of former boarding students. Köhler writes the following about the conflict between Bach and Ernesti:

Both men from that time forth became foes. Bach began to hate the students who devoted themselves entirely to the humaniora *and pursued music only on the side, and Ernesti became hostile toward music. If he came upon a student practicing an instrument, he would exclaim, "Do you want to become a beer-fiddler, too, then?" Thanks to the high regard in which he was held by Burgomaster Stieglitz, he managed to have himself relieved of the duties of special inspector of the school and to have them assigned to the Fourth Colleague. Thus when Bach's turn came to do the inspection, he invoked the precedent of Ernesti and came neither to table nor to prayers; this negligence had the worst possible influence on the moral formation of the students.*[115]

It is doubtful that Bach passed unscathed through this last major conflict with the authorities of which we have knowledge. The year 1737 is also when Johann Adolph Scheibe's first public attacks on Bach's method of composition are launched. It would not be surprising if Bach's withdrawal from public life began around this time—for instance with his temporary resignation from the directorship of the collegium musicum, whose importance in the middle period of Bach's work must now be discussed.

The crises of the 1730s can also be seen as having positive effects: Bach's conflict with officialdom helps liberate him from the kind of civil servant's loyalty that could prove an obstacle on his path to creative autonomy in his later works.

DIRECTOR OF THE COLLEGIUM MUSICUM
AND COMPOSER OF SECULAR MUSIC

MUSICUM COLLEGIUM is a gathering of certain adepts of music who come together for their own practice, both in vocal and instrumental music, on dates certain in designated places, under the leadership of a certain director, and perform musical pieces. One finds such collegia in various places. In Leipzig Bach's collegium musicum is renowned above all others.[1]

Even this dry entry in Zedler's *Universallexikon* from the year 1739 gives a sense of the importance of such an enterprise for Leipzig. The institution of the public concert is still in its infancy, at least in Germany; once the opera season ends, even a city like Leipzig, with its famous trade fair, has no musical events for which people must pay admission. That means that the collegium musicum becomes as crucial to the cultivation of musical taste as the concerts at court in the royal seat.

In 1729, when Bach assumes direction of the collegium musicum, which meets in Zimmermann's Coffeehouse, he is continuing a great tradition associated at the time with names such as Adam Krieger and Georg Philipp Telemann. In a sketch of his life written in 1718 for Johann Mattheson, Telemann speaks enthusiastically of an institution he himself established in 1700, following a new organizational model: "This Collegium, although it consists exclusively of students, of whom often as many as 40 come together, is nonetheless a great pleasure to listen to."[2] Looking back on his own era, Telemann praises the artistic quality of the singers, some of whom also belonged to the opera company; and he maintains that no instrument was missing from this ensemble. He considers it worthy of special mention that he performed quite often for the Saxon elector, Friedrich August I, and other high-ranking dignitaries. When Telemann's successor, Melchior Hoffmann, dies in 1715, an obituary lauds him for keeping "the public concert" "most particularly flourishing."[3] And recalling his time at the University of Leipzig between 1707 and 1710, Gottfried Heinrich Stölzel, the Gotha kapellmeister, estimates the group's membership at fifty or sixty, and comments:

> *The collegium musicum, which he [Melchior Hoffmann] directed, drew me to it in the very first days after my arrival…Although [the ensemble] at that time was heard only on high feast days, and during the fair, at Leipzig's New Church: should it come as any surprise that, invigorated by Hoffmann's refined taste, it attracted many listeners?*[4]

Thirty years later, Stölzel can still name a whole series of members, who even in those days were notable virtuosi, or developed into such, or ended up in solid bourgeois professions. Among others he mentions the violin virtuoso Johann Georg Pisendel, whose debut is described in 1784 by one of Bach's successors as cantor at St. Thomas's, Johann Adam Hiller:

> *When Pisendel, shortly after his arrival in Leipzig, wanted to be heard for the first time in the collegio musico there, a current member of the collegium, Götze, who later became his faithful friend, looked at him askance, for Pisendel, both in his appearance and his garb, seemed to promise nothing extraordinary. "What does the lad want?" Götze asked with his usual vivacity: "Yes, yes, he will give us a fine show of fiddling." Meanwhile Pisendel laid his concert music on the stand, a piece by his master Torelli, and he had scarce begun to play the first solo when Götze laid aside his violoncello, which he was accustomed to play at all times, and gazed at the new student in amazement.*[5]

Hiller shows a sure sense of the telling anecdote when he goes on to describe how, during the adagio, the future *Handelsgerichtsakteur* (commercial court official) Johann Christoph Götze was so astonished that he ripped his wig from his head. Yet the story is sufficiently documented to provide insight into the nature of the new evening concerts: the musicians are interested in the most recent music and open to surprises. They usually sight-read, rehearsing only for special occasions. The coffeehouse patrons sit over their coffee or hot chocolate and listen; the more knowledgeable among them discuss the music with the musicians during the intermissions. All in all—if for a change we can posit the ideal case as the norm—we have here a wonderful early example of cultivation of music by the middle class, with connoisseurs and dilettantes equally represented among both performers and audience, and both groups talking about music in a more relaxed atmosphere than the later "symphonic concerts," with their strict rituals, would ever allow.

After Hoffmann, the directorship of the collegium musicum passes to Johann Gottfried Vogler, who however soon moves to a second collegium, founded by Johann Friedrich Fasch. In 1718 Balthasar Schott succeeds him. Schott began as a student, then became the organist and musical director at the New Church. Under his direction the collegium musicum meets in the following years in Herr Hemm's Ratskeller, in Herr Helwig's coffeehouse on the market square, and finally "at Herr Gottfried Zimmermann's Coffeehouse, in summertime on Wednesdays, on Wind-Mill Alley, in the garden from 4 to 6 o'clock, and in wintertime on Fridays in the coffeehouse on Cather[ine] Street, from 8 to 10 o'clock."[6]

Zimmermann, who in 1721 already owns an impressive collection of instruments, will host the collegium—directed by Bach after 1729—until the time of Bach's death in 1741.

It would be surprising if the former kapellmeister Bach had not established contact with Schott's collegium musicum shortly after his installation at Leipzig. In fact, a trace of evidence exists to show that he did just that: the score containing Bach's orchestral overture in C major, BWV 1066, may have been prepared for Schott's collegium musicum, which would indicate that Bach's orchestral music was performed there.[7]

Yet in his first Leipzig period Bach must have been less concerned with the occasional performance of his orchestral works than with the challenge of finding suitable musicians, beyond the core of council musicians and city pipers, to perform his church music and music for important occasions. Initially it was probably singers for solo parts that he needed most, then increasingly instrumentalists. The *drammi per musica* already mentioned could not have been performed without such additional musicians. For "Vereinigte Zwietracht der wechselnden Saiten," BWV 207, we have a score calling for twenty-five voices; with the musicians assigned to him in conjunction with his official position, Bach could not possibly have mustered this many performers. A performance of the *St. Matthew Passion* would have benefited from this kind of augmentation as well.

For Bach to be able to count on a larger stable of performers, an official act is needed. He may have thought that in taking over the collegium musicum he was cutting the Gordian knot: "P.S. The latest is that the Lord has now also provided for honest Herr Schott, and bestowed upon him the position of Cantor in Gotha; wherefore he will take his leave next week, as I am willing to assume his *Collegium*."[8]

We find this postscript in a letter from Bach, usually not much of a letter writer, to his pupil Christoph Gottlob Wecker, dated 20 March 1729. Bach's obvious glee stems not only from his satisfaction at seeing his friend Schott promoted from organist and cantor at the New Church to a cantorship but also from the prospect of finally heading an ensemble that at least numerically equals his kapelle in Cöthen.

Of course Bach's accession to the directorship cannot come about solely on the basis of a private arrangement with his predecessor; traditionally the directorship of the collegium musicum goes with the organist's position at the New Church, and the combination makes good sense to the city council; for one thing, the overlap is a great boon to the performance of modern music at the New

Church, important for sustaining the city's musical reputation; for another thing, it saves money. If the director of music at the New Church can call on his collegium and the instruments stored at the Zimmermann Coffeehouse, he needs less funding from the council; and in fact during the subsequent years considerable extra appropriations became necessary for the New Church to acquire instruments and improve the organist's situation.

Fortunately 1729 happens to be the year in which Lange is in office, a burgomaster who is well disposed toward Bach. When it comes to the selection of the organist for the New Church, Lange backs twenty-four-year-old Carl Gotthelf Gerlach, Bach's pupil and assistant with figural music. Gerlach has a recommendation from Bach and is certainly willing to renounce his right to direct the collegium musicum in favor of his teacher. From this time on, if not earlier, Gerlach performs in the collegium as an alto singer, a violinist, and a harpsichordist. Bach will later reward his loyalty by installing him as his deputy and successor.[9]

The four other candidates, who, like Gerlach, audition with cantatas, one of them even with a Brockes passion, seem to have all performed creditably. But Lange recommends Gerlach, with the interesting comment that he "could play the organ, which the others could not."[10] May we speculate that behind this comment lies the expectation that once Bach has the performers from the collegium musicum at his disposal, vocal music at the New Church will no longer be so important? Lange helps expand Bach's circle of activity; he furthermore sees to it that in the first months of 1729 a complete set of stringed instruments is acquired for St. Thomas's; these are now available to Bach, in addition to the instruments from Zimmermann's Coffeehouse. To be sure, the council adds a drop of bitterness to the joy he will feel at this "restructuring" of Leipzig's musical life.[11] From 1730 on, the council's appropriation for assistants to help with the church music will go only to the New Church, no longer to St. Thomas's.

But Bach does not know of this change when in the early summer of 1729 he draws on his new resources with evident delight: on 6 June, the second day of Whitsun, he performs at St. Thomas's the cantata "Ich liebe den Höchsten von ganzem Gemüte," BWV 174, with a really large ensemble. Up to the day before the performance the copyists are busy writing out the parts for at least twenty-two voices, and Bach himself is working at the last moment to revise the introductory movement of his Third Brandenburg Concerto to serve as an initial sinfonia for this cantata, that is, to provide it with a sort of "harmony music."[12] Whereas the original had only three violins, three violas, and three cellos above the basso continuo, he adds two corni da caccia, three oboes, and ripieno strings. The choir is called for only in the final chorale; the important feature of this cantata is a display of magnificent sound, and perhaps during the performance Bach glances over at August Lange, who has helped make this possible.

The large-scale instrumentation of two other cantatas from the Picander annual cycle—"Man singet mit Freuden vom Sieg," BWV 149, and "Gott, wie dein Name, so ist auch dein Ruhm," BWV 171— may likewise be connected with Bach's taking over the collegium musicum; the same is true of the three festival cantatas "Singet dem Herrn ein neues Lied," BWV 190; "Gott, man lobet dich in der Stille," BWV 120b; and "Wünschet Jerusalem Glück," BWV Anh. I, 4a. These works are performed on 25, 26, and 27 June 1730 for the two-hundredth anniversary of the Confession of Augsburg.

Because the documentation of Bach's composing of sacred cantatas in this period is less complete than that of his early years in Leipzig, we must be careful about drawing such conclusions. But there is no doubt that as director of the collegium musicum Bach increases his production of congratulatory cantatas for the Saxon royal family and more often than before plays the role of artistic intermediary between the Leipzig university and the ruling house. When the Elector or his legates come to Leipzig to receive congratulations of various sorts, it is often Bach who receives them as the master of ceremonies.

Using texts by Picander for the most part, in 1732 Bach composes his *dramma per musica* for the Elector's name day, "Es lebe der König, der Vater im Lande," BWV Anh. I, 11, and in the following year the cantata "Frohes Volk, vergnügtes Sachsen," BWV Anh. I, 12, for the same occasion. For the birthday of Prince Elector Friedrich Christian, he composes the *dramma per musica Hercules at the Crossroads,* BWV 213, and for the birthday of the Electress Maria Josepha, in the same genre, "Tönet, ihr Pauken! Erschallet, Trompeten!," BWV 214. Only a month later he has to come up with a *dramma per musica* that begins "Blast Lärmen, ihr Feinde," BWV 205a; Elector Friedrich August II is being crowned king of Poland as August III.

In 1734, Bach wants to perform with his collegium musicum the cantata "Schleicht, spielende Wellen," BWV 206, at a birthday celebration for the Elector on 7 October. To his surprise, an evening concert is ordered for 5 October; the Elector has suddenly decided to come to Leipzig with his family—not to celebrate his birthday there but to attend the Leipzig Fair. But since 5 October is the first anniversary of his election as king, the serenade must allude to this event. At lightning speed, Bach adjusts his plans, puts aside for two years the birthday cantata he has started, and instead composes the *Dramma per musica overo Cantata congratulatoria,* "Preise dein Glücke, gesegnetes Sachsen," BWV 215, in which the following lines appear:

> Hear, hear!
> God and his help to us is near
> And watches o'er King August's throne.
> At his sign, all the peoples of the North
> Rejoice that he's our chosen king henceforth.
> Must not the tossing Baltic's zone
> Through Vistula's conquered tide
> To August's land
> By stroke of hand
> Its waters join beside?
> And lets he not that haughty town
> Which long defied his mighty crown
> Feel more his mercy than his rod?
> Our Lord, you see, finds pleasure great
> In showing subjects love, not hate,
> Nor riding o'er his foe roughshod.

This excerpt from the libretto, hastily penned by Magister Johann Christoph Clauder, makes it clear that this work expresses not only the deepest devotion but also the intention of explaining important political matters to the citizens by way of celebratory music. Cynicism or education? Under time pressure, Bach does not compose a new introductory chorus but borrows music from the name-day cantata "Es lebe der König, der Vater im Lande," performed a good two years earlier; at the time, the father of his people certainly did not hear it himself.

The city chronicler Johann Salomon Riemer has left us the following detailed account:

> *Toward 9 o'clock in the evening His Majesty was serenaded most respectfully by the students residing in this place, playing a work for trumpets and drums, composed by Herr Kapellmeister Joh. Sebastian Bach, Cant. of St. Thom., whilst 600 students carried wax torches, and 4 counts serving as marshals led the musicians. The procession commenced at the Blackboard and wound along Ritterstrasse, up Brühlstrasse and Catharinenstrasse all the way to the King's lodgings, and when the Music reached An der Wage, drums and trumpets joined in there, as did a choir at the Rathaus. As the Carmen was proferred, the four counts were admitted to kiss the sovereign's hand, and then His Royal Highness, as well as His Royal Consort and the Royal Princes, did not depart from the window for as long as the music continued, but graciously heard it out, and it well pleased His Majesty.*[13]

No fewer than seven hundred copies of the text are printed. Bach receives an honorarium of fifty talers from the university—almost a month's income. Alas, one of the musicians must pay for the evening with his life:

> *On this very day the experienced and most artistic Musicus and town piper Herr Gottfried Reiche Leucopetra-Misn. [i.e., from Weissenfels] and senior of the musical compagnie in this city, when he wished to go home, was felled by a stroke in City Piper*

Alley, not far from his house, such that he sank down, and was carried home dead. And this is said to have come about because earlier in the day he strained himself greatly blowing during the royal music, and also the smoke of the torches caused him much grief.[14]

With Gottfried Reiche, Bach loses his best town piper, an artist on the trumpet to whom he assigned important duties in connection with his Leipzig liturgical music from the very beginning. In his inaugural piece "Die Elenden sollen essen," BWV 75, he gave him prominence with the trumpet part in the chorale "Was Gott tut, das ist wohlgetan." And now, on the last day of his life he played the trumpet in the eight-part double chorus "Preise dein Glück, gesegnetes Sachsen," which Bach in later years would use as the Hosanna of the B-Minor Mass, to the greater glory of God.

The report also reveals indirectly that the town musicians are by no means excluded from performances of such celebratory music— as they also possibly participate now and then, on Bach's invitation, in the normal rehearsals of the collegium musicum. It is typical of early bourgeois concerts that musicians in civil service positions and dilettantes perform together. The city chronicler Riemer expressly documented this blending for the Great Consort, established in 1743.

The events honoring the Dresden royal family continue. We have records of performances of a cantata for the Elector's name day with the title "Auf, schmetternde Töne der muntern Trompeten," BWV 207a, and the previously mentioned Birthday Cantata BWV 206. On 28 April 1738, the celebratory music commissioned by the university and remunerated with fifty talers, "Willkommen! Ihr herrschenden Götter der Erden!," BWV Anh. I, 13, is performed for the impending nuptials of Princess Maria Amalia and King Carl IV of Sicily. On 7 October 1739, BWV G25, a birthday cantata whose title is lost, is performed, and finally, on 3 August 1740 a repeat of BWV 206, with changes to the text, for the occasion of the Elector's name day.

Complete scores of some of these works have been preserved, while others can be reconstructed more or less comprehensively from parodic versions. Some have disappeared completely, unfortunately including the *Abendmusik* to Gottsched's text "Willkommen! Ihr herrschenden Götter der Erden!" performed "amidst sounding trumpets and drums in front of Apel's house on the market square."[15] As will be discussed later, this particular work was cited by contemporaries to defend Bach against Johann Adolph Scheibe's charges of Baroque excess.

Bach's collegium musicum does not of course perform only for particular celebrations but rather draws attention by its weekly rehearsals. In 1736, Lorenz Christoph Mizler characterizes it matter-of-factly as a "public musical concert or gathering" in his *Musikalische Bibliothek*. The gatherings continued to be held "at Zimmermann's Coffeehouse," specifically "once each week, excepting during the fair, Fridays of an evening from 8 till 10 o'clock on Cather-Strasse, but twice a week during the fair, Tuesdays and Fridays at the same time." The concert directed by Johann Gottlieb Görner is also mentioned. Summing up, Mizler comments:

> *The members who make up these musical consorts consist in the majority of the gentlemen studying here, and there are always good musicians amongst them, so that often, as is known, later they develop into famous virtuosi. Every musician has the right to make himself heard in these musical concerts, and usually there are also listeners present who can appreciate the worth of a skilled musician.*[16]

What Bach and Görner accomplish in their respective collegia musica is highly significant in the history of music and at the same time prepares the ground for the establishment of the so-called Great or Merchants' Consort in 1743. This is not the first but certainly the most important institution of its kind in Germany, a forerunner of the Leipzig Gewandhaus concerts, the epitome of this specifically bourgeois cultural form.

Fortunately Bach's assistant and successor in the collegium musicum, Carl Gotthelf Gerlach, is also involved with procuring and copying scores. Parts of Bach's musical legacy that turned up in the archives of the Breitkopf publishing house can be linked to performances of the collegium musicum: overtures by Johann Friedrich Fasch, string symphonies by Melchior Hoffmann, chamber cantatas by Nicola Antonio Porpora, but also Handel's chamber cantata "Armida abbandonata." These lucky finds can be supplemented by copies of scores in Bach's own hand: around 1730, copies were made of overtures by Johann Bernhard Bach, with an added movement by Agostino Steffani, and in 1734–35 copies of Pietro Antonio Locatelli's Concerto Grosso in F Minor. Around 1731 Bach had Christoph Nichelmann make a copy of Antonio Vivaldi's A-Minor Concerto for Four Violins, which Bach himself arranged for four harpsichords.[17]

Such fortuitous discoveries—for that is what we are dealing with here—confirm what we would suspect in any case: Bach is familiar with his contemporaries' music, examines and performs it—when it appeals to him and fits a particular occasion. It would be more exciting to learn which of his own compositions he offered in the weekly "concerts" of his collegium musicum. Let us begin with the instrumental compositions: it is plausible that the period around 1730 sees him writing out the scores for the different parts of the Violin Concerto in A Minor, BWV 1041, the Double Violin Concerto in D Minor, BWV 1043, and the Overture in D Major, BWV 1068; the period 1738–39 seems likely for the Flute Overture in B Minor, BWV 1067. The collegium musicum probably performed these pieces, but, as explained above, they need not have been composed around the same time.

We know more about Bach's arrangements for the collegium musicum than about his compositions for this ensemble. We have scores for the different parts, or copies of complete scores for six concertos for two, three, or four harpsichords, probably from the years 1730 to 1736. They include the already mentioned arrangement of the Vivaldi Concerto for Four Harpsichords, BWV 1065. As for the two

Concertos for Three Harpsichords in D Minor and C Major, BWV 1063 and 1064, scholars still are not sure whether the original form, presumably scored for three solo violins, should be attributed to Bach or to an unknown composer. On the other hand, there is no doubt that the two concertos in C minor for two harpsichords are based on compositions by Bach: BWV 1060 is thought to have originated as a concerto for oboe and violin, and we know that BWV 1062 is based on the Double Violin Concerto BWV 1043. The Concerto for Two Harpsichords in C Major, BWV 1061, constitutes a special case; only the individual parts for the two harpsichords still exist. The string ripieno was added later and need not have been composed by Bach himself.

The scoring of these works raises the question of whether Bach preferred to work with harpsichordists as his soloists because the collegium musicum was short of outstanding string and wind players. The works just mentioned do not allow any such assumption. It seems more likely that he wanted to give his two eldest sons the opportunity to perform in concerts before they left home—Wilhelm Friedemann going to Dresden in 1733 as the organist at St. Sophia's, Carl Philipp Emanuel departing a year later to continue his studies in Frankfurt on the Oder. Bach must have wanted to equip his sons with the same kind of confidence that he nurtured in his pupil Johann Ludwig Krebs, attesting in 1735, "that he need not hesitate to have others hear him play."[18]

Around 1734 Carl Philipp Emanuel seems to have transformed a violin concerto in D minor into the harpsichord concerto BWV 1052a,[19] before his father went to work on the same piece a few years later; around 1738 Bach brought together in one volume (P 234) the scores for seven arrangements as harpsichord concertos of works written for other instruments, some of whose originals are known while others have disappeared. We know that BWV 1054 was based on the Violin Concerto in E Major, BWV 1042; BWV 1057 derives from the Fourth Brandenburg Concerto, and BWV 1058 originated as the Violin Concerto in A minor. In three other cases scholars agree on the nature of the lost original: as previously mentioned,

BWV 1052 was probably based on a violin concerto in D major, likewise BWV 1056, and BWV 1055 on a concerto for oboe d'amore.

Whereas the editors of the *Neue Bach-Ausgabe* felt so confident about the originals of these three concertos that they published reconstructions of the original scoring, the Concerto in E Major, BWV 1053 left them puzzled: the solo part for harpsichord does not allow one to draw any definitive conclusion about the instrument that served as the model. Nonetheless, recent reconstructions for viola, oboe, and oboe d'amore have been performed, recorded, and published; the last word has not yet been spoken.

What reasons could Bach have had for combining BWV 1052–58 into a complete score? Perhaps these seven keyboard concertos—plus BWV 1059, of which only a nine-measure fragment exists—were inspired by Handel's organ concertos, which appeared in 1738, and represent written versions of performances in which Bach improvised on the harpsichord, basing his performances on the solo parts of concertos he had composed earlier. These versions may have been intended to provide an example of his famous skill at improvisation. It is also conceivable that he intended the manuscript to serve as a handy supply of music for concerts in places such as Dresden. He may have performed as a soloist in the last years of his life with a work like the Triple Concerto in A Minor, BWV 1044, arranged from earlier works, for instance during his visits to Berlin and Potsdam.[20]

While old sources reveal that the sonatas for organ BWV 525–30 were used by Bach as instructional materials for Wilhelm Friedemann, comparable works for other instruments can be linked to the collegium musicum, even though the dates of the original compositions cannot be established with any certainty; this is true in particular of the sonatas for flutes BWV 1030 and 1032 and for the viola da gamba BWV 1027–29.

Some of the vocal music presented during the regular evening performances by the collegium musicum may also have been composed by Bach, but we have no precise information on this matter. At first glance, a work like the *Coffee Cantata* "Schweigt stille, plaudert nicht," BWV 211, would seem perfect for the setting of Zimmermann's Coffeehouse and for literary Leipzig in general; humorous or satiric allusions to the vice of coffee drinking were the order of the day: "If I must pass the day without coffee, you shall have a corpse on your hands by eventide," says Dame Nocaff in the *Good Wives' Trial* by Picander, who also wrote the libretto for the *Coffee Cantata*.[21]

The cantata "Ich bin in mir vergnügt," BWV 204, written in 1726 or 1727 in a tradition that Telemann too had cultivated, that of the Italian *cantata morale*, used texts from Christian Friedrich Hunold's *Academische Neben-Stunden* and also suits the coffeehouse setting. If Bach had not performed there as a guest before 1729, he certainly had the opportunity to present similar works in later years. The richly scored *dramma per musica* "The Contest between Phoebus and Pan," BWV 201, would seem to have a direct connection with Bach's installation at the collegium musicum.

Between the summer of 1737 and the fall of 1739 the collegium musicum must manage without its director at its weekly gatherings; Bach assigns Gerlach to substitute for him. We have already discussed Bach's absence as an indication of his gradual withdrawal from public involvement. Yet in October 1739 Bach resumes direction of the collegium and makes a public announcement that he is doing so. Otherwise, the number of news items in the Leipzig papers concerning the collegium musicum declines appreciably; after Bach's appointment as composer to the court in Dresden, he apparently feels he does not need such publicity.

The scarcity of regular reports in the press makes it difficult for Bach scholars to establish the end of his participation in the collegium musicum. Perhaps he gave it up as early as 1741, the year in which Zimmermann, the coffeehouse proprietor, died, or perhaps not until 1744, when Gerlach was first mentioned as his successor. In the meanwhile, the Great Consort has been established, on the initiative of the merchants' guild;[22] Bach has fulfilled his obligation to Leipzig's concert life, and perhaps he is weary of the daily routine.

We have direct confirmation from Johann Friedrich Wilhelm Son-nenkalb, a boarding student at the St. Thomas School, that in the years after 1746 Bach hardly performed outside his own house.

This testimony makes it unnecessary to speculate whether those responsible for the Great Consort might have been able to secure Bach's assistance if they had wished to. The reports from the first years of the consort reveal that from the beginning this was a more prepossessing institution than Bach's collegium, and that the audi-ence—"an assemblage of Leipzig families"—exercised a greater in-fluence over its performing musicians than was customary.

The secular cantatas from Bach's middle Leipzig period cannot be definitely linked to performances by the collegium musicum but certainly belong to its social context. In many cases Bach may have been suggested as a composer by Picander, who wrote the libretti for most of the cantatas we are about to discuss.

The celebratory cantata "Erwählte Pleissen-Stadt," BWV 216a, which cannot be dated precisely but was certainly composed after 1728, expresses local patriotism: the unknown librettist pits Apollo against Mercury in a debate over whether Leipzig owes its fame and fortune to its learning or its commercial prowess. Perhaps the librettist is merely fulfilling his obligation to praise his native town.

Two cantatas written to be performed at manor houses give ev-idence of Bach's involvement with the petty aristocracy in the envi-rons of Leipzig. In 1737, Picander and Bach pay tribute to Johann Christian von Hennicke as the hereditary lord of Wiederau with the cantata "Angenehmes Wiederau," BWV 30a, transformed a year later into the church cantata "Freue dich, erlöste Schar," BWV 30. In 1742 Bach composes the Peasant Cantata, BWV 212, which will be discussed at length later.

Bach adapted many secular cantatas from his Leipzig period to different purposes, sometimes changing the text slightly, sometimes making major alterations in the music. A prime example of this procedure may be found in the works he dedicated over the years to the governor of Leipzig, Joachim Friedrich von Flemming. On 25 August 1726 he presents the cantata "Verjaget, zerstreuet, zerrüttet, ihr Sterne," BWV 249b. Yet this is not an original composition; considerable portions of the music appeared a year earlier in the celebratory cantata for Duke Christian von Weissenfels, "Entfliehet, verschwindet, entweichet, ihr Sorgen," BWV 249a, written for 23 February 1725. Bach had used the same music for the first version of the Easter oratorio "Kommt, fliehet und eilet," BWV 249, composed for 1 April 1725.

For 12 January 1729 Bach composes the birthday music "O! angenehme Melodei," BWV 210a, for Duke Christian, who visits Leipzig for the New Year's fair and is described in the text as a patron of learning and the arts. Erasures in the surviving handwritten scores for individual parts show that Bach used the same work, with slight revisions to the text, to congratulate Count von Flemming—and for the anniversary of yet another "honored Patron," whose name is unfortunately not mentioned. Bach also used significant portions of the same music for the wedding cantata "O holder Tag, erwünschte Zeit," BWV 210, whose parts were scored sometime between 1736 and 1741.

In 1731 Flemming may have finally received an original composition, the birthday cantata "So kämpfet nur, ihr muntern Töne," BWV Anh. I, 10. Bach subsequently recycled its opening movement for the church cantata 248/VI, which in turn served as the basis for the sixth part of the *Christmas Oratorio* in 1734–35.

Newly discovered printed texts and intelligent analyses have enabled Bach scholarship to shed more and more light on the reciprocal borrowings among Bach's cantatas from the Leipzig period. Although these revelations by themselves do not allow us to recover lost works, they do give us insight into Bach's "workshop," specifically into the way he mined a limited amount of material for use in ever-new contexts. His economical practices do not imply indifference toward the creation of occasional works. We shall discuss in a separate chapter how the tension between composer and arranger actually stimulated his creative productivity rather than stifled it.

An anonymous polemic against Bach's compositional style, dated 14 May 1737, appears in the first section of Johann Adolph Scheibe's *Der critische Musicus;* it sparks a paradigmatic debate over musical aesthetics. *Der critische Musicus* is not a journal that treats current events but rather an encyclopedia of music that appears serially. In the eyes of Scheibe, a Gottsched pupil, contemporary poetry and rhetoric have achieved such perfection that good taste is triumphing almost everywhere: "Music alone remains to be included. This noble branch of knowledge requires as much effort as has been devoted to those others."[23]

Scheibe calls for a heightened sensitivity to composing in tune with nature. The foundation of all music, according to him, is not harmony or counterpoint but a flowing melody: "Each and every composer must sing in his thoughts." Simple rules, derived from those of modern poetry and rhetoric, will guarantee the production of compositions in which the melodic ideas are merged into an engaging and memorable ensemble. Not the composer's artistry but rather a "noble and lofty entertainment of the human spirit" should be foremost.[24]

Scheibe values contributions to his encyclopedia that in his eyes make for particularly pleasant reading. Thus in installment 6 he prints a letter from a friend who reports on a grand tour that took him to the places where important musicians plied their trade. Their names are not mentioned—not to protect their identity but to awaken the readers' curiosity as to who was the intended target of this or that jibe. Scheibe pretends to have had initial doubts about publishing the letter: "But since no one was named by name, I finally saw no compelling reasons to suppress this account." In a later supplement to the first of four installments of *Der critische Musicus,* he admits to at least one element of his shadowboxing: of course Bach in Leipzig was one of the examples mentioned. But not until the second edition of the encyclopedia appears in 1745 does he dare to reveal that he himself was the author of the entire letter.

Scheibe is not a pupil of Bach's, but he certainly is a Leipziger. Born in 1708, he learns to play the organ and masters the basics of composition, teaching himself for the most part. He often listens with the greatest admiration to Bach's performances on the organ and other keyboard instruments. After his father suffers major financial reverses, he must interrupt his studies of poetics under Gottsched. He fails to secure a position as an organist; in 1729 he is passed over after an audition at St. Thomas's, presided over by Bach, among others. Telemann encourages him to move to Hamburg, a city that has two musicians committed to the Enlightenment—himself and Johann Mattheson—and an enlightened press, to which Mattheson contributes by publishing a steady stream of books and periodicals that aim to educate the general public in the modern spirit. In 1767 Gotthold Ephraim Lessing will come to Hamburg to write his *Hamburgische Dramaturgie*, worthy of mention in this context because Lessing was sponsored as a young man by Gottsched and developed his ideas through productive criticism.

Presumably Scheibe, barely thirty at the time, is urged to embark on a career as a proponent of an up-to-date musical aesthetic. Telemann probably argues that an active debate on musical aesthetics is necessary, and it should be permissible to name names. Telemann is primarily a musician, hardly a theoretician; in addition, it is difficult to conceive that he would criticize his friend Bach, even if he saw reason to do so. Mattheson, on the other hand, is a faultfinder, who also snipes at Bach from time to time but sees himself as a mediator among the social classes.

Thus it falls to the "young man" to explicate what a "natural compositional style" is and how even the great Bach violates its principles. This is no mere cheeky defiance of the great authority Bach, whose preeminence no one knowledgeable about music would deny; it is the unavoidable parricide, which only a younger man can commit. Bach's own sons committed it de facto—simply by composing in a more modern style than their father, in spite of all their respect for him; at the same time, as advocates of a "mixed taste" they did not reject their father's legacy but rather assumed it.

*Herr ＿＿, finally, is the most prominent among the musicians
in ＿＿. He is an extraordinary artist on the clavier and on the
organ, and at present he has encountered only one who can contest his preeminence. I have heard this great man play a number
of times. One is astonished at his skill and can hardly grasp how
it is possible that his fingers and his feet cross each other and
stretch so marvelously and quickly, and thereby make the broad-
est leaps without striking a single false note or tying his body in
knots through such violent movements. This great man would be
the wonder of entire nations, had he but a more pleasing character, and if he did not deprive his pieces of all naturalness through
excessive and confusing ornamentation and obscure their beauty
with a surfeit of artistic effects. Because he judges according to his
fingers, his pieces are most difficult to play; for he demands that
the singers and instrumentalists execute with their voices and
their instruments what he can play on the clavier. But such a
thing is impossible.*

*He expresses in actual notes all the mannerisms, all the little
ornaments and everything that can be played in this method; and
that not only deprives his pieces of the beauty of harmony but also
makes the singing inaudible. All the voices are supposed to work
together, and in the same degree of difficulty, and no leading voice
can be made out. In short, in music he represents that which formerly Herr von Lohenstein represented in poetry. The bombastic
ornamentation led both from a natural style to an artificial one
and from the lofty to the obscure; and one admires in both the
strenuous work and extraordinary effort, which, however, is exerted in vain because it clashes with nature.*[25]

A careful reading of this classic piece of musical aesthetics reveals that the criticism is not directed wholesale at Bach but at his
vocal and instrumental music, his cantatas, passions, and oratorios,
whether secular or liturgical. In recommending Mattheson's *Kern
Melodischer Wissenschaft* (The Heart of the Melodic Art), a work
published in January 1738, Scheibe emphasizes the genre-specific

aspect of his criticism, perhaps on the advice of the editor: "Religious works by Bach are uniformly more elaborate and difficult, but by no means as impressive, convincing, or conducive to rational reflection as those by Telemann or Graun."[26]

In a response, also published in 1738, to criticism he has already received for taking this position, Scheibe articulates the paradigm shift even more clearly: the keyword in the new music is not "art" but "taste": "The so-called newfangled taste, which, according to the mature judgment of the impartial gentleman... may be spoilt, may in actuality be far better grounded and more natural than the old-fashioned taste of those who, with this gentleman, prefer that which is forced to that which is natural."[27]

The Gottsched disciple further makes it clear that he has no objection to a well-crafted piece but must denounce as confused a work in which the comprehensibility of the text suffers because the "voices are most wondrously mixed up" so that "one cannot distinguish which is the leading voice." The resulting effect is like "hearing nothing but a strange, indistinct, muddled, and unpleasant sound."[28]

Bach probably reacted with bitterness to this polemic, which is launched the very year after his appointment as court composer and collides with his efforts to garner praise outside Leipzig. Now people are finding fault with his art, too! Such indignation would be understandable. Of course Bach composes with an artistry that may be described as "old-fashioned," for heaven's sake, or as "Lohensteinian excess," a reference to the Baroque dramatist and novelist Daniel Caspar von Lohenstein. This topic has already been framed by Gottsched, in whose *Beyträge zur Critischen Historie der deutschen Sprache, Poesie und Beredsamkeit* (Essays on the Critical History of German Language, Poetry and Eloquence) the following judgment can be found on the philosophic Germany of his day: "Without doubt it also sees in this Englishman [Milton] the predominance of Lohensteinian excess, uncontrolled imagination, pretentious forms of expression, and wrong-headed judgment."[29]

Yet Bach composes flexibly and does not view art and nature as incompatible. As evidence we have not merely the one concerto "according to the Italian *gusto*," BWV 971, of which Scheibe reports almost with relief that it can be seen "as a perfect example of a well-structured one-part concerto."[30] Far more evidence can be found in Bach's development as a composer in the vocal and instrumental genres, which after all are primarily at issue in the whole debate. The path Bach takes from the combinatory technique of the first and second annual cantata cycles to songlike structures in later cantata works, and from there to the *St. Matthew Passion* and the *Christmas Oratorio*, reveals an unmistakable tendency to respond to current demands for an emphatic and catchy style—in other words, to the new "taste" that the majority of his contemporaries prefer.

It must have been around the year 1736 that Bach produced a final handwritten version of the *St. Matthew Passion*, which incorporates small but delicate rhythmic changes—for instance in the flute part in the opening chorus, starting with measure 26: he changes the rhythm of long–short–short to a highly modern Lombard rhythm of short–long–short.[31] That is something Scheibe cannot know, but is he familiar with the first version of this opening chorus? This version already has something of the gestic force and emphasis that people are demanding of a compositional style that is natural and provides direct expression of physical and spiritual sensations. To be sure, as naturally as this movement is structured into statement and counterstatement, the cantus firmus "O Lamm Gottes unschuldig" is woven in with the greatest artistry; and furthermore Bach includes in the definitive version of the *St. Matthew Passion* the difficult choral chorale "O Mensch, bewein dein Sünde gross." This part may indeed have struck his contemporaries as obscure or confused; but in his greatest works one can never have the natural without the difficult!

What works is Scheibe thinking of in 1737 when he describes Bach from his perch in Hamburg as the Lohenstein of music? Is it primarily the early Leipzig cantatas, which over the years are heard time and again in Leipzig's churches? Does he understand that Bach by no means considers these works the ne plus ultra, but rather since the 1730s has begun to make clear distinctions: as we have described, the ideal of the full-voiced and simultaneously obligato movement tends to gravitate toward liturgical music; correspondingly the genre of the cantata—now cultivated primarily as a secular *dramma per musica*—is opened up for modern styles of composition. It is interesting to see what a knowledgeable observer of the Leipzig scene, the music scholar Lorenz Mizler, writes in his *Musikalische Bibliothek* under the date of 5 March 1739 against Scheibe and in favor of Bach:

> *Herr Telemann and Herr Graun are excellent composers, and Herr Bach has produced equally excellent works. But when Herr Bach sometimes scores the middle voices more fully than others, he is taking his cue from the musical styles of twenty and twenty-five years past. Yet he can also do otherwise, when he so wishes. Anyone who heard the music that was performed by the students last year for the Easter Mass in Leipzig, in the most gracious presence of His Royal Majesty of Poland and composed by Herr Kapellmeister Bach, will have to grant that it was entirely constructed according to the newest taste, and lauded by all and sundry. That is how well the Herr Kapellmeister knows how to direct his efforts to suit his listeners.*[32]

Unfortunately, the composition mentioned by Mizler has disappeared: it is Bach's celebratory wedding cantata "Willkommen! Ihre herrschenden Götter der Erden," BWV Anh. I, 13. Mizler's comments attest to his good judgment: instead of insisting that Bach is an innovator, he sees him as a composer who opens himself to the new and knows how to use it when he wishes. At the time, Bach has just subscribed to Telemann's flute quartets, published in Paris in 1738—a sidelight on his multifaceted understanding of music.

A second defender of Bach cites the same work, presumably in reference to Mizler, calling it—in the terminology of the opposing camp—"moving, expressive, natural, orderly."[33] It is Johann Abraham Birnbaum in his *Verteidigung Bachs gegen Scheibes Angriffe* (Defense of Bach against Scheibe's Attacks)—a now vanished single printing from March 1739, which has come down to us only in a version reprinted in the second edition of Scheibe's *Der critische Musicus*. At the beginning of January 1738, Birnbaum took up the verbal cudgels under the pseudonym of Horatius, in a twenty-eight-page tract entitled *Unpartheyische Anmerckungen über eine bedenckliche stelle in dem sechsten Stück des Critischen Musicus* (Impartial Observations on a Controversial Passage in the Sixth Issue of the *Musical Critic*).

This Magister Birnbaum, who according to Mizler had "good insight into music, and himself plays the clavier most delightfully,"[34] has an appointment as an independent scholar at the University of Leipzig to lecture on jurisprudence, philosophy, and rhetoric. In addition to several works in Latin, he publishes a two-volume edition of *Deutsche Reden* (German Speeches), a tract titled *Angenehme Vortheile einer vernünftigen Einsamkeit* (Pleasant Advantages of a Reasonable Solitude), and another called *Von der Gewohnheit der Verlobten, bei der Trauung einander die Hände zu geben* (Of the Custom in Which the Affianced Take Each Other's Hands at the Wedding). It is possible that Bach enlisted this experienced lecturer and writer to respond to Scheibe.

At any rate, Bach arranges for the printing of Birnbaum's second tract himself. In an inquiry dated 3 March 1739, Bach's relative Johann Elias Bach, at the time serving as his secretary, asks an informant in Jena whether, despite the impending Easter fair, it might still be possible to have printed "a small treatise of 7 to 8 sheets, specifically in the typeface that the printers call Cicero-small, in octavo" in time for the fair. Four days later the same man, in the name of his cousin and of Magister Birnbaum, asks a cantor called Johann Wilhelm Koch in Ronneburg to organize the printing of two hundred copies on medium-quality paper.[35] He specifically directs that the nouns not be capitalized—a style that can be found already in Birnbaum's first treatise.

Bach probably supplied Birnbaum with the ammunition he considered suitable for his defense against Scheibe's attack. Thus Birnbaum's first piece launches the story of the keyboard competition between Bach and Louis Marchand at the court of Dresden.

Making this story known may have been important to Bach, whom Birnbaum at every possible juncture thenceforth addresses as "His Eminence, the Court Composer."

Bach may also have been the source of Birnbaum's references to the clavier and organ composers Nicolas de Grigny and Pierre Du Mage, in whose published compositions all the mannerisms and little ornamental devices were written out in notes, as Scheibe charged in the case of Bach. One insight Birnbaum records, citing Palestrina and Antonio Lotti, reads like an idea from an unwritten treatise on music theory by Bach: "Harmony becomes far more complete when all the voices work together and each one carries a melody of its own that harmonizes perfectly with all the others."[36]

The mention of the contemporary composer Lotti constitutes a kind of inside tip from the workshop of Bach the composer: between 1732 and 1735 Bach, as already mentioned, copied a short mass of Lotti's in four to six parts—perhaps in connection with the composing of his own short mass BWV 232[I], the lead-in to the B-Minor Mass, or at least in clear reference to the current situation with masses at the Dresden court: Lotti was active there from 1717 to 1719, and there Jan Dismas Zelenka prepared a score of the G-Minor Mass that in turn can be identified as the basis for Bach's own copy.[37]

In 1775, Carl Philipp Emanuel told Forkel, insatiably eager for information about his father, "*ad IImum:* in his last years he greatly prized: *Fux, Caldara,* Handel, Kayser, Hass, the two Grauns, Telemann, *Zelenka, Benda,* & altogether everything that was particularly praiseworthy in Berlin and Dressden."[38]

Was this already true in the thirties? It is conceivable that when it came to music, Bach increasingly saw the Leipzig brand of Protestantism as provincial, or even confining, and directed his gaze toward those courts whose cultivation of music seemed broad-minded and multifaceted. Of course he wants to be, and remain, a thoroughly German composer. In this sense he can take pleasure in a passage in a letter of 1737 written by Lotti (now living in Venice) to Georg von Bertuch, a major general in the fortress of Akerhus near Oslo, then engaged in composing twenty-four sonatas in all the keys. In his letter Lotti remarks, "My fellow countrymen have good ideas, but are no composers; the true composing one finds in Germany."[39]

Bach is using Birnbaum to convey a veiled message to Scheibe: the ideal of the full-voiced and simultaneously obbligato style was adumbrated not only by a classical composer of the past, Palestrina; it also receives legitimation from an Italian highly respected as a church musician. Besides, it corresponds to the current practice in liturgical music at the court of Dresden, to which the court composer Bach sees himself as belonging.

Other passages in this text seem to have been viewed by Bach scholars as having marginal significance only, because they ostensibly originate with Magister Birnbaum. Yet the description of the relation between art and nature reflects Bach's own thinking:

> *If art aids Nature, its only purpose is to preserve Nature, indeed to improve her better condition, not to destroy her. Many things are supplied by Nature in a most grievous form, which receive the most beautiful aspect when art has shaped them. Thus art furnishes Nature with her missing beauty and enhances that which is present. The greater the artistry, that is to say, the more industriously and painstakingly art works to improve on Nature, the more perfectly glows the beauty brought forth thereby. Accordingly it is impossible that the greatest art could obscure anything's beauty.*[40]

Against this background it becomes understandable that Birnbaum, perhaps inspired by Bach here as well, should take offense when Scheibe characterizes the court composer as a "music maker"— albeit the most outstanding one in Leipzig. The magister distinguishes sharply between practitioners who should be called mere "musici" and virtuosi and great composers. But here the Young Turk Scheibe might agree: he meant no disrespect, merely expressed himself carelessly. Besides, his intention is not to belittle Bach but to declare his era past—in the name of progress.

This agenda necessitates portraying the situation in black and white. Indeed most debates on musical aesthetics have been conducted in a manner emphasizing binary oppositions, as a way of keeping the positions clear. Here "excessive and confused ornamentation" is contrasted with "pleasing sound," "obscurity" with "nobility," "overexertion" and "exaggerated artifice" with "beauty" and "Nature"—in sum, "art" versus "taste." Modern musical aesthetics can be proud of having given rise, in the first decades of its existence, to a discourse that would still be pertinent a century later: in 1844, Carl Kossmaly, a kapellmeister and critic not, on the whole, ill-disposed toward Robert Schumann, condemned Schumann's Piano Fantasia in C Major, opus 17, with words that might have been written by a Scheibe redivivus. To him, the contrary examples are no longer Telemann or Graun but Mendelssohn or Chopin:

> The eccentric, willful, vague, and blurry nature of this music can hardly be exaggerated—the exuberance he loves above all sometimes degenerates in this piece into excessive ornamentation and complete incomprehensibility, just as the striving for originality here and there loses itself in shrillness and unnaturalness. The composer reminds us—to use a simile—of a rich, dignified gentleman who, out of aristocratic arrogance, wants to make himself inaccessible to any claims, and to that end selfishly and stubbornly barricades himself from the world, has deep moats dug around his entire territory and towering hedges of thorns planted, has warning shots fired and traps laid for the feet of intruders, and walls himself off to such an extent that people abandon all thought of seeking to make his closer acquaintance.[41]

Although Bach is isolated from the Leipzig city council at least from the 1730s on, this does not mean that his artistic activity is isolated. His praises are sung everywhere, and even his former rector, Johann Matthias Gesner, now a professor at Göttingen after five years at the St. Thomas School, includes in his 1738 annotated edition of Quintilian's *De institutione oratoria* a long footnote in which he celebrates Bach in Latin as a modern citharoedus, who can not only sing and play the harp at the same time, like Apollo, but also conduct thirty to forty musicians and hear any false note, no matter how loud the music.[42]

At forty-seven Gesner is not yet old, but of course also not as young as Scheibe; the latter's criticism primarily represents that of the younger generation, advocates of the Enlightenment, but not that of all musically knowledgeable circles. Even Johann Mattheson, an envoy of the musical Enlightenment, at least relativizes Scheibe's attacks in his *Vollkommener Kapellmeister* (Compleat Kapellmeister) of 1739. Among the various "styles of composition" he, too, mentions the "excessively ornate" but says it should be rejected only when it "does not fit the persons, things, thoughts, and actions to be portrayed" and, for example, "too greatly adorns items of little import."[43] In this context, composing naturally means to Mattheson not simply but in the style appropriate to the subject.

This argument dovetails with that of Birnbaum, who rejects Scheibe's accusation that Bach's intensive use of dissonance robs his pieces of appeal:

> *The true appeal in music resides in the combining and alternating of consonance and dissonance without damaging the harmony. The nature of music requires the same. The various passions, especially the sorrowful ones, cannot be expressed adequately without this alternation, which accords with nature.*[44]

Apparently this intervention shook Scheibe's certainty. In the second edition of his *Der critische Musicus*, which appeared in 1745, the term "Nature" is replaced by "reason" in a decisive spot, the last sentence of his first commentary of 1737. He seems to have learned in the meantime from contemporary French philosophy that reason must on occasion correct nature, when nature stands in the way of aesthetic appeal.

Allow me to insert here a personal observation, directed more to the Bach lover than to the Bach scholar: I cannot imagine that Scheibe really disliked Bach's church compositions—which are primarily at issue here. No one who truly appreciates music could or can escape the fascination they exert on the listener. The nub of the problem lies in matters of belief: it is not the musician Scheibe but Scheibe the man of the Enlightenment who resists the mysterious profundity of this music. Its profundity is that of myth, as deeply grounded as it is unfathomable, defying all attempts at rationalistic explanation. This phenomenon is bound to threaten the weak ego of a man who has emancipated himself from the old faith but whose new belief is still in mere progress. How can an old man, with a single cantata chorus, send the entire melody-plus-one euphoria of the Enlightenment packing, along with its demand for a music for all!

In the judgment of Theodor W. Adorno, not someone you would usually think to mention in the same breath with Scheibe, we can hear an echo of Scheibe's criticism. Adorno ascribes to Bach's music "an element of heteronomy, of not being gripped by his subject,"[45] even when his composing subjects of course have to work far harder, following Beethoven's example, than a composer of odes in accord with Scheibe's taste. No—Bach's church music is not entirely gripped by its subject, but it gives the subject a voice that originates in faith. "When I hear the *St. Matthew Passion*," Adorno says, "when I hear great music, I am sure that what this music expresses cannot be untrue. But that this truth should manifest itself again in the forms of traditional religion is something I cannot accept. Yet perhaps that is a limitation and a failing on my part."[46]

For the Bach historiographer today, the question of how to assess his middle Leipzig period, extending into the 1740s, is one of perspective: is Bach already in retreat, on the defensive, turning inward? Some evidence supports this interpretation. Or is he respected as a conservative, in the positive sense, as one who does not reject the new but wants to preserve the old values—an artist who allows the ideas of the Enlightenment to pass through him more than he actively seeks them? There is evidence for this view as well; and part of his great historical significance for us today can be found in this direction. Into the nineteenth and twentieth centuries, he provides legitimation for a kind of music that does not succumb to trendiness but dedicates itself to the difficult task of keeping an eye on the whole, of moving forward without abandoning the past, of pleasing its hearers yet creating meaning. His contemporaries recognized this universalism, at least in part. It is in this spirit that Friedrich Wilhelm Marpurg writes in 1749 in his journal *Der critische Musicus an der Spree*, "Thus foreigners perceive for example the taste of an immortal Bach of Leipzig as a special original taste, not a taste originating in imitation of a foreign nation."[47]

At the time, Marpurg is thirty years old, with an affinity for the Enlightenment and therefore for the French aesthetics of imitation. In 1753 he will publish *An Essay on the Fugue* and in it refer with gratitude to Bach. Marpurg has fewer preconceptions than Scheibe and can recognize how Bach's art transcends any specific era; indeed, he calls Bach an immortal in his own lifetime. In the same Berlin tradition, the writer E. T. A. Hoffmann, discussing in 1814 Johann Friedrich Reichardt's Piano Sonata in F Minor, mentions Bach along with Handel, Haydn, Mozart, and Beethoven as one of the "most noble, mighty spirits" whose music "fills one's breast with unutterable longing" because it conveys something of the absolute and purely romantic essence of this art.[48] For Hoffmann, too, the contrapuntalist and powerful harmonist Bach is no bugaboo but a witness to the "inner riches" of music. Here the Enlightenment is overcome more quickly than Scheibe could imagine; Bach is one of the founding fathers of German classical music.

There is one creative project during his Leipzig period in which Bach can pursue his ideas about the universality of music without anyone's attempting to interfere—that of the *Clavier-Übung*. It has already been mentioned that Bach places considerable emphasis, even during his early years in Leipzig, on having a presence not only as a church composer but also as the author of keyboard music; and this desire makes sense in light of the high value this genre held for him in Cöthen. Yet for understandable reasons the undertaking at first advances slowly. The first partita, BWV 825, appears in 1726 with a dedication to the hereditary prince of Cöthen. It is the first score whose publication Bach oversees himself. The engraver is the young Balthasar Schmid, a student at Leipzig who probably gave Bach a reasonable price. In the *Leipziger Post-Zeitungen* Bach announces to all "lovers of the clavier" that he "intends to issue an Opus of Clavier Suites," and has "already made a beginning with the first partita."[49]

In the years 1727, 1728, and 1730, the second through fifth partitas, BWV 826–29, appear one at a time. In 1731 the moment has come: Bach publishes six in one edition, with the designation "Opus I." The title page indicates that they are "Published by the Author" and commissioned by "the Orphaned Daughter of Seel Boetius, below the Rathaus."

He calls the work an exercise for the clavier—apparently alluding to the successful partitas and sonatas published by Johann Kuhnau. It is from his predecessor that he also borrows the prudent measure of publishing the works himself. The "preludes, allemandes, courantes, sarabands, gigues, minuets, and other gallantries" referred to on the title page are intended to "delight music lovers." Bach wants to create the impression of accessible music. With this first attempt at publishing his music, the composer seems determined, in a fit of petit-bourgeois commercialism, to leave nothing to chance. He also takes the distribution into his own hands; the printed version can be obtained not only from him and at the Leipzig fair but also from colleagues in Dresden, Halle, Lüneburg, Wolfenbüttel, Nuremberg, and Augsburg.

When Bach chooses the term "gallantries" on the title page to refer to the nontraditional dances in the collection, he is using a word that appears in the titles of numerous fashionable poetry collections appearing around that time in Leipzig. There are the *Gallant Poems* of Johann Burchard Mencke, whose name we encountered in connection with the wedding cantata "Auf, süss entzückende Gewalt," BWV Anh. I, 196. Mattheson, too, publishes his *Beschütztes Orchester* in 1717 for the "homme galante."[50]

Yet the suites in opus 1 are anything but light fare. On 30 May 1730 the poet Louise Adelgunde Victorie Kulmus writes to her fiancé Gottsched, "The pieces for the clavier by Bach that I am dispatching to you…are as difficult as they are lovely. Even when I have played them through ten times, I still seem to myself an utter beginner."[51] Several years later Mizler advises anyone who does not know how to place his fingers with great precision that he would be better off avoiding "the partitas for clavier of our famed Herr Bach of Leipzig."[52] This is virtuoso music, and at the same time an expression of a highly systematic attempt to demonstrate all the compositional possibilities represented by the clavier suite.

In the second part of the *Clavier-Übung*, which appeared in 1735, Bach goes to even greater lengths to provide compositions à la mode: he offers a "concerto in the Italian *gusto*," BWV 971, in tandem with an "overture in the French style," BWV 831; the following year a second edition follows, with previous mistakes in the engraving corrected. The work is received with enthusiasm. We have an early version of the overture in BWV 831a, in the hand of Anna Magdalena Bach, perhaps intended for sale to a private patron before the printed version can "gladden the spirits" of the rest of the public, as the title page emphasizes. An early version of the *Italian Concerto* probably existed as well.[53]

These works mark the end of Bach's involvement in publishing keyboard music of his own that takes its cue in some sense from contemporary taste. The next two parts of the *Clavier-Übung* can hardly be viewed as works for ordinary consumption geared to a broad audience; they mark, rather, the beginning of Bach's last phase of production.

THE LATER LEIPZIG YEARS: THE UNIVERSALIST

The Bach of the last phase is no old man gathering his waning strength to bring in a last harvest. He is, however, increasingly weary of his post as cantor of St. Thomas's, and would perhaps have already resigned if such a step were feasible or customary in those days; one cannot help thinking of his eldest son, Wilhelm Friedemann, who at fifty-three will in fact resign from his position in Halle, although afterward he will never find a firm foothold anywhere.

Johann Sebastian is around fifty-three himself when he picks up the gauntlet thrown down by Scheibe; takes a break from his collegium musicum; engages in last skirmishes with the elector over his right to select the school prefect; receives an official commission from the university to compose the wedding cantata "Willkommen! Ihre herrschenden Götter der Erden!", BWV Anh. I, 13, described as particularly gallant; is temporarily enjoined by the city council from performing a passion; auditions town pipers and writes evaluations of them; makes music at his house with court and chamber musicians from Dresden; travels to Altenburg to perform on the organ as a visiting artist; resumes his work with the collegium musicum; witnesses the birth of his daughter Johanna Carolina; accepts the role of godfather to Cantor Koch's new baby in Ronneburg; and so on and so forth.

In short, Bach's activity is by no means dwindling in 1738. Yet there is a remarkable decrease in the number of documents referring to external involvements, and extensive records of squabbles are entirely absent from now on. Thus it is dictated less by the chronicler and more by the state of affairs that in the report on Bach's last years factual material takes a backseat to reflections on his standing and the character of his late works. This approach corresponds to Bach's own assessment, as it does to the life of many an aging artist, who must no longer struggle to secure his place but turns toward putting his house in order.

It is not resignation in the face of external circumstances that causes Bach to turn to works like the third part of the *Clavier-Übung*, to the *Goldberg Variations*, to the second part of the *Well-Tempered Clavier*, to *The Art of Fugue*, or to the canon and variations on the song "Vom Himmel hoch." The *Musical Offering*, which also belongs to this group, owes its composition to a very worldly occasion: Bach's visit to the court of Frederick the Great of Prussia.

It is tempting to see Bach at the end of the 1730s as laboring to save the *ars musica* as a speculative system from the Enlightenment, which has issued a challenge in the person of Johann Adolph Scheibe. But that implies too strongly that Bach is on the defensive and does little more than repeat Albert Schweitzer's judgment, formulated, however, in reference to Bach's Protestant church music:

"Thus Bach represents an end point. Nothing starts with him; everything merely leads up to him."[54]

We can do justice to the contrapuntal works of the last years only if we view them on the one hand as a logical continuation and culmination of Bach's lifelong systematic thinking about music, on the other hand as a new beginning, in the sense of a conscious decision: Bach is setting out to find a form of musical expression beyond established genres and styles, or the essence of music itself. Ultimately, the canon and the fugue are neither genres nor styles but compositional methods, though of a special kind: they are perfectly suited to represent his ideal of perfect harmony. As Birnbaum has explicated, this ideal finds its realization when, in an ensemble of independent, euphonious voices, each works together perfectly with every other.

The instrumental works of Bach's late period are not merely the culmination of medieval and baroque conceptions of order and harmony; they contain much that is modern and exciting, contradictory and fragmentary. This body of work resembles a laboratory—yet not merely that of an alchemist who thinks he is on the trail of ancient wisdom. Here experiments are also conducted with the newest material. Bach has an established station, but he does not remain stationary. As drawn as he is to the ethereal, he displays at the same time an obvious desire to compose recognizable music—recognizable and therefore endowed with aesthetic properties in tune with the times. The abstract philosophy underlying the canon and the fugue becomes an entirely new concrete expression of pathos, melancholy, sensitivity, humor; and the preestablished harmony of a contrapuntal movement occasionally manifests tensions that already hint at the sonata form as it will develop in Viennese classicism.

Here the genres and styles again come into play that make it possible for music to move from a self-contained existence to one within a context and translate its beauty from the realm of systematic philosophy to that of social and personal experience—genres such as the choral arrangement, the song and variations, the quodlibet, the sonata, the invention, the prelude, the ricercar; likewise styles such as Italian, French, gallant, or old-fashioned. Thus Bach's late art is not only an *ars combinatoria*—a term Gottfried Wilhelm Leibniz will introduce to describe his project of creating an artificial universal language based on mathematical principles. At the same time, Bach's music mirrors the art of *melopöie*, which according to Johann Mattheson consists of "adeptness in inventing and formulating singable phrases in which the human ear can find delight."[55]

Bach's decision is wise. Genres and styles come and go; if one wishes to stand the test of time, one can do so only with works that transcend contemporary taste. With the definitive manuscript versions of the *St. Matthew Passion* and the B-Minor Mass, Bach aspires to leave the world a few masterful works in the oratorio genre; but it seems to him more important and above all more practical to publish printed music that will reflect in durable fashion his conception of "the essence of music,"[56] without appearing excessively erudite. Using ever new points of departure, these works would display the relation between objective and subjective forces, between poiesis and mimesis, between order and expression, between music that exists for its own sake and music that exists for others.

Bach thereby assumes a pivotal role in history. He sums up what went before him and at the same time lays the foundation for important developments that will come after him. Above all, the notion of voices working together will be critically important for the so-called absolute music of the era of Beethoven and Brahms, where it will reappear as the guiding concept of compositions based on motifs and themes. In Bach, the universalism of the Middle Ages and the baroque merges into modern idealism.

We resume our chronicle of Bach's life and career with the fall of 1739, when the *Leipziger Zeitungen* published the welcome news for "those who love Bach's keyboard exercises" that "the third part thereof is now complete and currently to be obtained from the author in Leipzig, at 3 talers apiece."[57] What other publications of clavier and organ music do the Leipzig papers announce during this period? In 1733, they mention choral preludes in two to four voices by Georg Friedrich Kauffmann; in 1737, chorales, preludes, and variations by Johann Caspar Vogler, intended for rural organists; in 1739, caprices and courtly pieces by Gottlieb Moffat, as well as a keyboard concerto in a lighter style by Christian August Jacobi; in 1740, six light organ preludes arranged according to the current taste by Bach's pupil Johann Ludwig Krebs. In 1743, keyboard pieces by Johann Christian Roedelius should be mentioned, "composed according to today's *goût*, which fall lightly but pleasingly on the ear, for which reason they are suitable both for the ladies and for other music lovers, who enjoy playing such light and agreeable works."[58]

The pieces in the third part of the *Clavier-Übung* are light-years removed from all these works—not only with respect to the difficulty of playing them but also in their compositional, theological, and philosophical ambitions, to which we return later. Bach must have recognized that he was breaking the bounds he had set for himself in the first two installments of the work. The dedication on the title page makes this distinction: "Written for those who love and most especially those who appreciate such work, to gladden their spirits." The work is intended "chiefly for the esteemed organists" and is "exceedingly well composed," as Bach's nephew and secretary, Johann Elias Bach, informs someone who expresses interest.[59]

The printed version contains not only twenty-one "different preludes on the catechism and other hymns for the organ," BWV 669–89, as the title page announces, but also the four duets BWV 802–05 and the Prelude and Fugue in E-Flat Major, BWV 552. Bach seems to have begun work on this third part soon after completing the second. Painstaking analysis of the title, pagination, paper, and engraving of the original printed version has revealed the stages of its creation: he first planned to produce a series of "great" chorales on the catechism; then he decided to add four instrumental duets and to give the work an elegant frame with the Prelude and Fugue in E-Flat Major; and finally he included the arrangements of the catechism chorales, to be performed on the organ.[60]

The additions to the work, not mentioned on the title page, which must have been engraved earlier, reflect Bach's sense that a collection of compositionally, emblematically, and technically demanding arrangements of Protestant hymns for the German mass and the Lutheran catechism might scare off people interested in his *Clavier-Übung,* whose numbers have grown with the publication of the relatively popular second part, containing the *Italian Concerto* and the *French Overture.* He therefore includes "small" arrangements of chorales that can be performed on the organ keyboard, and thus also on the cembalo, as well as duets free of cantus firmus; with the duets, as well as with the Prelude and Fugue in E-Flat Major, he also expands the scope of the genre.

It is interesting that in this process he takes into account precisely "those *puncta* with which a righteous organist should and must be familiar"—at least according to a representative of the Danzig organists' guild, a certain Johann Jacob Hamischer, who in 1673 stipulates that an organist should be capable of playing a prelude "in any musical tone," "to treat any chorale or sacred psalm...*per fugas*...in the *manuali et pedali,*" and to "elaborate it with four voices at least ex tempore."[61] Does Bach aspire with this collection to present music of the highest order for regular use in worship services? Perhaps not precisely that, but he very likely has in mind music for an organ virtuoso of the sort he performs in his own concerts. Accordingly, on 1 December 1736 he may have performed pieces from the third part of the *Clavier-Übung,* to the extent that they were completed, when he inspired "the greatest admiration" with his concert on the new organ in Dresden's Church of Our Lady.[62] Not only the Prelude and Fugue in E-Flat Major would have fit this setting but also the chorale arrangements, full of artistry yet with a modern sheen.[63]

It would not be even a half-truth to ascribe to Bach the desire for success. Here Mattheson comes to mind, who in 1739 publishes his fifty-third book, the *Compleat Kapellmeister,* which has become his best known. In the chapter "On Melody," we find a small but harmless jab at Magister Birnbaum and the latter's reply to Scheibe's attack on Bach. In the chapters on the different types of fugues Bach then receives high praise as a master of the genre.

Mattheson initially treats at length the puzzle canon for Ludwig Friedrich Hudemann, BWV 1074, composed in 1727. In his *Getreuer*

Music-Meister (Faithful Music Master) of 1728, Telemann already suggested one solution to the puzzle, and Mattheson now proposes two more; the third part of Lorenz Mizler's *Neu eröffnete musikalische Bibliothek* (Newly Opened Musical Library) of 1747 will offer three more. Even more interesting than this remarkably widespread response to the Hudemann canon is a passage in which Mattheson seems to address Bach personally:

> *So far as is known, of double fugues with three subjects, nothing more has appeared in engraved copper than my own work, under the title "The Sonorous Language of the Fingers," Parts One and Two, 1735 and 1737, which out of modesty I do not wish to praise to anyone; but would rather wish that something of the same sort might be brought to light by the famous Herr Bach in Leipzig, who is a great master of the fugue. In the meantime, the lack of such works reveals on the one hand the carelessness and the passing of thorough contrapuntalists, but on the other hand the slight demand on the part of today's ignorant organists and composers for such edifying things.*[64]

Should it surprise us that this book, with more than five hundred pages and musical examples often extending over several pages, was printed in Leipzig? Since it must have taken considerable time to set the work, it is by no means out of the question that Bach may have seen the proofs while he was preparing his own *Clavier-Übung* for publication. It is doubtful that he felt particularly flattered by Mattheson's well-intentioned challenge. First of all, he does not view himself as a mere producer of "instructive works" with a small circulation. And then, too, without necessarily thinking of his own "passing," he is contemplating a work, perhaps as a fifth part of the *Clavier-Übung,* that will again brilliantly display his skill as a contrapuntalist.

But he accepts Mattheson's challenge, according to the Canadian Bach scholar Gregory G. Butler, and rushes into print the E-Flat Major Fugue, perhaps written earlier.[65] This magnificently complex composition contains a five-part simple fugue, a four-part double fugue on a new theme and the first one, as well as another five-part double fugue on a third theme and the first one; so here is the double fugue with the three subjects Mattheson called for. Whether one might even characterize it as a triple fugue, although the three themes are not brought together, is a question we shall not attempt to answer.

More must be said, however, about the third part of the *Clavier-Übung:* in Bach's hands it becomes a compositional confession, with a complexity unprecedented even in the context of his other work. In the formulation of Christoph Wolff, who is profoundly informed on Bach's late work, Bach now sees "not only his efforts and goals as a composer but apparently himself as well in a historical framework."[66] He finds his historical position as a mediator. His compositional style displays both traditional and modern features; the antithesis between gallant (courtly) and scholarly (characteristic of his time) seems to have been defused, and the stylistic contrasts cut across all the genres. Thus, for instance, the great arrangement of "Vater unser im Himmelreich," BWV 682, as a chorale reveals both extraordinary complexity and a thoroughly French modern element, while the first part of the E-Sharp Major Fugue belongs to the *stile antico*.

Bach's private students have no doubt already experienced their master's many facets. But now, not least in response to Scheibe's provocation, Bach lays all his cards on the table, by sleight of hand transforming a tidy little private project, his *Clavier-Übung*, into a forum for discussion. This technique suits him better than the expository written word. In this sense the third part of the *Clavier-Übung* becomes the first step toward a body of work in print with which he creates in his last years a public presence for his thinking and practice as a composer. He is no longer addressing the citizens of Leipzig or the court at Dresden; not even, as in the first two parts of the *Clavier-Übung*, the "hommes galantes." Without becoming old-fashioned or closing himself off from the taste of the day, he is now writing for the initiates.

The editions are small, of course: of the one hundred printed copies of the "Prussian Fugue"—by which he means the *Musical Of-*

fering or its six-part ricercar—he will "give away most to good friends, gratis."[67] Yet this is less an act of squandering than one of purposefulness. If the copies reach the right recipients, their meaning and intention are fulfilled: the enrichment of the musical world through concentrated exposure to his art.

Like Bach's knowledgeable contemporaries, we are overcome with respect for the brilliant syntheses he achieves in his late works, yet we have no need to make a mystery of his accomplishment. Presumably Bach thought in terms of large projects all his life: the *Orgelbüchlein* and the Cöthen keyboard works, including the *Well-Tempered Clavier* and the *Inventions and Sinfonias,* belong here, as do the works for violin and solo cello, the *Brandenburg Concertos,* the keyboard suites, the two first Leipzig cantata cycles, the passions, and the *drammi per musica.*

Bach's late work is a similar project—and of course not one chosen at random; after Bach has expressed many things in a variety of styles and genres, he is now concerned with the "core" of music. Yet that does not mean that he withdraws like a monk into his cell to work only on the one, true music. He also composes, in addition to other works, the *Peasant Cantata,* BWV 212; the Schübler Chorales, BWV 645–50; the German arrangement of Pergolesi's *Stabat mater,* BWV 1083; and finally the last great project, the B-Minor Mass.

Furthermore, Bach can draw on a broad tradition in the history of composing, a tradition of basic instructional and practice pieces whose content presents itself both as appealing music and as examples for students. Many such works accompanied Bach from the beginning: in his early apprenticeship and journeyman years in north Germany, he may well have encountered works of this sort by Adam Reincken and Dietrich Buxtehude. In Weimar he perhaps made the acquaintance of Buxtehude's contrapuntal arrangement of the hymn "Mit Fried und Freud fahr ich dahin" through Johann Gottfried Walther; he also may have seen Walther's copy of Johann Theile's *Musikalisches Kunstbuch* (Manual of the Musical Art)—a collection for instructional purposes of fifteen exercises in multiple counterpoint, with examples ranging from excerpts from masses to sonata movements. As late as the mid-1730s Walther copied the *Kunstbuch* for his epistolary friend Heinrich Bokemeyer, later a member of the Mizler Society, thereby demonstrating that even in the era of the later Bach this work was still considered significant by those who knew counterpoint.

Scholars have seen Buxtehude's *Contrapuncti* as the models for the mirror fugues from *The Art of Fugue*,[68] and Theile's *Kunstbuch* as a forerunner of the *Musical Offering*.[69] It is hardly conceivable that in Weimar Bach did not also take Samuel Scheidt's *Tabulatura* out of his cousin's bookcase and study it. Evidence from that period suggests that he also studied Frescobaldi's *Fiori musicali* and Nicolas de Grigny's *Premier livre d'orgue*.

The great musical thinker Bach is fulfilling an obligation imposed both by his life and by history when he now turns to creating his own *Kunstbücher*, which combines traditional ideas with new ones; he is neither fossil nor loner, but rather a sort of treasurer of the *ars musica*. As such he is certainly capable of acting "politically." We must consider here not only the *Art of Fugue* project, which he, blind and dependent on assistants, must leave unfinished at his death, but also his purposeful joining of the Mizler Society and his brilliantly staged entry into Potsdam. But let us take things in order...

Perhaps it was at Michaelmas in 1739 that Bach approached the Nuremberg engraver Balthasar Schmid, who had already helped produce the three first parts of the *Clavier-Übung*, and asked him whether he would be willing to engrave and print an entire work for him; this would be another *Clavier-Übung*, to be precise the *Aria mit verschiedenen Veraenderungen vors Clavizimbel mit 2 Manualen Denen Liebhabern zur Gemüths-Ergetzung verfertiget* (Aria with diverse Variations for Clavicembalo with Two Manuals, written for the Delight of Lovers of the Instrument). Since the printed version in all likelihood appeared in 1741 at Michaelmas, Bach did not have much time to spend on his *Goldberg Variations*, BWV 988.

Schmid did indeed become the engraver and publisher of part 4, and he provided this publication with the first and only decorative title given to any work by Bach that appeared during Bach's lifetime.

On the title page one finds *Clavier Übung* at the top, but no mention of its being the fourth part: presumably Schmid thought it might hurt sales to allude to the three previous parts, which had not appeared under his imprint.

Today we can still put our hands on eighteen printed copies—a remarkably large number. They include Bach's own copy with a handwritten supplement, which contains fourteen circular canons, arranged in order of increasing difficulty, based on the beginning of the bass aria BWV 1087. Two canons turn up in other sources from his later years in Leipzig: the six-part canon composed for the Mizler Society, BWV 1076, of which Bach is holding the sheet music in the 1746 portrait by Haussmann, as well as the canon BWV 1077, which he inscribed in Johann Gottfried Fulde's album that same year.

The aria, which can be identified as a dance movement clothed in the fashionable garb of a saraband or polonaise, has thirty-two measures that constitute the beginning of the composition. Around 1740 Anna Magdalena Bach transcribed this passage into her *Klavierbüchlein*. We have good reason to assume that it was composed by Bach, even though other models exist—for instance in the form of a minuet by Jean-Henri d'Angelbert, a classic composer of keyboard suites. The series of eight basic notes in the bass, from which Bach's so-called circular canons are also formed, is prefigured in examples widely disseminated in the seventeenth century: even then variations on ostinato bass figures were popular, derived from folk music and improvisational practices.

Johann Nicolaus Forkel ascribed the composition of the cycle, known from then on as the *Goldberg Variations,* to Bach's acquaintance with the Russian ambassador to the court of Dresden, Hermann Carl von Keyserlingk, the man who in 1736 bestowed on Bach the appointment of court composer:

> *The count once remarked to Bach that he would like to have a few*
> *keyboard pieces for his musician Goldberg, pieces so gentle and*
> *somewhat merry that the count could be a bit cheered up by them*
> *during his sleepless nights. Bach thought he could best fulfill this*

wish with variations, something he had previously considered a thankless task because the basic harmony remained always the same.... The count thenceforth referred to them only as his variations. He could not get enough of them, and for a long time, whenever sleepless nights came, he would say, Dear Goldberg, do play me one of my variations. Bach was perhaps never rewarded so well for one of his compositions as for these. The count bestowed on him a gold beaker filled with a hundred louis d'or.[70]

This anecdote is so lovely and in every sense so humane in spirit that it is a pleasure to be able to confirm that it has a credible core. The Johann Gottlieb Goldberg mentioned by Forkel was sent to Bach by Keyserlingk for training in 1737—though as a boy of ten![71] This fact alone makes it highly unlikely that Bach would have composed such an intricate work primarily for the little hands of Goldberg. It is easy to imagine, however, that Goldberg played the work often for Keyserlingk once he became the count's house cembalist; it is also conceivable that Bach dedicated the work to the Reich count—informally rather than officially—and received acknowledgment in hard coin.

The fourth part of the *Clavier-Übung* might be seen as intended not to keep Goldberg's hands busy but to stick in Scheibe's craw. Scheibe's attack came so unexpectedly in 1737 that in the third part of the *Clavier-Übung* Bach could parry only incidentally, by expanding a basic concept already in existence. The full response comes in 1741. It is entirely intentional when Bach uses in the title the German word for "variations" in an aria instead of calling the work an *aria variata*, as he did with his earlier variations, BWV 989, or, following current usage, "partite diverse." In using the German term, he indicates that he is establishing a specifically German genre of variation, a synthesis of elements from song, dance, concerted and strict style.[72]

The relation between nature and art that Magister Birnbaum attempted to clarify in philosophic abstractions when he defended Bach against Scheibe is portrayed here with wonderful lucidity, and at the same time with dialectical complexity, and yields beautiful sound. What is nature: a little air like the one from the concluding quodlibet, a prettily formed and highly singable aria, or the structure of a cycle based on a readily recognizable numerical series, that is, multiples of three—to the extent that every third variation is a canon, while the interval mounts from the initial note to the ninth?

And what is art? Is it the contrapuntal sophistication exemplified in every individual canon, the compositional skill that allows different simple airs to be heard simultaneously; or is it the ability to conceal and disguise these airs in such a way that they present not merely a semblance of pleasing music but the phenomenon itself? How else—if we take Forkel's anecdote at its word for a moment— could a sleepless Count Keyserlingk have been "cheered up" by this music?

While Bach is publishing the fourth part of the *Clavier-Übung*, he is working on a collection that would certainly make a suitable continuation: the second part of the *Well-Tempered Clavier*. The first part, finished in Cöthen, can no longer be considered for publication—not because it has become outdated but because it has now been disseminated so widely in manuscript that a printed version cannot be expected to sell. A second part allows Bach to kill several birds with one stone: he can give "homeless" individual pieces a home; he can also offer his students, and perhaps even a patron willing to pay, a new collection of preludes and fugues; and finally, he can bring to the musical marketplace a title that, thanks to the first part, already has a significant reputation among connoisseurs.

The so-called London manuscript offers a source for the second part of the *Well-Tempered Clavier*, most likely composed between 1740 and 1742. The manuscript, most of it in Bach's hand but with portions in Anna Magdalena's, consists of large sheets of paper, folded once, usually with a prelude on the front and the corresponding fugue on the back. This collection of loose sheets, intended to allow for additions and substitutions, found its way from Wilhelm Friedemann Bach, Muzio Clementi, and other private collectors to the British Museum in remarkably complete form; only three pairs are missing. Another important source is a manuscript prepared in

1744 by Bach's son-in-law Christoph Altnickol; it does not derive directly or indirectly from the London manuscript but rather represents the second part of the *Well-Tempered Clavier* in a version that allows us to conclude that Bach did not work consistently on one manuscript but made his revisions in different versions.

Eleven preludes or fugues exist in older forms, some of which were transposed into a different key before being included in the second part of the *Well-Tempered Clavier*, to fill certain gaps; thus Bach transposed BWV 872a from C major to C-sharp major because he had at hand no other suitable compositions in this key. He certainly used older material in other cases. Yet we should not be too quick to conclude that the second part of the *Well-Tempered Clavier*, like the Eighteen Chorales in the original Leipzig manuscript, BWV 651–68, is basically a collection that offers old wine in new bottles. It speaks for the importance this work had, at least in Bach's circle, that in the 1740s each of his older sons and also each of his students had his own copy.

We do not know precisely when Bach started his *The Art of Fugue* project. The first date that can be established is 1742, when he composes major portions of the Berlin manuscript Mus. MS Bach P200. Whether he intends to compose a fifth or even a sixth part of the *Clavier-Übung* cannot be determined. But clearly *The Art of Fugue* is designed as a work for the keyboard, and at least the first version is suitable not only for the study of counterpoint but also for performance as a complete work. We should not be misled by the fact that the work is transcribed as a score rather than given in keyboard notation; there was a long tradition of this practice in works designed for the study of keyboard instruments. In the sixteenth and often in the seventeenth century, an organist would obtain a considerable portion of his repertory by rewriting vocal compositions in strict style for his instrument.

In those days the learned cantor was the composer and guardian of pure musical theory, while the organist functioned primarily as a reproducing artist, at least as far as strict style was concerned. In the course of the seventeenth century, organists like Frescobaldi, Froberger, Poglietti, Muffat, Scheidt, Buxtehude, and Reinken

achieved distinction as composers in the strict style; they often constructed contrapuntal works intended for instruction and practice as
scores. On the one hand, this practice showed that they viewed their
art as a continuation of a motet tradition that they wanted to maintain; on the other hand, the score made study of the structural connections easier. It took an experienced performer to transpose such a
score for performance on the clavier or organ; yet it was precisely this
skill in which he could take pride.

Choosing to write *The Art of Fugue* as a score, Bach places himself far more emphatically than in his previous compositions in the
tradition of learned organists who wish to preserve and develop a
music theory that is anchored in counterpoint yet can also be expressed on a keyboard instrument. The publication of the previous
parts of the *Clavier-Übung* can be seen—in a formal sense—as incidental to Bach's activity as cantor and music director; it parallels
similar undertakings by his predecessor Kuhnau and his colleague
Telemann. But with *The Art of Fugue* Bach becomes what he was
once in reality, an organist. This change occurs at a time when he is
increasingly withdrawing from his official and public functions.

We may speak of a "self-imposed quasi-retirement,"[73] or simply
of intensified involvement in a professional arena from which Bach
never really absented himself. His desire to become active as an organist and theoretician—not merely in his own study or in Mizler's
musical society—manifests itself at the latest during his visit to Potsdam; there he performs in a manner reminiscent of the great papal
organist Frescobaldi and the imperial court organist Froberger. To
put it differently: if his secret wish for a "*praedicat* from the Court
Kapelle" of the Prussian king had been fulfilled, the letters patent
would have referred to a court organist rather than a court kapellmeister or composer.

In mentioning Bach's relation to the tradition of strict style
among recent organists and its bearing on virtuoso keyboard practice,
I do not mean to imply that the horizon of *The Art of Fugue* did not
extend farther back—to the contrapuntal art of the old Dutch composers. It is probably no coincidence that around 1742—when

according to current scholarship Bach is working on the first manuscript of *The Art of Fugue*—he writes out a score for Palestrina's *Missa Sine Nomine* that includes parts for cornet, trombones, and continuo. This arrangement indicates clearly that Bach performed the mass, but perhaps the performance came about precisely because he was engaged in theoretical study of Palestrina at the time.

Bach is not the only one to be so engaged in Leipzig. The year 1742 also marks the publication by Mizler of a German translation of Johann Joseph Fux's *Gradus ad Parnassum*—at the time the authoritative textbook on strict style. But Fux considers Palestrina a teacher "to whom I owe all I know of these matters, and whose memory I shall never cease to revive with most profound reverence all the days of my life."[74] That Bach's library contained the 1725 Latin edition is documented by the existence of a copy with his book stamp; it may have been Bach who urged Mizler to undertake the translation.[75] Presumably he is aware of what Mizler writes around the same time in his *Musikalische Bibliothek,* about "systematic musical composition" and its foundations, "which rest upon the unalterable rules of harmony, which have always existed, and still exist today, and shall continue to exist, so long as this world remains in its place and the rules according to which it is made do not alter, although for the rest, its musical garb may alter at will."[76]

No further explanation is necessary for Bach's undertaking *The Art of Fugue;* on the basis of the many contrapuntal works he has composed hitherto, he seeks to find the essence of a compositional style that will express the hidden order of nature in the most graphic manner possible. The entire project takes place under the heading "All from One," which means it will be monothematic, proceeding from a single *soggetto.* But this *soggetto* is not historical material that he elaborates, like the aria of the *Goldberg Variations;* it is raw material, so to speak, a reduction to the potential energy of a twelve-note series.

This series is allowed to reveal its full potential—in accordance with Magister Birnbaum's entry on the topic of nature and art, certainly inspired by Bach: "Many things are furnished by Nature in most unprepossessing form, which acquire the most lovely appearance once art has shaped them." One can speak of such art only "when all parts work together." But this should occur "without the slightest confusion": "each part distinguishes itself from the others by means of a particular variation, even though they often imitate one another."[77]

"It would appear that for Bach revealing the secrets concealed in harmony was practically a mania,"[78] Christoph Wolff comments in reference to this passage in the obituary: "Once he had heard a particular theme, he could grasp, as it were instantaneously, almost anything artistic that could be brought forth from it."[79]

Great though the temptation may have been for Bach to develop the *soggetto* of *The Art of Fugue* as variously as possible, he seems to have been content with twelve variations in the first version, to judge from the Berlin manuscript Mus. MS Bach P 200 (BWV[2a] 1080/1–3. 5–11. 15 and 16): three simple and three counterfugues, two double and two triple fugues, and two canons. That, at least, is the view of Pieter Dirksen, who has subjected the manuscript to painstaking analysis.[80]

The number 12 has a long tradition in works of this sort and especially in music printed between the sixteenth and nineteenth centuries: it can be found for instance in Vincenzo Ruffo's *Capricci in musica a tre voci* of 1564, described as essentially the "sixteenth-century art of the fugue."[81]

Let us leave Bach alone for a moment with this first version and turn our attention to his daily life. When the new rector of the St. Thomas School is introduced on 12 February 1742, his absence is noted; the cantor, who does not have to present any choral music during Lent, is probably traveling. On 30 August of that year he is a guest at the Klein-Zschocher estate, where Carl Heinrich von

Dieskau's accession is to be honored. Bach conducts a performance of a "cantate burlesque," "Mer han en neue Oberkeet," the so-called *Peasant Cantata*. This multilayered work, rich in explicit and subtle humor, is the last secular cantata by Bach that has come down to us—a little jewel sui generis.

It is unfortunate that in February 1743, when the city of Zeitz commissions a composition to be used in testing candidates for town piper positions, the choice falls at the last moment not on Bach, as originally planned, but on Johann Gottlieb Görner. Otherwise we would know how the late Bach envisions parts for the trumpet, the alto trombone, the cornet, the violin, the oboe, and the horn that will be playable by ordinary *musici* yet at the same time honor the musicians' guild. As an organ inspector and teacher Bach continues to be in demand; pupils in a steady stream provide accounts of their training by Bach. Altogether, his reputation is growing: around 1745 Georg Andreas Sorge dedicates eighteen *Sonatinas for the Clavichord Set according to Italian Taste* to the "great and world-renowned virtuoso and prince of keyboard players."[82]

Yet there is little to report of Bach's everyday life in Leipzig. We therefore turn again to his creative work, first to *The Art of Fugue*. In a second phase of work dating from 1746 or 1747, Bach adds to the twelve-part first version the two mirror fugues BWV 1080/12 and 13, whose concept may be taken from Buxtehude's *Fried- und Freudenreicher Hinfarth*. In addition, he composes a new version of the augmentation canon BWV^{2a}1080/15.[83]

The work is interrupted by his journey to the court of Frederick the Great in Potsdam. We owe our earliest information about the events of this trip to a press report that appears 11 May 1747 in the *Berlinische Nachrichten von Staats- und gelehrten Sachen* and is reprinted a short while later by the *Leipziger Zeitungen*, the *Hamburger Relationscourier*, the Magdeburg *Privilegierte Zeitung*, and possibly also by a Frankfurt paper:

> *From Potsdamm one hears that on Sunday last the renowned*
> *Kapellmeister from Leipzig, Herr Bach, arrived there with the*

intention of taking in the excellent music at the royal court. In the evening, about the time when chamber music is customarily played in the royal apartments, His Majesty was informed that Kapellmeister Bach had arrived in Potsdamm, and that he was in His Majesty's antechamber, awaiting His Majesty's gracious permission to hear the music. His Majesty promptly gave orders to admit him forthwith, and upon his entrance went to the so-called forte *and* piano, *and was gracious enough to play himself for Kapellmeister Bach, without any rehearsal, a theme he wished Bach to perform as a fugue. This was accomplished so felicitously by the Kapellmeister that not only His Majesty deigned to express his most gracious satisfaction but also all those present were filled with astonishment. Herr Bach found the theme given to him so exceedingly lovely that he proposed to commit it to paper as a proper fugue and thereafter have it engraved in copper. On Monday this famous man let himself be heard at the organ in the Church of the Holy Spirit at Potsdamm, and harvested general applause from the many listeners foregathered there. In the evening His Majesty again prevailed upon him to perform a six-part fugue, which he executed to His Majesty's delight and to general admiration, as skilfully as on the previous occasion.*[84]

The memories Bach's eldest son, Wilhelm Friedemann, had of the Potsdam visit are captured in Forkel's biography of 1802:[85]

His second son, Carl Phil. Emanuel, entered the service of Frederick the Great in the year 1740. At this time the reputation of the extraordinary art of Johann Sebastian was so widespread that the King likewise often heard it spoken of and praised. He therefore became desirous of hearing and making the acquaintance of so great an artist. At first he subtly intimated to the son his wish that his father might come to Potsdam someday. But little by little he began to ask quite insistently why his father did not come. The son could not avoid conveying the King's utterances to his father, who, however, could not attend to them at first because he was usually overwhelmed with a multitude of tasks. But when the King's utterances were repeated in several letters from the son, in the year 1747 he finally took steps to make this journey in the company of his eldest son, Wilhelm Friedemann. Around this time the King had a chamber concert every evening, in which he usually performed several pieces on the flute. One evening, when he was just readying his flute and his musicians had already gathered, an officer delivered to him the written report of strangers newly arrived. With his flute in his hand, he perused the paper, but at once turned to the assembled members of the Kapelle and announced in some agitation: Gentlemen, old Bach has come! He thereupon put down his flute, and old Bach, who had betaken himself to his son's lodgings, was summoned to the palace forthwith. Wilh. Friedemann, who escorted his father, told me this story, and I must say that to this day I recall with the delight the manner in which he told it. In those days it was still customary to make rather lengthy salutations. Thus the first appearance of Joh. Seb. Bach before such a great monarch, who did not even give him time to change from his traveling clothes into a black cantor's coat, had of necessity to be accompanied by many apologies. I shall not rehearse the nature of these apologies here, but merely remark that in Wilh. Friedemann's mouth they became a veritable dialogue between the King and the apologizer. But what is yet more important is that for this evening the King renounced his flute concert, instead urging Bach, at that time already known as old Bach, to try out his Silbermann fortepianos, which were located in several rooms in the palace. The members of the Kapelle went along from room to room, and everywhere Bach had to try out the instruments and improvise. After he had tried them out and improvised for a while, he asked the King to give him a theme for a fugue, which he would then perform without any preparation. The King admired the learned fashion in which his theme was developed on the spur of the moment, and now expressed the wish to hear a fugue with six parts obligato, presumably in order to see how far such artistry could extend. But because not every theme is suitable for such development in many voices, Bach chose one of his own and promptly performed it, to the greatest admiration of all those present, in as splendid and learned a manner as he had previously displayed with the King's theme. The King wished as well to become acquainted with his skill on the organ. Therefore on the following days Bach was conducted by him to all the organs in Potsdam, as previously to all the Silbermann fortepianos. After his return to Leipzig he worked out the theme he had received from the King in three and six parts, added various highly artistic canons to it, had it engraved in copper under the title "Musical Offering," and dedicated it to its originator.

Despite the small contradictions between the two accounts, one can distinguish between the historical core in Forkel's version and anecdotal embroidery. But let us reconstruct the chronology of the most significant events. On Sunday evening, 7 May 1747, Bach appears at court in time for the chamber music that is regularly played between 7:00 and 9:00 o'clock, on this day probably not at Sans Souci Palace, which had just been completed, but rather at the old City Palace of Potsdam. He is certainly introduced to the court officials by his son Carl Philipp Emanuel; whether a special personal invitation is received from the king remains an open question. In any case, Bach listens to the evening concert from the antechamber before being invited in by the king.

First he tries out some of the new Silbermann pianos and then asks the king to give him a theme on which he can improvise a fugue. The following day he gives an organ concert at the Church of the Holy Spirit, and in the evening he has another opportunity to perform a six-part fugue at court on a theme of his own choosing.

The groundwork and preparations for the visit to Potsdam were probably handled by Carl Philipp Emanuel, court cembalist to Frederick II, but certainly at Bach's own wish; it would be strange indeed if Bach had not long since wanted to take advantage of one of his visits to his son to be introduced to the king and to demonstrate his artistry. Frederick the Great is not some random potentate but the new star in Europe. Allied with Austria, Bach's own prince elector has just lost the second Silesian War against the Prussians; all eyes are on the king of Prussia. It is conceivable that Count Keyserlingk, the Russian envoy to the court of Dresden and Bach's patron, may have served as intermediary, making it possible for Bach to perform for Frederick.

In view of the years of conflict in Leipzig, Bach is evidently always on the lookout for recognition in other settings, and this time he goes about it skillfully—as the newspaper reports, perhaps planted by his own family, attest: he enters Berlin modestly, as a potential admirer of the modern taste the thirty-five-year-old king has made de rigueur for his court kapelle; he returns home with head held high, as a splendid representative of the old style.

It is in this essentially public forum that Bach finds the defining role for his old age: it is the role assigned to him by Mattheson, that of a superb contrapuntalist who can also perform brilliantly in the modern style. This interpretation receives support from the manner in which Bach reacts to his Potsdam visit, with a printed work consisting of thirteen compositions on the *thema regium* and bearing the rather histrionic title *Musical Offering*.

This work includes a three-part ricercar, certainly based on the Potsdam improvisations; a further one in six parts; ten intricate canons; and a four-movement trio sonata for flute and violin, intended to pay tribute to the king's flute playing and his musical taste. But some of the learned canons, which are accompanied by symbolic annotations, also show characteristics of the gallant style.

Bach probably chose the designation "ricercar" for the aura that already surrounded the term at that time. The word also lent itself to an acrostic, which Bach wrote in by hand on the title wrapping for the ricercar intended for the king: **R**egis **I**ussu **C**antio **E**t **R**eliqua **C**anonica **A**rte **R**esoluta or, freely translated, "The piece performed on the King's command, along with further examples of the art of the canon."

It cannot be established whether the "royal theme" on which Bach based his *Musical Offering* is the one given to him in Potsdam as a *soggetto* for improvisation. As suggested previously, it is unlikely that Frederick the Great could have come up with such a sophisticated theme at the drop of a hat, musical though he was. Perhaps his court musicians made the recommendation, or perhaps the theme initially had a simpler form. Far less credible is the suggestion that Bach "planted" the theme by way of Carl Philipp Emanuel; he certainly had no need to take such precautions.

Both ricercars are written to be performed on instruments without pedals; the canons 1 and 8 call for two violins, or a flute, a violin, and continuo instruments, respectively. The other canons were probably composed for the cembalo, but perhaps also for melodic instruments at the discretion of the performer.

Johann Georg Schübler from Zella does the copper engraving, and the work is printed by Breitkopf in Leipzig. For an edition of two hundred copies Bach pays an advance of two talers and twelve groschen.[86] The work appeared in time for Michaelmas, in September 1747, and can be purchased from Bach and his two eldest sons for a price of one taler. The layout is somewhat awkward; the score, the individual parts, and the puzzle notation have to be included in the same edition, which therefore appears not as a bound volume but as three separate fascicles made up of varying numbers of folded double and single sheets, alternating between portrait and landscape layout.

This lack of consistency is symptomatic: the *Musical Offering* is not a cycle intended for performance but rather an artistic compilation in Theile's sense, although it has the advantage of being based on one *soggetto*. In response to a specific situation Bach has created a collection unique unto itself. It does not display the character of an opus; the creation of a work of that nature will preoccupy him during his further work on *The Art of Fugue*.

When Bach dedicates the *Musical Offering* to Frederick the Great on 7 July 1747, has he perhaps done more than find the defining role of his old age as a great contrapuntalist? Is he positioning himself for an actual appointment? Several works of this period—including the trio sonata in the *Musical Offering,* the Flute Sonata in E-flat Major, BWV 1031 (whose authenticity many scholars question), and the Concerto for Three Harpsichords, BWV 1063—have been described as late adaptations of the Berlin style established by Quantz, Graun, and Hasse.[87] But we must wonder what a sixty-two-year-old could have become in Berlin—where Quantz and Graun hold sway. Even the honorary post of a court composer is difficult to secure!

It is far easier to join the Corresponding Society of the Musical Sciences, founded in 1738 by the previously mentioned Bach pupil Lorenz Christoph Mizler. Bach takes nine years to make up his mind before he joins the society in June 1747, as its fourteenth member. Meanwhile the following well-known or less well-known persons have joined: an officer and lover and patron of music called Giacomo de Lucchesini; Mizler himself, as secretary; Georg Heinrich Bümler, the kapellmeister in Ansbach; Christoph Gottlieb Schröter, organist in Nordhausen; the Wolfenbüttel cantor, Heinrich Bokemeyer; Georg Philipp Telemann; Gottfried Heinrich Stölzel; Georg Friedrich Lingke, who owns an estate near Weissenfels; the musical prior of the Irsee Abbey near Kaufbeuren, Meinrad Spiess; Georg Venzky, the rector of Prenzlau; George Frideric Handel as an honorary member; Father Udalric Weiss from the Irsee Monastery; and Carl Heinrich Graun.[88]

Of the projected twenty memberships, four are reserved for foreigners and six for honorary members, which includes patrons. The society is described as corresponding, because it focuses less on individual exchanges of views than on a common interest in promoting recognition of the historical, philosophical, mathematical, and poeticological dimensions of music. In this spirit, before he enters the service of a Polish count in 1743, Mizler gives lectures at the University of Leipzig not only on philosophical and mathematical topics but also on the history of music and on Johann Mattheson's *Newly Launched Orchestra.*

Mizler, who aspires to become the first instructor in musicology at a German university, has the goal of "giving music completely the character of a scholarly field, researching its history and putting it into an orderly form."[89] As a pupil of Gottsched and an admirer of Mattheson, he is not hostile toward the Enlightenment, only toward superficiality in an allegedly enlightened approach to music. In this respect he and Bach, whom he venerates, must be in agreement. We should not ascribe too much significance to Bach's joining Mizler's society so late in the day. There may have been circumstances of which we have no knowledge; after all, Johann Gottfried Walther, who would have fit into this circle perfectly, never did join.

Then, too, although Bach has immense musical knowledge, he is neither a scholar in the sense of the society's bylaws nor a man given to expression in words or writing: "Bach did not engage in profound theoretical observations on music," the obituary tells us.[90] Nonetheless, in 1747 it seems advisable to him to go public, so to speak, as one of the learned composers. It is no disgrace to belong to an institution that counts Telemann, Stölzel, Handel, and Graun among its members. Nor can it hurt to join an association whose bylaws obligate the members to come to one another's defense in case of unjustified public attacks.

Speaking of Handel, it should be mentioned here that Bach never met his great rival in person. In 1719, when word reached him that Handel was in Halle, Bach jumped into the post chaise but arrived too late. When Handel visited his hometown again ten years later, Bach was in bed with a fever. And Handel did not respond when Wilhelm Friedemann Bach delivered Bach's invitation to Handel to come to Leipzig. Carl Philipp Emanuel commented later that it pained his father greatly "not to have been able to meet Handel in person, this truly great man whom he particularly admired."

Each member of the society had to provide a portrait of himself and also submit a theoretical or practical work each year, which Mizler then sent "postpaid" in a "packet" to all the other members to be evaluated and considered for a prize.[91] Since this procedure did not work perfectly, it is all the more notable that in the last years of his life Bach showed himself to be a model member. In 1747 he supplies the portrait of himself painted the previous year by the Leipzig painter Elias Gottlob Haussmann, known for portraying prominent citizens. He also submits an offprint of the six-part puzzle canon BWV 1076, the sheet music of which he is holding in the portrait. He also submits the version printed by Balthasar Schmid in Nuremberg of Canonic Variations on "Vom Himmel hoch." His annual contribution for 1748 is the *Musical Offering,* and for 1749 he may have intended to give *The Art of Fugue.*

The Canonic Variations, BWV 769, occupy a dual context in Bach's late work: on the one hand they belong, with the *Goldberg Variations,* the *Musical Offering,* and *The Art of Fugue,* to those last series of works in which the composer demonstrates his mastery of the canon with the most brilliant intensity. On the other hand, they document the late Bach's love for the organ chorale—a genre he cultivated from youth on. The third part of the *Clavier-Übung,* actually a collection of organ chorales, does not stand alone; in the years 1739–41, 1746–47, and again in 1749 he is occupied with a project that entails bringing together the organ chorales written largely during his Weimar period, which—as we know from the Leipzig manuscript of the so-called Eighteen Chorales, BWV 651–68—forms a representative collection, possibly for publication.

We can see the importance this undertaking holds for Bach from the fact that in 1749, perhaps already aware that he is going blind, he commissions Johann Christoph Altnickol, his son-in-law, to add to the collection, already up to number 15, further works from those on hand. These are numbers 16 and 17, which Altnickol cannot have got around to copying until after Bach's death.

Along with the Leipzig manuscript of the Eighteen Chorales, a work in print further reflects Bach's preoccupation with this genre in his late years: the Schübler Chorales, BWV 645–50, brought out around 1748 or 1749 as *Sechs Choräle von verschiedener Art* by the publisher Johann Georg Schübler in Zella (Thuringia) but also available from Bach and his two older sons. We can see that over and above his work on *The Art of Fugue* and the B-Minor Mass, Bach remains very active and, in this case, certainly motivated to look through those of his cantatas that contain chorales to see if he can extract solo numbers from them, arrange them for the organ, and put them into a new context. What will endure, he seems to be saying, is not settings of fashionable poetry but highly complex versions of the chorale.

Altogether, things are by no means quieting down around him. A report by the Nuremberg historian Christoph Gottlieb von Murr, written somewhat later, tells us that in 1747–48 Bach also receives a visit from the gamba player Wolfgang Carl Rost.[92] This information jibes with other evidence that during these late years Bach is very interested in chamber music; we have not only a manuscript from his circle of the previously mentioned Flute Sonata in E-flat Major, BWV 1031, but also a note, probably by Johann Christoph Friedrich Bach, on the score of the sonatas for violin and keyboard, BWV 1014–19: "This trio he composed before his death."[93]

The information is incorrect, since these particular works probably go back in large part to the Cöthen period, but the note itself is valuable because it indicates that Bach's second-youngest son was aware that near the end his father was busy revising this material.

Another indication that up to his final illness Bach fulfills his obligation to perform cantatas is the sheet music prepared afresh for later repeat performances—for instance, the cantatas 34, 82, 91, 118, 137, 170, 185, 40, 168, 186, 96, 82, 69, 195, 16, 187, and 29. As already mentioned, works in Latin and oratorios are also on the program. Even an ambitious work like "The Contest between Phoebus and Pan," BWV 201, is revived in 1749, for an unknown occasion. At the last moment Bach changes the "raging Orbilis" in this *dramma per musica* into "Birolius—perhaps a dig at the Dresden politician Heinrich Count von Brühl."[94] Von Brühl persuaded the Leipzig city council to allow forty-six-year-old Gottlob Harrer, the director of his private kapelle, to audition on 8 June 1749 as a possible successor to Bach in the cantor's position:

On the 8th, on orders from the noble and most wise council of this city, most of whose members were present, in the great musical concert hall in Three Swans on Mount Brühl, a sample performance

for the future cantorate at St. Thomas, in case the Kapellmeister
and cantor, Herr Sebast. Bach, should expire, was offered by Herr
Gottlob Harrer, the Kapelle director of his Excellency the Privy
Councilor and Prime Minister Count von Brühl; and received for
the same great applause.[95]

The city is in debt to the Saxon prince elector and therefore also indirectly to his powerful prime minister, having fallen into arrears on its share of the enormous sums that Saxony must pay the King of Prussia as reparations after the lost war. The council thus has little choice but to accept the Dresden court's wishes when it comes to filling the cantor's position, thereby choosing as Bach's successor a musician who is in no sense a real cantor and schoolmaster but rather a kapellmeister, who promises to comply with the court's desire for Leipzig to become a center of modern, worldly church music.

Those members of the Leipzig city council who constantly criticized Bach's performance as cantor thus find themselves jumping from the frying pan into the fire. It is not, by the way, appropriate to speak of a slight to Bach, as is often done in the Bach literature, for it is perfectly normal at this time to fill a position during the lifetime of an incumbent; many parallels can be cited. Thus Telemann is promised that he will succeed Kuhnau almost two decades before Kuhnau's death; and in 1722, when he actually applies for the cantor's position at St. Thomas, this old commitment still figures in the negotiations.

It could even be interpreted as a sign of respect that the audition takes place not at one of the principal churches, which are Bach's stamping ground, but at the site of the Great Consort, a choice that does not lack for symbolism. Does Bach intend to take a bit of revenge on his successor's patron by enriching the old cantata text with the Birolius–Brühl play on words? Or is it, as Philipp Spitta assumes, a different affair to which Bach is alluding: in May 1749, the Freiberg rector Johann Gottlieb Biedermann launches a polemic in an essay entitled *De vita musica* against what he views as the excessive emphasis on musical education in the schools, whereupon Bach asks a fellow member of the Mizler Society, Christoph Gottlieb Schröter, to respond with a critical review.

The reply turns out to Bach's complete satisfaction, as can be seen from a letter to the Frankenhaus cantor, Georg Friedrich Einicke. The original has been lost, but Johann Mattheson printed a copy in which Bach comments that he has no doubt but that the rector's "dirty ears" will be cleaned out and "rendered more adept at the hearing of music."[96] Bach cannot resist the temptation to disseminate Schröter's response in an anonymous special printing—but with certain comments made more acerbic in a way that underlines the author's ire. In a letter dictated after his eye operation on 26 May 1750, he says that he "is by no means to blame, but that the fault should be imputed only to him who saw to the printing."[97] We may wonder whether he would have been so combative around the beginning of 1750 as to insert such changes into another's writing.

Having examined this last little satyr play in Bach's life, let us return to his last major projects: *The Art of Fugue* and the B-Minor Mass. The former work Bach resumes in the first half of 1748, but with a dual strategy. First, he makes preparations for the engraving, using the handwritten version, P200, as his basis; perhaps the immediate purpose is to have his annual contribution to the Mizler Society ready in time. As in the case of the organ chorales BWV 645–50, the engraving is entrusted to Heinrich Schübler. Bach delivers pages with notes on one side, the so-called *Abklatschvorlagen,* or stereotype templates. The paper has been soaked in oil and thereby made transparent. When these pages are laid blank side up on the prepared copperplate, the notes can be traced onto the metal for engraving.

As Wolfgang Wiemer has determined through detailed examination of the printing,[98] some of the stereotype templates (as they are numbered in the printed version and in BWV²) were prepared by Bach—numbers 1, 3, 4, 11, 12/2, 13/2, and 15–18; the others, numbers 2, 5–10, 12/1, and 13/1, were prepared by other copyists, for instance his son Johann Christoph Friedrich. Bach's writing ability deteriorates rapidly from August 1748 on. Numbers 14, 19, and 20 were not engraved until after his death, and these are the pieces whose authorship is dubious or at least problematic.

The second aspect of Bach's strategy helps explain why Bach has not made more progress by August 1748 in preparing the templates for engraving. Apparently no longer satisfied with his original concept for *The Art of Fugue,* he has decided to compose additional pieces: Contrapunctus 4 as well as Canons 17 and 18. He revises parts of other pieces, for instance giving Contrapunctus 1 four new measures at the end, which in turn affects Contrapuncti 2 and 3, which also receive new conclusions. Contrapunctus 10 grows out of a significant expansion of Contrapunctus 4, which occupies the sixth place in manuscript P200; Canon 15 even undergoes two stages of revision.

The composition from scratch of two more canons may reflect his experience with working on the *Musical Offering.* The expanded endings of the first three contrapuncti indubitably render them more dynamic; it is as if he wants these pieces to end with a bang.

It is difficult to determine in what other ways Bach reconceived these works while preparing the edition for printing, for the publication as it appeared in 1751 or early 1752 was not authorized by him. We do not even know who was involved in pulling it together. Possibly Anna Magdalena Bach had her hand in the matter.[99] After her husband's death, she may well have needed the money this publication could be expected to bring in. We know that she presented the Leipzig city council with several copies in May 1752 and received fifty talers in remuneration.

It is obvious that those who assumed responsibility for the printed version after Bach's death, including the engraver, had no real insight into Bach's plans for the work; otherwise an older version of number 10 would not have been included as number 14. Furthermore, it can hardly have been Bach's intention to have the three-part mirror fugue, number 13, also appear as number 19, this time in an arrangement for two harpsichords. The handwritten version of this arrangement does form part of the original manuscript, but it was probably written down primarily for instructional purposes.

Even more puzzling is number 20, the unfinished *Fuga a 3 Soggetti*, with the series of notes B-A-C-H as its third theme (in German notation, B meant B-flat, H meant B-natural). The handwritten original, composed between August 1748 and October 1749, does exist, but it remains a matter of conjecture whether Bach meant to include this section in *The Art of Fugue.* The indications to that effect in the first printing, in the obituary (perhaps based on the first printing), and in the comments of Wilhelm Friedemann are not proof. The composition of this fugue never reached the point at which one could verify whether the *soggetto* from *The Art of Fugue,* held in reserve until then, was intended to appear as the fourth theme.

Is it possible that the *Fuga a 3 Soggetti* remained unfinished only in the clean copy that has come down to us but was completed in concept, without the knowledge of those responsible for the printed version?[100] We should also mention the contrary theory: that Bach left this fugue a fragment, not because his strength failed but because the piece did not satisfy him in the form it was taking.[101]

Today the overwhelming majority of Bach scholars are convinced that as a quadruple fugue the *Fuga a 3 Soggetti* belongs to the corpus of *The Art of Fugue* (although Gustav Leonhardt disagrees).[102] Yet they find it difficult to assign the piece a definitive position in the work. We may ask with Pieter Dirksen whether this fugue remained unfinished not only in form but also in concept—perhaps as an improvised placeholder for a fourteenth and final contrapunctus that Bach intended to compose when preparing the collection for engraving.

Also, more than just this contrapunctus may be missing—perhaps Bach did not get around to composing other fugues or canons. The handwritten version of *The Art of Fugue* from the year 1742 contains twelve pieces; might the final version have been intended to contain twenty-four? As impossible as it seems at first to justify such speculation,[103] it forces us to admit how little we know. Perhaps Bach himself never came to a final decision on the matter.

But there is little doubt that *The Art of Fugue* was intended for a keyboard instrument and for performance with two hands. When the work is offered for subscription in the *Berliner Nachrichten aus dem Reiche der Gelehrsamkeit* of 1 July 1751, issuing from the Berlin circle around Carl Philipp Emanuel Bach, reference is made to a score, while it is also noted that "at the same time everything is specifically composed for the use of the clavier and the organ."[104] That there are almost impossible reaches of a tenth in the mirror fugues need not mean that these two contrapuncti must be performed on two harpsichords.[105] Some fudging in the performance of impressive contrapuntal works on the keyboard belongs to a venerable tradition. The organ should not be considered the primary instrument on which these works were intended to be performed, not least because of the smaller range of the keyboard; the reference to the organ in the subscription offer should be understood as a marketing ploy.

"If Bach had been a builder and if only one city hall that he built were still standing, it would be classified as a historic structure, with a prohibition on altering so much as a single stone. But he was only a composer!" In 1975 Walter Kolneder uttered this lament, responding to the innumerable attempts to establish the "definitive" order of *The Art of Fugue* and to rearrange the work accordingly, and he backed it up with a quotation from Rousseau: "Everything is good in the condition in which it leaves the hands of the Creator; everything disintegrates in the hands of man."[106] When applied to a work in progress like *The Art of Fugue,* this notion sounds no less shortsighted for being voiced by an expert. In the meantime, the new Bach edition, edited and annotated by Klaus Hofmann according to the newest principles, includes both the handwritten and printed versions. Hofmann's excellent "Critical Review" encourages people to give further thought to what Bach intended. Such reconsideration does not diminish the composer but promotes the discourse necessary for any vital engagement with his music, an engagement that cannot take place without some friction and variations in quality.

It is certainly true that the process of hunting down and interpreting the truth about Bach has long since become a sort of mythmaking, but that is inevitable when one is dealing with great art.

Likewise, there should be no objection to adaptations of *The Art of Fugue* for the organ, string instruments, a saxophone ensemble, and so on, so long as it is recognized that these arrangements are merely one possible encounter with the music. May we not assume that Bach would have wanted us to approach his works by paths that make sense to us as individuals? It is to be expected that a work will change when its audience grows from a few hundred connoisseurs to a worldwide community of music lovers.

During the last phase of work on *The Art of Fugue*, Bach must have realized that the time remaining to him was limited. Perhaps the dramatic decline in his ability to write, which is unmistakable in his handwriting after August 1748, was the deciding factor. From that time on, the fugue project had to step back in favor of another, the composition of the B-Minor Mass.

In the early nineteenth century Bach's "great Catholic Mass," as it is called in Carl Philipp Emanuel's listing of the unpublished works,[107] probably echoing a customary family description going back to Bach himself, was considered his major supradenominational work—before the rediscovery of the *St. Matthew Passion*. In 1847, Carl von Winterfeld, one of the first historiographers of Protestant church music, counted it among the "entirely self-sufficient" works by Bach, by which he meant that it was an original composition, but he did not suspect[108] that this work had had a long gestation and also consisted to a significant degree of "self-borrowings."

In the twentieth century these facts became increasingly clear to Bach scholars, and by the time the volume in the *New Bach Edition* devoted to the B-Minor Mass appeared in 1954, it was no longer possible for the public at large to ignore them. Friedrich Smend, the editor at the time, refused to call the work the B-Minor Mass; instead he listed on the title page all the headings Bach himself had used for the separate sections of his original score: *Missa, Symbolum Nicenum, Sanctus, Osanna, Benedictus, Agnus Dei et Dona nobis pacem.*

Smend established that the Berlin original score, Mus. MS Bach P180, combined "four separate compositions," which Bach "treated as individual works even once they were brought together": the Missa, composed in 1733 and consisting of a Kyrie and a Gloria; a Credo, which Smend assumed to have been composed in 1732; a Sanctus, which he thought went back to 1736; and the sections ranging from the Hosanna to the *Dona nobis pacem*, which he saw as having been composed last, in 1738 or 1739. Smend theorized that Bach put these sections together not in order to "create a coherent work that could be performed straight through" but rather to present in one representative volume "individual compositions that were similar in type and related in form and content."[109]

Not only a Bach scholar but also and primarily a Lutheran theologian, Smend may have been mightily disturbed by the notion of Bach's composing a great Catholic mass. Yet he was correct in his observation that Bach's score consisted of discrete elements. He was mistaken in his dating, however—except for that of the Missa—and seems to have been blind to the place the B-Minor Mass occupies in Bach's life and work.

We see the situation very differently today: in the period after August 1748 Bach feels an overpowering longing to offer a complete mass, from the Kyrie to the *Dona nobis pacem*. One may speculate about external circumstances: in Dresden the dedication of the court church is in the offing, an ideal opportunity for him to remind people of his position as composer to the court. In the summer of 1747, shortly after his visit to the court of Frederick the Great, word comes from Berlin that the cornerstone for the Catholic Church of St. Hedwig has just been laid. Perhaps he hopes to write a grand mass for its dedication, which, however, will not take place until decades later.[110]

Vague though these two indicators are, we must take such possible occasions into account, for in Bach's day—and not only then—it would be a complete anomaly to compose a major choral work without a commission. Does Bach intend to have the mass printed as evidence of what he can do? Given the costs involved, that seems highly unlikely. But he must have drawn from somewhere the prodigious energy it took to compose a full mass on a scale unprecedented in that period—not composing all of it from scratch, to be sure, yet conjuring it out of thin air! This is no *Art of Fugue,* with which a genius of a genre shows his mastery anew. This is conquest of entirely new territory.

In the absence of any concrete indications of the occasion, we must make do with a somewhat sentimental explanation: Bach does not want to die without having written a grand Catholic mass. He is, as we have said, an artist with a great sense of himself and of history, and in his last years in Leipzig he is shaping his image for posterity. When it comes to compositions for the keyboard, he has worked the field thoroughly; he will leave the printed editions of the *Clavier-Übung,* and both parts of the *Well-Tempered Clavier* and the *Chromatic Fantasy* have been disseminated quite widely in handwritten copies; the *Fantasy* would "remain lovely through all saecula," as a source quoted by Johann Nikolaus Forkel will write.[111] As for samples of artistry, the *Musical Offering* is already in existence, and *The Art of Fugue* is on the way.

But exemplary pieces of vocal music are to form part of the legacy as well. The *St. Matthew Passion* can represent Protestantism. And the B-Minor Mass? We should explore the idea that the late Bach wants to give expression to a theology that transcends the denominations and to do so in a magnificent work of religious music. He is not cozying up to Catholicism. The term "Catholic mass" should be understood ecumenically, in the sense of the words from the Credo: "et unam sanctam catholicam et apostolicam ecclesiam ("I believe in one holy, catholic, and apostolic Church").[112]

Bach takes the Kyrie, Gloria, and Sanctus entirely from compositions he has on hand, and the final movement, the *Dona nobis pacem,* recapitulates the *Gratias agimus tibi* from the Gloria. Most of the other sections consist of older pieces with new texts or in new arrangements. Yet the B-Minor Mass is not simply cobbled together. To be sure, by 1748 it would be difficult for him to compose a mass entirely from scratch; in London, Handel is struggling at the same age to come up with new ideas and on one occasion does not shrink from mining the printed *Philomena pia* by the minor composer Franz Habermann.

There is another way to refute the charge that Bach's mass consists of piecework: the multipart formula he adopts provides the ideal framework for inserting a range of compositional models, and the Latin prose is adaptable enough to lend itself to settings of the most varied origins.

By the end of 1749 at the latest, Bach has brought the work on the B-Minor Mass to a conclusion and with it possibly his composing altogether, for we have nothing indisputably written by him at a later date. Even receipts for money were signed in the last months of his life by Anna Magdalena or Johann Christian Bach, though they are written out to "Johann Sebastian Bach." A letter dated 27 December 1749 to Count Wilhelm von Schaumburg-Lippe, which Bach sent along when his son Johann Christoph Friedrich was appointed as court musician in Bückeburg, bears a signature in someone else's hand.

We know that as late as May 1750 Bach is still able to pay attention to correspondence; Johann Mattheson quotes an excerpt from a letter dealing with the Schröter–Biedermann dispute. In May of the same year the court organist from Schwerin, Johann Gottfried Müthel, arrives at Bach's house in order to "perfect himself in his métier."[113] To what extent he succeeded, given Bach's declining health, cannot be determined. Müthel may have been one of the "friends" to whom Bach "dictated on the spur of the moment" the organ chorale "Wenn wir in höchsten Nöthen sein," BWV 668a, as the preface to the first printing of *The Art of Fugue* describes.[114] But this role has also been ascribed to eighteen-year-old Johann Christian Kittel, who was living in Bach's house at the time.[115] A different account asserts that the chorale was dictated to Christian Friedrich Penzel, a student at St. Thomas School who was only thirteen at the time of Bach's death.[116] Forkel names Bach's son-in-law Johann Christoph Altnickol as the one to whom the work was dictated, which gives us four candidates for the "friend" who was taking dictation from Bach "a few days before the end."[117] The dictation seems to have become the stuff of legend,[118] the more so since a piece of evidence that would seem at first to speak for the legend must ultimately be cited against it. The last entry in the handwritten version of the Eighteen Chorales, BWV 651–68, refers to a choral movement with the textual notation "Vor deinen Thron tret ich hiermit," BWV 668: the notation, which is ascribed by Bach scholars to a scribe known as "Anonymous 12," breaks off at measure 26; up to that point it is essentially identical with the piece "Wenn wir in höchsten Nöten sein," BWV 668a, from the first printing of *The Art of Fugue*.

This incomplete version of BWV 668 transcribed by Anonymous 12 is not, however, a piece of dictation but a clean copy, with nothing that points to Bach's approaching end. We may assume that the organ chorale "Wenn wir in höchsten Nöthen sein" or "Vor deinen Thron tret ich hiermit" was available some time before Bach's death in a source that could be used as the basis both for Anonymous 12's transcription and for the score of the chorale in *The Art of Fugue*.

This presumptive common source consists in turn of a reworking and expansion of the organ chorale "Wenn wir in höchsten Nöthen sein," BWV 641, already part of the *Orgelbüchlein*. What we know of the sources fits the picture of a Bach who returned to older compositions during his last years, revising them and situating them in a new, meaningful context—for instance, that of the Eighteen Chorales. That this late collection breaks off with a fragment belonging with the choral text "Vor deinen Thron tret ich hiermit" surely has symbolic value when it occurs in the work of a devout Christian such as Bach. In this sense, those responsible for seeing to the engraving of *The Art of Fugue* launched, no doubt at least partly in good faith, a legend with some truth at its core.

We can only speculate about the nature and course of Bach's last illness. From the fall of 1749 on he must have suffered so greatly from the loss of his eyesight that at the end of March and the beginning of April he twice put himself in the hands of the English oculist John Taylor, who was visiting Leipzig at the time. On 4 April, the *Berlinische Privilegierte Zeitung* reports on the first operation:

> On Saturday last and yesterday evening Sir Taylor delivered public lectures in the concert hall, in the presence of scholars and other persons of rank. Remarkable numbers of people flock to him, seeking his help. Among other things, he has operated on Kapellmeister Bach, who through frequent use of his eyes had almost robbed himself entirely of their use, and the operation achieved the most wished-for success, such that he regained the complete acuity of his vision.[119]

But this report of a successful operation must have originated with Taylor's entourage, for it did not match the truth. The obituary gives a different account:

> Not only could he no longer use his eyes, but his entire body, otherwise thoroughly sound, was completely cast into an uproar by the operation and by the administration of harmful medicines and other things, such that he was almost constantly ill for a good half a year thereafter. Ten days before his death his eyes suddenly seemed to improve, so that one morning he could see quite well and could also tolerate the light again. But a few hours thereafter he suffered a stroke, which was followed by a raging fever, with the result that, despite the greatest care given him by two of the most skillful physicians of Leipzig, on 28 July 1750, shortly after a quarter past eight in the evening, in the sixty-sixth year of his life, he calmly and peacefully, through the mercy of his Redeemer, departed this life.[120]

Up to now, the skill of the respected oculist Taylor has not been seriously called into question by medical historians; Bach's death has been attributed instead to an infected wound, which brought on a stroke, followed by pneumonia, the immediate cause of death. More recent scholarship has ascribed Bach's death not to complications from the eye operation but to untreated diabetes. It was already known to medical science in the nineteenth century that diabetes could cause blindness and strokes.[121]

On 22 July 1750 Bach received private Communion in his house from the archdeacon of St. Thomas's, Christoph Wolle; six days later he died. The notice quoted at the very beginning of this book was recorded in the sexton's book for 30 July 1750.[122]

The burial took place in St. John's cemetery with the appropriate honors, but in full accordance with the rules that applied to persons of his station. By 8 August, Gottlob Harrer had been named his successor; as previously mentioned, the city council was more or less compelled to select the one among the six candidates favored by Reich Count Brühl. "Herr Bach had been a great musician, it is true, but not a teacher, so that as his replacement as Cantor of the St. Thomas School a person must be chosen who was skilled in both capacities; he believed that both would be found in Herr Harrer," is the euphemistic explanation given by Mayor Christian Ludwig Stieglitz, who is well aware that Harrer has no pedagogical training. When Harrer dies in 1755, the city council will demand anew "that the cantor's office be restored to its previous footing under Herr Kuhnau, and that the new cantor pay heed not only to music but also to instruction, seeing as much *désordre* had occurred with Herr Bach."[123] Harrer, too, seems to have been no paragon; but he probably comported himself more tactfully than Bach, about whose conduct in office the former burgomaster Jacob Born splutters again with great indignation.

In the fall of 1750, Bach's estate is inventoried; to the dismay of later Bach scholars, the musical material is omitted, having apparently been divided up earlier, for reasons unknown. The detailed listing attests to a well-equipped bourgeois household, whose value is estimated at 1,122 talers and 12 groschen, including outstanding debts to the family; money and coins (382 talers); silver vessels and other valuables (251 talers); musical instruments (371 talers); tin, copper, and bronze articles (16 talers); clothing and housewares (61 talers); and religious books (38 talers). The widow receives a third of the inheritance, and two-thirds goes to the nine surviving children from the two marriages.

In November 1750 the Dresden violin virtuoso and concertmaster Johann Georg Pisendel, who had many connections to Bach and his work, writes to Georg Philipp Telemann: "Now three members of the Mizler Society have died, namely Herr Stelzel, Herr Bimler, and Bach, yet I have not seen a mourning ode: Quare [Why is that]?"[124] Where Bach is concerned, Telemann does not wait to be asked again; in January Pisendel can print in the *Neu-eröffnete Historische Correspondenz von Curiosis Saxonicis* the following "Sonnet on the Late Kapellmeister Bach" from Telemann's pen:

> Let foreign lands their virtuosi laud
> Who through their lovely sounds have earned great fame,
> On German soil we need not look abroad
> To find musicians worthy of the name.
> Departed Bach! Alone thy splendid organ-playing
> Long since earned thee the title of "the Great,"
> And what thy quill hath writ, the highest art displaying,
> With joy and envy masters contemplate.
>
> So sleep! For ne'er forgot shall be thy fame;
> The pupils thou hast schooled, and those they school in turn
> Shall forge a crown of honor for thy name.
> Thy children's hands add jewels that brightly burn,
> But what shall truly make thee prized in times to come
> Berlin now shows us in a worthy son.[125]

Johann Sebastian Bach the Great and the "prized" Carl Philipp Emanuel—with such epithets Telemann must have hit the nail on the head in the minds of many contemporaries: at his death, the father has almost become his own monument, while his son represents all that is new in northern Germany.

The detailed obituary that appears in 1754 in the fourth volume of Mizler's *Musikalische Bibliothek* remains to this day one of the most valuable sources on Bach's life. We owe most of it to Carl Philipp Emanuel Bach, although Bach's pupil Johann Friedrich Agricola and

Mizler himself also contributed. The school director of Halberstadt, Georg Venzky, Bach's "colleague" in the Mizler Society, offers a poem intended to be sung.

There is nothing spectacular about Bach's death and burial—no magnificent funeral as for Handel, no actual or legendary pauper's grave as for Mozart. A highly respected cantor of St. Thomas dies at an age not unduly young for those times—such is the way of the world. His influence never reached the public at large. For a good half century he will live on among music lovers as a mighty virtuoso on the keyboard and the organ, as an outstanding contrapuntalist and fine harmonist. Then his day will dawn, bringing great admiration for his universality: but no one will ever truly be able to appreciate its full measure.

THE BACH HOUSEHOLD

Although we know very little about Bach's living conditions in the years before he came to Leipzig, we have ample information on his circumstances in that city. Like the rector of St. Thomas, the cantor has living quarters in the school itself. Bach lives in the south wing, the rector in the north wing. The wide central core of the building houses the classrooms, the dining hall, a rehearsal room, and a conference room. The more than modest dormitory for the fifty-five boarding students occupies the attics.

After the school is renovated in 1731 and a fourth floor added to the original three, Bach can walk from the third story of his cantor's apartment down a corridor to the rehearsal hall and conference room—but also to the rector's living quarters; the cantor thus lives in proximity not only to his students but also to his superior. It is an agreeable arrangement for bringing the two families together and providing godparents for the children. But it can be oppressive when conflict arises.

After the renovation, Bach must have plenty of room, with the ground floor and three upper stories,[126] for house guests and pupils. An early photograph, taken before the building was torn down in

1902, shows a room on the second floor of the school traditionally known as the Composing Room. It is by no means a fancy space, but Bach's study, when furnished, must have looked quite comfortable, and the view out the window onto the tree-lined promenade could have been delightful.

> *Now I must mention something of my domestic circumstances. I am married for the second time, for my late first wife died in Cöthen. From my first marriage I have three sons and one daughter still living, whom Your Honor will recall having seen in Weimar. From the second marriage I have one son and two daughters living. My eldest son is a* Studiosus Juris, *and the others are still in school, one in the prima form and the other in the second, and the eldest daughter is as yet unmarried. The children of my second marriage are still little, and the firstborn, a boy, is 6 years old. But they are all born musicians, and you may believe that I can already put together an ensemble both* vocaliter *and* instrumentaliter *from my family, since my present wife sings a fine, clear soprano, and my eldest daughter chimes in not badly. I shall almost exceed the bounds of courtesy if I inconvenience Your Honor with further information, and so I hasten to conclude, remaining with the most humble lifelong respect*
> *Your Honor's most obedient and devoted servant*
> *Leipzig, 28 October 1730*   *Joh. Sebast. Bach*

That is the conclusion of the Erdmann letter, the beginning and middle of which have already been quoted. It is evident that Bach's family is a source of joy to him. Anna Magdalena impresses him with her ability as a singer. When he is invited to perform in other towns, as he is at least five times in Cöthen and twice in Weissenfels, she is documented as accompanying him quite often and enhancing the ensembles he puts together in those places. At home she busies herself as a copyist; her writing so closely resembles her husband's that even an expert like Philipp Spitta at first attributed a manuscript of the violin solos to Johann Sebastian, an error he corrected in the supplement to the second volume of his biography.

The most significant copies prepared by Anna Magdalena were completed between 1727 and 1731 and perhaps intended for sale: the violin solos BWV 1001–06 and the cello solos BWV 1007–12, archived in the Berlin Staatsbibliothek as Mus. MS Bach P268 and P269. She also helped with the copying of the first part of the *Well-Tempered Clavier*, the so-called Müller Autograph P202; with the so-called London Autograph of the second part of the *Well-Tempered Clavier*; as well as with a copy of the organ sonatas BWV 525–30, begun by Wilhelm Friedemann.

In a pinch, Anna Magdalena, like Bach's sons, helps by writing out parts for a composition. Thus she writes parts for the cantatas "Es ist das Heil uns kommen her," BWV 9, "Meine Seufzer, meine Tränen," BWV 13, "Wär Gott nicht mit uns diese Zeit," BWV 14, "Liebster Jesu, mein Verlangen," BWV 32, "Ach Gott, wie manches Herzeleid," BWV 58, "Alles nur nach Gottes Willen," BWV 72, "Was mein Gott will, das g'scheh allzeit," BWV 111, "Meinen Jesum lass ich nicht," BWV 124, "Süsser Trost, mein Jesus kommt," BWV 151, but also for the *St. Matthew Passion*, the B-Minor Mass, the motet "Der Geist hilft unser Schwachheit auf," BWV 226, and the concerto for two harpsichords BWV 1061.

In 1722, shortly after their wedding, Bach puts together a collection of pieces for his wife, of which only a fragment, with the original versions of the *French Suites*, BWV 812–17, and a few individual pieces, has survived. He soon takes this notebook apart and replaces it with another begun in 1725 and added to until some time in the 1740s.[127] He provides material for pages 1–41 with early versions of the partitas BWV 827 and 830 from the later first part of the *Clavier-Übung*, and then Anna Magdalena adds a few smaller pieces: dance movements by such composers as the Dresden court organist Christian Petzold and François Couperin, as well as the chorale "Wer den lieben Gott lässt walten," harmonized by Bach.

On page 56 a younger member of the family attempts writing a bass part to the melody "Gib dich zufrieden und sei stille," BWV 510; Father Bach uses the facing page to write a new composition in G minor to the same text, BWV 511, then transposes this work into the key of E minor, more comfortable for his wife to perform, and makes small improvements, as is his wont (BWV 512). On pages 60–67 young Carl Philipp Emanuel enters marches and polonaises that he has composed himself. After that, on two facing pages, we find two versions of the song "Sooft ich meine Tobackspfeife." On the left side, one of Bach's sons is trying his hand at the melody and bass; on the right, Anna Magdalena transposes this attempt into a singable key, and Father Bach adds a new, moving bass.

After several more dance pieces, on pages 75 and 78 Anna Magdalena copies Gottfried Heinrich Stölzel's aria "Bist du bei mir"; the two pages in between are first left blank on purpose; later she fills them with the aria from the *Goldberg Variations*. On pages 79–81 she enters an early version of the opening movement of Carl Philipp Emanuel's piano sonata Wotquenne Listing 65/7; then a polonaise by Johann Adolph Hasse; the C-major prelude from the first part of the *Well-Tempered Clavier*, mistakenly shortened by five measures; and numbers 1 and 2 of the *French Suites*, BWV 812 and 813. The next piece, written in a very awkward hand and marred by a large ink blot, is an attempt at a marchlike piece, perhaps by the youngest son, Johann Christian.

The last part of the notebook, from page 102 on, is chiefly filled with Bach's vocal compositions, most of them transcribed by Anna Magdalena for her own use. They include the religious songs "Warum betrübst du dich," BWV 516, "Schaffs mit mir, Gott, nach deiner Güt," BWV 514, "Wie wohl ist mir, o Freund der Seelen, wenn ich in deiner Liebe ruh," BWV 517, "Gedenke doch mein Geist zurücke ans Grab und an den Glockenschall," BWV 509, "O Ewigkeit, du Donnerwort," BWV 513, but also the recitative and aria "Ich hab genug" / "Schlummert ein, ihr matten Augen" as a shorter version of the corresponding sections in the cantata "Ich hab genug," BWV 82. The chorale "Dir, dir, Jehova will ich singen," which also occurs in the Schemelli songbook, appears in a four-part version by Johann Sebastian (BWV 299) and a two-part reduction by Anna Magdalena (BWV 442). Here, too, it is astonishing to observe how her hand comes to resemble her husband's.

The famous *Aria di Giovannini* "Willst du dein Herz mir schenken," transcribed by an unknown person who obviously knew Italian, was temporarily removed from the notebook but then put back in. In the pages at the back, where no music is recorded, from page 122 on, we find a wedding poem in Anna Magdalena's hand, as well as rules for the general bass, first in an incomplete version penned by Johann Christoph Friedrich, then noted in fifteen points by Anna Magdalena.

In this lively notebook representing two generations of Bachs, vocal works can be found next to instrumental works, religious next to secular, light next to serious, clumsy next to perfected, solemn next to cheerful, didactic next to entertaining, homegrown next to imported. One can hardly form a better picture of the Bach family in Leipzig than that afforded by this notebook, which at the same time reveals a good deal about Anna Magdalena: she is not only her husband's helpmate but at the same time her children's music teacher, a singer, and a performer on the harpsichord.

The songs and arias display the piety typical of the time, although it needs Bach's creative genius to come into its own musically. The song focusing on Jesus and the soul plays an important part. Such songs, cultivated in particular by the Pietists but not exclusively by them, were often sung at prayer services conducted in people's homes. Characteristic of their content is the notion that one must be ready at any moment for death, a reality in the lives of Christians in this period. Perhaps the anguish of everyday life could be borne only because it was accompanied by the belief that God would shield his children from the worst and, when they cried, "I have had enough," would redeem them from earthly suffering.

The Stölzel aria occupies a place between Jesus worship and conjugal love. The text goes, "Bist du bei mir, geh ich mit Freuden zum Sterben und zu meiner Ruh. Ach, wie vergnügt wär so mein Ende, es drückten deine schönen Hände mir die getreuen Augen zu" ("When thou art with me, I go with joy to death and to my final repose. Ah, how contented would be my end, if thy fair hands my eyes did close"). Does the Savior function here as an allegorical figure, alluding to the spouse? Although the song comes from an opera by Stölzel, the question cannot be answered, because it is precisely the blurred line between the secular and the religious spheres that gives the *Klavierbüchlein* its charm. Also "Erbauliche Gedanken eines To-backrauchers" (Edifying Thoughts of a Tobacco Smoker) should be interpreted as a morality poem combining serious and humorous elements. The second stanza, not recorded in the *Notenbüchlein*, can be found in another source:

> The pipe is made of earth and clay,
> And so am I; I too someday
> Must turn to earth from whence I came;
> The pipe may fall, or in my hand
> It breaks in two; you understand:
> Its fate and mine are just the same.[128]

This poem, which Telemann also set to music, follows the pattern of a "canapé song" much loved at the time and also used for the "Lied eines Frauenzimmers über den Schnupftaback" (Song of a Lady on the Subject of Snuff), from the collection *Sperontes Singende Muse an der Pleisse*, which appeared in several parts and editions, starting in 1736:

> My pinch of snuff's my greatest pleasure,
> My pastime, my belovèd treasure.
> My pinch goes with me everywhere,
> 'Tis dearer than my head and hair.
> It heals what pains may come my way,
> The one effective panacée.[129]

Such mockery, irony, and ambiguity would not have been appropriate for Anna Magdalena's *Notenbüchlein;* so far as can be determined from the documentary evidence, she, like her husband, was committed to traditional values. Because we have drafts of a few letters written by Bach's relative Johann Elias Bach between 1737 and 1742, while he was serving as tutor and secretary to the family, we know something about Anna Magdalena's predilections. Thus Johann Elias writes to his mother at the end of April 1738, asking her to send special presents for his hosts, the Bachs:

> *If possible, I would like to have for Monsieur my cousin a bottle of the brandy made with excellent yeast and a few carnations,* notabene, *yellow, for our Madame Cousin, a great lover of the gardener's art; I know I should surely please them mightily and insinuate myself all the more with both, wherefore I entreat you once more, and remain, as above.*[130]

Johann Elias also asks a Herr von Meyer in Halle for carnations for Anna Magdalena, saying she is already looking forward to them "as a small child looks forward to the Christ Child, and I must apologize that I am compelled to importune Your Honor so often on her behalf."[131]

In a letter written in June 1740 to Cantor Johann Georg Hille from Glauchau, whom he met a few years earlier in the Bach household, the subject matter is a songbird:

> *...the aforementioned Kapellmeister, when he returned from Halle during Lent this past year, reported to his most beloved wife, along with many good things, that Your Honor possessed a linnet which, thanks to the skill of its instructor, sang most winningly. Since my honored Madame Cousin is greatly fond of such birds, I feel I should inquire whether Your Honor would be disposed to relinquish this little singer to her for a modest price, and to send it to her by secure means.*[132]

On this occasion we learn not only that Anna Magdalena is fond of songbirds but also that her husband likes to use the Lenten period between Invocavit and Palm Sunday, the so-called *tempus clausum*, when no cantatas must be performed, for travel. During one journey, which, however, does not take place during Lent but in the summer of 1741, Bach receives word that his wife has fallen seriously ill. On 5 August, Johann Elias writes of a "violent gush of blood," from

which "an insidious fever or some other evil consequences may arise."
After Bach announces his return for a date that seems too late to the
concerned family in Leipzig, another letter, dated 9 August, reads:

> ... we feel nonetheless great pain at the growing weakness of our
> dearly beloved Mama, who for a fortnight now has not had one
> hour's rest for a single night, and can neither sit up nor lie down,
> such that last night I was summoned, and we could not but think
> that, to our great grief, we should lose her. The most urgent ne-
> cessity thus compels us to dispatch this most dutiful report, that
> Your Honor may perhaps hasten your journey without delay...[133]

Anna Magdalena recovered and was once more able to attend
to her household duties, which included caring for the numerous
pupils and guests, who—if we may trust the surviving evidence—
frequented the house day in, day out. Of particular interest to the
music historian are the visits paid to Bach by fellow musicians, as described, for instance, in a letter by Johann Elias of 11 November 1739
to Cantor Johann Wilhelm Koch of Ronneburg:

> ... and I certainly hoped to have the honor of speaking to my
> Brother soon, for which I wished all the more eagerly since at that
> time something especially fine in the way of music took place, for
> my honored Cousin from Dressden, who was present here for
> more than four weeks, along with the two famous lutenists Herr
> Weise and Herr Kropffgans, could be heard several times per-
> forming at our residence.[134]

The cousin referred to here, who performed several times with
the chamber virtuosi Silvius Leopold Weiss and Johann Kropffgans,
is Wilhelm Friedemann Bach, and we may well believe the writer
when he suggests that at that time "especially fine" music could be
heard in the Bach house, and surely not only on that occasion; indeed Carl Philipp Emanuel reports on a visit paid to Leipzig by the
famous Dresden flautist Pierre-Gabriel Buffardin. No doubt many
of the musicians from Bach's collegium musicum also made music
with him at home. There were plenty of instruments for the thor-

ough bass; according to the inventory of Bach's estate, he owned five cembalos, a *Lautenwerk* (lute-harpsichord), and a spinet.

But to return to Anna Magdalena: her chief concern had to be her children. She became mother to four of them from her husband's first marriage, and she bore thirteen of her own, eleven during the first thirteen years of the marriage. Six of her offspring survived beyond early childhood. When her husband, who was sixteen years older than she, died in 1750, the two eldest children from the first marriage, Wilhelm Friedemann and Carl Philipp Emanuel, had already left home, but Catharina Dorothea, born in 1708, was unmarried and still lived with the family. The eldest of Anna Magdalena's own children was Gottfried Heinrich, born in 1724 and apparently feeble-minded from youth. Elisabeth Juliana Friederica, whom the family called Liesgen, married Bach's pupil Johann Christoph Altnickol in 1749. Two other sons were on their way to becoming fine musicians: eighteen-year-old Johann Christoph Friedrich and fourteen-year-old Johann Christian, later known as the Milan or London Bach. The youngest were twelve-year-old Johanna Carolina and eight-year-old Regina Susanna.

In 1749 Johann Christoph Friedrich received from his mother a Luther bible for Christmas—apparently in anticipation of his installation as musician at the court of Bückeburg. She inscribed it as follows: "As a lasting reminder and for Christian edification this magnificent book is given to her dear son by Anna Magdalena Bach, née Wülcke, your faithful and well-disposed mama."[135]

At forty-nine, upon Bach's death, Anna Magdalena assumes guardianship of Johann Christoph Friedrich and his three younger siblings, and with it complete responsibility, attesting on 21 October 1750 to the Leipzig city council that she does not intend to remarry. In addition to her third of the estate, she receives the share of those children who will continue to live with her. The council pays her a "half-year's grace,"[136] after which she moves to Haynstrasse, presumably to the house of the jurist Friedrich Heinrich Graf, a friend of the family who provided legal assistance with the settling of the estate. In the burial book of the Leipzig council we find the following notation on her death, dated 29 February 1760: "Almswoman, 59th yr., Anna Magdalena, née Wilke, widow of Herr Johann Sebastian Bach, Cantor at the Thomas School, on Haynstrasse."[137]

"Almswoman" has harsher connotations to us than to Bach's contemporaries: as the widow of a municipal employee, Anna Magdalena is entitled to financial support that can be seen as "a combination of widow's pension and welfare."[138] If we include the money she received directly from the estate or from the sale of her husband's music up to and including the first printing of *The Art of Fugue*, it seems likely that she did not suffer want during the ten years by which she outlived her husband. To be sure, her daughter Regina Susanna later experienced such financial distress that in 1800 Johann Friedrich Rochlitz, in his capacity as editor of the *Leipzig allgemeine musikalische Zeitung*, issued a call for donations, to which Ludwig van Beethoven intended to respond.

Should one of Bach's sons from his first marriage have taken in his stepmother and her daughters after his father's death? We do not know why this did not occur. Carl Philipp Emanuel did bring Johann Christian to Berlin, where he remained for six years before trying his luck in Italy.

If we think about Bach's swarm of children from his point of view, we must admit first of all that we have no information about his relationship with his daughters. Any concern for the children's professional well-being is directed entirely toward the sons, as we would expect for that era, but in Bach the concern is intense. We have already mentioned the musical instruction the two eldest sons receive from their father in the Cöthen period. In Leipzig their musical training continues, but Bach also pays close attention to their academic development; in the year of his installation in Leipzig he preregisters Wilhelm Friedemann, who is barely thirteen, at the university. He also gives Carl Philipp Emanuel the opportunity to study at the university, first in Leipzig, then in Frankfurt an der Oder.

In 1733, when Wilhelm Friedemann applies for the position of organist at St. Sophie's in Dresden, his father pens two petitions in his name. One is addressed to Appellate Councilor Paul Christian Schrödert:

> *To the Highborn, Noble, and most Erudite Lord Appellate Councilor, Most gracious Patron: May the excessive temerity with which I undertake to dispatch the enclosed to Your Excellency be excused? The undersigned need only recall the munificence which Your Excellency has showered upon his humble servant for it to appear almost irresponsible to extract more of the same; yet it suffices to remark that especially clients (among whom I am not the last) have always been granted access most freely to Your Excellency. For it cannot be unknown to Your Noble Excellency that Herr Pezold, quondam organist at St. Sophie's, has passed into the Beyond and his station is presumably left vacant. Therefore I most humbly take it upon myself to draw the attention of Your most noble and wise Excellency, as a most competent judge, through this reminder. And herewith submit to Your Excellency my most humble request that you graciously deign to bestow your high patronage on your insignificant servant. In confident expectation that this my humble petition shall find favor, I shall endeavor all the more earnestly for the rest of my life to show myself*
> *Your Noble Excellency's most humble and obedient Servant*
> *Leipzig, 7 June 1733*   *Wilhelm Friedeman Bach*[139]

Bach seldom adopts such an obsequious tone on his own behalf; but for his son it seems entirely appropriate. Wilhelm Friedemann indeed receives the position—but on the strength of his ability, for "according to the declaration and *judicio* of all the musicians" he is "the best and most skilled."[140] We may wonder whether part of Wilhelm Friedemann's success at his audition may be attributable to the fiery Prelude and Fugue in G Major, BWV 541, of which his father makes a very handsome copy around this time.

Carl Philipp Emanuel seems to have secured his position with the Prussian crown prince, later King Frederick II, without his father's help. It is Johann Gottfried Bernhard who turns out to be the problem child. On 2 May 1735 Bach recommends the almost twenty-year-old for employment as the organist at St. Mary's in Mühlhausen, where he himself played in his early years. Johann Gottfried Bernhard gets through the audition successfully, and takes up his post, but he is so badly received that Bach recommends him in letters to Councilman Johann Friedrich Klemm in Sangerhausen, dated 30 October and 18 November 1736, for the vacant organist's position there. This time, too, his son proves successful, being voted in on 14 January 1737, although his appointment is not confirmed by the consistory until August.

But Johann Gottfried Bernhard leaves his new post in the spring of 1738; in a letter to Klemm, dated 24 May 1737, Bach has to admit "with pain and regret" that he does not know his son's whereabouts. After the young man's departure from Mühlhausen, he, Johann Sebastian, has not only paid a draft "but also...a few ducats to settle some debts." Yet he hoped in vain that thenceforth his son would "embark on a new mode of life":

> But now I must hear again, with great consternation, that he has once more borrowed here and there, not changing his way of life in the slightest, but even absenting himself and not giving me to date any inkling of his whereabouts.
>
> What shall I say or do further? Since no admonition nor even any loving care and assistance will suffice anymore, I must bear my cross patiently and leave my miscreant son to God's Mercy, doubting not that He will hear my sorrowful pleas and in the end so work His Holy Will upon him, that he shall learn that a change of heart can come about wholly and solely through Divine Grace. Since now I have revealed myself to Your Honor, I have all confidence that you will not impute the evil conduct of my child to me, but will be convinced that a faithful father, whose children are close to his heart, seeks to do all that is possible to promote their well-being.[141]

This rather heartrending letter tells us a good deal about Bach as a father: on the one hand, he loves his son, does not condemn him, and continues to hope that the young man can change his ways. On the other hand, he does not want to consume himself in lamentation or sorrow for this son, for life makes other demands on him.

Johann Gottfried Bernhard Bach seems to move in next with his relative Nikolaus Bach in Jena, where he enrolls at the university to study jurisprudence. On 27 May 1739 he dies "of a high fever"—the capitulation of a young man who was unwilling or unable to comply with the expectations of his times?[142] He must have been a good musician, but so was his older brother Wilhelm Friedemann, who also had trouble meeting external expectations, the more so the longer he lived.

We have already mentioned the letter Bach wrote at the end of 1749 in an attempt to help his second youngest son, Johann Christoph Friedrich, obtain a position at the court of Bückeburg. The youngest, Johann Christian, made his way entirely without intervention. His father is reported to have applied a quotation from Gellert to him: "Jörg will surely succeed through stupidity."[143] Although we have no confirmation for this anecdote, it has the ring of truth—if we substitute for stupidity a carefree attitude otherwise foreign to the Bach family. Caring not a fig for his father's values, this same Christel even converted to Catholicism in Italy, a step that caused his half brother Carl Philipp Emanuel to note next to Christel's name in the family chronicle written by his father: "*Inter nos,* conducted himself differently from honest Veit"—referring to the legendary Protestant ancestor who fled from the Catholics into German territory.[144]

In 1727 Bach composes the cantata BWV 84, which begins with these words: "Ich bin vergnügt mit meinem Glücke, das mir der liebe Gott beschert" ("I am contented with the blessings a loving God on me bestows"). He may have identified with the text, which he perhaps modified himself—but hardly with the version the librettist Picander published a year later: "I am contented with the station a loving God on me bestowed."

Bach can hardly have been content with his station as cantor of St. Thomas. But as his letter to Erdmann, the friend of his youth,

From the Argentine writer Jorge Luis Borges comes a poem called "Inventarium": Someone takes it upon himself to draw the whole world. In the course of the years he peoples a room with provinces, kingdoms, mountain ranges, bays, ships, islands, fishes, rooms, instruments, heavenly bodies, horses, human beings. Just before his death, he discovers that this painstakingly constructed labyrinth of lines is the image of his own face.[145] Bach's face does not bear the features which the Leipzig celebrity painter Elias Gottlieb Haussmann drew in 1747. His real face is the labyrinth of lines that make up his work.

allows us to conclude, he was personally happy: his was the happiness of a blessed husband and father, and also that of a great artist. Nonetheless he must also have identified with the sentiment in the opening line of his cantata BWV 146: "Wir müssen durch viel Trübsal in das Reich Gottes eingehen" ("We must enter the kingdom of Heav'n through a multitude of sorrows").

PART TWO

THE VOCAL MUSIC

THE EARLY AND WEIMAR CANTATAS

Of the roughly two hundred surviving Bach cantatas, scholarship has classified six as early, that is, assigned them to the years Bach was in Arnstadt or Mühlhausen. The dates of two of the six are unproblematic: in the autograph of the cantata, "Aus der Tiefen rufe ich, Herr, zu dir," BWV 131, Bach signs himself as "Org. Molhusino"; the printed text of the *Ratswahl* Cantata "Gott ist mein König," BWV 71, is dated 4 February 1708. The four other cantatas, of which only later copies exist, can be considered early works based on considerations of style or genre: "Nach dir, Herr, verlanget mich," BWV 150, a work difficult to classify liturgically; the choral cantata on the Easter hymn "Christ lag in Todesbanden," BWV 4; the cantata "Der Herr denket an us," BWV 196, which had been characterized somewhat prematurely by Bach scholars as wedding music;[1] and the famous *Actus tragicus*, BWV 106, "Gottes Zeit ist die allerbeste Zeit." We are dealing here with occasional music, and our information regarding the circumstances and purpose of their composition is imperfect. A seventh work should not be excluded from this group of early cantatas solely because its authenticity is disputed: the New Year's Day cantata "Lobe den Herrn, meine Seele," BWV 143.

In the years around and after 1700, the church cantata with several movements is still a new genre. In the century of Martin Luther, the single-movement Gospel or choral motet was predominant; in the seventeenth century the motet had been supplanted or at least complemented by the sacred orchestral *Konzert*—likewise primarily based on Bible texts or hymns. The congregation did not want simply to receive God's word in passive devotion and respond in standardized forms like the Credo or in chorale; they wished to enter into a living dialogue with the divine message, and wanted this dialogue to reflect their dynamic and spontaneous emotional response to it. In other words, aesthetic values played a role in creating the style of the seventeenth century—dynamics, structure, and individual expressiveness—and increasingly characterized how church music was understood; they took their place alongside the more objective function of setting Bible texts to music with choral transcription.

Thus, in the last third of the seventeenth century, devotional elements start to enter into the *Konzert*, which up to that time had been a single movement: flowingly lyrical but at the same time emotional strophic arias, with poetical texts often closely related to early Pietism. An example of this change can be found in a composition of Dietrich Buxtehude, where the certain faith of the apostle—"Ich halte es dafür, daß dieser Zeit Leiden der Herrlichkeit nicht wert sei, die an uns soll offenbaret werden" ("I hold this time of suffering to be unworthy of the glory that will be revealed unto us")—is followed by an emotionally charged transformation of this message by an individual soul, fearful by nature but comforted by faith in Jesus:

> Was quälet mein Herz mit Trauer und Schmerz,
> was ängstet mein Leben, mit Trauern umgeben,
> was heißet mich trauern, die Welt zu bedauern?
> Nur, Jesu, zu dir steht mein Begier.

> Why is my heart tormented with grief and pain,
> my life made fearful, surrounded with sorrow,
> why do I grieve for the world,
> all my desire, My Jesus, is for thee.

By the turn of the eighteenth century the sacred *Konzert*, now expanded to include the aria, gradually develops into a multipart cantata; in this earlier form it is a mixture of various textual elements. When Bach made his pilgrimage to Buxtehude in Lübeck in 1705, he could hear works of this new type—for example, the cantata "Alles, was ihr tut," still a favorite of Protestant church choirs today. It opens with the concerted setting of the Gospel text beginning with these words; is followed by a strophic aria set for several voices, "Dir dir Höchster, dir alleine," then an *arioso* setting of the Psalmic words "Habe deine Lust am Herrn"; and concludes with the homophonic chorale "Gott will ich lassen raten."

Of course this is only one of several possible models; at the start of the eighteenth century, the form as a whole is in an experimental stage. One person contributing to the general though by no means unfruitful instability is the preacher and poet of the Court of Weißenfels, Erdmann Neumeister, who in 1704 publishes a cycle of texts for the year, *Geistliche Cantaten statt einer Kirchen Music* (Spiritual Cantatas in Place of Liturgical Music): this is meant to encourage the composition of sacred cantatas modeled on Italian opera, that is, a series of recitatives and arias on freely composed, madrigalic texts.

The ensuing controversy within the Protestant church is in no way solely an aesthetic one; it involves questions of theology, piety, and tradition. There is the question of whether the so-called madrigalic cantata, considered the spawn of worldliness, has any role in a religious service. There is the more general question of whether a sacred work should have multiple parts and thus encourage the trend toward a multiple perspective in the worship service—or whether to respect the tradition, by which each musical composition had its specific place in the liturgy: for the Introit, an Introit motet would be heard; for the reading of the Gospel, a *Konzert* on the relevant Bible text; for the Credo, a musical setting of that part of the Latin mass or the Lutheran Credo; and so on.

In other words, at the very heart of a movement arising in the Enlightenment we see a debate taking shape: Should the arts, including works commissioned by the Church, be allowed to develop autonomously, or should they be controlled by prevailing social ideas?

Against the background of this tension, the young church musician Bach comes of age, and in his unique way he will make productive use of it in his work. His effort to mediate between autonomy and church orthodoxy occurs at the highest intellectual and compositional level; his striving is less mediation than constant innovation.

It is not difficult to establish in general, and in detail, how the young Bach came in contact with the sacred cantata form in its *status nascendi*—at a time when he must have been particularly receptive to everything that was new. He encountered it at his older brother's house in Ohrdruf, certainly in his Lüneburg period, and finally in the Lübeck of Buxtehude. In his application for discharge in Mühlhausen in June 1708, he can point out, as mentioned earlier, that he is in possession of a "goodly supply of the most exquisite pieces of music for the church," by which he might have meant the more traditionally oriented Old Bach Family Archive.

Specialists have naturally attempted to pin down what models the young Bach used in writing his cantatas.[2] Their finding is not surprising: he does not compose like a talented pupil; nor does he flaunt a "progressive" style by, say, adapting the overly "smooth" composition of the Italian manner. Even in the utilitarian genre of the cantata he very quickly developed his own style of composing, which combined a variety of perspectives on the autonomy and functionality of art.

This varied approach applies only partially, of course, to what may be the oldest surviving cantata: "Nach dir, Herr, verlanget mich," BWV 150. Bach could have performed it in Arnstadt during the Communion service. It became familiar only in the nineteenth century, when Johannes Brahms used the four-bar passacaglia theme of its final chorus as the basis for the finale of his Fourth Symphony. Recently the theory has arisen that Bach in turn borrowed the theme from Johann Pachelbel, to honor Pachelbel on the occasion of his death in March 1706.[3]

To add to the body of conjecture that forms an indispensable part of any description of Bach's early work, here is another thought:

Bach could have composed the cantata on the Luther chorale "Christ lag in Todesbanden," BWV 4, while still in Arnstadt, as a test piece for Mühlhausen, Easter, 1707:[4] this idea assumes that as an organist he was also required to compose and present vocal music. The same text had been chosen by Pachelbel, organist in Nuremberg, who was a generation older, as the basis for a cantata. It is interesting to note that Bach's work is no more progressive than that of his brother's teacher at Ohrdruf. On the contrary, his style is more motet-like than concertante, and in general less polished than that of the older maestro.

The imitative cantus firmus treatment of the fourth strophe, "Es war ein wunderlicher Krieg, da Tod und Leben rungen" ("It was an awesome thing, that strife, when death and life did wrestle"), sounds downright antiquated.[5] At the same time, it has "figural" traits that one would characterize as neither old nor new but typically Bachian: for example, in the canonic voice line, the phrase "ein Tod den andern fraß" ("one death devoured the next") is indeed devoured by the next repetition, in which "ein Spott aus dem Tod ist worden" ("death is made a mockery")—this passage is composed in a spirit that Bach may have absorbed from the starkly pictorial, almost woodcarved words of Luther. Pachelbel too alludes to the "wunderlicher Krieg" between life and death but depicts it more as an instrumental "battaglia," in the modish Italian fashion.

Bach makes full use not just of the imagery of the Luther chorale but also of its inherently musical qualities, exhibiting particular fascination with the head motif of the cantus firmus: the descending second. In contrast with the original hymn melody, and also with Pachelbel, he takes it not as a major Dorian second but as a minor, that is, a chromatically sharped second. This is most daring, for a young musician to alter a melody line of one of the most traditional Luther chorales, a melody that had been sacrosanct for generations.

In truly paradigmatic fashion, at the start of his sacred music career, Bach demonstrates that he will not simply take up the tradition but actively change it, and not arbitrarily: the descending minor second, a fragment split off from the head of the melody, is a rich interval for motivic composition. He makes it the key interval of the entire cantata and uses it as such even in the introductory sinfonia.

The more attentive churchgoers in Mühlhausen may have been surprised at hearing the minor second interval following the sinfonia, then immediately again in the first strophe of the cantus firmus, and after that in all the other strophes—particularly evocatively in the second: "Den Tod niemand zwingen konnt" ("No man can conquer death"):

This telling connection with the text points out the fact that for Bach the falling minor second was not just a structural element but possessed semantic qualities as well, which a century earlier Cantor Joachim Burmeister of Rostock described, in his discussion of the possible rhetorical devices in music, with the term "pathopoeia": this would be a "figure" with which, as the Greek name says, passions could be aroused, using, among other things, semitones alien to the mode.[6] Bach proceeded in exactly this way, putting a sharp on the fourth step of the Dorian scale, raising A to A-sharp.

This is not an arbitrary half step foreign to the scale but a compactly evocative opening motif, in which the melody descends a halftone, then rises again. Nor is it just a musical rhetorical figure; at the same time it is a gesture—comparable to a sob—that evokes the type of melody found in lamentations for the dead. In different tonal, harmonic, and metric contexts in Western music, it is associated with the emotional fields of longing, suffering, adversity, and death. This interval occurs in the first of Heinrich Schütz's *Kleine geistliche Konzerte*, "Eile mich, Gott, zu erretten"; at the start of

Mozart's G-minor Symphony; in the song "Die Krähe," from Schubert's *Winterreise;* and in the "Vox" aria from Penderecki's *St. Luke Passion,* to cite just a few examples.

It is not in itself remarkable that Bach places his composition in this semantic context: there are enough instances of it in his music and in that of his contemporaries. The significance is, rather, that he modifies the Lutheran cantus firmus to give the music a "semantic" meaning: he thus stands at the intersection of the vectors of tradition and innovation, of figural order and artistic self-determination.[7]

The descending minor second can be understood not just structurally, figuratively, and emotionally but symbolically as well. When Bach modifies the Dorian mode by raising the A to A-sharp through the use of the symbol # (the sharp is known as a *Kreuz,* "cross," in German), he is setting up not just an audible but also a visible sign— quite conceivably a symbol of Christ's suffering, which in fact plays a central role in Luther's Easter hymn. I record this thought with some reservation, since it could put even more speculative ammunition into the hands of overzealous, theologically minded Bach scholars than they presently have. Still, it must be mentioned here: as one can see from this single musical phrase, the young Bach was obviously already composing with a kind of contemplation, profundity, and complexity to an extent previously unknown in music history: he is looking for both textual and musical dialogue with his historical model, the chorale. From this model, through conscious intervention, he derives a motif that can speak both structurally and semantically; this in turn enhances the composition with additional meaning. As a result of such complexity, the musical texture is open to further interpretation.

Interpretations can be structural as well as semantic. On the structural side, it would be possible as an experiment to trace the descending minor second through the entire composition. On the semantic side, this "elevation by the cross" that Bach accomplishes in the musical texture could be seen as a symbol of the greatest Christian "skandalon": with the crosslike sharp functioning to intensify the central image. In later chapters I discuss instances where Bach beyond doubt made intentional use of sharp accidentals or two vocal lines written to intersect in a cross. But one last thought for now on the descending minor second, without making too much of it.

Bach was on familiar terms with this interval, since it occurs, as B-A and C-H, twice in his own name. Naturally he did not scribble his name all over his music, but as the scion of a large, widely dispersed family he would have had to come to terms with it musically. So it is of some significance that his modifications to a traditional cantus firmus are accompanied in this case by the inclusion of his name cipher: composing thus takes on an a priori significance, almost in the sense of a self-fulfilling prophecy. Once again, caution must be used: from this aspect we are concerned primarily with a *structure* in which we can consider Bach's music, and a discursive context in which we can reflect on it, and not with tortured attempts at finding meaning. To appreciate the delicate balance of Bach's music one must not try to impose on it an inherently formal logic or delve overly into esoteric theories in which aesthetic pleasure is reduced to a negligible quantity.

Those who would see already in the young Bach the first traces of those "strange perfections" that Magister Johann Abraham Birnbaum ascribed to the court composer in 1739[8] should not succumb to the temptation to make him into an artist who towered above his age in every way. In fact, the cantata "Christ lag in Todesbanden" makes it clear that Bach came only gradually to full mastery of his craft, regardless of any flashes of genius. By basing his cantata's large-scale form on the choral transcription pattern "per omnes versus" (a pattern familiar to every organist), he was on solid compositional ground. Many details in fact attest to an almost naive adoption of organistic practice, for instance the pedal bass in the first verse.

Nonetheless, two decades later, the work still had enough appeal for Bach to have it performed in Leipzig in connection with the choral cantata cycle of 1724–25, which reflects his concern at the highest level with vocal choral music as a form. In the rearrangement, by reinforcing the choral voices with an antiquated-sounding brass ensemble of cornet and trumpet, he takes up the tradition of the Leipzig town band and thus emphasizes in this new version the backward-looking impetus of the first version. Of course neither version should be seen as consciously "historicizing" but rather as a way, quite characteristic of Bach, of using historical styles occasionally in a larger context.

Seen from the point of view of genre history, the cantata "Aus der Tiefen rufe ich, Herr, zu dir," BWV 131, perhaps chronologically the third but in any event certainly composed in Mühlhausen, is a transition from the traditional, psalmic, concerted works of the seventeenth century to the multipart cantatas of the early eighteenth century; as an individual work its concentrated diction is impressive. Again Bach jettisons the original lyrics: he sets in full Psalm 130 of the Luther Bible. The solo parts are kept more monodic instead of being in the modern recitative or aria style. To avoid completely any sense of Italian "suaveness," a strophe of the hymn "Herr Jesu Christ, du höchstes Gut" is included in both vocal solos, as so-called "choral troping" (variations)—a procedure uniquely suited to demonstrate the multilayered quality of Bach's thinking and composing, which characterizes all his sacred vocal music. He could rely on tradition here,[9] but he goes far beyond it in scope and style. The *Actus tragicus* and the *Ratswahl Cantata* (Town Council Electoral Cantata) "Gott ist mein König" also make use of choral troping. The fact that three of the five early cantatas under discussion here use this innovative technique speaks for itself.

BWV 71, "Gott ist mein König," quite in contrast to the compact musical material and rather "quiet" orchestration of cantata BWV 131, is not only splendidly and richly orchestrated but also much more varied in its movements. The text, which was certainly assigned for Bach to set to music, stems more likely from a pastor than an experienced poet. Published at municipal expense, the composition became the first and only printed edition of a Bach work to exist until the Leipzig period, aside from a subsequent work published under similar circumstances, which has been lost. The publication of BWV 71 attests to the self-promotional bent of the free imperial city of Mühlhausen, and the commissioning of Bach attests to the esteem in which the twenty-two-year-old musician was held.

He shows himself even in his first "strong music" (*starcken music*) unmistakably an organist—for instance, in the duet "Ich bin nun achtzig Jahr," composed from start to finish with organ obbligato and the other continuo instruments tacit. In all likelihood he played the organ himself, which figures prominently in the foreground to the end, and also enjoyed the skilled leading voice. Woven into the tenor's vivid account of an old man's difficulties in the maintenance of his duties, and of his readiness for death, is a soprano voice that sings the religiously confident hymn strophe "Soll ich auf dieser Welt mein Leben höher bringen" ("If I should in this world / My life extend yet longer"), using the technique of the ornamented north German organ chorale, changing from the beginning key of E minor to a reassuring G major. Since the organ bass line is innovatively set as a quasi-ostinato, the result is a quartet of highly idiosyncratic voices that shows the complexity, if not yet the density, of Bach's later compositions.

The vocal-instrumental ensemble movement "Du wollest dem Feinde nicht geben die Seele deiner Turteltauben" ("May'st thou to the foe not deliver thy turtledoves' own very spirits") radiates the charm of its uniqueness. While the words in themselves are not particularly sensational, coming as they do from the same Psalm 74, which probably was the author's source in other cases, the music is a showpiece. As if snatching a butterfly from the air, Bach captures a genre composition on paper that for its time, more clearly than any of his other early vocal compositions, has no models.

The singers express their ten-word appeal for sanctuary in a quasi-homophonic movement, carefully marked "affettuoso e larghetto," which largely dispenses with motivic or thematic material and is composed totally of passages of heightening emotion and harmonic asperity. At the end the voices unite in a monotonic, now almost passionless recitation in Phrygian psalm mode. The model for this style of composition is the lament, which in the seventeenth century played a significant role not only in opera but also in instrumental music—not least in the form of the *tombeau*, which in turn is a threnodic variant of the allemande. An allemande can clearly be heard in the melody-leading instrumental part as well, and a comparison with an allemande from Georg Böhm's Harpsichord Suite in F Minor seems plausible.[10]

The "chorus" is embedded in a three-layered instrumental movement: in the higher register a sighing figure is heard, often with an echo effect, carried by oboes, recorders, and violins: this figure soon defines the vocal setting as well. In the middle part an arpeggiated sixteenth-note figure is heard in the cellos, which is imitated by the bassoon in quasi-heterophonic fashion. A staccato passage of quarter notes in small intervals marks the bass register throughout.

Thus, at an early point in time, we have a model for a movement, a model that Bach later used again and again—for instance in the opening chorus of the *St. John Passion:* a nuanced instrumental sound with three characteristic levels and a chorus clearly declaiming in the foreground. Spitta admires the movement as "tone painting,"[11] Schweitzer as "perfect mood music."[12] In anticipation of the nineteenth century one could almost speak of "composition with sound layers" (*Klangflächenkomposition*), a term that seems justified in view of the doubling of cello and bassoon, done not to achieve structure but for color. This heterophony provides a soft, blurred effect, as was then the mode with keyboard instruments. Daniel Vetter, organist of St. Nicholas's Church in Leipzig, deemed it a sign of good taste when "all was sweet and polished" (*alles douce geschleiffet*).[13] But this is only one aspect of the composition: keeping in his mind's eye the turtledove as a symbol of the anxious congregation of the faithful singing through their fears, Bach writes a movement with obvious illustrative and emblematic qualities.

The chamber music style of the movement contrasts with the larger-scale scoring of the outer movements. The opening has an imposing architectural solidity: between two *concertante* sections, whose several vocal and instrumental choruses point to Buxtehude and seem almost traditional, a section is set in which the voices flow polyphonically. The concision of this movement is deliberate, as shown by the end: Bach closes not with the festive sound of trumpets and timpani but in an almost mannerist style, with the quiet echo first of paired oboes, then flutes, unaccompanied even by continuo.

The final movement, on the text "Das neue Regiment," begins *concertante* with several choruses, like the first movement, but then moves into a permutation fugue on the text "Muß täglich von neuem." Carl Philipp Emanuel Bach's statement that it was simply his father's "own peculiarly meditative nature" (*blos eigenes Nachsinnen*) that made him into a "pure and skilled fugue maker even in his youth"[14] is warranted here, for the permutation fugue has something of the puzzle about it: a thematic model is devised whose four parts are interchangeable (see musical example on page 290).

In a second step, the simultaneously sounding voices are fitted horizontally together, as in the first soprano entry of the fugue. Then, once alto, tenor, and bass have entered in sequence in the same manner, and once the responses at the interval of a fifth have been made (the fugue form requires that successive entries alternate in the tonic and dominant), then the first exposition is complete.

Further expositions are essentially the result of rearrangements of the component parts. Interludes in a permutation fugue are rare. This type of fugue was not Bach's "invention" (as, surprisingly, was stated in recent literature);[15] it was already present in Johann Theile's *Musicalisches Kunstbuch*, for example, as well as in instrumental and vocal works of Nicolaus Bruhns. It is possible that Bach approached the permutation fugue largely through self-study—but such an accomplishment should not be overrated either: the "false polyphony" of the permutation fugues can be worked out diagrammatically and are in no way on the same level as a skillfully wrought polyphonic fabric, nor do they meet the specialized requirements of the art of counterpoint, which uses stretti, amplifications, reversions, crabs, and so on.

The fact that Bach writes fugues of this type in his early cantatas, and indeed that he does not eschew them even in his Leipzig period, does not by any means imply that initially he was not up to more exacting methods of this kind of composition. Still, the permutation fugue has its advantages, vocally speaking: it is easy to sing and, because of the frequent vocal entries, enables inexperienced listeners to perceive the imitative principle, without lessening their enjoyment of a clearly, audibly structured work primarily oriented about song or dancelike sections with harmonic underpinnings.

The cantata "Gottes Zeit ist die allerbeste Zeit," called in the sources the *Actus tragicus*, BWV 106, is the best-known early vocal work of Bach. Although it has come down to us only in posthumous copies, the most important of which was completed in 1768 in Leipzig, its authenticity has never been in question: in view of the many technical characteristics typical of the young Bach, there is little reason to doubt that authenticity.

In this cantata there is a total absence of rhyming verse in the style of the madrigal cantata then becoming popular. In the *Bach Compendium* the conjecture is made that the cantata is part of a planned or even completed larger oratorical work. But the compilation of texts comes from traditional devotional works—it consists mainly of biblical text and hymn verses; it appears in similar form among other places in the *Christliche Betschule* of Johann Olearius, printed in 1668.[16] The title line, "Gottes Zeit ist die allerbeste Zeit" (in Latin, "Dei tempus optimum"), comes from neither Bible nor hymnbook; it may have been the motto of the deceased person for whom the work was composed. There were a great many such mottoes in use at the time: "In mortem praeproperam" ("I rush headlong into death") goes a comparable motto in the famous emblem book of Andreas Alciatus.[17]

For Bach experts and enthusiasts of the early nineteenth century, the *Actus tragicus* was *the* rediscovery among the Bach cantatas. They liked the biblical language, which was both earthier and at the same time more intimate than all the rhyming works of the Baroque or Romantic eras: they were moved by the depth of emotion, which they could feel all the more clearly because of the thoroughly old-fashioned form of the work, which avoided completely the da capo aria. To put it briefly, they were excited by a find that beneath its patina of age revealed a youthful freshness and a naive, heartfelt religiosity—qualities on the verge of being lost to Romanticism—a Romanticism that even in its own view was succumbing to exhaustion.

Moritz Hauptmann, who wrote a beautiful transcription of the work in the spirit of the nineteenth century,[18] sees it, from the "musical-architectonic" viewpoint, as a "curious *monstrum* of inter-twining movements heaped on top of one another, just as the phrases of text are similarly cobbled together totally without any grouping principle or high point."[19] Nonetheless, he was rapturous in his praise to the singer and Bach lover Franz Hauser: "It is beautiful beyond all measure, and I know of nothing I would place above the F-minor chorus 'es ist der alte Bund' with the soprano section 'o komm' and the ending—it, too, is so daring and profoundly imaginative, that it reminded me of Beethoven, but never getting out of control."[20]

Felix Mendelssohn Bartholdy also called certain parts of the work "heavenly," "sublime," and "profound."[21] In a letter to his father of 23 March 1835 he shows an astonishing degree of musicological-historical insight:

> *There is something peculiar about this music;—it must fall very early, or very late [in Bach's work], because it is completely different from his usual style of writing in the middle period, and the first choral sections and the final chorus are such that I should never have taken them for Sebastian Bach, but for someone else from that period, whereas no one else could have written one measure of the middle sections.*[22]

Even though the cantata, in its choral framing movements, does not rise above the general run of Protestant church music at the beginning of the eighteenth century, it nonetheless has moments of original-ity, if not genius—even in the opening sonatina. The sonatina brings to mind a pastorale, not just because of the melody played by the recorders but most particularly in view of the heterophony that is carried through more consistently in this passage than in the movement discussed ear-lier from the *Ratswahl Cantata*, "Du wolltest dem Feinde nicht geben." This heterophony clearly recalls practices from the folk idiom and in places could be meant to portray a duet of shepherd flutes.

If its gentle tone reminds us of a pastorale, then this pastorale is surely a sacred one: after taking its leave of this world, the soul finds peace in the pastures of the divine shepherd. In the Weimar cantata "Komm, du süße Todesstunde," BWV 161, a pair of recorders plays to these verses:

> [...] das kühle Grab wird mich mit Rosen decken,
> bis Jesus mich wird auferwecken,
> bis er sein Schaf führt auf die süße Himmelsweide,
> daß mich der Tod nicht von ihm scheide.

> The cooling grave will cover me with roses
> Till Jesus shall me re-awaken,
> Till he his sheep
> Shall lead forth to life's sweetest pasture
> That there e'en death from him not keep me.

In this connection it does not seem beside the point to revisit a hypothesis dating from early Bach scholarship, namely, that the *Actus tragicus* could have been composed on the death of Bach's Erfurt uncle Tobias Lämmerhirt (i.e., "lamb-herd") on 10 August 1707: stylistically the work is a good fit for this period. Indeed, in view of the baroque era's love of all kinds of meaningful allusions, even the suggestion of one of Lämmerhirt's descendants that the scoring with "shepherdlike" recorders is an allusion to the name of the deceased[23] cannot be dismissed out of hand—though of course neither can it be taken as fact.

Bach did not do himself a great favor with the traditional, "quiet" orchestration—a pair each of recorders and violas da gamba. This scoring and its retention throughout the entire work turn out to be a confining choice; for the powerful numbers "Bestelle dein Haus" and "Glorie, Lob, Ehr und Herrlichkeit" in particular, the recorders do not appear to be the ideal instrumentation. This fault obviously does nothing to alter the cantata's moments of true genius, as found especially in the chorus "Es ist der alte Bund, Mensch du mußt sterben." Here Bach brings together four compositional and semantic levels; yet the movement does not seem at all constructed or "worked out"; at each hearing it remains arresting, almost frightening in its immediacy: whoever is touched by music such as this must be mindful of his own death.

With its urgent eighth-note ostinato, the ground bass impresses upon the senses the inevitability of death. In similar fashion at the end of the century, Wolfgang Amadeus Mozart would conceive the "Gesang der Geharnischten" (Chorus of Men in Armor) from *Die Zauberflöte*. Over the implacable forward march of the instrumental bass line the three low voices of the choir, with austere melodic and harmonic changes, give voice to the moral, "Mensch, du mußt sterben," within the formal framework of a fugue. The descending theme can be seen as a "saltus duriusculus," a "hard leap," as it was known in the figural theory of the baroque, while it functions harmonically as a diminished seventh chord. But this point is merely evidence of the work's craft—an awareness of which is sometimes useful or even required, to be sure, but it in no way deprives the work of its mystery.

Despite the demanding polyphony, the phrase "Mensch, du mußt sterben" and in particular the word pair "du mußt" is brought out repeatedly with precise articulation. When the lower voices pause in their moving lament on the coming of death, the basso continuo continues unwaveringly, but the choir's soprano voice enters with the ecstatic plea "Ja komm, Herr Jesu." To keep the whole from dissolving into an erotically charged mystic Pietism, the small instrumental ensemble intervenes with a wordless rendition of the hymn tune "Ich habe mein Sach' Gott heimgestellt," but presented in the richly ornamented fashion of north German organ chorales. The lower voices return, still warning ominously, "Mensch, du mußt sterben," but now with less intensity. The last word comes in a sigh of longing, "Ja komm, Herr Jesu," after all the other voices are gradually muted, a freely lilting coloratura cry against the silence of death, yet an echo too of heavenly joys to come—a *"jubilare sine verbis"* ("rejoicing without words"), as St. Augustine termed the most beautiful legacy of the church music sung by the people of his time.[24]

Some have looked at the entire *Actus tragicus* from the standpoint of its formal symmetry and even found a detailed key plan, an "interference pattern" of textual and musical motifs in the sense of a "theology of form."[25] While the former idea is obviously justified, the latter is at least partially the product by wishful thinking. One can imagine that the young Bach had an inborn sense of form as well as an acquired feel for theology, but it seems unlikely that he would have built this composition, impressive precisely for its liberality of spirit, around an outline that he had worked out to the last detail. Aside from that, for those who love Bach's music for aesthetic reasons, such considerations are secondary in their appreciation of this work, which contains so many different kinds of beauty. Also, an overemphasis on uncovering systems and meanings could lead to the slighting of that organ most important to musicians: the ear.

Bach's early cantatas are actually late, in that they come late in the seventeenth century.[26] In their formal irregularity, the "landscape" of the older mixed cantatas resembles an English park, in which Bach insists on planting his own trees—among them some rare, even exotic. He does not yet indulge himself in the French park of the madrigal cantata, which is then becoming fashionable; its system of regular paths—recitative, da capo aria, second recitative, second da capo aria, and so on—does not for the time being appeal to him.

Initially Bach is not a court composer in the way the librettist Erdmann Neumeister is a court poet. He comes from a tradition of Lutheran sacred music that was distinctively municipal; accordingly, the guiding principle was to craft a musical setting for Bible texts and chorales. He grew up in the town band (Stadtpfeifer) headquarters and loves its colorful settings. He is an organist, which leaves traces in his vocal music. Only on special occasions does he have the chance to produce a sacred cantata and so cannot even start to develop a specific style.

In Weimar, this situation changes. An express condition of

Bach's appointment to the post of concertmaster is the obligation to compose new church pieces every month. Possibly four of the Weimar church cantatas predate his appointment: "Gleich wie der Regen und Schnee vom Himmel fällt," BWV 18; "Mein Herze schwimmt im Blut," BWV 199; "Nun komm, der Heiden Heiland," BWV 61; and, in its earlier version, "Ich hatte viel Bekümmernis," BWV 21. Despite the fact that he included these works in his performance schedule for Weimar immediately after he took up the post of concertmaster, we will look at them now as a little preview of later experimentation in the field of the cantata.

The libretto for "Gleich wie der Regen und Schnee" was written by Erdmann Neumeister in 1711; the mixture of Bible passages, Lutheran litany, chorale, and original texts for recitatives and arias may reflect the poet's attempt to moderate the radicality of his earlier conception of the cantata. Bach provides this motley libretto with an even more motley composition: he opens the work with a sinfonia, the original scoring of which (four violas!) is reminiscent of the Sixth Brandenburg Concerto; in its musical style there is the sense of influence from the Italian concerto style, as well as the extent and detail of a concerto movement.

After the sinfonia comes the cited title words of the prophet as recitative—in a setting part secco, part arioso. This could be the first extant "modern" recitative from a Bach church cantata, while secular examples date from a little earlier: the *Hunt Cantata*, BWV 208. From the start Bach makes clear that in his church recitatives it will not be the familiar parlando of opera or secular cantatas that dominates but a kind of composition that strives for dignity, expressiveness, and lucid presentation of the text—especially in all kinds of biblical texts set for solo voice.

Third is a movement in which Bach, tending to accord with the set text but with a notable heightening of contrast, brings a tenor recitative together with the Lutheran litany. Known as the German Prefatory, in Bach's time this was still common Sunday practice in most churches, but clearly not in Weimar.[27] In Bach's composition, the tenor, in increasingly virtuoso coloratura passages, makes his personal plea, so to speak, for faith and resoluteness against all manner of obstacles, while the chorus imperturbably intones the separate sections of the German Prefatory. The special pleas for intercession fall to the soprano, while the other voices have the repeated refrain "Erhör uns lieber Herre Gott" in the tradition of a false bourdon passage. The four violas participate intensively in all this, and Bach has written an active part even for the basso continuo, which at times positively rages—for example, in asking to be spared the "murderous cruelty, wrathful frenzy of Turk and Pope" or when recalling the persecutions that caused so many Christians to fall away from the faith "like rotten fruit."

A comparison with the like-named cantata of Telemann (for which Erdmann Neumeister's libretto might originally have been written, since the two men were in close contact) shows striking differences. While Bach formally adopts the liturgically customary performance of the prefatory, which has the prayers of intercession sung by a single voice and the chorus enter only at the refrain, Telemann cannot quite manage the realistic assimilation of a segment of everyday liturgy into his cantata: he sets the whole litany as a four-voiced movement but makes it livelier by using a recitative that approximates the pattern of speech. The tenor recitative, on the other hand, is much more conventional:

Glau-ben und fal-len ab wie fau-les Obst, wenn sie Ver-fol-gung sol-len lei-den.

The two composers react quite differently to the task of musically uniting the old and new textual elements of the libretto. While Telemann avoids extremes and in fact attempts to bring liturgical psalmody and modern recitative closer together, Bach highlights the contrast, almost as in a genre painting: with, on the one hand, the liturgical *schola* quietly performing its work, and, on the other, a soloist entering in almost theatrical fashion with his "modern" recitative. What seems in the libretto to be a harmless combination of litany and recitative Bach makes the centerpiece of the entire cantata.

In the following short section on the words "Mein Seelenschatz ist Gottes Wort," he enters what is still new ground for him, the da capo aria, by repeating the eight-measure introductory ritornello at the end of the normally two-part number. The way the four violas are combined in a single, concerted voice has an unusual effect. The cantata ends with a four-voice choral section, "Ich bitt, o Herr, aus Herzensgrund," surely one of the earliest examples of the "typical" Bach final chorale, since the one we have in "Christ lag in Todesbanden," BWV 4, was probably composed later, for Leipzig.

The cantata "Mein Herze schwimmt im Blut," composed for soprano solo and small instrumental ensemble, presents a completely different picture. Though influenced by a hymn verse, the libretto by Darmstadt court poet Georg Christian Lehms consistently follows the recitative-aria pattern. His poetry shows strains of Pietism, not just from the linguistic but also from the theological point of view, in its depiction of the Christian's *mortificatio* and *vivificatio*, that is, the path from mortal consternation at one's own sins, to the confession of guilt, to the happy certainty of faith. This progress is shown as a psychological process, the emphasis placed more on the human change of heart than on God's act of salvation.

It may not be coincidental that Bach specifically chooses this text for one of his first "modern" religious cantatas, that is, a work defined by a regular sequence of recitative and aria, assuming (as above) that in one out of four cases the response to a recitative is not a da capo aria but a hymn strophe. The steps to salvation methodically presented in the text lend themselves well to a series of recitatives and arias, giving emotional weight to each of the situations depicted. Each da capo aria has its own character, but they fit together into a kind of suite. "Stumme Seufzer, stille Klagen," with its flowing sixteenth-note melismata, is oriented on the song style of the Pietist strophic aria but is also close to the slow, melancholy allemande. "Tief gebückt und voller Reue" has the rich tone of a saraband reminiscent of a Handel vocal chaconne; one cannot rule out that the court composer, then not quite thirty years old, may have had his eye on Handel. Bach ends the cantata with the lively gigue "Wie freudig ist mein Herz."

Coming between the saraband and the gigue, the soloistically set hymn strophe "Ich, dein betrübtes Kind," as a trio for soprano, viola obbligato, and basso continuo, is a little gem. While the organ chorale structure shows through, Bach also writes the viola part in a completely *concertante* style: using diminished harmonies (perhaps provoked by the word "Kind" ["child"]), he makes the first line of the hymn the head motif of a ritornello, which the viola elaborates. Thus we have three characteristic musical activities: the unwavering eighth notes of the basso continuo, the sixteenth-note pattern of the viola, and between them the quiet quarter-note motion of the voice. This is a model of the "everything from one" idea that Bach would use repeatedly in the course of his creative work—particularly in arias and organ chorales.

An early version of the cantata "Ich hatte viel Bekümmernis," BWV 21, could have first been heard as a sample piece of Bach's work at Advent 1713 in Halle. But this is speculation, as is the idea that Bach presented another version of the work at the end of 1720 in

Hamburg. It may have been there that Johann Mattheson first heard the cantata. In any event, he subjects it in his *Critica Musica* of 1725 to a thoroughgoing analysis, particularly on the question of the acceptability of textual repetition of the type: "Ich, ich, ich, ich hatte viel Bekümmernis" ("I, I, I, I was in great distress") or, "Komm, mein Jesu, und erquicke (Pause) und erfreu mit deinem Blicke (Pause) komm, mein Jesu, (Pause) komm, mein Jesu, und erquicke, und erfreu…mit deinem Blicke diese Seele…" ("Come, my Jesus, and refresh [pause] and gladden with your gaze [pause] come, my Jesus, [pause] come, my Jesus, and refresh, and gladden…with your gaze this soul…").[28]

Most readers have taken Mattheson's text as a condescending and lightly sarcastic criticism of Bach. On closer reading, though, it turns out that Mattheson is defending Bach's work against a rule of composition proposed by Heinrich Bokemeyer, the cantor of Wolfenbüttel, which set the strictest conditions on textual repetitions, even forbidding them altogether "if pauses are inserted between them."[29]

So the citation does not at all fit the popular complaint that torrents of criticism were poured on a misunderstood Bach, because of his supposedly "meaningless verbal stutterings";[30] on the contrary, it highlights a lively musical aesthetic exchange then taking place on the genre of the religious cantata. We do not know to what extent Bach's church music was debated; but the fact that it was is attested to not only by occasional public discussions but also by copies of the music that circulated among his pupils and friends and were certainly not always received with reverent awe. There exists a copy of the Weimar cantata "Widerstehe doch der Sünde," BWV 54, made by Bach's pupil Johann Tobias Krebs the elder, with the help of Johann Gottfried Walther, probably soon after its composition. We shall see what special features may have encouraged discourse on Bach's compositional style: sacred music was a subject not just for musical but also for theological discussion.

Particularly in the case of "Ich hatte viel Bekümmernis," we today can still profit from taking part in yesterday's discourse by examining the cantata's head motif: is it a lucky inspiration to place the three exclamations, "Ich, ich, ich," at the beginning and to let the complete phrase "Ich hatte viel Bekümmernis" be heard only afterward? Can this compositional choice be compared with the grandiose beginning of the motet "Komm, Jesu komm," where the thrice-repeated "Komm" prepares the listener, with the help of a rhetorical climax, for that fervency of feeling that saturates the whole work?

Bach's intent, so goes the answer, is different: he is appropriating the head motif of a typical Italian concerto movement into religious vocal music; one experiences the main theme of the introduction instrumentally, indeed organically. It appears again in similar form, not just in his mentor Buxtehude but also in his own organ fugue BWV 541, a fair copy of which comes down to us from the 1730s, but which probably dates from the Weimar period.[31] Later in the course of the movement, in an almost experimental fashion, Bach strings together musical segments as a canon; the beginning of thinking in large thematic, harmonic blocks, as in the modern concerto style, is evident here.

As a whole the cantata has a rather motley sequence of movements, which in many places harks back to the older mixed cantata, but this feature can probably be explained by the work's history. There is speculation about an earlier version that included neither the opening sinfonia nor the final chorale, "Das Lamm, das erwürget ist," with its conspicuously incongruous trumpet scoring. The core of the work would have been the dialogue between Christ and the soul,[32] interesting enough in itself. For example, the da capo aria

"Seufzer, Tränen, Kummer, Not" is remarkable in its mixture of brevity and motivic density; nearly all the movement's material derives substantially from the top of the opening ritornello.

Nonetheless the effect of the movement is due not so much to its craft as to its emotional impact, from the traditional topoi of suffering, to be found in the dissonant suspensions in ninth and second intervals and the descending minor second. This succinct combining of form with emotional content is without doubt the mature Bach, while one can still find much of the young Bach in the choral setting "Was betrübst du dich, meine Seele, und bist so unruhig in mir," which follows soon after: the start of the text is set in the sense of a madrigalic motet of the seventeenth century; the instruments initially reinforce an air of unrest with irregular complementary rhythms.

After a brief, mostly homophonically set plea, "Harre auf Gott; denn ich werde ihm noch danken," there follows a permutation fugue on the words "daß er meines Angesichtes Hülfe, und mein Gott ist." Here Bach is using the religious musical tradition of his predecessors, in the loosely connected series of segments as well as in the motet-like movement "Sei nun wieder zufrieden, meine Seele," which is enriched by the addition of the cantus firmus "Was helfen uns die schweren Sorgen." The opening sinfonia, with its refined chamber-music quality, strengthens the impression of a work in progress combining old and new.

With the Advent cantata "Nun komm, der Heiden Heiland," BWV 61, we have a different situation: Erdmann Neumeister's libretto, probably printed in 1714, inspired Bach to an individual yet stylistically homogeneous composition, in which the desire for modernity and courtly grace is apparent throughout. In the first movement he starts with a French overture with its traditional formal sequence, providing for a solemn beginning with dotted bass rhythms, a dance-like fugal central part, and a return to the beginning. This movement is an overture not in the usual sense but in a vocal-instrumental sense: the chorale strophe "Nun komm der Heiden Heiland" is incorporated both textually and musically, such that this savior is received like a triumphant ruler. This device had been used in opera for ages,[33] but to hear it with such effect in church music is something new. A refined tone is retained in the recitatives and da capo arias that follow, and the violin figures give even the traditionally worked-out final chorus an air of virtuosic brilliance.

After Bach is appointed concertmaster on 2 March 1714, in light of his commitment to the monthly creation of sacred works, a new era of cantata composition begins. But is it really a new era? Bach's penchant for experiment and variety continues, even if it is kept within bounds by the need to follow preset libretti. The poet of the court is consistory secretary Salomon Franck, whose duties also include the library and the coin collection. Today we know that Bach composed seventeen cantatas from Franck's *Evangelisches Andachts-Opffer* (Protestant Worship Offering). Some anonymous cantata texts that Bach set in Weimar may have come as well from Franck, who was not so faithful, admittedly, in the fulfillment of his duties that Bach could avoid the occasional need to revert to the libretti of other poets.[34]

The libretti that Bach set in Weimar can be described as patterns for "moderated" madrigalian cantatas: their texts are as a rule freely composed verses that serve as the basis for the opening chorus, recitatives, arias, and in exceptional cases the final chorus. Now and then Bible texts appear set as solos—as the Vox Christi, for example; at the end there is usually a chorus, performed in a simple setting note for note, in the Middle German tradition. For Bach, these preset texts could have been both confining and inspiring. He had to do without the choral setting of Bible words at the beginning; nor would there have been much opportunity for large-scale choral treatments. (He would turn to both of these forms in the Leipzig cantata cycles of 1723–24 and 1724–25.)

On the other hand, a concentrated focus on "free" poetical texts would have had distinct advantages. The least obvious is that the choral "poverty" of the texts induced Bach repeatedly to "smuggle" instrumental cantus firmus into his settings of free poetic texts, thus allowing him to create a compositional fabric more richly allusive in both music and content. A good example of such smuggling is the cantata "Alles, was von Gott geboren," BWV 80a, on a text of Salomon Franck. The pattern for the opening statement is a five-verse text, which apparently Bach neither wishes nor is able to set as a sufficiently impressive choral movement. So, as elsewhere, he must make do with a small solution, that is, start with an aria on the text:

> Alles was von Gott geboren, ist zum Siegen auserkoren.
> Wer bei Christi Blutpanier in der Taufe Treu geschworen,
> Siegt im Geiste für und für.

> All that which of God is fathered
> Is for victory intended.
> What by Christ's own bloodstained flag
> In baptism hath been promised
> Wins in Christ for evermore.

But here it seems to him too small a solution: to increase the importance of the aria as an opening statement, he adds an impressive instrumental cantus firmus, namely, that of the chorale "Ein feste Burg ist unser Gott." This was in accord with the libretto, ending as it did with the strophe "Mit unsrer Macht ist nichts getan," which comes from precisely this Luther chorale. Those attending church services at the Weimar court must surely have wondered which strophe Bach likely had in mind (if they recognized the music at all) in this purely instrumental reference within the introductory aria. Today we know more, for Bach gave a text to the instrumental cantus firmus when he revised cantata BWV 80a in Leipzig, putting to it that exact choral strophe that had been the conclusion of the Weimar version:

Mit unsrer Macht ist nichts getan, wir sind gar bald verloren.
Es streit' für uns der rechte Mann, den Gott selbst hat erkoren.
Fragst du, wer er ist? Er heißt Jesus Christ, der Herr Zebaoth,
Und ist dein andrer Gott, das Feld muß er behalten.

With our own might is nothing done, we face so soon destruction.
He strives for us, the righteous man, whom God himself hath chosen.
Ask thou who he is? His name: Jesus Christ, The Lord of Sabaoth,
There is no other god, the field is his forever.

In retrospect it is clear that with his interpolation of a cantus firmus, the Weimar Bach has given us a proper exegesis of his librettist's aria text: we ourselves, he emphasizes, are in no way "destined to be victorious"; rather we are weak human beings who would "soon be lost" in our struggles if Christ were not fighting for us; it is not we but he who is victorious! Franck had first expressed this idea in the final chorale; Bach brings it out, in the Lutheran sense of "simul iustus et peccator" from the beginning.*

One might ask whether an artist and thinker as great as Bach might not occasionally have been able to write librettos of the same quality as the ones given him to set to music, and whether there was anything preventing this other than guidelines of hierarchical authority, professional restrictions, or lack of time. For now the question seems moot; however, the process described above suggests that Bach often engaged himself intensively with the theological implications of the libretti presented him. At the risk of overinterpretation, one could speculate that in this instance he wanted to give an account

---

*"righteous and sinning at the same time": a phrase coined by Luther to describe the state of the Christian believer.

of his own religious beliefs to the Weimar Ducal Consistorial Secretary, about whose theological training little is known.

Against this background, the revision history of the cantata deserves further comment. When Bach was in Leipzig, perhaps even during work on the cantata cycle of 1724–25, he needed a cantata for the Feast of the Reformation and so made use of a practice by no means unusual for him—revising an already completed work for a new situation. In this he refers back to his Weimar cantata, which admittedly was meant for the Oculi (third) Sunday of Lent and was connected only superficially to the Reformation by the fact that the final choral uses one strophe of "Ein feste Burg," traditionally heard at the Feast of the Reformation. But there is also that hidden connection, namely, the instrumental cantus firmus in the opening aria.

Apparently this connection is enough to prompt Bach to rework a cantata for Oculi Sunday into a choral cantata for Reformation Sunday, although further steps are necessary: the aria, "Alles, was von Gott geboren," which came first in the Weimar version, now becomes number 2; the head movement is now a still simple choral setting of the first strophe of the chorale "Ein feste Burg." He also adds a choral aria on the strophe "Und wenn die Welt voll Teufel wär," and finally he needs a new final chorale, since the strophe "mit unserer Macht ist nichts getan" has already been used (in the instrumental cantus firmus). Bach selects the regular final strophe of the Lutheran hymn: "Das Wort sie sollen lassen stahn." In this version, the new cantata BWV 80, BC 183a, was completed by 1727–31. Later (perhaps not until 1744–47) he visits the work a third time, composing as the opening movement that lengthy and splendid choral setting of "Ein feste Burg" by which the work has remained known to the present day.

What a long way this cantata journeyed before reaching its definitive version—not only compositionally but theologically as well! From a cantata predominantly for solo voices, as was determined for Bach by the Weimar libretto, has come a concerted work that starts with an imposing choral setting. From a work primarily devoted to the individual Christian soul has come one that encompasses the religious experience of the entire congregation. In contrast to the Weimar version, the more subjective solo numbers, such as "Komm in mein Herzenshaus, Herr Jesu, mein Verlangen" and "Wie selig ist der Leib, der Jesu dich getragen," no longer occupy a central place in the work but are retained with minor textual adjustments in a more comprehensive context. All in all, a cantata whose words and music were tinged with Pietism has been transformed into a document of genuine Lutheran church music.

It was apparently heralded as such among Bach's circle and after his death—not by Wilhelm Friedemann Bach, who set the opening theme to a Latin text, "Gaudete omnes populi," for a performance in Halle, but probably by pupils like Johann Christoph Altnickol, whose copy of the score became the basis for the first printing, arranged by the Dessau cantor Friedrich Schneider in 1821, to the delight of the influential music scholar Friedrich Rochlitz. Rochlitz devoted an extensive article to the work in his *Allgemeine musikalische Zeitung* the following year, where he particularly emphasized the "wonderful combinations" of the opening chorus and recommended that "the congregation join in" in the final chorale.[35]

A person looking at the history of this one work only might ask whether the findings of source research, which itself has a hypothetical bent, have perhaps been too intensively mined to allow far-reaching conclusions. But in the light of comparable cases we can speak of a *structure* to Bach's compositional strategy, elements of which can meaningfully be brought out, even if one or another individual instance proves invalid. In the present case, one could even pursue further the influence of this element in Bach's theological and compositional thinking: the salient point with the Reformation cantata is not that, to save work, he resorted to revision but that he wanted to create a model for Lutheran church music that would endure.

As a church composer, Bach did not merely survive in the byways of musical tradition, relying on the merits of his "dated" madrigalian cantatas, only later undergoing a powerful renaissance. He was always alive and regarded as a classic figure in Lutheran liturgical music, which by the nineteenth century was no longer seen as confessional music but understood in the sense of its own musical mythology. Bach, transcending his personality, contributed to the creation of this mythology. His B-Minor Mass is one of the crowning achievements of his life and was his bid to write himself into liturgical music history with all the stylistic variety and power of musical language available to him. There will be more discussion later of this kind of universal thinking. But cantata BWV 80 shows Bach already on the way to a Lutheran universalism.

We return to the advantages that Bach at Weimar could have found in focusing on freely composed texts, and consider the opening choruses. In the seventeenth century choruses on scriptural texts or hymn melodies tended to be composed either as motets with continuo accompaniment or as fully concerted works for instrumental-vocal groups; of course there were various mixtures and special forms. In all cases, the structure would be determined in large measure either by the scale of the scriptural text or by a cantus firmus that had to follow the text line by line. The resulting sequential structure was in direct opposition to the sense of form of the modern Italian concerto, which dealt in well-defined harmonic blocks, achieved contrastive effects by alternating solo and tutti sections, and imparted an overall formal symmetry through the frequent use of da capo passages.

But if the text came from a librettist, the composer was generally guaranteed at the start that it comprised only a few lines, making a da capo structure possible and giving the composer an opportunity to plan a modern concerto movement. The first three cantatas that Bach composed after his appointment as concertmaster put this idea to the test. The respective head movements all have texts composed by Salomon Franck:

> Himmelskönig, sei willkommen,
> laß auch uns dein Zion sein!

Komm herein!
Du hast uns das Herz genommen. (BWV 182)

King of heaven, thou art welcome,
Let e'en us thy Zion be!
Come inside!
Thou hast won our hearts completely.

Weinen, Klagen, Sorgen, Zagen,
Angst und Not
sind der Christen Tränenbrot,
die das Zeichen Jesu tragen. (BWV 12)

Weeping, wailing
Grieving, fearing
Dread and need,
Are the Christians' tearful bread,
Them the sign of Jesus bearing.

Erschallet, ihr Lieder, erklinget, ihr Saiten!
O selige Zeiten!
Gott will sich die Seelen zu Tempeln bereiten. (BWV 172)

Resound now, ye lyrics, ring out now, ye lyres!
O happiest hours!
God shall all the souls to his temples now gather.

One sees at a glance that the composer does not have to accommodate long, unwieldy texts. The verses are flexible, well suited to the da capo form, which Bach makes use of in all three—for the first time in the Weimar church cantatas. What is more, the opening chorus of "Erschallet, ihr Lieder," BWV 172, turns out to be so sleekly "Italian" that some have suspected it was originally modeled on a secular tribute (or congratulatory) cantata, which has been lost.[36] It is of course conceivable that Bach, eager to experiment with new forms, threw himself into the religious cantata possibilities present in the new Italian concerto style; this effort could be seen as a parallel to the *concertante* garb he gave to certain organ works of this period.

But whichever interpretation one prefers, "Erschallet, ihr Lieder" is almost the prototype of a certain type of D-major chorus, secular here but later recycled in spiritual works of the Leipzig period—for example, the opening chorus for the *Christmas Oratorio,* "Tönet, ihr Pauken, erschallet, Trompeten" / "Jauchzet, frohlocket, auf, preiset die Tage."* The grouping of trumpets and timpani makes for a particularly festive impression; melodically, the main section is triadic, essentially chordal, and clearly structured in extended harmonic cadences as well as brief, *concertante* instrumental intervals. The contrasting middle section is set in the relative minor key of one of the major segments; freely polyphonic, more motet-like than *concertante,* it accordingly allots only a secondary role to the instruments.

In the opening choruses to the two cantatas composed immediately before this one, Bach shows that he can treat da capo form quite differently from the modern concerted style. In "Himmelskönig, sei willkommen," BWV 182, he picks up on his mentor Buxtehude's exuberance and writes a permutation fugue that might have been meant as a welcoming round dance—in any case it has a thoroughly dancelike character. If this movement creates the impression that the kapellmeister in his first work was cautiously staying with familiar compositional styles, then his opening motive in "Weinen, Klagen, Sorgen, Zagen," BWV 12, performed four weeks later, seems all the more daring. Above a four-measure ostinato figure known in musical figure theory as a passus duriusculus—that is, a sequence of hard or chromatic descending fourths—a freely polyphonic ex-

---

*"Sound, all ye drums now! Resound, all ye trumpets!" (BWV 172) / "Triumph, rejoicing, rise, praising these days now" (BWV 248, I). The former is a lyric from a secular work, the latter from a Christmas oratorio.

change characterized by harmonic frictions is developed between instruments and voices: the voices introduce a sort of lament with a chromatically sharped melody, which the instruments answer with stereotypic figures of implacability:

Bach meets the poet's challenge to realize in musical terms the variety of his text, with its use of rhyming asyndeton, a rhetorical device of loosely linked ideas derived from the same conceptual area: at the start of a movement, unusually for Bach, each word of the opening phrase is sung by a different voice. Toward the end of the motet-like middle part of the chorus, at the words "Zeichen Jesu" there is a conspicuous voice leading that is not strictly called for by the musical context. In extended note values, this tonal sequence appears: F–B-flat–E-flat–A-flat. If we combine the two outer with the two inner note heads, we get a figure in the form of an X, which could stand on the one hand for the cross—note "Xisten," Bach's shorthand usage in the score for "Christians"—and on the other hand for the letter chi, in Christian symbolism the often used first letter of the Greek word "Christ."[37]

No matter how important it is for Bach in the context of artistic creativity to follow the meaning of a text in every detail, his music is hardly ever exhausted by its representational or symbolic function. It works with figures per se, figures that, while not semantically neutral, are open, their sources more remote than it might at first seem. Thus he could transform the gesture of subjective lamentation—by descending from the minor sixth to the fifth—years later in the B-Minor Mass, underlaying it with other texts and phrases, into the objective process of the Crucifixion:

Bach also set the chorus "Christen, ätzet diesen Tag," from the like-named Christmas cantata BWV 63, splendidly and unusually scored for four trumpets and three oboes, in da capo form. It is related to the chorus "Erschallet, ihr Lieder," which also is written in a courtly-secular tone and conceivably for a place beyond Weimar; it may be a parodic use of a secular template.[38]

In the opening choruses of the four other Weimar cantatas, Bach dispenses with true da capo form, although the textual patterns here too might have suggested it. Instead, he experiments with combinations of fugal, motet-like, and *concertante* motifs, but neither does he reject the symmetry of the da capo or the rondo form. Three of these opening choruses—"Der Himmel lacht! Die Erde jubiliert," BWV 31; "Ärgre dich, o Seele, nicht," BWV 168a; and "Herz und Mund und Tat und Leben," BWV 147a—contain extended fugal sections that are not based on the permutation principle. In the fourth of the choruses mentioned—"Wachet! Betet!" from the cantata of the same name, BWV 70a—at the end of his Weimar period, for the first time he tries out the technique of incorporating the chorus within a free-standing instrumental section, where sometimes the orchestra, sometimes the choir, is dominant.

The remaining Weimar cantatas make do without introductory choruses: perhaps Bach had himself decided to give up his original idea of beginning every cantata with a large chorus; or perhaps the attitude of the court made this idea seem inadvisable or impracticable. In any event, in the religious music of Bach's Weimar period there are many solo cantatas in which the chorus does not appear until the finale, being preceded by recitatives and arias in various sequences.

But occasionally in these solo cantatas we can see Bach's will break through: his desire to replace the missing choral introduction, by turning the opening aria into a significant head motif: an example of this is the opening aria "Widerstehe doch der Sünde" in the cantata of the same name, BWV 54. The work could have been meant for Oculi Sunday 1715, but there are no concrete indications of this. The brief libretto, limited to a succinct listing of numbers in the form aria-recitative-aria, was not written by the Weimar court poet Salomon Franck, nor is the score in Bach's hand. But as mentioned above, there was a special interest in this cantata among the students and friends of Bach's Weimar circle—understandable in the light of its opening section alone, which Wilhelm Rust, the cantata editor of the old Bach *Gesamtausgabe,* had already deemed an "historic event."[39] Bach starts with the seventh chord, which "frightened" Albert Schweitzer: "Through the quavering basses and violas and the sighing violins the piece takes on a distinctly uncanny sense; in this way it attempts to portray the horror of...sin, the menacing curse throughout the text."[40]

Arnold Schering sees the score from another perspective:

This introduction doesn't contain even a hint of the horrific image of sin: rather, it is the portrait of a soul, gaining energy but initially weak, in agonizing and unceasing struggle to free itself from heavy shackles. Bach does not paint sound portraits here; he is dealing in psychology. With that chord whose sharply dissonant second has its effect even without coarse emphasis, Bach gives us something like the sinner's first reflexive movement in his attempt to throw off the devil, and thus he leads us straightaway into the agonies of conscience. If sin appeared to human eyes as something unspeakably horrible, the struggle against it would not be a heroic deed. But unfortunately sin is "wondrously beautiful seen from without." And Bach stresses this by giving the whole work in melody and sound a sort of "lustful" quality (in the idiom of the period), making it at the same time seem alluring, blandishing. Surely a portion of Bach's incredible genius resides in his artfulness at this kind of double symbolism—here, shown in the heart's opposition and will to resist, as against the snares and temptations of sensuality—capturing this all in one and the same musical selection.[41]

We may find Schering's interpretation of the dual symbol of resistance and temptation more precise than Schweitzer's notion of an uncanny, threating curse; we may even recall the plausible conjecture of some Bach scholars that, in his Leipzig period, Bach took up the section again in the *St. Mark Passion*, BWV 247 (now lost), setting to it the new text "Falsche Welt, dein schmeichelnd Küssen ist der frommen Seelen Gift" ("Untrue world, thy fawning kisses / Are to righteous souls a bane"), thus documenting that even without detailed precise connection to a specific textual meaning, his music had enormous linguistic power.

But it is more productive to look at the compositional means Bach uses to achieve his effects. It is of course not remarkable that he finds musical images and symbols for key textual concepts—sin, temptation, resistance—for such was routine procedure for a baroque master composer working in the tradition of *musica poetica*. More fascinating is how he deals with these topoi: seen harmonically, the introductory ritornello is composed as a single, ten-measure-long resistance against the tonic—the key, that is, where a piece normally begins.

That Bach begins with a dissonance is in itself remarkable; however, the same sound—namely, dominant plus dominant seventh chord—also comes at the start of another cantata, "Nun komm der Heiden Heiland," BWV 61, composed around the same time, where the voice of Christ in *recitativo accompagnato* sings, "Siehe, siehe, ich stehe vor der Tür und klopfe an," here too with the intention of rousing Christendom to rise up in the struggle against sin. More exciting is that Bach begins with a form that, structurally speaking, one might have expected to hear only after the composition had attained a critical tension, leading either to the reprise, or, acting as an extended suspension, go into the final key.

In his *The Compleat Capellmeister* of 1739, Johann Mattheson recommends that beginning composers structure their works in six sections in accordance with the rules of rhetoric: Exordium, Narratio, Propositio, Confutatio, Confirmatio, and Conclusio, or, in his words, "Introduction and Beginning, Narrative, Content or Purpose of the Tonal Discourse (*Klangrede*), Resolution (*Auflösung*) of Objections (Rebuttal of Counterarguments), Reinforcement of the Argument, Outcome or Conclusion." The author demonstrates what can occur within the Confutatio using an aria of Benedetto Marcello: the composer works with "allied ideas (*Bindungen*) and opposed ideas (by which is meant dissenting and dissonant objections) until he happily frustrates the Confutation, resolves it and brings his 'Periodum' to an end a fourth from the tonic; at which point the Continuo takes up the complete theme, by means of another repetition at a fourth interval, and changes it all around anew..." After further Confutationes the theme returns in the da capo section as Confirmatio and Conclusio.[42]

To date there has not been sufficient research to know how much Bach was in agreement with Mattheson's suggestions for the "disposition," that is, the "nice arrangement of all parts"of a piece.[43] But in the aria "Widerstehe doch der Sünde," it can be seen that he uses one section, which in an aria one would ordinarily assume to be a Confutatio, as an Exordium. This departure should be noted by those who want to find Bach in agreement with contemporary systems of rhetoric, poetics, emblematics, and composition. In creativity, inspiration is apt to contradict the norms of the time. One type of musical genius lies in the ability to set imagination and technique in opposition in ever new combinations. Unlike norms, such oppositions cannot be repeated constantly in the artistic realm.

It was to be three generations before Beethoven would begin a work with a dissonance—the First Symphony. But here too it is not just a single dissonance; the seventh chord heard at the outset is the first link in a chain of chords that in the truest sense of the word searches for the tonic; it is not, as in Bach, an expression of resistance but of seeking, feeling one's way. There are not many such beginnings in music history. Johannes Brahms, who as a young man criticized Robert Schumann for beginning a movement with a seventh chord ("wie glückich sie wandeln, die seligen Geister" from the oratorio *Das Paradies und die Peri*),[44] himself structured the opening of his First Symphony, in many ways modeled on the opening chorus of the *St. Matthew Passion,* as a kind of meditation on the question of how to begin, although he did not begin with a dissonant chord.

Brahms acts with great respect for the tradition of Beethoven's structural thinking, of Bach's courageous exegesis, forgetting his musical craft to intensify the meaning of the given text—intensified because the demand Resist! is not just conveyed through symbols or images but is experienced directly on the plane of energy: even before the singer starts the line "Widerstehe doch der Sünde," the opening ritornello has brought into the listener's consciousness the process of resistance, through its drawn-out eighth-note figures in the bass and spasmodic eighth-note viola passages. At the same time the gestures of flattery in the violin, and later sung by the alto, presumably standing for the beguiling words of Satan in serpent form, are present but less obvious by comparison: they do not violate convention either compositionally or in the impression they make on the listener. This contrast corresponds with the text: the temptations a Christian is subject to enter on light feet; resisting them requires an effort whose musical equivalent bores into the listener's ear.

We would have been satisfied if Bach had composed an aria portraying both aspects of Satan—the flattering and the corrupting— at once, the latter perhaps through the diminished triad, as in fact it is used several times in the cantata on the theme of sin. But here, once again in Bach's work, we come upon a particularly fine jewel, whose radiance is the result of a principled willingness to transgress the traditional boundaries of composition.

Another novelty is the middle section on the three lines "Laß dich nicht den Satan blenden; denn die Gottes Ehre schänden, trifft ein Fluch, der tödlich ist" ("Be thou not by Satan blinded, / For God's glory to dishonor / Brings a curse of fatal doom"). In the first appearance of this text the vocal part is so simple and songlike that it could almost have come from a Pietist hymnal of the time, were it not for the continuo. The continuo does not provide a simple harmonization of the melody; in deliberate disharmony it grates with the alto voice, and even then surprises us with a false ending at the words that speak of God's deadly curse.

Nonetheless the basso continuo line does not seem too alien, for it takes up faithfully the flattering theme of the ritornello, also present all through the middle section, which is sensible both musically and textually: the ritornello theme, as so often in Bach, acts to identify and unify the entire aria, even in the traditionally contrastive middle section; at the same time it is clear that the seductiveness of sin remains the issue.

From this one example, certain basic things about Bach's relation to the da capo aria can be seen: he doesn't use the pattern to highlight the A-B-A form, which lets the singer make an effective presentation. As a composer who is writing not primarily for singers, he does not care to fill a preset and unchanging symmetrical formal structure with constantly new and interesting content. Even the da capo form, which he only approximates here, is solely the basis for a musical statement, a statement characterized less by general form than by individual structure. The structure grows out of motives and themes musically immanent in the work, clearly, but that also derive special meaning from the text. Conversely, the text profits from both the organizing and emotional power of music through the application of these motives and themes.

The cantata's next recitative shows in exemplary fashion what Bach even in his Weimar period could do with a secco passage. In the first part, exciting harmonic changes and combinations of sounds suffice for ideas such as "distress," "vain shadow," "whited sepulchre," and "apples of Sodom" to emerge vividly without need of further rhetorical effort. In the final part, the image of sin, as a sharp sword that passes through body and soul, sets off an agitated sixteenth-note figure in the continuo.

Even in the final aria, the librettist Georg Christian Lehms, who usually favors warmer, Pietist tones, cannot let go of the theme of sin and judgment: "Who commits sin is of the devil, for he has brought sin into the world" ("Wer Sünde tut, der ist vom Teufel, / Denn dieser hat sie aufgebracht"). It continues on a more conciliatory note, though still didactically: "But when we resist its evil bondage with righteous reverence, sin is put to flight directly" ("Doch wenn man ihren schnöden Banden / Mit rechter Andacht widerstanden, / Hat sie sich gleich davongemacht").

What can a composer do who wants to stay close to the text? In the first aria he has already presented a tableau of sin, temptation, and resistance; the set text rules out the possibility of a lively, dance-like ending that reflects the conviction of the Christian. But Bach is equal to the task: he composes a strict fugal aria—his first, as far as we know today—and so gives the exegetical and compositional needs of the work their due. The strict form of the fugue calls attention to the warning against sin—particularly where the subject of the fugue traces an abrasive, chromatic course, which has traditionally been expressive of suffering and straying: in it the continuo moves almost constantly in eighth notes, relentless and inexorable. Particularly with Bach, fugues have their individual character. As a text, "Himmelskönig sei willkommen" demands a different type of fugue than "Weinen, Klagen, Sorgen, Zagen" or even "Wer Sünde tut, der ist vom Teufel."

Inspiration gives Bach a chance to make progress in the fugue form. While the section is essentially based on permutation, it has many idiosyncrasies: the fugue's opening statement also serves as a ritornello-aria; the middle section of the aria, in a free da capo form, displays *concertante* elements, especially in its vivid portrayal of sin in retreat, but has stretto string passages and interesting harmonic digressions as well. Albert Schweitzer said succinctly, "Harmonically this piece is of unequaled harshness."[45] In the last five measures of the aria, the appearance of the fugue theme in the exposed bass register, like an organ pedal part, reminds us that here is a professional organist at work. We wonder whether the entire cantata might not be meant as a three-part work analogous to the prelude-adagio-fugue form Bach tended to use in Weimar. The cantata is a masterpiece *sui generis*.

"Widerstehe doch der Sünde" is, moreover, one of the few Bach Weimar cantatas to do without a chorale or choral citation. Many other cantatas on freely composed texts contain arias with instruments that quote from chorales—as for example the head section "Komm, du suße Todesstunde" from the above-mentioned cantata of the same name, BWV 161. Bach provides an organ obbligato and expressly requires the sesquialtera register for performing the hymn "Herzlich tut mich verlangen nach einem sel'gen End." This obbligato is interwoven with the alto part, whose tone is taken from the

Pietist aria, and is softly accompanied by two recorders. The whole has a mystical, gentle feeling that continues even when the recorders, with the strings, persistently mark a tolling death knell, in the recitative heard later, "so schlage doch, du letzter Stundenschlag."

The next number shifts the movement and intensity of feeling of the strophic aria, usually a solo, to the chorus:

Wenn es meines Gottes Wille, wünsch ich, daß des Leibes Last
Heute noch die Erde fülle, und der Geist, des Leibes Gast,
Mit Unsterblichkeit sich kleide in der süßen Himmelsfreude.
Jesu, komm und nimm mich fort! Dieses sei mein letztes Wort.

If it is my God's intention, I wish that my body's weight
Might today the earth make fuller, and my ghost, my body's guest,
Life immortal take for raiment in the sweet delight of heaven.
Jesus, come and take me hence! May this be my final word.

Bach has set this strophe of Salomon Franck, orthodox but with a Pietist spirit, in a manner both movingly simple and very artful: the "chorus"—in Weimar, probably an ensemble of four voices—intones this spiritual minuet in a loosely homophonic setting, alternating with the strings, which are given a kind of ritornello to play in straightforward fashion. The pair of recorders provide a pastoral overlay, and their rapid figures, played quietly and tranquilly, not overly *concertante,* act as a filigree frame to surround this movement, which is saturated both with the longing for death and the expectation of heaven.

During his Leipzig period, the unique chamber-music intimacy of the Weimar version was compromised by replacing the recorders with transverse flutes throughout, supporting the cantus firmus of the head motif with a text and reinforcing the flutes with violins. But no matter how appropriate it may be to clarify the text and reinforce the sound in a different situation, the later version, which may have been done without Bach's collaboration, does not preserve the charm of the Weimar setting.

For a librettist touched with Pietism, as was Franck, even an Easter cantata can express a soul's desire for imminent union with Jesus—as in the cantata BWV 31, "Der Himmel lacht! Die Erde jubilieret," with the aria "Letzte Stunde, brich herein" ("Come unto me, final hour"). This time the strings introduce the melody, "Wenn mein Stündlein vorhanden ist," in the aria segment, where Bach, with some effort, successfully combined the formal principles of strophic song and da capo aria. The result, for Heinrich Besseler, is a "spiritual lullaby," an example of "expressive melody" for which the Weimar Bach led the way.[46]

Choral tropings of this type have a special connection to the musical traditions of the Bach family; at the same time they are an important component of Bach's own compositional style. When later on he inserts the instrumental cantus firmus "O Lamm Gottes unschuldig" into the eight-part introductory chorus of the *St. Matthew Passion*, requiring once again the use of the sesquialtera register on the organ, we can see him learning how to compose from his own experience from multiple perspectives.

Toward the end of his Weimar period, Bach again achieves a great success in the genre. In the cantata "Wachet! Betet," BWV 70a, possibly written for the second Sunday of Advent, 1716, he uses the biblical report of the second coming of Christ, thematized in his libretto, to make a powerful, even theatrical presentation of the terrors of the Last Judgment and blessed salvation in Christ. The above-mentioned introductory chorus represents an extended wake-up call, which starts with an ordinary trumpet call and soon leads to a dramatic surge of voices. As if in anticipation of the people's choruses in the great passions, Bach has the singers use a variety of gestures, sometimes driving the musical process ahead, sometimes retarding it, setting up a dynamic that goes well beyond the norm of a well-proportioned concert movement.

Excitement builds in the bass aria "Seligster Erquickungstag, führe mich zu deinen Zimmern." Bach sets these words with a mixture of Pietist simplicity and Handel-like calm, but then lets loose a true theatrical storm in the central portion, to the text "Schalle, knalle, letzter Tag, Welt und Himmel, geht zu Trümmern!" The closing lines, "Jesus führet mich zur Stille, an den Ort, da Lust die Fülle," find their way back to the rapturous tone of the beginning. Seldom indeed is the Bach lover made so aware, not just of how much Bach is personally involved in his compositions, but also of the naive joy the baroque artist takes in moving the "levers of fear, of awe, of horror," to insert here, somewhat anachronistically, E. T. A. Hoffmann's thoughts on Beethoven's Fifth Symphony.[47]

The dynamic, abruptly alternating moods of the above aria have been compared with the drama of an opera scene of Keiser,[48] which implicitly raises the question of what Bach may have known of early German operas, such as those of Reinhard Keiser or George Frideric Handel. In any case, despite his commitment to compose "unoperatically" ("nicht opernhafftig"), he presented this cantata in Leipzig, not only on multiple occasions but with the addition of two strongly gestural, contrastive, and powerfully scored recitatives, which visibly strengthen the dramatic quality of the work. Did he compose the new texts as well? Here would be a good starting point to find out more about Bach the librettist!

In the first part of this chapter, we presented in full the beautiful and interesting parts of those few "early" cantatas that have come down to us. We will not be able to do the same with the Weimar cantatas: there are too many beautiful and interesting works with too many beautiful parts.

The Bach we see in 1713, nearly thirty years old, is already a master as a composer of cantatas, but thank goodness not self-satisfied; he is a master who is subject to the most varied influences, constantly learning, and obviously confident enough to have a wide field of interest. Though as a rule he is given a specific libretto to set, by commission, the religious cantata is never a utilitarian form for him but a large frame in which a composer can work out all the things that can be done in this genre.

Bach is constantly finding the new but without discarding the old. Thus it would be wrong to speak of the canata as an "experimental" field: these are valid works but do not form a unified group. Even if it had been his intention eventually to compile a complete year's cycle of cantatas as the consequence of his official obligations in Weimar, they certainly would never have been the sort that could be printed together like Telemann's *Harmonischer Gottesdienst:* the scoring and structure were too miscellaneous. How could a cantor or kapellmeister have been able to adjust his calendar to a new musical caprice every Sunday? Bach is not writing just for colleagues or for the Weimar court; he is also writing a piece of compositional history—his own, but in time of course part of musical world history.

The German Lutheran legacy of the chorale, motet, and religious concert, the now international tradition of counterpoint, Italian innovations in the area of the instrumental concerto and the aria—Bach takes all these into account, in shifting combinations, and makes them his own. Keeping this creative principle in mind, it would be dangerous to try to work out a linear progression in his craft. Of course once certain structural problems have been solved, a composer will never return to earlier solutions, but such a rule is useful with Bach only in narrowly defined areas. Finally, we must never underestimate how many threads this composer can hold in his hand at one time.

In general the old isn't bad because it's old, nor is the new better because it's new. Age as well as history can be an intentional part of composition: long before Beethoven, Bach in Weimar was writing from this experience. Between the old-German, motley, almost unwieldly sequence of movements in the choral cantata "Gleich wie der Regen und Schnee," BWV 18, and the deft Italianate presentation of changing emotional effects in the solo cantata "Mein Herze schwimmt im Blut," BWV 199, lies an entire world. And yet if Bach philologues can be relied upon, both works were created at the same time.

In Weimar, Bach develops his models according to the motto "concise and complex," and they retain their effect in his Leipzig cantatas, more evident in the arias than in the choral sections (even though the Crucifixus of the B-Minor Mass came out of the introductory chorus "Weinen, Klagen"). But in the aria, Bach sets new standards that are of a dizzyingly higher level compared not just with his own earlier cantatas but with those of his contemporaries as well. There is a great variety of concise and nuanced arias: all are controlled by a peculiarly Bachian dialectic, which will be described more fully later. Semantic and structural components are sublated—that is, combined into one conception; they are mutually dependent, mutually enhancing, two sides of the same thing.

Even if Bach in his Weimar cantatas cannot be said to have followed specific strategies, styles, or compositional methods, one trait deserves emphasis, a trait that Heinrich Besseler sees particularly manifest in those arias and duets that are "based on a lyric tone and seek new poetic-musical symbols for old mystic themes. Ideas of death and the hereafter, flight from the world, and the dream of bliss form the core. The soul's loving union with Christ, its dance with the heavenly bridegroom call a dreamlike, tender musical language into being."

In the context of relevant, Pietistically tinged texts, Bach attains that "soulful, expressive melody for which the eighteenth century was searching" and in this respect prepares the way for that century. As long as one does not overstress his inclination to the "personal and intimate,"[49] and one can see that the whole breadth of his musical thoughts and deeds is already present in the Weimar period, then this insight is correct.

Bach does not give up these views in Leipzig but integrates them into a conception that allows more space for the sublime. But on the subject of Bach in Weimar, let it be said that this inclination for the sublime, when active in the adaptation of a work from the Weimar period, did not necessarily benefit that work. Hans-Joachim Schulze doubts whether the monumental motet movement from the definitive version of the above-mentioned cantata "Ein feste Burg ist unser Gott," BWV 80, with its instrumental cantus firmus canon, "can be seen as a linear improvement in all parameters."[50]

THE LEIPZIG CANTATAS

On 30 May 1723, the first Sunday after Trinity, Bach presents his inaugural composition in St. Nicholas's Church in Leipzig: the two-part cantata "Die Elenden sollen essen," BWV 75. That the previously mentioned Leipzig chronicler speaks of a reception with "good applause" does not necessarily mean that Bach was greeted with enthusiasm; but it does show that his debut was understood as a noteworthy cultural event—the new leader of Leipzig's official musical life is making a name for himself.

Bach has several things to consider before this premiere: since in his first year he does not want to present the citizens of Leipzig with a series of random separate pieces, he needs to plan out an entire cantata cycle. Normally such a cycle starts with the beginning of the church year, the first Sunday in Advent. But he makes his plan synchronous with the year of his office, which starts on the first Sunday of Trinity, and he evidently keeps to this schedule in his later Leipzig cantata cycles.

At the outset he has some decisions to make on the textual form of the cycle. In Weimar, he was largely, though not completely, relieved of this decision by the person responsible for such matters, court poet Salomon Franck; in Leipzig, however, there is no official librettist. Bach does not choose to use one of the numerous printed text series that are already in existence and that would be generally available in and beyond the immediate vicinity: collaboration with those familiar with the local scene is a better way of meeting both the Leipzigers' expectations and his own. It makes sense to proceed cautiously here, and not just because the texts must be submitted in batches to the superintendent of approval; Bach has theological and artistic ideas of his own, as do the clergy, aldermen, and congregation.

The first thing to establish is which type of libretto should be followed in the first cycle. Bach decides on the "mixed" cantata, where traditional elements of the Bible and choral passages are included with modern elements, recitative and aria. This type of cantata usually starts with an impressive chorale based on biblical citations but occasionally on a hymn verse. The ending is a chorale finale, which is by now traditional in other towns as well; as a rule its chording is simple. The solo numbers—recitatives, arias, and duets on freely composed texts—find their place between these two framing pieces. But "inside" the cantata too there is always room for a choral adaptation of one sort or another.

In his first Leipzig cycle, Bach chooses the purely madrigalian cantata form with choral finale only as the exception: for one thing, he wants to reuse the mixed cantatas that he composed in Weimar. A second reason is the occasional need to lighten his workload. Third, he has to avoid making too many demands on the choir; accordingly, he dispenses with an opening chorus, beginning instead with a sinfonia, recitative, or aria.

In his preference for the mixed cantata, with its impressive choral opening movement based on Bible passages or hymns, Bach is an exception to the trend of the day. There are other towns and courts where the mixed cantata takes its place alongside cantatas with specifically written and freely composed texts, but none where the choral and biblical Lutheran are given the same emphasis as they are in Leipzig.

But that is precisely the point of Bach's new obligations. He was appointed to secure the traditional principles of the choir of St. Thomas—a choir to which Heinrich Schütz, the musical Praeceptor

Germaniae, had dedicated his *Geistliche Chormusik* seventy-five years earlier: as a passionate plea for a serious choral art, which was now in danger of being lost in an age of basso continuo and upper-voiced melodic lines. The clergy and town councillors particularly, in their aversion to an overly modern art, may have insisted on having the singers of the St. Thomas School perform in Leipzig truly as an ensemble, for it was specifically for the choir's sake that the St. Thomas School was maintained and subsidized as a school for the poor in the first place.

Bach was expected to create for his inaugural appearance "such *compositiones* as would not be *theatrical*" and to put his church music together in such a way that "it not appear too *opera*-like, but rather move the listeners to silent devotions." The implicit caution here may have been against having too many solo numbers.

In conspicuous fashion, many of the first movements set to Bible texts open with impressive phrases: "Die Himmel erzählen die Ehre Gottes," "Erforsche mich, Gott, und erfahre mein Herz," "Schauet doch und sehet, ob irgend ein Schmerz sei," "Siehe zu, daß deine Gottesfurcht nicht Heuchelei sei," "Du sollst Gott, deinen Herrn, lieben," "Es ist nichts Gesundes an meinem Leibe."* Bach might have asked his librettist to start the cantata texts with mottoes like these. In any event, he uses them to place tonal "signs" at key words like "elend," "Himmel," "Schmerz," "Gottesfurcht." These are complex units of combined musical and semantic meaning: they are neither figures of musical rhetoric nor tone painting (*Tonmalerei*) in Albert Schweitzer's phrase; they are in a dialectic way both text-related and text-independent. The common factor uniting text with music is the gestural element inherent in such signs at the beginning of a cantata.[1]

---

*"The Heavens are telling the Glory of God," BWV 76; "Examine me, God, and discover my heart," BWV 136; "Look indeed and see then if there be a grief like to my grief," BWV 46; "Watch with care lest all thy piety hypocrisy be," BWV 179; "Thou shalt thy God and master cherish with all thy bosom, with all thy spirit," BWV 77; "There is nought of soundness within my body," BWV 25.

The shape these works will eventually take is conditioned by decisions about the texts; Bach presumably made such decisions together with his librettist(s). The inaugural cantata BWV 75 demonstrates this interaction of music and text. At the start is the psalm citation "The wretched shall be nourished till they be sated, and they who desire the Lord shall tell his praises. And your heart shall evermore flourish." It is the message of the story of the rich man and poor Lazarus told in the Sunday gospel reading: not the rich man living in excess but the "wretched" Lazarus will receive the heavenly food, which in the end is all that matters. In all succeeding numbers, the motto is paraphrased poetically:

RECITATIVE:
What use the greatest store of wealth
Since all things in our vision
Must disappear?
What use the stirring of vain yearnings,
Since this our flesh itself must perish?
Alas, how swiftly doth it happen
That riches, pleasure, pomp,
The soul to hell condemn!

ARIA:
My Jesus shall be all I own!
My purple is his precious blood,
Himself my most exalted wealth,
And this his Spirit's fire of love
My most delicious wine of joy.

While the recitative is instructive, the aria gives the Christian's soul the opportunity for an emotionally charged response. Arias of this type often let the "I" turn to address Jesus directly. The second pairing of recitative and aria is set up similarly:

RECITATIVE:

God humbleth and exalteth
Both now and for all time.
Who in the world would heaven seek
Shall here be cursed.
However, who here hell's pow'r overcometh
Shall there find joy.

ARIA:

I take up my sadness with gladness to me.
Who Lazarus' torments
With patience endureth
Be taken by angels above.

In a third pairing, the recitative provides a key word for the choral strophe closing the first part of the cantata:

RECITATIVE:

A conscience clear hath God provided
So that a Christian can
In simple things find great delight and pleasure.
Yea, though he lead through long distress
To death,
Yet is it in the end done right and well [*wohlgetan*].

CHORALE:

What God doth, that is rightly done [*wohlgetan*];
Must I the cup soon savor,
So bitter after my mad plight,
I shall yet feel no terror,
For at the last
I will find joy,
My bosom's sweetest comfort,
And yield will ev'ry sorrow.

The second part of the cantata is similar in form; but the theme of poor versus rich becomes more generalized and is treated in the context of an emotional devotion to the figure of Jesus: "Jesus makes my spirit rich. For Jesus' flames of sweetness, from which mine own have risen, engulf me altogether," and so on.

The librettist knew that his libretto would be submitted for approval to the consistory and afterward be available in printed form to worshippers. This was both honor and obligation: honor, because his theological ideas could appear in a form that would receive more attention than a transitory sermon; obligation, because his formulations had to be theologically correct and appropriate for the conditions which then obtained in Leipzig—in a period dominated by the conflict between Lutheran orthodoxy and Pietist fractionalism.

This conflict would only seldom be aired publicly, since most princes—including the sovereign prince of Saxony—wished to avoid unrest in their respective states, expressly forbidding it by edict. But everyone privately knew who and what were considered orthodox or Pietist, and the differences between them were reflected in sermons, songs, and cantata texts. In the didacticism of a given text, how fervently or even ecstatically expressed was the reverence for the figure of Jesus? Did the text's veneration of the blood and wounds of Christ overstep the bounds of Lutheran mysticism? Where did the Pietism of the text become overly effusive? To what extent was the expression of Enlightenment theology acceptable?

In other words, we cannot look at Bach's cantata libretti as a unified body expressing one consistent set of theological ideas. They must have provoked many private and even public discussions. Even in his inaugural Leipzig cantata Bach may have touched off controversy: the song "Was Gott tut, das ist wohlgetan" (the fifth and the last strophe of which each closes a segment of the cantata) is not a traditional Lutheran chorale but a current spiritual song, which was in fact "a characteristic example of the early Pietist aria."[2]

According to a note in the Nordhäuser *Gesangbuch* of 1687, it was written in 1675 by the conrector Samuel Rodigast in Berlin, when a musician friend in Jena, Severus Gastorius, was seriously ill; the latter composed the music. When Gastorius recovered, the Jena "Cantorey" was charged with performing the aria every week "at his front door...to make it better known."[3] By 1708 it was famous as a "hymnus suavissimus & per universam fere Evangelicorum ecclesiam notissimus," that is, as one of the most beautiful and best known songs[4]—an opinion shared by Johann Caspar Wetzel in his 1721 biography of famous lyric poets.

Is it coincidence that Bach uses a melody that first appears in Johann Georg Christian Störl's *Gesangbuch* of 1710 but at the word "ist" substitutes the "sentimental sixth interval" for the fourth—"in an accommodation to modern [Pietistically influenced] taste"?[5] He uses this version only once again, in the cantata "Nimm, was dein ist, und gehe hin," BWV 144, but uses the traditional version on seven other occasions:

Almost no research has been done on the details of text and song selection in Bach's Leipzig cantata libretti, but there are plenty of questions. For the third Sunday after his appointment, that is, the fourth Sunday after Trinity, why did Bach compose the cantata "Ein ungefärbt Gemüt," BWV 24, using a text published in 1714 by Erdmann Neumeister? It begins with the words:

ARIA:
Ein ungefärbt Gemüte
nach deutscher Treu und Güte
macht uns vor Gott und Menschen schön.
Der Christen Tun und Handel,
ihr ganzer Lebenswandel,
soll auf dergleich Füßen stehn.

REZITATIV:

Die Redlichkeit
is eine von den Gottesgaben.
Daß sie in unsrer Zeit
so wenig Menschen haben,
das macht, sie bitten Gott nicht drum.
Denn von Natur geht unsers Herzens Dichten
mit lauter Bösem ümb.
So muß es Gott durch seinen Geist regieren
und auf der Bahn der Tugend führen [...]

ARIA:

An undisguised intention
of native faith and kindness
Doth us 'fore God and man make fair.
For Christians' work and commerce
Throughout their whole life's compass
Should on this kind of footing stand.

RECITATIVE:

Sincerity
Is one of God's most gracious blessings.
The fact that in our time
There are but few who have it
Comes from not asking God for it.
For of itself proceeds our heart's contrivance
In nought but evil ways;
If it would set its course on something worthy,
Then must it be by God's own Spirit governed
And in the path of virtue guided...

As the text goes on, the dry theological tone little by little is transformed into an old-style sermon of thundering oratory:

Gott seis geklagt!
Die Redlichkeit ist teuer

Manch teuflische Ungeheuer
sieht wie ein Engel aus.
Man kehrt den Wolf hinein
den Schafspelz kehrt man raus.
Wie könnt es ärger sein?
Verleumden, Schmähn und Richten,
Verdammen und Vernichten
Ist überall gemein.

O God, forfend!
Sincerity is precious.
And many fiendish monsters
Appear in angel's guise.
We bring the wolf within,
Sheep's clothing don without.
What could be worse than this?
For slander, spite and judgment,
Damnation and destruction
Are ev'rywhere now found.

Here there is nothing left of the balance that the librettist took pains to maintain in the cycle's first two cantatas. If Bach identified with his "mixed" theological outlook, what caused him to choose the Neumeister text, as faithfully *deutsch*-patriotic as it is theologically fierce? Some help comes from sources' revelation that Bach premiered two cantatas on that fourth Trinity Sunday of 1723: the Neumeister cantata and the cantata BWV 185, "Barmherziges Herze der ewigen Liebe." Its text, by the Weimar court poet Salomon Franck, is obviously very close to Pietism; at least the opening aria is:

Barmherziges Herze der ewigen Liebe,
Errege, bewege mein Herze durch dich,
Damit ich Erbarmen und Gütigkeit übe,
O Flamme der Liebe, zerschmelze du mich.

O heart filled with mercy and love everlasting,
Stir up and arouse now my spirit with thine;
So that I may practice both goodness and mercy,
O thou, flame of loving, come soften my heart.

Just as obviously, Bach's setting is inspired by strophic aria form with continuo accompaniment in bouncy triple time. The voice leading of the two parts is characteristic: it is not *concertante* style but tends more toward the homophonic song, as in some Bach duets structured as dialogues of the soul with Jesus. The trills and slurs in the melody give it a soulful, yearning sound: one is reminded of the judgment of the theological faculty at Wittenberg in 1716, which condemned the Pietists' hopping, skipping, lighthearted songs and the "rapturous enthusiasms" some of them tended to evoke.[6] On closer inspection, of course, we see that Bach lets the melody instrument in this ostensibly "Pietist" duet play individual lines taken from the cantus firmus of the Reformation chorale "Ich ruf zu Dir, Herr Jesu Christ"; in this way he combines in his unmistakable way various theological, stylistic, and associative levels.

On the previous Sunday, Bach had performed "Ich hatte viel Bekümmernis," a work with highly Pietist connotations; now, for another Pietist Weimar cantata, did he need an inarguably "orthodox" companion piece? Did the Leipzig librettist beg off, forcing Bach to scan through the printed libretti, finally hitting on the Neumeister text for the fourth Sunday after Trinity? We do not know whether Bach liked its tone or simply tolerated it. We can only make conjectures about the sources and the reasoning behind the selection of texts for those cantatas in the first cycle that were actually composed at Leipzig.

The author of the texts for BWV 75 and 76, the two double cantatas that start the cycle, may be identical with the librettist of the two audition pieces Bach and Christoph Graupner submitted in applying for the *Kantorat* (cantorship) of the Thomaskirche some months before; the six libretti have similarities.[7] Hans-Joachim

Schulze considers the mayor of Leipzig, Gottfried Lange, as a possible candidate; when a young magister in Leipzig, Lange wrote an opera for the court at Weißenfels, which was even staged in Hamburg with music by Johann Christian Schieferdecker.[8] It is quite conceivable that applicants for the cantor's position were given cantata texts, of which one was to be composed, like an examination, in seclusion, and that Lange, who as burgomaster considered himself in charge of matters artistic, showed his colors in this way.

Lange may have written the first two libretti of Bach's Leipzig cycle, serving him as well as adviser generally; it must have been important to him that his protégé make a good impression at the start. He certainly would not have been willing to write Bach an entire year's cycle of texts: Bach's librettist needs not only to make use of and enlarge already existing Weimar cantatas but also to convert secular ones from Cöthen for church use—a tedious, humdrum kind of work not suited to a sitting mayor. Bach probably required the services of several librettists, serially or simultaneously, in his first year at Leipzig.

The assumption that Bach himself wrote some of the still unidentified texts can also be eliminated. We do not even need to consider whether Bach's theological training or poetic abilities were up to such a task, since there are enough other counterarguments. First, he would not, particularly in his first year, have had time to create libretti for months in advance, given all the other work he had. Second, at this time there was strict separation of the functions of librettist and composer: it would have raised eyebrows if Bach, without having even attended the university, had tried to take on the role of theologian and poet. Third, the principle would have applied, even to Bach, that a vocal composer (if he is not Richard Wagner) needs the stimulation and challenge of a set text: only material that comes from outside can inspire the necessary creativity.

We leave this matter to make a few further remarks on the libretti of the first cycle: for the new St. John's Day cantata, BWV 167, "Ihr Menschen, rühmet Gottes Liebe," performed on 24 June 1723, Bach may again have been able to call on a local librettist; this work is shorter, beginning with an aria; as in BWV 185, the chorus appears only in the final chorale. To make up for this, the cantata performed for the Feast of the Visitation on 2 July has an extended opening chorale and larger dimensions overall: this was originally the Weimar cantata for the fourth Sunday of Advent, "Herz und Mund und Tat und Leben," BWV 147a, to which Bach adds three new numbers, so that the original one-part work is now two-part and suitable for performance at the Feast of the Visitation. We have no reports on the cantata performances on the fifth and sixth Sundays after Trinity, 1723; for the seventh Sunday, we do know that Bach adapted his Weimar cantata BWV 186a, "Ärgre dich, o Seele nicht," originally composed for the third Sunday of Advent; by making minor changes to the text and including new recitatives, he makes it into a two-part work appropriate for its new place in the liturgical calendar.

From the eighth Sunday after Trinity on, there is a clear preference for one-part form, predominantly "nested," in one of three variations: Bible passage, recitative, aria, recitative, aria, chorale; Bible passage, recitative, chorale, aria, recitative, aria, chorale; Bible passage, aria, chorale, recitative, aria, chorale. Appearing in the middle, a one-part chorale was nonetheless performed in two parts, before and after the sermon. Bach became clearly less eager to offer two-part cantatas. (The possibility that he occasionally performed two shorter cantatas instead, as on the fourth Trinity Sunday, has been referred to above in connection with the theory of a double-cantata cycle.)

Bach continues his effort to integrate his Weimar cantatas into the Leipzig series. On the eleventh Sunday after Trinity he presents both the newly composed "Siehe zu, daß deine Gottesfurcht nicht Heuchelei sei," BWV 179, and the solo cantata "Mein Herze schwimmt im Blut," BWV 199. The libretto of the former is heavily didactic; with its menacing atmosphere it could be classed alongside the Neumeister text "Ein ungefärbt Gemüte":

> Falscher Heuchelei Ebenbild
> können Sodomsäpfel heißen,
> die mit Unflat angefüllt

und von außen herrlich gleißen.
Heuchler, die von außen schön,
können nicht vor Gott bestehen.

Likeness of false hypocrites,
We could Sodom's apples call them,
Who, with rot though they be filled,
On the outside brightly glisten.
Hypocrites, though outward fair,
Cannot stand before God's throne.

The rather drastic orthodoxy of the explicit images chosen by the unknown librettist here may find its justification in the wish to form a counterfoil to "Mein Herze schwimmt im Blut," where Georg Christian Lehms's text, in its veneration of the blood and wounds of Christ, has obvious traits of Lutheran mysticism and Pietism. One might conjecture similarly on the musical setting here: the opening theme set over the words "Siehe zu, daß deine Gottesfurcht nicht Heuchelei sei" has great structural rigor, compared with the more sentimental sound of the Weimar cantata; it is no accident that Bach was able to reuse it as the Kyrie of his short Mass in G Major, BWV 236.

In his planning the cantata BWV 69a, "Lobe den Herrn, meine Seele," meant for the next (twelfth) Sunday after Trinity, Bach apparently had to do without a creative librettist: the text is a revised and abridged version of a libretto published in 1720 by the Schleiz pastor Johann Oswald Knauer, and it was written for a relation of his, Gottfried Heinrich Stölzel, court kapellmeister at Gotha. On the one hand, Knauer borrowed from Neumeister's texts; on the other, he quite empathized with the Pietist tendencies of the Gotha court. Interestingly, Bach and his editor do not continue with the two-part structure of their model: Knauer's libretto is shortened to the standard six-part sequence of chorus, recitative, aria, recitative, aria, and final chorale. The text of the cantata for the next (thirteenth) Sunday after Trinity, "Du sollst Gott, deinen Herren, lieben," BWV 77, derives from a text of Knauer's but with certain conspicuous changes, for instance, in the first aria:

Knauer	Bach
Mein Gott, ich liebe dich	Mein Gott, ich liebe dich
von Herzen,	von Herzen,
mein ganzes Leben	mein ganzes Leben
Hängt dir an.	hängt dir an.
Laß mich doch dieses	Laß mich doch dein
Glück erkennen	Gebot erkennen
und meine Liebe	und in Liebe
so entbrennen	so entbrennen
daß ich dich ewig lieben kann.	daß ich dich ewig lieben kann.
My God, with all my heart I	My God, with all my heart I
love thee,	love thee,
And all my life depends on thee.	And all my life depends on thee.
But help me fathom this great	But help me thy great law to
happiness,	fathom
And let my heart be so kindled,	And with love to be so kindled
That I thee evermore may love.	That I thee evermore may love.
(Trans. J. Hargraves)	(Trans. Z. Philip Ambrose)

That mankind on his own was capable of knowing where "his happiness" (*Glück*) lay is an Enlightenment idea and could not have been expressed openly in Leipzig.[9] The librettist has already touched on the idea of human reason in the phrase "das Licht der Vernunft" ("the light of reason"), in the cantata for the second Sunday after Trinity, "Die Himmel erzählen die Ehre Gottes," BWV 76, and explicitly rejected all those who refuse to honor God; however, this reason is not innate in man but is the gift of the Son of God. Only through Him can man, by nature unreasoning and sinful, come to true knowledge:

Fahr Hin, abgöttische Zunft!
Sollt sich die Welt gleich verkehren,
Will ich doch Christum verehren,
Er ist das Licht der Vernunft.

Get hence, idolatrous band!
Though all the world be perverted,
Will I still Christ render honor,
He is the light of the mind.

For the fourteenth Sunday after Trinity, for the cantata "Es ist nichts Gesundes an meinem Leibe," BWV 25, again Bach looks outside for his text: a poem from 1720 by Johann Jacob Rambach, who was at that time a theology student.[10] Even more strongly than Knauer's libretto, the text fashioned from Rambach's work employs an even more baroque, extreme language, particularly in its description of mankind's sinfulness:

Die ganze Welt ist nur ein Hospital,
Wo Menschen von unzählbar großer Zahl
Und auch die Kinder in der Wiegen
An Krankheit hart daniederliegen.
Den einen quälet in der Brust
Ein hitzigs Fieber böser Lust;
Der andre lieget krank
An eigner Ehre häßlichem Gestank;
Den dritten zehrt die Geldsucht ab
Und stürzt ihn vor der Zeit ins Grab.

Now all the world is but a hospital,
Where mortals in their numbers passing count
And even children in the cradle
In sickness lie with bitter anguish.
The one is tortured in the breast
By raging fever's angry lust;

Another lieth ill
From his own honor's odious foul stench;
The third is torn by lust for gold,
Which hurls him to an early grave.

In the text of the cantata for the fifteenth Sunday after Trinity, "Warum betrübst du dich, mein Herz," BWV 138, the complaints of material poverty are highly unusual:

Wie kann ich nun mein Amt in Ruh verwalten,
Wenn Seufzer meine Speise und Tränen das Getränke sein?
. . . .
Gott sorget freilich vor das Vieh,
Er gibt den Vögeln seine Speise,
Er sättiget die jungen Raben,
Nur ich, ich weiß nicht auf was Weise,
Ich armes Kind,
Mein bißchen Brot soll haben.

How can I now my post maintain in calmness
When sighing is my portion and tears are all I have to drink?
. . . .
God clearly careth for the kine,
He gives the birds their proper nurture,
He filleth the fledgling ravens.
But I, I know not in what manner
I, wretched child,
My bit of bread shall garner.

The "poor child" does indeed know it is ultimately in God's keeping; so the complaints about the lack of food are surprising. Was Bach sighing sympathetically or winking privately to himself as he set these lines? Or, less likely, did he just register this text as one among many, with no particular feelings about it?

In any event, with this work Bach is setting to music for the first time, in his first Leipzig cantata cycle, a text that can be classified as a chorale cantata—an indication that this libretto was also probably not written ad hoc for the first Leipzig cycle. The cantata for the sixteenth Sunday after Trinity, "Christus, der ist mein Leben," BWV 95, is also a kind of chorale cantata; and this time the poet has found room not just for this chorale but for three others as well.

But by the seventeenth Sunday after Trinity, this little interlude of chorale cantatas has come to an end: the libretto of BWV 148, "Bringet dem Herrn Ehre seines Namens," begins with a psalm citation but also is very like a poem of Picander that starts "Weg, ihr irdischen Geschäfte." Still, it is doubtful whether this cantata was actually written for the year 1723.

Toward the end of the first cantata cycle—that is, Easter and Whitsuntide of 1724—for the first time Bach makes extensive use of parodies of his own work, by setting new words to the secular congratulatory cantatas from his Cöthen period. He may have been fatigued from the composition and performance of the *St. John Passion;* with the Easter and Whitsun workload of three cantata performances apiece looming, he may have fallen back with relief onto existing compositions. Further, here was an opportunity to place the music from those occasional pieces from Cöthen into a new, more enduring context.

Regarding the art of parody, Picander will be a skillful aid to Bach in later years; whether he was already working for Bach by the spring of 1724, and perhaps even collaborating on the text of the *St. John Passion,* we can only guess. Was it his help that made, from the secular "Der Himmel dacht auf Anhalts Ruhm und Glück," BWV 66a, the cantata for the second day of Easter "Erfreut euch, ihr Herzen," BWV 66; from "Die Zeit, die Tag und Jahre macht," BWV 134a, the cantata for the third day of Easter, "Ein Herz, das seinen Jesum lebend weiß," BWV 134; and from "Durchlauchtster Leopold," BWV 173a, the cantata for the second day of Whitsuntide, "Erhöhtes Fleisch und Blut," BWV 173? The original for the cantata for the third day of Whitsuntide, "Erwünschtes Freudenlicht," BWV 184, is not known but is certainly a Cöthen cantata.

Closer examination of the libretti for Bach's first Leipzig cantata cycle yields a few basic insights. We are dealing not with a closed series of texts of the same kind but with a heterogeneous sequence of individual pieces, some interrelated, others quite varied and separate from one another. But this miscellany cannot be equated with randomness; it is more a reflection of the situation Bach faced in Leipzig at the time. First, he was in a dialogue with authorities and the congregation and was surely learning one thing at a time; second, he had to use the texts that were available to him in Leipzig; third, he wanted to find a place in this Leipzig cycle for cantatas from Weimar and Cöthen—in original form, in revision, or as parodies. The result is that the quality of these works is "motley" on three different levels.

But it would be a mistake to underestimate the effect of these libretti on the listener simply because they don't have the force of a consistent dogmatic viewpoint or the consistency of a closed cycle of sermons. Printed versions of the texts were available to worshippers; they could read and reflect on them beforehand while listening to the performance or afterward, in assessing the service: at that time, theology and piety were guiding principles of life far more than we can imagine today. Bibles, prayer books, and hymnals were not just sold but read. Bach himself, who certainly did not need any extra work, nonetheless was an avid Bible reader, as we know from the marginal jottings in his household bible.

So it would be misleading to see these libretti merely as hurdles on the path to Bach's music, to be vaulted as elegantly as possible, or as a negligible quantity. Rather, they are a key to understanding Bach; and the greater the value one ascribes to them, the more one will understand about the Bach who did not compose absolutely but in context. This context is far more than a single textual topos, a pretext for the composer to work out a device of musical rhetoric or try a bit of tone painting. It is Bach's faith—not an abstract but a concrete faith. It is in faith that he deals with his texts, in faith that he gains his creative insights, and to the extent that his listeners have not completely subscribed to Enlightenment ideas, they interpret these insights in similar faith.

Though Bach's will to create autonomous musical meaning was powerful, his desire was just as great to engage himself deeply with the meaning of a text and its actuality for a life of devotion. The—occasionally—astringent appeal of his cantatas is the direct result of the tension between the otherworldly remoteness of their form and the urgent quality of their meaning.

One facet of this tension may be illustrated by a comparison of two arias premiered in 1724: one by Bach, the other by Handel. For the cantata "Herr Christ der einge Gottessohn," BWV 96, Bach composed the bass aria that begins, "Bald zur Rechten, bald zur Linken lenkt sich mein verirrter Schritt":

Only a few months earlier Handel wrote the aria "V'adoro, pupille," for the opera *Giulio Cesare in Egitto:*

The arias may well be compared since both can be understood as a type of saraband. Looking at the settings of the first line of the text given in the examples, one can see for oneself that the order of their phrases is the same: Stollen—Stollen—Abgesang. But how differently the two composers treat this bar form: for Cleopatra's love hymn, Handel shapes a pleasant melodic arc based on the cadence I-IV-V. Bach, on the other hand, uses the two *Stollen* to emphasize the straying, stumbling pace thematized in the text: the steps deviate first to one side of the path, then the other; the swaying pattern in the voice, and the dissonant harmonic passage ending indecisively on the word "Schritt" ("step"), illustrates that this path is the way of error; the above example shows just the beginning of the twists and turns of Bach's musical line. The accompanying instruments have different functions as well: whereas in Handel they hardly amount to more than a continuo, albeit one of great feeling, with Bach their role can be understood more symbolically, with the chorus of strings "stumbling" one way and the oboes the other.

This music has none of the elegance and elemental, immediate appeal of the Handel—it is not even beautiful: in the nineteenth century the gesture Bach selected here would have been called "characteristic," in the sense of the concession beauty must make to a certain ugliness in the depiction of unbalanced characters. Bach is illustrating here not characters that are interchangeable but a topos central to his Christian life: the embattled state of the individual Christian existence. Against this he contrasts, in the aria's middle section, the peace the soul is granted in the knowledge that the Savior is at its side:

(Klavierauszug)

To compose music like this meant that Bach constantly had to rise to the challenge of each new libretto given to him. With the text in front of them, even the most knowledgeable of his listeners would have followed the daring harmonic changes with bated breath, changes that only the text at hand could legitimate; they heard and were moved by the calming rhythmic meter to which he set the words "Gehe doch, mein Heiland, mit" ("Walk with me, my Savior, still").

Handel's attitude toward theater and his liking of pure beauty and immediate effect are directly opposed to Bach's striving for truth and precise textual interpretation. The melody of the aria "V'adoro, pupille" is heard first as an instrumental serenade played against the backdrop of a starry Egyptian night, then Cleopatra sings it: its classical form makes it adaptable to multiple applications. Bach's "Bald zur Rechten, bald zur Linken" cannot so easily be moved into a different context; it is specifically part of an interpretation of the Gospel for the eighteenth Sunday after Trinity, the goal of which was to bring the figure of the Messiah closer to the listeners—and not just any listeners but those Leipzigers who were in church on 8 October 1724.

At the same time, this piece of music is autonomous, not simply composed to fit the text but dominated by a rhythmic motive (dotted eighth, sixteenth, and quarter notes) that is never stilled, continued even in the central section, where the text speaks of Jesus as unfailing preparer of the way. Even though the aria shows thematic developments and formal processes, Bach engages with the issues of the text but is not completely taken up by them: having set himself a theological theme, he still creates music that as a composition can stand by itself.

What we have sketched here in looking at a single aria can be applied to Bach's entire cantata output and particularly to the first Leipzig cycle: there is a dialectic between a creative impulse using autonomous forms, on the one hand, and a flexible engagement with theological messages and actual performance considerations, on the other. This dialectic does not detract from the music; it makes it more alive, gives it multiple perspectives. Similarly, the Passions do not suffer from their wide variety of texts and mixture of forms. Indeed, the Bible itself is an example of such multiplicity: it is not cut from one cloth like a theological textbook but is an extremely diverse collection of literary forms, points of view, and modes of representation.

Therefore Bach's first Leipzig cantata cycle cannot be compared, for example, with Telemann's *Harmonischer Gottesdienst* of 1725–26, a cycle composed to entirely madrigalian texts. The widespread commercial success of Telemann's cycle is due precisely to its standardized nature: text, orchestration, and the sequencing of numbers and movements all follow a single pattern. The user knows to expect music that will be easy to perform anywhere: beautifully and expertly composed, but without any corners or sharp edges, especially with regard to real-world situations.

Bach's situation is more like a laboratory: with no complete libretto cycle at hand, he is living more or less hand to mouth; he has to deal with the particular conditions of Leipzig and can hardly have a composition ready more than a few weeks ahead. His increasing time pressure is evident even in the source documents of the first two cantatas of the cycle: while the original manuscript of "Die Elenden sollen essen," BWV 75, his inaugural cantata for Leipzig, is carefully worked out and notated, since he could prepare it at his leisure while still at Cöthen, the score for the double work "Die Himmel erzählen die Ehre Gottes," BWV 76, meant for the very next Sunday, is more like a rough draft, with a great many corrections: just one week after taking office, he has not the time to complete a fair copy; and this will be the rule from now on.

But the laboratory is no obstacle on the path to a great idea—if the idea is understood as a work in progress: after each Sunday performance, Bach can reconsider how a particular work sounded, how it was received, and draw the appropriate conclusions for the next cantata. He is a master at balancing the demands of art and the necessities of daily life. Of course, a system that leaves him little time for composing and forces him to employ revisions of older works takes its toll. But he will not adapt too much to the pressure, not accept the notion that a man in his position must manufacture cantatas by the dozen, come what may—he stubbornly maintains a sense of himself, and that sense enables him to produce new cantata settings that, despite the day-to-day background, are like polished, multifaceted, shimmering jewels: miracles of compositional organization, musical expression, depth of theological symbolism, and existential vitality.

Music history contains no other case in which a composer could work productively under such tension: the will to conceive on a grand scale in the face of quotidian realities that make compromises of all kinds inevitable. One might think of Haydn, who came up with his contributions to the "classical style" in the genres of symphony, string quartet, and piano sonata in his laboratory, as one might refer to the musical life of the far-off court of Prince Esterházy; but Haydn's work on this great idea stretched over decades and had to take fewer externals into account.

Bach generally must respond from week to week. All the more astonishing, then, is the confidence with which he immediately sets out to compose opening movements to Bible texts and choral verses—a challenge he seldom took on before. Of course, there are choral passages set to Bible texts and choral cantus firmi in the Weimar cantatas; but even a chorus such as "Ich hatte viel Bekümmernis," from the eponymous cantata BWV 21, which he deemed worthy of inclusion in his first Leipzig cycle, is not set up as the large-scale vocal and instrumental concertized setting that he is now trying out in ever new variations.

In that first Leipzig cantata cycle, by expressly giving the heading "concerto" to the opening chorus of each cantata (and thus in a sense to the whole work), Bach is giving a signal. In Protestant church music of the seventeenth century, this term was reserved primarily for musical settings of Bible passages and chorales, as a successor to the term "motet." The term continued to be used as this one-movement concerto was expanded to include aria strophes and gradually evolved into the older mixed cantata, but then it no longer applied to the introduction of the purely madrigalian cantata.

Since Bach, for his first two Leipzig cycles, consistently chooses to set his opening movements to a Bible citation or choral strophe, thereby keeping the relevant traditions alive, he is also able to bring the term *concerto* back into favor. And in fact, from now on he will distinguish *concerto* from *cantata:* the first term is applied to church cantatas that begin with Bible passages or chorales, the second to both sacred and secular cantatas whose text is primarily free rhymed verse. So we should see Bach's decision to use the heading "concerto" first of all as an affirmation of the Lutheran and specifically Leipzig tradition of sacred music. It also is evidence of the composer's self-confidence: the point is not to revive the large-scale sacred *Konzert* of the seventeenth and early eighteenth centuries, with its rather formulaic assignment of roles to vocal and orchestral choruses. Rather, Bach is taking on the task of blending, with the greatest finesse, the older contrapuntal style with the new *concertante* method of composition, to create an ecclesiastical form of art that is both modern and traditional at the same time.

Bach's reflections on past and present, and his attempts to create a so-called classical style, are evident not only in instrumental cycles like *The Well-Tempered Clavier,* the *Goldberg Variations,* or *The Art of Fugue* but also in vocal series such as the first and second Leipzig cantata cycles. Bach gives the Protestant church cantata an unmistakably new look, solely through transforming its vocal-instrumental introduction into an entire opening movement, the importance of which is no less than that of the main sonata movement of Viennese classicism. The compositional processes here are different, but comparisons can be drawn as to the importance of the opening theme as a subject for philosophical discussions in the medium of composition.

The range of possibilities Bach conceived of for the vocal-instrumental *Konzert* goes far beyond the norm of utilitarian or occasional music. The great variety of form evident in the opening movements gives a clear view of his efforts, in constantly changing patterns and configurations, to blend chorus and orchestra, to meld the polarities of counterpoint and *Konzert,* cantus firmus adaptations and ritornello technique, and to combine the syntax of set texts with the logic of autonomous musical form. Most astonishing is how rapidly he increases his skill at composing grand settings of these kinds.

The opening chorus of the inaugural cantata "Die Elenden sollen essen," BWV 75, consists of two movements, modeled on the French overture pattern, whose accented rhythms drive the first part:

an instrumental setting of elegiac splendor carried by oboes and strings, in which the polyphonic choral setting devoted to the *Elenden* ("the wretched") is incorporated such that two more or less independent structures are interwoven without losing their separate integrity. The movement's second part (on the words "Euer Herz soll ewiglich leben") is a choral fugue sui generis: the instruments with continuo do not follow the vocal lines colla parte but in turn create a *concertante* framework; this framework is not structured as consistently as in the first part, but there are thematic entries of the two oboes in stretto passages.

Even in this first Leipzig choral movement, Bach has succeeded in squaring the circle: not only has he taken to heart the Leipzigers' expectations that their cantor produce for the choir motet and fugue settings that are contrapuntally solid; at the same time, he treats his audience to an amazing feat, a work that links the motet and the modern *concertante* styles. "Just what is this new cantor and *director musices* giving us, a choral fugue or an instrumental concerto?" the more sophisticated of his listeners might have asked.

The technique of embedding a chorus in an instrumental movement is not completely new for Bach: he used it in the 1716 Weimar Advent cantata "Wachet! Betet!," BWV 70a, if far more simply: for one thing, there the rhyming text with its regular lines was considerably easier to fit into the framework of a *Konzert* setting; for another, the choral setting in BWV 70a is homophonic over long intervals and thus less difficult to synchronize into the harmonic flow of the movement. In Leipzig, however, Bach attempts far more difficult combinations; and despite the opinions of some scholars, he did not make things easier for himself by simply instrumentalizing the voice parts: thematic openings, at least, often take their cue from the text, even if they are not necessarily derived from the words directly.

The challenge is especially clear in the opening movement of the twin of this work composed for the following Sunday, "Die Himmel erzählen die Ehre Gottes," BWV 76. In the fugue "Es ist keine Sprache noch Rede," Bach makes the fugue form function symbolically: at the words "Es ist keine Sprache noch Rede, da man nicht ihre Stimme höre" ("There is no speech or language, where their voice is not heard"), tenor, bass, soprano, and alto enter separately, in succession. This procedure illustrates in clear musical terms the passage of the divine message in stages from one nation to the next.

As in BWV 75, the structure of the opening chorus of BWV 76 can be compared with a prelude and fugue, though here the "prelude" is modeled not on the French overture but on a concerto movement with solo trumpet. Unlike BMW 75, the instruments in the fugue do not function independently, with one important exception: the trumpet—surely played by Johann Gottfried Reiche, at the time probably the best musician in Bach's ensemble—is given the fifth splendid entry.

In this case Bach wrote a permutation fugue, the simplest but most effective form of fugue to set words to. So it is all the more surprising to note the technical complications in the cantata that was composed for nine weeks later, the eleventh Sunday after Trinity, "Siehe zu, daß deine Gottesfurcht nicht Heuchelei sei," BWV 179. Although the fugue written to this text is almost totally without *concertante* characteristics (aside from the continuo, which is sometimes autonomous), the pairing a mirror fugue (where each entry is an inversion of the previous one) with canonic imitation represents almost a quantum leap in approaching the art of the *stile antico*.[II]

One Sunday later Bach tests combining concerted music with a double fugue, in the opening chorus of "Lobe den Herrn, meine Seele," BWV 69a. And again, one Sunday later, in the opening chorus of "Du sollst Gott deinen Herren lieben," BWV 77, he composes a movement that has attained such fame in the literature that it might itself inspire a chapter in the history of Bach scholarship. Philipp Spitta, praising in 1880 "a completely new, cleverly conceived, and masterfully executed form," noted that this setting of the Gospel on love should be seen not just as a motet but properly as an "organ choral," where the cantus firmus of the chorus, "Dies sind die heil'gen zehn Gebot," is blared right into the vocal movement by the trumpet and then enlarged and treated as a canon in the continuo. Spitta did find it "odd," however, that Bach had broken apart the fourth line of the chorale into two pieces: "Neither a poetic nor a musical reason for this procedure can be found."[12]

In 1925, in his programmatic essay "Bach and the Symbol," Arnold Schering thinks he has found a reason: in order "to bring out the number ten," the composer resorted to

> *means which were only justified by the purely external require-*
> *ment of giving the trumpet ten separate entries. It is entirely*
> *probable that Bach's congregation, having recognized the master's*
> *consistency on this point, would at such moments faithfully count*
> *off the entries, and thus respectfully appreciate the numeric sym-*
> *bolism along with the multitude of other kinds of symbolism.*[13]

Above and beyond this numeric symbolism, Schering sees the "symbolic fabric" of the movement on four levels, expressly acknowledging Albert Schweitzer's earlier ideas on the subject.[14] The joyful emotion expressed in melismata on the word "heart" is seen as "symbolism of the first order." The trumpet sound signaling majesty is thus of the second order. The third order of symbols is technological: the fact that the cantus firmus of the hymn "Dies sind die heil'gen zehn Gebot" (the Ten Commandments) is a canon in the fifth interval, "per augmentationem," refers to the strictness of the law. Finally, there is a fourth order of symbols: by having the chorus invoke the New Testament commandment to "love thy neighbor" while at the same time singing the hymn tune standing for Old Testament law, Bach forges an "ideological bond" between the old and new laws.

The American Bach scholar Gerhard Herz (1974) even sees ten symbolic levels, woven together into one of the most complex sound structures in music history.[15]

George von Dadelson cautions us against chasing after symbols (1980), especially numeric symbols, and this caution applies particularly to the attempt to interpret symbolically the ten choral entrances of "Das sind die heil'gen zehn Gebot": there is, after all, a precedent in contemporary hymnals for the hiatus in the fourth line that Spitta found so puzzling. For Dadelson, what matters finally is "that beyond all these symbolic connections the piece presents an organic musical whole. What matters is not the symbols, not the figures, but the completed unit in which they play a part."[16]

Accordingly, in looking at the opening movement of BWV 77, Friedhelm Krummacher intends explicitly "to better understand Bach's music in the context of its own structure." He is not content simply to note that Bach—like his cantoral predecessors Knüpfer, Schelle, and Kuhnau—mediates between the genres of motets on biblical mottoes and choral adaptations; nor is he overly impressed by the fact that Bach set—rather artlessly—the cantus firmus as a canon at the fifth and then motivically linked the choral parts to it:

> *Obviously the course this music takes is not completely determined by its abstract framework. The layers of the movement cannot be explained by a single schematic pattern. However, there are three perceptible vectors defining the process: first, rhythmic differentiation between the voices; then, tonal development of the contrapuntal section; and finally, the harmonic tensions to be found in the choral canon.*

In Krummacher's view, Bach starts with a "dialectic model" that lends the abstract framework of the movement an "exciting inner development," systematically leading to the coda at the words "thy neighbor as thyself," this coda being "the contrary quintessence" of the movement; in this way Bach achieves "esthetic qualities that the nineteenth century discovered and to which we remain indebted today." As an interpretation of the text, too, the music retains its "autonomy—an autonomy that has nothing to do with schematics or purely formulaic calculations, but has some of the characteristics of a fantasia, which is why it is unanalyzable."[17]

In the course of their history, works of art gradually lose their connection to their creator and become open to interpretation—the longer the history, the more interpretations. Bach's many-layered oeuvre has, a priori, an oversupply of interpretative possibilities; so there is nothing wrong in principle with looking at the BWV 77 opening movement from the systematic viewpoint of the nineteenth century. Nonetheless, one might ask whether Bach thought that the systematic quality that we now observe was the driving force of the movement or just an incidental result. This quality does not explain the impact on the listener, at any rate: the Leipzig churchgoer, whose perceptions live on in us today, at least in part, most likely first heard, without words, the five-line tune of the hymn for that particular Sunday's feast day, as it is played in the chorale "Dies sind die heil'gen zehn Gebot," and immediately identified it as such—not in the bass line (though it appears there in its original form) but in the soprano trombone.

Despite Dadelsen's and Krummacher's reservations, we may assume that Bach intended the ten entries to be understood symbolically; this idea is more plausible when we observe that the first of the excess trumpet entries (measure 9 of the example) was not part of the original score but added later.

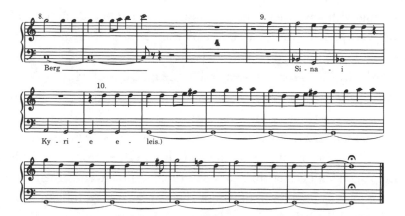

Yet surely Bach could have arranged for the trumpets to enter in a less bizarre fashion. We look in vain for a rationale that might explain the trumpet entries. Instead, we are left to conjure up fantastic images: Moses with the tablets, having come down from Mount Sinai to try to interest his people in God's commandments, when they have fallen away from faith and lowered themselves to dancing around a golden calf; imploringly he turns this way and that, beseeching them and holding up first one, then the other of the tablets to heaven.

Bach's churchgoers could have imagined similar biblical images as they listened to Reiche, "their" trumpeter, seeing him as well as hearing him (at least from the good seats), or as they read their prayer books. At the same time, did they appreciate Bach's audacity in incorporating a vocal motet into an adaptation of a cantus firmus? And do we think it succeeds aesthetically, or was it just an experiment with transitory appeal?

Bach continues his experimenting. For the very next Sunday, the fourteenth Trinity Sunday, he writes an opening chorus for the cantata BWV 25 to the gloomy Psalm verse "Es ist nichts Gesundes an meinem Leibe vor deinem Dräuen und ist kein Friede in meinen Gebeinen vor meiner Sünde" ("There is nought of soundness within my body, for thou art angry, nor any quiet within these my bones, for I am sinful"). Once again he crosses a vocal motet setting with a wordless cantus firmus, to which one mentally adds words—perhaps the first stanza of the *Sterbelied* ("hymn for the dying"): "Herzlich tut mich verlangen nach einem sel'gen End" ("Ardently I long for a blessed end"), the final line of which is "sehn mich nach ew'gen Freuden; o Jesu, komm nur bald" ("I long for eternal joy; O Jesu, come, but soon"). But this time the motet is worked out much more strictly, and the chorale is heard in a four-part setting: a cornet playing the melody and three trombones. The Leipzigers appreciate this: they see the brass quartet of their own town pipers in the flesh, of whom Bach's predecessor Johann Kuhnau had written in his novel *Der musikalische Quack-Salber:* "If on a feast day they play a hymn from the tower with trombones alone, we are moved beyond measure, and we ween we hear the angels singing."

By fitting the brass passages (which match the four couplets of the *sterbelied*) into the motet structure in four large blocks, Bach works as a genre composer, applying "local color" so conspicuously that it takes something away from the motet principle: whenever the brass enter, the carefully worked out canonical theme and the imitative leading of the motet get a bit shaky; moreover, there are continual harmonic frictions. Did Bach find it stylistically too difficult or just unnecessary to keep the canonic idea going underneath the brass passages? Or, as a particular interpretation of the psalm text, did he want these places to depict the frailty of human existence, its helpless abjectness before God?

Taking a broad view of Bach's music, the musicologist Gerd Rienäcker speaks of a "consciousness of catastrophe," located in Luther's theology but also finding an echo, perhaps, in the catastrophic visions of a composer like Gustav Mahler. He recalls for us the

> ... *longing and fear of those human beings who most have to endure earthly suffering, who must live with disease and misery while confronting the prosperous bourgeoisie and aristocracy, accompanied only by their hope for another, better world, by their*

prayers, by never-ending labor, and by their search for God, who accepts them or condemns them, a God whom they see and grasp, before whom they must stand or fall, a God who ultimately and finally is drawn into their earthly conflicts.[18]

A few years before Rienäcker, the composer Hans Werner Henze had written in an essay called *Johann Sebastian Bach und die Musik unserer Zeit*:

There are things said in this music which up until this point no one had ever dared to say with sounds, had ever been able to say, or ever even tried to say. With unparalleled realism, here we have the birth of a universal language, a plain language, and through its help and mediation, human emotions and conditions are revealed in which—and only now can we see and think on it this way—not just the traditional Christian bourgeois audience sees itself, but also the modern, lonely, doubting human being, who has lost faith, who has no firm foothold in society, and whose life must primarily be spent (like Büchner's Woyzeck) "without the church's blessing."

In the dolorous plaints of the oboe d'amore and the shawm, we recognize our own weeping and wailing as children, and later, too, we heard these sounds again, when we were hungry and cold in the gray, northern church naves, where the joys and tortures of sin and sinners were revealed to our souls, by all those toccatas and chorales, O lamb of God, comfort and punishment, atonement and penitence, existence, and pain. This music forgives us poor wretches, it promises us new joys, it weeps for us with all the world's souls.[19]

This brief excursion into the musicological background of BWV 77 has brought us to its sister work—and to an insight usually more proper to the feuilletonist or, ideally, the philosopher. But this insight too belongs to our theme; it is not some subordinate type of reception history but part of an inclusive history of Bach discourse.[20]

To deal sensibly with a phenomenon like Bach, we must consider not only empirical research results but also underlying subjectivities and the trends that cause changes in them. Obviously, research affects opinion, but opinion also affects research, and every piece of analysis that has scientific value is nourished by the dialectic between research and opinion.

Let us return to the plan of the first Leipzig cantata cycle. Bach paid particular attention to the opening phrases composed for the chorus and demonstrated in them how he envisaged a Lutheran church music that was rooted in tradition but also included the forms and possibilities of the modern orchestral work. Accordingly, the cantata year was as diverse as the various problems and solutions that were to be found within it.

"The beautiful young woman and the graying contrapuntalist, bent over the score, hear his works with equal pleasure." This entry in the *Tonkünstler-Lexikon* of Ernst Ludwig Gerber (1790), though found under "Haydn," would apply equally well to Bach if "beautiful young woman" were replaced by "devout Christian." The Christian finds as much satisfaction in Bach's cantata settings as the connoisseur who has been educated in the musical tradition. For all the evident artifice of Bach's music, one cannot fail to hear the many religious symbols that for his contemporaries were very easy to understand. This is especially true of the chorales, which could definitely be heard not just in complicated renditions but often in totally unadorned, original form—and not just in the simple final chorales but also in many opening sections.

For example, in the *Dialogue between Fear and Hope,* as the cantata "O Ewigkeit, du Donnerwort," BWV 60, is known, presented on the twenty-fourth Sunday after Trinity, 1724, where Hope sings the chorale "O Ewigkeit, du Donnerwort, o Schwert, das durch die Seele bohrt" ("Eternity, thou thund'rous word, O sword that through the soul doth bore") without any ornament at all, reinforced by a cornet, everyone in the congregation understands what it is about, no matter how operatic and agitated the accompaniment may sound. And in the cantata "Liebster Gott, wann werd ich sterben,"

BWV 8, for the sixteenth Sunday after Trinity, when the death knell is tolled, there may well have been a "shiver [...] running through Bach's congregation," as Arnold Schering suspects.[21]

The experience of the churchgoers of Leipzig may have been similar to that of modern concertgoers, who often have little awareness of the structure of the work they are hearing, paying more attention to individual "events" that stand out from the flow of sound. Wasn't a Bach cantata much more understandable than many a sermon that the Leipzigers had to submit to? Were they ever dissatisfied with his music? We know about Scheibe's rebellion, but Scheibe was an Enlightenment partisan and a purist regarding "natural" and "reasonable" modes of making music. Did the worshippers at St. Thomas and St. Nicholas think like Scheibe, or were they impressed by Bach's music, which admittedly they may not always have understood in its complexity but which they revered for its sublimity despite all the slogans of the Enlightenment?

Unquestionably, in his early and middle Leipzig years, Bach moves closer to his audience: if we look at the opening chorus of the *St. Matthew Passion*, which even in 1727 was presented in the form it has today, we are impressed by the classicism and intelligibility of its design. The diversity and fantasia-like qualities of the first cantata cycle seem a thing of the past: there is a double chorus, with a shape determined by the text's simple dialogue; thus it is easy to hear; we can orient ourselves within its comprehensible, da capo–like musical flow, and finally we hear a cantus firmus that is fitted almost perfectly into the architecture of the work—or at any rate without harshness or dissonance.

The "great" events of the first Leipzig cantata cycle take place in the opening choruses. Nonetheless there is much one could say about the solo parts—that is, the recitatives and arias on freely composed texts. Clearly, Bach is cultivating the forms of recitative and aria with a modernity that need not fear comparison with those of his contemporaries but that still bear the hallmarks of authentic sacred music.

His treatment of recitative speaks for itself. Study of early sketches of scores, later abandoned, reveals that he made a surprisingly large number of changes to the recitative parts. He doesn't see the recitative as an operatic parlando, with the function merely to move the plot along and prepare for the next aria; nor is the recitative just the routine setting of a didactic text, a "lesson," as is often the case in Telemann's church cantatas. Every text is given a fresh look and a new form.

The very first recitative of the inaugural cantata BWV 75 is a good example. It contains no peculiarities or extravagances, but the rhetorical implications of the text have been considered carefully: the dignified theme set as a string accompaniment is meant to be a little homily; the passage that speaks of *Majestät* that *vergeht* ("passes away") is carefully articulated; *Überfluß* ("excess of wealth") is clearly illustrated. Bach depicts the passage "denn unser Leib muß selbst von hinnen" ("since our flesh itself must perish") with a descending melody and diminished seventh harmony, and he contrasts against the accented sounds of *Reichtum, Wollust,* and *Pracht* ("riches," "pleasure," "pomp") the final descent into hell, where again the diminished seventh shows the way.

she-hen   daß Reich-tum,   Wol-lust   Pracht   den Geist zur Höl-le macht!

One Sunday later, in cantata BWV 76, Bach sets to music the following recitative text:

> So läßt sich Gott nicht unbezeuget!
> Natur und Gnade red't alle Menschen an:
> Dies alles hat ja Gott getan,
> Daß sich die Himmel regen
> Und Geist und Körper sich bewegen.
> Gott selbst hat sich zu euch geneiget
> Und ruft durch Boten ohne Zahl:
> Auf, kommt zu meinem Liebesmahl!
>
> Himself doth God leave not unproven!
> Both grace and nature to all mankind proclaim:
> This, all this, did, yea, God achieve
> So that the heavens waken
> And soul and body have their motion.
> God hath himself to you inclined
> And calls through heralds passing count:
> Rise, come ye to my feast of love!

He sets these last words of direct discourse as an aria, and the original tenor part contains—for the first time in his vocal works—the term "arioso." With few exceptions, from then on he uses the general heading "arioso" only in passages where the Vox Dei or Vox Christi speaks directly: the divine voice must not be heard in profane recitative but only in more significant passages. In the present instance, the miracle of creation, which causes the heavens to awaken and sets the human spirit and soul in motion, is presented as a little "study in motion":

Two Sundays later, in the cantata "Ein ungefärbt Gemüte," BWV 24, Bach sets the close of the recitative "Die Heuchelei ist eine Brut" as a heartfelt, even simple prayer, in aria style.

Four days after that, in the St. John's Day cantata "Ihr Menschen rühmet Gottes Liebe," BWV 167, Bach composes a recitative of such daring that Franz Wüllner, publisher of the cantatas in the old *Bach-Ausgabe,* questioned the accuracy of his sources. The philosophical key to the second part of the recitative, marked adagio, in which some observers have discovered a veritable trove of twelve-tone writing, is the text passage where Jesus leads lost sinners who "are truly repentant" to Paradise.[22] Bach demonstrates the difficulty of this path in a number of different ways—mounting dissonances, jarring chromaticism, unconventional melodic progressions. One gets the impression that since he had to do without a big opening chorus for this holiday cantata coming between two Sundays, he wanted at least to provide a movement whose harmonic refinement would go beyond what the text alone required and be more or less free-standing.

Bach composes the second recitative of the cantata with an arioso closing as well. This time, at the words "und stimmet ihm ein Loblied an" ("and raise to him a song of praise"), he anticipates the first melody line of the succeeding final chorale, "Sei Lob und Preis mit Ehren." This was a small foretaste of a practice he would repeatedly follow, as he had already done at Weimar, and finally most skillfully in the audition piece BWV 23, "Du wahrer Gott und Davids Sohn": weaving hymn tunes into his recitatives and so enriching them with additional meaning.

The most spectacular example of this weaving is the bass recitative "Ach, soll nicht dieser große Tag," which Bach incorporated along with four more numbers in the Weimar cantata "Wachet! Betet!," BWV 70a, before repackaging them in the BWV 70 version on the twenty-sixth Sunday after Trinity in 1723: the trumpet blasts the chorale "Es ist gewißlich an der Zeit" ("Now is in truth the time at hand") right in the middle of a dramatic invocation of Judgment Day. In a section of the New Year's Day Cantata, presented about five weeks later, "Singet dem Herrn ein neues Lied," BWV 190, he inverts the relation of recitative and chorale: the chorus intones the Lutheran Te Deum "Herr Gott, dich loben wir" one verse at a time in a four-part *falso bordone* setting, while between these lines the solo bass presents *in recitativo* the reasons for praising God.

The arias of the first cantata year are just as variously structured as the recitatives. Of course, the modern da capo aria form is on the horizon; but Bach barely follows this pattern: he deals with the form in reflective, multiple ways. This approach is clear even in the first aria he must set for BWV 75, "Mein Jesus soll mein alles sein." Right at the start he lays out the entire thematic and motivic material, which comprises a two-measure pattern with a moving bass part, autonomous in itself, but is still derived from the melody part. Both voices immediately swap themes:

This pattern will define the whole aria—even the middle section at the words "Mein Purpur ist sein teures Blut" ("My purple is his precious blood"), which of course normally would contrast with the sections framing it. So the form is not A-B-A' but A-A'–A". With such narrowly determined material one might expect a rather academic composition. But the feeling is dancelike, clearly taking its lead from the polonaise, and even the voice part does not slavishly follow the set two-measure model but starts with a free-swinging rhythmic theme that derives from the Pietist aria and perfectly suits the character and expressiveness of the text, which is about the love of Jesus. The strictly thematic model seems to have been forgotten, but not quite, of course: the quintessential motif of the aria ritornello can be heard in the bass:

Here we see profiled one of Bach's basic principles of creativity, the idea of making much from little—and not just in this one aria: coming as it does at the start of the whole year's cycle, it seems to have been the determining factor in his conception of the aria per se. One of its characteristics is the continuous use of the quasi-ostinato bass figure. In BWV 76, he works this figure into as many numbers as possible—not just in the arias but even in the homophonic four-part settings that close the first and second parts of the cantata:

In the aria "Hört, ihr Völker" from the same cantata, Bach employs a distinctive rhythmic motif, as a quasi-ostinato in the bass and also imitatively in the two other parts of the trio section.

That Bach made use of a technique that in the music theory of the time was sometimes known as *perfidia*[23] is a clear indication that he viewed his work for the first year's cycle as experimental, not just in the big opening choruses but in the aria form as well. The autograph score of BWV 76 contains considerable changes and corrections specifically to the aria "Hört, ihr Völker": only while actually composing the work does he decide to make consistent use of the *perfidia* technique.[24] He may have been inspired to do so by the text: just as the brief rhythmic motif is quickly passed from voice to voice, the nations with similar alacrity shall hearken unto the voice of God! But a more compelling reason may have been Bach's desire to subject the form of the aria to an overriding and rigorous compositional principle.

Examples of *perfidia* can be found occasionally in the works of Bach's contemporaries—for example in the duet "Dio pietoso" from Alessandro Scarlatti's oratorio *Il primo omicidio* (1706) or in Handel's psalm *Dixit dominus,* written about 1707. But generally speaking, a trio setting organized around a characteristic motif and structured throughout by a contrapuntal setting is not the ideal form for an aria. Bach did not give up this ideal in the arias for the *St. John Passion,* which he composed the following year, but he was able to make the result sound a little less unwieldy.

Bach's experimentation is not confined to structure. He is also concerned with bringing variety to his instrumentation: for the inaugural cantata BWV 75, in the aria "Ich nehme mein Leiden mit Freuden auf mich," he brings in the oboe d'amore, an instrument unfamiliar to most Leipzigers at that point. The trumpet is employed for the solo numbers in the cycle not only in the operatic *stile concitato,* as in the aria "Fahr hin, abgöttische Zunft" from BWV 76, but also, rather more unusually, in the alto solo "Ach, es bleibt in meiner Liebe," from BWV 77. Despite the generally demanding trio setting, the melodic feeling here is more of a religious song than of an aria; so it is all the more surprising that Bach entrusted the elaborately elegiac obbligato part to the trumpet.

Another factor that plays a role in the structuring and scoring of the first cantata cycle is the need to spare the boy soprano voices as much as possible in the coldest part of winter. Thus, in most of the works performed between the second day of Christmas and the first Sunday after Epiphany, there are no soprano arias (e.g., in BWV 40, 190, 153, 65, 154).[25] An examination of the cycle as a whole reveals Bach's tendency to reinforce the choir generally through the use of ripieno (orchestral) instruments. In Leipzig he could no longer fall back on the mature voices of female sopranos as he could in Weimar and Cöthen; but even the altos, tenors, and basses of the St. Thomas choir cannot always have possessed fully trained voices. A detailed study of the Leipzig performances of Weimar cantatas compared with their original Weimar versions might yield more precise information about the special conditions Bach had to deal with in Leipzig.

The systematic Bach may have had misgivings about the great variety of form used in the first Leipzig cantata cycle. Was it possible to create Lutheran church music of a more concentrated form and in the process promote the idea of a cycle? He explores this possibility in his second cycle, the chorale cantatas, and in so doing is actually reinforcing a local tradition. In 1690 the pastor of St. Thomas's, Johann Benedict Carpzov, published his *Lehr- und Liederpredigte* (Sermons Spoken and Sung), where he remarked that in his recent sermons he had not only explicated the respective Sunday's Gospel reading but in each instance had interpreted "a good old-fashioned Protestant Lutheran hymn" as well, and after the sermon he had the whole congregation join in and sing that hymn. He intended to continue this in the following year, and the cantor Johann Schelle promised to provide "pleasant music to every hymn" to be performed before the sermon.[26]

Carpzov was no longer living when Bach took office and so could not have been the instigator or librettist of the chorale cantata cycle Bach began on the first Sunday after Trinity in 1724. Is Bach's author perhaps the former *Konrektor* of St. Thomas, Andreas Stübel, whose chiliastic, that is, radically Pietist views caused his removal from office?[27] Hans-Joachim Schulze considered this scholarly and poetically gifted man a possibility because (among other reasons) he died after a three-day illness on 31 January 1725, just at the point when the last three libretti of the chorale cantata cycle set by Bach were due. Schulze conjectures that Stübel's death could have been the crucial factor causing the cycle to remain incomplete.[28]

There was probably only one author involved, who would of course have allowed Bach to make alterations. In the inner sections of the libretti, the author at first remained so faithful to the original words of individual hymn verses that his texts lack originality, but later on—perhaps at Bach's behest—he made his words more descriptive and emotionally affecting, then finally followed a kind of middle road. The outer portions of the cantata did not need tailor-made texts: the first strophe of a hymn appropriate for the Sunday in question would serve as both the textual and musical basis of the head motif, and one of the later strophes would likewise be the basis of the final chorale.

In this second cycle, the chorale cantatas, there are new impulses for both composer and listener. It gives Bach the chance to address a basic problem more systematically than in the first cycle, a problem that might loosely be described as the blending of mythos and logos in art. The chorale is mythos in the sense that it is religious practice and theology realized in sound, and as such it is more mythic than, say, the reading from the Bible: it is symbol made sound, and in each new realization it achieves its effect even without words.

When Johann Mattheson says in his *Compleat Kapellmeister* of 1739, "true choral song is not properly classified as music," he does not mean to disparage the chorale: the comment simply follows a statement he made just before this, that for music "two sorts of people" are required, namely, "compositeurs," whose task it is to create "figured" music, and "executeurs," who more or less "read,"or "recite" in a sense, what they find in the musical notation.

Since the chorale is not something composed, it does not meet the criterion of music. Nonetheless even the "most simple of psalms" can acquire the "quality of figured song" when a composer sets it.[29] Here the logos as creative impulse enters the picture, to confront mythos and shape it into a rationally planned and executable form. The process brings about a structure in which artistic creativity and the message of myth work as one. This dialectical relation between transcendence and the autonomy of art is inscribed in the heart of Lutheranism. Since the Reformation, Lutheran churches have cultivated the genre of choral musical treatments in whatever forms, such as motets or concertos, were current at the time.

With the start of the eighteenth century and the triumph of modern standard musical forms defined by their own inner logic, as exemplified by the instrumental concerto of Vivaldi or the da capo aria, the problem increases: How can the composer make use of the inaccessible and immutable nature of myth in musical forms that are becoming more and more autonomous?

Bach sees this problem with great clarity in the chorale cantata cycle. He must present the inherently heteronomous in an autonomous work of art and, accordingly, accomplish the "connection of integral musical forms with the chorale and its line-by-line melodic changes."[30]

In this cycle, in those first movements where he does not consciously follow the traditional sequence of the motet, he composes from multiple perspectives: he might build his "house" with an overture- or concerto-like form, or he might tell a story. In contrast to a concerted form, the chorale is not firmly established at the start but is constructed line by line in varying configurations.

An illumination called *The Building of Twelve Abbeys* from the late-medieval manuscript of Girart de Roussillon shows the different stages of work on buildings dedicated to God.[31] The illustrator does not mean to document any particular stage of construction, in the sense of modern photography, but to appreciate in pictorial form projects honoring God as sacred works of art. The hymn in a chorale setting is a re-creation wrought with a similar feeling of reverence; in the chorale cycle, when Bach structures his opening movements purely as motets, he functions much like an artist of the late-medieval period. But in those cantatas where he contrasts the chorale setting with a concerted or overture form, he is injecting tension into the work: to stay with the metaphor, this tension is that between a respectful copy and a modern creation, between heteronomy and autonomy.

In the first cantata, "O Ewigkeit, du Donnerwort," BWV 20, performed on the first Sunday after Trinity, the chorus replicates the bar form of the set chorale, the verse sequence a-a-b-a-a-b-c-c. Written as a modified *Kantionalsatz* (simple homophonic four-part setting) with the verses blocked in clusters, the chorale is clearly audible in the vocal-instrumental structure, particularly since the soprano melody voice is reinforced by a soprano trombone (*Zugtrompete*). Still, the chorale does not exercise complete control over the section, which is set up along the lines of the modern French overture in A-B-A' sequence: grave in 4/4 time, fugal vivace in 3/4, and again a final grave in 4/4.

The chorus of the chorale, as unwieldy as it may seem, must adapt itself to this framework and in the faster middle section let itself be overtaken by the 3/4 rhythm. In the final grave, even the lower voices participate in the thematic elements of the overture style. After the vivace middle section has ended in a dramatic diminished seventh chord, the grave motif from the first section does not start in again, as one might expect; rather, during an exchange between oboes and violins, we hear several dramatic orchestral chords, then another dotted motif, quite different from the beginning. The chorus enters immediately, and its lower voices take up both these elements, with the intention of providing further textual interpretation. The elements that suit the style of the French overture fit just as well with the "ganz erschrocken Herz" ("frightened heart") that the chorale makes mention of here.

Or is the entire thing driven by the chorale? Has Bach introduced these motifs in his overture only to help explicate the chorale? In any event, the entry motif of the overture is substantially derived from the first line of the chorale. To go a bit further: did Bach decide to use the overture form to give the new cycle a dignified opening—as he did in the first cycle—or because the inherently dramatic impact of the overture seemed best suited for bringing out the iron voice of Eternity? He must have discussed this with his librettist; for the chorale does not exactly fit the story of the rich man and poor Lazarus in the Gospel for the first Sunday of Trinity—it is more suited to the readings of the last Sundays of the church year, which deal with death and the last judgment. Accordingly, he used the chorale in the prior year at the top of cantata BWV 60 on the twenty-fourth Sunday of Trinity.

The opening movement of BWV 20 is certainly not the most technically difficult that Bach wrote for the chorale cantata genre, but it is a little marvel in its integration of heterogeneous elements like the chorale and French overture—far beyond the first attempt he made in Weimar with "Nun komm, der Heiden Heiland," BWV 61.

In the chorale cycle, his experimenting with the tension of two stylistic levels was not confined to one opening movement, of course; it is also apparent in a comparison of two cantatas. The motif opening the cantata, "Ach Gott, vom Himmel sieh darein," BWV 2, performed only a week later, on the second Sunday after Trinity, looks backward, inasmuch as it is a choral motet without instrumental obbligato. But we should not be too quick to see this motet as a composition in *stylus antiquus*—for there is a largely independent basso continuo that in the very first choral line adds a chromatic ascending fourth to the diatonic descending fourth of the Phrygian mode:

This "exposition" to a contrapuntal harmonic structure[32] cannot be explained simply by baroque compositional and figure theory, for it also anticipates some traits of concentrated motivic-thematic work, such as are found in Beethoven's *Große Fuge*, opus 135. The compositional historic bridge might be represented by Mozart's "Song of the Men in Armor" from *The Magic Flute*, which recalls Bach's set text "Ach Gott, vom Himmel sieh darein," with its strophe "Das Silber, durchs Feuer siebenmal bewährt," but at the same time also shows some traits of strict style.[33]

In Bach, the backward reference to the chorale and its theological meaning, and thus to mythos, is unmistakable. For this reason, cantata BWV 2 is the utmost expression of the tension between heteronomy and autonomy. We see this tension, of course, throughout

Bach's work: the vocal and instrumental works cannot be conceived of as separate from each other in this sense, the thinking of Theodor W. Adorno notwithstanding.[34]

Adorno is thinking primarily about the instrumental works, especially *The Well-Tempered Clavier*, when he praises Bach as the first composer to raise motivic-thematic work to the level of "universality," thus preparing the way for the concept of the integrated art work.[35] It is more with respect to Bach's vocal music when Adorno suggests that "the voice of a fully independent subject, its emancipation from myth simultaneous with a reconciliation with myth, and thus, with its truth content" was more fully developed with Beethoven than with Bach.[36]

But neither praise nor censure from Adorno's historical-philosophical viewpoint does Bach justice: it is precisely in his medial position between the ages that his significance lies, both in the vocal and the instrumental area. A choral adaptation like "Ach Gott, vom Himmel sieh darein" is not just a heteronomous work in the service of mythos—no more than a fugue from *The Well-Tempered Clavier* is just a harbinger of the fully independent subject and the integral work of art.

Let us now return to this thought: the overall concept of the chorale cantata cycle not only gave Bach the composer new momentum; it also gave his listeners in Leipzig more access to his art. Surely the large majority of worshippers could not comprehend his composition in every detail, but they could certainly follow a work that was organized about the text and strophic sequence of a well-known hymn repeated throughout the work: there was, despite all the compositional craft, a clearly perceptible thread to follow.

It was no arbitrary thread: the congregation had grown up with church hymns; they heard them not just in church but also from the itinerant student choirs known as *Currende;* they sang them and read them in their devotionals at home. They had their favorite chorales, and on the appropriate occasions selected special wedding or funeral chorales. They were more familiar with the hymnal even than with the Bible. A performance practice of Bach in later years shows just how important it was to him that worshippers be able to pick out the hymn tune of the cantus firmus, even in complex compositions. In individual voice parts added later on, in the chorale cantatas particularly, he reinforces the soprano voices of the choir with parallel instrumental accompaniments.[37]

The chorale cycle contains a remarkable mixture of old and new hymns. Of course, the traditional Lutheran hymn is predominant. But there are numerous newer ones of the Pietist aria type, among them "Was frag ich nach der Welt," BWV 94; "Was Gott tut, das ist wohlgetan," BWV 99; "Liebster Gott, wenn werd ich sterben," BWV 8; "Mache dich, mein Geist bereit," BWV 115; "Ich freue mich in dir," BWV 133; and "Liebster Immanuel, Herzog der Frommen," BWV 123. This mixture gives the impression of a conscious attempt to satisfy both the orthodox and quasi-Pietist factions in the religious community. Even more than that: the inclusion of the songs "Liebster Gott, wenn werd ich sterben" and "Ich freue mich in dir" underscores Bach's wish to take part in the topical musical and religious discourse of the day.

The first of these two melodies, the foundation of BWV 8, was included by the organist at Leipzig's St. Nicholas's Church, Daniel Vetter, in the second part of his *Musikalische Kirch- und Hauß-Ergötzlichkeit* (Musical Delights for Church and Home) in a four-part vocal setting, but not without making a few comments on its history: the Breslau theologian Caspar Neumann had composed the text, and Vetter, a Breslau native, had written the melody for it at the request of the Breslau cantor Jacob Wilisius, who wanted a funeral hymn for himself. After Wilisius's death in 1695, the hymn quickly became popular, although in *verstimmelter*—that is, mutilated—form. So Vetter desires now to publish a corrected version, "for the sake of many devout souls in this city [Leipzig], who though blessed with good fortune are all this notwithstanding ever mindful of their death."[38]

Eleven years later Bach appropriates Vetter's setting with a few changes as the final chorale in his own cantata BWV 8, thus clearly showing his acceptance of local traditions of piety. He takes a similar position two years later when he uses the setting "Welt ade, ich bin dein müde" by the former organist of St. Nicholas's Church Johann Rosenmüller as the final chorale for cantata BWV 27, "Wer weiß, wie nahe mir mein Ende." Both chorales have death as the subject: the singing of such chorales outside, and inside, the houses of certain citizens, not just when someone had died but as a sign of constant readiness for death, was an important duty of the *Currende,* who took the preferences and traditions of certain prominent families into consideration—as did their cantor.

An interesting case is the hymn "Ich freue mich in dir," which Bach used for BWV 133, the first strophe of which goes:

> Ich freue mich in dir
> Und heiße dich willkommen,
> Mein liebes Jesulein!
> Du hast dir vorgenommen,
> Mein Brüderlein zu sein.
> Ach, wie ein süßer Ton!
> Wie freundlich sieht er aus,
> Der große Gottessohn!

> I find my joy in thee
> And bid thee hearty welcome,
> My dearest Jesus-child!
> Thou hast here undertaken
> My brother dear to be.
> Ah, what a pleasing sound!
> How friendly he appears,
> This mighty Son of God!

The text is by the Leipzig poet, literary scholar, and jurist Kaspar Ziegler and was published in the *Geistreiches Gesangbuch* (Halle, 1697) and again in another *Geistreiches Gesangbuch* (Darmstadt, 1698)—two decidedly Pietist hymnals. Bach jotted down the melody he used for it in BWV 133—neither of these two collections had it— in the margins of the first page of the score for the Sanctus BWV

232^{III}, which was heard along with the cantata in one of the Christmas services of 1724. No printed version of the melody has been found dating before 1738![39] So Bach seems not to have known the song, and to have based it on a special, perhaps oral Leipzig tradition—further indication that the second Leipzig cantata cycle should be seen in the context of the local situation.

Today the most impressive thing about the cycle is the strictness with which Bach kept his composition within his theme: the integration of old and new. It is fascinating, for example, to see how he continues to deal with the *stylus antiquus*. While in BWV 2 it seems, outwardly at least, to have been the controlling force, in BWV 101, the cantata for the tenth Sunday after Trinity, "Nimm von uns, Herr, du treuer Gott," the antique style conforms to the modern concerted principle: the daring interweaving of choral motets with the very eloquent musical material first heard instrumentally in the introduction results in "a unique, very complex and almost inaccessible composition," in the opinion of Siegfried Oechsle.[40]

Bach's treatment of the opening section of the cantata for the fourteenth Sunday after Trinity, BWV 78, "Jesu, der du meine Seele," amounts to a tour de force.[41] He sees that the hymn tune can be combined with a well-marked ostinato: the familiar bass *lamento* from earlier music history appears in his own works—among other places, in the cantata BWV 12, "Weinen, Klagen," and in parodic form again later in the Crucifixus section of the B-Minor Mass. He uses the ostinato figure twenty-seven times in all, sometimes in other keys and parts, and once in an inversion.

Two even more distinctive features of this movement are the combination of choral melody with ostinato and their incorporation into the framework of a *concertante* setting with a very idiosyncratic ritornello. And, as if this were not enough: for every choral line Bach devises preimitations: these independent motifs vividly anticipate the message of each verse. The result is a many-layered composition that speaks on all levels—a work whose subtleties cannot be absorbed on first hearing but in which the chorale is unambiguously prominent.

One of the high points of the second cantata cycle is the "Herr Jesu Christ, wahr' Mensch und Gott," BWV 127, written for Quinquagesima (Shrove Sunday), 1725. The opening theme so impressed the generation after Bach that it was incorporated into the passion pastiche "Wer ist der, so von Edom kommt" (BC D 10), probably compiled after 1750, mostly from compositions of Carl Heinrich Graun. It is worth noting that Bach used material from no fewer than three chorales in this composition setting: "Herr Jesu Christ, wahr' Mensch und Gott" is the basis of the choral section; the tune "Christe, du Lamm Gottes" is interwoven here too—its first line in the opening ritornello; finally, in the continuo, one hears the start of a chorale repeatedly, in slightly altered rhythm, which can be identified as "O Haupt voll Blut und Wunden" or "Herzlich tut mich verlangen nach einem seel'gen End."

The ritornello that gives the movement its structure is distinctive: its head motif is derived from a diminution of the first line of the hymn "Herr Jesu Christ, wahr' Mensch und Gott"; it continues with a figure that is essentially a series of dotted sixteenths, which not only is a further development of the head motif but also is heard simultaneously with it. So even before the chorus has begun, the instrumental introduction has a structure of great density. A pair of recorders starts the development; an eighth note later an oboe duo comes in with the head motif; by the third bar the recorders take up this motif, which now is swapped among the instrumental parts and line by line becomes the material for the imitative voice setting that embellishes the cantus firmus.

At the very beginning, along with the recorders, two violins and a viola have also come in with the chorale line "Christe, du Lamm Gottes." Although this part is unmistakably harmonized with tonic, dominant, and subdominant, Bach has composed the first three measures of the continuo as a pedal point. After it, the continuo takes up from the oboes the head motif of the ritornello (i.e., the shortened first line of the chorale "Herr Jesu Christ, wahr' Mensch und Gott"), but after only two bars it transitions into the line of the chorale "Herzlich tut mich verlangen."

The attempt to describe just the first eight measures of the introduction puts one in the role of a reporter trying to describe a major event from several different angles simultaneously. But one should not conclude that this complexity makes the music difficult or incomprehensible. For Bach bathes this introduction in the bright light of a pastorale: when the recorders begin their lovely melody in thirds—in the typically pastoral key of F—over the extended tonic pedal point in the continuo, the impression is of the easy charm of a pastoral painting.

Beyond the emblematic level—Christ as the good shepherd, heaven as the ideal pasture—the symbolic meaning of the three choruses also merits the listener's attention. Here the cantus firmus of the main chorale is conspicuously foregrounded, especially its first line, "Herr Jesu Christ, wahr' Mensch und Gott" ("Lord Jesus Christ, true man and God"): as the subject of the head motif it is audible almost at every moment. Along with this, a central article of Christian faith, Christ's mediating role between God and man, is constantly invoked through repeated references to the three topoi: Jesus Christ, man, and God.

One could write a chapter on the compositional and theological significance of the rest of the cantata.[42] For Friedhelm Krummacher, even a book was not enough to plumb the depths of the chorale cantata cycle. We forgo further analysis here and simply describe the further course of this cantata, the recitatives and arias of which are exemplary for the whole cycle. First, a simple yet carefully worked out secco recitative interprets in musical terms such characteristic words as *entsetzet, nichts, Seufzer,* and *Ruhe* ("strikes terror," "nought," "sighing," and "repose," respectively); this recitative is followed by an aria whose exquisiteness is the equal of Bach's greatest creations in the genre and whose orchestration and form are unique in his work.

A solo oboe's soaring lyric melody contrasts with an almost static accompaniment, eighth-note staccato figures of the recorder duo and regular plucked quarter notes in the basses. The vocal line merges with the *vox humana* of the oboe. We could almost be hearing the kind of chamber music that can be found in the slow movements of

Bach's sonatas and concerti. A solo part introduces an elegiac, free-ranging melody; the other instruments provide a respectful, measured, almost motionless accompaniment. After this introduction another solo voice enters, the soprano, and immediately becomes intertwined with the instrumental solo. That such an arrangement is typical more of instrumental than vocal settings does not necessarily mean that Bach composed these structures out of autonomous musical thinking, with no connection to the text at hand.

Of course he had both specific models and individual details in mind before he would get involved with a set text. But he obviously calls them up and applies them with reference to the text. The oboe here surely stands for the soul, and the accompanying ensemble stands for the heavenly "idyll"[43] that this soul can expect after death. This textual reference gets even more specific in the middle of the aria, when the voice exclaims in the "Jesus tone" of a Pietist aria, "Ach ruft mich bald, ihr Sterbeglocken" ("Ah, call me soon, ye deathly tolling bells"), and the strings, silent till now, come in for four measures and two and a half beats to imitate the tolling bells with an undulating *lamento* pizzicato:

Krummacher is right that Bach did not intend to divert the listener with a figural imitation of tolling bells, knowing that a skillfully wrought "compositional structure" would ensure that such a setting has an emotional impact.[44] But if this composition had been purely instrumental, would Bach have found the nerve or even the justification to score a mere four and a half measures (out of ninety-six) with strings, to have them play a figure that does not appear anywhere else in the movement? Autonomous and figural viewpoints cannot be separated here: Bach does not need a textual justification to decide how something will sound. Which elements should be included is not just for the autonomous composer to decide: it is always an issue for the interpreter of the text and its meaning as well.

The aria "Die Seele ruht in Jesu Händen" in some of its idiosyncratic traits represents a dimension of composition that was new at the time: great feeling expressed in sound. Before that point in musical history, instrumentation of such delicacy was rare; the sound of bells tolling, especially, is an early and subtle example of composition using sound clusters (*Klangflächen*).

Nor does this observation complete the inventory of the cantata's figurative images; Bach appends a number modestly called "recitative," that is in fact like a little opera scene: blaring trumpets and string tremolos all in *stile concitato* depict Judgment Day, when heaven and earth are obliterated and Christ appears to render final judgment. The setting of the literal words of Christ, which could be called an arioso, contrasts His benevolence when addressing the faithful against three alternating invocations of the horrors of final judgment and death. The words "Verily I say unto you," addressed to the redeemed sinners, are underlaid with the ritornello theme from the introduction, thus recalling the line "Herr Jesu Christ, wahr' Mensch und Gott." The line lends its symbolic power to this genre picture, which in a different context might also connote secular struggle and strife.

The extent to which the cantata, from start to finish, is stamped with the sign of the chorale is shown not just by the ending chorale as such but by its final chord. This chord is C major, though the entire cantata is in F major: for the cantus firmus dictates it thus. Understood from the point of view of harmonic function and not modally, the piece ends with a false cadence on the dominant and not the tonic.

Here, if anywhere, Bach found his way to a classically balanced style in the chorale cantata form. On the one hand, strict form and variety of material dominate his treatment of the chorale; on the other, he uses modern tonal language to paint vivid images: a pastorale, the sound of bells tolling the hymn for the dead, and Judgment Day. All this is done by combining structural and figurative details into a collective whole that is not randomly or casually conceived, as it sometimes seems with Handel, but that makes clear distinctions for the listener between foreground and background.

It is not surprising that with this work the chorale cantata cycle nears its end: the various possibilities of the form have now been tried out and put into practice. Six weeks later, at the Feast of the Annunciation—with the cantata "Wie schön leuchtet der Morgenstern," BWV 1, which impressively combines a choral adaptation with concerted form, and with the "revival" of the early cantata "Christ lag in Todesbanden," BWV 4, on the first day of Easter, 1725—the cycle is complete for the time being. Did the Leipzig city council act in wise anticipation of what lay ahead when it refused to purchase Johann Kuhnau's musical testament from his widow? At any rate, with the completion of the first two Leipzig cantata cycles, Bach has most decidedly put his predecessor into oblivion.

However much we may admire Bach's highly sophisticated way of treating the church hymn, in the chorale cantata cycle in particular, we should be mindful of the fact that he plies his craft not in some theoretical hothouse but in keen awareness of real-world circumstances. The opening themes of those very cantatas that share a tendency for simple four-part vocal harmonic settings are those based on modern church hymns (e.g., BWV 94, 99, 8, 115, 133, and 123). Despite his treatment of genuinely Lutheran cantus firmi, Bach had no wish to "arrange" these arialike tunes or alter their metrical flow. This forbearance was a help to those listeners unfamiliar with complicated music and also met the expectations of the Pietists among them.

Although there is a large number of outstanding individual cantatas composed after the two Leipzig cycles, Bach did not compose any more cantata cycles of comparable uniformity, as far as we know today. He had solved the two main problems of the Protestant church cantata: presenting both the word of Scripture and chorales in a suitably dignified manner. In the discussion that follows, then, we speak not of large-scale successes but of individual trends.

First, we should take note of the works composed as supplements to the chorale cantata cycle. After the summer of 1725, Bach gradually composes a half dozen works, eventually to include them, one by one, in the still incomplete cycle. From 1725 to 1735 eight choral text cantatas are written.[45] Most of these are not meant to fill a gap in the cycle, nor can they be matched with any particular Sunday in the liturgical calendar. They may have been composed for the Sunday worship service, but as a small corpus of works they testify to Bach's intention to make a specific contribution to the genre of choral arrangements *per omnes versus* ("for all occasions"), a task he had attempted only once in the cantata cycle itself, with "Was willst du dich betrüben," BWV 107.

In a chorale text cantata, of course, there is no freely composed verse: the strophes of the hymns must serve as the textual basis for both arias and recitatives. This requirement makes the composing of the recitative sections difficult and the use of da capo forms almost impossible. It would be nice to know which aesthetic aspects of this special genre particularly appealed to Bach. Antecedents of the genre can be found in the choral concerted work *per omnes versus* and in his own early cantata "Christ lag in Todesbanden," BWV 4. For these Leipzig chorale text cantatas, instead of choosing Reformation chorale texts, he tends to pick hymns that are more the aria type, with flowing meters—quite likely intentionally.

Despite the significance of each work on its own, when they are performed serially, there is an undeniable risk of monotony. The text of a chorale provides less opportunity for the vivid presentation of images and emotions than does a good madrigal. The omnipresent form of the cantus firmus is also confining. Maybe Bach wants to prove that a church composer can succeed without using modern verse, and also save himself the trouble and expense of literary permissions. Or perhaps he had enough of madrigal texts, given that they played such a dominant role in the third cycle and even the "fourth"—so far as it can be reconstructed.

Any pronouncements on the overall profile of these last two cycles, each composed over a longer period of time, must be cautious, since the many gaps in our sources allow only a glimpse of general tendencies. With the third cycle, Bach's eagerness to start every cantata with a brand new choral movement has disappeared. Now there is often an aria at the top; this spares both his compositional labors and the St. Thomas choir voices, but at the same time it means giving up an impressive opening. Consequently, in this period he experiments with incorporating a chorus or an aria into an already existing instrumental movement, or he replaces the opening with a movement from an instrumental concerto.

He delivers a masterpiece for the first day of Christmas, 1725: the opening movement from the overture BWV 1069 is the basis for the opening section of the cantata "Unser Mund sei voll Lachens," BWV 110, but a four-part chorus ("unser Mund") is worked into the instrumental fabric. For the first time, he uses movements from solo instrumental concertos in the cantata "Wir müssen durch viel Trübsal in das Reich Gottes eingehen," BWV 146, which was probably written for 12 May 1726. He turns the first movement of the violin concerto BWV 1052a into the opening movement of the cantata and gives the violin solo melody part to the organ. He inserts a choral section ("Wir müssen durch viel Trübsal") into the slow movement of his concerto model. In the cantata "Geist und Seele sind verwirret," BWV 35, it is likely that he fell back on a concerto movement (i.e., the head motif of the lost D-Minor Concerto, BWV 1059) for the beginning and possibly made use of its other movements too: its slow movement might have served as the basis for the aria "Geist und Seele sind verwirret," and its finale may have been used as the instrumental introduction to the second part of the cantata. No less remarkable an example of this borrowing is the cantata "Gott soll allein mein Herze haben," BWV 169, performed 20 October 1725: its opening sinfonia is essentially identical with the opening movement of a concerto that has survived, not in its original setting for a solo melody part, but in its later arrangement as the Concerto for Harpsichord in E Minor, BWV 1053.

Bach inserts a new aria into the concerto's slow movement, its melody set to the words "Stirb in mir, Welt, und alle deine Triebe" ("Die in me, world and all of thy affections"). The poignant sweetness of the concerto's enchanting siciliano becomes even more meaningful as it is transformed into a farewell to false worldliness and a hymn in praise of divine love: a striking example of Bach's ability to make new and sometimes even greater works out of already finished pieces.

Just two weeks later Bach returns to the concerto BWV 1053, this time taking its unused final movement and placing it at the top of the cantata "Ich geh und suche mit Verlangen," BWV 49. Three weeks after that, the opening movement of the First Brandenburg Concerto serves him as the introductory sinfonia of the cantata "Falsche Welt, dir trau ich nicht," BWV 52.

What little remains of a presumptive fourth cycle, the Picander cantatas, contains three more adaptations of instrumental concerto movements. The fragmentary version we have of the introductory sinfonia, from the cantata "Ich habe meine Zuversicht," BWV 188, is evidently the final movement of a lost Violin Concerto in D Minor, which later became the clavier concerto BWV 1052. The model for the sinfonia of the cantata "Ich steh' mit einem Fuß im Grabe," BWV 156, is the middle movement of the Violin Concerto in G Minor, also lost, which Bach adapted into the clavier concerto BWV 1056. Already mentioned above is the first movement of the Third Brandenburg, recycled into the head movement of the cantata "Ich liebe den Höchsten von ganzem Gemüte," BWV 174.

The first performances of the last three works most likely took place between October 1728 and Whitsun 1729—the period when Bach took over the collegium musicum and significant new responsibilities. The obvious dominance of instrumental writing is a signal that the cantor Bach, except for a few exceptions in the area of chorale text cantatas, now finally bids farewell to the systematic and scheduled composition of cantatas, and in his place the kapellmeister Bach now takes the stage.[46]

THE PASSIONS

In its historic and aesthetic significance, the *Passion according to St. John* suddenly appears in the heavens like a new comet. Of course, the genre is not without precedent. In the free Hanseatic city of Hamburg, as early as 1705, for a small entrance fee one can attend a performance of a passion oratorio given in the municipal almshouse—with a text by Bach's later librettist Christian Friedrich Hunold and music by Reinhard Keiser, director of the Hamburg opera. Although conservative circles and the clergy are alarmed at this intrusion of the decadent element of opera into the realm of religious music, Hamburg becomes a center for performance of passions in a way that anticipates our modern concert world: the texts of the works performed are largely freely composed and are set essentially as in modern opera—as recitative, arioso, and aria.

In 1712 the Hamburg patrician Barthold Heinrich Brockes stages a private performance of his libretto *Der für die Sünde der Welt Gemarterte und Sterbende Jesus* (Jesus, Martyred for the Sins of the World) to Keiser's music: a major social event attracting some five hundred listeners. Four years later, Georg Philipp Telemann, who had just been called away to Frankfurt am Main as director of church music, has his own version of Brockes's Passion performed there in the Barfüsserkirche—not in the municipal almshouse, as originally planned, because of the anticipated crowds, "to which event many of the most renowned foreign musicians decided to come," including "Her Serene Highness the Princess of Hesse-Darmstadt."[1] Telemann writes in his autobiography of a further performance of this passion, where "guards were posted at the church doors, allowing no one to enter who did not have a printed copy of the passion."[2]

Events such as this may have encouraged Johann Mattheson, that champion of enlightened music appreciation for the bourgois class, to put on four different settings of the Brockes passion in the same year, 1719, one each by Keiser, Handel, Telemann, and himself. The paradigmatic importance of this event can hardly be overstated: that the audience could compare the stylistic merits and peculiarities of the competing composers' musical settings of an identical text makes it clear that it was musical pleasure and education of the bourgeois' musical tastes that mattered here. The event was not religious or even liturgical in the narrower sense.

In Leipzig, things are not this far along. Operas are occasionally presented—the local authorities want to convey an impression of cosmopolitanism, particularly at trade-fair season—but in introducing musical passions that are operatic, one must be careful. As mentioned earlier, Telemann's setting of Brockes's passion is presented in 1717 in the New Church—a secondary setting but also a tryout venue for contemporary religious music. Bach's predecessor Kuhnau first presents passions at the Thomaskirche in 1721 and 1722, which are straightforward, making do with songlike, simple choruses and solos.

But now Bach enters the scene with his contribution to the form. Perhaps he did not get quite this far in Weimar; we know little about the Weimar or Gotha Passion, previously mentioned. In Cöthen he lacked the opportunity to position himself at the vanguard of the form, but here in Weimar he starts to take control. He finds a basic text in the Brockes passion: seven of nine ariosos and arias are based on Brockes's texts, but these appear in more or less greatly altered form in the *St. John Passion*. Their general tone is unmistakable: gone is the overly florid speech and "high" style, replaced with simpler, more heartfelt language.[3] A comparison of two versions of the bass aria, "Eilt, ihr angefochtnen Seelen," shows the difference:

Brockes's Passion Text

Eilt, ihr angefochtnen Seelen,	Haste, O sorely tempted spirits,
Geht aus Achsaphs	Fly from Achsapus'
Mörder-Höhlen,	murderous caverns,
Kommt!—Wohin?	And come—whereto?
—Nach Golgatha!	To Golgotha!
Nehmt des Glaubens	Put ye on of faith the pinions,
Taubenflügel.	Flee—whereto? To the Hill
Fliegt! Wohin?	of Skulls.
—Zum Schädel-Hügel.	For your welfare bloometh there.
Eure Wohlfahrt blühet da.	

Bach's Passion Text

Eilt, ihr angefochtnen Seelen,	Haste, ye, O sorely tempted
Get aus euren	spirits,
Marterhöhlen,	Go forth from your torment's
Eilt!—Wohin?	caverns,
—Nach Golgatha!	Haste—where to?—to Golgotha!
Nehmet an des Glaubens	
Flügel.	Put ye on of faith the pinions,
Fliegt! Wohin?	Flee—where to?—the cross's
—Zum Kreuzes-Hügel.	hilltop,
Eure Wohlfahrt blüht allda.	For your welfare bloometh there!

The source of the words for the aria "Ich folge dir gleichfalls mit freudigen Schritten" has not yet been discovered; the text of the remaining ninth madrigal number, the aria "Ach, mein Sinn," comes from a textbook (1st ed. 1675) by the long-deceased Christian Weise, the Zittau school principal, poet, and teacher of poetics: *Der grünenden Jugend nothwendige Gedancken [...] in gebundenen als ungebundenen Reden* (Necessary Thoughts for Young People in Verse and Prose). The aria's text serves as an example of how a purely instrumental introduction can be given a "madrigalian ode" as an underlay.

But who would have been thumbing through an almost fifty-year-old text on poetics? Hardly Bach himself, who surely had other things to do, but perhaps his librettist Picander, whose bourgeois name was Christian Friedrich Henrici, then just 24 but already well known in Leipzig as an enterprising creator of occasional poetry for weddings and the like. The first hard evidence of their collaboration dates to 1725, but Picander might still have been given the job of adapting the libretto for the *St. John Passion*. A more experienced librettist would not be so quick to attempt improving a text of the highly esteemed Brockes oratorio; but a young, self-taught poet would not think twice about taking an aria text from an older didactic work.

By offering the revised Brockes text, Bach is serving up the latest thing in the genre. He is also doing something else, quite purposefully: basing his passion on Bible quotations and chorales. He is definitely not creating an aesthetically unified, freely composed passion-oratorio, as later musicologists will come to name the genre. Rather, it is an "oratorical passion" in which there is a place both for the liturgically traditional elements of Bible citation and chorales and for freely composed aria texts, so that theology and poetics shake hands, so to speak. This decision may have been in accord with his instructions as St. Thomas cantor not to compose "theatrically," but it is, most important, *his* decision.

This matter would be of interest only to historians of music and Pietism were it not for Bach's imaginative power, able to create the contours of a great work from a collection of texts that, seen objectively, could be termed a clever compromise between tradition and invention. This power is evident right from the opening chorus, with the words:

Herr, unser Herrscher, dessen Ruhm in allen Landen herrlich ist.
Zeig' uns durch deine Passion, daß Du, der wahre Gottessohn,
Zu aller Zeit, auch in der größten Niedrigkeit, verherrlicht worden bist.

Lord, thou our master, whose repute
In every land majestic is!
Show us through this thy passion
That thou, the very Son of God,

In every age,
E'en in the midst of deepest woe,
Art magnified become!

The selection of texts alone is extraordinary: it is consistent, of course, with the theology of the Gospel according to John in presenting not a patient, suffering Christ but Christ as an omnipotent ruler. This youngest of the Evangelists also emphasizes more clearly than the others that Jesus himself sovereignly decides, as the incarnate word of God, on his own martyrdom, never losing his majesty or dignity. Still, there is no other passion in the history of the form that deals, as this one does, primarily with the Savior's suffering in the opening movement and where the music is meant to portray emotion, the emotions chosen are those of pain and suffering.

Also remarkable is the text of the opening chorus. Its first half is based on Psalm 8.2 (and perhaps also a liturgical formula), but its second half is free verse, which, in its linguistic simplicity, even conventionality, does not offer the composer any special reason to indulge in tone painting. Bach's intellectual power alone forms from this text a movement that, with one stroke, is the artistic fulfillment of the promise that the Hamburg settings of Brockes's passion only hinted at: it is the gateway to modern concerted music.

Where else, in all the eighteenth century, besides Bach's *St. Matthew Passion*, does there exist a similarly large-scale vocal-instrumental construct, sublime in character, with such powerfully interpretative language and such symphonic scope? The form is defined by an opening orchestral movement, whose essentials are set forth in the first eighteen bars. It becomes a foil for the choral section but could stand alone. The choral setting is strongly related to the instrumental setting; essential portions of it are composed over sections of the instrumental introduction.

The way in which three characteristic semantic motifs are interwoven in the stand-alone instrumental movement is unique for its time. No doubt a symbolic intent, conceivably to represent the Trinity, lies behind this compositional method. The basso continuo line stands for God the father; the woodwind instruments, sometimes in strict canonic leading, often playing dissonances on the accented beats, remind us of the sufferings of his son, through the use of the "painful" intervals—that is, diminished second, augmented second, tritone and major seventh intervals; the Holy Ghost is heard in the surging movement of strings.

Because Bach's composition is always grounded in multiple perspective, we can ignore such Trinitarian speculation and look at the work in purely symbolic terms, without detracting at all from the profundity of meaning. In such a view, the basses represent calm, the strings a self-contained circular motion, while the winds ultimately depict that dynamic force that gives a direction to these elements of calmness and self-contained motion, making them "historical":

Into this complex orchestral movement, filled with tension and dissonance, Bach introduces a large-scale vocal setting, which in a rhetorical gesture—short chordal outbursts and surging melismata—appeals to God the Son as a sovereign ruler (*Herrscher*). This could be seen as a kind of crowning of Jesus, triumphant even in suffering. Then, in an imitative gesture, at the words "größten Niedrigkeit" ("greatest humiliation"), the music sinks to an extremely low register, in the sense of the traditional musical-rhetorical device called catabasis.

In its details and as a whole the passage offers many interpretative possibilities but also provokes questions concerning its form. On the surface we are dealing with da capo form; but the fugue motif of the central portion, at the words "Zeig' uns durch deine Passion" ("Show us through thy passion"), does not constitute the expected contrast to the motif of the framing sections (the words "Herr, unser Herrscher" ["Lord, thou our master"]) but is almost exactly the same. Although this duplication does not diminish the power of the movement, it is a little less convincing than, for instance, the solution Bach came up with in the opening movement of the *St. Matthew Passion:* the beginning of the *St. John Passion* seems more untamed, still "fermenting," as it were.

The enormous artistry here, which for Bach was identical with profundity, continues to be evident in the ariosos and arias of the *St. John Passion.* Of course Bach had already written many beautiful arias in his church cantatas. But his first truly great work seems to have spurred him on to greater efforts, to set himself new standards: aside perhaps from "Mein teurer Heiland," every aria is unmistakably a treasure.

Their instrumentation is sophisticated: the respective arias are scored for two oboes, two unison flutes, strings, two violas d'amore, strings, viola da gamba, continuo, flute, and oboe da caccia. The setting of the two ariosos is similarly refined, with two violas d'amore and lutes, two flutes, two oboes da caccia and strings, respectively. Wide-ranging instrumentation such as this can hardly be found in the church music of Bach's predecessors or contemporaries; it evokes the small ensembles of the courtly households, and particuarly those of early German opera, whose composers favored settings with characteristic, striking instrumentations.[4]

The arioso "Mein Herz!"—a mere nine bars—alone makes clear that it would be misinterpreting Bach to see his thinking just in structural, symbolic, and representational terms. Sound, and how it is achieved, is no less important. First, the static winds are followed by the strings with their ragged, dark, low-lying tremolo: as they pause, the tenor sings his first "Mein Herz!," and the strings take up their tremolo once more. The first measure brings in the agitated, trembling heart, and the next six measures reveal the world's response: the sun in eclipse, the rending of the temple curtain, the earth quaking, the graves giving up their dead. As this unfolds, the static winds start to surge, and the tremolo strings grow more violent and expansive.

The voice part describes the events occurring with all sorts of augmented and diminished steps and jumps. Wild tone clusters take form as well, and their tension is the product of an extended bass G, held through almost six bars, while chords, dissonant in themselves, are played by the winds in their meandering transformation from G major toward A major. This extended G takes on new and surprising functions in the harmonic fabric, even while simply being there. The predominant sense here comes from the sound alone, notwithstanding the density of the narration: the descant of the bass beneath the slow progress of the winds, a mixture of two different colors, and against this the harsh unison tremolo of the strings—played on an open G in the violins, thus without any refining vibrato from the left hand.

We must remember that Bach could not select his Leipzig musicians but had to adapt *nolens volens* to conditions as they were. Even the scoring of the ariosos and arias described above is not always that of the first performance, which possibly took place without any transverse flutes: in light of the various versions of the *St. John Passion,* such a scoring would rather be a "best case."

Each of the arias shows its character not just through the instrumentation but by a process, taken quite far here, of reducing the text to a single idea that can be captured in musical tones—symbolic, representational, and absolute all at once. A wonderful example is the aria "Ach, mein Sinn." Bach understands this text as an expression of desperation and distance from God and thus works doggedly with a single compositional pattern, constantly repeating a descending chromatic *lamento* in the bass. While the basic structure, a chaconne, calls to mind the ineluctability of fate, its string writing evokes a feeling of confusion: the individual voices have discontinuous rhythms, written more or less against one another, with short and long note values in abrupt alternation; the stresses of meter and measure are constantly shifting.

With all the devices of musical rhetoric, the tenor articulates Peter's despair at having denied his savior. The indecisive lingering on the dissonance E#-G#-B-C# at the words "Ach, mein Sinn" can be seen as the rhetorical figure *dubitatio,* the subsequent explosive major sixth B-G# is an *exclamatio,* and so on. At the same time, the tortured, assaultive sound of the tenor part has both a rhapsodic immediacy and a theatricality. Once again we see Bach's double perspective, as Janus-like he gazes back to the scholarly tradition of humanism and ahead into the Sturm und Drang to come.

Works of this concentration, difficult yet comprehensible at the same time, did not fall into Bach's lap; he considered and reconsidered appropriate models, and took his time in working out the details, his daily duties notwithstanding. This consideration is shown by comparing, for example, the soprano aria "Ich folge dir gleichfalls mit freudigen Schritten" from the *St. John Passion* with the bass aria "Ich folge Christo nach" from the cantata "Weinen, Klagen, Sorgen, Zagen," BWV 12. Bach composed the cantata in 1714 for the Weimar court church services and presented it again ten years later in

Leipzig, a few weeks before the *St. John Passion*. It would be pointless to stack the two works up against each other, as a whole, but this particular comparison demonstrates that he often did not settle for one solution, even if it succeeded, but continued to search for a better answer.

In the bass aria of the Weimar version, the theme of following was already a key concept: right at the start, the string part is written as a canon, as if to symbolize this idea; later the vocal part is also brought into the canon. Compare this graphic but relatively unsophisticated device with the craft Bach brings to the soprano aria of the *St. John Passion*. First he changes the meter from a spirited but not very characteristic 4/4 to the 3/8 rhythm typical of a lively passepied. The dancelike character of the aria is underscored by the conventional (though highly unusual for Bach) periodic structure of part A; its forty-eight measures can be easily grouped into four-measure, eight-measure, and sixteen-measure patterns.

Bach is just as consistent in his development of the idea of following as he is with the dance element of "die freudigen Schritte" ("joyful steps"). In the Weimar bass aria, the ritornello theme illustrates the idea of "Schritt für Schritt" ("step by step"), and the canonical entry of instruments and voice illustrates "Folgen" ("following"). But now he is not content with this simple construct: not only does each melodic step follow the last, the second flute measure follows the first one exactly, and in bar 5 a series of sequences begins in the flute voice. In contrast to the Weimar aria, the basso continuo moves independently of the "Folge" motif. The flute and voice parts are sinuously interwoven in various ways—they don't just follow each other in canon. The message of the text is that the souls of the faithful need sometimes to be pushed and pulled into following; the middle section brings this out clearly. Toward the end of the aria, the two voices have reached a state of near-perfect harmony: they no longer simply follow one another in docile canon but proceed together, intimately linked in thirds.

There are only a few Bach arias in which the continuo and the instrumental obbligato maintain their respective rhythms with such persistence. Donald J. Grout spoke of a "moto perpetuo" here: it is meant to give an impression of unstoppable continuity, both musically and in the sense of the continuity of the Christian religion.[5] All in all Bach uses many subtly different means to portray the idea of succession. He is somehow able to let the different aspects of this idea appear as a motif in a thematic development and still give the movement a closed structure. A da capo is suggested, but its repeated section overshoots its assigned goal of mere repetition—it turns the finale into the real high point of the aria. The fact that this aria, purely instrumental for long stretches, could be performed as a trio movement, unlike its Weimar counterpart, shows clearly the extent to which Bach, in his first great passion, was testing his ability to concentrate and integrate different perspectives in a comprehensible form.

Comprehensibility does not necessarily imply the use of conventional da capo arias. Bach does not reject this form wholesale, but in the arias of the *St. John Passion* we can gauge how much he has moved away from its formulaic nature. He expressly writes a da capo only for the aria "Erwäge" and in "Eilt, ihr angefochtenen Seelen," where the opening ritornello is repeated anyway; but the other arias evidence a nondogmatic approach to da capo form. Throughout the despairing course of "Ach mein Sinn," it is completely omitted, and in "Es ist vollbracht" it is skillfully worked into the dramaturgy of the aria: after the segment "der Held aus Juda siegt mit Macht und schließt den Kampf" ("The man of Judah wins with might / And ends the fight"), where the fanfares of victory introduce an almost operatic quality, the setting of the last half line "es ist vollbracht" ("it is fulfilled") leads back to the beginning.

To the audiences of the day, if they considered only the music and not the text, did music of this kind seem religious or secular? In 1721, a few years before the *St. John Passion* was first performed, Gottfried Ephraim Scheibel, in the previously mentioned *Zufälligen Gedancken*, writing on setting religious texts to secular arias, had opined: "the Affect remains / it is only that the *Objecta* vary / in that, e.g., here one feels spiritual pain, there, a worldly one [...]

just as I am saddened by secular things / so I can also be saddened by spiritual ones / as I rejoice in the one / I can rejoice in the other. The Tone which pleases me in an *Opera* can do the same in a Church."[6]

This work, which appeared in the trade-fair cities of Frankfurt and Leipzig, may have been known to the Leipzig superintendent, who in his notes spoke of the "musical arias" of the *St. John Passion* that Bach had circulated. Whether he was being a bit condescending or skeptical toward the self-referential art Scheibel was promoting, we do not know. But it is a fact that Bach not only employs an artful, expressive writing style in the freely written portions of his passion but devotes the same attention to his setting of biblical citations and chorales—regardless of whether he is setting the "soliloquies," the *turba* choruses, or the cantus firmus movements.

It is not just respect for the ecclesiastical tradition, particularly in Leipzig, that causes Bach, unlike Brockes, to leave untouched the prose biblical portions of his passion narrative—the decision is also artistically inspired, as can be seen throughout the score. Rhymed adaptations could not have even approximated the immediacy and liveliness of Luther's text, and Bach had no reason, even musically, to set the parts of the Evangelist, the Savior, Peter, and so on—the soliloquizers—as direct speech. Bertolt Brecht, the master of epic theater, was fascinated two hundred years later by the "model of dramatic music" shown in the Evangelist's first words, "Jesus went with his disciples over the brook of Kedron." Brecht: "He gives us the precise location of the stream."[7]

This does not mean that in setting the words Bach was particularly concerned with the location of the brook of Kedron. But he gives the music, in its unadorned directness, a vividness and availability to the senses that lets us see the events in their historical facticity and yet also having a significance that goes beyond it. These are not opera recitatives, condensations to advance the plot and give the singers their cue for the next aria. He is setting the doctrine of salvation in the actual words in which it was spoken. This kind of direct yet profound speech is in the tradition of Heinrich Schütz's *Kleine geistliche Konzerten:* the music is organized around the text being performed but has at the same time an order of its own. Music could be compared to human gesture: from a distance, it seems to have structure but remains something apart; up close and in the context of specific words, it communicates a concrete message.

The opening recitative of the *St. John Passion* shows this double character. On the one hand, the declamation is set up with great care: like a good orator, Bach organizes the statements around smaller units of meaning; he emphasizes key words like "Jesus," "Jünger," "Kidron," "Garten," "Judas," "verriet," and "wußte" ("disciple," "Kidron," "garden," "Judas," "betrayed," and "knew") by having them appear on the downbeat of the measure or sung on the high notes. In general the voice leading is livelier and so more expressive than in an ordinary secco recitative. But he is careful to maintain logical musical organization. The first section of this example is framed in C minor; the second section has a harmonic center of F minor; he begins each section with a descending third, giving it a heading: "Jesus," "Judas."

This *parallelismus membrorum* contains a third element of Bach's style: the music has symbolic qualities. Jesus is given the major third, Judas the minor third, and the frame in which it is set is a tritone lower. This interval (the tritone) was unnatural to the ancients, the "diabolus in Musica"; even in Bach's time, when given a significant placement, it signified something unusual if not uncanny.

Occasionally Bach employs a style for the Evangelist's part that, in Mattheson's Enlightenment view, should be permitted only in an aria and even then only for a "special reflection"; but for a recitative, "where the material is just rendered more or less as speech," it seemed to him "silly and tasteless."[8] However, in Bach's passions, for example in narrating the scourging of Jesus, the graphic tonal description is a reflection of the direct emotional involvement of the passion audience, sublimated though it may have been, especially in the artfully worked-out arias:

Da nahm Pi - la - tus Je - sum und gei - - - - - ßel-te ihn.

As a rule, for the *turbae*—that is, the exclamations of the soldiers, disciples, Jews, et cetera—Bach writes directly out of everyday speech patterns and the dramatic situation. Many are masterpieces of figural writing as well, polyphonic, but having both emotional punch and symbolic qualities. Looking at the "Kreuzige" ("Crucify") chorus, one wonders what inspired Bach to write such a perfect genre piece. More than the other outstanding numbers in this passion, it has kept its dramatic power down to the present day—one can plausibly hear it as a modern tone-cluster work. There is nothing like it in the works of his contemporaries, nor are there any known relevant preliminary works by Bach himself.

He made the single word "kreuzige" the dramatic center and theological high point of the passion. In a compositional style approximating fugal form, that is, skillfully polyphonic but not rigidly contrapuntal, the key word of the passion is heard against rhythmic masses of sound and mordant dissonances, a pandemonium of howling, cursing, and wild gesticulating. Very seldom in musical history has the expression of passionate hatred been so tellingly translated into music.[9] Naturally, this style is not without its theological-historical background: one interpretation of the passion story made popular in Bach's time by the Rostock theologian Heinrich Müller, presented here as *pars pro toto*, called the "Kreuzige" cries the "murder song of the Jews," continuing that "even today the world is possessed by a murderous rage like that of the Jews."[10]

Musically the chorus may represent the genre picture of a charivari in an anti-Semitic context.[11] According to another interpretation, in the stereotypical instrumental figures found in the Jews' chorus "Wir dürfen niemand töten" and the soldiers' chorus "Lasset uns den nicht zerteilen," Bach falls back on the traditional musical technique of *perfidia* (literally, "faithlessness"), which is the persistent retention of one figure or compositional technique.[12] The three matched pairs of *turba* choruses could be a reversion to the idea of *perfidia:* the Jews' and soldiers' adamant repeating of the phrases "Sei gegrüßt, lieber Jüdenkönig" and "Schreibe nicht: der Jüden König," "Kreuzige, kreuzige" and "Weg, weg, mit dem, kreuzige ihn"; and "Wir haben ein Gesetz" and "Lässest du diesen los" ("Hail to thee, king of the Jews," "Do not write 'king of the Jews,'" "Crucify, crucify," "Off, off with him, crucify him," "We have with us a law," "Let this one go free").[13]

Finally, the "Kreuzige" chorus can be interpreted symbolically: the diagonal leading of individual voices results in crossing of the voices: the free composition makes crossing almost unavoidable, but the text seems to demand it. The movement from the G minor of the opening to the final D major—that is, opening to the dominant—can be seen as the breakthrough to a "cross"-key.[14]

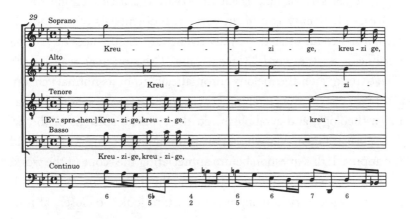

There are no polyphonic renditions of church hymns in the first version of the *St. John Passion,* apart from the inclusion of the choral section in the aria "Mein teurer Heiland." So Bach takes all the more trouble with the twelve hymn verses, distributed more or less evenly throughout the work, which constitute the congregation's response to the Word of the Bible, and with their reflection in the ariosos and arias. Despite the homophonic compositional mode, note against note, he still finds places to insert different colors, in the sense of characteristic "harmonizing styles," to use Werner Breig's terminology.[15] For instance, the relative simplicity and restrained use of notes foreign to the key, as in "Er nahm alles wohl in Acht," reflect the sermonlike consolations of the text, while the chromaticism of "Petrus, der nicht denkt zurück" mirrors Peter's anguish at his denial of Christ. In the very first chorale, "O große Lieb," the path of suffering that Jesus must take is illustrated by the accumulating dissonances: only twenty-two of the forty-two downbeats of the melody are normal triads or sixths—fully twenty are dissonances of varying harshness. At the word "Marterstraße" ("the martyr's way") Bach even dares to alter the melody chromatically from its normal version.

If we consider overarching criteria such as composition, dramaturgy, theology, and symbolism, do the separate sections of the *St. John Passion* taken as a whole constitute a large form? One should not approach this question before appreciating the scope of the work, its wealth of wonderful detail. It is true for the *St. John Passion* as it is for every great, rich, living work of art: to look too closely at how the masonry is joined may detract from the pleasure and emotional impact of the edifice.

Nonetheless, the question regarding general principles of order and structural sense in the work is justified and should be answered in a nuanced way. There is a case for skepticism here. This form in particular, the passion oratorio, does not allow much leeway for thinking in formal or symmetrical terms, even though theological (or perhaps Neoplatonist) Bach scholars will insist on searching for it. But the highly colorful drama of biblical testimony is the passion oratorio's one fixed and unchanging measure, and it is difficult enough to arrange arias and chorales so that they "answer" as precisely as possible the preceding Bible passage, let alone allow of being spaced evenly throughout the work.

Bach dismantles the passion's symmetrical framing of opening and closing choruses, which had become a firm tradition, by following the actual final chorus with the simple chorale "Ach Herr, laß dein lieb Engelein." This need not have been his artistic decision; it could have been the wish of the Leipzig cleric whose task it was to vet the text. As a general rule, vocal works of this scale were composed for a specific performance, a situation that could change from time to time and indeed often did. It is hard to imagine that Bach would have held any preconceived notions about using a large-scale format.

On the other hand it should be kept in mind that Bach always wants to secure some kind of logic for his compositions on a larger formal level, as the last mentioned example illustrates. Even where he does not explicitly wish to achieve cyclic organization in a larger work, he is a great artist of form, with the ability to impose overarching order almost casually—that is, perhaps not with ultimate consistency but with an inclination toward unity throughout. Klaus Hofmann has taken a look at the *St. John Passion* arias with this in mind: he finds the keys chosen such that they "form a series of thirds; up to the fifth of the ten aria settings, they are descending, then ascending."[16] This calculus is not perfect: "Durch dein Gefängnis, Gottes Sohn ist uns die Freiheit kommen" doesn't fit well into this series; as Hofmann says himself, not only was it composed as a chorale but its words are more like a hymn.

We need not be disturbed by small irregularities such as this: there is evidence of an underlying principle that played a role in a more extensive tonal organization of the *St. John Passion* but that was evidently not of paramount importance: Bach eliminated it in his revision the following year. In any case, he arranged the arias in the passion with care. Also, this work should in no way be considered more naively dramatic and eclectic in nature than the *St. Matthew Passion*—although this was once the unanimous judgment in the literature dominated by Spitta and Schweitzer.

The more open-minded we are to other theories on the large-scale form of the *St. John Passion,* the more benefit we can derive from them: they prompt further thought and research. In 1926 Friedrich Smend saw the "heart" of the passion consisting of numbers 16e to 27a of the *Neue Bach-Ausgabe.*[17] Expanding on the above-mentioned correspondences of the three pairs of turba choruses, Smend postulates a mirror-symmetrical arrangement of these numbers about a central axis formed by the chorale "Durch dein Gefängnis." In a work appearing a few years later, Hans-Joachim Moser postulates a similarly symmetrical arrangement of "tonal surfaces."[18] Picking up this idea and criticizing it at the same time, Eric Chafe (himself criticized in turn)[19] differentiated three tonality centers that Bach used in symmetrical arrangement: one each for the flatted keys, the sharped keys, and the "natural" key of C major / A minor.[20]

Bach's passions are unequal sisters. Robert Schumann found the *St. John Passion* so much "more daring, more powerful, more poetic" than the *St. Matthew Passion:* "How dense, how totally brilliant in the choruses, and how masterfully done!"[21] But even this original view does not obscure the fact that in the *St. Matthew Passion* Bach takes a giant step toward classicism. This can be seen even in the libretti: while the *St. John Passion* is a compilation based on the well-known Brockes text, the libretto of the *St. Matthew Passion* exhibits a structure that was planned and conceived from the outset. Bach himself may have set the theological direction and asked his librettist Picander to work from Heinrich Müller's *Geistreicher Passions-Schule* of 1688, which is visibly present throughout as the model.[22] Here is an example:

Heinrich Müller	**Matthäuspassion**
Am Abend /	Am Abend da es kühle war,
da der Tag kühle worden war /	
kam die Sünde der Menschen	Ward Adams Fallen offenbar;
ernstlich ans Licht /	
am Abend nimmst sie Christus	Am Abend drücket ihn [den Satan]
wieder mit sich ins Grab /	

daß ihr nicht mehr
gedacht werde.
Um die Vesper=Zeit
kam das Täublein Noah
zum Kasten / und siehe /
ein Oel=Blat hatte sie abgebrochen
und trugs in ihrem Munde.

der Heiland nieder

Am Abend kam die Taube wieder

Und trug ein Ölblatt
in dem Munde.

At evening, when the day had
become cool,
The Sin of Man was first revealed.
At evening, Christ took it down
with him into the grave,
That it never again be thought of.
And at vesper-tide, the dove
returned to Noah's ark,
And lo! It had broken off an
olive branch,
And bore it in her mouth.

At eventide, when it was cool,

Was Adam's fall made manifest;
At eventide the Savior
overwhelmed him.

At eventide the dove returneth,

Its mouth an olive branch now
bearing.

Picander may well have used other models for individual numbers. He bases the final chorus in particular on his own previously
published passion libretto of 1725: *Erbauliche Gedancken auf den grü-
nen Donnerstag und Charfreytag* (Edifying Thoughts for Maundy
Thursday and Good Friday). But his new passion verses are superior
in every way: only now is Picander in a position to create a libretto
that is poetically deft, replete with images and ideas, a libretto that
meets totally modern criteria. So with his introduction featuring the
allegorical figures "The daughter of Zion and the faithful," he is in no
way grounding his work solely in the older Brockes passion. He is
also in agreement (for a change!) with Johann Christoph Gottsched:
in his famous poetics, *Versuch einer Critischen Dichtkunst* (1730),
Gottsched expressly wanted the oratorio genre to have not just
biblical characters but also "allegorical figures from religion; such
as faith, hope, charity, the Christian church, the spiritual bride,

Sulamith, the daughter of Zion, or the faithful soul."[23] Should these last two figures, which indeed appear only in the printed libretto and not in Bach's score, have even been mentioned in Gottsched's poetics with reference to Bach's *St. Matthew Passion*?

Picander uses the pair to give his text a consistent structure and to give the composer a chance to compose in dialogue or multiple choruses. Of course his verses represent only one textual level of the *St. Matthew Passion:* the other level is that of the Bible passages and chorales. These two levels meet in the opening chorus: the singing of the chorale "O Lamm Gottes unschuldig" is built right into the middle of the eight-voice double choir, where the daughter of Zion and the faithful come together. All this, including the instrumental voices, is a highly differentiated construct. Yet when the passion is rediscovered in 1829, Adolph Bernhard Marx can still say, "This rich work of art is as simple in its total combined effect as the Strasbourg cathedral, which Goethe taught us how to see."[24]

Would Marx have said this about any single section of the Chorale Cantata cycle, or has the opening chorus of the *St. Matthew Passion* attained a new quality? Despite its basic polyphonic structure, nowhere is there the impression of strained contrapuntal work; instead, the section flows along with an elegiac expansiveness, and the seven lines of the cantus firmus fit in very naturally. The secret is not so much the section's clear form as its dialogic principle. Bach uses the two choruses in brilliant fashion to lay out the text's fundamental message. The diction is conversational, direct, and clear, and the text is easy to understand, despite the several moving voice parts. It is hard to imagine that librettist and composer did not discuss the music-text fit in detail:

> Tochter Zion: Kommt, ihr Töchter, helft mir klagen, sehet!
> Die Gläubigen: Wen?
> Tochter Zion: Den Bräutigam. Seht ihn.
> Die Gläubigen: Wie?
> Tochter Zion: Als wie ein Lamm

Cantus Firmus (als Bestätigung hinzutretend): O Lamm Gottes unschuldig. Am Stamm des Kreuzes geschlachtet.

Daughter of Zion: Come, ye daughters, share my mourning...
See ye!
The Faithful: Whom?
Daughter of Zion: The Bridegroom there, behold Him.
The Faithful: How?
Daughter of Zion:...just like a lamb
Cantus Firmus: O Lamb of God unspotted
Upon the cross's branch slaughtered.

Even more than the opening chorus of the *St. John Passion*, the movement is a piece of great vocal-instrumental symphonic music. Doris Finke-Hecklinger sees it as the embodiment of "pure pastorale,"[25] in a minor key, of course, and in contrast to the pastorale's light, dancing quality almost every melody note is harmonized. The cantus firmus, whose text deals with the Lamb of God, fits marvelously smoothly into the rolling 12/8 meter. The opening pedal point invokes ideas of nature, but the nature is that of a primal landscape. It is the impulse of a fundamental new beginning, such as Brahms sought for decades before he could give it new expression in the first bars of his first symphony.

But we are getting ahead of ourselves. Bach's audience probably took little notice of new departures but was immediately struck by the musical gesture of restrained grief, which, compared to the opening of the *St. John Passion* or the earlier Leipzig cantatas, has traits of gallant-courtliness. But there is a great deal more. In the cantus firmus, written into the score in red ink, is the symbol of belief, like a shining rescue ship sent out onto a surging sea of grief. Archaically bright G major is sent into battle against elegiac E minor. The visual power of this genre scene, the immanent logic revealed as it unfolds, becomes relativized; another force takes the helm, opens up the closed form, crosses the frontier of the aesthetic norm, and steers a new course. In the theology of Bach's day, the cantus firmus points to a heavenly Jerusalem as a counterpart to the earthly one, from which the lamentations of the two choirs are heard.[26]

After these metaphysical thoughts, let us return to the music itself, to observe some of its fine points. Bach does not repeat the pedal point of the orchestral prelude at the choral entry: now it must yield to the ritornello theme, which moves from the woodwinds to the basses and then the tenors, while the soprano and alto in turn begin a soaring lament, with melismata sometimes extending over six bars—a small detail in a score whose depths cannot be plumbed fully even in many pages.

With the decision to use a double choir in the *St. Matthew Passion*, Bach has created a great deal of freedom for himself. Not only does the introductory chorus attain a dimension previously unknown, but also the final chorus, "Wir setzen uns mit Tränen nieder," gains in importance where the choirs call out to each other, "ruhe sanfte" and "sanfte ruh" ("rest thou gently" and "gently rest"). Of course, this section is largely defined by the melancholy rhythm of the saraband, which can be heard more clearly here than in the final chorus of the *St. John Passion*. Both rhythmically and formally, the final part of the *St. Matthew Passion* approaches that kind of dance that, in Johann Mattheson's words, needs "lauter steiffe Ernsthaftigkeit" ("nothing but upright seriousness").[27] The instrumental framing portions may be stylized, but they are still quite real dance movements with congruent halves of twelve bars each, and the choral insertions fit smoothly into the dance's periodic pattern.

Amazingly, Bach gave his great work a finale whose musical connotations are secular. The work's outer sections one could almost take to be from an orchestral or keyboard suite,[28] while he ends three of the four versions of the *St. John Passion* with a chorale. So the *St. Matthew Passion* has an ending as refined as it is modern, and one in which neither a Mattheson nor a Scheibe could have found anything to object to.

Did Bach later feel the need for a counterbalancing force? When he takes up the *St. Matthew Passion* again, in the 1736 version, instead of the simple chorale "Jesum laß ich nicht von mir" he uses the wide-ranging chorus "O Mensch, bewein dein Sünde groß" to end the first part. This grandiose but difficult movement, originally used in 1725 to start the *St. John Passion,* thus gets its final placement. Clearly here Bach not only abandons the principle of multiple ensembles in the great commentary choruses but also explodes the dimension of "reasonable" architecture à la Mattheson and Scheibe. This process could attest—in the context of the purely chorale-text cantatas of the same decade—to a new, late-blooming fondness for skillful choral adaptations.

The double choir plays a modest role in the turba choruses. Did Bach realize at the first possible opportunity—the chorus of high priests in "Ja nicht auf das Fest"—that setting up two choruses might not make the setting more dramatic but rather tend to weigh it down? He avails himself only modestly of this option in the other turbae, mostly in brief interjections and choruses of essentially syllabically declaimed, emotionless statements: "Weissage uns," "Was geht uns das an," "Gegrüßet seist du," "Der du den Tempel Gottes zerbrichts," "Andern hat er geholfen" ("Foretell it to us," "What has that to do with us," "My greetings to thee," "Thou who dost God's own temple destroy," "He brought others salvation").

The central idea of murder in the two almost identical "Kreuzige" choruses is written as a dense four-part setting. Here we do not have a confusion of howling, cursing voices as in the *St. John Passion;* rather, the *soggetto* traces the figure of a cross as it is led up from below through all the voices, "in accordance with the rules, so to speak, like the pitiless cruelty of the ultimate punishment," as Emil Platen sees it.[29]

An eighteenth-century composer wishing to create a modern passion but one that avoids the danger of being theatrical faces the question of how to deal with those forms that dominate opera, the recitative and the aria. Bach sticks to the path he took in the *St. John Passion.* The Evangelist's message is set neither to the old lesson tones nor as an opera secco, but more in the *stylus luxurians,* already distinguished from opera secco by musicologists of the seventeenth century for its greater rhetorical emphasis. For the moment let us not speak of the many figural, pictorial, and symbolic elements but of a subtle nuance: the Hebrew-Aramaic words spoken by Jesus on the cross: "Eli, Eli, lama asabthani" are translated into German: "Mein Gott, mein Gott, warum hast du mich verlassen?" ("My God, my God, why hast thou forsaken me?"). Bach wants to make it musically clear that the German words present a translation, so he translates his musical text from B-flat minor to E-flat minor.

He does this in as literal a way as possible: except for the special phrasing of the word "warum" and the fact that the original notation starts above the first auxiliary ledger line, while the "translation" (in the tenor clef) starts on it, the notation of each is identical down to the accidentals and the continuo numbering! It would have fit the normal flow of composition to set the translation as an unconscious variation from the original. But for this case Bach went to conspicuous lengths to make both text and notation of the translation identical to the original.

Moreover, there is no "halo,"[30] that is, the string quartet accompaniment that Bach normally set around Jesus's words in the *St. Matthew Passion*. He could have found a model for this instrumentation in Alessandro Scarlatti's Latin *St. John Passion* (ca. 1700). Also around this time, in his *St. Matthew Passion* performed in Riga, Johann Valentin Meder accompanied the Vox Christi with two violins that provide a tremolo lament for long intervals. A little later, Reinhard Keiser does the same in his *St. Mark Passion*.

In his *St. Matthew Passion*, Bach is at pains to keep his secco recitative free from any associations with secular music: he reserves the secco for relating the biblical events only, the words of which are written in red ink in the definitive score. Thus he had to find another compositional form than the secco to set the ten freely composed recitatives that Picander had planned. He took the opportunity to create a new method, known in formal terminology as "motivic accompagnato."[31] The voice leading is recitative-like, so it would be wrong to call them ariosos, as they often are nonetheless. But the accompaniment to the voice has an ostinato rhythmic motif and such a speechlike sound that the corresponding numbers could be described figuratively as symbols or genre pictures, and some could be given specific titles like "river of tears," "suffering," "bowing down before," "silence," "scourging," or "Good Friday evening."

Bach's style of composing in one sense is rooted in the emblematic art of the baroque: the voice delivers the epigram, and the instruments present the *pictura*. It is both highly modern and almost an anticipation of the Schubert song with its characteristic stereotypical gestures in the piano accompaniment:

The increased importance of the madrigalian recitative, first made evident in the *St. John Passion* with the two numbers (there called arioso) "Betrachte meine Seel'" and "Mein Herz," has consequences for the whole aesthetic concept of the *St. Matthew Passion:* in no fewer than ten cases, this work dispenses with the idea coming from opera that the recitative is simply a musical passage to an aria. Instead, Bach gives the two a linkage in which the first can be understood as an introduction to the second. This represents inherent progress in the work, when compared with the *St. John Passion,* where (except for the two ariosos just mentioned) the arias are scattered like set pieces, and the rapid sequence of numbers from "Von den Stricken meiner Sünden" to "Ich folge dir gleichfalls" does not seem well thought out.

In contrast to this, the ten pairs of motivic accompagnato plus aria can be seen as regular chamber music interludes, for which by and large a sophisticated set of instruments is selected. Thus, the soprano recitative "Er hat uns allen wohlgetan" is accompanied by two oboes da caccia, which then combine with a leading flute to form a three-voice accompaniment for the next aria, "Aus Liebe will mein

Heiland sterben." This admittedly unusual tone color evokes another world more strongly in a passion oratorio than it would in an opera or secular cantata. In the rush of events of the passion, the Evangelist has just had Pilate say, "What evil has he done?," and a curtain opens on to a scene of meditative music: one could almost be in a cloister or a baroque painting. Then the events of the outside world break in again: "They shouted all the more, 'Let him be crucified!'"

It speaks for Mendelssohn's artistic insight that in his representation or revival of the *St. Matthew Passion* he retained this pairing of recitative and aria, although he had to substitute A clarinets for the oboes da caccia: the recitative is untouched, and in the aria, the instrumental introduction is left intact too. It was not only Mendelssohn who sensed something of the magic of the aria. Breslau's music director Johann Theodor Mosewius learned of Mendelssohn's feat in the newspapers and hastened to Berlin in time for the third performance on 17 April 1829, after traveling day and night. He rehearsed the work a year later with his Singakademie in Breslau and wrote a "musical-esthetic interpretation" of the *St. Matthew Passion* in 1852, in which he discussed the lyrical dimension of the aria "Aus Liebe will mein Heiland sterben":

> *Here there is not a hint of anything external, one must engage oneself completely with music like this, one must seek out and explore its atmospheric mood, in which, I might almost say, such musical still-life paintings are opened up to our inner feelings, and where the emotions can attain true inner understanding. Once this is allowed to happen, once the core of deep poetry hidden within is revealed, and flows into the realm of senses and feelings, then one returns to it again and again, with ever greater joy and pleasure.*[32]

What Mosewius called atmosphere comes mostly from the basset horn section with the second oboe da caccia as the lowest voice. Only rarely does Bach write a vocal section without a continuo, which means there is nothing in the bass register, often for symbolic reasons: in this case he wants to signal that the Savior, his death imminent, no longer stands firmly on the earth but already is nearing a higher plane. Thus the basset horn passage can be considered as a "baroque topos of innocence."[33]

Besides the establishment of a firm coupling of the aria and the motivic accompagnato, the new forms of dialogue given by the libretto add to the importance of the arias. Bach uses them repeatedly through the passion, having the chorus of faithful women break right into the recitatives and arias of the Daughters of Zion—as in the numbers "Ich will bei meinem Jesu wachen / so schlafen unsere Sünden ein"; "O Schmerz! Hier zittert das gequälte Herz / Was ist die Ursach aller Plagen"; "So ist mein Jesus nun gefangen / Laßt ihn, haltet, bindet nicht"; "Ach, nun ist mein Jesus hin? / Wo ist denn dein Freund hingegangen"; "Sehet, Jesus hat die Hand, uns zu fassen, ausgespannt, kommt [...] /wohin?"; and "Nun ist der Herr zur Ruh gebracht / Mein Jesu, gute Nacht."*

The name "Jesus" appears mostly at the midpoint of the above texts: they are modeled after the dialogue between Jesus and the individual soul (*die Seelenbraut*) from the tradition of baroque mysticism and Pietism. Picander and Bach use this topos to make the freely composed texts of the *St. Matthew Passion* seem less like an arbitrary sequence of texts and more like a subplot providing a meaningful paraphrase of the biblical narrative.

Does the corpus of arias here show compositional skill on a higher plane than in the *St. John Passion*? The level of quality of the *St. John Passion* could hardly be improved on—but even in the arias, an element of classicism can be found in the *St. Matthew Passion* that the earlier work simply cannot claim. In the arias of the *St. John Passion*, the figurative and thus spiritual element is in the foreground; the later work has an almost sensual sound. Perhaps this difference

---

*"I will be with my Jesus watching / That slumber may our sins enfold"; "O pain! Here trembleth the tormented heart / What is the reason for all these great torments?"; "Thus hath my Jesus now been taken / Free him, hold off, bind him not!"; "Ah, now is my Jesus gone! / Where is then thy friend now departed?"; "See ye, Jesus hath his hand, us to capture, now outstretched / Come! [. . .] Where to?"; "Now is the Lord brought to his rest. My Jesus, now good night!"

is the result of a more intensive study of Italian music. Many arias of the *St. Matthew Passion* have a cantabile tone, almost supersaturated with pure sound.

Let us compare two numbers based on a dotted saraband rhythm: "Ach, mein Sinn" and "Können Tränen meiner Wangen." In the first aria (described above) from the *St. John Passion,* the expression of anguish and despair is almost unpleasant to listen to, while the line of the alto voice in the second is suave and sensual. The melody stays oriented about a vertical axis with a descending bass line, and the mordent-like sixteenth-note figures make one think of Mediterranean, almost folk music. The dotted eighth figure that defines the aria's ritornello and doubtless depicts the scourging of Jesus clearly expresses melancholy, but the general effect is more moving than harsh.

In "Ach, mein Sinn" there is not even a hint of da capo: it would not fit the aria's turbulent emotional gesture. But in "Können Tränen" the da capo seems almost a matter of course: the impact of the aria on the listener is that of an autonomous form. It still has figurative elements: the whiplike sound of the scourge, the sound of teardrops, the sound of the sobbing Daughter of Zion. But these figures could easily be generalized: the music would lose none of its expressive power if it were being set to another text of equal emotional impact. The combining of powerful figural language with a rich, sensual musical effect does not result in a work that is difficult to absorb (as elsewhere in Bach it does); the work is pleasurable. This change may be seen as part of a trend toward the classical, where no one element comes to the fore but rather where the flow of the music itself is always in control.

In 1729 Bach incorporated important parts of the *St. Matthew Passion* into his funeral music for Prince Leopold of Anhalt-Cöthen

(BWV 244a). It has been asked whether he felt any scruples at putting such a sublime work to other uses. There may have been practical reasons: the music had to be ready soon after the prince's death. The music had to be approved in advance and rehearsed well to avoid problems; so it is possible that there was not time to complete a large new four-part composition.

Apart from this, the idea that the music from ten beautiful arias of the *St. Matthew Passion* and its final chorus would once again be heard in a religious rite may have pleased the composer more than it worried him. The noble pathos of these sections in particular was well suited to the courtly traditions of mourning. The original composition lost none of its greatness through such adaptation. How much more blithely did Bach's contemporaries transport their more successful arias from one opera to the next!

SECULAR CANTATAS AND THE *CHRISTMAS ORATORIO*

In the same year as the *St. Matthew Passion,* Bach creates another vocal work of mourning: the *Ode on the Death of the Queen, Christiane Eberhardine:* "Laß, Fürstin, laß noch einen Strahl," BWV 198. The refined courtly sound, which had played a role in setting the character of the *St. Matthew Passion,* here dominates the entire work. It is no accident that the university chronicler emphasizes the composition's "Italian style": it lacks any element of genuine Lutheran church music, making use of neither Bible passages nor hymns nor large-scale concerted or extensive fugal development; instead, the score contains a sequence of chamber-music-like recitatives and arias and predominantly homophonic choruses. The chorus "An dir, du Vorbild großer Frauen" is something of an exception, but the fugue beginning each of its halves has a theme with a lyrical quality and transitions quickly into a homophonic final section. So the impression of musical flow that dominates the work is not obscured.

The instrumentation is exceptionally refined: for the aria "Wie starb die Heldin so vergnügt," in addition to the two gambas and two lutes planned in the score, Bach calls for two recorders, probably to brighten the sound.[1] In the recitative "Der Glocken bebendes Getön," to portray the sound of bells tolling the death knell in all pitches, he employs two oboes d'amore and strings as well as the above-mentioned gambas, lutes, and recorders.

Viewed both chronologically and aesthetically, this *Trauerode,* which is known to be the model for the missing *St. Mark Passion,*

BWV 247, forms a bridge between Bach's Lutheran and secular music. The work, alternating between sacred and profane mourning, represents a paradigm shift. The occasions for which Bach creates innovations in his Leipzig vocal compositions tend less and less to be the Sunday and feast-day services in the Thomaskirche and St. Nicholas's Church and more and more another kind of function: ceremonies in connection with academia and musical tributes to members of the electoral ruling house and other high-ranking persons. Of course *Æolus Propitiated*, BWV 205, and "Vereinigte Zwietracht der wechselnden Saiten" ("United Division of Strings Ever Changing"), BWV 207, had already appeared (in 1725 and 1726, respectively). Still, the years after the completion of the first two cantata cycles can be seen as a time of transition, when the emphasis in Bach's life gradually shifted from the role of *Thomaskantor* to that of *director musices* and future leader of the collegium musicum.

With the two last-named compositions we come to Bach's secular vocal works. Current scholarship identifies the *Hunt Cantata*, BWV 208, of 1712–13 as the earliest of these: one of Bach's earliest efforts at Italian cantata style and da capo aria. The last of these is the burlesque *Peasant Cantata*, "Mir hahn en neue Oberkeet" (dialect for "Wir haben eine neue Obrigkeit" or "We've got a brand-new governor"), BWV 212, a work of cryptic humor. Among these dozen other works can be identified—mostly lost cantatas in praise of personages at the courts of Cöthen, Weissenfels, and Zerbst—around nine festival pieces for Leipzig University and school occasions; twelve festival pieces for the Saxon electoral house; eight other cantatas of various types; and four wedding cantatas, to which should be added the high-spirited *Wedding Quodlibet*, BWV 524, an extravagantly suggestive work probably meant for a Bach family occasion (assuming that the fragmentary score was not just written out but actually composed by Bach).

The two Italian solo cantatas "Amore traditore," BWV 203, and "Non sa che sia dolore," BWV 209, occupy a special position: both come down to us in manuscripts of dubious authenticity. The music does not point to Bach as its author—it was likely written by a German composer who was at home in the Italian cantabile style.

It would be pointless trying to construe a stylistically unified corpus of any degree from the works that have survived; even sketching lines of development is problematic, since the original occasions that gave rise to them, and thus the types of work Bach considered writing for them, are so various. The general term "secular cantata," which was first used in the nineteenth century, cannot do justice to this great variety.[2] To keep from bogging down in detail, we restrict the term only to the *drammi per musica* that originated mainly in the period between the *St. Matthew Passion* and the *Christmas Oratorio.*

Bach's selection of the term *drammi* makes clear that the works are in no way lyric solo cantatas but impressive and substantial works of a genre most closely related to chamber opera. Besides the two above-mentioned cantatas, BWV 205 and 207, this group includes the following works presented between 1728 and 1736: "Erwählte Pleißenstadt," BWV 216a ("Leipzig the Chosen City"); "The Contest between Phoebus and Pan," BWV 201 ("Geschwinde, geschwinde, ihr wirbelnden Winde" ["Now hasten, ye winds of confusion"]); *Hercules at the Crossroads,* BWV 213 ("Laßt uns sorgen, laßt uns wachen" ["Let us tend him, let us watch him"]); "Tönet, ihr Pauken! Erschallet, Trompeten," BWV 214 ("Sound, all ye drums now, Resound, all ye trumpets"); "Blast Lärmen, ihr Feinde," BWV 205a ("Blow uproar, opponents"); "Preise dein Glücke, gesegnetes Sachsen," BWV 215 ("Praise now thy blessings, O fortunate Saxony"); "Auf, schmetternde Töne der muntern Trompeten," BWV 207a ("Resound, pealing notes of the vigorous trumpets"); and "Schleicht spielende Wellen," BWV 206 ("Glide, glittering waters"). (Works with numbers having the suffix *a* come from earlier settings.)

In most of the *drammi per musica* the characters come from Greek antiquity: Apollo, Pallas Athena, the wind gods, Pan, Midas, Hercules, and so on. They retell the myths, relating them to the present day—for instance, in *Æolus Propitiated,* a cantata performed on the name day of the Leipzig professor August Müller. The date is 3 August 1725, and the wind god feels once again like loosing the raging autumn winds from their enclosure. But Zephyrus, the gentle summer wind, is afraid of rough autumn, and Pomona, goddess of the orchards, fears for her harvest. Finally Pallas Athena begs for a delay, so that she can hold her celebration on Mount Helicon, home of the muses, in the warm summer air. But Æolus is appeased only when he is told that Müller will take part in the muses' celebration. The chorus, which at first depicted the raging winds, is transformed into a students' choir: "Vivat August…blest be thou, O learned man!"

One might be tempted to smile at this, yet the work is exemplary of the new arena Bach is entering, exchanging the gallery of the Thomaskirche and St. Nicholas's Church for a secular podium—a move from Christianity to humanism. He is dealing now not with gospel, hymn, Lutheranism, Christian doctrine, the repentance of sin, the preparation for death, or the certainty of faith but with Greek mythology and its translation to Ovid's *Metamorphoses* and Virgil's *Georgics*. He is also dealing with an interior world, with grace, beauty, culture—and not least with questions of aesthetics, as in "The Contest between Phoebus and Pan," about the right kind of music: King Midas, setting himself up as judge of matters he knows nothing about and in his total ignorance preferring the harsh natural tones of Pan to the "lovely lays" of Phoebus, is given ass's ears in punishment.

Bach may have enjoyed having some influence on the life of academe through his involvement with humanistic themes and commissions for works associated with them: as composing sacred cantatas and passions constitutes participation in religious discourse, so setting the *drammi per musica* signifies participation in the current discussion of education and culture—with its high and low points.[3] One can imagine him relishing the composition of a libretto that deals with the punishment of someone who thinks himself an expert on questions of art, music in particular.

The libretti of the *drammi per musica* offer a composer like Bach all sorts of enticements to enter emotional and performative areas that would not be so accessible to works with spiritual texts. The central idea is the "charm of melody" in Phoebus's song or, more generally, a middle style, which by its very nature is uncomfortable when compared to the high or sublime style reserved for sacred subjects. In the secular works of his Leipzig period, Bach is able to make this genre completely his own, and thus can be receptive, more than in his sacred music, to a gallant and sentimental style.

An example: the bass aria "Rühmet Gottes Güt und Treu," which in its similarity to the operatic style of Johann Adolph Hasse can be considered an "extremely rare concession by Bach to popular taste"—was it originally composed for the sacred wedding cantata "Dem Gerechten muß das Licht," BWV 195, or did it stem from an older, secular context?[4] Let us remember the comments of Lorenz Christoph Mizler and Johann Abraham Birnbaum in 1738: both writers feel that they can prove Bach's ability to write "perfectly in the latest fashion" by pointing to a secular work, namely, the cantata "Willkommen, ihre herrschenden Götter der Erden," BWV Anh. I, 13, which unfortunately is lost.

It was not the be-all and end-all of composing for Bach to write in the latest fashion, but it is definitely one aspect of his work. And such writing was done more easily for an audience that expected secular music than in the church, where opinions—even Bach's own— were divided in this regard. So what is the musical gain in writing *drammi per musica*?

Without becoming an opera composer, Bach is contributing to the dramatic genre and thereby opening up further dimensions of musical expression. Even the first of the Leipzig *drammi, Æolus Propitiated,* has one of the most powerful instrumental settings in all his work. The choral introduction was composed practically for a complete baroque orchestra: besides strings and continuo there are two flutes, two oboes, three trumpets, timpani, and—uniquely for Bach in this setting—three horns. In the martial final chorus, this total ensemble is used over and over again as a single mass of sound. It is almost as if the *director musices* wanted to make a big impression at the beginning by using an ensemble worthy of an opera.

The recitative after the chorus is dramatic as well; it has Æolus as lord of the winds appearing in impressive musical decor. To the powerful entries of the brass instruments, Bach adds swift runs in the flutes and strings, including the basses. Other musical elements of the plot are painted in musical terms: the raging winds of the opening chorus, Æolus's fierce laughter, the murmuring zephyrs, Athena's joking. That these emotional effects and genre pictures are meant more for the opera stage than for the choir stalls of the church does not rule out stylistic overlaps between the two. The choruses in the *drammi* are free of strained contrapuntal passages; they are homophonic or loosely polyphonic. Bach relies on catchy themes and natural articulation, as in the opening "Tönet, ihr Pauken! Erschallet, Trompeten!," BWV 214: the first line is sung unison by the chorus, not a particularly artful setting but nonetheless a lively exclamation taken up by all voices together.

First, the choral motif is played by the timpani; Bach has taken the imperatives of the text literally; the timpani, which after all can play only intervals of a fourth, are thought of thematically with this limitation in mind: their interval is transformed into the basis of the whole section. This is a new kind of figured writing: Bach does not employ musical rhetorical figures, does not compose symbolically or in pictures but naturally—taking the sound of the instrument in question and turning it into a phrase that is as memorable as it is engaging:

This is a language understood even by the musically unsophisticated; the listener can follow without sorting through subtle levels of meaning: the text speaks of drums and trumpets as the representatives of courtly ceremony—and lo! these representatives appear.

This kind of music could be called "easy to like," and it is composed to be just that. We see here another paradigm shift: the composition's aesthetic orientation changes from object to listener. No longer is the music wiser than the listener. Instead of reflecting philosophically or laying out agendas, it wants to give the listener the chance to enjoy music by making it a part of himself—simple enjoyment for its own sake.

As far back as 1722, in a discourse on nature and reason in music with the Wolfenbüttel cantor Heinrich Bokemeyer, Johann Mattheson demanded that melodies be "original," simple, and pleasant.[5] A generation later, Bach's son Carl Philipp Emanuel declares it to be the "obligation" of the composer "to be able to feel all the emotions he wants to arouse in his listeners."[6] The highest art is to be able to realize in musical language the listeners' feelings: thus the epoch was called the "era of feeling" (the literary genre *Empfindsamkeit* epitomized by Klopstock's poetry)—and not because the music of this trend necessarily reflected what the word means today, sentimentality.

Old father Bach did not share this broadly subjective view of music. When he declares himself open to a sensual, listener-oriented style, he does not mean that this is all he wants, that this is the essence of art. He can write in the latest style, to be sure, but doing so is not his goal. Note that even the works of his theatrical or middle style retain a fair degree of figuration and development. The chorus "Tönet, ihr Pauken! Erschallet, Trompeten!" is not just an introduction scored for these instruments but a sophisticated construct of all kinds of motifs. The master composer cannot be denied!

We return to the two *drammi per musica* of 1733, "Laßt uns sorgen, laßt uns wachen" and "Tönet, ihr Pauken! Erschallet, Trompeten!" On 27 July of that year Bach dedicates the Kyrie and Gloria of his B-Minor Mass to the Elector of Saxony—not least in hopes of an appointment as court composer. The performances of 5 September and 8 December reinforce Bach's wish to be remembered at the

Dresden court not just as a religious composer but as a secular one as well.

In composing the two *drammi,* was it his intention from the outset to recycle essential sections as parodies for a major sacred work, perhaps even asking his librettist Picander to consider an alternative religious text while composing the original verses? Whatever happened, for each of the six feast days between 25 December 1734 and 6 January 1735, he produces a major sacred work consisting to a large extent of parodies—especially of the above two *drammi.* He expressly calls it an "oratorium," a term that is not unusual for the time. But in his musical lexicon of 1732 Johann Gottfried Walther defines "oratorium" as "a religious *Opera,* or *musical* representation of a religious story." This definition can hardly be stretched to define a cycle of six cantatas.

Historically the merging of two not particularly well-known genres created a new genre that could be termed an oratorio in Bach's sense: the Christmas "history," known primarily through Heinrich Schütz's composition, and the institution known as *Abendmusiken*— the evening concerts of Lübeck that Bach's teacher Dietrich Buxtehude had brought into existence. These took place on several Sundays each year during Advent, providing a framework for the occasional performances of cyclic works like the five-part *Himmlische Seelenlust auf Erden* (The Heavenly Soul's Earthly Bliss) or *Das Allererschröcklichste und Allererfreulichste* (The Most Dreadful and the Most Wonderful).

Bach keeps this generic term as well in composing his *Ascension Oratorio,* BWV 11, for the Feast of Ascension in 1735, a work of about the length of a cantata, and in 1738, when he republishes the Easter cantata "Kommt, fliehet und eilet," BWV 249, as the *Easter Oratorio.*

Superficially, the *Christmas Oratorio* owes its creation to a clever calculation on Bach's part: putting earlier secular works (besides BWV 213 and 214, one aria is derived from BWV 215) to new use for cantata performances during the Christmas season. Thus music composed for a specific event is saved from oblivion and given a permanent context that the original occasion could not offer.

The new context is the *de tempore*, that is, the church calendar: each one of the six cantatas of the *Christmas Oratorio* can in future be performed on the Sunday or feast day for which it was written. But Bach also provides a larger context: a story with a continuous narrative. Calling it *oratorium*, he presents the people of Leipzig with a great new work that took the form of texts specially printed for the occasion.

Here Bach shows himself to be a composer who thinks theologically, using his beautiful new secular music as a key to open the portal to a new genre of sacred music, one long associated with charm, sweetness, nature, and joy—namely, Christmas music. The form that this type of music often took was the pastorale or shepherd's music.

Bach employed the greatest artistic discretion, moreover, in the way he approached parody, that is, the reworking of existing vocal music. From the *drammi* BWV 213, 214, and 215 he uses the opening choruses for the first, third, and fifth part and a total of eight arias. This is a small body of secular music, written at more or less the same period of time, integrated in style and well suited to the festive, warm, and generally bright tone associated with Christmas. What Bach had tested out in the secular realm he soon applied to the religious realm as well.

This process was not mechanical. In the second part, instead of using an opening chorus, for which he could certainly have found something to create a parody from, he wrote a new instrumental pastorale. In similar fashion, he wrote a new final chorus for the fifth part. Originally he had intended to parody the final chorus from BWV 213, "Lust der Völker, Lust der Deinen, blühe, holder Friedrich"; his librettist had come up with a rewrite of this to fit the strophic pattern. But clearly Bach had second thoughts about whether the original form, a gavotte-like round song, was an appropriate foundation for an opening chorus on the words "Ehre sei dir, Gott, gesungen" ("Let thy praise be sung, O Lord") and instead composed something new, and more ambitious, for the new text.

The madrigalian recitatives introducing the arias of the first five parts are also new: "Nun wird mein liebster Bräutigam," "Wer will die Liebe recht erhöh'n," "Was Gott dem Abraham verheißen," "So geht denn hin, ihr Hirten," "Immanuel, du süßes Wort," "Wohlan, dein Name soll allein." In the *St. Matthew Passion* tradition, they are accompagnati carefully worked out with an eye for textual and musical unity. If the musical quality of an aria still retained any traces of its original secular character, it was put into a spiritual context by the preceding recitative, most particularly in four cases, where Bach wrote choral recitatives combining original verses with hymns, thus emphasizing the liturgical association of words and music.

In five instances he goes a little further with the madrigalian recitative than he has gone before: he uses the recitatives to integrate the chorales, more clearly than he did in the passions, into the narrative. Thus, the bass comments on the hymns of praise sung by the heavenly hosts: "'Tis meet, ye angels, sing and triumph, / That we today have gained such fortune! / Up then! We'll join our voice to yours, / We can as well as ye rejoice." This is the cue for the final chorus, "Wir singen in deinem Heer." Perhaps because of the experience he gained in composing the *drammi per musica* (and perhaps with the help of his librettist), Bach took an additional step: with the exception of the sixth cantata (which is almost completely a work of parodies), the numbers in the *Christmas Oratorio,* despite their variety, are more carefully balanced against one another than in the *St. John* or *St. Matthew Passion.* Beyond the effort to distribute recitatives, arias, and chorales appropriately thoughout the Bible story, we sense the care that each number proceed logically from the preceding one and that the different text and music genres be divided up evenly throughout the libretto. This is less a concession to Enlightenment fashion than Bach's acceptance of it: Scheibe's criticism of Bach as essentially chaotic and bombastic simply does not apply here.

On the contrary: along with those numbers adapted from secular works, some new ones composed especially "for Christmas" sound remarkably natural. Especially natural is the sinfonia in siciliano rhythm, a pastorale in 12/8 time. With its inspired double chorus, this piece is one of the outstanding examples of the pastorale genre: against a rural shepherds' idyll[7] invoked by four oboes playing a bassett-horn section with folksy melodies over a bourdon bass, one hears a more refined, "angelic round" played by flutes and violins.[8]

Bach is a length ahead of his contemporaries even on their home turf: not only does he know how to depict an earthy pastorale in keeping with the passion for nature just then coming into fashion, but he links his depiction of real scenes to a reference to the fields of paradise, that one place where mankind's yearning for nature and peace can be finally satisfied. As Albert Schweitzer has noted, Bach combines here, in one topos, the adoration of the heavenly hosts with that of human shepherds, in a theologically convincing way, without the need of outside biblical expertise.[9] Musically, the thematic linking of these two realms, the salient compositional feature of the section, anticipates sonata movement structure with its two contrasting themes, exposition, development, and recapitulation.[10]

In the *St. Matthew Passion*'s mighty double chorus "Sind Blitze, sind Donner in Wolken verschwunden?," Bach has already offered a little nature portrait. But though impressive, this tone painting remains more an abstract figuration: the text speaks not of actual thunder and lightning but of the shock that the Savior's betrayal and arrest does *not* unleash a storm from heaven! The "storm chorus" makes sense only as the portrayal of the anguished emotional state of Jesus's disciples.[11] The pastoral sinfonia from the *Christmas Oratorio* can be understood without taking such logical detours: it is the backdrop for the shepherds in their field, the angel, and the heavenly host. Here the music is not so much important for its figuration as for its sound: it supplies "local color" in the clearest possible way— not just for the earthly but also the heavenly locale.

One cannot value the philosophical and musical importance of the sinfonia too highly. In "Great German Music of the Eighteenth Century" (1907), Wilhelm Dilthey wrote that this movement contains "every possible depiction yet to come of our love of nature."[12] Of course there are a great number of instrumental pastorales in the seventeenth and eighteenth centuries. But surely no composition exists that so explicitly combines the pastoral topos, the local color, with a real idea—the idea of peace—resulting in a sinfonia movement of the highest level that is at once painting in music and consistent form throughout. It is a musical character presented as the process of musical thinking.

One cannot compare something like the graceful Pifa (shepherds' dance) section of Handel's *Messiah* with a work of this level; an apter comparison would be Haydn's portrayal of Chaos in *The Creation* or Beethoven's *Pastorale* symphony, which point to German idealism, or even illustrate it, in that they imbue sensual experience with something spiritual. The pastoral bells in the first movement of Mahler's Sixth Symphony should be heard as a last reminiscence of this transcending of nature.

Pastoral local color dominates the whole second part of the *Christ-mas Oratorio*—another novelty for Bach! In the ritornello lines of the final chorus, "Wir singen dir in deinem Heer," he does not revert to the introductory sinfonia just to give a clear and logical completion to the thematic cycle of Shepherds; but for the two accompagnati that deal with the shepherds' chorus he again picks up the scoring with four oboes, repeating once more the bourdon bass line and ostinato. The aria "Schlafe, mein Liebster" has a particularly sensitive and subtle in-strumentation: while the original, secular ritornello was played by the strings, here it is given to the oboes. In contrast to the original, and quite unusually, he accompanies the voice with a flute that doubles the melody one octave higher, brightening the whole sound.[13]

After the pastorale, the previously mentioned chorus of the heavenly host, "Ehre sei Gott in der Höhe," is probably the most im-portant new composition in the *Christmas Oratorio*. It is a turba cho-rus, but Bach uses it only in part to advance the plot; he sees it more significantly as the bearer of a universal message that is also anchored liturgically in the Gloria of the Latin mass. The section is remark-ably rigorous in a formal sense, despite the emotion in the individual voices. The continuo part consists largely of running eighth-note figures, continuing until the words "und Friede auf Erden" ("peace on earth"), when it is replaced by a pedal point similar to the basset-horn section from the pastorale.

The former symbolizes the power and eternity of God; the lat-ter provides a hint of the peace that man could have in God but sel-dom finds on earth. The instruments are introduced in different ways: the opening staccato phrases have a sharply stimulating effect, while the legato at the words "und Friede auf Erden" contributes a great deal to the sudden shift of mood. In the final section "und den Menschen ein Wohlgefallen," written as a canon, the instruments' only function is to support the voices. The continuo calls to mind one of the two sections, "Credo in unum Deum" and "Confiteor" from the *Credo* of the B-Minor Mass, composed later. But the "Ehre sei Gott in der Höhe" chorus is not at all in the *stile antico;* it is composed in a pleasing and varying fashion, somewhere between the middle and high alla breve style.

We turn again to the opening choruses, which are composed almost in the gallant style, and to the arias, this time in their original form:

> Tönet, ihr Pauken! erschallet, Trompeten!
> Klingende Saiten, erfüllet die Luft!
> Singet itzt Lieder, ihr muntren Poeten!
> Königin lebe! wird fröhlich geruft.
> Königin lebe! dies wünschet der Sachse.
> Königin lebe und blühe und wachse!

> Sound, all ye drums now! Resound, all ye trumpets!
> Resonant viols, make swell now the air!
> Sing now your anthems, ye vigorous poets,
> Vivat regina! How happy the shout!
> Vivat regina! the hope of the Saxons:
> Long live the Queen, may she flourish and prosper!

Thus the opening chorus of BWV 214. Bach takes the exhortations of the text at face value and composes music expressly coming out of those words. Is anything lost when another, religious text is substituted—namely, the words with which the *Christmas Oratorio* begins?

> Jauchzet, frohlocket! auf, preiset die Tage,
> Rühmet, was heute der Höchste getan!
> Lasset das Zagen, verbannet die Klage,
> Stimmet voll Jauchzen und Fröhlichkeit an!
> Dienet dem Höchsten mit herrlichen Chören,
> Laßt uns den Namen des Herrschers verehren!

> Triumph, rejoicing, rise, praising these days now,
> Tell ye what this day the Highest hath done!

Fear now abandon and banish complaining,
Join, filled with triumph and gladness, our song!
Serve ye the Highest in glorious chorus,
Let us the name of our ruler now honor!

Is it a loss that the instruments mentioned in the text—timpani, trumpets, strings—are no longer expressly apostrophized in the sacred text, now merely appearing "in person"? Bach may originally have thought so: deleted text lines in the score invite us to surmise that he wanted to start the religious version as well with the words "Tönet, ihr Pauken." But then he opted for a text that accounted far better for the festive mood of the music than did the original birthday tribute to a Saxon queen.

Bach's tonal language is well suited for the use of parodic adaptations, because it has a depth unaffected by superficial connections of word and sound, and an openness that allows linguistic additions of varying specificity. As music it is precise but cannot be assigned to any detailed portrayal of a particular emotion or image. Ludwig Finscher (1969) put it this way:

> The wealth and complexity of even the simplest composition of the Thomas cantor create a musical connection above any textual interpretation and any parodic adaptation, a "surplus" of musical craft extending beyond the set text. Wealth and complexity— and not lack of definition—give the work a multivalent quality making it open to various texts, different interpretations, and a shifting accentuation of meaning.[14]

Not all the parodies are equally successful. Did the original words of the aria "Bereite dich, Zion, mit zärtlichen Trieben, den Schönsten, den Liebsten bald bei dir zu sehn!" ("Prepare thyself, Zion, with tender despatch / Thy fairest, thy dearest soon with thee to see") cause problems? Surely many a listener must have wondered, hearing the words "Deine Wangen müssen viel schöner prangen" ("Thy cheek must now this day bloom forth more fairly"), why the cello at just that moment begins to labor and trace serpentine patterns. The answer to the puzzle is of course in the original text of *Hercules at the Crossroads,* the *dramma per musica* where Hercules, wavering between Virtue and Lust, forswears the latter:

Ich will dich nicht hören,
Ich will dich nicht wissen,
Verworfene Wollust, ich kenne dich nicht.
Denn die Schlangen,
So mich wollen wiegend fangen,
Hab ich schon lange zermalmet, zerrissen.

I will never heed thee, I will never know thee,
O decadent Vice, thy face I know not!
For the serpents
Which within the cradle sought me
Have I long since dealt destruction, dismembered.

Finscher sees no problem in wriggling serpents and blooming cheeks finding shelter under the same musical roof: the music was indeed "composed to the words, but is by the same token a composition of intrinsic value." An idea such as this invites contradiction: it is doubtful Bach would have ever composed the conspicuously serpentine bass line if it had not been called for by the text. That even in this exceptional case there is disagreement demonstrates how receptive his material is generally to alterations of text and changes of meaning.

This receptiveness in no way means that Bach the vocal composer was indifferent to a set text. On the contrary, the text was an extraordinarily important source of inspiration to him. As the music scholar Hermann Kretzschmar pointed out three generations ago, the text served the *ars inveniendi,* the art of invention. The inventions Bach made in this way derive their meaning not from being an image of something else but from within themselves.

Consider also that the system of parody sketched here was aesthetically workable only because there were sufficient works at hand that Bach might use. When working on an important project, he obviously selected his parody original with great care. But there is an exception to everything: for all its beauty and detail, the sixth part of the *Christmas Oratorio* is not wholly convincing as the keystone of an otherwise very carefully wrought work—probably because Bach, suddenly less fussy, decided to use a complete cantata that he had just written, down to the recitatives and final chorus. In this effort he did not even have to rewrite the original instrument parts to this cantata (BWV 248/VIa, since lost) but through insertions, cross-references, and erasures was able to put the entire thing in the oratorio.[15] Toward the end of his work, he was apparently short on time or resources and so had to make sure he could complete his great project without expending further energy on it.

In estimating the extent of Bach's use of parody overall, Friedhelm Krummacher's observation, following Werner Heumann, that "almost half the extant vocal work" is affected by it,[16] seems a little biased: here "model" and "copy" are added together. Of the original works alone, at most a quarter of them were affected; and in this quarter there are cantatas, for example, that contribute merely a single aria as a parody original.

Let us turn now to two chamber cantatas: the *Coffee Cantata*, BWV 211, and the *Peasant Cantata*, BWV 212. Musically these works are quite different from the works that Bach himself called *drammi per musica*. Here we do not find splendid, gallant compositions but carefully drawn and imaginative character studies with an element of farce. Once again we note that in music history he alone created works like this. In the plastic arts, one finds parallels to them not so much in Dutch genre painting as in the drawings or etchings of artists such as Jacques Callot, in his Capriccio series. The aria sequences of both cantatas could be seen as such a series: one could even see these cantatas as part of a group. Both works are humoristic almost in the Romantic definition of the concept: to quote Jean Paul, they attest to a "higher comic universal spirit, which is neither the denouncer nor the gallows priest of individual fools"[17] but a spirit that loves and despises the world at once.

The *Coffee Cantata* was written around 1734 to a text of Picander, and Bach in all likelihood presented it in Zimmermann's Coffeehouse with his collegium musicum. Even Schlendrian's first aria, "Hat man nicht mit seinen Kindern hunderttausend Hudelei" ("Don't one's children cause one endless trials and tribulations"), indicates this. The father, growling like a honey bear about his daughter's coffee addiction, begins with repeated eighth notes; the strings accompany with sixteenths, and their inexact unison reflects with genial strokes of the pen Schlendrian's bumbling, bull-in-a-china-shop style:

But one should not think that the sixteenth-note figure in the strings is just an accompaniment to the voice part: it is intrinsic material, turning up in the introduction to the aria and later in the continuo as well. Schlendrian's tic becomes a theme and is maintained continuously. It also goes with the words "Was ich immer alle Tage meiner Tochter Liesgen sage" ("What I'm ever daily saying to my daughter Liesgen praying"), but only because Bach was aiming not for a likable, gallant style but rather a good-humored caricature. Schlendrian's slightly pathetic lament is perfectly illustrated by the wavering cadences on the word "Hudelei," with no one cadence quite like another.

Schlendrian's clumsy continuo aria, "Mädchen, die von harten Sinnen," suits the text; but it would also be usable for a religious text like "Sünder mit verstockten Sinnen!" In fact, the aria "Empfind ich Höllenangst und Pein" from the cantata "Ach Gott, wie manches Herzeleid," BWV 3, and the aria "Ach, wo hol' ich Armer Rat!" from cantata BWV 25, are both similar in this respect. Meanwhile, the aria's charm results directly from the obstinacy with which it lavishes a figuratively and harmonically strict theme on a trivial subject. The exclamations "Mädchen," "leichte nicht," and "trifft man," all separated by pauses, are certainly meant to be parodistic.

The composer has given his daughter Liesgen two flattering arias—"Ei! Wie schmeckt der Coffee süße"—and an elegant minuet with flute accompaniment, but with the intent also to show how affected the girl is. The aria is in three-bar, not four-bar groupings. Moreover, metric, musical, and verbal accents are in constant conflict with each other—at least until the strict trochaic meter changes into triple time! The other aria, "Heute noch," accompanied by strings and harpsichord *concertante,* has a special charm. On one hand, the music is a proper, lilting pastorale in itself; on the other, the meter, something approaching a French gigue, lends the song a coquettishness, given a certain emphasis by the delighted cries of "Ach, ach, ach, ein Mann!"

Did Bach have a secret sympathy for a Liesgen who wants a man not just for pleasure but because it is more satisfying to exercise the rights and duties of a wife and mother than to be a spinster sitting with her sewing at the window, envying every woman walking by in a "fashionably wide whalebone skirt"? In any event, he adds a positive ending not foreseen by Picander. Liesgen gets her "trusty sweetheart" and can continue to swill down coffee, for "Die Katze läßt das Mausen nicht" ("the cat won't stop catching mice") and "Wer will nun auf die Töchter lästern" ("why should anyone criticize our daughter now") when Granny and Mama get away unscathed? Bach sets the closing bourée as a rondo with figured variations, in the folk music tradition; so the finale ends quite simply but still retaining the now familiar playful three-bar divisions.

We can read the *Coffee Cantata* as we might read a book for fun, but the *Peasant Cantata* (1742) presents us with many puzzles. Here two middle-class men (Bach and Picander) put their heads together, in part to honor a nobleman, the local district captain and revenue officer Carl Heinrich von Dieskau, on the inheritance of his estate at Klein-Zschocher, but in part to describe in detail the wretched conditions of the peasants with key words like "Armut," "Strafen," and "Militärdienst" ("poverty," "punish," "military service") and to make pointed jokes about their new lord. This is all done within the genre of a burlesque cantata, the text of which the honoree presumably approved in advance.

Given the work's many enigmatic details, we do not know how the collaborators in this "social play" viewed their respective roles. It is only certain that Bach was taking aim not just at peasant music but at town and even court music as well, without openly taking sides. Does he make the "Flicken" overture purposely bad to mock the "low handiwork of his social inferiors, the 'Beer Fiddlers' heedlessly playing away undaunted, incapable of either imagination or elaboration?"[18] Or is this a case of virtuosic play with allusions, references, and citations "full of sympathy and—that rarity in serious music— full of humor"?[19]

None of the seven song or dance fragments can be positively identified as folk music, but there can be no doubt that here Bach is taking a hard look at the folk and their music, while still managing to write an attractive and endearing work of music. In this he is one of the few who took the trouble to study in depth the peasant music of his time and also promote its value. But everything he approached he took seriously.

Despite the many sections with dancelike or songlike qualities, the *Peasant Cantata* is not merely a collection of genre pictures; it is more concerned with thematizing a section of the social world of the period, seen in musical terms. In this sense it is music about music, a musicophilosophical commentary on society and a discourse on composing styles—as Picander's text is a discourse on peasant life. This seemingly harmless composition is a transition to the late work: from this point on, Bach is less concerned with reflecting social aspects of music and more concerned with the essence of music. This essence is the purpose of *The Art of Fugue,* which Bach is working on intensively at the time of the *Peasant Cantata.*

Compositions that could be compared with this would not be works like Leopold Mozart's *Bauernhochzeit* (Peasants' Wedding) but the third movement of Beethoven's *Pastoral Symphony* or the *tempo di minuetto* from his Eighth Symphony. In the first of these two, the peasants playing away on their fiddles are obviously a part of the nature that the composer is calling up; the minuet in the latter, with its distractions and false entries, shows the sarcasm of a symphonist who despite his lofty ideals still cannot save the world, and so here he just shows it as it is.[20]

References to the *Pastoral* of course cannot explain the meaning of the *Peasant Cantata:* while we are well informed, from Beethoven's own testimony, about the joy and religious inspiration that he derived from nature, we know nothing of the motives that caused Bach to see the peasant musicians as poor but not unsympathetic cousins. We do know why the quodlibet, an amalgam of folk-song melodies, was placed at the end of the *Goldberg Variations.*

Amazingly, Philipp Spitta, who after all had an expert's insight into Bach's greatness, relegated the *Coffee Cantata* to the "same genre" as Johann Nicolaus Bach's student work *Der Jenaische Wein- und Bierrufer.*[21] But this work is more properly placed in the company of the Quodlibet, BWV 524, for which Bach, as noted earlier, wrote out the manuscript and perhaps composed. In exactly the years when it might have been presented at a Bach family wedding, Erdmann Neumeister wrote in his introduction *Die allerneueste Art zur reinen und galanten Poesie zu gelangen* (The Latest Method of Writing Pure and Gallant Poetry) that the quodlibet was coming into fashion as "the gallant successor of the old drunken litany...a sung potpourri of proverbs, sayings, and dirty jokes" all thrown together.[22] This is not a bad description of the little occasional work, even including the word "gallant." We would be missing something, not musically, but biographically, if we did not have this fragmentary collection of notes, probably richly larded with allusions to members of the Bach family!

THE MAGNIFICAT AND THE MASSES

"One need only look at the masses of Stölzel, who died only recently, or the masses and the Magnificat of Bach, who died a few days ago in Leipzig…to discover that we have men in Germany who could easily take on a composer like Perti."[1]

These remarks of a certain anonymous A., who we have good reason to think was Johann Friedrich Agricola, make clear that at least in Bach's circle of students there existed quite specific ideas about his Latin church music, although it is unclear—with the exception of the Magnificat—who commissioned them and to what extent they were performed during his lifetime. Agricola lived in Leipzig from 1738 to 1741, the same time that Bach was absorbed with composing his own Latin masses and adapting those of others.

Thus Agricola could see for himself how much importance Bach attached to this genre at that time. Was it Bach who compared himself, with regard to Latin church music, to the renowned Italian mass composer Giacomo Antonio Perti? One particular issue will not be missed by any scholar engaged with Bach's Latin church music: at every step of the way, one will confront the topic of parody, that is, setting older music to a new and quite different text. To put it more pointedly, in his Leipzig period Bach was drawn to the form but wrote fewer and fewer original compositions for it.

The Magnificat in E-flat Major, BWV 243a, probably wholly original, is marked by the verve of the early Leipzig years. With its festive scoring for three trumpets, timpani, and a pair each of oboes and flutes, it is impressive, with a *concertante* energy that leaves no room for the *stylus gravis* one often finds in this form. The very first theme makes it clear that this is no Leipzig sacred cantata: despite all its contrapuntal decorum, it seems worldlier even than most of the opening movements of the first cantata cycle. The style points to the later *drammi per musica*. Even the first chorus is clearly not the musical adaptation of some religious dictum—it is, rather, a hymn being sung, with all the loveliness and joyfulness that go with singing.

The *omnes generationes* chorus reminded the British Bach scholar Sanford Terry of the corresponding section of a Magnificat[2] ascribed to Tomaso Albinoni; the American Bach scholar Robert L. Marshall points out parallels between Monteverdi's and Bach's choral settings of "sicut erat in principio."[3] But the question of putative appropriations of other works by Bach is less important than the fact that he was aiming for an Italian sound, which would be modern to Leipzig ears and audibly distinguish the work from the cantatas. Of course the Magnificat does not use da capo form: Bach generally avoids using it in his Latin sacred music. This text, like that of the masses, obviously does not lend itself to repetition driven purely by considerations of musical form.

In "sicut locutus est" the work has an a capella section in *stile antico*, but this remains an exception. The trio "Suscepit Israel," where oboes, in the D major setting, play the traditional recitation sound of the Magnificat in long valued notes, like a cantus firmus, is not as strict as it looks—there is a gallant quality in phrases like this one:

Soprano II 21

re - cor - da-tus mi - se - ri - cor - - - - di - ae.

The flexible diction of the Latin line and the clarity of detail are surprising. The tenor aria "deposuit potentes," equally passionate and dramatic, describes how the exalted shall be humbled and the humble exalted. Hanns Eisler was so impressed by this that he openly modeled a song for his Brecht cantata *Die Mutter* on it: "Arbeite, arbeite, arbeite mehr" ("work, work, work more") is the bitter message, for simple work is not enough. The powerful must be kicked off their thrones: that is the answer revealed in Bach's music![4]

Do the four choruses relating to the feast of Christmas constitute a foreign body in the total liturgical context? Marshall thought that bringing these things together in one work was "a Lutheran composer's challenge" and that it worked both theologically and musically.[5] At the same time, Bach confronted, and met, an even greater challenge: he wrote his first major Latin church work—not in the traditional style of the Roman church or of the German Lutheran heartland but as a composition sui generis: fresh, worldly, figural music, but of great emotional power.

We have already discussed individual movements from masses of the early Leipzig period. Like the earlier version of the Magnificat, they were written for the worship services of Leipzig. But as early as the Kyrie and Gloria of the later B-Minor Mass, Bach's aspirations go beyond Leipzig and its churches, even if that is where they got their first hearing: the short mass of 1733 is dedicated to the Prince Elector of Saxony. Obviously Bach wanted to expand the horizon of his authentically Lutheran church position—in the secular as well as the religious realm.

In Bach's Latin masses the question of parody is perhaps not critical for an aesthetic evaluation but still of great relevance. It was already known in the nineteenth century that the B-Minor Mass, from the Credo on, consisted largely of parodies and adoptions from other works. In the meantime we have also had to give up the idea that the Kyrie and Gloria are original compositions. Bach essentially honored the Saxon Elector with a bouquet of parodies. Partly on the basis of corrections shown in the autograph score, Joshua Rifkin postulates that the first Kyrie, from the fifth measure on, could have been a parody of a C-minor section of a cantata.[6] Earlier, Christoph Wolff suggested that a work of Johann Hugo von Wilderer may have served as the model for the first Kyrie, a G-minor mass that Bach could have known in Dresden.[7]

The duet "Christe eleison" can also hardly have been original, and so its first soprano part cannot have been composed for the voice of

Faustina Hasse, court singer at Dresden.[8] Seizing on Rifkin's idea, Klaus Häfner discusses the duet "Seid zu tausen Mal willkommen" from the lost celebratory cantata "Entfernet euch, ihr heitern Sterne," BWV Anh. I.9, as a possible model.[9] Rifkin and Häfner surmise that the original for the second Kyrie was a cantata chorus on German Bible texts. Picking up on their ideas, Alfred Dürr considers the lost chorus "Ehre sei Gott in der Höhe," BWV 197a, as the model for "Gloria in excelsis Deo" and "Et in terra pax."[10] While scholarship has largely kept the next section, the "Laudamus te," out of the parody discussion, it has determined that the opening chorus of the *Ratswahl* Cantata, "Wir danken dir, Gott," BWV 29, is the original for the "Gratias agimus tibi" and also that the opening theme of the cantata "Schauet doch und sehet, ob irgend ein Schmerz sein," BWV 46, is the original for the "Qui tollis peccata mundi." Moreover, the "Domine deus," "Qui sedes," "Quoniam tu solus sanctus," and "Cum Sancto Spiritu" are all suspected of being parodies.

Parodies or adaptations of older works are also found in the four short masses BWV 233–36, which were certainly composed in the late 1730s. In the Kyrie of BWV 233, Bach apparently fell back on a vocal piece from the Weimar or Mühlhausen period, in which the first soprano sang the Lutheran Kyrie "Christe, du Lamm Gottes." Since German could not be sung in a Latin mass, in the revised version Bach scored it as a cantus firmus to be played in unison by horns and oboes.

Bach relies mostly on sacred cantatas composed between 1723 and 1726, among them "Gott, der Herr, ist Sonn und Schild," BWV 79, "Herr, deine Augen sehen nach dem Glauben," BWV 102, "Siehe zu, daß deine Gottesfurcht nicht Heuchelei sei," BWV 179, and "Es wartet alles auf dich," BWV 187. He considers choruses in strict style especially apt for Kyrie settings as well as for more modern arias. In the process of adaptation, entire sections are composed anew, voice leadings and harmonic progressions are improved, vocal parts are made instrumental and vice versa, proportions are changed, and occasionally a piece will acquire a new character through tiny changes to the melody line.

All this offers us a view, indirectly but with great clarity, of what composition meant to Bach: continuous development, in many different directions, using an original, open-ended model that exists only as an idea in the final result. Seen in this way, the five short masses profit from the experience Bach gained in the 1730s in working with existing material. Of course, the text of the mass makes his job easier: the Latin language, with its short phrases, can be molded to fit almost any model. It is of primary importance that the original version of a section is defined by a basic emotion that fits the mass text. To clarify this with an example, Marshall compared the "Qui tollis" from the B-Minor Mass's Gloria with its original:[11]

Out of the noble and dignified stride of the original "Schauet doch," Bach creates a more exciting and passionately articulated tonal sequence for "Qui tollis." The *soggetto* that they share, incidentally, is not unknown: it points ahead to *The Art of Fugue* and the *Musical Offering*.

Some transformations go further. As a pattern for the Gloria of the A-Major Mass, BWV 234, Bach selected the section "Friede sei mit euch" from the cantata "Halt im Gedächtnis Jesum Christ," BWV 67. It was originally called an aria, but this term was hardly appropriate, since "it presents a scene of operatic explicitness unique in Bach's work."[12] After nine bars of instrumental prelude, the Vox Christi begins in measured tones with the blessing "Friede sei mit Euch!" ("Peace be with you"); the chorus answers energetically, "Wohl uns, Jesu, hilf uns kämpfen und die Wut der Feinde dämpfen,

Hölle, Satan, weich!" ("Oh, Joy, Jesus, help us battle and dampen the foes' great rage, Hell and Satan, yield!"). This is followed by an antiphonal exchange between the Vox Christi and the chorus.

The most sharp-eyed scholar would never suspect that a movement structured in this way could be the parodic model for a Gloria, if the original work were not extant. But it is, and we can follow Bach's method in detail. He uses the nine-bar orchestral prelude to the aria for the opening choral section "Gloria in excelsis Deo." Thus, the original's "Friede sei mit Euch" sung by the Vox Christi is available for setting the words "et in terra pax hominibus voluntatis." Then the chorus comes in with "Laudamus te" instead of "Wohl uns, Jesu, hilf uns kämpfen."

Did Bach show here, as Philipp Spitta thought, that "no task was too hard" for him, except that he "almost utterly destroyed the splendid poetry of the original"?[13] This is seen too much from the viewpoint of the original. If we knew only the new creation, we would be astonished by the gestural richness, the freshness, even the drama of the composition—elements that especially help the transition from the Gloria to the "et in terra pax" and that are anything but standard fare in mass settings.

Nor is this the end of the parody story. Its last chapter concerns those parts of the B-Minor Mass that Bach had been working on since early fall of 1748, trying to make a full mass from the short mass of 1733 dedicated to the Prince Elector in Dresden: the Credo, Hosanna, Benedictus, and Agnus Dei. Let us start with two movements in the *stile antico* from the Credo, "Credo in unum Deum," and "Confiteor." In view of their idiosyncratic qualities, one might think them original compositions. Each text emphasizes the element of unity: "Ich glaube an einen Gott" and "Ich bekenne mich zu einer Taufe zur Vergebung der Sünden" ("I believe in one God," "I believe in one baptism for the remission of sins"). Bach expresses this thought musically by basing both parts on the respective Gregorian melody: the Credo from the start, the Confiteor conspicuously from bar 73:

It cannot be maintained with certainty that he did this first in 1748–49. Knowing that he favored the *stile antico* particularly in the years around 1740 brought Wolff to consider an earlier origin.[14] Peter Wollny thought an earlier version of the "Credo in unum deum" was also likely.[15] In contrast, Wolfgang Osthoff takes the view that the "Credo in unum Deum" of the B-Minor Mass finds its chief model in the F-Major Credo, BWV 1081,[16] which Bach probably composed in 1747–48 as an addition to a mass by Giovanni Battista Bassani. But more important than detailed considerations like these is the general observation that Bach's setting of the "Credo in unum Deum" is not a classic Palestrina setting (though Wolff thinks it self-evident), but rather a highly sophisticated combination of traditional and modern elements. Such a style assumes not only two hundred years of musical development after Palestrina but forty years of Bach's composing as well. As Siegfried Oechsle showed, such a style, which combines a motet cantus firmus treatment with running instrumental bass and modern harmonic thinking, cannot be the result of a naive traditionalism. The complexity of the piece is actually the compositional expression of the universality that characterizes the B-Minor Mass as a whole.

"Patrem omnipotentem" is an adaptation of the opening chorus of the cantata "Gott, wie dein Name so ist auch dein Ruhm," BWV 171. A sketch fitting the music of "Et in unum Dominum" turns up in the 1733 autograph for the *dramma per musica* BWV 213. The Crucifixus has its original in the choral segment "Weinen, Klagen, Sorgen, Zagen" of the eponymous Weimar cantata BWV 12. "Et resurrexit" is modeled on the chorus of a secular work—perhaps identical with the lost homage cantata "Entfernet euch, ihr heitern Sterne," BWV Anh. I.9.[17] An aria from the lost cantata "Wünschet Jerusalem Glück," BWV Anh. I.4, has been claimed as the parody pattern for "Et in Spiritum Sanctum."[18] The original for "Et exspecto resurrectionem" is the second section of the *Ratswahl* Cantata "Gott, man lobet dich in der Stille," BWV 120.

For the Sanctus of the B-Minor Mass Bach took a Sanctus movement he had composed for Christmas 1725. The "Osanna in excelsis" is based on the head theme of the lost cantata "Es lebe der König, der Vater im Lande," BWV Anh. I.11. To date there has been no conclusive evidence in support of early speculation that the music of the Benedictus originally belonged to another work. But it has been documented extensively that the alto aria "Agnus Dei" is patterned after the aria "Entfernet euch, ihr kalten Herzen." The aria "Auf, süß entzückende Gewalt," BWV Anh. I.196, originally part of the *Wedding Cantata,* had already been transplanted by Bach to the *Ascension Oratorio,* to the words "Ach bleibe doch, mein liebstes Leben." The "Dona nobis pacem" is a reversion to the "Gratias agimus tibi" of the B-Minor Mass, itself a parody of the cantata section BWV 29/2.

Are there any parts at all that are original compositions from the years 1748–49? Perhaps the "Et incarnatus est": Bach wrote it on a loose sheet of paper and inserted it into the score later. He garnered the words from the previous duet "Et in unum Dominum," lengthening its text as needed. What caused him to change his original intentions for "Et incarnatus est" and make it a section of its own? And is there a chance that he borrowed the movement from another composer?[19] There are remarkable similarities with the "O clemens" segment of Giovanni Battista Pergolesi's *Salve Regina* in C minor, composed in his later years. Yoshitake Kobayashi holds the view that the "emotive expressivity" of Pergolesi's music prompted Bach to his "partial borrowing."[20]

"To improve something already existing seemed to the late Bach, and perhaps even the 'middle' Bach, easier than creating something totally new." This is how Hans-Joachim Schulze respectfully phrases one of the truths about Bach's work.[21] But is it *the* truth? Another truth is that Bach stayed with and continued to work on tried-and-true models. One of many examples of this is the solo "Agnus Dei, qui tollis peccata mundi, miserere nobis," from the B-Minor Mass. The alto sings the entreaty "Lamm Gottes, das der Welt Sünde trägt, erbarm' dich unser" ("O Lamb of God, who taketh away the sins of the world, have mercy upon us"), with a gesture of impassioned, intimate pleading, to music of almost unearthly beauty. This comes from a piece composed for a wedding, with this text:

> Entfernet euch, ihr kalten Herzen.
> Entfernet euch, ich bin euch feind.
> Wer nicht der Liebe Platz will geben,
> Der flieht sein Glück, der haßt sein Leben
> Und ist der ärgsten Torheit Freund.
> Ihr wählt euch selber nichts als Schmerzen.

> Go far from me, ye cold-hearted ones.
> Go far away, I am your foe.
> Who ever will not make room for love,
> he flies from happiness, he hates his own life.
> He is the friend of the worst kind of madness.
> Ye choose for yourselves nothing but sorrows.
> (trans. John Hargraves)

The original music for this aria, which is reminiscent of Vivaldi's "Piango gemo," has been lost; as mentioned, though, Bach used it ten years later with another text in the *Ascension Oratorio*, "Lobet Gott in seinen Reichen." In the new text, Jesus, departing from this earth, is implored with these words:

> Ach bleibe doch, mein liebstes Leben,
> Ach fliehe nicht so bald von mir!

Dein Abschied und dein frühes Scheiden
Bringt mir das allergrößte Leiden,
Ach ja, so bleibe doch noch hier;
Sonst werd ich ganz von Schmerz umgeben.

Ah, stay with me, my dearest life thou,
Ah, flee thou not so soon from me!
Thy parting and thine early leaving
Bring me the most egregious suff'ring,
Ah yes, then stay yet here awhile;
Else shall I be with pain surrounded.
(trans. Z. Philip Ambrose)

Again, more than ten years later, Bach transforms the music into the Agnus Dei. Given the totally different liturgical context, he must have made structural changes to the music that go far beyond the elimination of a few coquettishly sighing figures. It was only logical for him to eliminate the da capo form here, which had already done some damage to Gottsched's symmetrically arranged verses and to their adaptation for the *Ascension Oratorio.* Since Bach as a matter of principle rejected the use of da capo form in his Latin sacred works, it would be out of place in the B-Minor Mass. But the adaptation goes further: against his own model, he has the voice begin with a broad legato address before returning to the original ritornello theme at the words "qui tollis":

It was probably easier for him to keep working on an old model than to write a new composition. But that could be put another way: initial attempts need to be finished and put into a definitive final context. The gesture of pleading supplication, which was directed at cold hearts in the *Wedding Cantata,* and at Jesus as he departs this world in the *Ascension Oratorio,* is now directed at the Lamb of God as the heavenly mediator who decides on eternal salvation or damnation. Jesus is the final authority to which this plea of all pleas must be addressed, and this authority is ultimately the best repository for Bach's musical gesture of supplication.

To put this idea more generally: Bach cannot conceive of a better context for his music than the universality of a large mass. So he selects from the wealth of existing works and individual sections those that are particularly deserving of "promotion."[22] In this late survey of his own work, everything that worked well or was "characteristic" found its place—whether from Weimar or Leipzig, erudite or gallant. In what other genre could stark contrasts be so well integrated, or so many different facets of style brought together, than in a large mass! Despite the work's variety, Bach, from the beginning, consciously composed with the aim of spiritual unity in mind.

Is it a sign of diminishing creativity that at the very end of the mass he completely repeats the music of the Gratias to the words in the *Dona nobis pacem,* or is it good theological sense?[23] Stylistically, is it a problem that he places far more importance on the preludes and interludes in the Kyrie and Gloria than he does in other parts of the B-Minor Mass?[24] With the Hosanna and the "Pleni sunt coeli," are two insufficiently contrasting sections run together, which a composer with a more sovereign plan would not have done?[25] And what are we to do with the fact that the portion of the B-Minor Mass composed earliest, the Sanctus, is the very part where word and sound, theology and music, come together most powerfully?

Despite such questions, the B-Minor Mass is both Bach's theological and compositional legacy—the summa of his work in honor of God, and in honor of himself: what composer before or since him has with such supreme confidence extracted the quintessence from his own work? Seen from this perspective, the meaning of the B-Minor Mass could never be exhausted by a single performance, even if Bach had intended such a thing. His last, great, crowning achievement is the expression of his universality; it illustrates that he composed not for any one situation or listener. His music comes from a wider perspective and so speaks a language that we understand but in which we also sense another language, one that transcends our ability to evaluate it aesthetically.

The music of the B-Minor Mass is in no way retrospective. Of course it does not have the lightness of Pergolesi's *Stabat Mater,* which is also a work of revisions and one that Bach obviously thought much of. He is not alienated by the modern church style but does not greet it with open arms either; he remains in between. He is probably more uncompromising, more polarizing than, say, his Dresden colleagues, in the way he sets various styles against one another in his "great Catholic mass." But even by Bach's time, the mass form positively shimmered with every conceivable variety of stylistic facet, and it would continue so through the history of music—one need think only of Mozart's *Requiem* or Beethoven's *Missa Solemnis.*

With regard to the timelessness of the B-Minor Mass, Bach was a participant in an aesthetic discourse that was being carried on in France at the time, known as the Querelle des Anciens et des Modernes. The "ancients" insist on the primacy of the old: its value must remain; all the new can do is imitate it.[26] Here "old" means exclusively classical antiquity. But just a few years after Bach's death, the term *Gothic* underwent an upgrading.[27] To be "a real Goth in the art of music,"[28] as Johann Adolph Scheibe saw Bach's antirationalism and antinaturalism, became a compliment before the century was over. Even Friedrich Wilhelm Zachariä, librettist of sentimental oratorios, is overcome by a "holy Gothic shudder"[29] at the sight of the city of Goslar with its "old-fashioned walls and towers," and Johann Friedrich Reichardt in 1782 transposes Goethe's view of the Strasbourg Cathedral onto musical history: to him Bach represents a Gothically sublime human art, though not yet in the most highly developed sense.[30] Finally in 1821, Carl Maria von Weber speaks glowingly of Bach's "sublime spirit," which has erected a "truly Gothic cathedral of art."[31]

When Felix Mendelssohn rediscovered the *St. Matthew Passion*, motivated not least by the spirit of Prussian Protestantism, the "great Catholic mass" had long been around: Carl Philipp Emanuel Bach had brought the work into public consciousness through his preparation of the Credo for performance as early as 1786. A score is discovered in Haydn's estate; in 1810 Beethoven requests a copy from his publishers Breitkopf and Härtel. Eight years later the Swiss musician and publisher Hans Georg Nägeli announces the printing of the "greatest musical art work of all times and nations."[32]

Today there is a double aspect to the B-Minor Mass. It appears to us on one hand as the epic work of an ancient poet for which more and more sources are being discovered—the difference being that Virgil, for instance, took his inspiration from foreign sources, while Bach falls back on his own production. On the other hand, we experience it as myth, whose origin we do not question; we take it as it is and interpret it in the light of our own existence.

This response is similar to our twofold experience of the Bible: some test it with historical derivations and textual analyses; others look for God's message. But what is the message of the B-Minor Mass? Is it the work's spiritual and theological unity? Is it the universality of its tonal language? Is it a mysterious order of measure and number available only to those who believe? Here is a view of the Credo that tries to reconcile these perspectives.

Bach subsequently made the "Et incarnatus est" into an independent section. Moreover, in the B-Minor Mass there is emphasis not just on the central Christological messages of crucifixion and resurrection but also on Jesus's incarnation as a human being. The formerly eight-part Credo now has nine parts, and the statement "Crucifixus etiam pro nobis," which one can look at as standing apart from the other movements, moves to the center.[33]

Chorus: *Credo* (*stile antico* with liturgical cantus firmus)
Chorus: *Patrem omnipotentem* (concerted)

Duet: *Et in unum Dominum* (concerted)

Chorus: *Et incarnatus est* (modern motet movement)

Chorus: *Crucifixus* (strict style)

Chorus: *Et resurrexit* (concerted)

Aria: *Et in spiritum sanctum* (concerted)

Chorus: *Et expecto* (concerted)

One can take pleasure in this symmetry and imagine that Bach intended it. It makes the work a dimension richer, but does the revelation contribute to the music's fascination? That we experience music not in an instant, as we might the well-proportioned facade of a chateau, but over time makes it almost impossible for our senses to take in symmetries that were developed on paper. Hearers of the Credo will notice mainly that the two solo numbers, which in an ideal overall plan would assume subordinate positions, take the longest, while the two solemn sections in *stile antico* pass quickly.

Most important, the audience has to deal with an enormous variety of styles, which are more difficult to assimilate than in the passions or the *Christmas Oratorio,* owing to the lack of a continuous dramatic thread. This is true even of a single, liturgically coherent portion of the mass like the Credo. *Stile antico* alternates with *stile moderno* in a breadth of variations unusual even for Bach, and in between are character pieces like the specially composed, totally meditative section "Et incarnatus est," which itself brings together different linguistic levels, in just as simple yet fascinating a way. Above a bass written as a continuous organ pedal point or a calmly striding line arise two different voices: the choir and the violins. The choir presents the liturgical text in categorically objective language, illustrating the incarnation of God as a descending third, seventh, or other widely spaced interval. The voice of the violins maintains, through a series of modifications, from beginning to end, a motif of lamentation. It speaks[34] as if it came from one of Haydn's Sturm und Drang symphonies; the allocation of function to the voice and orchestra melodies acts almost like a road sign pointing to Wagner's much later music dramas.

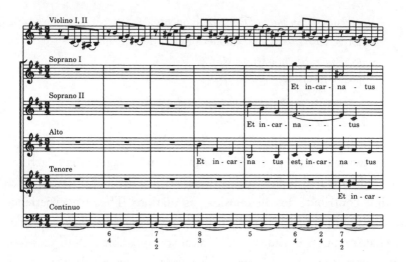

There may be comparable patterns in earlier works of Bach; but seldom have two such different characteristics been brought together in one movement, in so concise and classical a manner. Was this meant to be Bach's final compositional legacy? It would attest to a sympathetic relation of Bach to the incarnation of God in Christ: his Cross had already been composed into the piece! Or was Wilhelm Dilthey right, when he described his impression of the "Incarnatus" as the "middle-point of the whole mass" in these words: "no color, but like a light in which all colors are one: it has no change, everything quietly set in the same quavering tones. Here there is no suffering, and no joy."[35]

Bach and the Dance of God, a book by the English musicologist and composer Wilfried Mellers that appeared in 1980, devotes much space to the B-Minor Mass. To compare Bach's *ultimum opus* with a dance before God is a wonderful insight. It brings out many different aspects of the work: in the space of the church, the timeless formula of the mass, the quintessence of the worship service, is raised up like a symbol. The composer lets his music dance before this symbol. Its individual parts need not be strictly attuned to one another; they are connected by the *formula Missae,* and their purpose is to meet the theological richness of the mass with a wealth of musical forms, styles, and expressions.

But we should not look for a cyclic idea in the B-Minor Mass in terms of the structural-analytic categories of modern musicology. Such an idea was an alien concept for the time: it is hard to find it in Beethoven's *Missa Solemnis*! The cyclic idea of the B-Minor Mass is theological and thus also musical-philosophical: Bach puts his mark on a genre spanning ages, nations, and confessions. The work of art he has extracted from the formula of the mass is autonomous, yet at the same time this work finds its ultimate authentication precisely in the truths of that formula.

In 1907 with respect to the B-Minor Mass, Dilthey declared wonderingly that Bach "excludes the chorale [from the mass], contradicting the architecture of all his other sacred music," to immerse himself in the "universal, objective character of the mass." In and for the Protestant culture of his age, he construes the Kyrie of the mass formula as an expression of the need for salvation and the Gloria as celebrating God's guarantee of it.[36]

This point of view, hardly ecumenical—indeed, almost too narrowly concerned with the phenomenology of religion—was and remains a thorn in the side for advocates of a renewed Reformation theology. All the same, in resorting to the mass, Bach realizes one of his creative goals: the objectification of a subjectively created work. In this context, the full mass offers better opportunities than genuinely Protestant sacred music, which in Lutheran theology must give precedence to proclaiming and interpreting the word of God. Bach, who concerned himself over a lifetime in his sacred cantatas, passions, and oratorios primarily with the Sundays and feast days of the church calendar, with concretizing in music the message of the day, here finally finds his way definitively to the essence of the worship service, an essence that Luther never regarded lightly.

Of course, the desire to objectify subjectively created art is always intermingled with another desire: to give subjectivity to a form (here the mass) that transcends ages, nations, and styles. *The Art of Fugue* gave Bach the chance to play out this dialectic in the instrumental realm. The B-Minor Mass is its counterpart in

the vocal realm. These two splendid examples of his late work ensure his place in Western musical history: centered between the
categorical thought of the Middle Ages and the individualistic
thought of the modern age. What follows is for the former a fall
from grace; for the latter, a road of no return to the promised and
accursed land of freedom.

THE MOTETS

The verdict of history on Bach's music has often been right: the motets are an example. In November 1789 the choir of St. Thomas's surprised Mozart on his way though Leizpig with a performance of "Singet dem Herrn ein neues Lied," and he reacted with these words "Now here is something one could learn from!"[1] In his 1860 essay "The Music of the Future," discussing this motet, his "favorite," Richard Wagner praises its "lyrical verve of rhythmic melody," which roars along "as if through a sea of harmonic waves."[2]

In the mountain range of Bach's work there are many peaks: places in which, beyond all considerations of time and form, the essence of a thing is revealed. The purely a capella double chorus motet of 1727, "Singet dem Herrn ein neues Lied," BWV 225, is a pinnacle of absolute vocal music. The text, taken from Psalm 149, provides a matchless opportunity for the composer:

> Singet dem Herrn ein neues Lied, die Gemeinde der Heiligen
> sollen ihn loben. Israel freue sich des, der ihn gemacht hat. Die
> Kinder Zion sei'n fröhlich über ihrem Könige, sie sollen loben
> seinen Namen im Reigen; mit Pauken und Harfen sollen sie ihm
> spielen.

> Sing ye the Lord a new refrain; the assembly of saints should be
> telling his praises. Israel joyful be in him who hath made him.

Let Zion's children rejoice in him who is their mighty king; let them be praising his name's honor in dances; with timbrels and with psalt'ries unto him be playing.

The whole work is one great exhortation to sing, play, dance, praise, and rejoice—the listener need not understand the exact words, since the singers are doing all these things with the music! Bach has one of the two choruses repeatedly interrupt the continuous text and simply cry out, "Singet, singet." This is like the jubilation that to Saint Augustine was the essence of veneration for God, the concept of "absolute" singing.[3] One is reminded of a marginal note Bach made in his bible in Exodus 15.2021: "First prelude, two choruses to sing in praise of God."[4] The passage concerns the prophetess Miriam and the women following her, who form a train "with timbrels and dancing" in honor of the Highest.

In contrast with his other motets, Bach dispenses for the most part with detailed textual interpretation, except for the varying nuances in how the singing, playing, dancing, praising, and rejoicing are expressed. There is certainly no setting the theology of *Romans* to music or of taking the "stony road." Theology and music flow together from a single impulse: the *laus Dei,* praise of God. In the tradition of Luther's psalm readings, *laus Dei* does not just mean the congregation praising God: God also praises his own actions through the hearts and mouths of mankind.[5]

The first section in particular expresses the original conception of multiple choruses. Bach seems to call forth what we have in our collective unconscious: surges of sound, directed yet infinite, tranquillity in motion. We see at once that this is not two choruses singing, sometimes together, sometimes in alternation, but two choruses in collision. There is hardly another case in music history—not even in the brilliant eight-part *Magnificat* of Heinrich Schütz—where two choruses are vested with such individuality and yet so artfully interwoven. On the formal level, this work is superior to Bach's other multiple-chorus motets, though they are hardly weak in this regard.

How subtly, almost imperceptibly, the dance fugue "Die Kinder Zion" is worked into this polychoral setting, though it defines the structure of the entire movement. At the fourth entry of the theme, the fugal setting extends into the second chorus. The result is a conglomeration of voices extending across eight parts, then compressed into four; the result of this concentration is that in just five dense bars Bach brings this segment to an end, thus freeing the work from what Wagner jokingly called its *Mückengeschwirr* ("swarm of buzzing gnats").[6]

Bach's formal mastery is evident not just in this first section of the motet but in all its architecture. In the second section, the chorale "Wie sich ein Vater erbarmet" and the aria "Gott, nimm dich ferner unser an" alternate. The third section begins at the words "Lobet den Herrn in seinen Reichen" ("Praise the Lord in all His doings") with blocks of homophonic double-chorus singing and ends with the four-part fugue "Alles, was Odem hat, lobe den Herrn, Halleluja." Thus Bach has taken the three-movement Italianate instrumental concerto, which he already translated into his organ works in Weimar, and adapted it to his vocal music in an original fashion. "Singet" constitutes the extensive opening movement; the combination of chorale and aria then takes the place of the slow, lyrical middle movement; "Lobet den Herrn in seinen Reichen" is the relatively uncomplicated introduction to the dancelike final movement, faintly reminiscent of a passepied, "Alles was Odem hat."

Of course, Bach would not be Bach if he did not turn all this into a work of many layers. The head movement displays the principle of double choruses in every imaginable variation. Using the medium of architecture as well as pure sound, he opens up new musical space in a way not previously known. Quite different from the comparatively naive Venetian use of multiple choruses, this new alternation between the expansion and the contraction of the body of sound is what gives rise to this truly spatial dimension in the music. The second movement is not content with just one song: two different types of lyric are presented in choral opposition. The final movement unites the two choruses in a four-part fugue, making it quite clear that the end of all music, if not its beginning, is always to be found in a pure, harmonious setting.

Bach's sense of proportion is always evident: the motet begins and ends in triple time, not just to lend a dancelike flair but because of the originally theological context of triple time, or *tempus perfectum*. His proportionality goes further: the sixteenth notes of the first movement and of the final fugue are in the same tempo, so the motet retains a kind of kinetic symmetry.[7] In view of his liking for clear and obvious proportionality, it should not be overlooked that he wrote a note in the autograph score asking that the middle section—using another verse, and with the two choruses swapped—be sung a second time.

Among the score's many niceties are the nuanced section endings. The last measures of the first movement all but drag onto center stage the psalm text's drums and harps. The second movement does not end with the choruses united but with the first chorus singing an *Abgesang*, that is, the last two lines of its final aria, for the second choir has already bid farewell with the words of the chorale "Sein End, das ist ihm nah" ("his end is near"). A quiet ending, perhaps—

but at the same time it is the upbeat to the flashy final movement "Lobet den Herrn in seinen Taten." Bach saves the soprano's high note, B-flat, for the third-to-last measure of the closing fugue: only after this risky stunt is complete can the final note of jubilation be sounded.

The second movement is remarkable for its combination of texts: it pairs a traditional Lutheran chorale with a modern strophic text, which was either written for this occasion or was a fragment from some other religious text adapted by Bach. This combination is unusual for the genre but offers some interesting possible theological interpretations: the two choruses seem to juxtapose the church at large, represented by the chorale, with those in the community who personally struggle with their faith. The *Ecclesia* is not played off against the *ecclesiola* (the "little church," or smaller community of saved within the church), as the Pietist view would have it; both are tellingly characterized. The chorale goes confidently forward, while the aria brings the generalities of faith down to the level of the individual believer, beseeching God personally for His protection.

Bach sharpens the contrast between chorale and aria on a musical plane. He gives the aria, whose text is far from Pietist, a melody that the orthodox would criticize for sounding like the flirtatious, warbling tunes of the Pietists—at least in the beginning. As the composition goes on, he moves the aria in a more hymnlike direction, approaching the chorale both musically and theologically.

Why does the motet contain a strophe that begins with the words "Wie sich ein Vater erbarmet" ("As doth a father mercy show") but ends with "Also der Mensch vergehet, sein End, das ist ihm nah" ("E'en so is man's life passing, his end to him is near")? Was it meant to be a New Year's service in which one should sing a "new song" but at the same time remind the listener of the transitoriness of earthly life? We do not know, but no matter: may this model of a motet remain for us the epitome of divine praise, a pure work of art with no other purpose!

The other three double-chorus motets, understandably, suffer in comparison with "Singet dem Herrn ein neues Lied"—particularly the funeral piece "Fürchte dich nicht, ich bin bei dir" ("Fear not, I am with you"), BWV 228. The first part, having extended homophonic sections, contrasts with the second part, which is set for only four voices but contrapuntally: the three lower voices sing the prophet's words "denn ich habe dich erlöset" ("for I have redeemed you"), while the soprano sings two verses of the chorale "Warum sollt' ich mich denn grämen" ("Then why should I grieve"). Bringing a chorale tune into a motet movement is a familiar practice in Lutheran church music, and a Bach family tradition besides. But this particular motet stands far above the norm of the genre by specifically reflecting on this contrast,[8] and its counterpoint distinguishes it as being anything but music written casually for an itinerant student choir to sing at a funeral. The attempt to distill various aspects of the motet form into a single piece is typical of Bach—though probably of a younger Bach: the strained chromaticism of the second part of the motet doesn't quite fit the text "Ich habe dich erlöset" ("For I have redeemed you") and indicates the labored quality of the work as a whole.

This work could date from Bach's Weimar period, especially since the chorale inclusion is reminiscent of that in the motet "Ich lasse dich nicht, du segnest mich denn," BWV Anh. III.159. This anonymous motet comes from a score of 1712–13, the first fourteen bars of which Bach wrote in himself—perhaps as a compositional model for his pupil Philipp David Kräuter, who (apart from a few revisions by Bach) wrote the rest of the work.

The motet "Komm, Jesu, komm," BWV 229, has a much more mature sound. While the polychoral structure of "Fürchte dich nicht" seems forced and the counterpoint strained, this work is charming, with its supple diction and almost gallant quality. For this period, *gallant* most of all implies singability (*Sanglichkeit*) and expressiveness, as opposed to structure and counterpoint. Singability, in the modern sense, is evident throughout the work. The words "ich sehne mich," with their parallel thirds and sixths, demonstrate this, as does the second, longer half of the motet, on the text "Du bist der rechte Weg." This is composed as an aria in 6/8 time for two choruses, and its modernity is manifest in part by the long series of trills performed twice by the alto in the second chorus on the word *leben*, in part by the strophe "Drum schließ ich mich in deine Hände und sage, Welt, zu guter Nacht!" appended to the main section. The addition is not a final chorus in the sense of a *Kantionalsatz* (simple four-part harmony) but—highly unusual for Bach—an aria in the 3/4 time of a minuet, with all the small declamatory, rhythmic, and melodic piquancy[9] then befitting a modern religious or secular strophic song in the style of Pietism.

The earliest known source of the motet is a manuscript copy of the score written out by Christoph Nichelmann in 1731–32. Over twenty years later, in his book of 1755 on the nature and characteristics of melody, this same Bach scholar praised the harmonic originality of the closing aria: it is seen as capable of expressing the "passion required by the text," not only because of the composer's artistic expertise but also because he was so "moved" by "impressions" that the harmonic sequence made on him, that the melody flowed out of a preexisting "feeling" as if from a "spring."[10]

It is no accident that this writer, who is arguing from the musical-aesthetic vantage point of sentimentality (*Empfindsamkeit*), chooses just this aria as an example of expressive and easily comprehensible music. In hardly any other of his major vocal works does Bach so consistently keep to a style that is both singable and expressive in the sense meant by his Enlightened contemporaries— whether we call it gallant or merely a temporary response to a trend.[11] Also ear-catching is the music's rhetorical drama: the four-fold exclamation "Komm" given to both choruses is meant not just as a climax in the traditional figurative sense but also as a gesture of direct verbal power. He could certainly have found this type of thing in the motets of his day, and there are parallels in the opening choruses of the *St. John Passion* and the B-Minor Mass. Of course Bach's rhetoric is architecture, too: the question "Wie fange ich an?" ("How do I begin?") is answered in a way that points ahead to the classicism of Vienna.

Compared with the counterpoint section "denn ich habe dich erlöset" from "Fürchte dich nicht," even the depiction of the "bitter path" is direct and clear, despite its labored chromaticism and diminished seventh intervals: the voice pairs in a canon on fourths, as well as the steep path they seem to be climbing, come to an end after only ten bars. Then the contrapuntal figural style gives way to a style that is more oratorical and amenable to the senses. The second chorus asserts, once again, "Der saure Weg—wird mir zu schwer," but now in a homophonic phrase; the first chorus sings during its seemingly breathless pauses the words "zu schwer—zu schwer." There are comparable subtleties in Bach's polyphonic chorus parts, but they are easily lost in the vocal fabric; here they are audibly brought out.

Bach wrote funeral motets largely on commission. In this case, was he composing for someone who was aesthetically in tune with the Pietist aria and therefore wished a simple but expressive, indeed, a modern composition? Perhaps it was a person who wanted something totally different from, say, the late-sixteenth-century motet with texts in Latin and German, "Turbabor sed non perturbator / Mein' Sünd'n mich werden kränken sehr," which could still be heard at Bach's time, thanks to an endowment. Bach once performed one at a memorial service for Johann Maria Kees on 18 July 1723.[12]

Although the rhetorical quality of "Komm, Jesu, komm" may be superior to that of its sister work, "Singet dem Herrn," it is architecturally not in the same league. The analytically trained eye may detect bar form in the structure as a whole,[13] but the progress from section to section is really felt more in psychological terms: from the melancholy yet rapturous invocation of Jesus to the deep sighs over the travails of life to the lively conviction of faith in the dancelike final refrain.

"Der Geist hilft unser Schwachheit auf," BWV 226, the only precisely dated motet of Bach, takes a middle road. Bach wrote it for the burial of his rector, Johann Heinrich Ernesti, which took place in the university church on 20 October 1729. Since the funeral sermon, at the wish of the deceased, was to be on the eighth chapter of Romans, it seemed appropriate to choose that text for the music. Though not unexpected, the rector's death came quickly;[14] thus one can assume that Bach began the composition only the evening of the day the rector died. If this was the case, then Bach had a mere four days to write and rehearse the piece.

Given the time constraint, it would not be surprising if he adapted previously existing work. This has indeed been conjectured: the model for the opening double-chorus movement "Der Geist hilft," it has been thought, was a secular composition for just two voices.[15] Revising such a composition would of course have taken time. Nor can it be ignored that the distinctive opening phrase describes the moving of the spirit in a fashion that occurs in other vocal works dealing with the Holy Ghost, as in the motet "Jesu, meine Freude," at the words "der Geist aber ist das Leben" ("the Spirit still yet is living").

The third section of the motet, the four-part fugue "Der aber die Herzen forschet," contains corrections in the autograph, especially in the text chosen for the music. These are not always happy choices, even in the final version, particularly at the words "Denn er vertritt die Heiligen" ("Because he intercedeth for the Saints"). Stylistically, the model for this section in strict style could have come from a cantata from the Leipzig period.[16] Finally, the second section, on the words "Sondern der Geist selbst vertritt uns aufs beste mit unaussprechlichem Seufzen" ("rather, the Spirit himself intercedeth for us, ineffably sighing"), was evidently written down in the conceptual sketch and thus should be considered as original.[17]

There are indications that Bach wrote this middle section last and that he wrote the Bible text he set to it from memory: he forgot the word "selbst." In correcting this error afterward, he had to change the tonal sequence of the theme, thus destroying its original symmetry. Nonetheless, the section marked "Fugato" (a highly imperfect characterization) is the motet's showpiece: a five-to-six-part genre piece on the theme "Seufzen" ("sighing"). The total of nine theme entries are commented upon in such variety by the sighing melisma figures of the countervoices that the whole section has the effect of a single unutterable sigh. The graphic effect of so much groaning and sighing is somewhat lessened by its being embedded in a contrapuntal section. The compositional style hearkens back to the expressive madrigal art of the old Italians, but with its less flowing and rather more figured melody, and the consistent use of motifs, this is authentically Bach.

It is odd that Bach went to the trouble of writing down the four-part final fugue "Der aber die Herzen" separately for each chorus. There was a ready supply of score paper available for such purposes, but is that a sufficient explanation, or did Bach originally intend to end the work in eight parts? The final chorale, "Du heilige Brunst," probably taken from a lost Pentecost cantata, constitutes the end of a motet[18] that cannot conceal its motley ancestry, nor, given its greatness and rhetorical power, does it need to.

What the perfect form of "Singet dem Herrn ein neues Lied" is for composers, the perfect architecture of "Jesu, meine Freude," BWV 227, is for theologians. Form is the goal of a composition, its telos; it is realized in time, and its attainment can bring aesthetic pleasure. Architecture is a sort of design survey of a composition; it exists on paper and is perceived only as an abstract plan, not as a process in time. Throughout its reception history, the form of "Jesu, meine Freude" has been less admired than its architecture. When we look at its form, we find variously set strophes of the hymn "Jesus, meine Freude" appearing in alternation with variously set texts from St. Paul's Epistle to the Romans.

An observation of the work's architecture shows that its eleven sections are arranged in axial symmetry: the opening chorale is musically identical with the finale chorale (1 = 11); the two five-part *Spruchmotetten* (proverb motets), "Es ist nun nichts Verdammliches" and "So nun der Geist," are as musically identical as their differing texts allow (2 = 10); the two *Spruchmotetten* "Denn das Gesetz des Geistes" and "So aber Christus in euch ist" correspond in that both are three-part (4 = 8); the other four chorale arrangments fit into the symmetry only because they are all the same genre (chorales); the center of the work consists of a great five-part fugue on the text "Ihr aber seid nicht fleischlich, sondern geistlich" (6).

The grand old men of Bach biography, Philipp Spitta and Albert Schweitzer, had little to say about motets and did not feel that any of this was worth mentioning. After World War I, when the architecture of Bach's keyboard music, in particular *The Art of Fugue*, was beginning to be noticed—by August Halm, Fritz Jöde, Wilhelm Werker, Wolfgang Graeser, and Erich Schwebsch, among others—enthusiasm began to grow for the miraculous structure evident when one started to examine "Jesus, meine Freude." Of course those music scholars and lovers of Bach with more of a musical-aesthetic orientation will always maintain that the order of a composition, while not unimportant, is secondary compared with the composition itself—but even they will appreciate, if not admire, the music's cyclic element.

For this is clearly a cycle—where a hymn setting *per omnes versus* and a setting of five verses from Romans 8 are not merely spliced together but transformed into a structure of nuance and sophistication. What brought Bach to write something like this? It is a funeral motet, although the complete work comes down to us only as a later copy and thus it cannot be dated. But who commissioned it?

One might almost think that Bach commissioned it himself. He worked on it for decades. That there is much switching between four and five voices and that the "Gute Nacht, o Wesen" section presents the cantus firmus in a different version from that of the other hymn sections, which was the normal version in Weimar, suggest that the composition was not created in one piece. The three choral movements, numbers 1, 3, and 7, are to be found in a copy dating from 1735: were they copied from an already existing score, or was the motet at that point incomplete? Bach may not have created this textually and symmetrically unique work until late in life, basing it on already existing materials. This work has its counterpart in the *Goldberg Variations*, where a series of canons is interleaved with free variations.

The text is impressive for its theological intensity. Its stern yet impassioned delivery of the apostle Paul's doctrine of justification is coupled with intensely felt choral verses, imbued with the joy and love of Jesus, that were written by the lay poet and burgomaster of Guben, Johann Franck. The melody is by the Berlin cantor Johann Crüger, publisher of the widely known hymnbook *Praxis pietatis melica*. That the concerns of orthodoxy and Pietism are thus brought together in unique fashion does not imply that Pauline theology here is to be aligned with orthodoxy, or that the poetry is to be aligned with Pietism. Rather, the combination provides an adequate sampling of the theological currents of Bach's time.

Combinations of this kind are to be found in many of Bach's cantatas but seldom with such dramatic effect that Schweitzer could speak of "Bach's sermon on living and dying."[19] It is a sermon conceived by Bach himself, not just musically but also theologically: if the motet in fact derives from preexisting materials, then only he could have undertaken compiling the final text. He may not have been a master poet, but he could certainly produce a series of densely theological texts, which in form could be compared with an opulently structured yet symmetrical garden or palatial estate.

If we look at "Jesu, meine Freude" as baroque representational art, as a likeness of worldliness, a symbol of divine order and the secular order of the state that derives from it, we should not forget that in Bach's day emblematically arranged works of prose and poetry were published and read in great number. For the musician, what is and remains important is what the composer does with his textual models.

One notices immediately that Bach is not focused simply on the idea of symmetrical arrangement—he brings his entire repertory of genres and styles into play. Only the first and last chorales are in fact musically identical, which makes good sense, since the poem closes with the motto it opened with: "Jesu, meine Freude." The second and next-to-last section are nearly identical, and this could easily be for formal as well as architectural reasons: eleven sections, a rather long span, need a clearly marked frame.

In the inner sections (3–9), variety is the guiding principle. Each choral strophe is unlike the others. "Unter deinen Schirmen" might be read as a *Kantionalsatz* (simple four-part harmony), even though the "Krachen" und "Blitzen" ("thunder and lightning") in the text is depicted graphically by the independently led voices accompanying this section. And although the soprano presents the melody simply in "Weg mit allen Schätzen," the alto, tenor, and bass parts lead lives of their own, as if they were the accompanying voices in a figured organ chorale.

The section "Trotz dem alten Drachen" is motet-like to such a degree that Johannes Brahms was proud of being the first to have "discovered" its cantus firmus "binding."[20] This text has provided a treasure trove for rhetorical musical figures and tone painting: the words "Trotz," "Furcht," "Toben," "Singen," "sich're Ruh," "Abgrund," "Verstummen," and "Brummen" ("spite," "fear," "rage," "singing," "sure peace," "abyss," "fall silent," and "complain") are brought out and interpreted with great intensity, but the strophic pattern is not destroyed in the process.

The choral adaptation "Gute Nacht, o Wesen" is a little miracle. Bach largely dispenses with rhetorical and coloristic touches and devotes himself wholly to the valedictory mood of "Gute Nacht." This four-part basset-horn section with the tenor part as foundation suggests a mood of weightlessness; the two sopranos *concertante*, often in thirds and sixths, paint an intimate picture of the Christian soul as it bids a final farewell to the world and its pomp. The alto part weaves the cantus firmus, transposed down a fifth, into the fabric of the whole, and the result is painful harmonic frictions. The movement is reminiscent now of an organ chorale of the Weimar period, now of the gallant style of the Leipzig motets. It was probably based on a model that Bach used in various different contexts[21]—for example, in the third movement of the violin sonata BWV 1021.

The five numbers composed on the Romans text do contain thematic material derived from the cantus firmus of the chorale, but their main concern is presenting the words clearly. The Pauline message "Es ist nun nichts Verdammliches an denen, die in Christo Jesu sind" ("there is therefore now no condemnation to them which are in Christ Jesus") is sung at the outset in an expressive, syllabic style.

Why does Bach emphasize the word "nichts" ("no") with such pathos, by having the chorus exclaim it three times in a row, inserting grand pauses between the repetitions? He is composing rhetorically, not argumentatively: it is not so much Paul's reasoning as his passion that is being underscored. Bach takes on a very modern look here, by forcefully using such suggestive effects in setting a prose text.

For all its textual concerns, the musical setting has its own immanent logic; this suits this music well for its later (tenth-section) setting of the words "So nun der Geist des, der Jesum von den Toten auferwecket hat" ("The spirit of him that raised up Jesus from the dead"). This time it is the word "des" ("of him") that is emphasized; since the reference is to God, the emphasis is justified.

Further on in these two related sections, imitative and homophonic parts alternate. For the sake of rhetorical emphasis Bach's writing gets more discontinuous, not to say wilder, than one usually encounters in seventeenth-century *Spruchmotetten*—for example, in Schütz's *Geistliche Chormusik*. But in the meantime, the traditional norms for the motet genre have lost some of their validity. So Bach can move more freely in this field than in, for instance, the cantata.

That he made use of this freedom is seen in the two numbers with matching orchestrations: "Denn das Gesetz des Geistes" and "So aber Christus in euch ist": both are trio settings with *concertante* touches—hardly motets in the traditional sense. Along with their neighboring chorale strophes, they form brief episodes flanking the broad middle section of the motet, the setting of its central message, "Ihr aber seid nicht fleischlich, sondern geistlich" ("Thou art not of the flesh but of the spirit").

While the four above-mentioned Bible-passage settings have significant portions devoted to direct discourse and textual presentation, this center is composed as a five-part fugue, and so it is a piece of absolute music: its fugal structure, which is not at all according to the book, determines the form, and the text is fitted in. Werner Neuman was not incorrect in calling it an "organ fugue for the voice."[22] The

key words "fleischlich" and "geistlich" ("fleshly," "spiritual") are prominently displayed: so although Bach does not think twice about inserting a fugue—the queen of musical forms in his eyes—into the center
of his motet, he still takes great care in his treatment of the text.

As we conclude these observations, it is evident that the architecture of the motet is just as important as its form. Bach is able to
introduce a great variety of ways to handle chorales, texts, and language in the medium of pure choral composition, because he frames
this variety with a total concept that, while formally extrinsic, objec-
tifies it. Just the regular alternation of choral strophes with Bible-text
settings provides a necessary stability in view of how different the individual movements are. At least with repeated hearings of the cycle,
its subtler symmetries are able to clarify its consistency as a whole.

We can speak of two high points in Bach's motet output: the one
is defined by the direct and sensual perception of form in "Singet
dem Herrn," the other by the formal architecture reflected in "Jesu,
meine Freude." These are the two complementary great qualities of
all Bach's creative work.

The motet volume of the *New Bach Edition* contains two other
motets besides the ones mentioned already: "O Jesu Christ, meins
Lebens Licht," BWV 118, and "Lobet den Herrn, alle Heiden," BWV
230. Each falls somewhat outside the norm for this genre. "O Jesu
Christ, meins Lebens Licht" is a funeral work written in 1736–37 and
is something between a cantata movement and a motetic choral transcription: it should be seen in the context of the late choral text
cantatas. Its original scoring—two horns known as litui, one cornet,
three trumpets—implies that the work was performed outdoors, either in a funerary procession or at a graveside. This practice does not
accord with the normal ritual of Leipzig obsequies and indicates that
the occasion of composition was out of the ordinary.

The four-part song "Lobet den Herrn, alle Heiden" has come
down to us only from nineteenth-century sources, and its authenticity is in doubt on stylistic grounds. It does not fit the image we have
of Bach's motet style. While possessing some gallant traits, it gives
one more the sense that it was meant to be a retrospective on the

motet form in general. The author of this work, which is in places very skillfully composed though without evidence of great deliberation, may have been a son or student of Bach's—Friedemann Bach or Johann Gottlieb Goldberg.

It may not be entirely due to the vagaries of transmission that the core of Bach's motet work consists of only five pieces. In other genres, too, that did not demand regular production of new works—as did the cantata or organ choral forms, for instance—he left a moderate number of exemplary pieces.

PART THREE

THE INSTRUMENTAL WORKS

THE ART OF THE TOCCATA

As a composer of sacred vocal music, Bach took his place in a long tradition. For nearly nine hundred years composers had been setting Bible texts, ornamenting Gregorian cantus firmi, or transcribing hymns. Even those hallmarks of the modern passion and religious cantata—recitative and aria—did not come out of the blue but were borrowed from opera, where by Bach's time they had already flourished for two generations.

Even an acreage that has been so long and intensively cultivated can yield one great final harvest, one that puts earlier results under critical and productive scrutiny, one after which nothing radically new can be created. Against this background, Bach is truly, in Albert Schweitzer's phrase, "an ending."

Systematic thinking about music has limits when applied to the vocal forms: to the extent that a given set text is taken seriously as a reflection of social reality and not just as musical material, it forces music into its service—if not in every particular, surely in the assumptions that surround the act of composing: texts and socially determined contexts dictate its forms, general outline, and matters of time and timing. A composer can relativize these matters or make us unaware of them, but he can never ignore the fact that a text will insist on its own rights, that it wants something from the composer. No one would contend that Schubert's genius was constrained by the poems of the *Winterreise;* but we can still be happy that he also produced works without any obvious textual connection: impromptus, sonatas, quartets, symphonies.

The instrumental genres of music are still relatively young in the age of Bach. An instrumental ensemble music totally independent of vocal models, and on the same level as the vocal music of the period, comes into being only with Corelli, Albinoni, and Vivaldi. The arts of modern keyboard and organ music of Cabezon, Gabrieli, Byrd, Sweelinck, Frescobaldi, or Froberger are no more than three or four generations old. Bach likely felt, or instinctively knew, that here there lay a challenge, that he would one day far surpass his most immediate models and teachers—Pachelbel, Böhm, Buxtehude.

The music of the keyboard instruments in particular is young Bach's home turf. Whether out of necessity or desire, he has decided against a university course, which would certainly have smoothed the way to a cantoral position. Instead he accepts, at age eighteen, an organist's position—not in order to relax in a modestly compensated but comfortable post but to pursue a career as a keyboard musician.

As organist he can claim a perquisite that he would hardly have been granted as cantor: three or four months' leave to go to Lübeck to visit the greatest living organist, there "to understand [*begreiffen*] various things about his art." *Begreiffen* means more than the study of Buxtehude's compositions, which may well have been known in manuscript form to the young Bach; it means to find out as much as he can about the professional life of a leader of the new music in north Germany. Certainly, after taking this journey, the longest of his life, he better understood what was required to become an important organist. Such a person would see himself as a virtuoso; he would write works for his own repertory and thus play a role as a composer in defining keyboard and organ music; finally, from the perspective of the instrument, he would get to the essence of music per se.

That even in his early years Bach was an expert on organs and later a teacher, and that Johann Christoph Bach incorporated his younger brother's keyboard and organ works in his collection of manuscripts for study, is concrete proof, as it were, that people generally thought that Bach would have a career as an organist. He could have been thinking of Dietrich Buxtehude and Adam Reinken as models—but also of the internationally famous Girolamo Frescobaldi, who like Bach was not just a keyboard expert and writer of virtuoso pieces for clavier and organ but also a composer trained in the writing of instrumental music of all types. Thus his famous *Fiori Musicali*, which Bach would copy down in 1714, contains both toccatas and canzones of a very clavier-like nature within his "organ masses," as well as classic examples of a strict style that originally evolved for vocal music but that now invested instrumental music as well with prestige and dignity.

Performing for an audience is part of the job of every practicing musician, but it has a special significance for lutenists and keyboard musicians: soloists have the chance to produce an entire work of music on their own, to give their fantasy free reign without concerning themselves with other players. Inspiration, invention, and execution meet in ideal fashion.

The simplest kind of performing traditionally comes at the start of a recital: the artist introduces himself and the possibilities of his instrument. At the same time, like the rhapsodes of antiquity, he "prepares," testing his finger dexterity with rapid runs and the tuning of his instrument with lightly struck chords. In Italy since the middle of the sixteenth century this improvisational art was known as the toccata, and Frescobaldi was its master. It became widespread in south Germany as well, particularly through the efforts of his German pupil Johann Jakob Froberger. It was brought to north Germany, where south and traditional north German styles were being combined in different ways around the middle of the seventeenth century, probably by Matthias Weckmann. Typically, toccatas and preludes classed as *stylus phantasticus* are full of contrasts, surprising changes, and alternating segments of "free" (without bars) and "bound" (*gebunden*—i.e., having bar lines and meter) imitative play. Another important feature is the pedal obbligato, a north German innovation.

When Bach was young, the toccata and organ prelude were at their zenith as the epitome of the fantastic style. There are famous examples of the genre by Buxtehude and Nicolaus Bruhns, among others, which in manuscript form quickly became widespread in central Germany as well. The so-called *Möller Manuscript* (compiled by Bach's older brother Johann Christoph between 1703 and 1708) contains examples: a prelude in A major by Buxtehude and two by Bruhns, one in E minor and one in G major. The same volume contains preludes by the young Johann Sebastian; he is measuring himself, as it were, against his models.

Bruhns's Organ Prelude in E Minor begins in toccata-like fashion, namely, in an exploration of the tonic. The composer first sketches out an initial figure, unruly and theatrical, containing eleven of the twelve tones of the chromatic scale on the tonic; then he bores into it harmonically and stays there. This music is both concise and manneristic: for its time, it was the very best kind of composing.

Bruhns follows the toccata-like introduction with a veritable fugue on a chromatic, strikingly active main subject and a playful countersubject. After another toccata-like interval comes a second fugue with a bizarre subject and a very idiosyncratic exposition. A mere seven free-form measures form the final segment.

Over a clear structure (toccata beginning, fugue 1, toccata-like middle, fugue 2, toccata ending) and in a very compact space, Bruhns has assembled a whole arsenal of forms and compositional modes appropriate to the fantastic style: intonation, pedal point, arioso, pastorale, siciliano, recitative, sinfonia, chaconne, *fuga pathetica;* on top of all this is an original arpeggio figure borrowed from violin practice.[1]

Bach cannot yet compete with this mixture of comprehensibility, elegance, and fantasy, even though there are hints of his ability in the opening of his Prelude in G Minor, BWV 535a, composed 1705–08 and added (in autograph form) to the *Möller Manuscript:*

This piece, one of the oldest surviving preludes of Bach, already shows a typical characteristic: an emphasis on consistency, even within the fantastic style. The figured opening is shaped more clearly as a sequence than in Bruhns; the tonal space is explored more completely; the tone clusters between the two pedal points are more systematically expanded from one part to four parts, in the harmony of the diminished seventh chord.

Moreover, Bach gives the beginning toccata section only twenty-one measures; then comes the fugue. It is modeled on a type of north German canzone and closely resembles a theme of Adam Reinken, which is preserved in the *Möller Manuscript* as the model for a fugue by Peter Heidorn. The scope and consistency of this fugue's motivic work go far beyond what one usually sees from north German organ masters.

Bach makes impressive use of the pedal in presenting the theme. Before, when his preludes were in the central German tradition, there was only incidental use of the pedal. He was probably impressed, during his visit to Lübeck, by Buxtehude's pedal use. From now on, he will arrange the themes of his organ fugues with great skill, in order to make striking pedal entrances possible, without being hampered by any of the limitations that thematic invention normally imposes.

The young Bach keeps revisiting previously drafted work. As early as 1710–11 (at least in the opinion of Jean Claude Zehnders and Werner Breig) he started a complete rewrite of this composition, probably in the course of his teaching.[2] In this rewrite, the prelude loses its multicolored fantasia quality, but its length grows. Bach retains the beginning and ending but inserts an impressive new middle section. This middle section is characterized not by the rapid, fantastic, episodic changes such as those in Bruhns's prelude but by a stereotypical thirty-second-note figure, which sequentially descends all twelve steps of the chromatic scale and goes even a bit further. Hermann Keller writes that Bach here is making "his first explorations in the labyrinth of chromaticism and enharmonicism," still not completely sure how to write in this style.[3] For instance, he uses two different notations in a row for the same tones:

Bach needed to write an intermediate version—preserved among others by his pupil Peter Kellner—before he could convincingly set up this long sequence of broken diminished seventh chords. Aesthetically speaking, this sort of chord sequence is nothing unusual; to modern ears it sounds even obsolete. But the compositional process reflects Bach's effort to find his way from an arbitrary arrangement of tones, such as existed in the traditional toccata, to coherent harmonic systems. To be sure, the chromatic descent as such does not define a structure; but since it is loosely organized about an implied dominant pedal point at the center of the movement, it provides the prelude with a large-scale form. In the introduction, the composer arrives at the dominant; in the middle section, under the cover of the dominant he penetrates the depth of the harmonic space, returning to the tonic in the final part. It need hardly be mentioned that this is reminiscent of sonata structure.

Speaking in general terms, one could say that a musical composition is seen no longer as a chain of linked ideas but as the fulfillment and architecturing of time. A paratactic structure becomes a syntactic one. When looked at in this way, a movement or section is like the audible expression of a hierarchic system. The rudiments of this idea already existed in the older forms of dance, song, and aria, insofar as these are based on functional-harmonic principles; the modern Italian-style concerto in particular set the direction for Bach.[4] Still it is noteworthy that the young composer picked precisely the genre that seemed most appropriate to a simple array of fantastic ideas—the toccata—to overlay with ideas of this kind.

For Bach to write music covering a larger harmonic territory, he must have not merely a functional harmonic system but also a modern harmonic system of equal temperament, one that allows unlimited modulation through the use of enharmonic tonal ambiguity. In Arnfried Edler's view, Bach had worked out the use of functional harmonics on harpsichords, which tended to be tuned with equal temperament. Also, he had the opportunity on his Lübeck visit of 1705 to get to know the organ of the Marienkirche there, which was possibly tuned to an approximate version of equal temperament.[5] The range of possibilities is established early on: coherent large forms independent of a set text or cantus firmus can be created only if the musical material is absolutely versatile—which does not necessarily mean that an artist like Bach would always make use of these possibilities.

It is no wonder that Bach undertakes to rework the BWV 535a fugue as well; but he changes neither the theme nor the basic pattern of entrances. By being a bit stricter with the rules of composition and cutting back on the fantasy character of the countervoices, he does reduce some of its overly abundant inventiveness and playfulness in favor of logical and linear voice leading. The increased virtuosity required by the pedal part is not an extrinsic change but an indication of his wish that in a well-balanced setting all the voices play an equal role.

We can generalize a bit from a comparison of the two versions of the Prelude and Fugue in G-Minor. In Bach's organ and keyboard works, there is a tendency to damp down the essential fantasia quality of the toccata, wherever it works against larger structural forms, forms that Bach advanced through his lifelong occupation with the binary prelude and fugue. It is no accident that he was the first in music history to elevate the prelude-fugue form to canonic status. It is less significant that his first efforts in this new form are not on the same level as Buxtehude and Bruhns, who brought the old form of the north German toccata to its highest point, and to its end. Bach saw it as his historic mission to bring new order into the landscape of organ and keyboard music, and not least to impose a new standard on the fantasia style, for the sake of the larger form that he was advocating—this binary form.

He was the first to cultivate this form and make it a specialty. Before, the free and bound styles were informally united in varying combinations in the fantasia style, but with him they become polar though closely interrelated: they allow the emergence of the kind of tension required for the creation of any large-scale form. For us today the combination of prelude and fugue is a given, but it is largely his achievement, and it is linked in an almost mysterious way with his work. Without the will or the way to yoke these two unequal brothers together in the service of an ideal third, they will shake off their bond and break away from each other. What other historically important musical form is linked with a single name? Bach alone was impassioned in his pursuit of that ideal third. After him only Beethoven, not by accident, in his opus 133 harnessed overture and fugue together in the spirit of Bach. *The Well-Tempered Clavier* did not come as a bolt from the blue.

But it would be a distortion to see the young Bach as on the path toward large-form structure only. That there are compositions under the category of prelude and fugue where he revels in the toccata element does not mean that he did not also enjoy both the fantastic and the virtuoso style. A good example is the pairing of the Prelude and Fugue in D Major, BWV 532, composed at about the same time as the Prelude and Fugue in G minor, BWV 535. Spitta called the D Major "one of the master's most brilliant organ works"—probably because of its supremely virtuosic pedal part,[6] which prompted one copyist to remark, "In this fugue, the feet have to do some serious pedaling" ("Bey dieser Fuge muß man die Füße recht strampfeln lassen").[7]

While the middle section of the prelude is written as a long and quietly flowing alla breve, which lends stability to the form, there are quite individual characteristics in the outer movements. Bach begins with an ascending scale in the pedal part: the performer is meant to explore the tonality not with ten fingers, as usual, but with both feet. The initial motif (given to the right hand in the roughly contemporaneous toccata BWV 912a) is set in the pedal, and with brio. Later these octave passages are also played in the manual, in the final section of the prelude where the double pedal lends further excitement to the rhapsodic *Abgesang*, which has a bracingly dissonant accompaniment.

In contrast, the fugue follows with a theme that recalls Buxtehude's affable canzone introductions—but only just recalls it: Buxtehude did not write themes this fantastic.[8] Given the seemingly unending sequence of sixteenth notes, it is ill-suited for an imitative musical style. And in fact the typical opening motif of the countersubject appears not simultaneously with the theme but in the interval that splits the theme in two—not just once but several times.

This example is taken from the revised version BWV 532: Bach has meanwhile modulated into more distant keys like C-sharp minor and E major. The distinguishing characteristic of the fugue is its playfulness: he writes an almost *concertante* dialogue of theme and countersubject, with the pedal gamely accompanying. The final measures fit the fugue's capricious mood: a pedal solo, broken into by the upper voices, falls back on the beginning and gives the opportunity for an uninhibited reintroduction of the theme and countersubject; then suddenly the movement ends, like the punch line of a joke.

Wit is indeed part of the nature of the fugue. Bach wants to show not simply that he can write a fugue but all the things he can do in that form. The theme is like Buxtehude and like Pachelbel, but is Italianate and violinistic at the same time. Edler points out a violin part from Marco Uccelini's *La gran battaglia* that is identical with the first half bar of the fugue in BWV 532.

By setting the subject in such various keys even in the pedal part, Bach demonstrates the modernity of his technique, which here would seem to require the use of both heel and toe of the left foot.[9] The young composer is wielding all the means at his disposal to create an original performance piece—truly a fantasy on the theme of fugue.

That there exists an earlier version of the BWV 532 fugue without a prelude suggests Bach's desire to join prelude and fugue as basically paired movements and yet still look on the fugue as a completely independent form. In the early Weimar period, these ideas are just taking shape. For that reason the keyboard work BWV 911 in C minor found in the *Andreas Bach Book* is entitled "toccata," although the work underneath this heading is both a prelude and fugue.

With the Prelude and Fugue in D Major, BWV 532, even in his early Weimar phase, Bach has already arrived at a level of sustained mastery, before he did in all the other genres he employed. At this point he is an unrivaled organ virtuoso: this is demonstrated by the number of students he has in Weimar as well as by the number of copies of his organ works that are circulating. While there are relatively few manuscript copies of Bach's vocal music that are not autographed or authorized, copies of his preludes and fugues exist in abundance. His keyboard works are generally known and at the same time are models of the form.

The word "model" is appropriate, since Bach composed no more than two dozen great toccatas. Given the many different paths these works took in coming down to us, it is unlikely that many were lost. In contrast to the realm of the religious cantatas, he composed his preludes and fugues not serially for everyday repertoire use but as singular showpieces, meant more for concert use than for Sunday services. It was not wrongheaded for a Viennese publishing house in 1812 to collect the six preludes and fugues BWV 543–48 into a first edition, nor was it wrongheaded forty years later for Franz Liszt to produce his famous transcriptions based on this edition. Granted, this collection does not contain all the significant ones; but as a concentrate of the essential characteristics of the toccata, it works, and at the same time it points to an idea that may never have occurred to Bach's pupils and contemporaries: to gather works of the same type into two or three series, like the *Brandenburg Concertos*.

One of the great musical challenges of the day is the Italian concerto style. On the one hand, Bach is attracted to this style: it offers crucial beginning points for the creation of a musical architecture, or, to use the previously mentioned terminology, it creates movements that are not an array of small units of meaning but have a coherent syntax throughout. On the other hand, with his predilection for complexity, he does not have confidence in the boldness and simplicity of a concerto movement by Albinoni or Vivaldi. It becomes Bach's lifelong project to bring the possibilities of the modern large musical form into line with his own ambitions, in a way that becomes a new and unique solution of formal problems in each of his works.

The Toccata in F Major, BWV 540, represents a remarkable achievement of the middle Weimar period—the fugue was probably written later. For Felix Mendelssohn Bartholdy, who tried out the work for himself on an ill-tuned organ one cold and rainy day in a little Swiss village, the modulation at the conclusion sounded "like it would make the church collapse."[10]

The ending is indeed remarkable: after a pedal point of thirty measures on the dominant, Bach does not go into the tonic but brings in a false cadence that had been avoided earlier (in bar 270); then, after a major second chord, he indulges via C-flat major in a "Neapolitan" chord in G-flat, finally landing so abruptly in F major that one is reluctant to take this as the definitive reconfirmation of the tonic. This is all the more surprising, as the toccata begins with the tranquillity of a pastorale: a pedal point in F, fifty-four bars long, is held underneath the gaily festive canon in the two upper voices. Then comes an extended pedal solo of twenty-eight bars, whereupon the long first section is repeated from the beginning, this time in the dominant and with the upper voices switched in the canon, again with an extended pedal point and pedal solo after. This twofold exposition ultimately encompasses 170 bars and ends in the dominant, but the piece cannot end there: it needs something new, something surpassing the old. Indeed, it soon becomes clear that the naive beginning was only a foil for a development that would be the equal of a sonata movement in every way.

Bach's adamant dwelling on an ostinato F or C in the exposition is matched by his systematic approach in conquering harmonic space, handling dissonance and chordal progression with great boldness. The fanfare theme, which he contrasts with the opening theme, is played on almost every step of the chromatic scale, in the service of a large-scale modulation plan. The second part of the toccata is laid out on the concerto principle. The catchy fanfare now acts like a ritornello, even though constantly modulating. But the scattered citations of the introductory theme, heard as episodes, are bound to fixed key signatures. So the form Bach has chosen does not really correspond to a Vivaldi-type concerto movement. It is impossible to say whether he is "toying with the conventions of the *concerto grosso*"[11] or following a variation of the type, as did Giuseppe Torelli, among others, in his opus 8.[12]

Fanfarenthema

The self-confidence with which Bach applies the principles of the Italian concerto to organ music is impressive. While eager to have the advantage of its large form, he resists the imposition of the concerto's transparent structure with its regular alternation of tutti and solos, of its clear distinction between ritornello and episode, and so on. The word *toccata* is apt here: for all the brevity of its melodic phrases, the whole flows like a broad river: calm at first, then wildly agitated, and finally, after a long journey—we are speaking, barwise, of Bach's longest organ movement—it empties, with great suddenness, into the ocean.

Bach brilliantly combines the toccata's tendency toward rhapsodic forward motion with the concerto's architectural organization of parts—that is, its linear and structural elements, not in the sense of a clean and unified work, in which elements of different size are reduced to their lowest common denominator, but more as a kind of constructed wildness. In cases such as this, musicologists are justifiably proud of detecting, through analysis and description, the combination of toccata and concerto styles. Significant as such insights are, a composer like Mendelssohn was no less sophisticated when he remarked, in his reflections on the end of the Toccata in F major, "That was one fearsome cantor." A statement like that does justice to the elemental force with which this organist, a youth no more though still in his twenties, dealt with the tradition of Buxtehude, Bruhns, and Reinken and at the same time with the challenges of Corelli, Torelli, Albinoni, and Vivaldi.

On the basis of his experience as an organist and orchestra conducter, Reinhold Birk has compared this force with that of the *Eroica:* Bach shares Beethoven's predilection for long developments at brisk tempi and for heroic-dramatic action.[13] One should not overlook Bach's penchant for the large and symphonic simply because it appears here "only" in a toccata: in the Germany of that time, there were great organs but no great symphony orchestras. With advancing age, even Bach's organ writing became clearer and more proportioned (alas, one almost could add). But who would take the late Prelude in E-flat Major from the third part of the *Clavier-Übung* over the Toccata in F Major? We would not want to give up either.

A work of the size and expressive power of the F-major toccata calls for speculation on how it came into being. Jean-Claude Zehnder links it with the *Hunt Cantata* of 1712 or 1713 and suggests that Bach composed both the vocal work and the toccata for the court and the hunting gentry of Weißenfels.[14] Indeed, the episodic theme played in the pedal at first makes one think of some courtly ceremony, perhaps even a hunting signal. The organ in the Augustusburg at Weißenfels, with its unusually large pedal, going all the way to f′, was perfectly suited to the demands of this work.

Peter Schleuning interprets the toccata as a "sublime pastorale" and a symbol of the annunciation of Christ's birth: the first part shows the peaceful shepherds in the field making music, the agitated second part their fright on hearing the heavenly message.[15] Interpretations like this are useful when presented not as the final word of the experts but as a spur to further thought. The views of Zehnder and Schleuning are complementary: if we accept the idea that such works were performed not just routinely at church services but also for special ceremonial occasions, then we should examine their semantics.

There is good reason to take a fresh look at formal and compositional subtleties. For instance, in the false cadence episode at bar 204f the shift from A major to D minor is drawn out through fifteen bars of deft modulation. It is a paragon of the fantastic style yet with a well-thought-out plan, all the more so considering that each of the fifteen bars has thematic relevance as well. The episode is perceived less as an obstruction than as a rock around which a stream flows.

By the rules of musical logic, in bar 270 this false cadence should be repeated along with the entire preceding section. But something else happens: Bach squares the "deception" (*Betrügerey*), as his contemporaries called it, by shifting the false cadence in the repetition from its expected place to bar 318, shortly before the end, thus achieving the tremendous effect that Mendelssohn described.

In such cases an analyst might question whether a particular anomaly was in fact intended by the composer, but here he can be quite sure: Bach is playing with elements of form and their functions—and he does this so well that the question again arises as to whether the Toccata in F Major in fact dates from 1712–13, and thus is experimental, or whether it belongs to the later Weimar period. The sources do not allow a definitive answer.

If the toccata BWV 540 is like an endless stream, the nearly contemporaneous Toccata in C Major, BWV 564, is more like a panorama of organistic possibilities—we are not just looking at the toccata head motif alone but keeping its three-movement form in mind: toccata, adagio, and fugue. Written during the Weimar period, it is one of Bach's attempts at three-part form, such as are found in the sonata and concerto, and documents his concerns with modern Italian music in large form.

The first movement opens with a long manual solo, its running passages typically toccata-like, but at the same time it borrows from the fantastic violin style of the Italians. The following pedal solo, even longer in number of measures, does not come off as elegantly as the introductory manual part: to make the rapid succession of sixteenth notes, sixteenth triplets, and thirty-second notes audible at all in this low register requires the use of powerful reed stops, which give an effect more of gravity than of brilliance. The young Bach may have tested the capabilities of new organs with traditionally north German pedal parts like this, to the pleasure of listeners and the horror of organ builders—since the entire work was generally understood as a test piece for organ.[16]

The second section of the toccata's first movement could have been the continuation of such an organ test, to check the balance between manual and pedal. The section is interesting musically in that it combines two ideas of form: Bach is first writing a dialogue between two characteristic themes, which perhaps were to be performed on two different manuals; but to present this dialogue, he selects the framework of the Italian concerto with its elements of ritornello and episode.

Lothar Hoffmann-Erbrecht sees works like the Toccata in C Major as "prestudies" for Bach's stand-alone instrumental concertos. This view is supported by the second movement of the toccata, which had earlier made Spitta think of "a solo adagio with harpsichord accompaniment."[17] Slow concerto or sonata movements of Corelli, Torelli, or Vivaldi are the obvious godparents here; and Bach himself incorporated this type as the second movement of his *Italian Concerto.* But analogies and associations should not stray too far from the organ repertory: after all, the north German masters of the seventeenth and early eighteenth centuries cultivated the genre of expressive, highly colored organ chorales, to which Bach contributed masterpieces such as the adaptation of "O Mensch, bewein' dein Sünde groß," BWV 622, from the *Orgelbüchlein.*

The ending fugue exhibits no concerto-like traits but is still divided into clear sections and is broadly narrative. While the pauses that are embedded in the north German theme would be routine matters for Buxtehude or his contemporaries, Bach positively revels in them. Claus-Steffen Mahnkopf has seen in BWV 564's "elements of rhetorical self-referentiality, its tendency toward overwrought gesture, its love of virtuosity and boldness" the signs of mannerism in Bach's early Sturm und Drang works.[18] But mannerism is always the signal of an approaching end: with fugues like this Bach is saying farewell to the north German organ style. Even the most rollicking fugues of *The Well-Tempered Clavier* will be set in a more focused way.

Likely composed a few years later, the incorrectly captioned "Doric" Toccata in D Minor, BWV 538, presents us with a completely different picture. It is probably the last of the older, four-phased type of Bach organ fugue that reveals the theme more through additive than structural form in various tonal steps.[19] Still, it is not without structural devices: interludes on a single motif are transposed into various keys as in a concerto, taking on the rank of thematically linked episodes. This results in a structure that is anything but transparent and concerto-like: the theme in strict style, worthy of a ricercar, aided by two obbligato voices in counterpoint, is woven into a dense and complicated fabric. As Hermann Keller noted, there is not a break in the tension anywhere in the 222-bar movement; indeed, the four stretto passages only intensify it.[20]

The compositional rigor of the BWV 538 fugue's strict style is matched by the consistent form of the preceding toccata movement. While the Toccata in F Major, BWV 540, despite all its urgent forward momentum, was still divided into various sections, here we find one continuous sixteenth-note motion from beginning to end on the thematic material introduced at the outset:

There is no playing around with manual or pedal solos; nor is there any of the fantastic sectional structure of the old toccata. The great variety of changes evident throughout the piece are in the service of the concerto principle, which, while treated unconventionally,[21] still amounts to a breakthough in Bach's organ works. The ritornello does not appear in one and the same form, yet the stages of ritornello and episode are set unambiguously, and the changing forms taken by the ritornello, which can be heard as derivations from a single underlying motive,[22] allow the listener to hear the scheme of theme, elaboration, and cadence, as the above example clearly shows.

The word "unambiguous" is inaccurate, if we accept (along with Werner Breig) the existence of an earlier, lost version of the toccata,[23] in which the function of the episodes was not yet completely clear. In Weimar, Bach is wrestling with the concerto form: yet no one setting is a way station on the path to perfection of this form; each is a work in its own right. His difficulties with form do not detract from the worth of his works; on the contrary, they liberate the creative power to find ever new solutions. In the Toccata in D Minor, what is fascinating is the tension between two modes of time: time rushing by and time hierarchically captured.

One cannot speak of Bach's toccata art without mentioning the toccatas for clavier, of which the most important, the *Chromatic Fantasy and Fugue* in D Minor, BWV 903, was probably composed in Weimar, but perhaps not until Cöthen, possibly in 1720 as a *tombeau* on the death of Maria Barbara Bach.[24] It was preceded by other examples of the form: BWV 913 could have come from Arnstadt under Buxtehude's influence; an earlier version of BWV 912, preserved in the *Möller Manuscript*, could date from this time. Toccatas BWV 914 and 915 already show signs of the Italian sonata style, and end with virtuoso fugal passages with violinistic style themes. Toccatas BWV 910, 911, and 916, all from the *Andreas Bach Book,* have been dated to the Weimar period.[25]

That Bach often employed his early toccatas for teaching, even in later years, indicates that despite their stylistic heterogeneity and occasional excesses, for him they were models of their type. But during his life, and more after his death, the *Chromatic Fantasy* was considered the unrivaled pinnacle of the form. Only once in the history of music, in Arnfried Edler's opinion, "were such different structural and expressive elements like figuration, free-floating improvisational arpeggios, and instrumental recitative so compellingly combined."[26]

All the sources call this work a fantasy, never a toccata, primarily because of the word *recitativo* written over the final movement. This section is presented as a cleverly arranged harmonic maze with a wealth of dissonances, false cadences, and enharmonic ambiguities. The harmonic scheme was known as the Devil's Mill[27] in the music theory of the day. Bach attempts in a very small space—in time-lapse motion, as it were—the systematic traversal of the keys of the chromatic scale, as he does in *The Well-Tempered Clavier* on a much larger scale. As early a critic as Forkel linked the two works by noting with admiration—probably based on the reminiscences of Bach's sons—how Bach had effortlessly "fantasized" through "all twenty-four keys":

> He linked the remotest keys together as easily and naturally as the nearest; it was almost as if he were modulating in the inner circle of a single key. Harshness was totally alien to his modulation; even in transitional passages his chromaticism was as gentle and flowing as if he had remained in the related diatonic keys only. His so-called chromatic fantasy, now in print, can prove what I am saying here.[28]

But the chordal progressions, superficially random yet obeying a strict if hidden organizing principle, are merely the background for the voice of lamentation that soars above them. The *recitativo stromamento,* an expression of deepest agitation and despair, was part of

opera even in the seventeenth century; but it was Bach who introduced it to instrumental music. The *Chromatic Fantasy* is probably
the first instrumental work consciously to attempt the portrayal of an
emotional state—grief—from a first-person perspective. Vivaldi's
concerto *Grosso Mogul,* opus 3, has a recitative section that is similar
in this regard, and Bach himself set a version of it for organ as BWV
594,[29] but this is at most a hint of what is to come.

The melodic line of the section titled "Recitativo" cannot be cate-
gorized as in the recitative style, for it is not singable, metrically free, or
harmonically open—it is on many levels a calculated work of art.[30] But
clearly there is a subject here, speaking wordlessly. One is reminded of
Dorothea Ertmann, a Bach interpreter and a student of Beethoven
in Vienna, who recalled her teacher's visit after the painful loss of her
son: "Instead of expressing his sympathy with words, he sat right
down at the piano, without a word, and extemporized at length."[31]

Connecting these two ideas might seem forced, if we did not
know that Beethoven knew the *Chromatic Fantasy,* which since 1802
was widely available in Vienna in print as well as in manuscript; indeed, he copied parts of it himself in 1810.[32] Beethoven also composed the *Hammerklavier Sonata,* opus 106, and the Piano Sonata in
A-flat Major, opus 110, as a kind of lively conversation with the
Chromatic Fantasy.[33] The *Klagender Gesang* ("Song of Lament"), in
particular, from the adagio of opus 110, finds a model there:

Beethoven found in the *Chromatic Fantasy* an intense linkage of
subjective emotional expression with formal rigor.[34] We can see the
work in the baroque tradition as the "presentation of pathos per se,"
as does Rolf Dammann, and celebrate the recitative in particular as
a high point of baroque rhetoric in the world of instrumental
music.[35] Or, like Peter Schleuning, we might point to features that
anticipate Sturm und Drang.[36] Bach has created a paragon, classic
and unique, on the theme of restraint and freedom, pointing the way

to what was later called absolute music—in its struggle for both authentic subjective expression and objectifiable form.

It is not coincidence but necessity that links Bach's model piece with the expression of suffering and despair: the essential structure of absolute music is that of melancholy. With Theodor W. Adorno's music theory as background, we can say: the subject is articulated as suffering; its authenticity inheres in this alone, but the subject remains powerless against the systems that have created its suffering.[37] When art succeeds, its imaginative power dispels the individual sense of impotence that knowledge triggers; art makes the inability to act an occasion for utopian thinking. Nietzsche, that "philosopher of life," in ridiculing Brahms's music as "the melancholy of impotence,"[38] made this point all too clearly.

As productive as it might be to trace patterns of historical influence, we must not define Bach the composer through his reception history. With Bach, fugue follows fantasy. Thus the fugue is an objectifying act, tempering the passion of the fantasy preceding it: the subjective must not overpower. Granted, this fugue is not moderate in character: the *fuga pathetica* matches well the tone of the *phantasie*—the bombastic octave doublings at the end make it clear that the subject has not disappeared. The liberties that Bach takes in working out its movement are analogous to those he took in the fantasy, as Friedrich Wilhelm Marpurg noted in his two-volume *Abhandlung von der Fuge* (1753–54).[39] His having the countersubject enter on the seventh seemed so outlandish to Hans von Bülow, a century later, that he corrected it.[40]

Johann Nikolaus Forkel received the *Chromatic Fantasy* in the second decade after Bach's death through Wilhelm Friedemann. Included in his package were these lines of a mutual friend, who "liked to write doggerel":

> Anbey kommt an
> Etwas Music von Sebastian,
> Sonst genannt: *Fantasia chromatica;*
> Bleibt schön in alle *Saecula*.[41]

In this package you can see
Some of Sebastian's pages,
Called *Chromatic Fantasy*,
'Twill be lovely through all ages.

If a classic, perfectly balanced style exists anywhere in Bach's work, it is to be found in the Prelude and Fugue in B Minor, BWV 544. The work, coming down to us as an autograph in fair copy from the years 1727–31, may have been written in the Leipzig period, when Bach was composing organ works no longer for his immediate needs (as he had at Weimar) but to produce masterpieces, each work a deliberation on a specific idea. With all due respect to the preludes of *The Well-Tempered Clavier*, the B-minor organ prelude leaves one astonished, so great is Bach's art in bringing together a small ensemble of ideas into an integral, self-generating form that avoids every stereotype.

But no gain is made without some loss: the toccata principle has now been abandoned. With its dramatic nature, oriented about the player as subject, and featuring a rhapsodic flow of ideas, the toccata is not the best vehicle to present a work of all-encompassing organization and self-contained structure. Bach now uses the concerto form exclusively—although no longer in the comparatively naive fashion he favored in Weimar and integrated into the toccata form. His approach is highly reflective and subtle.

The organist as interpreter is the first to sense this: if he tries to distinguish between tutti and solos as in a regular organ concerto movement, switching from one manual to another, he quickly discovers that such change is not possible, for the solo episode does not lead immediately back to the ritornello. Furthermore, the episodes are dovetailed with the subsequent ritornellos in a way that brings out the work's idea of unity rather than contrast. The piece is arranged on this pattern:

Ritornello with cadence on the tonic (16 bars)
Episode with motif 1 plus ritornello with cadence on the
    dominant (26 bars)

Episode with motif 1 plus ritornello with cadence on the tonic
  parallel (13 bars)
Episode with motif 2 plus ritornello with cadence on the
  subdominant (13 bars)
Episode with motifs 2 and 1 plus ritornello with cadence on the
  tonic (16 bars)

The most meaningful element of the traditional concerto movement, the ritornello, loses significance in the course of this movement: while at the first and second appearance it is in its full glory for sixteen bars, by the third and fourth appearances it is reduced to six and eight bars, respectively. Even at the end the ritornello does not return for a final bow, as it were: it is put to rest, headless, in just six measures.

This ritornello is not a ritornello in the usual sense of the word: though the pattern of Vivaldi-type themes is recognizable—that is, head motif, development, epilogue—Bach has composed a highly sophisticated structure of melody and counterpoint in four to five voices, into which the pedal is thematically interwoven with great ease. Just a glance at the score reveals what a compositional gem we have before us:

The first episode is easily identifiable: while the pedal is silent, the solo part unfolds. But in the second half of the section, the plot thickens. Segments of episodes combine with shortened segments of the ritornello; there is more development, intensity, and complexity. But it is not sufficient merely to note that here he is composing more procedurally in the sense of Viennese classicism than in the concerted style of the age of the continuo. He is visibly concerned with establishing an almost mathematical balance among the nine parts of the prelude. Ulrich Siegele has proposed the theory, and proved it in many cases, that in his later years Bach laid out his forms according to mathematical ratios.[42]

The prelude is divided at bar 43, by the cadence to the dominant, exactly in half. Assuming the form has five parts, Christian Martin Schmidt has found further symmetries: the two framing sections of 16 bars each embrace a second part of 26 bars, and a third and fourth part of 13 bars each—that is, again 26 bars together.[43]

Another proportionality is that of the golden section. This is calculated using the Fibonacci sequence, named after the thirteenth-century mathematician, in which each term is the sum of the preceding two: 1, 1, 2, 3, 5, 8, 13, 21, 34, and so on. The further along the sequence one goes, the more closely the ratio of the two preceding sections approximates the ratio one would get by dividing the entire span by the golden section. Even the 8:13 ratio comes passably close to this ratio; but 8:13 is the same as 16:26. Thus the first part relates to the second (16:26) as the fifth does to the combined third and fourth (16: 13 + 13) in the ratio of the smaller part to the larger in the golden section. The two frame portions together are 32 bars, the three middle sections comprise 52: this, too, is in the ratio of 8:13.

One could argue at length whether Bach consciously worked with proportions from the visual arts, or whether this use of his eye was unconscious. It would be hard to see the proportions of the prelude's five parts as a coincidence: instead of adopting standard concerto movement structure and its more or less arbitrary alternations of tutti and solos, he created a sequential form with a proportional scheme expressly designed for this unique work. It may be that this allusion to the golden section will at least prepare the ground for the idea of proportion in Bach's works.

The classic aspect of the B-minor prelude is not limited to its architecture; another critical element of the work is its highly organized relation of order and expressiveness. Seldom are these qualities seen together at such a level: the prelude possesses extraordinary rhetorical power. One can hardly find another organ movement of Bach with such extensive vocal structure throughout. While the voices do not quite sing, to an unusual degree they speak, and with detailed articulation. So many gestures with such varied nuance are otherwise found only in the vocal-instrumental choral and aria settings.

Hermann Keller reveals an instinct for such associations in his observation that the B-minor prelude brings to mind the Kyrie from the B-Minor Mass and the aria "Erbarme dich."[44] Such comparisons can be pushed too far, but this reference to the aria from the *St. Matthew Passion* shows the prelude's affinity with the sentimental gallant style. Above a dancelike pedal part that is just a bit ponderous, there are note patterns that might be understood as overlay, as regression, syncopes in the sense of shifted notes, and that stylistically all sound remarkably modern. The tied legatos and suspensions in the pedal voice precisely match Jacob Adlung's concept of modern organ playing.[45] But despite such contemporary touches, the piece still is not in accord with the zeitgeist's ideal of naturalness: the contrapuntal setting is too complex, the filigree work of the voices is too intricate.

Bach never surpassed the level of classicism that he attained in the B-minor prelude—that is, the union of diverse formal ideas with expressive means, resulting in a harmonized whole. But he probably equaled it in the Prelude in E-flat Major, BWV 552, which opens the third part of the *Clavier-Übung*. Though this piece also has some traces of the gallant style, by and large it is a more austere conception—more like the French overture form that inspired it.

Despite its length—after the F-major toccata, BWV 540, it is Bach's longest organ prelude—the overall design is never obscure. One last time, with the help of Italian concerto form, Bach demonstrates not just how it helps regulate simple passages so that they are easily understood but also how it helps create structures that are the equal of those in the future sonata movement. The fugue in E-flat, which closes the third part of the *Clavier-Übung*, is divided in three parts, and its overall design is the height of perfection. With Bach's earlier fugues it might have been possible to separate and remove this or that exposition passage without toppling the whole structure; here it is no longer possible. He has overlaid so many elements of symmetry, key arrangement, musical procedurality, and rhythmic transformation, that removing one stone would bring the whole edifice down.

It is more than mere speculation to see references to the Holy Trinity, both in the tripartite structure of the fugue as well as in the three themes of the prelude—Bach likes to appropriate organizational ideas from outside the field of music. Compositions like this are not written primarily for the listener—as were the toccatas and fugues of the immediate past—but are meant to be a legacy of the artist's own artistic philosophy. Yet this music is not a bit abstract. The three themes, two of which are paired throughout the movement, run the scale of beauty from sublime to charming. The third at first sounds like a dance finale, but toward the end it returns to its initial *stile antico* theme, now with different rhythmic figures, which are symbolic of the *coincidentia oppositorum*, the sign of the divine essence.

In this chapter, the organ toccatas and preludes were presented in chronological order. Having finished our presentation, we do not apologize for this approach, but qualify it to this extent: the sources give us little support for an absolute chronology and clues only for a relative one. Thus caution is advisable. We should not claim, positivistically, that Bach progressed in a straight line. After all, for him, what was progress?

As mentioned earlier, there may be musical standards that, once he established them, became a Rubicon he did not want to cross again—but were they the ones we imagine they were? The many different versions of these works for keyboard instruments prove that he kept refining models, not dropping them. One striking example is the Prelude and Fugue for Clavier in A Minor, BWV 894, dating, without dispute, from Weimar. In his final years, he revised the work and adapted it for the first and last movements of the Triple Concerto for Flute, Violin, and Harpsichord in A Minor, BWV 1044, showing what he could do when he wanted to. Typical characteristics of the original are seen again in his rewrite but are presented more coherently and at greater length.[46] Generally speaking, a Bach biography cannot avoid attempts at a chronology; but where there are no fixed points of orientation, the biography can offer only suggestions for a historical approach to his art.

THE ORGAN CHORALES

More than two hundred chorales arranged for organ have come down to us under the name of Johann Sebastian Bach. Much of the art of composition he learned through arranging chorales for organ, and later he used the genre for teaching composition to his students. Although he was actively a professional organist only until his thirty-third year, he continued to arrange hymns for organ until the end of his life. It may be just a legend that the chorale "Vor deinem Thron tret' ich" was the last composition he worked on, but the hymns of the church and their skillful adaptation were as defining for his life as a Christian and composer of sacred music as the Bible and its interpretation were for a Protestant theologian of the time.

There are serious questions about the transmission of Bach's chorales, starting with the authenticity of many pieces that exist only as secondary manuscripts: a 1997 catalogue of organ chorales of dubious provenance lists 198 numbers![1] A critical examination is also needed for partially corrupt versions, some of which are a complete muddle, where Bach's pupils scribbled down their teacher's chorale transcriptions and continued composing them for their own purposes.

In this situation, we must abandon the idea of reconstructing versions that are authentic. It is better to look at the entire field of source transmission as evidence of a productive engagement with Bach's organ works. Some of his chorale transcriptions came down to the nineteenth century via their use in church services, where they underwent further "composition." *The Well-Tempered Clavier* also did not need to be rediscovered: Bach's cantus firmus music remained in continuous use among the cognoscenti.

In the organ chorales, the authentic Bach can be found primarily in the collections he created himself: the *Orgelbüchlein*, BWV 599–644; the chorale transcriptions BWV 669–89 from the third part of the *Clavier-Übung*; the Eighteen Chorales, BWV 651–68, from the Leipzig original manuscript; the Canonic Variations on "Vom Himmel hoch," BWV 769; and the organ transpositions, BWV 645–50, known as the Schübler Chorales. The early chorale adaptations BWV 1090–1120 from the Neumeister Collection, as well as the fifty or so chorales in the range BWV 690–765, which are beyond all doubt authentic, cannot be considered here, even though we thus give short shrift to Bach's early forays in composition, as well as to a number of important engagements with central and north German models.

But we will at least touch on the hymn accompaniments of the Arnstadt period, which earned Bach the criticism mentioned earlier in the biographical section—that is, that they did more to confuse the congregational singing than to keep it together. The accompaniments to "Allein Gott in der Höh sei Ehr," BWV 715, to the four Christmas chorales "Gelobet seist du, Jesu Christ," BWV 722, "In dulci jubilo," BWV 729, "Lobt Gott, ihr Christen, allzugleich," BWV 732, and "Vom Himmel hoch, da komm ich her," BWV 738, as well as to "Herr Jesu Christ dich zu uns wend," BWV 726, have come down to us in complete form, though largely through his Weimar and Leipzig pupils. Meanwhile, in view of the mischievousness of these pieces, there is little reason to deny that he accompanied the Arnstadt congregation in the manner that caused complaint.[2] Later in his teaching and practice he may have seen this style as one of his early trademarks. Perhaps, winking an eye, he entertained his students with stories of his earlier wranglings with the Arnstadt church authorities.

A good example of Bach's Arnstadt hauteur can be found in the opening of "Herr Jesu Christ, dich zu uns wend," BWV 726. At the end of the first line, instead of the expected D major there is a six-five chord in G major in false cadence, which at the start of the second line is resolved to C major—but only after the two lines are connected by a tonal garland of thirty-second notes. The rather astringent harmonizations of the final line probably "confounded" congregations outside Arnstadt as well.

We might see such works as the attempt to secure maximum independence and virtuosity even for that simplest of musical forms, the accompaniment. The young Turk wanted to show his musical mettle as much as possible.

The rigorousness of the *Orgelbüchlein*, the first large project of Bach we know of, goes much further: for the first time in music history, there appears a cycle of works that pursues and reflects the idea of an integral work of art. The structural integrity of a composition derives not only from a high degree of consistent form and coherence. The idea, in the tradition of Theodor W. Adorno, is relevant only when an aesthetically plausible dialogue can be perceived between the subject that shapes the work and the material that is being shaped.

One example is the first movement of Beethoven's Fifth Symphony: on the one hand, it is defined by motivic-thematic, harmonic, and dynamic processes, with their own intrinsic disciplines; but its life, its vitality, comes from a dialectical relation between the ordering of the tones and the intention of the composer.

Of course, everyone, including Bach, has forerunners. In their cantus firmus masses both Guillaume Dufay and Josquin Desprez aimed at compositions that in modern terminology might be called integral works of art. In his *Gradualia* of 1605 and 1606 William Byrd expressly tried a similar idea in an even more comprehensively cyclic work.

But much of these gains in the philosophical dimension were lost as the seventeenth century wore on. So one is justified in seeing in Bach's *Orgelbüchlein* a new beginning for this philosophy—astonishingly, with a series of small pieces that are little more than accompaniments to a cantus firmus that could be sung like a song. Seen in this way, the *Orgelbüchlein* is a direct continuation of the Arnstadt organ chorales. Yet the integral quality of the work was achieved by dispensing with a full working out of the cantus firmus. This phenomenon deserves a brief digression.

By Bach's time, instrumental variations or figurations on the melody of a sacred or secular song had a long tradition that originated in folk music. They gave the accompaniment of strophic music more variety, and perhaps provided commentary on it as well. By the sixteenth century, similar practices gave rise to written variations for keyboard instruments. For music making in the home, variations on secular songs provided an educational transition from mere competence to expertise in playing an instrument. In the church context, chorale arrangements *per omnes versus* were suitable as music to be performed in *alternatim* fashion during Communion: the congregation or choir sang the hymn verse, the organist played his first partita, followed by a second hymn verse, a second partita, and so on. Since the verses performed by the organ were not meant strictly as accompaniment to the congregational singing, the chorale melody could assume new forms from verse to verse.

Four chorale partitas, as they came to be known, are attributed to Bach: "Christ, der du bist der helle Tag," BWV 766, "O Gott, du frommer Gott," BWV 767, "Sei gegrüßet, Jesu gütig," BWV 768, and "Ach, was soll ich Sünder machen," BWV 770. They exist only as copies and so are difficult to date exactly, but are generally assigned by Bach scholars to Arnstadt or the early Weimar period. Bach largely relied on traditional central and north German models and is expectably less original here than in other forms.

There may be particular reasons for this traditionality: the sequential patterning of the chorale partita does not lend itself to a writing style aimed at creating a logical structure. During the several phases of his work on "Sei gegrüßet, Jesu gütig," considered the last of the chorale partitas, Bach may have come to feel uneasy with the form, finally abandoning it to give his compositional efforts a different focus: a series of chorale movements, each of which could be considered a model of its type.³ He does not take up hymn or chorale arrangements *per omnes versus* again until his last years—under other circumstances and on the highest plane: in the *Goldberg Variations,* BWV 988, and the Canonic Variations on "Vom Himmel hoch," BWV 769.

This new concept did not come out of the blue and was not realized all at once: Bach took some of the chorale arrangements for the *Orgelbüchlein* from an existing collection of them⁴ and gradually added the others. He may first have considered writing a book of chorales for everyday use, and then gradually formed a plan to turn his efforts systematically to a more clear-cut compositional project.

Klaus-Jürgen Sachs has looked closely at the subtitle, which points out that the *Orgelbüchlein* offers the "beginning organist" instruction in "developing a chorale in many diverse ways." He sees in it Bach's "compositional-didactic intent" to offer "examples of an advanced school of figuration."⁵ Actually, the pieces of the *Orgelbüchlein* not only pick up the long tradition of the chorale partita and secular song variation but also add to the tradition with new figural ideas such as those suggested by Friedrich Erhard Niedt in the second part of his *Musikalische Handleitung,* published in 1706. The following three-note figure of Niedt's⁶ could be taken as a preliminary version of the five-note figure in Bach's chorale "Alle Menschen müssen sterben," BWV 643:

Niedt Bach

While for Niedt "figuration" means filling out a bass line with figured note patterns that are rhythmically and melodically congruent, Bach goes much further. A glance at the pedal part reveals that he too followed the normal practice of his craft in embellishing the bass line, which moves largely in quarter-note values, with eighth- and sixteenth-notes figures. He confines himself to a single figure, however, and this is not formulaic but in Heinrich Besseler's terminology "characteristic,"[7] that is, appropriate for this particular melody.

More, Bach consistently works for a setting that takes this omnipresent motif, which occasionally includes even the hymn tune, and utilizes it as the material for a dense contrapuntal structure. At the same time this setting is more or less transparent, so the motif's characteristic quality is not lost in the fabric of the different voices; it is brought out with rhetorical emphasis. In the context of the chorale's message—human mortality—it can even be taken as a laconic commentary: "God knows that is so"—these words could be set to the motif.

Because of its "picturesque" qualities, Albert Schweitzer called the *Orgelbüchlein* a veritable "lexicon of Bach's tonal language." Without it, Schweitzer thought, it would be impossible to understand what Bach was trying to express in the themes of his cantatas and passions.[8] In fact, though, Bach made extensive use of comparable short motifs even in his vocal works—and of course in the most various semantic contexts.

A half century later, Heinrich Besseler set out to trace a direct link from Bach's "organ songs without words" and their "distinctive accompaniment" to Franz Schubert's *Lieder* with piano accompaniment: "What we have before us is nothing less than the prototype of the romantic song, as it appeared with Schubert one hundred years later. 'Gretchen am Spinnrad' and 'Erlkönig' move in a very different emotional world, but their forms follow the same principle."[9]

One can make judgments like those of Schweitzer and Besseler only by emphasizing the work's poetic element over its structure. Robert Schumann would never have thought of doing such a thing: to him, the preludes and fugues of *The Well-Tempered Clavier* were "character pieces of the highest order"; but he also praised their "profoundly deductive, combinatory nature."[10] The *Orgelbüchlein* was probably provided to Schumann by Felix Mendelssohn Bartholdy as a partial manuscript; he would presumably have described a work like "Alle Menschen müssen sterben" as an arabesque, a romantic metaphor for the intertwining of order with expression.

We can understand the *Orgelbüchlein* as the product of the music theory of its era, or interpret it against an aesthetic backdrop that takes into account the musical experience of the nineteenth century—both viewpoints have merit. But there is a third approach: seeing the settings of the *Orgelbüchlein* as evidence of a dialectical engagement with specific rules and liberties.

The rules are self-evident: the organ must perform a hymn tune in such a manner that it could be silently sung along during the piece and, given the tempi of the Bach era, even out loud. There is no room for an artfully wrought framing device: aside from small deviations, the setting begins with the first note of the hymn tune and ends with its last note.

Some restrictions are not dictated by the form but arise from the free will of the composer. Bach's aim here is a setting for four voices that do not divide the functions of melody and accompaniment among themselves but, with the pedal as an equal partner, fuse to make a greater whole, a well-articulated and thoroughly worked out contrapuntal structure: the voices remain freely improvised when they are not carrying the cantus firmus. We never lose sight of the cantus firmus, but the setting has its own intrinsic logic: the socially determined aspect of music is obvious throughout, even as it seems to free itself from it.

This is an advance over the chorale partitas: there, the cantus firmus was clearly primary and its figuration secondary; here, there is an exciting tension between the melody and its characteristic setting. From this viewpoint, Besseler's suggested comparison of the *Orgelbüchlein* settings to Schubert's songs seems less apt: the characteristic accompaniment that Bach provides the chorale tune is no perpetuum mobile, as in *Gretchen am Spinnrad* or Mendelssohn's *Lieder ohne Worte;* it is an essential part of the structure, not ornamental—it has an expressive meaning of its own as well.

Composers like Beethoven, Schumann, Brahms, Schönberg, and Webern studied settings such as these instead of Schubert's songs: they are the philosophers of the guild, as opposed to the singers like Monteverdi, Schütz, Handel, Telemann, Mozart, Schubert, and Verdi (if we may oversimplify). Bach's art fascinates the philosophers, because even in a short and formally unproblematic setting (not unlike a formula) it still embraces the tensions of order and expressiveness, of poiesis and mimesis, autonomy and heteronomy—thus the whole of music itself.

This quality is seen not just in the work of the mature or late Bach; it is apparent very early on, vividly in the *Orgelbüchlein.* In the organ chorale "Der Tag der ist so freudenreich," BWV 605, each of the three figured voices has its own character yet also complements the others.

The material being used for the figuration has two functions: structural and gestural. In other ways, the setting is less elegant than that of "Alle Menschen müssen sterben": the middle voices are stereotypes, and the bass line is formulaic; the line endings are overemphasized, to the disadvantage of the flow of the whole. The work, possibly one of the older pieces of the *Orgelbüchlein,* documents

Bach's inclination to pursue the integral work of art; it is present throughout if not perfectly realized in every measure.

A number of settings put traditional counterpoint techniques on display—for example, the canonic leading of the cantus firmus. This method requires particular skill with voice leading in the accompaniment and is a technique at which Bach was not expert at the outset (even though he had tried it in a few chorales of the Neumeister Collection), as dissonances inevitably crop up between the two voices of the canon; examples of this are BWV 600, 608, 618–20, 624, 629, and 633. In chorales like BWV 614, 622, and 641, the cantus firmus has the coloration of the north German tradition, or the arrangement of "Christum wir sollen loben schon," BWV 611, with the cantus firmus in the alto voice.

The "picturesque" element that so fascinated Schweitzer plays a role in almost all the pieces in the *Orgelbüchlein*. The beginning of the setting "Durch Adams Fall ist ganz verderbt," BWV 637, shows just how much Bach enjoyed "bringing out" this exceedingly simple, even formulaic hymn tune through daring harmonies and bizarre motifs. Not only the Arnstadt chorales but settings like these as well may have struck many listeners more as examples of artistic high-handedness than as respectful interpretations of the hymn texts. Adam's fall is imitated not only in the diminished sevenths of the pedal but also in the downward movement of the tenor voice and the labored efforts in the alto to rise back up again. Diagonally intersecting voice leadings, hard dissonances, and rapid changes in harmonic direction make the listener uneasy.[11]

We could apply traditional figuration theory to the many harmonic and compositional liberties taken here[12] or see them as expressive dissonance, to use the language of modern emotive music theory. But any attempt to deal with this musical material will encounter an element of radicality that is difficult to reconcile with the simple concept of accompanying and interpreting a chorale. The leading of the quite unsingable pedal voice part, although it remains perfectly symmetrical to the final affirmation, is reminiscent of the twelve-tone compositions of Arnold Schönberg—for instance, the song "Tot" from opus 48. It is usually the late Bach's strict and uncompromising style that is vaunted; but the style appeared as early as Weimar, and in a work with a title as harmless as "Little Organ Book."

The many other chorale arrangements of the Weimar period are no match for the concentrated power of the *Orgelbüchlein*. Bach himself may have taken this view; in his last years, he made a point of collecting a number of them into an anthology. This collecting probably had a purpose similar to that of the second part of *The Well-Tempered Clavier*: in the absence of a printed work, to provide his students and admirers with a manuscript compilation of works typical of the genre. The collection was supposed to contain perhaps twenty-four pieces; however, the so-called Leipzig Originalhandschrift Mus. MS Bach P271 contains only the Eighteen Chorales, BWV 651–68, of which the last—"Vor deinem Thron tret ich"—is generally conceded to be incomplete. Almost all the pieces also exist in older versions stemming from the Weimar period, so it is appropriate to view the collection as exemplary of Bach's Weimar organ chorale writing outside the *Orgelbüchlein*; we shall therefore discuss them at this point, shuttling at will between the Weimar and later Leipzig versions.

With the Eighteen Chorales, the variety of detail that the pieces of the *Orgelbüchlein* exhibit in the frame of an unchanging form is extended to embrace a multiplicity of different compositional styles. To underscore the collection's ambition, at the very beginning comes the great chorale fantasy "Komm, Heiliger Geist, Herre Gott," here in the Weimar version BWV 651a. This should be thought of as a manual three-part fugue on a theme from the first line of the chorale;

here and there, bits of the cantus firmus are played in the pedal in long-value notes.

The word *fugue* does not imply a dense contrapuntal structure in *stile antico*. In its fantasy element, the movement is reminiscent more of a concerted toccata, perhaps the toccata BWV 540 in the same key, which was discussed in detail earlier. The concerted element is most evident in the middle of the movement, where the cantus firmus pauses for nine and a half measures: Bach takes advantage of this opportunity to insert a *concertante* episode with a sighing motif that, with its many thirds, sounds almost flirtatious.

The later Bach of Leipzig was no longer happy with his Weimar version, with its truncated cantus firmus. To remedy this he lengthened the movement by more than half, although only a quarter of the bars were new composition; the rest derived from the text of the earlier version. Without question he wanted to show his respect for this venerable Lutheran chorale: it is no accident that this invocation of the Holy Ghost is the first piece in the collection.

The second piece, BWV 652, also shows the extent of Bach's ambition in his approach to the Eighteen Chorales. It too is devoted to the chorale "Komm, Heiliger Geist, Herre Gott" but composed *alio modo,* a sign that Bach was reaching into his musical storehouse to give a demonstration of the art of chorale arranging. This longest of all his organ chorales is more traditional than its predecessor; it may even be a historical model in the image of Böhm, Buxtehude, Bruhns, or Reinken. Each line of the hymn appears sequentially in an imitative setting in the tenor, alto, pedal; finally it is colored in the soprano. Bach's observance of this principle outdoes that of his predecessors, but consistency does not give this didactic work quite the spark of the BWV 651: its *concertante* verve has yielded to a saraband-like gravity.

"An Wasserflüssen Babylon," BWV 653, the third work, is also in the north German tradition, but it is doubtful that this meditative piece had anything to do with his Hamburg debut in 1720, when he is said to have improvised "almost a half hour" on this chorale, moving the nearly hundred-year-old Adam Reincken to make the tribute: "I thought this art had died out, but I see that it lives on in you."[13] The version in the Eighteen Chorales works its charm through its subtle ornamentation in the French mode.

The next piece, the arrangement of the Communion chorale "Schmücke dich, o liebe Seele," BWV 654, has its own reception history. Felix Mendelssohn Bartholdy loved it and wrote to his sister from Munich in the fall of 1831:

> *In fact, Fanny, here I have found the proper registration to play Seb. Bach's "Schmücke dich, o liebe Seele." It is as if it were made for it, and sounds so moving, that every time I start to play it, I shudder all over. I use a flute pipe (8 feet) for the moving voices, and a very quiet 4-foot one which floats above the chorale throughout—you know that from Berlin. But for the chorale there is a manual which consists wholly of reed stops, and there I use a gentle oboe, a clairon, very soft, 4 feet, and a viola. This imbues the whole chorale with a peaceful sound, as though they were far-off human voices, singing the chorale from the bottom of their hearts.*[14]

Mendelssohn enjoyed performing the work in Leipzig as well. In an essay entitled "Monument für Beethoven" appearing in his journal *Neue Zeitschrift für Musik* in 1836, Robert Schumann under the *nom de plume* "Jonathan" addressed Mendelssohn with these words:

> *And then you, Felix Meritis, a man of both great mind and heart, played one of the Chorales with variations: the text was "schmücke dich o meine Seele," and there were gilded garlands hung about the cantus firmus, and you poured such blissfulness and joy into it, that you confessed to me yourself, "if life were to rob you of every hope and belief, this one chorale would restore them all to you."*[15]

Four years later, in the Thomaskirche at Leipzig, the rediscoverer of the *St. Matthew Passion* held an organ recital that was unusual for the time, since it was devoted exclusively to Johann Sebastian Bach, to benefit his promotion of a Bach memorial. The concert included "Schmücke dich, o liebe Seele." Schumann was enthusiastic, saying that the concert provided "the pleasure of double mastery, with one master interpreting the other," and he characterized the organ chorale as "a priceless, profoundly felt work of music, such as comes from a true artistic temperament."[16]

Philipp Spitta was not far behind: for him, the work's formal peculiarities, completely understandable in terms of the genre history, were mere colors to help "present and complete an inner portrait of solemn, subdued heavenly rapture."[17] In his last years, Albert Schweitzer wrote, on the basis of old manuscripts:

> *Truly, the portrayal of atmosphere in this Communion piece is one of a kind. A strain of mystical sensuality runs all through it. The idea of the soul as the loving bride of Christ, which the text borrows from the Song of Songs, and from the concept of the celestial banquet, plays into the portrayal of eucharistic bliss, and lends this languorous music a movement of shuddering ecstasy.*[18]

Certainly the eucharistic mysticism attaching to the chorale has helped give it its special rank. But for us today, it is difficult to decide whether the saraband-like setting is due to the chorale's being an enlarged and elevated rendition of the north German "colored" chorale, or due to its solemn and meditative mood—a mood that can be realized completely only in the context of the Eucharist.

There are few organ chorales of Bach that combine hymn settings and four-part counterpoint so unpretentiously. This is one piece from the *Orgelbüchlein* that has been raised to the level of the monumental, but invested with motifs that are not so much figurative or figured as flowing and expressive. The lovely passages in thirds and sixths can be seen, in Schumann's phrase, as gilded garlands entwined about a cantus firmus, which itself has become an arabesque or hieroglyph.

The fifth chorale arrangement, "Herr Jesu Christ, dich zu uns wend," BWV 655, is not a hymn setting but a sonata movement. This composition, described as a trio, anticipates the trio movement of an organ sonata—but here it is assigned a particular task: to make audible the material of the cantus firmus. This happens in two ways: in a structure of Italianate grandeur, the *concertante* opening section presents a ritornello that takes up the triad fanfares of the chorale's beginning; a shorter final section adds to the upper voices, which play on undeterred, a ground bass composed of nothing less than the entire cantus firmus.

This conception could have originated in the Weimar court: there was lively interest there in the Italian arts of the sonata and concerto, and so the court organist may have felt it would add a little luster to his image if he showed what he could do with these forms on the organ. The local princelings must have perked up their ears and then nodded approvingly, when one day, in a festive court service, Bach introduced the German Gloria with a modern trio movement, which in a spirited ending segues into the hymn in its last few bars.

To this experiment with the trio, Bach added another: "Allein Gott in der Höh sei Ehr," BWV 664fa/b. After an extended opening section, which gives the first line of the chorale its opportunity to have a word, at length, and in the pedal, the middle section allows strictly *concertante* elements to take the stage, with brilliant triad figures and trill sequences. The final reminiscence of the opening section is relatively short: although only two lines of the hymn, it is still enough to remind the congregation which hymn is to be sung next.

This procedure is in the opinion of Werner Breig "not beyond reproach."[19] Indeed, the Leipzig Bach would probably not have composed anything more along these lines. The primary consideration in the numbers of the *Clavier-Übung*, part 3, for him was the presentation and profound reflection on the cantus firmus. Another trio on "Allein Gott in der Höh sei Ehr," BWV 676, that is also included has a classical balance. Soon after, Bach incorporated this piece of Weimar boldness without great change in the Eighteen Chorales, showing that he stood by it.

As Franz Schubert is supposed to have "paved the way to the large symphony" through the chamber music he created in his circle of friends,[20] so Bach at Weimar may have found the way to the concerto a century earlier by experimenting in areas that formed the core of his professional activities...a remarkable idea for music history to conjure with. He is temperamentally incapable of taking over the modern Italian concerto form without distance or reflection; he simply must adapt it to his style in order to make it his own. Doing this via the chorale is only superficially a detour. In reality it allows him to enhance the basic ideas of the sonata and the concerto, forms with an emphasis on melody, with those features that played a critical role in his own art: skillfully worked out motifs and themes and obbligato, largely contrapuntal settings.

Bach was at his best as a composer and interpreter of cantus firmus arrangements. By transferring the potential of this art form, already over a century old, to the idea of concerted music, he established the foundation for the absolute music of Viennese classicism, whose sonata movement, while not identical with a formal-harmonic scheme, contains the above-mentioned elements of motivic and thematic work and a coherent compositional style. Not just the miniature pieces of the *Orgelbüchlein* but also one-of-a-kind experiments like the chorale trio "Allein Gott in der Höh sei Ehr" were extraordinarily successful from a musical history perspective. The same applies to the expressive melodic work of the thirty-year-old composer of cantatas: Weimar's Bach was up to it.

The variety of forms of the Eighteen Chorales might even include works dating from before the composition of the *Orgelbüchlein.* Given its loose form and lack of overall structure, "Jesus Christus, unser Heiland," BWV 666a, could be the earliest, followed a bit later by the chorale "Nun danket alle Gott," BWV 657a, an amazing amplification of the four-part organ chorale with pre-imitations in the style of Pachelbel. The 1714 cantata "Himmelskönig, sei willkommen," BWV 182, has a final chorale of similar construction, "Jesu, deine Passion."

In other movements the compositional techniques of the *Orgelbüchlein* are continued. In "Komm, Gott Schöpfer, heiliger Geist," BWV 667a, the setting of the first verse is identical with the organ chorale of the same name, BWV 631, from the *Orgelbüchlein.* Then after an interlude, Bach gets his breath back again, to execute the cantus firmus in the pedal, in long-note values. But there is a noticeable lack of an overall scheme, and the two sections barely relate to each other.

The chorale "Wenn wir in höchsten Nöten sein," BWV 668a, gets a treatment going far beyond the customary revision. The original version in the *Orgelbüchlein* is a colored organ chorale of the north German type (BWV 641). Late in his Leipzig period, most scholars think, Bach produced an expanded version that appeared both in the posthumous publication of *The Art of Fugue* and as a fragment under the heading "Vor deinen Thron tret ich" as the last of the Eighteen Chorales.

In the Leipzig version, the hymn melody, traditionally meant to be performed on a solo manual, is largely stripped of ornament, made more objective and "demoted" more or less to the *prima inter pares* voice of a contrapuntal section. But this demotion is balanced by an enhancement: Bach now precedes each line of the hymn with a pre-imitation figure longer than the line itself.

The trend is clear: while the *Orgelbüchlein* version, despite the counterpoint accompaniment, had something of the subjective sound of a "soul" tune from early Pietism, the Leipzig version documents a thorough working out of the cantus firmus in the style of the *Clavier-Übung*, part 3, and shows Bach's desire to display the objectifying power of the chorale. The use of techniques like this does not really fit our image of the late Bach: by the 1730s the technique of pre-imitation (where each line is preceded by a shortened and then an inverted form of itself) was almost ancient history, and could be justified only for use in work of the highest level.

It is just that—the level of the work—that has provoked recent inquiry,[21] and the critic Peter Williams is right in suggesting that there are divergences in the work between old and new segments with respect to harmonic development. The arrangement of the "Aus tiefer Not" chorale, BWV 687, from the *Clavier-Übung*, similarly constructed, is decidedly more convincing. So in addition to the biographical, there are technical and aesthetic questions regarding Bach's supposed funeral chorale. Did arrangements such as this possibly arise from teaching situations? Did Bach mean to document how the character of an organ chorale can be altered with a few little tricks?

We leave this question open and turn to the third part of the *Clavier-Übung*, a collection in which Bach announced his philosophy of the organ chorale in authoritative published form. Like the two previous parts of the *Clavier-Übung*, this collection, through use of model examples, represents a special field of keyboard music: the organ prelude. "As if it were a practical, yet theoretical handbook, the organist can select individual works according to need, whether it be for use in the worship service, or for technical instruction and demonstration of all the various possibilities of liturgical organ music"[22]—so Christoph Wolff describes the work's function. It was deliberately dedicated not only to "those who love" this kind of music, as were the previous two parts of the *Clavier-Übung*, but "especially to the cognoscenti of this kind of work." Bach obviously knew he was presenting the listener with demanding music, both technically and compositionally.

"To build a house requires a frame; but it would be odd indeed to seek, let alone find, the builder's honor not in the house but in the frame!" These words of E. T. A. Hoffmann, quoted by Wolff in his search for organizing principles in the original printed editions of Bach's works,[23] could shed light on the third part of the *Clavier-Übung:* is its order in the frame or in the house itself? As we showed in the biographical section, Bach was making changes to what went to print right up to the last moment. First it was only supposed to have the great organ chorales; then the small chorales came in, stage by stage; then the framing pieces, the Prelude and Fugue in E-flat Major; and finally the four duets BWV 802–05. This does not invalidate the idea that Bach had some organizing principle in mind during all these preprinting phases, but it seems unlikely that he meant to construct a musical cathedral.

The word "cathedral" is not used casually here: since 1930, the organ mass has continually been associated with part 3 of the *Clavier-Übung.*[24] But it does not follow in any way "the order of the Protestant mass in its layout."[25] Bach is setting, as he says in the title, "the Catechism and other vocal works," and the importance of the latter should not be underestimated. With the prelude, the vocal works make up the first part of the edition: the German Kyrie, "Kyrie, Gott Vater in Ewigkeit," in two settings and the German Gloria, "Allein Gott in der Höh sei Ehr," in three. That is a respectable short mass, but in the title only the "catechism chorales" that follow are mentioned as such, each one in two settings: "Dies sind die heilgen zehn Gebot," "Wir glauben all an einen Gott," "Vater unser im Himmelreich," "Christ, unser Herr zum Jordan kam," "Aus tiefer Note schrei ich zu dir," and "Jesus Christus, unser Heiland, der von uns den Zorn Gottes wandt."

It must remain an open question why Bach chose or permitted a title that imperfectly described the content of the work, but we should not conclude from the title's vagueness that his selection of key Lutheran hymns was arbitrary or even subjective. He likely had a fixed canon of hymns in mind, such as those that existed in Andreas Reyher's *Schulmethodus* for primary school use in the principality of Gotha in 1642. On the subject of his "Catechismus-Gesangs" (Catechism Songs), Reyher, whose *systema logicum* was verifiably Bach's introduction to logic, gives specific instructions, one of which is of particular interest here: he lists the songs the schoolchildren were to use for their workday morning singing sessions.

This list is almost identical in content and sequence with Bach's six "Catechismus-Gesaengen." Only the Friday morning hymn, "Erbarm dich mein o Herre Gott," is replaced in his collection by "Aus tiefer Not schrei ich zu dir." Perhaps Bach remembered a different order from his school days, or perhaps he preferred "Aus tiefer Not" for some other reason.[26] If the German Kyrie and Gloria are included, the third part of the *Clavier-Übung* could be described as the organistic portrayal of Lutheran religious belief. In 1739, the two hundredth anniversary of the Reformation in Albertine Saxony, there would have been good reason for such a musical representation.

But Bach probably did not so much intend to do that as to present his *summa* of liturgical organ playing. If at the time of publication he had any musical renown at all, then it was as an organ composer and organ virtuoso, so it would have been natural to choose this field in which to make his profession of faith. The third part of the *Clavier-Übung* is a profession of faith, whether seen from a theological or compositional point of view. No one asked Bach to exhibit his skill at chorale arrangement in such a theologically formal, ceremonial fashion. We clearly see his conviction that the chorale prelude is a part of the divine worship service and that its foundation is the Lutheran faith.

As the Halle organist Johann Gotthilf Ziegler reported in 1746, Bach advised his students "not to play the hymns offhand but according to the sense of the words."[27] He advocated not only a musically expressive approach to organ playing but also an organist who was devout and dedicated. By giving his collection of cantus firmus–based compositions the formal framework of the Prelude and Fugue in

E-flat Major, he enhanced the standing of the form. The difference in structure and characteristics, when compared with the *Orgelbüchlein*, the Leipzig Eighteen Chorales, and the Schübler Chorales, is obvious.

These comments have given appropriate attention to the work's theological dimension. We could go beyond this, and indulge in theological speculation on the individual chorale arrangements. We could apply numerology—noting, for instance, that the three great kyrie settings total 163 bars in all: a prime number, "which as an indivisible number expresses the indivisibility of the Trinity." The multiple occurrences of the number 42 might be a reference to Jesus,[28] who in Matthew's Gospel is said to have been born in the forty-second generation after Abraham. And so on.

If Bach indeed thought kabbalistically, which can neither be proved nor disproved, it would mean that he made the art of composition a bit more difficult for himself. Some basic observations on this appear in the final chapter, "Bach's Art." Looking at the chorales of the *Clavier-Übung*, we merely mention here the danger of such speculation: with a focus on counting, it is easy to forget what great art Bach produced. Of course this art is speculative, but the speculative element is largely within the compositions themselves.

We see this right at the beginning of the chorale arrangements, in the double kyrie triptych BWV 669–74, Bach certainly had something in mind by setting the first of the "little" manualiter arrangements in 3/4 time, the second in 6/8, and the third in 9/8: the number three, symbolic of the Trinity, appears doubled and squared. Meanwhile these three "great" arrangements of the kyrie are all written in alla breve rhythm, and for a thoroughly musical reason. *Alla breve* here is almost a synonym for *stile antico* and thus a writing style in the vocal polyphonic tradition of Palestrina. In his organ works back in Weimar, Bach had been able to study this style in the kyries from Frescobaldi's *Fiori musicali*, among others. Later, in Leipzig, he became intensely involved with the masses of Palestrina, Lotti, and Caldara. The organ chorale "Aus tiefer Not schrei ich zu dir," BWV 686, is set in the *stile antico*, and Bach adopts the Phrygian modal key from the given cantus firmus, an indication of his awareness of tradition.

The true organist, Bach means to announce at the outset, must be at home in the tradition—in that of strict style as well as in that of the cantus firmus and the church tones. It was no accident that Johann Philipp Kirnberger, in the second volume of his *Kunst des reinen Satzes* ("The Art of Strict Musical Composition"), mentions the treatment of church tones, among other things, using the third part of the *Clavier-Übung* as an example: at the time of its publication, he had just become a Bach pupil, and Bach would surely have trained him thoroughly in the use of church tones.

But what do we mean by "use"? In the kyries, Bach is quite high-handed in his treatment of the Phrygian mode. In Pierre Boulez's view, his harmonic language dismantles the modal or church-tone functions even more boldly than Schönberg's twelve-tone language dismantled tonality![29] This means that Bach is writing anything but a sleek Palestrina setting. Rather, into the three- or four-part *stile antico* counterpoint he inserts another element: the Phrygian cantus firmus of the Gregorian kyrie.

The melodicism of the accompanying setting is derived from this material in a very artful fashion, to be sure. Still, these two elements, each with its own claim to greatness, stand in strange juxtaposition. Bach's contemporaries must have heard the composition almost in double refraction. They heard an artfully arranged setting in *stile antico*, into which the Gregorian cantus firmus is woven, giving it an almost archaic character. The cantus firmus does not in itself seem archaic, since the Leipzig audience knew it from their liturgy, but paradoxically, its archaic effect comes from its modern, dissonance-rich harmonization, which casts it in a new, alien light. Bach has the opening line of the cantus firmus in BWV 669 start with the word "kyrie" in E-flat major, and end in D major, although the key of D major is (cautiously put) not provided for in G-Phrygian. Even greater confusion for the listener results when, at the D-major harmony, Bach starts the alto voice on a′, as if to repudiate the minor second of the Phrygian mode. At the same time, this entry is in itself purely Phrygian.[30]

Melodic consistency and a flowing Palestrina-like setting lessen the impression of harmonic tension, but tension is unavoidable in an alla breve setting that is both flexible and complicated in its harmony and counterpoint—particularly when something as unwieldy as a Phrygian cantus firmus in long-note values is interwoven with it.

This does not mean that Bach first composed the alla breve and then added the cantus firmus. The tension between the two elements is a deliberately planned structural element. One sees the difference between this structure and the impressive canonic skills of the old Netherlandish masters and their ability to bind together multiple contrapuntal parts variously derived from one or more cantus firmus. Bach does not start out thinking of the parts but of the whole, which must satisfy certain conditions: it should be in *stile antico* and draw its material from a set cantus firmus; it must bring out the artless and archaic cantus firmus as such, contrasting it with skillful counterpoint work, all the while making use of modern functional harmony's ability to provide a form.

Similarly complex thinking, with a constant awareness of musical history, speaks from the great chorale arrangements of the catechism—"Dies sind die heilgen zehen Gebot," BWV 678, and "Vater unser im Himmelreich," BWV 682. In each, Bach sets himself the task of incorporating the plain cantus firmus, in the form of an unbroken canon, into a strictly constructed trio movement. His success in meeting this compositional challenge is not in itself remarkable: theory teachers and composers know that the task is difficult but not impossible. What is astounding is Bach's sure-footed selection of completely different solutions. "Dies sind die heilgen zehen Gebot" picks up on traditional compositional methods of the seventeenth century and displays the canon on the cantus firmus on a separate manual. Thus, despite its prodigious demands on player and listener, it is historically part of the tradition of the form and to some extent comprehensible to the listener. One can always follow the cantus firmus.

In comparison, "Vater unser im Himmelreich" is bizarre. Because the canon voices of the cantus firmus are divided over two separate keyboards, they are not acoustically separated from the other parts. The fabric of constantly intersecting voices is nonetheless barely comprehensible, because Bach has overlaid the contrapuntal layer with its traditional opposite. The two voices "accompanying" the cantus firmus canon are expressive solos taken from the slow movements of his sonatas and concerti and tricked out with modern mannerisms and gallant rhythmic changes.

The gallant element is transcended in a unique fashion: the accompaniment parts are suffused with strange, one might even say occult, motifs. It is as if something sacred needs to be protected from profane eyes. God is concealed by musical figures that speak but in a manner hard to interpret.

Bach's use of a frankly obtrusive Lombardian rhythmic pattern, unusual for chorale arrangements, within a highly complex and unstable rhythmic structure, demands so much concentration that it is almost impossible to appreciate the larger-scale progression of the work. Whether to go beyond the "sighing" melodic line, which seems to suit the text, and see any symbolic significance in the many variously articulated smaller motifs, is the listener's choice.

Was it Bach's intention that this arrangement, which has been called the most difficult of his chorales to perform,[31] be heard not only as a musical Our Father or even as the symbol of "groanings which cannot be uttered," as Romans 8.26 has it,[32] but as a modern trio movement at the same time? This purely instrumental way of listening is easier with the arrangements of "Allein Gott in der Höh sei Ehr," BWV 675 and 676: in these works the concerted trio structure, in which the cantus firmus is embedded, is foregrounded. But here again Bach could not resist offering two trios in addition to the manualiter version: BWV 675 could be called a gallant invention and BWV 676, with its cheerful ritornello, a sonata movement that is winsome. The formal symmetry of the latter makes up for what Bach, in his daring Weimar setting of "Allein Gott in der Höh sei Ehr," BWV 664, perhaps felt he owed "the cognoscenti of this kind of work."

With the third part of the *Clavier-Übung* he goes so far beyond the first two parts, and beyond the *Orgelbüchlein* as well, that its contents can no longer be thought of as utilitarian. The cantor of Leipzig's St. Thomas's Church, "already a legend during his lifetime,"[33] is here putting his *fiori musicali* on view: a work for demonstration and study both, which one of course can also use for playing—or better yet, concertizing. But most important, the work conjures up once and for all the spirit of the Protestant organ chorale. In the world of the Enlightenment, the listener no longer wants to be steeped in a chorale, reflecting devoutly on every line. What is wanted now are chorale preludes to preview the congregational singing, not chorale arrangements that are a world in themselves.

The genre no longer fits any of the dominant styles: along with the gallant style of writing, the strict style was still tolerated, but only for masses and fugal compositions. There is less and less room in the culture for the increasingly luxuriant offshoots of the organ chorale that flourished for nearly two centuries. Still it should be noted that extended, fantasy-like chorale arrangements were once a Dutch and north German specialty and probably continued to be heard in special organ recitals and evening concerts. With his hybrid forms, it was Bach himself who marked the end of the genre. His pupils are astounded by his art, attempt tentatively to carry it on, but do so pretty much alone.

The teacher will take one step further: to the Canonic Variations on the Christmas hymn "Vom Himmel hoch da komm ich her," BWV 769, which were in fact expressly composed for the organ but have, even more than the third part of the *Clavier-Übung*, the quality of demonstration pieces. Written on the occasion of Bach's joining Lorenz Mizler's Societät der Musicalischen Wissenschaften in 1747, they are a series of canonic masterpieces.

The high point of the printed version is the fifth variation. It contains in sequence the song's melody in a mirror canon and the second part following at intervals of a sixth, third, second, and ninth. The greatest density is at the end. As the fourth line is heard once more, the first line is set above it in sixteenth notes and reversed. Above the final pedal point of the last three measures, Bach presents as his *non plus ultra* all four lines of the song, one above the other.

This is more than a technical composing coup: the affective impact of the hymn—amazement at the events of the Nativity—is concentrated and summarized one more time. In the very last bar, the tonal sequence B-A-C-H can be heard (though spread over two parts). This of course did not escape the composer himself, and he likely regarded it, perhaps smiling to himself, as his hidden autograph to the work.

This is not witchcraft, since the underlying cantus firmus is quite flexible, but still the result of the most extreme care to develop from the simplest materials—the watchword being "all from one"—an ever more complex structure. For this reason the work fascinated twentieth-century composers. Paul Dessau celebrated the final section in his analysis as "a singular triumph of the composer's art."[34] Pierre Boulez admired the "strictness and logical consistency" of the compositional method, which created "musical architectonics" from within, which was itself a "structure generator."[35] Igor Stravinsky arranged the variations for mixed chorus and orchestra in 1956. Gerd Zacher wrote an essay on the variations, in which he contrasted the strictness of their structure with the wealth of musical rhetorical statements he found in them.[36]

It might seem logical to end this chapter with the Canonic Variations as the end point to Bach's nearly lifelong work with the Protestant chorale. But there is a postscript: the Schübler Chorales, BWV 645–50, named after Georg Schübler, who published them in 1748–49. This publication corresponds with that of the Canonic Variations but in a complementary way: the esoteric quality and contrapuntal complications of the latter are answered by the *concertante*, thoroughly accessible style of the former: though the four trios and two quartets are not simple to perform, they are easy to hear, lively and occasionally in the gallant style. This is hardly surprising, since five of the six pieces are verifiably transcriptions of arias and duets from sacred cantatas of the 1720s or 1730s; indeed, a vocal original may also lurk behind the sixth piece, "Wo soll ich fliehen hin," BWV 646.

The selection is not arbitrary. Given what was probably a modest store of suitable pieces, Bach would hardly have been able to come up with much more than a half dozen.[37] Compared with the above-mentioned original organ trios—"Herr Jesu Christ, dich zu uns wend," BWV 655, as well as "Allein Gott in der Höh sei Ehr," BWV 664, 675, and 676—these arrangements have advantages and disadvantages. For those who know them, they do not stand up to their originals—for instance, the trio "Wachet auf, ruft uns die Stimme," BWV 645, alongside its original, the tenor aria "Zion hört die Wächter singen" from the cantata "Wachet auf, ruft uns die Stimme," BWV 140. Based on works originally written for a mixed vocal-instrumental ensemble, these chorales have certain a priori vocal characteristics; and some of them are in da capo form, so they have an easier time finding the ear of the listener than their sister works composed for instruments only. Bach was certainly not ill-advised to agree late in life to a publication that picked up on his reputation as a specialist in the area of organ composition, but at the same time he preserved for posterity certain fine single pieces from his sacred music.

In 1788, Johann Friedrich Köhler, the author of a manuscript history of the schools of Leipzig, thought that these compositions would not age: they would "outlive every modish revolution in music," probably echoing a remark generally attributed to Carl Philipp Emanuel Bach (source anonymous).[38]

A handwritten copy of the Schübler Chorales, still in private hands, shows that late in life Bach was not only correcting printer's errors but also still working on the lifelong job of making nuanced improvements to his compositions.[39]

THE CÖTHEN DEMONSTRATION CYCLES: *INVENTIONS AND SINFONIAS, THE WELL-TEMPERED CLAVIER,* SIX SOLOS FOR VIOLIN

"You find everything in Bach: the development of cyclic forms, the conquest of the realm of tonality—the attempt at a summation of the highest order."[1] Anton Webern is thinking of Bach's work as a whole, but the first great proof of this idea is found in the demonstration cycles written at Cöthen. These were not the product of momentary inspiration but came out of that "meditative" temperament that his son Carl Philipp Emanuel thought had made Bach a great contrapuntalist.[2]

It might seem surprising that Bach could find time for such meditation, particularly in Cöthen, for the musical projects arising from it are not usually part of the duties of a kapellmeister and chamber music conductor. Nonetheless, completion of the demonstration cycles falls in the second half of the Cöthen years, a period of transition, when Bach, faced with the challenges of the next position he has set his sights on, wants to nail down securely the fundamental skills of his art. To put it another way: having arrived at an artistic pinnacle, Bach now, with *The Well-Tempered Clavier,* the *Inventions and Sinfonias,* the violin solos, and the *Brandenburg Concertos* (to be treated in the next chapter) presents the great, complementary cyclic works that could be understood as concentrated paradigms of all his composing.

Only a composer equally gifted as harmonist and contrapuntalist, with an overall "harmonic-polyphonic concept" in mind,[3] would be equal to such a task. In fact, his obituary praises him for having "employed the most hidden secrets of harmony with the most skilled artistry."[4] Johann Abram Birnbaum, on the other hand, praises the "voices [that]...work wonderfully in and about one another, but without the slightest confusion."[5] The two together "make up his strange [that is, unique] perfections."[6]

When we look in particular at the *Inventions and Sinfonias* and *The Well-Tempered Clavier*, the Cöthen demonstration cycles can be seen from three different aspects: as works of pedagogy, as works of art, and as contributions to a philosophy of music.

The pedagogical nature of the works is emphasized in their respective titles by Bach himself: the *Inventions and Sinfonias* were written for "those eager to learn" with the intention that they might "learn how to play purely" with two or three obbligato voices; the preludes and fugues of *The Well-Tempered Clavier* were composed, not least, for the "use and advantage" of "young musicians eager to learn." This pedagogical intent is just as clear in the works themselves and their context: almost all the *Inventions and Sinfonias* as well as a series of preludes from *The Well-Tempered Clavier* are found in early versions in the 1720 *Klavierbüchlein* for Wilhelm Friedemann Bach, allowing us a glimpse into the father's teaching of his eldest son.

Did the son not only learn from the father but also assist him with the composition of the two-part inventions, and even compose the last in B minor on his own? A 1972 thesis to this effect, while not very convincing,[7] might nonetheless bring us to look at the famous series in a new light.

Bach's instruction of his son was probably not fundamentally different from that which he gave to other students. The lexicographer Ernst Ludwig Gerber reports on the keyboard lessons his father received in Bach's house in 1724–25:

> *At the first lesson [Bach] set his Inventions before him. When he had studied these through to Bach's satisfaction, there followed a series of suites, then* The Well-Tempered Clavier. *This latter work Bach played altogether three times through for him with his unmatchable art, and my father counted these among his happi-*

est hours, when Bach, under the pretext of not feeling in the mood to teach, sat himself at one of his fine instruments and thus turned these hours into minutes.[8]

The Inventions, Sinfonias, and preludes are not a "school of dexterity" like Czerny's, yet have a decidedly technical element to them. The practice of the independent playing of both hands is presented in many different ways. Leaning on a remark of Carl Philipp Emanuel concerning Bach's use of the thumb in playing,[9] Henning Siedentopf makes the further point:

> *Bach is the first to use the hand in his keyboard music the way nature would like to have it used. The whole set of rules for the use of the hand herewith becomes accessible. From this combining of various technical principles of play arises the* Klavierübung *("keyboard practice"), a form of study that develops greater dexterity for the hand, in a manner suited to it. If we start with the contemporary concept of "signing" as a language of the fingers, Bach was the first to let the hand "come of age," so to speak, that is to develop a rich vocabulary and suitable syntax.*[10]

For Bach, out of physiological facts, out of the nature of those hand movements that make keyboard music possible comes the nature of music, which the composer makes visible through the perfection of his art. This nature should be understood as *concordia discors,* unity in multiplicity. Each voice of the musical statement is an obligatory, independent entity, as is stated on the title page of the *Inventions and Sinfonias;* at the same time, each voice combines with the others in perfect harmony. No matter how bold and independent of each other the voices may be, the principle of harmonic coherence rules them all. For Bach the thorough bass (continuo), seen as harmony in the modern sense, is the "most perfect foundation of music."[11]

But while it is possible to learn the thorough bass from the book *Musicalische Handleitung* by Bach's contemporary Friedrich Erhard Niedt, a work aimed at rapid mastery without the student's first having to deal with "cruelly long preludia, toccatas, chaconnes, fugues, and other such strange Creatures,"[12] Bach sets up a music theory structure that recognizes the thorough bass as an ideal foundation but has more in mind than merely a setting of the upper voices, in which the right hand details what the left hand sets for it. He wants instead a fabric of voices that are *obligat* and *cantabile* in equal measure.

The *Inventions and Sinfonias* convey a "strong foretaste of *Composition*," while *The Well-Tempered Clavier* serves as a special diversion for whoever "is already versed [*habil*] in this study." This last formulation points out the artistic character of the works, which we shall first examine in the *Inventions and Sinfonias*.

These works are original as a type of composition, even though their systematic arrangement *per omnes tonos* is not.[13] One is distantly reminded of the tradition of the *bicinium* and *tricinium,* which, in diluted form, was continued in the Latin schools of central Germany up to Bach's time. But the terms *bicinium* and *tricinium* were always understood to mean ensemble music for two or three singers or players. As models of strict yet *cantabile* composition arranged by key, the *Inventions and Sinfonias* are unique. They do not fit into any genre or style. Bach described the inventions of the *Klavierbüchlein* for Wilhelm Friedemann as "Praeambula" and the sinfonias as "Fantasias." His new nomenclature shows his awareness that he is breaking new ground.

The mixture of contrapuntal and figured rhetorical elements is unparalleled. The old and new senses of the *stylus phantasticus* intersect in an unmistakable way. While up until Athanasius Kircher this style was understood as "the uttermost concentration of strict style in the contrapuntal fantasy,"[14] three generations later Johann Mattheson described it as "the freest most liberal style of setting, singing, and playing music," which could only "be mastered by clever heads full of invention, and rich (sometimes even too rich) in figures of every kind."[15]

Mattheson's use of the terms *invention* and *figures* should be noted. *Invention* comes from *inventio*, a term of rhetoric. *Figure* is an even more concrete allusion to the doctrine of musical-rhetorical figures, originating in late-sixteenth-century rhetoric. This context makes clear that the *Inventions and Sinfonias* not only had a well-thought-out structure and a "cantabel" or singable quality to boot but also were meant to be artistic—that is, connected to musical rhetoric and poetics.

But what do these terms matter compared to the works themselves! Given the requirement of having two and sometimes three voices and a harmonious, largely imitative style, both cycles consist of exercises of all kinds: they are paragons of composition of the highest order. With the help of some of the more straightforward pieces, twentieth-century composers and many Bach scholars and interpreters have ventured to penetrate the mysteries of Bach's counterpoint and also to describe the aesthetic and philosophical context of these work cycles.

After Ferrucio Busoni published an edition of the two-part Inventions in 1907, with characteristic commentaries, Fritz Jöde used them barely two decades later in developing his idea of organicism in music. His aim was to replace the "mechanics" of traditional form theory with this idea and by proceeding along "the guidelines of psychology" and "by analysing individual phenomena" to come closer to understanding their "unity."[16] In 1951, Erwin Ratz, a student of Schönberg's, devoted a lot of space to the *Inventions and Sinfonias* in his *Einführung in die musikalische Formenlehre* ("Introduction to Musical Form Theory"), which in 1968 he reissued with the subtitle *Über Formprinzipien in den Inventionen und Fugen J. S. Bachs und ihre Bedeutung für die Kompositionstechnik Beethovens* ("Principles of Form in the Inventions and Fugues of J. S. Bach and Their Significance in the Compositions of Beethoven"). In his "functional form theory" Ratz, like Jöde, was interested in why a musical work of art is perceived as a "closed organism," as an "entirety."[17] Finally, in 1957 and 1959 Johann Nepomuk David devoted one short book each to the Inventions and Sinfonias, analyzing the musical notation of this "music with a purpose," to lay out their astonishing order, their purity of craftsmanship, and their correct use of materials—in sum, their "beauty of technique."[18]

Hermann Keller considered the three-part Sinfonia in F Minor, BWV 795, one of "the master's crown jewels."[19] Bach works with a two-bar counterpoint model that contains three themes that appear simultaneously. Since these are in triple counterpoint, he can develop a fugue from this model with three constantly interchanging subjects.

It is hardly possible to understand the piece purely as a contrapuntal structure. The beginning and the ending, at least, seem to be more an upper-voice setting. The listener's impression is less the perception of ten thematic entries than of a progression distantly resembling a suite: the arrival at the tonic parallel in bar 13 marks a kind of caesura, followed by a circuitous modulation back to the tonic.[20] Since the thematic figures do not change in any material way, the "sighing" motif dependably stays with the listener throughout despite the addition of interludes, and the movement is relatively short, it is possible to take in this trinity of contrapuntal density, harmonic tension, and gestural force with the ear alone. While often one needs the score to comprehend the wondrous structure of a Bach fugue, here the immediate impression is sufficient: the invention calls to mind a highly polished object that can be held in the hand and examined from all sides.

The rhetorical character of the movement is evident. The shape of the opening melody voice is exactly like a sigh, and it is supplemented by a countersubject with a descending chromatic quarter-note passage, a bass *lamento*. The second countersubject introduced in bar 3 adds detail to the theme's gestural sorrow, which is itself the rhetorical justification for the harmonic frictions that arise. Undeniably, the movement has a dramatically effective arc of tension, with its apex at the end of the middle third.[21]

Bach's pupil Johann Philipp Kirnberger, in his *The Art of Strict Musical Composition,* took issue early on with the composition's ample store of dissonances, which was unusual even for Bach.[22] And Philipp Spitta feared that "the distorted impression most listeners would perhaps get on first hearing" might prevent their realizing that behind the "daring intervals, changing notes, and harmonic cross-relations lay not just forced artifice but a truly imaginative vision."[23] In his *Tonsatzlehre* ("Craft of Musical Composition"), Paul Hindemith frankly dubbed it a harmonic "jigsaw puzzle." "The listener is continually being asked what he wants to listen to, independent chords or subordinate notes foreign to the chord.... The uncertainty this artifice causes goes so far that even in the first measure with only two voices, the listener does not know exactly what is meant."[24]

Siegfried Borris disagreed, assessing the F minor sinfonia as "a carefully thought-out piece rich in expressive suspensions," with a "typically Bachian harmonic progression."[25] But that is something of a gloss-over: even just to hear the tritone interval E-flat–A-natural (the last beat of the first measure) harmonically as the fragment of a dominant seventh or second chord takes effort.[26]

Is it perhaps more sensible to take this harmonically awkward interval as an example of a chromatic cross-relation, that is, parrhesia (a musical figure nearly obsolete by Bach's time)? There would have to be a reason for this "freedom of speech," as the term translates into English, and this would be the sinfonia's overtly sorrowful character. Hermann Keller compared it to the F-minor section "Weinen, Klagen, Sorgen, Zagen" from the eponymous Weimar cantata BWV 12, and Heinrich Besseler recalls the emotional realm "with which the expressive melody was originally associated: the contemplation of the suffering and death of Jesus Christ." In his view, the work thus requires "a fittingly emotional performance that brings out the inner coherence of the melody."[27]

Günter Hartmann takes the step from a figural or emotional interpretation to a symbolic one with his observation, following Walter F. Hindermann's lead,[28] that the sighing figure when transposed produces the tone row B-A-C-H. This fact is significant against the backdrop of his own "Bach emblematics": the sequence B-A-C-H contains the first two letters of the names "Bach" and "Christ" in a chiastic relation symbolizing Christ's cross. When Bach uses the sequence B-A-C-H, in Hartmann's view, he is trying to represent in terms of his own person what he wrote later in the Fulde family album, beneath his canon BWV 1077, these words in musical code: "Symbolum. Christus Coronabit Crucigeros," or, "Christ will crown the cross-bearers."[29]

A few years earlier Ulrich Siegele designed a "symbolic proportioning" of the F-minor sinfonia based on the number of entries and notes. As he sees it, the church doctrine of penitence and faith is fulfilled in the piece: ten entries of the theme stand for the law, that is, the Ten Commandments, as fulfilled by Christ; seven nonthematic sections stand for the Gospels, for the gifts of the Holy Ghost. Making use of a numeric alphabet, which he calls "traditional" but which is only one of many known to Bach's time, Siegele comes to further conclusions:

> *The thematic upper voice at the beginning, the second subject, has fourteen notes: BACH itself signifies contrition. The thematic setting, in its last entry, and only here, has forty-three tones. If we deduct from these forty-three tones of all three subjects the fourteen tones of the second subject, that leaves twenty-nine tones. This is Bach's artistic sign: SDG [Soli Deo gloria] = JSB. But the forty-three tones of all three subjects say: "CREDO, I believe." Bach is bearing witness, not abstractly but personally, to the church's doctrine of penitence.*[30]

In addition to symbolic proportions, one can find mathematical proportions. To take only one example, the piece's mathematical midpoint comes at bar 17, where actually a rather special event occurs with the reaching of the minor dominant,[31] even if it is not the most memorable from the listener's standpoint. The dramatic high point comes more or less at the dividing point of the golden section.

The great variety of opinions held by scholars and reception historians on this one small section gives some idea of the difficulty of reducing a piece like the F-minor sinfonia to a nutshell. For composers especially, it is a miracle; they know how difficult it is to cut a many-faceted jewel like this. It is difficult counterpoint yet succinct in form; it is based on modern thorough-bass concepts yet flouts the orthodox music theory of the day with its harmonic daring; it is an autonomous work, complete in itself, yet derives its authenticity from traditional conventions of figurative and affective music theory; it is a model of compositional form with three obbligato voices, yet, with its detailed articulation of gesture in the melodic line, it is the epitome of dramatic, almost emotion-driven writing. The work can be proportionalized in various ways and allows all sorts of symbolic interpretations. Given all this artistic richness, who could categorically exclude the possibility that Bach himself might have had some symbolic intention in mind?

While for teaching purposes Bach may have thought of the *Inventions and Sinfonias* as a preparation for *The Well-Tempered Clavier,* they are certainly of equal rank to it, since they embody the element of concentration versus the infinite variety of the universe expressed in the twenty-four preludes and fugues in all the keys. The latter are Bach's most convincing demonstration of the "bipolar principle" of prelude and fugue as "separate works, but cyclically and reciprocally connected." This being so, it is his most important contribution to the *stylus phantasticus,*[32] which traditionally always brought the strict and free styles together under one roof—though not with the systematic rigor that he requires for this work.

The principle of organizing keyboard music in ascending key order has a long tradition. Caspar Ferdinand Fischer, half a generation before Bach, produced his *Ariadne Musica,* a series of preludes and fugues dedicated to "magistris atque discipulis" ("teachers and pupils") that also takes the bipolar principle seriously. Closer inspection of course brings to light serious differences between this collection and *The Well-Tempered Clavier:* for one thing, Fischer's twenty preludes and fugues, or *fughette,* are so short that a pair of them usually fit on one widely spaced page.

What is new about *The Well-Tempered Clavier* is the radicality, breadth, and multiple perspectives of its artistic concept—in a word, its autonomy. There is a considerable difference between a composer creating a collection like the *Ariadne Musica,* who stakes out for his tonal territory only twenty of the twenty-four keys of the major and minor chromatic scale, and a composer who from the outset claims the entire range of tones for his use. Whoever would act like a modern composer and explore the whole realm of music in all its directions must set up his own laws. In place of the simple numeric series 1:2:3:4:5, and so on—the frequency ratios of the overtones—he must deal with the irrational number represented by the square root of twelve; using this number, he must rationally divide the octave into twelve strictly equal but no longer "natural" semitones.

Andreas Werckmeister, in his work of 1707, *Musicalische Paradoxal-Discourse,* thought this process not necessarily unnatural but hybrid: just as the square-root series "are the proper roots of perfect or pure *consonances,*" so is God "in His essence completely pure and perfect: even, perfection itself." But true Christians should not presume to attain this perfection; rather, they must take care "not to conceive of and ascribe to themselves a perfection that properly belongs solely to God."[33]

With this, Werckmeister acknowledges that the lack of practical know-how ruled out the possibility of balanced tuning at that time. But he also condemns the presumptuousness of trying to resolve the conflict between the natural sequence of the overtone series and the rational ordering of a twelve-tone system.

In practice Bach did not employ perfect tuning but literally "well-tempered" tuning. According to the necrologist, "in the tuning of harpsichords, he achieved so correct and pure a temperament that all the tonalities sounded pure and agreeable."[34] According to traditional key characteristics, C major may have sounded purer than C-sharp major. But such aesthetic considerations for performance do not alter the fact that *The Well-Tempered Clavier* brought equal temperament as a theoretical concept, or philosophical postulate, into the agenda of music history: the composer demands the authority to organize his tonal material according to his own will. This demand goes hand in hand with the final establishment of functional harmonic tonality, as theoretically set up by Jean Philippe Rameau in his *Traité de harmonie* in 1722, the year of the completion of the first part of *The Well-Tempered Clavier.*

Are both these achievements in line with Enlightenment philosophy, which gives free rein to humanity's inborn urge to explore but demands naturalness too? Or are they more the late-born offspring of medieval-baroque speculations about musical arcana? Even the sixteenth century produced compositions like Matthäus Greiters's *Fortuna* motet, which modulated in a circle of fourths from F minor to F-sharp minor.[35] By Bach's time musical puzzles such as this (called *Teufelsmühlen* or "devil's mills") had been succeeded by works like the *Fantasia durch alle Tonos* of one Friedrich Suppig, the *Musicalischer Circkel* in Johann David Heinichen's school of thorough bass, or the *Toccata per omnem circulum* of Andreas Sorge.[36] As always, Bach's music eludes such simple categorization.

While the structural principle of *The Well-Tempered Clavier* is quite strict, the characters of the individual pieces fit together in a somewhat loose ensemble. To be sure, in some cases the prelude and fugue are obviously closely connected,[37] and certainly there is clear evidence of keys having definite characteristics. But the element of variety is as essential as that of order. This is why Richard Wagner spoke of a "world-idea" here.[38] This idea is found in both parts of *The Well-Tempered Clavier,* which despite their disparate origins make up a unified whole and are absolutely of equal value. We thus deliberately choose to look at book 2, and in the following paragraph we examine the Prelude and Fugue in F-sharp Minor, BWV 883, which exhibits critical features of this two-part cycle.

The prelude, a perfectly articulated character piece throughout, can be looked at as a sinfonia—that is, as a meticulous three-part invention, as a sonata movement, or even as the andante movement of an instrumental concerto.[39] Divided into three parts, followed by a kind of reprise, it hardly repeats itself in the literal sense, playing instead with contrapuntal variations on motifs that for the most part are found in the opening melody.

Melody, a term that should be used with caution for thematic forms in the age of the continuo, in this case is fitting: the opening section, which sets the tone for the whole work, is not simply a device or ritornello but a song with a wide tessitura, ornately structured both horizontally and vertically—"sung from the depths of the soul," as Hugo Riemann writes in his *Handbuch der Fugen-Komposition*[40]— in contrast to his occasional dry style. Naturally, "song" is meant metaphorically, not literally. The theme is liberally endowed with syncopation, with doublets and triplets, and obviously written for the clavier. As the work goes along, despite a tendency for the melody to stay in the upper voice, there is a good deal of motivic development, which serves to disguise the simple periodicity of the piece.[41]

For all its gallantry, the musical diction is not modern in the Italian or French style but graced with a delicate liveliness all Bach's own. One reflexively imagines the gestures of a ballerina, not dancing ballet of course but, all unnoticed, just dancing for herself.

The motivic link with the fugue is clear: its first theme answers the syncopated descending fourth that started the prelude with an ascending leap of a fourth that is no less expressive. F# – C# becomes C# – F#, to mention just one example.

Prelude and fugue are not polar opposites at all but siblings. Just as the prelude is not only "expression" but "structure" too, the fugue is likewise not only "structure" but "expression" too. What the observer notices first, of course, is the complicated structure. Bach has written—a rarity in itself—a triple fugue for three voices, and in a double sense: the three themes are treated separately, and then they are combined. The last four bars show how the three subjects enter one last time in exquisite timing—at half-measure intervals—finally to speak "with one voice":

The notes in small print blur the entries somewhat but cast a distinctive light on Bach's writing style: he is not showing off his fugal skills but composing a movement where we do not notice the skillfully wrought counterpoint and certainly not the artful construction of a triple fugue. Instead, we admire the combination of motivic density and rhythmic-melodic flow. Each of the three voices speaks clearly and eloquently throughout, with no voice just being a counterpoint to a more prominent one.[42] And yet all three are subordinated to the idea of an unstoppable, flowing river of sound.

There is no distinction between important and unimportant passages, little that is unthematic, barely a pause or an interlude, and no important break between individual expositions. The river of sound flows inexorably but with occasional change in intensity: imperceptibly, the syncopated, almost lingering movement of the first subject becomes merged with the regular striding pace of eighth notes, and these in turn give way to the rhythmic dotted eighths of the second subject. Finally, with the appearance of the third subject in the middle of the movement, in sixteenth notes, the definitive pulse of the piece takes over; but it does not obscure the previous rhythms, which continue.

Bach is composing with a consciousness of history: a sequence of different rhythmic forms was de rigueur for seventeenth-century fantasies and fugues like those of Samuel Scheidt's *Tabulatura nova*. But where these might be considered an assortment of excerpts, Bach ventures to meld heterogenous rhythmic forms "by skillful arrangement into an intellectual as well as a structural unity."[43] This is the realization of Bach's credo "All from one, all in one"; it is also "the idea of a collective melody from the merged parts of a polyphonic setting." In Carl Dahlhaus's view, this idea fascinated the nineteenth century and especially Richard Wagner, beyond the classic era of the sonata.[44]

In *The Well-Tempered Clavier*, Bach summed up all the genre traditions of keyboard music but also introduced new formal types. In view of their variety and nuance of expression, Arnfried Edler is reminded of the genre of the French "pièce de caractère." Not forgetting that practically every piece deals with a compositional problem sui generis, Edler arranged the preludes and fugues of both parts of *The Well-Tempered Clavier* by genre and type:[45]

Arnfried Edler's Arrangement of the Preludes and Fugues of *The Well-Tempered Clavier*

		Prelude			Fugue	
BWV	Key	Time	Genre Type		Time	Genre Type
PART I						
1. 846	C	C	arpeggio		C (4/4)	hexachord fugue
2. 847	c	C	figured prelude		C	dance fugue
3. 848	C#	3/8	dance prelude, minuet		C	*fuga incomposta*, theme made of jumps
4. 849	c#	6/4	aria		C	ricercar fugue
5. 850	D	C	figured prelude		C	*fuga pathetica*, French style
6. 851	d	C	figured prelude		3/4	*fuga composta*, theme in steps
7. 852	E♭	C	figure prelude with double fugue		C	dance fugue

BWV		Key	PRELUDE Time	Genre Type	FUGUE Time	Genre Type
8.	853	e♭/d#	3/2	aria pathetica	C	ricercar fugue
9.	854	E	12/8	dance prelude, siciliano	C	*fuga sciolta* (free fugue)
10.	855	e	C	aria/figured prelude	3/4	Invention
11.	856	F	12/8	dance prelude	3/8	dance fugue
12.	857	f	C	*präludium ligatum*	C	*fuga pathetica*
13.	858	F#	12/16	dance prelude	C	dance fugue
14.	859	f#	C	sinfonia	6/4	*fuga pathetica*
15.	860	G	24/16 C	figured prelude	6/8	dance fugue
16.	861	g	C	*präludium patheticum*	C	*fuga pathetica*
17.	862	A♭	3/4	concerto	C	*fuga pathetica*
18.	863	g#	6/8	sinfonia	C	*fuga pathetica*
19.	864	A	C	sinfonia	9/8	dance fugue
20.	865	a	9/8	concerto	C	*fuga ligata* (fugue without interludes)
21.	866	B♭	C	figured prelude	3/4	dance fugue
22.	867	bflat	C	*präludium patheticum*	C	ricercar fugue
23.	868	B	C	sinfonia	C	*fuga plagalis* (theme moves in scale steps)
24.	869	b	C	sonata	C	*fuga pathetica*
PART 2						
1.	870	C	C	sinfonia	2/4	dance fugue
2.	871	c	C	sonata	C	*fuga ligata*
3.	872	C#	C	arpeggio, canzonetta	C	*fuga composta*
4.	873	c#	9/8	sinfonia	12/16	dance fugue
5.	874	D	12/8	sonata	C	canzone fugue
6.	875	d	3/4	figured prelude	C	chromatic fugue
7.	876	E♭	9/8	dance prelude	C	ricercar fugue
8.	877	d#	C	sonata	C	canzone fugue
9.	878	E	3/4	(trio-)sonata	C	ricercar fugue
10.	879	e	3/8	sonata	C	dance fugue, gigue
11.	880	F	3/2	sinfonia	6/16	dance fugue, gigue

			PRELUDE		FUGUE	
BWV		Key	Time	Genre Type	Time	Genre Type
12.	881	f	2/4	sonata	2/4	canzone fugue
13.	882	F#	3/4	concerto, French style	C	dance fugue, gavotte
14.	883	f#	3/4	sinfonia	C	ricercar fugue, 3 themes
15.	884	G	3/4	dance prelude, saraband	3/8	dance fugue
16.	885	g	C	prelude, French style	3/4	canzone fugue
17.	886	A♭	3/4	*präludium patheticum*	C	*fuga pathetica*
18.	887	g#	C	sonata	6/8	dance fugue, 2 themes
19.	888	A	12/18	dance prelude	C	*fuga composta*
20.	889	a	C	sonata	C	*fuga pathetica*
21.	890	B♭	12/16	dance prelude	3/4	dance fugue
22.	891	bflat	C	sinfonia	3/2	ricercar fugue
23.	892	B	C	concerto	C	ricercar fugue
24.	893	b	C	concerto	3/8	dance fugue

A lowercase letter indicates a minor key.

A whole world lies between the first C-sharp-minor fugue, which treats a *soggetto* in the extremely limited range of a diminished fourth, in the ricercar tradition, and the first A-flat-major prelude, which translates the modern concerto's solo-tutti contrasts to the clavier. A movement like the first prelude in E-flat minor seems to stand outside any idea of old or new style—a profoundly meditative piece, on which Wagner remarked, at hearing it played by Josef Rubinstein in the winter of 1878–79, "I play that with even more 'moonlight'—with me, the twilight never ends."[46] Cosima Wagner's diary reveals that the master of Bayreuth did not judge the pieces of *The Well-Tempered Clavier* solely on the basis of their atmospherics but on their compositional methods as well. She records his comment on the next fugue, one of the most erudite, powerful fugues of the whole work: "R[ichard] considers the fugue that follows to be most remarkable; it is extremely skillful, and yet so emotional; 'what strettos, augmentations, and accents it has!' For him, it is the epitome of the fugue."[47]

The fugues are not all equally erudite. There are *concertante* and dance fugues; eleven fugues of part 1 have only three voices, and one has only two. Thus Hugo Riemann's designation of *The Well-Tempered Clavier* as part of a "compositional catechism" is not unproblematic.[48] It tempts one to see it too much in the context of, say, *The Art of Fugue* and too little in relation to roughly contemporaneous compositions in other genres, for example, the *Brandenburg Concertos* or the *St. John Passion*. Like these works, *The Well-Tempered Clavier* is part of a discourse on the compositional and semantic characteristics of a type of music that was very important to the society of the time.

The students of Bach who came in contact with *The Well-Tempered Clavier* must first have been awed by the wealth of forms, types, and emotions they contained; but they soon came to understand how actively Bach approached and further developed both traditional and contemporary forms of keyboard art and not just counterpoint alone.

The preludes should never be thought of as lesser works than the fugues. They are sui generis character pieces, very often developed independently of, and not simply as preludes to, the fugue following. Bach had not yet written sonatas for the keyboard; but the quantity of material from his preludes that reappears in the fast and slow sonata movements written by his sons would be shown by any study that included the preludes of part 2.[49] Surely Bach was looking for perspectives that went beyond his time.

When the Dresden kapellmeister Johann Christoph Schmidt in 1718 required that a fugue be constructed like speech and adopt elements of the *stile moderno,* he was applauded by Johann Mattheson, who gave Schmidt space in his journal *Critica musica* to express his ideas.[50] One can also look through the fugues of *The Well-Tempered Clavier* to see whether they are built on rhetorical models like *exordium-narratio-propositio,* and so on. Gerd Zacher examined the

E-flat-major fugue, part 1, from this angle.[51] Bach's modernity does not come from any superficial resemblance to rhetoric, however, but from a fundamentally new concept of instrumental music. In Stefan Kunze's view, *The Well-Tempered Clavier* speaks an instrumental language that is characterized by its "deeply involving, contemplative articulation."

At this point, the formulaic approach to playing that dominated older instrumental music must abdicate; in its place comes a melodicism that by its very nature is nourished by decidedly interpretive impulses, and so it has semantic connotations.[52] This does not mean interpreting a text with musical means—an art perfected by Heinrich Schütz. Rather, the particular vocal-instrumental language so typical of Bach, the character of which is derived from its articulation and nuance, can give music meaning even without the context of words.

We can observe this phenomenon right in the first fugue of *The Well-Tempered Clavier*. It is obvious at first glance that its theme is a traditional musical figure derived from the ascending hexachord. The quarter notes are seen as the standard note value; eighth and sixteenth notes become mere figuration. But then the eighth note, undervalued at first, forms the major value unit, and now every one of them has weight: the theme speaks. To be sure, the theme can no more be linked with any emotive affect than can the fugue derived from it, yet clearly the music means something, alludes to something. This something need not be specified; it is enough to notice the contemplative way in which it is articulated and to follow its interpretative impulse.

One reason that not only Wagner, but Mozart, Beethoven, Schubert, Robert and Clara Schumann, the two Mendelssohns, Chopin, Brahms, Debussy, Busoni, Hindemith, and many other composers were fascinated by *The Well-Tempered Clavier* is its ex-

traordinary combination of strictness and freedom. The work allows
the inclusion of various genres and styles, and actually brings out the
idiosyncratic nature of each, but binds them together into a higher
kind of thinking. I say "thinking," for the unifying plan of a complete
progression through all the keys is a thought-out idea; and only a
performance attuned to this idea, and the listener's awareness of it,
can realize the work in its universal context. Can we imagine Johann
Caspar Ferdinand Fischer excitedly performing his *Ariadne Musica*
for his students from beginning to end? Bach does just this with his
Well-Tempered Clavier, to demonstrate the theoretically inexhaustible
variety of sensations contained in this "didactic" music.

The *Well-Tempered Clavier* could be called the first self-contained
cycle in music history. Bach did not just concatenate works that were
typical of a genre; he fused together various types of works that
would have a higher meaning in context with each other. Thus, individual pieces, each one in itself a microcosm, are best understood
when presented in an ensemble where one element brings the
uniqueness of the other into focus, at the same time helping demonstrate the higher context of the group.

Cycles of this type, whose elements are neither arranged arbitrarily nor held together by a musical idea, are historically rarer than one
might think. The middle ground between strictness and freedom can
be found only through intense concentration on each single element.
Take Schubert's *Winterreise* as an example: in that work, the ensemble
of individual songs, each representing an entire world in itself, is still
subordinate to a higher idea imposed by the literary subject.

Although there are pieces in *The Well-Tempered Clavier* that are
either erudite or tend to the gallant, the characteristic dichotomy of
the two then current does not exist in Bach as such. We may classify
his clavier suites as gallant and *The Art of Fugue,* also for clavier, as
erudite, but the world of *The Well-Tempered Clavier* is not described
with such categories. Its characteristics are universal.

Universalism is *the* theme of the scholarly world in the baroque
era. From the beginning, that world looked for and found generalities; it "stretched out its arms to the entirety of knowledge and

accomplishment."[53] Interrelations were sought everywhere—for the one in the many, for the system that could tame the multitude of individual phenomena. Karl Joël dubbed the seventeenth century the "classic century of the rational state," the cradle of the idea that all personal impulses and particular interests have to be subordinate to the universal reason inherent in the state.[54]

This idea is not foreign to the arts. The music historian in particular comes across it in the titles of works in which the universal scholars of the age attempted to fit the entirety of music inside the entirety of the world: for instance, Johannes Kepler with his *Harmonices mundi Libri V* of 1619, Marin Mersenne with his *Harmonie Universelle* of 1636–37, and Athanasius Kircher with his *Musurgia Universalis* of 1650.

With Gottfried Wilhelm Leibniz the universalist idea comes to fullest flower. Leibniz no longer thinks in traditional mechanistic and mathematical categories. His "best of all possible worlds," possessing "the greatest possible diversity and at the same time the greatest possible order,"[55] is no longer identical with Kepler's universe. It allows for human individuality and thus is in a state of constant change. Even the single thing—the monad—is in motion: "its only permanence is that law itself, which by its nature implies constant change, and which in each discrete substance is in harmony with the collective law of the universe."[56]

The entire world is expressed in every monad. The world can be defined as a system of vibrations, each vibration completely subsumed in the system. "On the highest level, a monad produces perfect major-key harmony"—this is French structuralist Gilles Deleuze's paraphrase of Leibniz's ideas,[57] referring to an image Leibniz borrowed from music in a letter to Arnault of 30 April 1687, where he tried to explain why monads would be in universal harmony, even while being totally ignorant of each other. The monads are like choral singers who perform their parts without knowing the parts of the others, and still must sing in harmony according to the composer's plan.[58]

Such discourses about universal world order were well-known in Bach's era. Those involved in this discourse did not always know of each other or have any influence on each other. Bach and Leibniz, like two monads, may each have gone his own way, and left it to a later age to take note of their resonances. But note that the *Monadology* was published posthumously in 1720 and *The Well-Tempered Clavier* was completed in 1722: it is hard to imagine a better, if coincidental, timing.

Certainly the separate preludes and fugues of *The Well-Tempered Clavier* can be seen as "windowless" monads, leading lives uninfluenced by their surroundings yet created by God in such a way that they display a marvelously shared order—the "pre-established harmony of all substances."[59] Within their own unique compositional, historical, and semantic context, they stand as individual compositions, but each has a fixed place in a tonal system where the relations among the intervals are all defined by the universal constant $\sqrt{12}$, that is, the square root of twelve.

Bach succeeds brilliantly in creating a cycle that corresponds to Leibniz's concept of a universe of individual creations with the rubric "unity, but in unrestricted variety." The individual pairs of preludes and fugues take no notice of one another and are not connected as are, say, the separate contrapuntal works of *The Art of Fugue*. But in their inevitable and unmistakable positioning in the whole they bear witness to a universal order that can be experienced as a model of the order of life—on a human scale, not on a mathematical-planetary Keplerian scale. In this manner *The Well-Tempered Clavier* offers a wonderful glimpse of what Leibniz was struggling to attain in his philosophy.

It does not matter whether we emphasize the speculative or the didactic elements in the Cöthen demonstration cycles: in the end, Bach is giving us the universal essence of music. He does this inwardly and outwardly free of his office and his duties as kapellmeister: he can concentrate on the task at hand. Nevertheless, these works differ from the late Leipzig instrumental cycles: while the

Cöthen works accentuate the *variety* that can come out of a single musical idea, the cycles of the last years emphasize the spiritual *unity* of all musical creativity.

In what follows, it may seem strange to include the six solos for violin, BWV 1001–06, in the Cöthen demonstration cycles. But it would not be fitting to treat them like the solos for violoncello, solely as sonatas and suites. These violin pieces show Bach's speculative and didactic ambitions—though in a form that hardly seems made for this purpose.

The violin is not Bach's chosen instrument for teaching or demonstration cycles, but the autograph manuscripts of these works strongly suggest that he felt very much at ease with the instrument: he seems to have wanted to transcribe the violinist's bowing motion directly into notes on the page. It is rare that a composer writes notes that are calligraphically perfect and also communicate the feeling of the music at the same time. Melody and harmony in one—that is the message of the six solos, which constitute as well an encyclopedia of the violin: prelude, fugue, concerto, aria, variation, dance—all are performable on it.

The violin solos were noticed early on, not so much because they were unique in Bach's work as because they had a special quality. They are conspicuous in the surveys of Bach's music that have survived from the second half of the eighteenth century. The Prussian princess Anna Amalia personally obtained a copy of them in 1873 for her Bach collection. Music lovers of the nineteenth century thought them quite the equal of *The Well-Tempered Clavier,* and were particularly enamored of the chaconne from the D-minor partita, BWV 1004. Composers such as Felix Mendelssohn Bartholdy and Robert Schumann added a piano accompaniment to the violin voice, not as a sign that they lacked confidence in Bach's linear setting but more in an attempt to open the concert hall to his violin solos. Johannes Brahms should be accorded special recognition, for instead of making an arrangement of it, he played it almost note for note on the piano with the left hand, commenting, "the chaconne to me is one of the most wonderful, incomprehensible works of music. On one staff, for one small instrument, this man has written a whole world of profoundest thought and deepest feelings."[60]

This chaconne, with its variations, has become the most famous piece of the cycle. By invoking various kabbalistic ideas, the work has been read as a *tombeau* on the death of Maria Barbara Bach,[61] but this is speculative at best. The overall feeling is incomparable: Bach appears in these violin solos as a musician of the highest order—not for any hidden messages but because of the fantastic mixture of playfulness and profundity, laughter and tears, joy and melancholy.

Even less than in *The Well-Tempered Clavier*, cold, clear analysis cannot explain or even support such expressions of wonder and admiration. It remains one of the mysteries of Bach how, in music for the solo violin, he combines and distills spirituality and sensuality, abstraction and tonal fullness, and musical language that is both universal and contemporary to his age, to illustrate his principle of "all from one and all in one."

It is easier to describe the novelty of the concept. Certainly in the generation preceding Bach there were compositions for violin without accompaniment—for example, those of Heinrich Ignaz Franz Biber, Johann Jakob Walther, and Johann Paul von Westhoff.[62] The last named was employed at the Weimar court in 1703, at a time when the young Bach was also employed there briefly, and so he had the chance to know the famous violinist's suites for violin solo from the year 1696. Technically they are more advanced than Bach's violin solos,[63] which are more in the line of Biber's expressive violin style.

The six solos consist of three sonatas and three partitas. The former follow the form of the four-movement *sonata da chiesa* ("church sonata"), the latter contain dance movements in various combinations and sequences. The key sequence of the six parts—G minor, B minor, A minor, D minor, C major, and E major—has a clever symmetry that escapes one at first: two major thirds (G-B and C-E) are connected by a fourth (A-D) whose tones are respectively the mid tones of the two thirds.[64] Thus all six tones of the hexachord are represented, but in an order that corresponds to the alternation of sonatas and suites.

Bach mixes popular and academic in the violin solos. One popular element is his inclusion of dance steps in the partitas—particularly in the structure of the B-minor partita BWV 1002, where each dance is followed by a *double,* allowing the soloist to play in a style that is virtuosic and yet easy to follow. The academic side appears mostly in the fugues, which are the second movement of each sonata. A real fugue is not possible on a violin, but one can hear entries of *dux* (first) and *comes* (second), for example, and one can hear interludes. Bach presents similar ideas in incomparable style in the 354-bar-long concert fugue from the C-major sonata BWV 1005: here he is able to suggest something beyond the audible and in the process give the listener the sense of participating in the performance of a demanding fugue.

The real significance of the six violin solos is not their virtuosic play with many voices, though this does give them access to a great deal of structural energy. The palpable new dimension of the compositions is their coherence. A work composed by Bach cannot just be divided up into one-voice and multivoice sections; even in its original, basic form, the entire thing has a polyphonic structure. Where a two-, three-, or four-part harmony transitions into a homophonic section, the polyphony is still there, lending the section a multivalent richness.

The tonal space that the quadruple-stopped chords open up at the start of the B-minor partita BWV 1002 does not disappear when the music becomes homophonic; it continues to influence the work's structural details. The composer Nicolaus A. Huber has pointed out comparable writing methods in works of Anton Webern and Pierre

Boulez, expressing the view that the homophonic violin solos resemble a multilayered organism, where homophony and polyphony, harmonic layers and horizontal rows relate to one another artfully, even cryptically.[65]

The uninitiated listener does not register these connections consciously but nonetheless reacts to them intensely. Bach's desire, coiled like a spring, to present the whole essence of music with just a single violin and the performer's struggle to satisfy this desire have an almost superhuman dimension, and they increase the listener's aesthetic enjoyment of the work by infusing it with that sense of the demonic, which, for the ancients, was the echo of the divine.

It may have amused Bach to revise the thoroughly undemonic (indeed quite playful) prelude of the E-major Partita BWV 1006 to be used as the opening sinfonia of the *Ratswahl* Cantata "Wir danken dir, Gott, wir danken dir," BWV 29, in 1731. The new setting, lavishly scored with strings, oboes, concertizing organ, trumpets, and timpani, exhibits a totally different character, but at bottom it is the same. He may have been thinking that every piece of music should initially keep its riches for itself; but then, later, at the right time, it should be allowed to show them off to the outside world.

THE CONCERTOS

Among Bach's surviving instrumental concertos, some give off a special radiance, while others have a lesser reputation in the public mind. In the first group are the *Brandenburg Concertos,* BWV 1046–51, the violin concertos in E major, BWV 1042, and A minor, BWV 1041, the Concerto for Two Violins in D Minor, BWV 1043, and the Concerto for Two Claviers in C Major, BWV 1061. In the second group are primarily the clavier arrangements of lost concertos originally composed for melody instruments, BWV 1052, 1053, 1055, and 1056, as well as the Concerto for Flute, Violin, and Harpsichord in A Minor, BWV 1044, also based on an older model.

Though one might regret that the focus of concerto performances is just on the original works, there is a good side to that situation: concentration on ten works makes it easier to understand each of them as unique and independent. This is all the more important, since for generations of Bach scholarship there has been a persistent tendency to evaluate Bach's orchestra concertos by a single standard, which might generally be dubbed the Vivaldi concerto form. The extent to which Bach followed this standard—wholly, partly, or not at all—is surely worthy of renewed study. He cannot intervene in the debate, but he would probably want to set the record straight.

As a young man, he was fascinated by the possibilities of the new instrumental concerto style of Albinoni and Vivaldi—as a century earlier Heinrich Schütz had been fascinated by the then-current concerted vocal style of Monteverdi. And just as one could not forever judge the religious vocal concertos of the great Sagittarius (i.e., Schütz, since *Schütze* means "archer") on how much they retained of the Italian concerted style, neither would Bach want to be lumped together forever with Italian models. We must look elsewhere to find that great "musical perfection" that Meister Birnbaum credited him with in 1738.

Having no intention to measure Bach's concertos on an imaginary model and recognizing their particular uniqueness, we begin with the *Brandenburg Concertos*. In gathering six concertos into a collection, Bach is following a convention but at the same time consciously privileging heterogeneity over formal unity. The publishers of his era are pleased when they can print music that was homogeneous in both orchestration and style, thus easier to learn and more salable, but Bach is looking for variety. He wants to explore, in the words of Nikolaus Forkel, what "can be done with many parts and few parts" in the realm of ensemble music. The intended audience for this demonstration is not his kapellmeister colleague at Brandenburg or even the dedicatee, the Margrave of Brandenburg himself: Bach is writing for the artistic world in general.

Compared with what was to come, the artistic world of Bach's time was small, so it is not surprising that there is no evidence of performances of the *Brandenburg Concertos* outside his immediate sphere. He could broaden the reach of his exceptional clavier and violin cycles through his students, but that possibility did not exist for orchestral music. Thus the *Brandenburg Concertos* remained, until long after his death, at most a topic for discussion among the initiated—discussion on the master's view of what an ensemble concerto should be.

At first glance it looks as if Bach's ensemble concertos did not come into bloom one by one but all together as a mixed bouquet—or is it pure coincidence that they and not the instrumental concertos form a closed, coherent collection? The instrumental ensembles of the concertos each have an individual quality to them: only when one takes a collective look at all six does it become clear that Bach has taken the sound of each instrument into consideration: recorder, flute, oboe, bassoon, trumpet, horn, violino piccolo, violin, viola, violoncello, violone, viola da gamba, harpsichord. This list includes most but not all the instruments known to his age—there are no trombones, for instance. Viewing the six concertos as a whole, he wields his *instrumentarium* as if it were multiply combined registrations of an organ, whose spectrum of sound is to be made visible in all its facets. It is the harmonious combination of the ensemble, and the way in which the sounds are arranged, that gives value and meaning to the timbres of the individual instruments.

Bach does not apply a rigid methodicism in this but aims more for a variety of tonal experience. The third and the sixth concerto are written for homogenous string ensembles with an expectably unified tonal color in various levels and nuances. The first two concertos, in contrast, have a colorful orchestration: the first is reminiscent of courtly ritual, and the second makes one think of the "tonal fantasy and concert form of the town pipers."[1] The orchestration of the fourth and fifth concertos lies between the tonal ideals of homogeneity and variety; in overall feeling, it approaches the courtly or gallant idea of a concerto.

Three of the middle movements show the close proximity of the *Brandenburg Concertos* to chamber music and the sonata. In the second concerto, recorders, oboe, and violins join the continuo; in the fifth, there are flutes, violins, and a concertizing harpsichord; and in the sixth, there are two violas and a cello line, whose livelier figuration contrasts with the continuo.

There is no lack of unusual instruments, exquisite tonal combinations, and difficult parts. The first concerto requires the violino piccolo to play a kind of dancing-master violin part. In the second concerto, the combination of recorder and trumpet is unusual: according to Johann Mattheson, a "practiced master" is needed to keep "a *flute douce* or other gentle *Instrument* from being drowned out by the trumpet."[2] The trumpet part is of the greatest difficulty: even at Leipzig, where Bach had a splendid trumpeter in the person of Johann Gottfried Reiche at his disposal, he never wrote another trumpet part of comparable difficulty.

In the fourth concerto, what is meant by the mysterious term "Fiauti d'echo," unique in Bach's work and very unusual in the works of the time? A recorder, one imagines—but in the second concerto, and elsewhere generally, Bach calls this instrument "flauto." In the second movement of the fourth concerto, the "fiauti d'echo" are asked to provide a constant alternation between forte and piano. Perhaps this way of writing explains the name of the instrument. It has also been suggested that he was thinking of two F sopranino instruments[3] or even of double flutes, whose two pipes would be suitable for switching from loud to soft playing.[4]

In the fifth concerto, two more instruments get their chance: the transverse flute, having just been introduced to the music world in 1717, when this concerto may first have been written, and the harpsichord as a concertizing instrument—a novelty as well. The violas da gamba in the sixth concerto are not as lucky: their challenge is to be background to the violas, an instrument not usually favored with solo parts. This arrangement is all the more astonishing, considering that Prince Leopold of Cöthen himself played the viola da gamba. Michael Marissen is of the opinion that Bach, in the context of an imagined conversation with his princely superior, was consciously, cleverly playing with these social roles.[5]

In contrast, Peter Schleuning wishes to see the movements of the Sixth Brandenburg Concerto as a "sequence of pastoral scenes," and in this special context to interpret the violas as "symbols of social inferiority," that is, as peasants' music.[6] An argument against both these theories is the fact that in Protestant church music before Bach's time, orchestrations like those of the Sixth Brandenburg Concerto were not unusual.[7]

There have been attempts to interpret the whole series of *Brandenburg Concertos* allegorically. In 1991 Philip Pickett offered the view that with these concertos Bach was paying homage to the margrave as a "classical hero" and saw the series as a "musical triumphal procession...in its structure and its content comparable to those allegorical marches, parades, acrobatics and festivals which used to be staged on important state occasions." In this interpretation, the concertos are given headings: "The Triumph of Caesar," "Fame, Homer, Virgil, and Dante on Parnassus," "The Nine Muses and the Harmony of the Spheres," "The Musical Contest of Apollo and Marsyas," "The Choice of Hercules," and "The Meeting of the Three Living with the Three Dead."[8]

Picking up on Reinhard Goebel's idea, Karl Böhmer introduced an idea that he thought more persuasive: that the concertos constitute an "allegorical illustration" derived from the "decorative program of baroque Residences." Without trying to take up a direct "reconstruction of Bach's compositional idea" or to explain "every detail in the course of the piece," he attempts to demonstrate "why Bach selected precisely these six concertos in praise of a baroque prince, and how and where this prince and his courtly society are represented in the music." Böhmer titles the six concertos, respectively, "The Prince as Hunter," "The Prince as Hero," "The Prince of the Muses," "The Prince as Shepherd," "The Prince as Lover," and "The Prince as Scholar."[9]

The guild of musicologists and the smaller guild of Bach scholars collectively pull a long face when asked to consider such (in their view) unserious excursions into the realm of fantasy. First, there is no evidence for any of it; second, readings like these shift the discussion of Bach's music from the fields of "pure" analysis into that of cultural and reception history and even everyday history. But whoever looks at music from a reception point of view will not find it odd that a courtly society perceived this ceremonial music, composed in its honor, very much as it viewed the Gobelins and portraits that hung in the concert hall, or the marble and sandstone sculptures that ornamented the palace garden.

There does exist evidence of specific ways of performing sonatas or suites in series. In the front of a deluxe edition of violin sonatas from the last third of the seventeenth century, by Heinrich Ignaz Biber, are copper engravings that offer a commentary on the fifteen mysteries in the life of the Virgin Mary. The set of ballet suites under the title *Florilegium* by Georg Muffat, published in 1695, bear the names of the virtues personified, such as Eusebia, Sperantis Gaudia, Gratitudo. Muffat's instrumental concertos from 1701 carry headings such as "Cor Vigilans," "Dulce Somnium," "Deliciae Regum," "Delirium Amoris," and so on. Dietrich Buxtehude composed a cycle, now lost, of seven clavier suites on the nature and qualities of the planets.

Those among the nobility who not only loved music but also played it themselves may occasionally have taken an interest in their kapellmeister's writing style and discussed, for example, to what degree he was conforming to more modern Italian or French tastes. As a rule, however, if they discussed music at all, those at court were probably more concerned with questions of instrumentation or interpretation.

At this point we have probably shown enough tolerance for theories that seek to place the *Brandenburg Concertos* in an emblematic context. For one thing, each concerto has its own history, so that such a theory can have traction only to the extent that it addresses the arrangement of the whole series. For another, the series has its own autonomous conception: as in his other important cycles, Bach is primarily concerned with making an unmistakable contribution to a historically developed musical imprint. The word "imprint" here mediates among categories such as genre, style, form, and compositional method; it is meant to address the way that music appears at a particular historical moment and in a specific social setting.

The *Konzert*—even the name has a double meaning—could function in this way as an "imprint," and the ensemble concerto more so. On the topic of ensemble concertos, Bach wants to say with his *Brandenburg Concertos* what in his view needs to be said. He reveals himself as a composer who is conscious of history, who confronts the present, and who at the same time is interested in systematically exploring all the compositional possibilities. It is more a virtue than a necessity that the cycle combines concertos from different creative periods. It is both a work in progress and a depiction of personal development.

Bach succeeded in creating a series unique in music history, which not even Telemann's *Musique de table* can approach. On the one hand, it is a comprehensible music that the senses can appreciate and that to this day can be considered a model of baroque classicism—concertos for amateurs of the art. On the other hand, this is music for the cognoscenti, for Bach is summing up. Particularly in the first, third, and sixth concertos he conjures up the spirit of traditional German ensemble musicianship influenced by the *stylus phantasticus*, which allowed the "transformation of conventional musical forms into unconventional variants."[10] He knows well how to use the modern, clear Italian concerto form, known simply as the Vivaldi style; it became a matter of pride with him never to repeat a form in the concertos but always to introduce a new one for group performance. In the process he invented thematic figures and forms of motivic development that anticipate most of all the "classical style" of Austro-German provenance.[11]

What these two different ages of music making have in common is the definition of the categories "composition" and "work." In the aesthetic view of Viennese classicism, music should be flowing, natural, and based in song, dance, or some other social entertainment form, and so take its shape from the human concept of grace. But at the same time its intrinsic worth should develop from its inherent possibilities—that is, it should represent a higher meaning. As Goethe put it, a Haydn string quartet could be seen as a conversation between four intelligent people,[12] or a Beethoven symphony, in a contemporary review, as a "Pindaric ode."[13] But Haydn's quartets and Beethoven's symphonies can be seen as attempts to build musical structure through the use of motivic-thematic development and variations; thus they allow the self-referential nature of the system to operate on an elevated, reflective plane.

To what extent the *Brandenburg Concertos* point the way to the compositional styles of Viennese classicism is not the issue; they laid the way for *the* music discourse of the classic-Romantic era. Bach's series of works for keyboard instruments or solo violin, and the sonatas, have an indirect connection here as well. But the all-important orchestral understanding of music and composition crucial to further development was advanced most of all by the *Brandenburg Concertos*, although naturally also by the great opening movements of Bach's passions and cantatas.

With all due respect for the *concertante* final fugue sections of the second, fourth, and fifth concertos, it is in the opening movements of the *Brandenburg Concertos* that the motivic-thematic work achieves a density, a critical mass from which proceeded Viennese classicism's sonata-form first movement in the true meaning of the term. They become the crystallization point for working out motifs, thematic process, and dynamic development and thus are paradigmatic of the individual and social undertakings of idealism in general.

The motivic material giving rise to all this is unassuming. Apart from the opening ritornello of the fifth concerto, which picks up the dramatic gesture of the Italian concerto form, and the thematically sophisticated exposition of the fourth concerto, Bach is essentially reverting to simple material that is transparently derived from seventeenth-century musical figures. Commonalities in the concertos' motivic materials are continually being construed by critics, most recently by Michael Talbot, but these are easily explained[14] by the fact that instrumental music of the seventeenth century repeatedly worked with the same simple figurations: with runs, broken triads, variations on a main note, and so on. In this kind of music, an original *inventio* was less important than a clever and variation-filled *elaboratio*.

The multiple ensembles of the opening movement of the third concerto find a precedent in the German tradition of the seventeenth and early eighteenth centuries: a sonata of David Pohle for eight strings survives, composed perhaps as early as 1660; sonatas with two and three separate instrumental ensembles by Johann Philipp Krieger, Johann Pachelbel, and Johann Michael Bach, among others, are documented but have not survived.[15] A glance at the instrumental chorale transcription "Gelobet seist du, Jesu Christ" from Samuel Scheidt's *Tabulatura Nova* of 1624 reveals that even the motivic work of the third concerto has its roots in the figurative practices of the seventeenth century: the compositional influence of Scheidt's work extended beyond the *Orgelbüchlein*! Examples closer in time to Bach's ensemble music can be found in Buxtehude's sonatas for violins and viola da gamba, the first set of which came out in 1696.

By including, as late as 1721, in his series of ensemble concertos a work that reflects the formal principles of traditional multipart ensemble music and that exhibits aspects of seventeenth-century-style thematic work, Bach reveals himself as a composer who is both conscious of history and highly reflective. The German tradition of ensemble playing is not to become lost in the excitement of enthusiasm for the modern Italian concerto style. Yet the Italian style turns up everywhere: even in the large-scale harmonic arrangement of the piece, the new structural pattern arising from the opposition of ritornello and episode, tutti and solo, is evident. The themes are not simply figurative in the seventeenth-century sense but oriented around the constructive thinking of the Italians. Like all the other first movements of the *Brandenburg Concertos*, this one too is defined by an opening ritornello divided into a prologue, a continuation, and a cadence. As the movement progresses, the ritornello becomes an important element in ordering the work.

Most interesting of all here are the specifics of this movement, as revealed even in the structure of the ritornello: it is neither simply an initial figure in seventeenth-century tradition nor—as in other Bach concertos—a complete exposition. Rather, it defines a course for the piece that, though hardly unthematic, is mostly driven by form. Its primary energy flows from the *figura corta*, as it is called in music theory,[16] here an anapest of two sixteenths and an eighth.

This movement bears out what Johann Matthias Gesner wrote in 1738 of his former colleague Bach, that is, he was a "homo membris omnibus rhythmicus"[17] or "a man attuned to rhythm in all his parts." More than any other of Bach's concerto movements, it is propelled throughout by the opening rhythmic impulse. It almost makes one think of Beethoven's Fifth Symphony, with its characteristic rhythm based on the opening knocking motif: not only are there the typically Bachian ritardandos and intensifications of sound before the entry of the final ritornello, the whole movement tends toward a development that anticipates Viennese classicism.

First we should note that the ritornello alternates between performing individual motifs in isolation and playing them in all voices at once. Distinctive renderings of single motifs, which are strongly brought out by the three separate ensembles, are followed each time by passages that bring them all together. Each complementary event increases the listener's sense of taking part in a process of accumulating energy and discovering patterns, a process that is "moving" in both senses of the word. Understood in this way, the final entry of the ritornello is not just mere da capo or recapitulation but a victory after long struggle—to use, for once, one of the literal meanings of the word *concerto*.

Another element recalls the first movement of Beethoven's Fifth: just before the reprise, a final solo cadence of the oboe articulates the subject's protest against the uncompromising nature of the thematic-motivic process, though ultimately it is absorbed into the whole. In the Third Brandenburg Concerto, the comparable moment is the entry of the first and only purely melodic idea, which appears following the ritornello ending in B minor in bar 78 in a renewal of the G-major key:

It is not enough simply to explain this idea as a derivation from the viola counterpoint to the ritornello theme or—taking the movement as a well-made rhetorical discourse—as an entry of the *confirmatio*,[18] which according to Johann Mattheson means "the artful reinforcement of the argument."[19] Starting in whole beats and ascending to the tenth of the G-major chord, it seems to offer opposition to the ritornello theme, which nonetheless retains the upper hand. Indeed, this little melodic glimpse of light emphasizes the ritornello even more—for example toward the end, where a figure derived from the ritornello rummages in the basses, venturing powerful melodic thrusts from low to high, and where the violin and viola ensembles sound the anapest figure with ever more intensity.[20] Similarly, François Florand writes that in the *Brandenburg Concertos* Bach

> *brings about a progression that proceeds organically out of the melodic flow, much like a river that seems to increase in size without any apparent outward cause, without glaciers or rainstorms, but solely from the inflow of mysterious underground springs. It is a process peculiar to Bach alone and is based on a pent-up internal reserve of power and effervescent energy, carried to the point where both creator and listener become sated, almost intoxicated, where the twisting and turning of the motif alone seems to have confused even the creator himself.*[21]

Comparing the Third Brandenburg's first movement with the opening movement of Beethoven's Fifth might be seen as a reaction against the tendency mentioned at the beginning of this chapter, namely, the analyses of Bach's concerto movements that piously tick off the different tutti and solo episodes or note how the motifs are developed but say nothing about the structure and spirit of the music.

It is impossible to get a sense of either from the viewpoint of Telemann or Vivaldi. The structural imagination of both these composers should not be underestimated, but much separates them from Bach's vision. For Bach, the concerto form is an idea constantly being refashioned. In these works, the dialectical meeting of form and content in a higher entity is conceived of for the first time from an orchestral perspective. The "accumulation of harmonic, chordal, and motivic effects" that Walther Vetter noted at the end of the movement, even though it is executed by eleven soloists, still sounds orchestral.[22] Bach had already learned how to mass ever larger numbers of instrumental voices yet by subtle composition techniques keep them clearly perceptible to the ear and, in so doing, make the listener also sensitive to the "unheard of" quality of the final climax.

The effect of these voices comes essentially from the decision not to follow any conventions in this setting for nine stringed instruments but to keep the desired tonal structure in mind. Since this decision applies to the entire movement, in fact to the whole work, it points even beyond Viennese classicism, recalling Wagner's invention of his eponymous tuba solely for the purpose of conjuring up Valhalla.

After a Phrygian cadence embracing only two chords, there follows a relatively short (48 bars) final allegro in the 12/8 meter of the gigue—the only known concerto movement of Bach to be composed in binary form. Has there been enough thought devoted to the question of why there is no slow middle section? Ultimately, we must place a question mark after Emil Platen's original suggestion that we imagine, instead, a 13-bar quasi-improvisatory group cadence:[23] if Bach had intended this, he would likely have left some indication in the dedication copy of the score as to how such a cadence was to be executed.

Ulrich Siegele, who has made a study of proportion as a compositional guide in Bach's concertos, pursues the idea that the outer movements of the concerto were originally planned for 2 × 48 bars, and the middle movement for 48; expansions in the first movement would then have largely eaten up the time planned for the middle.[24] While this idea may strike some as facile, since it comes from a speculation about the original plan of the work, it jibes with another observation: judged by the standard of the baroque ensemble concerto, the opening movement of the Third Brandenburg Concerto is a work of such concentration and discipline that it seems justifiable to follow it with a little treat, a dancelike, simple, if still imitatively worked-out refrain.

But are the first movements of the other concertos, which do contain middle sections, structured any more simply or worked out any less subtly? One would have to say no, while noting completely different solutions in each case. The opening movement of the first concerto, for instance, is enlivened by the tension between self-referential structural style and genre piece style. The whole work, which went through several stages before its final version was complete (and which even then cannot conceal its essential divertimento character), probably was written to accommodate the abilities of everyday court musicians. This is hinted at by the prevalence of oboes and horns in the scoring: in the *Residenz* courts of the eighteenth century, the players of these instruments, members of the "Hautboiste-Band," commanded comparatively little respect and did not perform chamber music; they played only for ceremonial and social occasions.[25] Johann Mattheson lamented in 1725 that "almost every one-horse Grand Seigneur and every Village Despot not only requires at least a pair of violons (basses), oboes, cors de chasse, etc. in his retinue but that the musicians wear year-round livery, polished shoes, powdered wigs, stand behind the coach, and receive the wages of a lackey and housing as well."[26]

This concerto's close proximity to everyday music making becomes evident, by the end of the concerto if not sooner, when oboes and bassoon or horns and an oboe tutti enter as a separate ensemble and, alone or with the strings, strike up a dance: we can actually hear musicians playing for a hunt banquet. The sounds of corni da caccia (hunting horns) and oboes were intended at least in part to sound this way. Beneath the obviously original caption "Grußruf mit Halali"[27] [*Halali* is hunting jargon for a horn flourish] Bach has written music for a horn call that is quite similar to the horn passages from the First Brandenburg Concerto:

Even if we leave open the question of whether Bach is imitating actual hunting calls, we can certainly assume that the two horn motifs are a concrete reference to the theme of the hunt and not just to ceremony in general. The opening sixth chord trill of the oboes both enriches the sound and accompanies the hunting scene. In Peter Schleuning's opinion, the whole section is a riding to hounds: "No painter could have brought the scene more vividly to canvas."[28]

"The entry [of the natural horns] into the intimate sphere of serious music must have been a sensation," Nikolaus Harnoncourt suspects.[29] But the idea that Bach would dedicate the first of the concertos to a hunt-loving prince, as a reflection of courtly life, is not so outlandish; therefore Schleuning's expansion on his idea is worthy of consideration: that the slow movement, characterized throughout by tones of deep sorrow and sharp dissonances, must have a programmatic background, offering perhaps a commentary on the suffering of the hunted prey. For all this, it should not be forgotten that any programmatic intent in the First Brandenburg, if one concedes its existence in the first place, is in sharp contrast to its structure.

Bach is by no means writing a hunt concerto, where everything is aimed at a pleasant rendering of blaring hunting horns and reedy shawms. With the first two movements he is instead introducing musically autonomous forms, into which associative elements are inserted like emblems: a particularly well-crafted art, meant for the cognoscenti. The horn calls alone do not, after all, really fit into the movement so easily as they often seem to in many an unthinkingly overpolished performance or recording. On the contrary, they sound clumsy, almost alien. Bach seems to want to prove to the court that integrating hunting horns into a chamber music ensemble can produce a work of art.

The music reveals a highly sophisticated familiarity with the concerto principle. Motivically and thematically, the first movement is not as subtle as the opening movement of the third concerto. But in the arrangement of its sections it is wildly creative, though not completely without order. Even the twelve-bar opening section is too complicated to be called a ritornello, and as the movement goes along, one cannot really distinguish tuttis from solos or ritornellos from episodes. For this reason, the six sections have been called six strophes,[30] but this designation does not take the work's overall structure into account. The structure is not readily perceptible, keeping the listener more or less in a state of permanent tension, but this tension is more or less a trademark of Bach's Weimar years, when the early version of the concerto, BWV 1046a, probably was written.

Let us now examine a contrapuntal argument. In the opening movements of the first, third, and sixth concertos, there are evident elements of the *stylus phantasticus,* which we know played an important role in Buxtehude's ensemble music.[31] But in the opening of the second concerto Bach gives a downright classical clarity to the balance between the individual parts and the work as a whole. Two-bar segments, sometimes slightly extended, are set together like building blocks, being combined to give the sense of a readily perceptible, largely symmetrical "choreography" of instruments.[32] He obtains almost kaleidoscopic variations through constant tonal changes and ends in a colorful unison. There are few elements of intentional confusion, and the musical equivalents of climax or drama are used sparingly. As Klaus Hofmann argues, there may have been an early version of this concerto *senza ripieno* (without full orchestra),[33] and this seems plausible from a structural viewpoint too: the four soloists, sufficient unto themselves, provide for one another an adequate mixture of tonal color.

While the distinction between ritornello and episode is clear in the second concerto, it is much less obvious in the opening movement of the fourth. Can the extended framing section, identical at beginning and end, even be called a ritornello? The eighty-three bars at the top are more an exposition, which "sets the scene with tension and excitement,"[34] brings about complex reactions in the rest of the section, and leads inevitably to a reprise at the end. In yet another way Bach is playing with the concerto movement model.

This time, the key instruments are the two recorders: they, not the ripieno strings, carry most of the thematic material. They also mediate between the ripieno and the concertizing violin, which has a demanding solo part, though not at a breakneck Vivaldi-like tempo. Bach seems to want to profile the solo violin; but he runs the risk of ending up with a virtuosic but structurally uninteresting piece by the insertion of some astonishing motivic-thematic and tonal subtleties in what at first glance is a nondescript flute duo. As the movement progresses, the violin undergoes a transformation: after its first two solos, consisting of virtuosic but unthematic runs, it takes part in the motivic-thematic process.

Perhaps Bach has reached the high point of his instrumental ensemble writing here, with a movement that meets two requirements at once: first, it should have the lucidity, liveliness, facility, and song-like articulation of a concerto, virtues that his contemporaries prized in Telemann; second, it must be limited to a few motivic-thematic idioms, must be densely contrapuntal, and, "by employing many parts and expanding individual sections in different ways," must be large in scale and varied in form.[35] In other words, the newly gained ability to write original, understandable upper-voice settings with natural articulation and phrasing can now be coupled with the centuries-old skill of working out structurally balanced and complex vocal settings or instrumental cantus firmus adaptations.

The high level of Bach's achievement in this and other aspects of the Fourth Brandenburg Concerto can be demonstrated by an arbitrary yet instructive comparison with Telemann's Concerto in E Minor for Two Flutes, the solo violin and string ripieno. The Telemann is not merely pleasant to listen to but also solidly worked out—the second movement even has occasional double counterpoint—yet it has no trace of Bach's multiple perspective and historical reflectivity. This first movement of the Fourth Brandenburg Concerto is a harbinger of the sinfonia *concertante,* not in the detail of its composition but surely in the way it brings together the two styles of the learned and the gallant.

The best evidence of this are the central measures 185–208, where both the virtuosic violin playing and the intensity with which the recorders and ripieno strings work out the motif and themes are taken to new heights. The splitting off of individual motifs, which Ernst Kurth noted in Bach's music generally, is not employed here for its own sake;[36] on the contrary, their progressive shortening and the manner in which they chase each other create a "strong inner accelerando"[37] and significantly increase the musical effect.

It is possible that Bach was put off by the strict Italian concerto form's simplicity, even as he acknowledged its usefulness in large-scale forms. If so, then every instrumental concerto must have seemed a renewed challenge to him, or arduous, if rewarding, toil. In any event, with the fifth concerto he is writing one more chapter in his ongoing discourse with the concerto form, by bringing together elements that no one else thought of bringing together: intimate solo keyboard performance with *concertante* ensemble playing.

The clavier itself shows that these opposites are to be reconciled. Although it must perform the continuo function—in the ritornello and elsewhere—it is split stylistically. First it is part of the concertino, to which the flute and violin also belong. Bach takes care with this concertino, distinguishing it more from the tutti than in other concertos. In this formal sense the first movement of the fifth concerto has the greatest degree of Italian clarity: the tutti are given the job of presenting the robust, eight-bar ritornello, with a theme quite typical of the period, and presenting it again at the proper moment. Of all the Brandenburg Concerto ritornellos, it is best suited to bring out the "modern, energized sound of the Italian-French string orchestra."[38]

The parts where the tutti accompany the concertino, on the other hand, are less motivic and not interwoven with it as much as in other concertos of the series; they serve mostly as a foil to the chamber music–like filigree of the flute, violin, and harpsichord. The charm of the scoring is partly that it anticipates the modern piano trio: the harpsichord is not just one voice, as in later transcriptions of solo concertos, but a complete harmonic setting. To meld the right- and left-hand clavier parts with the cantabile lines of flute and violin is a tricky business, accomplished in this concerto by a delicate combination of motifs and tonal effects.

The clavier's quasi–chamber music function is overlaid with the virtuosic: right at the start, the keyboard performer introduces elements of the toccata fantasia, which return triumphantly as a cadenza before the beginning of the final ritornello. While this cadenza took only a modest eighteen bars in the early version, BWV 1050a, the expanded later version contains a sixty-five-bar cadenza, apparently inserted into the dedicatory copy at the last minute, a showy climax that is the high point of the whole movement. In historical terms, surely we can speak of the "first foray in the direction of the piano concerto."[39]

Such cadenzas were popular in Italy. The German traveler and amateur violinist Johann Friedrich Armand von Uffenbach wrote from Venice in February 1715 on the performance of a violin concerto:

> *Toward the end Signor Vivaldi played an* accompagnement *solo admirably, to which he finally appended a Phantasie which quite frightened me, for it is impossible that ever its like was played before, or will be played again, for his fingers came within a straw's width of the bridge, so there was no room for the bow, and that on all four strings with fugues and a speed that was unbelievable.*[40]

In Germany such wizardry was more often than not met with disapproval. In his early autobiography from 1718, Telemann writes of the Italian violin concertos, finding in them "many difficulties and awkward jumps but little harmony and even worse melody."[41]

In the *Brandenburg Concertos,* Bach wishes to show his skill. Already famous as a keyboard virtuoso, he chooses his turf. He probably knew that the expanded cadenza would substantially alter the whole movement. Listening to the new version, it is difficult to decide whether one is hearing an ensemble or a virtuoso piece. The composer is no longer *primus inter pares* in an ensemble but a keyboard artist who uses the cadenza to summarize and reflect on the ideas the ensemble has already expressed; then, on his own, he ends the piece with a bravura musical feat on his chosen instrument. Heinrich Besseler viewed the fifth as the most modern of the *Brandenburg Concertos*—the one furthest along the path toward an artistic form that encourages identification in the individual listener.[42] But Bach did not walk this path in a straight line, nor did he walk this path exclusively.

In the second movement, the harpsichordist who played so brilliantly in the first movement is not above playing long stretches as an accompanist in a *concertante* trio sonata where the flute and violin take the melody. But he also does his part as a soloist in realizing a movement that is light and airy in structure, yet highly concentrated in motif and thematics.

The dancelike final fugue is more compact even than that of the fourth concerto. Bach gives us a flawless da capo form, but he derives the motivic material almost totally from the opening theme. There are quite distinctive solo passages for flute and violin. Pieter Dirksen, who has identified them as being in the French style, compares the movement with the fugal central part of a French overture, but also finds Italian elements in the middle section's gallant theme,[43] which Bach expressly marked "cantabile." All in all, in the Fifth Brandenburg Concerto, Bach shows himself in an elegant, worldly, and virtuosic light.

Is there no second violin part in the ripieno, because, as Siegbert Rampe assumes, Prince Leopold of Cöthen traveled with only six chamber musicians but still wanted to be the star of a concerto?[44] Or should we follow Dirksen's thinking, that Bach wanted to present this work at the Dresden court in 1717, for a competition with Louis Marchand (which never took place)?[45]

We have inadvertently arrived at a discussion of chronology, the current state of which is outlined here: most Bach scholars think that an early form of the first concerto may have been written in 1716, in the context of a performance of the very similarly scored *Hunt Cantata*, BWV 208, for the court at Weißenfels, although Michael Marissen rejects the thesis that the first movement served as the cantata's overture.[46] The third movement, with its solo violino piccolo, which was added later, could have been taken from a vocal concerto movement from the Cöthen period, which Bach adapted a third time in Leipzig, with new text, to become the head movement of the cantata "Vereinigte Zwietracht der wechselnden Saiten," BWV 207 ("United Division of Strings Ever Changing").[47]

The existence of an early version (*senza ripieno*) of the second concerto is not in doubt, although at present there are no ideas as to its date. The third concerto is also hard to date on stylistic grounds; but there are source-research reasons to date it before 1715—reasons that can be refuted only by positing a hypothetical intermediary source: in a Leipzig original manuscript, the adaptation of the first movement for use in the cantata, "Ich liebe den Höchsten von ganzem Gemüte," exhibits peculiarities of notation that Bach stopped using around 1715.

There are no recent chronological theories on the fourth concerto; an early version of the fifth, as mentioned above, has been dated to 1717. This leaves the sixth. The last concerto to be entered into the dedicatory score of 1721 is not without a prehistory: Bach took the middle movement from another work.[48] The concerto shows the spirit of the German ensemble tradition but exhibits a high degree of artifice in its composition and is thus not necessarily of early origin.

The tonal colors are noticeably dark, although clearly not meant to be somber; they do not prevent the liveliness of the first movement or the cheerfulness of the last. The sixth concerto could be called the sister of the third. Both are scored purely for strings, have the opposition of figure and tonal surface, and play with short motifs, especially the *figura corta*. But if the third concerto generally seems composed alfresco, the sixth has a chamber music–like filigree and more sophisticated sound effects. The ritornello at the opening of the third concerto, though not in unison, proceeds with a maximum of order and unity, while the ritornello at the start of the sixth is performed by a pair of violas linked in strict canon—and this above an ostinato figure in the continuo, a tonal flow of repeated single tones in the violas da gamba and bass.

The musical impression of the opening dominates the entire movement. During the episodes, even though the material is skillfully elaborated and combined, the listener is waiting for the next entry of the violas in canon, over the stamping ostinato figure. In the first movement of the third concerto, the dynamic force gets more intense throughout, but in the sixth it lets up during the episodes, which are largely free of the gravitational pull of the continuo, which then returns immediately after each episode. As with the third, Bach's instrumentation in the sixth is admirable, having a philosophical quality, particularly in the extreme combinations of instrumental sounds: not superficially tasteful or fantastic, they reach into ever more deeply felt layers of sound, corresponding to ever deeper levels of psychological experience.

The *Brandenburg Concertos* could be understood as an active coming to terms with the newest Italian orchestral writing; they are at once a tribute to it and a turning away from it. Bach is taking on not the Corelli concerto grosso here, as in the received tradition of Handel and Telemann, but the Vivaldi-style concerto. Of course, even this style offers no immediate stimulus to the earnest, reflective composing style that he preferred, no motivic thematic work on the level that we find in these *Brandenburg Concertos*. He always goes above and beyond his models.

The three surviving violin concertos offer a different picture. While they are not a reflection of the Italian style either, they do start from the viewpoint that the newer Italian solo concerto is an established, recognized musical genre. Bach does not adopt the virtuosic extremes of the Italian model, nor does he abandon his inclination toward a style that combines expressive delivery with his meticulous development of themes and complexity of form.

He is no longer concerned with theoretical discussions of concerto principles but is applying them in his own way—formally, classically, in a manner far removed from his youthful "wild ways"— Forkel's phrase describing Bach's early compositions.[49] The question must remain open as to whether the small corpus of violin concertos dates entirely from a period later than the *Brandenburg Concertos*. One can try to locate the roots of the *Brandenburg Concertos* in Weimar and of the major violin concertos in Cöthen or even Leipzig, but these guesses are as vague as they are rough. On the other hand, it is clear that their different orchestrations play a major role in the stylistic differences: a solo concerto follows rules different from those of an ensemble concerto. It deserves the name concerto only when it contrasts solo and tutti and gives the soloist sufficient opportunity for display.

Even the word "contrast" is debatable. Bach still reflexively composes his violin concertos according to a principle that adds a third element to the partners of solo and tutti—that is, a mention of the basic thematic material. This addition is evident in the loveliest of the three concertos, the E-major. The first movement presents a marked contrast between tutti and solo, but contrast is not the predominant element. More important for the structure and the overall impression is how Bach plays with the theme at the top of the movement. Only at the beginning does the theme give that sense of stability that would make it a good element in a traditionally structured concerto. In the extended, completely idiosyncratic middle section, it undergoes new reflections and refractions in the course of exciting harmonic passages, until finally, in the adagio cadence of the solo violin, it simply evaporates.

So when the theme comes back in the ensuing da capo, it seems more like returning home after a long development section than a final recapitulation in a ritornello movement. Clever and complicated arranging of the various sections of a movement is not Bach's purpose here, as it is in the *Brandenburg*s. Externally, the movement has the elementary stability of the da capo aria, which it resembles exactly in form. Internally, it revolves about the main idea, on which it meditates joyously in the outside sections and contemplatively in the central section. In this context, Stefan Kunze has spoken of "plumbing the depths of the material" and "exhaustive treatment."[50]

The solo violin part is like a bracket holding all the sections together; not only does it shine in virtuosic passages, but it leads the orchestra and stands for the intellectual idea behind the movement. It is probably unique to Bach that playing through the whole violin part, which is also in the tuttis, gives one a compact, yet complete picture of the entire movement. As in the six solos for violin, a single voice contains the whole movement *in nuce.*

The young Yehudi Menuhin had his Bach revelation while practicing the C-minor second movement this way, that is, a cappella: "I saw myself mentally as a peacemaker cutting Gordian knots, settling neurotic quarrels in an instant, saw mankind abandoning its entrenchments and embracing one another for my sake."[51] He probably would not have felt this way if he had played the semi-ostinato bass part instead of the violin's, because the bass, in dialogue with the solo violin, is no peacemaker; it trudges inexorably onward. In a most imaginative analogy to speech, Bach sets the constraints of law, expressed by the bass, against the freedom of grace, articulated in broad melodic arcs by the solo violin.

At the middle of the movement, for four bars the solo violin can plunge itself into the bright world of a pure E major and cast off its bass ostinato-like ballast. Accompanied only by the *bassettchen* (*petite basse*) ensemble, after its prior tentative, plaintive tones, it attains a freer diction and a more heavenward orientation. But then it must reconvene its discussion with its austere bass partner, which has the first word, the last word, and indeed the theme.

These poetic interpretations could be extended over many pages but would not be any more convincing than listening to the works, or comparing them with compositions from the generation after Bach, where his style has coalesced into a topos to be found in the solemn, meditative middle movements of late-eighteenth- and nineteenth-century piano concertos—most noticeably in Beethoven's Fourth, opus 58.

A comparison with the slow movement of the A-minor violin concerto shows what nuances Bach was capable of in a single genre. Here too there is a dialogue between solo violin and quasi-ostinato bass, but this time the two stand not opposed like two unreconcilable characters but like partners listening respectfully to each other and finally coming together in the final bars. This coming together may have inspired that Bach admirer Felix Mendelssohn to write his "Lied ohne Worte" in A-flat, op. 38, no. 6, titled *Duetto*, a hymn of praise to sibling affection.

The final movement of the E-major violin concerto leads back from the inner to the outer world. Bach writes a concluding rondo in the French style. Tutti and solo sections alternate with nice regularity, their functions clearly divided. The sixteen-bar ritornello returns five times in the tonic, in exactly the same form; in between, the *concertante* violin plays its couplets four times—three times over sixteen bars, the last time over thirty-two. Regrettably we know nothing of the date or origin of the work and can only surmise that its primarily French style, particularly the last movement, hints more at Weimar or Cöthen than Leipzig for its birthplace.

If the E-major concerto, despite its solemn middle section, makes more of an impression of amiability and "unconquerable joie de vivre,"[52] as Albert Schweitzer put it, the A-minor concerto is the epitome of composure. Here nothing stands out, nothing imposes. Motivic-thematic work is hardly brought out at all, is more a routine ingredient in a homogenous movement—but one packed with meaning and emotion in every detail.

The work seems like a counterweight to the individual *Brandenburg Concertos*. It has nothing of their interior colorfulness and variety, is more music per se—not like any of the counterpoints in *The Art of Fugue,* which has its own time and rules, but more like one great song, sung from the heart. With this in mind, Richard Wagner spoke of the "endless melody" that he saw "predestined" in Bach.[53] Its melodic progress is unbroken; the single tone is filled with meaning; there is nothing that is just construction, accessory, or filler—just tribute to conventional notions of form. We have such music all through Bach's keyboard works but not in the orchestral works to this degree—consider the two overtures in the D-major orchestral suites, with their almost clumsy, apparatus-like feel.

The concerto for two violins, BWV 1043, is written in the Sturm und Drang key of D minor: this represents the beginning, for the concerto, of a specific tradition of characteristics for key signatures, a tradition that leads, by way of Bach's own clavier concerto BWV 1052 and Mozart's piano concerto K 466 to Brahms's opus 15. Beethoven's demand that "something new and truly poetic must come into the traditional fugue form"[54] seems to have been anticipated by Bach in the introductory ritornello of the opening movement. This ritornello has the form of a full-blown fugal exposition with five theme entries, but at the same time it has a wildly impassioned expressiveness. In the episode sections, the solo violins enter with their own theme, which resembles a figure from Torelli's violin concerto op. 8, no. 8:

The trio sonata framework shines through. When a full ripieno is present, the solo violins have a hard time competing with the tutti in places like bar 30–31. In the central movement, these tutti support the harmony; the movement's beginning is similar to the aria "Gioie, venite in sen," from Handel's opera *Amadigi di Gaul*.[55] But to classify this movement as an "introspective type of Siciliana" says nothing about its power to speak to us. Whether we take note of its "wondrous peacefulness," with Schweitzer,[56] or of its "perspective on the vital stillness at the heart of existence,"[57] as did Rudolf Steglich, or see its "temple-like transfiguration," in Hans Joachim Moser's phrase[58]—this music, complex and sophisticated with its broad flow of different episodes, forms of articulation, and moods, is far beyond the reach of any literal metaphor.

The stretto theme of the allegro finale reminded Heinrich Besseler of the beginning of the Sixth Brandenburg Concerto;[59] but this movement, unlike the latter's quiet character, has extraordinary drama. The impassioned gestures of the beginning are not only taken up again but also strengthened. There is hardly another of Bach's orchestral concertos that ends as churned up as it started. Like the A-minor violin concerto, it is of the greatest concentration; but in the outside movements at least, the end result is not so much deliberation as stimulation.

Bach certainly wrote other solo concertos for one or several melody instruments. As was mentioned in the biographical section of this work, some of these can be reconstructed from the clavier concertos BWV 1052–59, which are either proven or highly probable arrangements of such works. Although the entire body of these clavier concertos, which have come down to us in a collection copied by Bach himself, should deservedly be honored as counterparts to the *Brandenburg Concertos,* here we can discuss only one original concerto for two claviers: the C-major BWV 1061a, perhaps written as early as Bach's Cöthen period, which he later revised by furnishing it with a string ripieno, BWV 1061.

The opening movement is the epitome of festive energy, and the three-part *concertante* concluding fugue has a youthful, Buxtehude-like, and certainly organistic playfulness. The irresistible charm of the whole work lies in the function of the two harpsichords: they are completely equal and thus constantly switch between them the assignments of tutti and solo. The result is an extraordinary degree of mobility—but also of density, both structural and tonal. Bach, who always considered the harpsichord *the* instrument for the concentrated display of complex relations, was fascinated by the possibility of doubling the potential here. Moreover, he would have enjoyed presenting the concerto with one of his sons, in which the two would not so much maximize their technical and musical skill as meld in complete partnership.

Another, even more famous clavier concerto of Bach survives, one *senza ripieno,* not as a sketch but in its final version: the Concerto in F Major, BWV 971, written "in the Italian *gusto* [...] for a Clav-Cymbel with 2. Manuals," as the printed announcement of 1735 put it.[60] In 1969 a probable early version of the first movement turned up and may shed special light on his method of composing. It is well known that he continued to do structural work on his compositions over the years, that when making new copies of the music he routinely undertook improvements as well to existing works.

However, there is little evidence to support the idea that Bach would give a characteristic theme its unmistakable Bach look only at a later stage of the composing process. We might have such a case here; but it is also possible that the version sketched out by the Nuremberg organist Leonhard Scholz is not older but simply corrupt. In Scholz's version, the opening theme of the first movement has none of the verve we know:

Italienisches Konzert:

Fassung Scholz:

Indeed, Walter Emery has conjectured that the *Italian Concerto* was first written during Bach's Cöthen period.[61] The Scholz version has encouraged Kirsten Beißwenger to wonder further whether the first movement was originally composed as a version with ripieno accompaniment.[62] It is hard to overlook the fact that the work's solo and tutti contrasts derive mainly from the acoustic potentialities of the two-manual harpsichord.

The first-movement solo parts have characteristics of the gallant style. The final movement's head theme, with its short-long-short rhythm, is modeled on the meter of the amphibrach, which Johann Mattheson said in 1739 "was nowadays most highly modish."[63] Nonetheless, the work is not properly a concerto in the Italian style but one that plays with Italian topoi. The outer movements, specifically, have an oversupply of subtle thematic and motivic work. Even the notion that one could clearly distinguish between solo and tutti, or solo voice and accompaniment, that parts could thus be assigned to one manual or the other of the harpsichord, is deceptive, despite the directives in the original print. In the quasi-development sections of the first movement, as in Bach's organ works, these parts overlap a good deal; in the third movement especially, to facilitate the contrapuntal work and thematic density, the ritornello and episodic parts have been made remarkably alike.[64] In Wolfgang Hirschmann's view, the concerto is comprehensible only in an "as if" mode, that is, only as a potentiality; the "system of convergences and divergences between the harmonic and motivic layout, the tonal differentiation obtained by changing manuals, and the ritornello structure," as Bach imagined it, make the work extremely demanding.[65]

August Halm has commented that Bach needs continually to be varying, veiling, toning down, or replacing his thematic figures with similar forms—to keep them flexible, alive in the rigid Italian concerto form that he has chosen. The "will of the form" opposes "the will of the theme" in the *Italian Concerto*.[66] Expressed another way: as in a Beethoven sonata, the composing subject, appearance notwithstanding, is really not in agreement with the empirical form but in fact wears itself out in the effort.

This need applies less to the middle movement, by its very nature: a two-part, broadly arching melodic aria richly ornamented, composed for affective impact and fitted out in the most modern manner. While the right hand plays the solo melody on the forte manual, the left plays the orchestra accompaniment on the piano manual. The piano part is based on an ostinato one-bar model, subtly arranged in a virtual three-part setting: lovely thirds in the upper line over a bass line. One thinks of the slow movement in Vivaldi's concerto *La Primavera* from "The Four Seasons" op. 8, no. 1.[67] Still, not everything is sleekly Italian: the primarily three-beat pattern of the ostinato is repeatedly broken by the binary pattern in the upper voice.

This work, which Bach's reverent critic Johann Adolph Scheibe praised as the perfect model of a keyboard concerto, found few direct imitators, although Johann Ludwig Krebs—with his teacher's *Clavier-Übung* clearly in mind—published an "Easy, Well-Arranged Concerto in the Italian *Gusto*" in 1743.[68] But there are many heirs, in spirit if not in letter: they can be found in the piano sonata form. With the *Italian Concerto*, Bach made a contribution to the establishment of this genre in the pre- and early-classic period that is no less important than that of Domenico Scarlatti.

THE SONATAS AND SUITES

At the beginning there is the *Capriccio on the Departure of the Beloved Brother*, BWV 992, written by Bach at about twenty. Clearly evident in this work is the influence of the *Musikalische Vorstellung einiger Biblischer Historien* (Musical Presentation of Several Bible Stories), which Johann Kuhnau publishes with great success in five editions for the keyboard-playing public, starting in 1700. As in Bach, there are *lamento* sections to express despair, for example, and fugues with a programmatic background. But Kuhnau means all this seriously: the *Vorstellung des Kampfes zwischen David und den Philistern* (Presentation of the Battle of David and the Philistines), for example, naively aims at musical leitmotivic effects but like an illustrated bible primarily tends to instruct and edify. Compared with this, Bach's composition, while not parodic, is humorous. The *Capriccio* is not for the larger public but for a circle of initiates, particularly his family, to whom Bach demonstrates, with enjoyment and reflection, how to have fun on the clavier with the baroque imitative aesthetic.

The Italian title—*Capriccio B sopra la lontananza del fratello dilettissimo*—leads one to expect an Italian elegance, and in fact Bach, while still in his youth, is working on the light touch of the Italians, for example when he copies out the secular solo cantata *Amante moribondo* of Antonio Biffi.[1] Thus he is all the more able to interpret the "General Lamentation of Friends" on his brother's departure, a type of composition with a solid keyboard tradition going back to

Johann Jakob Froberger, as a tragicomic event: the chromatic descending course of this section, comically titled "Adagiosissimo," is known in musical figure theory as a passus duriusculus. At this very early if not first appearance of the figure in Bach's work, it is allowed to wear the mask of comedy, although in the rest of his work it almost always appears in serious contexts.

The twelve-bar *Aria di Postiglione* plays in very characteristic fashion with the post-horn motif, a rising and falling octave. In the second bar, the postillion actually breaks abruptly into the musical proceedings, while later the falling octave motif is divided between both hands and thus more artfully blended into the piece. In the subsequent *Fuga all'imitazione die Posta*, one can almost hear the mirthful high spirits with which the young composer presents the post-horn octaves in ubiquitous counterpoint—for instance, in bars 48 to 51.

The *Capriccio*, a masterful work despite its lighthearted manner, finds an echo in Beethoven's piano sonata *Les Adieux*, opus 81a, and enjoyed great popularity in the nineteenth century. The "little trumpet piece," a phrase that Goethe used now and then in his oral and written conversations on Bach, probably refers to the *Aria di Postiglione* or the *Fuga all'imitazione die Posta*. Apparently it was part of the repertory of the *Badeinspektor,* or spa director, Johann Heinrich Friedrich Schütz, who also played from *The Well-Tempered Clavier* for Goethe in Bad Berka.[2] Franz Liszt, who had studied the *Capriccio* in a printed edition, classified it in his great essay *Berlioz and his "Harold-Symphony"* (1855) as part of the history of program music.

To this day we do not know what the original occasion of the *Capriccio* was. The catalyst for it must have been a concrete communicative situation, which links this early work with Bach's later sonatas, where communicative and even discursive elements are significant. In these works, the predominant setting is for one melody instrument and harpsichord obbligato: the set of six sonatas for violin and harpsichord BWV 1014–19, the sonatas for viola da gamba and harpsichord obbligato BWV 1027–29, and the two for flute and harpsichord obbligato BWV 1030 and 1032 all fall into this category. These works share a fascinating trait: they are trios and duos at the same time. Trios in a compositional sense: the melody instrumentalist takes one of the voices, and the hands of the harpsichord take the other two obbligato voices. And so Bach realizes his idea of three voices as his primal setting—but this should not call into doubt the significance of four parts in his concept of a musical setting. From a casting point of view, the sonatas for melody instrument and harpsichord obbligato are duets: only two players perform.

Ulrich Siegele has remarked that Bach seems to have been "an enemy of the continuo," and occasionally made a point of composing instrumental music where "adding a general bass was not only superfluous but impossible."[3] This comment, as clever as it is overstated, makes particular sense in the context of the sonata for melody instrument and harpsichord obbligato. By favoring the trio (meaning three-voice) sonata setting, Bach largely avoids continuo writing and at the same time rejects the role of mere accompanist for himself: in performance too, he is the central figure, though of course he has a counterpart in the player of the melody instrument.

In music history from the era of Viennese classicism on, the combination of melody instrument and keyboard obbligato is one of the most demanding, difficult, and intimate forms that serious music has to offer: namely, the dialogue. This form was already in existence at Bach's time. With a wealth of musical ideas and a style of composition that is as demanding as it is expressive, his sonatas for melody instrument and harpsichord obbligato have little in common with the trio sonatas of the baroque. No matter how important Corelli is as the father of the sonata for two violins and continuo, no matter how modern the style of continuo works composed by Bach's contemporaries—most of all Telemann—it is all still house and consumer music, a world away from what Bach means by a trio.

True, Bach wrote his sonatas for melody instrument and harpsichord obbligato as house music too—but as music for *his* house and under *his* leadership! A special element is at work here: he always picks his partner and makes high demands on his partner's abilities and musicality, but at the same time he is considerate of the other's individuality—it could hardly work otherwise. This was the situation at Cöthen, when Bach rehearsed with the chamber players in his home, and also in Leipzig, where he put up famous virtuosos—for instance, the aforementioned lutenists Silvius Leopold Weiß and Johann Kropffgans and the flautist Pierre-Gabriel Buffardin. Ensemble playing requires that partners react to the subtlest nuance if they are to have an enjoyable and sensitive dialogue.

Using the example of the Sonata for Viola da Gamba in G Major, BWV 1027, Laurence Dreyfus demonstrates how closely the composition, or at least the scoring, of a sonata can depend on outside contingencies. Some parts noted down by Bach were on the same type of paper that he had used to write out a gamba accompaniment for the recitative "Mein Jesus schweigt zu falschen Lügen stille," for a new production of the *St. Matthew Passion.* Back in the 1740s he could have had a gamba player available[4] who was proficient enough to make performing the sonatas worthwhile. Was this why he rewrote a sonata for two violins and continuo in G major—probably the original form of the Sonata for Two Flutes, BWV 1039— into this very gamba sonata?

Bach's sonatas were performed not only *by* able musicians but also *for* musical connoisseurs. The pieces rehearsed at Cöthen were surely heard by Prince Leopold and his court; the works first played in the cantor's home in Leipzig were most likely performed soon after that in the collegium musicum. But Bach always kept the music in his own hand—quite literally with the six organ sonatas BWV 525–30, for these trios are not even played by a duo; they are realized by a single performer, on a keyboard instrument with two manuals and a pedal. When played on a pedal clavier, they too can be seen as genuine house music.

This special situation explains why the study of Bach is so difficult: in the sonata, even more than in other genres, he is a composer who subjects his work to an endless process of revision. This for two reasons: first, he shifts from the sonata for one or two melody instruments and continuo to the sonata for one melody instrument and harpsichord obbligato, or to the trio for one keyboard instrument; second, he delights in revising already existing works or parts of works for a current occasion—say, to make music with a visiting virtuoso—either by rewriting or rearranging them.

Given the incomplete transmission history, this procedure, though presented as fact, is really conjecture, supported only by a clever edifice of hypotheses constantly in danger of collapse. One example: in 1966 Hans Eppstein, an authority in sonata research for a generation, reconstructed a complicated prehistory for the famed flute sonata BWV 1030. In his estimation, the generally known B-minor Bach manuscript version had a predecessor work in G minor: this theory is supported by a surviving harpsichord part in G minor. But Eppstein goes further: behind a G-minor version for flute and harpsichord obbligato, he suspects the existence of one for two flutes and continuo; and the first two movements here supposedly have their origin in a concerto movement for solo flute.[5]

A good thirty years later, Klaus Hofmann, no less an expert, suggested a far simpler descent for the work. In this view, the final version was preceded only by a trio for violin, lute, and a low string instrument—a "lute trio" in G minor.[6] There is something fascinating in both lines of thought, which need not be played off against each other here. Eppstein sketches for us a Bach who after repeated attempts eventually finds his way to a definitive version for posterity. Hofmann invites us to consider a Bach who would occasionally compose a trio sonata not for his own use but for three artists of his circle—but who in the end adapts the work for himself.

The proven or suspected early versions of movements from the sonatas for violin BWV 1014–19, for organ BWV 525–30, and for viola da gamba BWV 1027–29 cannot be presented here in detail. Instead let us take a brief look at the sonatas for a melody instrument and continuo not previously investigated. Today only a few of those sonatas once thought to be Bach's work are still considered authentic: the violin sonata BWV 1021 and the flute sonatas BWV 1034 and 1035. The other, disputed (or rejected) works for this setting should not be written off, however. They may reflect Bach's instructional practice, which naturally included learning how to play a general bass part. He could have given his sons and other students simple sonatas written by himself or others, and later reworked them. In this connection, the sonatas BWV 1021, 1022, and 1038 deserve special attention: they are written over the exact same bass line, which one would connect only reluctantly with Bach. Could they be interconnected studies from his pedagogical workshop?

The violin sonatas BWV 1014–19 were not all composed at the same time—which might well have been to their benefit: in its present form, the series does not have the unity and close systematic structure of the Cöthen demonstration cycles, but it has a variety and richness on the order of the *Brandenburg Concertos*. In the baroque period, we usually see the same style in a series of works set for the same instrument. This is not true of the violin sonatas. Except for the G-major BWV 1019, which has a particularly busy history, they all follow the Corelli *sonata da chiesa* scheme, that is, they have movements in the sequence slow-fast-slow-fast. But that sequence is the only typical trait they have.

Bach keeps to a strict trio part setting in the organ sonatas, in the viola da gamba sonatas (with few exceptions), and in the fast movements of the violin sonatas; but in the slow movements, the trio form is almost the exception. The very first sonata, in B Minor (BWV 1014), has its opening adagio, in effect the start of the entire series, set for as many as five voices. The adagio feels like the introductory sinfonia in a cantata, in that it adopts the expressive and meaningfully nuanced speaking style of vocal music, which is now for the first time gradually entering the realm of instrumental music, largely thanks to Bach himself.

Superficially, the cantilena line of the violin and the keyboard accompaniment appear to be quite different from each other. But if we look closer, it is clear that Bach was concerned with balancing the two parts. The emotionally charged thirds and sixths first played in the keyboard part, which have an especially innocent sound in the context of the surrounding dissonant harmonies, are later taken up by the violin—but only in the *Abgesang,* that is, the final stanzas that bring back the expressive, improvisatory cantilena of the introduction. It is only then that the importance of these thirds and sixths becomes evident: they are the motivic and thematic basis of the movement. This movement is inadequately explained either as a simple descant solo, in the tradition of monodic, coloristic, instrumental song, or as a three-voiced trio.[7] It is actually a duo in the Viennese classical sense: the parallel and opposite playing of both partners sets in motion forces that lend new and unaccustomed significance to the start of a sonata.

The dimensions of the following allegro go far beyond a traditional *sonata da chiesa.* The head theme is light and almost dancelike, and the whole movement is not difficult to understand, thanks to its da capo form. However, this very form denotes a new, larger-scale architecture: between two identical forty-bar framing sections there is space for a development section, which at sixty-one bars is proportionally longer than the equivalent part in many a classical violin-piano sonata. The term "development" can be used, since Bach takes the head theme, modulates it through the keys, and works with motivic fragments from elaborations on the theme. This motivic work has a pleasing thoroughness to it, the mark of a composer who is neither academic nor gallant, but wants to create a setting that is both well-proportioned and well-argued throughout—or, in modern language, integral.

The "Andante" heading of the third movement, at the time a relatively new term, should not be taken simply as a vague indication of medium tempo. Rather, *andante* means "that graceful and natural motion in music, rising from the bass, since the close of the seventeenth century."[8] Accordingly, the quasi-ostinato bass proceeds at a tranquil eighth-note pace. The rest of the action takes place in the two upper voices, which, led by the violins, move at times in melodious thirds, at times in interweaving legato arcs of sound. Spitta speaks of a "piece of wondrous loveliness, as if woven from garlands of flowers" and of an "organic" quality the equal of any Beethoven adagio movement.[9]

Spitta's remark is partly in praise of the work's poetry: the composition has a communicative power far beyond the baroque presentation of any single affect—it has both a joyful and sorrowful character, giving itself enough space for contemplation and resignation both. Spitta is also referring to formal qualities. In the first half, which has the shape of a two-part song, a secondary theme appears, but it is not just a corresponding melody in the Viennese classical sense, for it comes back in the second part, before the free-ranging coda. In this movement too, Bach does a great deal to ensure that a constructive musical form results from what is a merely plausible musical passage.

Besides the moderate contrast between elements in a single movement, there is also an emphatic contrast in the sonata's finale. The tranquil pace of the third movement turns into restless forward motion in the fourth. Still, double bars indicate that each section is to be repeated, rather like the stylized dance movements in the finale of the Third Brandenburg Concerto. But even in the turbulent rush to the end, Bach takes the opportunity to write both fugally and with all kinds of motivic detail. An important role is also played in this work by a rhythmic motif, introduced in bar 4, which urges the movement forward:

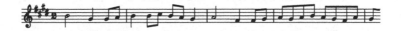

Bach does not let himself be restricted by the contrapuntal structure; he is even good for a few surprises. Just before the double bar he lands in the tonic but then jumps up again to the fifth—as if the spontaneous result of eye contact between the two performers. The work continues in the dominant after the double bar, with the opening theme now in the minor key. The driving rhythmic motif of the development disappears for a while but gives the movement a final twist in its last phase.[10] Bach ends up back in the tonic B minor a full six measures before the end. That too is only to tease—he quickly goes back to C major, then finally to the tonic.

Sonatas BWV 1014–19 as a group are fascinating not just in their wealth of forms but also in their richness of images and sounds. The second movement of the A-major BWV 1015 presents itself as a concert scene with a great collective cadence. Nor are these sonatas lacking in naive, folk tune–like themes, such as in the E-major BWV 1016:

There are tremendously expressive movements. The painfully impassioned siciliano from the C-minor BWV 1017 resembles the "Erbarme dich" aria from the *St. Matthew Passion:*

The adagio from the F-minor sonata BWV 1018 is one of the most thrilling examples of tonal layering in Bach's work: the endless series of eighth-note double-stops in the violin are combined with the filigree figures evenly divided between both clavier manuals. The result is a tone picture of compelling harmonic interest and mystic contemplation. The structure seems at first to lack contour, but it subtly draws extended bows of melody through the movement. A cantabile from an early version of the Sonata in G Minor, BWV 1019a, has a Handelian calm and radiance:

Although their BWV numbers might suggest it, the three viola da gamba sonatas should not be seen as an integral group: their origins and histories are all quite different. Within the group, the G-minor sonata BWV 1029 is somewhat special, in that it is not set up in *sonata da chiesa* form but rather is a "Sonata auf Concertenart"—a term Johann Adolph Scheibe uses in 1740 to describe a form[11] that was considerably older, that had adherents in central Germany, and that found its first important exponent in Telemann.[12] As a "sonata in concerto style," it has the tripartite form of an Italian concerto, from which it also takes over certain *concertante* characteristics.

The first movement begins with an eight-bar ritornello that has a family resemblance to the opening ritornellos of the Third and Sixth Brandenburg Concertos:

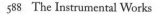

The right-hand clavier part begins its solo episode in the middle of the cadence. But what kind of solo episode is this? The new theme lasts only two bars and must be heard as counterpoint to the opening theme, which is performed in unison by the viola da gamba and the left-hand clavier part. By bar 11 the illusion of a solo episode is over: the ritornello is repeated in its entirety by the clavier, while the viola da gamba adds an independent part, which derives its theme in turn from the ritornello. It is not a new episode that is heard in bar 19 but the head theme of the ritornello once again, now in the dominant. New material is introduced in the middle of the movement, primarily between bars 53 and 95. The sections where it appears cannot really be called episodes; they are development sections preceding a kind of reprise.

Even a rough overview like this shows that it is no "sonata in concerto style" as defined by the enlightened Scheibe—that is, a piece transparent in form, modern in style and gesture. Instead, perhaps with a wink, Bach is importing into his sonata movement a foreign topos, the concerto ritornello, in order to play with the resulting possibilities and difficulties. We should keep in mind the communicative situation of the two players: as the theme of the movement, two players continuously perform a ritornello for each other, even though there is actually no concerto or aria structure to give the ritornello meaning.

Was this work written as early as Cöthen—as an intellectual discourse Bach was pursuing with his gamba-playing prince, as in the above-mentioned theory suggested by Michael Marissen (though based on the Sixth Brandenburg Concerto)? There is a little more evidence in support of Laurence Dreyfus's and Christoph Wolff's view that the work is from Bach's middle Leipzig period.[13] Its hybrid form would fit well with the *Italian Concerto* and with the overture with concertizing flute in B minor BWV 1067, to be described below.

It seems almost insulting to Bach's art to assume that the original form of the opening movement of BWV 1029 was a concerto movement. Of course, anything is possible. But accepting such a theory implies that the remarkably original structure of this work was actually the result of a retrospective manipulation. No matter how original John Hsu's idea may be, to say that this sonata's original form was a concerto orchestrated like the Sixth Brandenburg Concerto, with similarly clever voice leading, is nothing more than a gimmick.[14]

Philipp Spitta is less interested in this work's structure than in its gesture. Coming before the premiere of Wagner's *Ring*, his description provided a poetic context to the music—his prose turns Bach's piece into a veritable ride of the Valkyries—still of interest today: "Here is a composition of Magyar temperament: it roars across the plain on fiery wild steeds, rushing secondary motives sound like the blows of a whip, now the tone figures rattle downward in a diminished seventh harmony, and work their way up again beneath bright trills in the upper voice...."[15]

The middle movement of the sonata sounds oddly fragile and lost; it is a slow, two-part dance twelve and eighteen bars in length. The three obbligato voices have no connection with one another until the final part. The left-hand clavier part busies itself with a repeating, almost ostinato bass figure. The right hand adds an upper part that could be suitable for a saraband, but the tempo is too slow for the performer to play it that way: it is hard enough to bring life at all to the almost endlessly held half notes of the harpsichord.

The tempo of the movement is determined mostly by the viola da gamba, which indulges in a broad, sweeping melody, an adagio movement quite typical of Bach's sonatas. Of course the viola da gamba has the melody to itself for a time, and at the double bar briefly takes over the theme in the right-hand clavier part, which in turn takes over the lyrical elements of the viola da gamba. Only at the end do the three voices meet in harmony.

In rather original fashion, Dreyfus has seen the movement as "reconciling" saraband and adagio, uniting French and Italian style. But this reconciliation doesn't actually occur, since Bach's writing style in the end is not right for either form—even here his music keeps its distance from the dominant styles of the day.[16] Spitta is not writing flowery phrases when he hears "a clear premonition of

Beethoven" at the beginning of the movement, though surely not the "solemn, soulful" Beethoven he describes.[17] It is rather the Beethoven of the late bagatelles, when he no longer felt the need to bind disparate elements together but reflected on their differences instead. Bach is already doing this here—not alone at a piano but in dialogue with a partner.

To stay with Beethoven: the last movement of BWV 1029 might be compared with his cello sonatas opus 102. To describe the movement only as a fugue in concerted form fails to take note of a structure that is set up to deal with and integrate a variety of subtle motivic material. In the authoritative manuscript copy of the work, which was drawn up by a pupil of Bach's, the entry of a secondary theme in the harpsichord part is marked "cantabile," a rare occurrence in Bach manuscripts and eloquent in its way: this type of promotion of a secondary theme will be found in Viennese classicism.

The linkage between Bach's viola da gamba sonatas and Beethoven's cello sonatas is not arbitrary. At the premiere of opus 102 in 1818, a critic for the *Leipziger Allgemeine Musikalische Zeitung* wrote: "If we wanted to give to those unfamiliar with them some idea of the style and taste with which these sonatas are worked out, or at least their main movements, then we would say: think of the so-called clavier symphonies and similar works of Sebastian Bach."[18]

The term "clavier symphonies" refers to the three-part sinfonias, a copy of which was in Beethoven's possession, but also to other compositions *a tre*—hence the sonatas for clavier and an obbligato melody instrument.[19] Such a view does not explain Bach through Beethoven or vice versa, but it offers a wider perspective on Bach's art.

In the year of the first public performance of Beethoven's *Eroica*, an anonymous critic called it "an extensive, daring, and wild fantasy," thus betraying his own inability to explain the work's originality against the landscape of then-conventional symphonic and sonata models.[20] Yet another extensive, daring, and wild fantasy is to be found in Bach's sonata for flute and obbligato harpsichord, BWV 1030, whose opening movement is the longest Bach ever wrote for the sonata form. He may have gone over an early form of the sonata, written for violin in G minor around 1736–37, with a flute virtuoso, who encouraged him to transcribe it to B minor for the flute; in any event, that is when he rewrote the duet in this form and key.

The parallels between the B-minor sonata and the *Eroica* are as striking as their formal differences: in both works, traditional concepts of form fade and yield to rampant (though not formless) fantasy. Bach is not playing an intellectual game here with topoi of sonata and concerto forms, as he was in the BWV 1029 just discussed; no, he quickly makes us forget all about genre and form. There is hardly another movement in his sonatas so rich in ideas and yet with so little formal apparatus or figural padding. The opening fourteen bars line up one idea after another, and the flute, which is especially rich in inventive ideas, needs to rein itself in, for two bars at any rate, to let the harpsichord have a word.

The sonata's first bar is symptomatic: the right-hand harpsichord part is a sixteenth ahead of the flute and three sixteenths ahead of the left hand. It sounds like a work in rehearsal restarting after an interruption, or as if the listener has opened the door on a concert that has already started:

The flute in particular never seems to rest. The "far-reaching power of the melodic lines" that Ernst Kurth praised in Bach[21] is borne out in the first twenty-two bars, where the flute sings without interruption, though for a while it seemed that the harpsichord would be part of the dialogue. But no—an ironic moment in a "duo" context—bars 3 and 4 remain a one-time exception.

As the work proceeds, broad, sweeping (if ornately structured), melodic lines continue to dominate. There is little in the way of formal help for the ears, such as a contrasting ritornello and episode, theme and variation, or thematic section and interlude; instead, new ideas and old are fitted together in a long chain, with ever finer imitative figures toward the end. At the same time, the movement has a transparent architecture, is bipartite like the later classical sonata. The first part ends at bar 58, roughly the numerical middle, on the dominant; then a middle section, which form theory would call the development, bridges to the final section at bar 80, which, while not a reprise, does present an equivalent of the opening section.

The harpsichord functions in various ways. It accompanies elaborately, or just with simple chords; it performs in combination with the flute or concertizes independently—all of which is not set in a readily hearable pattern, more in the fantastic style, best described with metaphors: the harpsichord confidently guides the flautist through the movement but also knows when to take the lead itself, and even occasionally how to astonish his partner with spontaneous ideas—for instance, a little canon that starts out freely but then invites the flautist to imitate it:

The second movement cannot boast such refinements: an instrumental aria in siciliano time, its perfect balance and symmetry work like the calm after a storm. But even in the small framework of 8 + 8 bars, the harpsichord proves its worth by upgrading the gallant style of the flute with an exquisitely improvised accompaniment in the general bass.

After the rhapsodic flights of fancy in the first movement and the soulful meditation of the second, the final movement, consisting of two heterogeneous sections, runs over hill and dale. For eighty-three bars, without letup, a turbulent fugue is heard, until it stops suddenly—not for the stretto but for one more climactic episode in the shape of a 32 + 32 bar gigue. This gigue shows off its own idiomatic style perfectly, but, as if possessed, ramps up the excitement by doing away with the beat pattern. There is no comparable climactic passage in any other Bach movement: the whole sonata jumps out of the realm of the ordinary. To compare it with Beethoven's compositional style is more than just an aperçu: what they both share, expressed in philosophical terms, is "Romantic humor," which the writer Ernst Wagner expressly applied to the *Eroica* and which was also used by his friend and champion Jean Paul in 1804 with reference to Joseph Haydn's music: "Something like the cheekiness of withering sarcasm, expressing a kind of universal contempt, can be heard in certain music, for example Haydn's, where it destroys an entire series of notes with one strange one, and storms back and forth between pianissimo and fortissimo, between presto and andante."[22]

Bach may have wanted to compose organ sonatas as early as the Weimar period. Some combinations of movements have been dated from this time that follow a three-movement pattern rather than the binary prelude-fugue model. This is true, for example, of the *Piece d'Orgue* in G Major, BWV 572, its movements marked "Tres vitement," "Gravement," and "Lentement"; of the Toccata, Adagio, and Fugue in C Major, BWV 564; and of the Prelude, Largo, and Fugue in C Major, BWV 545.[23] This last piece is particularly informative, since the largo was later used as the middle movement in the organ sonata in C major BWV 529.

Bach was already playing trios in Weimar: on a two-manual organ he could perform and compose works for his favorite musical setting without outside help, with all voices intact. This kind of playing became more and more important to him, not just for performing the slow middle movements but for fugal composing as well. Evidence for this importance is found in the fast, partly fugal movements of the organ sonatas: here the three contrapuntal voices are distributed over the three organ manuals, while the Weimar organ fugues as a rule are written for one manual and pedal.

The organ sonatas exist as a manuscript Bach wrote around 1730, which is partly fair-copy notations and partly a conceptual sketch. According to Johann Nikolaus Forkel, Bach wrote down the collection "for his oldest son, Wilh. Friedemann, who then had to prepare himself for being the great organist he later became."[24] But to write down doesn't necessarily mean to compose from scratch. The head movement of the third sonata, BWV 528, is modeled on the sinfonia for oboe, viola da gamba, and continuo, which Bach used in 1723 to open the second part of his cantata "Die Himmel erzählen die Ehre Gottes," BWV 76. Older versions of other movements have also been proven to exist; an early form of the andante from the E-minor sonata BWV 528 was written, in the opinion of Peter Williams, as early as 1708, imitating French models.[25]

One way to investigate the variety of forms and styles of the sonatas is grouping them by age. As with comparable Bach groups of works, the only aesthetic point of view that matters is the principle of variation. One should not forget that as late as 1788 the organ sonatas were sometimes described as "gallant settings" and sometimes as works that "would survive every fashion revolution in music."[26] That this anonymously published opinion might have come from Carl Philipp Emanuel Bach does not reduce its value: the word *galant* in particular, Bach's son would not have used lightly.

In the narrower sense, there is a good deal that is gallant about the organ sonatas, in particular the middle movement of the G-major sonata, BWV 530—perhaps the only one completely composed from scratch. Its "lente" movement, in the form of a two-part song or dance of 16 + 24 bars, is a siciliano in the elegant style. At the outset we find much that was considered gallant at the time: short note values, large interval jumps, slurs, suspensions, syncopated notes, fast triplets, ties between longer melody groups.

The vivace that opens the sonata, despite certain gallant elements, appears to be a stable concerto movement on the older Italian pattern. In its extremely architectural working out of three thematic complexes it could be compared with the Organ Prelude in E-flat Major, BWV 552, but also with the third movement of the Flute and Harpsichord Sonata in A Major, BWV 1032. We might almost think that Bach added his own organ concerto to the Weimar ones BWV 592–96, which of course were transcriptions of the works of other composers.

This impression is erased by the last movement, which puts the concerto principle in opposition to the sonata principle. Despite the fugal style, it seems more modern and flexible than the opening movement; nor does it disdain to use a characteristic second theme. But the clearest anticipation of the classical sonata movement comes with the final movement of the Organ Sonata in C Major, BWV 529: the same main and secondary theme is found in both the exposition and the reprise, which starts in the subdominant, somewhat obscurely. The development contains both contrapuntal and highly motivic-thematic work. Even a final idea is present in the form of a stretto on the main theme.

The variety of forms and styles of the sonata BWV 530 is characteristic of the whole series. The overriding principle is a strict adherence to trio playing—that is, three voices. Since the presentation of a musical setting is limited to a single instrument (and Bach's own house instrument), much about these sonatas seems more concise and tighter than in the sonatas for a melody instrument with obbligato harpsichord. Yet they lack certain inventive characteristics of style, refinement, and delicacy that Bach would produce when challenged by the chance to play with a violinist, viola da gambist, or flautist.

Every genre Bach became involved with presented him with the same challenge: to confront productively a preset given—a text, a cantus firmus, a traditional style of writing, a current style trend. The suite model imposes its own restrictions. In the keyboard suites, the basic requirement of dance movements and their order (*meilleur ordre*) is cut-and-dried: allemande, courante, saraband, gigue. Bach largely kept to this order but took the normal liberties of the day by inserting other dance or song movements between the saraband and the gigue—one to four in number—such as the bourée, gavotte, musette, minuet, passepied, air, loure, polonaise, rondeau, burlesca, or scherzo.

But to preserve the essential nature of the form, the character of the dances must be identifiable: an allemande needs to be recognizable as an allemande, a courante as a courante. Bach observed this requirement for the most part; he adopted without question the opening figure of any specific dance type to make it immediately identifiable as such. The most obvious restriction on a composer of suites is in the musical structure itself: the models are always two-part forms, comprising 8 + 8, 12 + 12, 16 + 16, 8 + 16 bars, and so on; irregularities primarily result from the insertion of four-measure blocks. Bach largely conforms to this rule as well. So one might ask what it was about composing suites that seemed interesting to him? Let us look first at the *French Suites* BWV 812–17 from this vantage point. Early versions of the first five are contained in the little notebook for Anna Magdalena, started in 1722. While this fact says nothing definite about the date of composition, it does say something about the social context of the form: Bach's suites for clavier must have been meant for playing at home. Although he used them in his teaching, and located them, in order of difficulty, between the *Inventions and Sinfonias* on one side and *The Well-Tempered Clavier* on the other, they should be seen not as study or display pieces but as "gallantries," a term he famously used on the title page of the first part of the *Clavier-Übung*.

This characteristic coinage referred primarily to the freestanding dances betweeen the saraband and the gigue and could have been aimed especially at the gentle sex. Note that the *Klavierbüchlein* for Wilhelm Friedemann consists of the *Inventions and Sinfonias*, while that for Anna Magdalena is mostly suites. The basic outline of the first four *French Suites*, at least, is largely simple and conforms to the model, even if each is subtly and elegantly written; the allemande of the second suite, with its quietly flowing yet expressive movement, is a masterpiece all to itself.

But with the Fifth French Suite a new standard appears to be set. Bach uses the technique of "rhyming termination"[27] much more consistently than before: linking the two halves of each movement formally and thematically by giving them the same final groups or endings. Such rhyme is not superficial, as the allemande shows. The second half essentially is a development of the material of the first, and so it is quite logical that the last three bars of the first half return at the end as a kind of reprise.[28]

This work shows at a glance that Bach can work with structure and motivic themes even in a dance form of 12 + 12 measures. His son Carl Philipp Emanuel will take note of such possibilities and choose a compositional idea like that of the allemande in the Fifth French

Suite as the basis for his own sonata form, which he essentially stayed with from 1731 on. While Bach does not write any keyboard sonatas, he does follow the same path in the binary layout of his preludes in the second part of *The Well-Tempered Clavier*.[29]

Although he offers only the traditional dance sequence in the *French Suites*, along with the above-mentioned innovations, he starts each of the six *English Suites* with a prelude. Except for the splendid siciliano prelude of the first suite, these are rather extensive movements; they are longer than the inventions or the sinfonias or the preludes from *The Well-Tempered Clavier*. He quite openly imports the formal principles of the Italian concerto—as well as those of the da capo aria—to the clavier but keeps an underlying polyphonic, two-voice structure. The extroverted gestures of the concerto and the subtle motif-theme work in the prelude's interior are a mutually enhancing combination; these preludes all share sweeping legato melodies and continuous rhythmic drive.

Never again did Bach compose a series of such totally unified clavier sonata movements—and musically they can comfortably be classified as such, despite their concerto-like character—not even in the six partitas of the *Clavier-Übung*. But the dance movements of the *English Suites* also contain movements on the highest Bachian level. Ulrich Siegele comments on the gigue from the sixth suite, a double fugue followed by a mirror-image inversion:

> The last movement of the English Suites *bears the imprint of the master. And it seems that the master has gathered together the sum of his compositional powers for this signature piece, this paradigm of his work. He invents a theme that is essentially the musical pattern of the movement and the basis of its rhythmic continuity. With this he designs the nucleus of the movement, having a pronounced rhythmic quality, in double counterpoint. He develops this germinal theme sequentially in various ways. He transposes individual sections and swaps their voices within them. He inverts the tonal structure, and despite the restrictions of counterpoint, he is able to mirror the modulation based on the*

tonic, through time. He has mastered the twelve-step equal tem-
perament scale and learned how to bring the new material into
harmony with traditional tonal ideas.[30]

Although the first of the *English Suites* comes down to us in a man-
uscript from Bach's Weimar period and shows naive echoes of the
French suites of François Dieupar,[31] it still seems improbable that the
English Suites as a complete series are older than the *French Suites.*
But the last word has yet to be spoken on the chronology of either
suite.[32]

A new era indeed begins with the partitas that make up the first
part of the *Clavier-Übung.* The opening movements have an impressive variety of form: while the first partita opens with the prelude traditional to the form, the second starts with a sinfonia that can be
taken as a three-part cycle in itself: a slow introduction, its rhythm
approximating that of a French overture, is followed by a broadly
dramatic yet still meditative andante, which in turn gives way to a
concerted fugue.

An opening movement of these dimensions is unique in the
genre and represents a kind of acid test for the cyclic unity of the
suite.[33] At the risk of alienating any consumers who might be expecting "gallantries," Bach keeps coming up with new forms in his opening movements. Thus the introduction to the third partita, entitled
"Fantasia," is a continuous keyboard duet for two voices. The fourth
partita starts with an overture on the French model, but its fugal
middle section has elements of the *concertante* style. These elements
come more clearly to the fore in the Praeambulum of the fifth partita, a playful concerto-like setting; the main theme is reminiscent of
Viennese classicism. Such a medley of various types of first movements would have to have a toccata, and it does: at the start of the
sixth partita. But Bach chooses not to accent the extroversion and
the splendor of the form. Instead, he writes a lyrical, fervently
inward-looking piece of intellectual concentration.

It is the rule in such cases that the serious tone of the opening is
continued in successive movements. This is true for the saraband,

which picks up the free-ranging toccata character of the beginning, and shows, in a brief two-part dance movement with a fairly clear periodic structure, how to make the most of it. The next movement, inserted between the saraband and the gigue, isn't even titled "Gavotte"—it is marked merely as *tempo di Gavotta*—a hint that this is not an actual dance, merely a piece on the rhythmic model of a gavotte. The final movement, too, is not so much a gigue made fugal as it is a carefully worked-out fugue with the character of a rather unusual gigue. The formal convention of the suite is dissolving.

The "serious tone" of the sixth and last partita (though evidently one of the earliest to be written) is the result not solely of gesture and emotional content but also, as with the earlier numbered partitas, of its compositional structure: it has an element of composure and resolve rarely encountered in the genre. The individual dance movements have not only rhyme—that is, two sections which end similarly—but also many initial correspondences: after the double bar, the opening motif reappears, either in original or inverted form. Beyond this are motivic-thematic correspondences and developments within the halves. In the partitas Bach demonstrates even more systematically than in the *French* and *English Suites* that he understands perfectly, even in quadratic sequences of bar groupings and forms with largely preset meters, how to compose a movement in accordance with his unwritten motto, "All from one and one from all."

Certainly the partitas show that he is at home in the current national styles of the French and the Italians, that he can write in a sparkling, à la mode fashion, and that he is fluent in the gallant style. His effervescent flair is particularly evident in the gigue from the first partita, for example, or in the scherzo from the third, while the saraband from the fifth reveals his gallant style. In 1730, the year of the partitas' publication, Bach is without doubt composing in an even more gallant style than his son Carl Philipp Emanuel will in the slow movement of his *Prussian Sonata* in C Minor, published in 1742.[34] But this effervescence was not an end in itself—it was part of a strategy that became clearer in each of the four parts of the *Clavier-Übung:* first, to do justice to the encylopedic spirit of the age by giving examples for every current genre and style of keyboard music; second, with the help of this particular instrument, to demonstrate the universal essence of music from the point of view of one form.

In the two separately transmitted suites BWV 832 and 833, in the *English* and *French Suites,* in the partitas from first part of the *Clavier-Übung,* and in the second part of the *French Overture,* Bach wrote dance sequences for his home instrument and with them made indisputably his most comprehensive and wide-ranging contribution to the suite form. Closest to them in sound and arrangement of movements are the Suites and Partitas for Lute, BWV 995–97. The first is a transcription of the fifth suite for violoncello BWV 1011, but in the Bach tradition it has biographical interest, since Bach dedicated the autograph to a "Monsieur Schouster," who was perhaps the Leipzig publisher Jacob Schuster.[35]

The five-movement Partita in C Minor, BWV 997, is more ambitious as a composition than the E-minor suite BWV 996, although the latter should not be underestimated because of its early date of origin. Much of BWV 997 also can be found in a lute tablature prepared by a lutenist friend of Bach's, Johann Christian Weyrauch. Of particular difficulty here is a fugue arranged as a three-part sonata or song setting, on an unusually spiky theme, which has a simultaneous counterpoint. If Bach composed this partita in original form for lute around 1740, this would be a further, later proof of the consideration and affection with which he treated the instrumental virtuosos in his milieu: it ranks among the best of Bach's compositions of this time. Although not made to order for the lute, it is nonetheless composed very much in its honor. However, it may have been meant for the lute-harpsichord (a cembalo with double strings of gut, sounding like a lute).

The three partitas of the violin solos (BWV 1002, 1004, and 1006) adhere with some deviations to the traditional sequence of allemande, courante, saraband, and gigue but are very different from one another in the details of how they are put together, and as a group they exhibit a variety that rivals that of the Cöthen demonstration cycles discussed above. The six suites BWV 1007–12 have a more homogeneous feeling. While the first five were indubitably written for the cello, the sixth calls for a five-stringed instrument, behind which either a viola da braccio with a low C string or a precursor of the viola pomposa could be lurking.[36] According to lexicographer Ernst Ludwig Gerber, Bach thought of the latter as an instrument that would be easier to manage, as opposed to the "stiff manner in which the violoncello of his day was handled."[37]

In principle Bach keeps strictly to the sequence prelude, allemande, courante, saraband, gigue, but routinely adds a further dance, with a double, between the saraband and gigue: two each of minuet, bourrée, and gavotte. At that time, solos for cello were still unusual, brand-new territory; so it is not surprising that he sets up the suite sequence as a Gradus ad Parnassum, at the beginning particularly mindful of the specifics of the instrument. The second minuet of the first suite can be heard almost as the bass line to an imaginary melody part—a situation familiar to every cellist playing continuo.

Increasingly individual formal elements are combined with a gradual increase in technical difficulty.[38] By favoring a style typical for the genre and by breaking less new ground compositionally than he did in the violin solos, he allows the performers to take full advantage of his genius in writing music for a single voice, with its broad spans of melody, and thus to concentrate completely on their instrument. It would be incorrect, though, to think of the suites for cello as utilitarian art (Gebrauchskunst): the saraband of the fifth suite, for example, is the epitome of a setting in which a single, lonely melodic line has harmonic, polyphonic structural depth.

If we assume that the collection of cello solos, like its sister work for violin, were composed in the Cöthen period, it does not seem outlandish to date the partita for solo flute BWV 1013 in the temporal vicinity of these two series, even though, as mentioned above, like the cello solos, there are no extant manuscripts earlier than the

Leipzig period. Perhaps individual movements were originally written for another instrument and adapted for flute later on. In any event, every flautist has technical difficulties in performing them: often, no consideration is given to the need to breathe.

In the opening allemande, Bach has written an instrumental melody of extreme character. The two-section movement, in 19 + 27 bars, runs in linked sixteenth notes without any rhythmic variation; all the necessary information about this composition is given through changing pitch alone—but what information? The piece is neither amorphous nor periodic. Listeners flounder in their efforts to hear, in the chains of sixteenth notes, the regular repeated sections of a dance tune, but they are not left completely groping in the dark. Yes, Bach does follow every phase of "harmonic-metric consolidation" with an "episode of uncertainty and ambivalence,"[39] and he also avoids symmetrical correspondences, but he definitely places a value on order. But is this order melodic or harmonic? That the former serves the latter is apparently the special point of the movement.

The impossibility of conceiving of the orchestral overture of Bach's time with no French influence is borne out by the work's very name: *French Overture*. The compositional style of Jean-Baptiste Lully, court kapellmeister to Louis XIV, did indeed influence the genre. But the practice of composing an overture along with a series of dance movements, with no relation to an opera or any of its ballet scenes—in other words, creating orchestral works meant for concert performance from the outset—goes back to German composers. In 1682 Johann Sigismund Kusser and in 1693 Heinrich Erlebach published such works in the French manner and mode.

The reason for this development: despite the unwillingness or inability of the princely German admirers and imitators of the French Sun King to afford a permanent opera, they still wanted the aura of the musical splendor of Versailles in the form of concert or dinner music. To compose dinner music was a routine matter; therefore one can well believe Telemann's claim that at the little court of Sorau he composed some two hundred overtures from 1704 to 1708.[40] Thus it is all the more believable when he specifies in a letter from

1720 that he could set down on paper a half dozen four-part overtures in about eight days.[41]

The genre was standardized to a much greater extent than that of the concerto. Since no real thought was required about what form the impressive opening section should take—slow introduction with characteristic dotted rhythms, a faster fugal middle section, and a return to the introduction—for a composer gifted with imagination the dances that followed practically wrote themselves. A letter of a Bach pupil, Philipp David Kräuter, attests that at the Weimar court in 1713 (when Bach was there) there were performances not only of concertos in the Italian style but also of orchestral overtures in the French style.[42] The same was probably true at Cöthen.

Paradoxically, there was hardly a genre that gave Bach as much trouble as the orchestra overture. He was no mass-producer of occasional works; he wanted to give every opus his unmistakable profile. So the fact that only four of his orchestral overtures have survived is not necessarily explained by significant losses of original sources; another explanation would be that he turned to such assignments without great enthusiasm in his period as concertmaster and kapellmeister. It was not until Leipzig that he succeeded in extracting from this genre a work original in every way: the Concert Overture in B Minor, BWV 1067.

Of the three certainly older overtures, in C-major BWV 1066, D-major BWV 1068, and D-major BWV 1069, the first two are scored with a pair of oboes, which in tutti passages unite with the first violins to create the characteristic full sound of the French orchestra. The three-part oboe chorus of BWV 1069, on the other hand, has independent voice leading. To be sure, the orchestration of all three overtures presents problems, recently noted by Joshua Rifkin in particular: the oboe duo in BWV 1068 seems to be a later addition, as does the pair of trumpets here and in BWV 1069.[43]

This hint at possible early versions without trumpets or timpani or even oboes gives us a glimpse of a style of Bach overture that is more chamber-music oriented. With it we get a clearer view of the musical filigree work, particularly of the opening sections. Certain technical irregularities in the C-major overture come into sharper focus against this background, too. But this is not the place for detailed observations on these overtures or on the dance movements following them, one of which in particular, the air from BWV 1068, has always produced great delight in listeners. Let us take a last look instead at the B-minor overture with *concertante* flute, BWV 1067. It has been preserved in its original setting from the years 1738–39, although an earlier version for solo violin from about 1730 may have preceded it.[44]

While Handel was publishing his twelve Concerti Grossi in London in 1739, compositions that actually conjure up the old classic concerto style of Corelli and so do not attest to any innovative ambition, Bach, along with his German colleagues Telemann, Graupner, and Fasch, at the same time was taking part in the attempt to bring new ideas into the overture, a genre that from the beginning was encumbered with conventions. Among other things, it was an experiment to meld the form of the French overture with the Italian concerto and thus promote the "mixed style" propagated by Quantz. Christoph Wolff speaks of a "hybrid form" and a "fusing of genres" in the sense of a trend, which is noticeable in other Bach works of the time.[45] We have observed the unconventional combining of conventional genres before, with works like the *Italian Concerto* or the viola da gamba sonata BWV 1029.

How current such attempts were is revealed by the critical remarks of Johann Adolph Scheibe, who praised the "beauties" of orchestra overtures in 1740 while at the same time deploring the "all too precisely restricted sameness" of the form and the "very great similarity" in particular of the opening movements. He hopes for new impulses from "concert overtures" with "concertizing instruments."[46]

Bach meanwhile wrote such a work with his B-minor overture. It is true that the three older overtures in their opening movements also had concertizing voices, but there is an especially enlivening quality that comes with the solo instrument in the middle section of the opening movement, which sounds less like a concerted fugue than like a lively dialogue between solo flute and tutti strings—and so has a thoroughly pleasing quality with little of the genre's customary stiffness.

In the following dance sequence, the saraband, bourrée, and minuet represent the traditional element, the rondeau, polonaise, and badinerie the modern. The polonaise was especially fashionable then—and certainly in the Electorate of Saxony, allied through personal union with the Kingdom of Poland. For the brilliant flute solo in the polonaise, Bach writes a thoroughly gallant part, and in the closing "Tändelei," the German translation for *badinerie* ("dalliance"), he again gives the solo instrument the chance to bring the overture to a light and cheerful conclusion. Thus he shows himself to be a composer open to the new, in this, his last original orchestral work—as far as we know by current source scholarship.

So let the strict adherents of key signature characteristics take note: in the key of B minor, which Beethoven called the black key, Bach composed not only a kyrie and a fugue imbued with sorrowful emotion in *The Well-Tempered Clavier*, but also an orchestral work of bright character ending with a flirtation.

THE LATE CYCLES

The instrumental compositions in the last decade of Bach's life are defined by four cycles: the *Aria mit verschiedenen Veränderungen*, BWV 988, known as the *Goldberg Variations; The Art of Fugue*, BWV 1080; the Canonic Variations on "Vom Himmel hoch," BWV 769; and the *Musical Offering*, BWV 1079. In the area of vocal music, Bach was occupied with completing the B-Minor Mass, another work of cyclic character. All these projects spring from the same intention: his desire to articulate and summarize the essentials of his work. The result are cycles that go to the root of one particular subject, that demonstrate the richness of music through the use of one model theme.

We see once again a characteristic impulse expressly asserting itself: the will to compose in a concentrated and closed form. Up to this point Bach composed in the accepted musical genres for particular performance reasons, even if he was not particularly keen on them, and was able to meet the demands of the society around him with complete confidence. But here his thinking comes explicitly from the music itself. This is the context of Stefan Kunze's idea that in Bach's late cycles "music is now dealing only with itself, and no longer with its connection to the world."[1]

Of course Bach does not write his late cycles in a completely asocial context; but he is composing less for an audience interested in a specific genre than for a virtual public as the heirs to his musical legacy. He does this in the awareness of the artistic and social position he has attained by this time, not from any thoughts of his impending mortality.

He may have wanted to have the B-Minor Mass performed as a *missa tota,* that is, a complete Catholic mass. But more obvious is his desire to gather the best of his vocal creations into a single cycle that with its universal, underlying text will speak to the entire Christian world—the Christian world not just of his own time but of future generations as well.

In the case of the mass, the composer's efforts are concentrated on a model that has both textual and musical elements; in the instrumental cycles, the model is strictly musical: aria, hymn tune, *soggetto.* The second part of *The Well-Tempered Clavier,* though, cannot be included with these cycles: it too was "late," being first put together at the beginning of the 1740s, but it has no unifying thematic model.

The idea that Bach in his late cycles was thinking of any particular public should not be pushed too hard—the ways in which the cycles came into being are too different. Like parts of the *Clavier-Übung,* the *Goldberg Variations* were "completed for the delectation and delight of amateurs of music," thus were probably meant as music for everyday use. Of course the cycle has such strict structure and such large dimensions that it cannot be tossed off like a suite; its proper appreciation demands intensive study.

The Art of Fugue is meant to be played on the harpsichord but should not be thought of as keyboard music; its audience was those who, at least from the time of Johann Mattheson's pointed demands in his *The Perfect Kapellmeister,* were expecting a great contrapuntal work from Bach. The Canonic Variations, composed as an entrance requirement when he was accepted into the Mizler Society, are intended for a small fraternity of musical theorists. The dedicatee of the *Musical Offering,* Frederick the Great, was the greatest representative of secular power in the German-speaking lands: as such, he was being honored with a work which in Bach's view would be at the highest level of musical composition. Each of these works comes out of the attempt to go beyond conventional composition of the day and set new standards.

Each of the four late cycles has its theme in the compositional-organizational sense, which superficially justifies the use of the term "cycle." But *cycle* also implies a meaningful interconnection among the individual parts of the work: unlike in a suite or sonata, the ordering of the movements must be based not simply on convention but on an inherent logic. Bach has various ways of dealing with these ideas, as we shall show: the *Goldberg Variations* represent an ideal cycle, while the single movements of the *Musical Offering* are hardly more than a sequence of compositions of very different types, though carefully chosen, all on the same theme.

The *Musical Offering* is obviously not a less important work than the *Goldberg Variations* or the Canonic Variations solely because it imperfectly presents the true nature of a cycle. The question arises as to whether bringing out cyclic and symmetric structure, or looking for obscure systems of order, might sometimes be too much of a good thing. Music is an art in time: listeners can perceive features common to several sections, can follow motivic and thematic processes and intensifications developed over several movements, and can recognize musical elements heard earlier; they can hardly ever be aware of musical architecture.

For example, in *The Art of Fugue* the connection of four simple fugues at the beginning to a quadruple fugue at the end could have been part of Bach's plan, but such a plan is only comprehensible intellectually, not aesthetically, and adds marginally to the artistic character of the cycle. It is not the existence of four simple fugues and a quadruple fugue or their supposedly symmetrical arrangement but the beauty, richness, and denseness of the composition that determine its artistic significance. Gregory Butler doubts whether the quadruple fugue, preserved only as a fragment, really belongs at the end of the work—but if it doesn't, would its value be less?[2]

To be sure, music is in large measure an art of ideas, and for this reason alone it is important for scholarship to explore Bach's late cycles with a view to finding their ordering principles. But when, for whatever reason, a certain lack of focus in them becomes undeniable, the lack is not necessarily a fault—it may be a gift for listeners: no longer awestruck by the perfect order of the whole, they can concentrate on the particulars that are the special quality of art.

THE *GOLDBERG VARIATIONS*

One of the most beautiful literary tributes ever made to Bach's music is to the *Goldberg Variations,* in E. T. A. Hoffmann's tale, "Kapellmeister Johannes Kreisler's Musical Sufferings":

> *Then the Baron, my ancient tenor friend, came up to me and said, "Dear kapellmeister, they say you can improvise like an angel; please improvise something for us! Just a little, I beg you!" I answered drily, today I am just out of ideas; and while we were talking, a devil in the person of an elegantly dressed gentleman wearing two waistcoats spotted the Bach variations lying under my hat in the anteroom; he thought they were just any variations:* nel cor mi non piu sento—Ah vous dirai-je, maman *etc. and wants me to just sit down and play. I refused: they all fell upon me. "All right, then, listen and be bored to death," I said to myself, and started to play. By the third number, several women get up and leave, pursued by their mop-headed escorts. The Röderleins, since their teacher was playing, held out till number 12, though not without difficulty. The fifteenth drove the two-vested man to flee. Out of exaggerated politeness, the Baron stayed till number 30, guzzling all the punch that Gottlieb had placed on the piano for me. I would have happily stopped there, but this number 30, the theme, tore me irresistibly onward. Suddenly the quarto leaves spread out to a gigantic folio, on which a thousand imitations and developments of the theme stood written, which I had to play. The notes became alive, and glimmered and hopped all around me—an electric fire flowed through the tips of my fingers into the keys—the spirit, from which it gushed forth, spread his broad wings over my soul, the whole room was*

filled with a thick mist, in which the candles burned dim—and
through which peered forth now a nose, and anon a pair of eyes,
and then suddenly vanished away again. And thus it came to
pass, that I was left alone with my Sebastian Bach, attended by
Gottlieb, as by a familiar spirit.[3]

The Romantic author wrote this in 1810 in the name of his alter ego, Kapellmeister Kreisler, who was driven nearly insane by the shallowness of the materialistic, bourgeois musical world around him. He is not against but for something here, the *Goldberg Variations*, whose latest publisher, Nägeli, is mentioned in the story by name. The tale is not about musical phantoms but about a work of music with palpable notes that can actually be played. It is not the music that is illusion but the social antics taking place in the "charming home" of Privy Councillor Röderlein.

The "electric fire" of Bach's spirit shoots out of the notes. This idea describes not only E. T. A. Hoffmann's experience of Bach but Schumann's as well: it was no accident that Schumann named his piano cycle opus 16 *Kreisleriana*. Bach's contrapuntal skills here epitomize a fantastic imaginative power that does not spring from the subject but spurs it on in the search for infinite beauty. Infinity is an appropriate association for a series of variations: Hoffmann-Kreisler wants to continue the composition of the *Goldberg Variations*, making his own markings in his copy of the work after the thirtieth variation. Schumann *did* continue it with his *Kreisleriana*—as had Beethoven before him with the *Diabelli Variations*, opus 120.

Does the classic-Romantic reception of the *Goldberg Variations* amount to a productive misunderstanding? Are not these variations, which seemed to Hoffmann and Schumann an arabesque and thus an artistic manifestation of Nature proliferating, in actuality the complete expression of the "absolutist spirit," since their structural plan combines mathematical precision and numerical order with a tendency toward the "eccentrically large" and the "monumentally dominating"?[4]

It is fascinating to see what Bach does with the genre of the *aria variata* for keyboard instruments, a form dating from the time of William Byrd but still enjoying great popularity at Bach's time. One comes across many names in the history of the song variation: Girolamo Frescobaldi, Johann Jakob Froberger, Matthias Weckmann, Dietrich Buxtehude, Johann Pachelbel, George Frideric Handel. There even circulated among Bach's closer relations a relevant forerunner to the *Goldberg Variations:* the twelve variations, also in G major, on a saraband written by his uncle Johann Christoph.[5]

The aria forming the basis of the *Goldberg Variations* is also a type of saraband. Removing the melody's rich ornamentation in honor of the gallant style and looking at it together with its bass line, we find one of those descant-bass double frameworks that seventeenth- and early-eighteenth-century composers used as the foundation for composing their variations. The general pattern for Bach's aria is seen by Rudolf Flotzinger in the *Gagliarda Italjana*,[6] and by Günter Hartmann in something that he calls the "Bergamasca-Ruggiero double framework,"[7] which is based on song variations of Frescobaldi and Buxtehude. It can also be found in the *Klavierbuch der Jungfrau Clara Regina im Hoff*.[8]

This popular Bergamasca tune, which was sung in many versions and to different texts, is only faintly audible as the base of the artfully constructed melody in the aria; but in the final quodlibet it is unmistakable. The Ruggiero tune often paired with it is a well-known ostinato bass formula of the seventeenth century, originally used as the harmonic and metric basis for improvised dance music. How it differs from the *passamezzo* model is complex but not of great import in the case of the *Goldberg Variations*. The most significant difference is that Bach uses a pattern consisting of thirty-two bars and just as many "fundamental notes," as against the traditional practice of an eight-bar model. Bach's pattern allows space for more-extended forms.

We should not ignore his interest in the sequence of the "first eight fundamental notes" of the aria, as they are called in the handwritten appendix to the manuscript of the *Goldberg Variations*.[9] By sketching fourteen strict canons on this brief note sequence (BWV 1087), he gives a commentary on the real point of the variations. No matter how colorful and worldly the work is externally, its compositional core is a skilled examination of the basis of music: in a word, the seven tones of the diatonic scale. If this core could be called elementary, then the material used for the quodlibet is downright folksy: the two interwoven melodies there can have texts set to them. From Johann Christian Kittel, Bach's personal student in his last years, we have this reliable description:

> *In the final Quodlibet the melodies of two old folk songs ("Ich bin so lang nicht bey dir gewesen, Rück her, rück her" ["I've not been with you so long, come back, back"] and "Kraut und Rüben haben mich vertrieben" ["cabbage and beets drove me away"]) are deftly harmonized together. The theme of the former starts in the first-bar tenor part, and is imitated in the second bar by the descant, at the octave. The theme of the latter tune begins in the second-bar alto part and in the third bar is imitated by the descant at the fifth.[10]*

If we wanted to discuss all twenty-nine variations of the aria in this detail, we could fill a book; let us confine ourselves to the architecture. There are ten groups of three variations each. The last variation of each group is written as a canon—more precisely, variation 3 is a unison canon, variation 6 a canon at the second, variation 9 a canon at the third, and so on. Thus the twenty-seventh variation is a canon at the ninth, and the thirtieth and final variation is not a canon but a quodlibet.

Even a cursory glance at the notes reveals that the variations called canons are not studies in strict style and for that reason are not to be compared with those from the other late cycles. As expected with the genre of *aria variata*, and with only one exception, the cycles tend to be a continuo setting with canonic leading in the upper pair of voices. Their general character is that of dance or aria movements, slow sonata movements, or two-part preludes.

The middle variation of each group of three (2, 5, 8, etc.) is generally written in virtuosic style and meant to be played on two manuals. The performer can show off finger dexterity and the ability to intersect voices by the crossing over of hands. In view of the trend toward virtuosity exhibited in many song variations of the late eighteenth and nineteenth centuries, one is reminded of a statement from Schumann's *Musical House and Life Rules:* "All this business with difficult passage work will change in time; this skill is worth something only when used for a higher purpose."[11]

The first variations of each group of three (1, 4, 7, etc.) are, in the interest of greater variety, quite different from each other. Settings with a dancelike character predominate, so that the whole work has been called a "variation suite" or "suite of variations."[12] Also represented are a fughetta, a movement headed "alla breve" of the *stile antico* type, and an overture in the French style. This is the sixteenth and thus has the special function of opening the second half of the cycle, which Bach may have thought would not be clear without such a division.

Still, an overture cropping up in the middle of the cycle is not without its problems. The performer can see from the score that the sixteenth variation is mathematically the start of the second half and thus the justification of a new beginning, but the listener may not know. There is a hypothesis that the cycle was originally supposed to have only twenty-four variations, to which an overture did not belong: as a structural support the overture became necessary only when the number of variations grew to thirty.[13]

If this theory, proposed by Werner Breig, is right, there would need to be a plausible reason for the expansion—and there may be one. A series of twenty-four variations with the octave canon at the end would have been structurally and mathematically more perfect than the final version; in it the fughetta and the alla breve movement would have had a more special rank. Of course the cycle would have lacked, besides the overture, variations 25 to 30.

The overture seems to have a special experimental quality: the first of its two sections is a grave introduction in alla breve time, the second a fast fugato in 3/8. This combination of variation over a ground bass with a French overture recalls the hybrid forms that Bach sometimes favored in his Leipzig days.

The twenty-fifth variation stands out in a different way: it is based on the saraband, and scholars and music lovers have always counted it among the profoundest of all Bach's compositions. Unequaled as a model for similar pieces of music in the Sturm und Drang or sentimental style, its emotional impact is one of deep despair. As Rolf Dammann put it, its harmonic "processes," which do not shrink even from the keys of E-flat minor and A-flat minor and are the equal of the most daring harmonic progressions in the *Chromatic Fantasy*, lead us into "the darkest reaches of life: to Hell, perhaps, or Purgatory."[14]

Whether we like such metaphors or not, they give us a sense of how Bach's receptive contemporaries experienced this music. What matters is not that Bach wrote such a gloomy and grieving piece of music but how successfully he accomplished it: the traditional *stile monodico* is put into a completely modern setting yet still has an emotional intensity that only he knew how to create. A comparison with the *lamento* from the early *Capriccio*, BWV 992, shows the long road even a genius like Bach had to travel before he was able to write a movement with the intensity of the twenty-fifth variation. Beethoven, with his thirty-first Diabelli variation,[15] and Gustav Mahler, with the adagio from his Ninth Symphony, merely picked up where Bach left off.[16]

At this point, the series of variations again pushes into new dimensions: in terms of expression, Bach abandons once and for all the realm of the generic and the typical. Under the sign of melancholy, and in the final quodlibet under the sign of humor, the cycle ends not with perfect mathematical and musical symmetry in an academic octave canon but openly, as it were, with a mock canon on a popular tune. For the purpose of humor or caricature, the use of songs, song fragments, market cries, and the like in quodlibets was a time-honored tradition. The melodies he uses can be found in the four-part collection *Ohren-vergnügendes und Gemüths-ergötzendes Tafel-Confect* (Ear-Pleasing and Soul-Delighting Table-Confection) begun by Valentin Rathgeber in 1733. Bach tops off his scholarly house of marvels with a deliberately "popular" roof peak—but in his own way: the combination is witty but at the same time very skillfully done.

This inclusion should not be explained away by Forkel's report that the members of Bach's extended family were fond of singing quodlibets when they got together, laughing "heartily the while."[17] That Johann Sebastian in his youth once copied out, if not composed, a quodlibet himself, helps somewhat. "See, here are my roots," the mature composer might be saying. The necrologist's remark is even more informative, that Bach, "his serious temperament notwithstanding, when necessary seems to have deigned to assume a light and comic way of thinking, especially in playing."[18] Was this "way of thinking" necessary at the end of the *Goldberg Variations*?

Thinking back to Kreisler-Hoffmann in the Röderleins' salon: he remains stuck at the thirtieth variation—the theme pulls him irresistibly forward and inspires him to further flights of improvisation. The story does not explain whether the theme is one of the two songs quoted or the concluding theme. But it is indisputably the quodlibet movement as a whole that spurs Kreisler on. This need not happen in an atmosphere of guttering candlelight and Romantic fantasy; it is also possible as the consequence of a "light and comic way of thinking." In this last part of the *Clavier-Übung*, Bach has resolved to keep crossing new frontiers, whether in melancholy or in humor.

The twenty-fifth variation presents the emotion of grief with a realism that in the age of the bass continuo is usually associated with music set to a text. In the thirtieth variation, it is the reality not of grief but of everyday pleasure and disappointment that breaks into the rarefied sphere of art. We already know this phenomenon in Bach's vocal music. With respect to grief, we see it in the B-Minor Mass completed a few years later; with everyday emotions, we see it in the *Peasant Cantata*, written almost at the same time as the *Goldberg*

Variations. But these are forms in which the words can legitimate the transgressing of any musical boundary.

In the *Goldberg Variations,* on the other hand, we have the fledgling art of *instrumental* music taking wing—gaining musicological autonomy. No more is it the little sister of opera, song, and cantata, which up to then could say everything more clearly. It has found its way to a language, moreover, that can express what it wants; that can penetrate depths closed to spoken language; that can be humorous, ironic, or insinuatingly ambiguous: a language capable of double talk. Haydn's project of a classical instrumental music, which has much in common with the concepts of melancholic or humorous character, is unthinkable without the *Goldberg Variations*—whether Haydn knew them or not. It is almost too bad that Bach's pupil Kittel uncovered the textual background of the songs cited in the Quodlibet, thus bringing an intended guessing game to a premature end. In the final sections of Schumann's *Papillons,* opus 2, and *Carneval,* opus 9, when he weaves into the music the "Grandfather's Dance," a kind of "Good Night, Irene" final dance, in quodlibet manner, he limits his commentary in the second case to the ironic indication "Theme du 17. siècle."

But let us return to the idea of the open end. It is in opposition to the cyclical concept, which is responsible for the fame of the *Goldberg Variations* and certainly cannot be argued away. After the thirtieth variation the opening aria comes back—a cycle could hardly end more perfectly. For this reason, one cannot reject out of hand Otto Baensch's hypothesis that the song texts given to us by Kittel are words to be placed into the mouth of a personified aria, a figure who was driven away by the clamor of the twenty-ninth variation (not unlike the "cabbage and beets" of the text) but after the key phrase "Rück her!" ("come back") does return at the end.[19]

Running counter to this cyclic idea, whether taken seriously or humorously, is the vector of progressivity, the idea that instrumental music can be taken further than anyone has imagined—indeed, that it must be. It is part of the dialectic of Bach's creative career that this appeal takes place not in a genre that favors an open form, such as the toccata, but in the extremely closed form of the song variation. It is strange but true that here is where the breakout succeeds!

We end with a heretical question: Why does Bach give the aria that is the starting and ending point of his thirty variations a hypermodern, almost affectedly French form? For song variations, composers traditionally chose simple melodies, which allowed for the possibility of enhancement, ornamentation, and intensification in due course. According to Joseph Müller-Blattau, a simpler version of Bach's aria could have looked like this:[20]

But instead one could accept Robert L. Marshall's view that Bach's aria in its present form is written in a deliberate approximation of the newest fashion of the day.[21] Which then raises the question: Why, after this approximation, are the variations that follow so different from it? The gallant style rules supreme only in the aria; in the variations it is one of many styles, musical forms, and characters.

Responding to Marshall, Frederick Neumann has taken up the old theory that Bach did not compose the aria himself but included it in the little notebook for Anna Magdalena as the work of another composer.[22] For the time being, the truth cannot be settled through stylistic or scholarly arguments. The amazing fact remains that the aria effectively works as a frame around the variations devoted to it. This fourth part of the *Clavier-Übung* has a double ending: first, in the Quodlibet, the ending point as set by Bach, then the aria once again, as if nothing has happened.

A theory analogous to the "thema regium" (for Frederick) from the *Musical Offering* is that the aria was commissioned by someone who wanted to see if Bach could turn a dainty French theme into a composition completely his own. One candidate for this role is the Russian ambassador to the Dresden court, Hermann Carl von

Keyserlingk, for whom Bach traditionally is supposed to have composed the *Goldberg Variations*. This story, reported by Johann Nikolaus Forkel and already discussed in the biographical section of this work, is probably not made up out of whole cloth.

Keyserlingk was the Dresden court official who presented Bach with his appointment as court composer. Did he enter Bach's life again later with a French-style theme? Note that there are other possible sources for the *Goldberg Variations:* popular descant-bass models from the seventeenth century, and a minuet, in G major as well, by Jean Henri d'Anglebert, a court harpsichordist to Louis XIV whose works Bach knew well.[23]

THE ART OF FUGUE

The melancholy and the humor that speak from the *Goldberg Variations* can be interpreted as artistic responses to crises. Not personal crises but crises for a whole society, such as times of great change in values, which leave the artist unsure whether to cling to the old or to turn to the new. In constructing the *Goldberg Variations* as an *aria variata*, and quite systematically as a canonic work as well, Bach is choosing a traditional approach to composition. The fourteen canons inserted as a kind of appendix to the manuscript of the *Goldberg Variations* bear eloquent witness to his further thinking on strict ordering principles in music.

The "gallant sheen"[24] of both the aria and many of its variations present an unmistakable contrast to these principles. Perhaps as a result of this very contrast, Bach found his way to forms like the twenty-fifth or thirtieth variation, which more than elsewhere allow a personal quality to enter his music. Is this melancholy and humor a reaction to uncertain external conditions? The Italian musicologist Ugo Duse writes on the late Bach:

> He had been the Reformation's great cantor, and his problems
> were those of a man who was, in a way, quite defenseless against
> the crisis of culture and the Reformation. Bach may have experi-

enced this crisis in much more diverse ways than one might think;
he must have felt it as a collective crisis of hearing, a crisis of so-
cial relationships, a crisis of family relationships, a crisis of the old
political despotism; finally, in view of Frederick the Great's im-
partiality in the politics of religion, he must have experienced it
as an enormous crisis of faith.

Duse sees *The Art of Fugue* as an indicator of "consistency surrounded by opportunism, faith surrounded by skepticism, Reformation discipline and piety in the midst of expanding Jesuit
possibilism."[25] I have no problem approaching *The Art of Fugue*
under this speculative "key signature," but reserve the right to add
others as well.

The idea of a Bach who, in *The Art of Fugue,* is setting down
what he believes, fits superbly with the original concept, which in
Pieter Dirksen's view (cited earlier) is reflected in the first twelve
pieces of the Berlin autograph Mus. MS Bach P200, from 1742.
Bach's intense preoccupation at this time with strict style was discussed at length in the biographical section of this book. It was also
mentioned that a fugal work deliberately set up in twelve parts represents a virtually seamless connection with the traditional learning
and teaching works of the strict style. *This* tradition, Bach may have
thought, should not be allowed to fade away, should be brought,
through him, to its highest point.

A great contrapuntal work based on a single *soggetto* is new in
music history. There are any number of variations on a treble-bass or
ground bass framework, but these are not works primarily in the strict
style. Bach may have considered using the eight fundamental notes of
the aria from the *Goldberg Variations* and then decided against it. Instead he chose a theme in the tradition of the *soggetti* on which the
ricercare and fantasias of the seventeenth century were based, and
particularly in the tradition of the hexachord arrangements of Samuel
Scheidt, Girolamo Frescobaldi, and Johann Jakob Froberger.

Froberger's *Fantasia sopra Ut-Re-Mi-Fa-Sol-La,* which opens
the fantasia section of a magnificent autograph from 1649, was

considered an exemplary piece as early as 1650, when Athanasius Kircher included it in his great music theory work *Musurgia universalis*. The fantasy is named for its *soggetto,* the tone row of the hexachord. Since the Middle Ages, the tonal space of the various hexachords was the same as that available for multipart settings. In his contrapuntal works especially, Bach still composed in modes in the sense of hexachord theory rather than "functionally," according to the new precepts of Rameau. The *soggetto* of *The Art of Fugue* derives easily from this tradition, namely, from the tones of the *hexachordum molle.* The sixth tone, B, is missing; Bach resorts to the traditional rule governing exceptions, which says that the final tone of the hexachord in descending motion can be lowered by a half tone—in this case, to C-sharp:[26]

While the *soggetto* of *The Art of Fugue* is indeed descended from the old hexachord, in this particular form it has its own peculiar essence—but no individuality. It is, so to speak, not the composer's creation but a creation of nature, which keeps its secrets to itself. The composer will bring them to light. Here is perhaps the last appearance, and at the highest level, of the dialectic, speculative view of music from the medieval and baroque period: everything is already there, before it is revealed—it is only waiting for someone to reveal it.

If we follow Dirksen's argument, Bach's initial plan consisted of only three simple fugues, three counterfugues, two double and triple fugues, and two canons. The clarity of this concept would be suitable for the *Clavier-Übung*! The first three fugues, written in simple counterpoint, can be seen as a music course, if an unconventional one: they keep largely to the *stile antico,* and so demonstrate the structural principles of the form.

Reading further in the manuscript, though, shows that Bach really was concerned neither with setting up a course of instruction nor with depicting perfect order: numbers 4 through 12 are all written in double counterpoint, but beyond this each is quite different from the others in technique, style, form, and degree of expression.[27] Every additional counterpoint adds new structural or semantic elements, so that gradually the texture of the entire work gets denser, more layered, and richer in perspective and allusiveness.

One early high point of perfect yet eloquent counterpoint is number 8 in the autograph, which is the later Contrapunctus, 7 BWV 1080, 7. In the very first bars we hear the theme in original form, and as an inversion, but in three different note values—to name only the most striking features.

The effect is anything but intellectually perfect counterpoint. Hans Heinrich Eggebrecht discussed the ending of this movement under the heading "Dramatics": from a sort of "struck chord" on the first beat of measure 58,

> *a quasi recitative solo voice is heard in the first soprano, whose "fourteen" tones twice describe the leading-tone-root tone figure (C#-D); on the second repetition, the root tone gets defined as part of a six-four (second inversion) chord through repeatedly sounding this chord. Then the first soprano plays this leading tone to basic tone figure a third time, with emphasis, above the second (also recitative-like) soprano; at a fourth attempt, it spills over into a chromatic turn from C# to C, picking up the alto recitative once more through the "fourteen" tones, and finally coming immediately out of the diminished seventh chord into a bright major triad conclusion.*[28]

"Fugues," wrote Johann Mattheson in his *Perfect Kapellmeister* of 1739, "are quite pleasant and nice to hear; but a whole work of nothing but fugues expresses nothing and is quite horrible."[29] Bach may have agreed with this criticism when it was directed at *other* composers. In 1750 Friedrich Wilhelm Marpurg recalled his teacher's statements about old and new contrapuntalists, whose fugues were "dry and wooden" and had no "fire."[30] But Bach himself blazed new trails: *The Art of Fugue* is not just a strict contrapuntal edifice but a luxuriant garden of melody and harmony as well. This metaphor is not chosen randomly: the printed edition of the first part of the work is decorated with pictures of flowers and plants.

In their gallant ornamentation and more in the substance of their appealing harmonies and tonal effects, many of the counterpoints give the lie to traditional ideas about the ascetic quality of a typical fugue—as in the printed version of the Contrapunctus, 5 BWV 1080, 5.

But the more various and colorful the planting becomes, the more it is transformed into an enchanted garden or maze, even for its own creator. With the Contrapunctus 11, Peter Schleuning speaks of a "veritable thicket, an accumulation of extremes," and of the historically "trained luxuriant growth of chromatic lines." For the first time in his career, the composer sets himself the task of inverting a three-part triple fugue in all three themes. Even Bach does not succeed at this without some contortion, which appears quite graphically in the tenor-line bars 103–04. He leads the tenor along impossible paths, acting as an obliging helpmate who rushes here

and there, filling in whatever gaps are left in the harmonic texture of
the three other thematic voices.[31]

Donald Francis Tovey suspects that Bach experienced the writing of this Contrapunctus 11 as a kind of crisis, and that he afterward decided, among other things, to turn to composing correct
mirror fugues. This forced him to change his basic plan.[32] In a second attempt, which Dirksen dates to the years 1746–47, Bach did
compose the mirror fugues of 12 and 13 BWV 1080—perhaps after
studying Buxtehude's counterpoint work *Fried- und Freudenreiche
Hinfarth* (Peaceful and Joyous Departure). Probably in this connection he turned then to the inversion and augmentation canon 14 of
BWV 1080, which comes twelfth and last in the main section of the
Berlin autograph, but its somewhat unbalanced form apparently
was not to his liking.

For other scholars and interpreters the Contrapunctus 11 represents a crisis of a higher order. Erich Schwebsch, who described *The
Art of Fugue* in his 1931 book as a "mystical work," experienced it as
the "painful birth of the self": "cosmic forces" have "created man and
left him to himself, that he might gradually reform the world once
more, and imbue it with himself."[33]

Erich Bergel spins this thought out a bit more: "with mathematical precision, exactly at the midpoint of the fugue, the BACH
theme begins," thus signaling the cycle's turning point. While this
author concedes that the intermission "cannot of course occur in the
middle of the eleventh fugue,"[34] he is still persuaded that at this particular point "Christ's descent to earth" ends and His "ascension to
Heaven, and Bach's as well," begins.

Hans Heinrich Eggebrecht observes that the "lively" *soggetto* of *The Art of Fugue* "gives birth to the constrained and timid BACH countersubject, and from that point on is overshadowed by it." For him too the Contrapunctus II is

> *a high point, given the reversal that follows it, as the music is transformed into the statements of the mirror fugues, in which all this is erased: the sighing, the harshness, and the fear, the syncopations and the false intervals too: all that is mercifully wiped away, by that grace that through reflection allows the One to become the Other without human action, that grace that alone can justify the final fugue's subject of B-A-C-H-CIS-D, the connection of the self with the tonic key, the basic tone.[35]*

Since writing about *The Art of Fugue* has inevitably become a kind of "working on the myth," we must respect interpretations like this: they have grown to be part of the piece. Still, it is hard to believe that Bach intended from the beginning to divide the cycle into two sections out of philosophical and theological reasons. We would rather offer the theory that when he turned again to this work for the last time, after completing the *Musical Offering*, his project seemed to have got away from him, and that he had trouble finding his way again inside his own creation.

Not only did he have to take care of the suffering subject that had been brought into the world in Contrapunctus II. There were now two times two mirror fugues, which in a balanced cycle needed an appropriate counterweight. Finally, two canons seemed meager, given the new developments. But with each new piece the relations of the contrapuncti to one another were getting more complex and ambiguous; the situation could be compared to the mounting complication in the course of a game of chess.

Bach may have ended this game with himself in his own inimitable way, had he been granted more time. As it happened, the game was broken off. From what we can reconstruct from the preprint stages, he was working on three different levels. He set new endings to the three simple fugues that open the cycle. They need not end simply according to the rules of composition; rather, they should head toward a climax and conclusion set by the composer, who in this way creates a bridge connecting one contrapunctus to the next. A new, fourth fugue is added; it is more ordered and at the same time more sound-oriented than the first three. Peter Schleuning thinks it is plausible that with this fugue, Bach may have been trying to present the "contrapunto sincopato" that Johann Mattheson introduces through use of a very similar example in his *The Perfect Kapellmeister*.[36]

While the expansion of Contrapunctus 10, which was already part of the Berlin manuscript, seems hasty, there was clearly much care taken in the effort to promote the existing pair of canons to a foursome. Christoph Wolff rightly points out that the printed version presents not so much an "art of the fugue" as it does different "types of counterpoint."[37] The subgenre of the canon is well represented now: there are two canons each on the *soggetto* and on its inversion. The sequence that Bach intended but never completed was probably: canon on the octave BWV 1080,15, canon on the tenth BWV 1080,16, canon on the twelfth BWV 1080,17, augmentation and inversion canon B1080,14.

The canon on the octave, composed for the Berlin autograph, sounds both like a perpetuum mobile and like a study in counterpoint in the style of an invention. The canons on the tenth and twelfth, found only in the printed version, are well supplied with *concertante* characteristics. The special difficulties of this type of composition are noted with comments like "in contrapunto alla terza" and "in contrapunto alla quinta." The way Bach introduces this at the middle of the respective canon, the parts must harmonize in the octave as well. Of course, the highest degree of compositional skill is shown by the augmentation-inversion canon; he needed several attempts before completing this. This movement fascinates the uninitiated particularly: its emotional impact is at once gallant and melancholy. It shows how little justice is done to *The Art of Fugue* when one ignores the variety of genres, styles, emotions, climactic effects, and so on that are reflected in the mirror of counterpoint.

Still to be mentioned is the quadruple fugue with the B-A-C-H theme as the final crowning touch. But caution! At the end of the original printing—apart from the *"Sterbechoral"* ("Deathbed Chorale")—a triple fugue breaks off soon after the start of its third section, the part that develops the B-A-C-H theme, and the *soggetto* of *The Art of Fugue* is not heard at all. The extant sections have a fugue that offers nothing remarkable but is unique in its signature B-A-C-H, which appears here, completely undisguised, for the first and last time in all Bach's work.

We suspect but cannot say definitively that the *soggetto* of the cycle would have come in a fourth part of the fugue, nor can we say with certainty that this fugue would have belonged, possibly as a finale, in the cycle at all. But what is the point of this questioning? Those in charge of the printing of the work set the fugue at the end, and there it stands, once and for all a sign of the cycle's incompleteness. It is pleasant to imagine that Bach, with the B-A-C-H motif, set his signature beneath this work. Wilhelm Friedemann remarked that "his father was no fool; only in *The Art of Fugue* did he use his name as the subject of a fugue."[38]

But Wilhelm Friedemann is not a reliable witness for Bach's plans for *The Art of Fugue*. It is a fact that the "second part," whether beginning in or after the Contrapunctus 11, is a torso that rests on the currently known sources. All interpretations and attempts at reading the work as a two-part drama of "the development of the self" are speculation.

The question can still be asked as to whether Bach had more in mind than just presenting us with a rich book of art. Perhaps he strove to create a consciousness of both tradition and modernity. Schleuning reads in the printed version Bach's intention to create a "new kind of external clarity, uniformity, and simplicity."[39] He makes a connection between this and the age's passion for antiquity. Bach (in this view) recognizes that the homage to the vocal polyphony of the sixteenth century, inscribed into *The Art of Fugue,* is similar to the admiration for classical antiquity. So with his impressive array of counterpoints he was attempting to create an analogy to the orders of columns described by Vitruvius—that architect whose *De architectura* has survived the ages.

In the circle of the Mizler Society to which Bach belonged, the simple numerical relations on which architecture is based were compared with the numerical structure at the basis of music. Mizler himself, as an experiment, sets the Tuscular order of column to notes but finds "the melody all too sweet and insufficiently seasoned with dissonance."[40]

It is quite plausible that in Bach's day, in a society felt to be overly complex, even those in the realm of speculative music referred back to what they perceived as the simpler ordering systems of antiquity. It is probably impossible for us now to determine whether the source material for *The Art of Fugue* proves Bach's interest in antiquity. Schleuning's thesis seems plausible, that Carl Philipp Emanuel Bach dealt with this material—in the service of his father's work—in a way that amounted to "a masterful restaging, similar to Constanze Mozart's and Mozart's students' treatment of the *Requiem.*"[41]

Publishing the work as a torso and appending the alleged Deathbed Chorale helped create a Bach myth. With his idea of crowning the counterpoint series with an incomplete movement bearing the B-A-C-H signature, an inspiration that was both strategic and artistic, the son (to the extent that he was responsible) realized the concept of *non finito* that was current then—particularly in the realm of sculpture in the antique style. By adding the Deathbed Chorale, he also brings in the traditional *vanitas* motif in honor of his father.

One thinks in this connection of Giambattista Piranesi's *Roman Temple* from his *Antichità Romane* from 1756: low viewpoints and a perspective from underneath intensify the monumental effect and the quality of absoluteness that informs the architecture. The figures that naively populate the landscape in front of the temple, despite their small size, are not mere accessories: with fitting deference they have their place in this columned structure, which seems to come out of the past and to disappear into it.

The idea of *non finito* articulates the tension between the sublime infinite and human limitation. One need not stage *The Art of Fugue* to see it in this context: its highly complex intention never had a chance at a perfect and definitive form—that is the aesthetic message that puts it in the company of Beethoven's late work. Beethoven possessed a printed edition and a manuscript piano version of *The Art of Fugue,* whose contrapuntalism has echoes in the *Hammerklavier Sonata,* opus 106, but that occupied Mozart, Schumann, Brahms, and many twentieth-century composers as well.

One notes with pleasure the long history of the influence of *The Art of Fugue,* and the various attempts to define its proper order—published by, among others, Heinrich Rietsch in 1926, Hans Theodor David in 1927, Heinrich Husmann in 1938, Jacques Chailley in 1967, and Wolfgang Wiemer in 1977. But modern-day readers shudder at the mystification that Wolfgang Graeser produced with his 1924 essay in the *Bach-Jahrbuch.* The problem here was not the young musicologist's attempt to determine and circulate a plausible order for the counterpoints in *The Art of Fugue* but his use of the work to inspire connoisseurs and amateurs to participate in a patriotic struggle:

> *The disgrace of allowing one of the most precious of our national treasures to fall into oblivion has still not been erased; it has weighed on German music for a century and three-quarters. The German* Volk, *in a time of serfdom, of inner and outer poverty, must remember the spirits of its great, world-historic genius.*[42]

Graeser's scoring of *The Art of Fugue*—in part for full orchestra, with trumpets and trombones—was performed for the first time in the Thomaskirche in Leipzig by its likewise nationalistically minded cantor, Karl Straube, in June 1927, and afterward was continually repeated by important ensembles and interpreters—at least twenty times in 1928 alone.[43] The press reacted with enthusiasm. Although a self-described "warrior against false nationalism," the critic Felix Stössinger reveals himself pleased that now once again "the old, admirable German spirit has been resurrected."[44] *The Art of Fugue* documents Germany's position as one of the world's great powers. Its discovery is part of the "cosmic change" that the writer Wilhelm Schäfer, leaning toward national socialism, heralded in his address in the Bach memorial year of 1935.[45]

The educated bourgeois public took up the work willingly, if with an astounding lack of reflection, seeing it as a part of an essential Germanness that had the potential for and obligation to the highest level of achievement. When the violinist Hermann Diener performs *The Art of Fugue* with a small orchestra, his internationally respected collegium musicum, he precedes this "cultural act" each time with "Canons on a Theme by Frederick the Great, from the *Musical Offering*," for instance, in March 1939 in St. Peter's Church in Heidelberg, and air-raid alarms nothwithstanding, did so deep into the Second World War.[46] The Nazis' reverence for the Prussian king is a textbook example of how the military and musical arts, in large-scale strategic linkage, shook hands with each other in the key signature of nationalism.

The question of whether Bach, Beethoven, Wagner, and Bruckner are responsible for their exploitation by later generations has been endlessly debated in recent decades, with no conclusion. With respect to *The Art of Fugue*, one element is worth pondering: despite all the liveliness contained in the individual pieces of counterpoint and despite the creative way they are woven together, the work really represents less a flow of ideas than a system. Systems have the tendency to expand the reach of their own regulations. There is something deadly in this. In his poem "Death Fugue," which treats the lines "Death is a master from Germany" like a musical theme, Paul Celan establishes a structural relation between the strictness of counterpoint and the relentlessness of the machinery of murder.

No one needs to read *The Art of Fugue* in this sense. There are other things to admire about Bach's contrapuntal systems, as Schumann noted: elements of the fantastic and the arabesque and, with them, a mysterious bit of worldly wisdom. Whoever finds the signature of death in the notes of *The Art of Fugue* can be certain that life and death are a part of each other, that there can be no being with-out an order, even if that order sets limits to being. Death is a con-dition of life, and the loss of the moment is the only permanence. "It was a strange battle, where death with life did struggle," go the words of a Luther chorale set several times by Bach.

In a foreword he sketched in 1914 to part 2 of *The Well-Tempered Clavier*, Ferrucio Busoni wrote down these thoughts, which could also apply to *The Art of Fugue:* "For the important creator, the first period is that of his own seeking, the second that of his own discov-ering; the third and final period often seems to be a new search for something that only later seekers can interpret."[47]

THE *MUSICAL OFFERING*

For Philipp Spitta, the *Musical Offering* was a "tremendous work" but "without a lofty idea"; it was, moreover, "an omnium gatherum of piecework showing one single idea executed in as many different ways as possible."[48] In several articles published since 1979, Warren and Ur-sula Kirkendale have offered an opposing view, that the *Musical Of-fering* should be understood as the conscious application of certain parts of the *Institutio oratoria* by the classical rhetorician Quintilian:[49]

Quintilian's *Institutio oratoria*	Bach's *Musical Offering*
Parts of Rhetoric according to Kirkendale	Original Movement Headings
Exordium I	Ricercar a 3
Narratio brevis	Canon perpetuus super thema regium
Narratio ornata	[5] Canones diversi super thema regium
Egressus	Fuga canonica
Exordium II	Ricercar a 6
Argumentatio	[two enigmatic canons]
Probatio	Canon a 2
Refutatio	Canon a 4
Peroratorio in affectibus	Sonata sopr'il soggetto reale
Peroratorio in rebus	Canon perpetuus

This scholarly couple support their theory with the fact that the term *ricercar* was applied not just to music pieces but to the opening section of works of expert oratory. The theory further states, correctly, that Bach was acquainted with the rhetorical schemata of Cicero and Quintilian: rhetoric in the classical tradition was taught in schools at that time. The expectation that an educated composer of Bach's era would include elements of rhetoric in his compositions is reflected by Johann Mattheson's recommendation that "a careful arrangement of all the parts and details of the melody, or in the entire melodic work... should include the same six ingredients required of a speaker, namely, introduction, narration, proposition, confirmation, confutation, and conclusion. That is, *Exordium, narratio, propositio, confirmatio, confutatio, & peroratio.*"[50]

According to Cicero and Quintilian, this is the framework of a legal argument.[51] But although the devil is in the details,[52] Mattheson points out that an oration might be compared with a single aria but hardly with such a heterogenous combination of movements as is present in the *Musical Offering*. Indeed, it is incorrect to speak of a *series* of movements, since, thanks to Wolff's research, we have an outline of the order in which Bach composed the individual sections and gave them to the printer,[53] but it is still an open question to what extent he viewed his work in progress as an entity.

To speak of a collection rather than a series allows this different view of the work: the metaphor that leaps to mind is a display cabinet, which Bach gradually fills with treasures on a single theme—the "thema regium" or "royal theme." The viewer immediately sees that the sections of the printed edition, because of their three different formats, are less suited for being gathered together as a single bound set of music than they are for exhibition. The canons in particular can be seen as emblematic ornamental pieces.

Because of their mottos and musical notation styles, the canons are calligraphy and riddles at the same time, meant not just to be heard and studied but to be looked at as well. The dedication volume of the *Canones diversi super thema regium* contains the added text: "Notulis crescentibus crescat Fortuna Ascendenteque Modulatione ascendat Gloria Regis" ("With these notes may the King's fortune increase, and with this modulation, his fame"). This sentiment is more or less an epigraph to the picture presented by the image of the notes and thus a completed emblem (see page 636).

In the Middle Ages the writing down of a canon was often understood as a memento mori, as opposed to an art for the senses, which would offer only fleeting pleasure. The canons of the *Musical Offering* are not for transitory amusement. However, instead of reminding the listener of death, they point out that the happiness and fame of the ruler are symbolic values, which can be shown, among other ways, by a skillfully written canon together with a "symbolum"—the traditional term for the epigraph of a canon. Before being put off by the devout tone of his dedicatory text, we should understand that in his foreword Bach is paying homage not only to a ruler who was important "in all the sciences of war and peace, and particularly in music" but also to the general concept of sovereignty by the grace of God.

Bach's contribution to this ruler's fame is a new presentation of the centuries-old art of academic counterpoint. While the generations before him composed in this field primarily to honor God and only secondarily to honor their princely employers, Bach composes this work expressly as an "offering," laying it at the feet of a ruler who was known for his enlightened tastes but could also appreciate the old, when confronted by the artistic genius of a musician like Bach.

Frederick II's meeting with Bach was still fresh in his memory in 1774: as Gottfried van Swieten attests at the time, Frederick had not treated Bach as a fossil from a bygone age but respected him as an artist. He could even sing the "royal theme."[54]

Bach doubtless chose the obsolete term *ricercar* very carefully. He wanted to be more than a genial composer of fugues, that is, the peerless technician that his contemporary Mattheson made of him. Bach viewed himself as the trustee of a long tradition that practiced

The "thema regium" from the *Musical Offering*.

the art of counterpoint as applied theology blended with worldly wisdom. In the case of the "Ricercar a 3" the genre designation is technically correct: Bach writes a relaxed counterpoint, with passages that are downright pretty, in a style that the seventeenth century would have called "fantastic." But the second, the "Ricercar a 6," which was requested in Potsdam by the king but not delivered until the first printing, is a strict fugue in the *stile antico*. In fact, Bach, in his advertisement of the edition in the *Leipziger Zeitungen* of September 1747, does not hesitate to speak of both ricercars as fugues.[55] The original designation of "ricercar" was chosen only as a kind of brand name with the king in mind.

Let us go back to the exhibitory nature of the *Musical Offering*. The differing instrumentation of its parts point in this direction as well. It is no coincidence that the other three late cycles were written for keyboard alone and so have a rigor appropriate for the concentrated display of theory. With the "royal theme," which is not his own work, Bach's concern is not to show off his own invention but to demonstrate what a great artist can do with a theme of someone else's. He can improvise a counterpoint at the harpsichord, and still oblige the expected tastes of the listener with pleasing little turns of phrase. The three-part ricercar is the written documentation of the one performed at the Potsdam court. A ricercar can also be worked out in six voices; this demonstrates a contrapuntal art that needs a little more thought, but, as in *The Art of Fugue*, it can still be performed on the harpsichord.

One can also invent canons that offer not only something to the eye and the mind but also something beautiful for the ear—on the harpsichord, also in trio sonata settings, specifically required in the *Canon a 2 violini in unisono* and the *Canon perpetuus*. Perhaps Bach hoped that the canons of the *Musical Offering* would be played at the Prussian court and thus "exhibited" in the way most satisfying to a musician. In any event, to an astonishing degree he gave these compositions a speaking quality. In the *Canon perpetuus*, for example, the gallant style is audible in gesture and manner:

Bach most definitely wanted the king to play in a performance of the Trio Sonata for Flute and Violin. In his effort to please the king's taste, he reverts to the field of the basso-continuo sonata, which he had long abandoned, but writes a lively and unformulaic part, at least for the continuo performers. We do not know if his expectations were fulfilled or not. Even though Wolff sees "gallant phrase length and line shaping, as well as sensitive declamation and dynamics" in the slow movements of the trio sonata,[56] it is evident throughout that the "royal theme" itself, which is anything but gallant, demands its due, especially with regard to space. It runs through the long allegro movement six times, like a cantus firmus in all its dignity. In the other movements, in his voice leading and harmony, Bach makes no compromises in favor of agreeable sound or delicacy.

In artifice, the canons on the royal theme surpass everything in the field written by Bach's predecessors. In the *Canon a 2 cancrizans*, a "crab canon," the one notated voice must be played forward and backward simultaneously; in the *Canon a 2 per tonos*, the three voices spiral imperceptibly upward from C minor, until each voice, after the eight bars it takes to play through the ornamented "thema regium," reaches in turn the keys of D minor, E minor, F-sharp minor, G-sharp minor, B-flat minor, and C minor again.

In his 1979 book *Gödel, Escher, Bach*, Douglas R. Hofstadter was especially taken with this "endlessly reduplicating" canon. In this book the obvious inability of man to understand the nature of thought is the theme, and the *Musical Offering* is reflected on repeatedly. The *Canon a 2 per tonos* reminds Hofstadter of the illusionary paintings of M. C. Escher—the *Waterfall*, for instance, which plunges downward and yet flows back to its starting point.

This element of illusory infiniteness recalls the works of Netherlandish and German sixteenth-century composers, in which upward or downward modulations are executed through the sophisticated use of accidentals—often in connection with texts that speak of the wheel of capricious Fortune.[57] Bach may have known such works. Whether he did or not, one is struck by his having written by hand the words noted on page 635 into the dedication copy of the *Canones diversi.* Did he realize late in life that the ancient tradition of Fortuna could be revived and recycled for a modern use?

Aside from the degree of artistic skill, in which Bach cannot be outdone even by the old Netherlanders, there is a palpable element of stubbornness to these canons. It shows a strong personality that, the composer's deference notwithstanding, meets the king as an equal. That the age viewed the aristocracy as a part of nature was in accord with the idea of natural equality: the animal kingdom has its lion to rule it, humanity its king, said Calderon.[58] Such comparisons can easily go on: what the snake is to the animals, the sage is to humanity—including the composer of genius. In the third to last bar of the six-part ricercar, the note series B-A-C-H, though divided between two parts, appears simultaneously with the "thema regium." We should not make too much of this, but we should not ignore it either.

There is little reason to assume, with Michael Marissen, that the *Musical Offering* is actually dedicated to God.[59] It is more a confidently completed piece of journeyman work—an unlooked-for commission, as difficult as it was important. Only after this did Bach's attention turn to "last things": the printed version of *The Art of Fugue* and the completion of the B-Minor Mass. These are the great works that sum up Bach's compositional thought and work against the backdrop of his faith in God as the beginning and end of all music.

PART FOUR

HORIZONS

BACH'S ART

Insisting that Bach was unappreciated during his lifetime has become part of the Bach hagiography—mostly thanks to self-important commentators. Without question, he lived in almost continual conflict with the authorities in his middle and later Leipzig years. For this reason certain employers and members of the Leipzig Town Council may have lost their enthusiasm for his music. We have no written evidence to this effect. To the contrary, the few reports that have come down to us, despite the primitive state of journalism at the time, attest to the high esteem in which Bach was held during his lifetime. More than once he was deemed to be one of the most important composers of his time, alongside celebrities like Telemann, Handel, Hasse, and Graun. If measured by the number of significant students he had, he stands alone at the top.

Of course, Bach was never popular in a superficial sense. But his greatness was seen early on. In 1739 Johann Abraham Birnbaum spoke of the "strange perfections of Herr *Hofcompositeur*."[1] In 1782 Johann Friedrich Reichardt compared his experience of Bach with Goethe's impression of the Strasbourg Cathedral as a "work of eternal nature."[2] Two years later, Daniel Christian Friedrich Schubart, the Sturm und Drang poet, praised Bach's "gigantic intellect."[3] And in the last decade of the eighteenth century the London organist August Friedrich Christoph Kollmann had a "sun" engraved in copper, showing the German composers known to him, with Bach in the center.[4] This put Bach's artistic qualities into a religious light: the sun, according to ancient beliefs, is the embodiment of goodness and perfection. On the occasion of the rediscovery of the *St. Matthew Passion,* in 1829 Goethe thought he heard the roar of a far-off ocean. Rahel Varnhagen von Ense finds Bach to be "the equal of all of Kant." The historian Wilhelm Loebell invokes Shakespeare.[5]

Through such metaphors, and many more could be cited, Bach became transformed into a phenomenon of nature. Daniel Christian Friedrich Schubart, the first to call him an "original genius," tried to define more precisely that genius: "What Newton was as a sage of nature, Bach was as a musician."[6] The equation of Bach with Newton was not arbitrary: the English mathematician and physicist, who attempted to sum up all natural laws under a single principle and thereby derive the workings of God out of an order that could be observed in nature, remained a popular figure in the late eighteenth century, the age of the cult of genius.

When Schubart sees in Bach's work the meeting of "worldly wisdom" with "original genius," he touches the core of his musical thought: it is universal, balanced between the systematic thought of the Middle Ages and the subjectively oriented philosophy of the modern era. From the age of Pythagoras through the eighteenth century, music was considered a mathematical science. On the one hand, the numerical relations at the basis of music reflect the laws of how the world is built; on the other hand, music uses these laws in a unique way for the praise of God and the edification of mankind. While mathematicians and physicists can only calculate or demonstrate theoretically the "harmony of the spheres," music makes this harmony available to the senses through the medium of sound.

In the history of Western polyphony, it was primarily the rigorous forms of contrapuntal writing that were understood as the expression and symbol of the divine order of creation: the planets have their own orbits, yet are related to one another by obeying one and the same law. In this sense, the fugues of *The Well-Tempered Clavier* gave Wagner a glimpse of the "world-idea." The B-Minor Fugue for Organ, BWV 544, prompted his remark: "Here are elementary forces, like planets, with psychic life. That is the musician *katexochen* [par excellence]."7

This is not just about fugues and counterpoint in the narrow sense but about the principle Bach followed everywhere of the obbligato setting, which should be understood as independent and equal voices played with and against one another. "The harmony becomes far more complete if all the voices collaborate to form it...[and] where each one has a melody of its own that harmonizes quite well with the others." It was the pen of Master Birnbaum that recorded this guiding principle on paper in the 1730s.8

What is special about this obbligato principle becomes clear in the context of the prevailing compositional theory of the seventeenth and eighteenth centuries, which states that a musical setting has its harmonic foundation in the continuo. In short, the compositions of the baroque era tend to be reducible to a framework of melody and harmonic accompaniment. But Bach's compositions relativize the continuo and make sure that harmony comes as much as possible out of the voice leading.

Bach stoutly resists the modern, enlightened idea that the most natural and human way to experience music is in the form of melody plus accompaniment. For him, there exists not only human nature but also the nature of music itself: the composer must not take away from music's richness. The consequence for Bach is that every work of music has to be conceived as a perfect likeness of divine creation, as *concordia discors*, as oneness in the manyness of the world.

The principle of *concordia discors* at the same time points out why imitation and elaboration on only a few thematic figures play such an important role: in God's creation, of which music is a part, everything is connected to everything else. Any composition that does not show this connection is not doing justice to the idea of creation, is actually a betrayal of it. The principle in ancient Greek philosophy of "hen kai pan"—that is, "all out of one" and "all in one"—has a great tradition in Western music. But it was Bach who applied this principle to music with the greatest completeness and consistency. In this regard, cycles like *The Art of Fugue* are isolated peaks.

Schubart sets Bach alongside Newton because both men reveal the laws of creation and the existence of God. Thus both are models and guides for humankind in its search for order and meaning. That Bach is repeatedly called the "father of harmony," even by Beethoven, does not just refer specifically to the overwhelming musical richness of his polyphony, which he extended to the limits of the possible.[9] No, he is also the "father of harmony" because he took the art of composing to a level where it replicates to perfection the fullness and harmoniousness of Creation itself.[10]

The cycle is part of this idea, and it became more and more concrete to Bach during the course of his life: it fascinated him as it did no other composer in the history of music. Of course, the single work is a complete statement in itself, but always from the perspective of its own limited horizon. A series of works, or a cycle, offers the possibility of broadening this horizon, of casting one and the same idea into various expressive forms and thus treating it exhaustively. In such series as the *Orgelbüchlein,* the *Brandenburg Concertos,* and the choral cantata cycle, Bach goes beyond the tradition of grouping like things together; instead, he collects things of very different character on the same theme.

In the *Inventions and Sinfonias, The Well-Tempered Clavier,* the six solos for violin, the four parts of the *Clavier-Übung, The Art of Fugue,* and in the definitive form of the B-Minor Mass, there is a palpable endeavor to reveal the universal dynamic of music in cycles of a thorough nature. In the course of time, these cycles have taken on the character of demonstration or teaching pieces; they go beyond the creative subject to impart a kind of objectified information about music itself. Except perhaps for the passions, no single composition could have such historical influence. As stated in the chapter on the Cöthen cycles, Anton Webern speaks for composers from three centuries when he says, in 1933: "You find everything in Bach: the development of cyclic forms, the conquest of the realm of tonality—the attempt at a summation of the highest order."[11]

Such thoughts would have more philosophical than aesthetic relevance, would be aimed more at the sublime than at the beautiful in music, if they were grounded in the old mathematical-medieval-baroque understanding of music. But Schubart, our guiding spirit here, also invokes Bach's "original genius." He speaks as a contemporary of the young Goethe, whose Prometheus says, "Here I sit, forming mortals in my image; a race resembling me, to suffer, to weep, to enjoy, to rejoice!" We are dealing not with practical wisdom but with the creative power of genius! With respect to Bach, is this new understanding of music an anachronism or an insight?

First, the obvious: Bach is taking part in the general artistic discourse of the seventeenth and early eighteenth centuries, when music was shifting its position in the seven liberal arts, moving away from arithmetic, geometry, and astronomy and over to the side of grammar, rhetoric, and logic. At Bach's time music was becoming more attuned to its linguistic character, and composition was becoming the "melodic science." This science derived from a naturally flowing melody with continuo accompaniment; the melody could be worked into a powerful form of tonal speech. Musical time was no longer measured off by proportion but by how it was experienced. Musical themes took on their own life, and the sequence of movements became more dynamic. The important forms were the concerto movement and the aria, where the modern, predominantly Italian understanding of music was in the vanguard.

Bach is an original genius not so much as a participant in this discussion as in his distance from it. He is subject neither to the older categories of the quadrivium nor to those of the newer trivium; he stands outside and above them, and from there develops the idea of a balanced and reflective work of art. In this view, music is more than a utilitarian art, because every composition represents a harmonious and complete work in itself. In large forms like the passion or the cantata, he could not fully realize this concept, because of the variety of set texts; but in single vocal forms such as motets, concerto movements, and arias and in the instrumental forms, to a large extent he did.

With respect to instrumental music of the so-called classic-Romantic period, music criticism likes to talk about absolute music and the autonomous artwork: a piece is said to have autonomy when its structure is defined completely by the music itself. According to Carl Dahlhaus, the "triumph of analysis" consists in showing "that the sense of each part of a work is in its relation to all the other parts, and to the whole, and that the sole reason for each part is the function that it fulfills."[12]

When we speak of a balanced and reflective artwork, we do not mean this kind of autonomy, if indeed it exists at all. What we mean is Bach's ingenious ability to conceive of and to unite in one work all the different levels on which music is experienced. Bach is not a specialist for structure or genre, who thinks only about rhetoric, symbolism, or historical consciousness; he is a master of multiple perspective, of looking at the whole picture.

In the aria "Widerstehe doch der Sünde" from BWV 54 (discussed in the chapter on the Weimar cantatas), the pattern of the da capo aria is evident but combined with an idea alien to it. The introductory ritornello is not a positive device, but from a harmonic point of view it consists of nothing other than resisting reaching the tonic. Of course, this very resistance inheres in the text ("resist sin"), and so the ritornello is rhetorically justified. But it is also structurally significant: the musical characteristics of this resistance are not tacked on like an illustration; they are part and parcel of the movement from beginning to end, even if the text refers *expressis verbis* to resistance only at the beginning.

Historical reflection is apparent most of all in the final aria on the text "Wer Sünde tut, der ist vom Teufel." Bach writes it as a strict fugue, the theme of which traces that harsh chromatic path that the ancients called the passus duriusculus, to express the feeling of suffering, of losing one's way. Fugal writing here is adopted not as a historical method but as an expression of the harshness and difficulty inherent in the Old Covenant, in contrast to the grace of the New Covenant of Jesus Christ.

The combination of order and expressivity, structure and singability, structural autonomy and theological meaning, compositional rigor and social openness results in an enormous density of events: a lot is happening. This density does not come from a large number of instruments: we feel it even in the chaconne for solo violin. In general Bach tends not to favor major over minor parts, foreground over middleground or background, primary over secondary levels of meaning. He always has the whole in mind; and whatever is included as a part of this whole is taken seriously. The critic Scheibe's complaint that the great master wrote out all his ornamentation is a misunderstanding: anything Bach wrote out could never be an add-on; it is part of the work.

The density can be overwhelming. Bach's music, though rationally planned, sometimes seems an impenetrable, unsolvable myth, touching prelinguistic levels of meaning, where experience is not worked through but simply got through. When this occurs, what counts is not the argument but shock and awe, those emotions that take hold and move precisely those listeners who are incapable of decoding complex structure. The result can be laughter as well as tears: laughter over the infinitude of creation, and tears at one's own insignificance.

Bach stands at the center of Western musical thought. His music is totally of this earth: a passion is a passion, a minuet is a minuet. Each one of his works has its social setting: only *The Art of Fugue*, by definition, reaches for the stars. Even the religious element is rooted in the earth. Unlike Beethoven's, Bach's music has no need to seek justification within itself: it is based in faith. There is no impassioned, worldly ego but a deeply grounded spiritual self: vulnerable perhaps, but unshakable.

In the century before Bach there was one great composer who believed unwaveringly in the primacy of vocal music and in its mission of setting the word of God to music: Heinrich Schütz. For Bach, pure instrumental music was also of this order—but as *religious* music. With Bach, too, the way to a meaningful instrumental music, and beyond that to the autonomous musical work, proceeded naturally via the confrontation with theology and with religious texts. Instrumental music too has its meaning, because it is an image of Creation, made for the honor of God and the improvement of the human spirit. One cannot ignore the fact that the method used for the *Goldberg Variations*—that is, playing canons consecutively on the primary, the second, and third, and so on—was modeled conceptually on Johannes Ockeghem's *Missa Prolationum*.[13]

A generation later, Kant judged music without words an expression of "free beauty," but on a level with "foliage for architectural borders" and wallpaper.[14] After him, Hegel viewed purely instrumental music as "void, meaningless," and "not truly art."[15] These judgments come not from a lack of musical appreciation in the two philosophers but from the subsequent secularization of instrumental music. It was not until the age of Beethoven, when as part of the new religion of art, music was accorded rank and dignity, that a reevaluation of the art of music was possible—and this included the rediscovered keyboard and organ works of Bach.

So, while Bach's music is clearly anchored in traditional conceptions of art, it is also just as clearly a visible banner of modernity. Not until Bach does music enter history with all the full authority of high art. There were earlier composers and works of importance, but he was the first to show that beyond individual works, genres, and styles there lay *music itself*—not as a construct of musical theology and music theory but as a sovereign state where the composer ruled as artist and philosopher.

Bach asks questions about the essence of music. Can it be contained in *one* work—or in series and cycles like *The Well-Tempered Clavier, The Art of Fugue,* and the B-Minor Mass? How is meaning created—not just musical coherence but total meaning, in the medium which he expressly chose for it? He is the first musician to sum up the dialectic between the general and particular, the social and the individual in art; after him, only Beethoven could do this on the same level.

As mentioned before, Adorno ranked Bach "beneath Beethoven in a historico-philosophical sense, despite his greater 'success,' because there was attached to his music an element of heteronomy, of the subject not being totally in control of the material."[16] Instead of identifying with this bourgeois, individualist value system, we should appreciate Bach as the first composer who had major compositional strategies—strategies not relating to the ideal of absolute music but that were an exciting mix of demands made on the artist, confrontations with history, influence on the current social milieu, pursuit of personal and career goals: all transformed into sound. Adorno's idea that great music is nothing other than music, yet still a social act, could be proven true with Bach; here there is no difference between him and Beethoven.

There is something liberating about seeing Bach's music not just from a philosophical aspect but from a strategic one as well. While systematic philosophy is after one overriding truth, the thing about strategies is that they often fail. This is true for Bach's work: different tendencies and ambitions, though integrated, also collide with one another, conflict with one another. The universality of such work is due not to its perfection but to its multiplicity of perspective and outlook. So writes the philosopher Georg Picht: "The universality of Bach's music is not, as with Leibniz or Goethe, the demonstration of a unity complete in itself. Rather, the shattering of all earthly unity becomes the principle that creates its unity."[17]

This is what is modern about Bach: man himself must set about creating unity—against the backdrop of the *theologia crucis,* and in suffering and in overcoming. Like Luther before him, Bach has an ear for the tumult that is played out in the world and in the human soul, and he makes it his theme in his own way. Beauty is found in creation and in contradiction. It deals with the temporal but with a view of the eternal. He is idealist and realist at the same time. Idealist in his principle of "all from one and all in one," the idea that there must be a primal ground whence the essence of all music flows. Yet his writing is realistic in its details, in that it holds a likeness of the world in all its diversity and disparity.

Bach's music is not just order and hymn singing. In it, humanity cries out from the depths. In the skillfully woven polyphony, the Christian and his chorale singing are almost importuning. The sounds of the external world are here as well: post horn, hunting calls, pastoral music, and chiming bells are all set to music.[18] Bach represents a standpoint that is beyond medieval systematic thought, on the one hand, and yet still has the faith in progress that sees the good side of everything, on the other. I find this kind of universality, which goes beyond the opposites of autonomy and heteronomy, only in Pablo Picasso: the continual reduction of the visible world to its essentials coexists with the everyday, material things of life.

Bach's universality has one essential prerequisite: comprehensive mastery of the technique of composition. This mastery makes possible the conception of the work as a whole yet with all its characteristic elements in place. In music history, Bach's art is the first that has a share in the modernist aspiration to guide the social process through technological superiority. The ambition to find structures for the whole while still allowing detail to express subjectivity leads to the tensions that run through all modern art. This dialectic can be read particularly in *The Art of Fugue* and its themes: the *soggetto* stands for the whole, the B-A-C-H theme for the expression of subjectivity. The integration of the two remains incomplete.

Bach's philosophical and strategic thinking is, in the words of Michel Foucault, a part of the "discourse of masculine domination." The artist faces the world, creates forms to confront it, defines and concentrates things into language, sets standards. "Bach was a man, through and through; with him, no half measures, nothing feeble, everything was written as if for all time," remarked the twenty-two-year-old Robert Schumann in 1832; for him, studying *The Well-Tempered Clavier* had a "morally reinforcing effect."[19] Though the music of Handel, Mozart, or Schubert may be thought to have more soul and song than Bach's, it is Bach and Beethoven who have most influenced music history to the present day; they are the standard by which others judge their own work.

Bach always has his tools at hand—like Dürer's Melencolia, who while seated lost in contemplation still has all around her, in fantastic disarray, everything she needs to measure, discover, evaluate, and probe the forces that hold the world together. But this leads us to a further point: we can understand Bach's art only when we know the categories informing it. These are theology, rhetoric, and symbolism.

BACH AS A CHRISTIAN

The Lutheran faith is of the utmost significance for Bach's creative work. Theological erudition and piety do not make for musical genius, but they can help guide it. Still, it took special circumstances and turns of fate: Handel too was raised in the Protestant religion, received a theological humanistic education, and in his younger years was trained as a church organist, but his genius sought, and found, other avenues.

There exists one unambivalent proof of Bach's interest in religion: the index of his theological library.[1] It cites eighty-one volumes; in Robin A. Leaver's reckoning the number may be 112.[2] It would require almost twenty feet of shelving to hold it.[3] Martin Luther is represented by seven- and eight-volume editions—Latin and German—as well as by his speeches and the *Hauspostille*. Post-Luther writings show a broad spectrum of schools of thought and opinions. Writings of the Lutheran orthodoxy predominate; but theologians from the tradition of Lutheran mysticism, seventeenth-century reform theology, and Pietism such as Johan Arndt, Heinrich Müller, and August Hermann Francke are also represented. Since the devotional works are dominated by books on the church calendar, it seems likely that Bach used them to prepare for writing the Sunday scriptural cantatas.

There is almost nothing known about the secular books in Bach's library, since his heirs disposed of them even before the official probate of the will. We are happy enough to have a little further documentation of his theological inclination: a receipt from 1742 for his acquisition of a Luther edition from the property of the famous theologian Abraham Calov,[4] and Calov's bible. This so-called Calov Bible, a three-volume commented edition of the Luther text, came from the inheritance of Anna Magdalena and ended up in the United States, by ways unknown, where it was read carefully by the German immigrant Leonhard Reichle in the nineteenth century and given by his son to the Lutheran Seminary in St. Louis.[5]

As his notes and underlinings prove, Bach purchased the three volumes in 1733 and read a great deal in them. Since the bible went through many hands, it cannot always be determined which entries are his. But four commentaries dealing with the mission of church music are certainly from him. On the tale of the prophetess Miriam, who led the chorus of women with her drum, he writes the following marginal note in the book of Exodus: "First prelude to be performed in two choruses to the honor of God." About the regulations for services and singers, written down in the two books of chronicles, Bach wrote in three different places: "This chapter is the true foundation of all church music pleasing to God," "A splendid proof that along with other institutions of the church service, music from the spirit of God especially was also ordained by David," and "In a devotional music service, God is always present with his grace."[6]

Even those more interested in Bach's genius than in his personal piety are moved by such comments: here is a human being whose commitment to his biblical faith and to his art is total. Spitta, in his great biography, understated the oneness of art and faith in Bach. For Spitta, a secular Protestant, the difference was minor between Bach's daily life with the bible and Brahms's one-time compilation of Bible passages to use in his *German Requiem* (Brahms was Spitta's contemporary). But the difference is huge; and only those who understand this can gauge what it means that Bach did not use the words of the Bible just for a few oratorical works but Sunday after Sunday, year in, year out, and set to music its rhymed paraphrases with the utmost emphasis and unfailing energy: that was not craft or aestheticism but credo!

After his death, none of his sons showed any interest in his theological literature—times had changed. The passion with which he fought for using scripture and Lutheran chorales in his cantatas may have been welcomed in Leipzig by the traditionalists, but the extent to which he did this was not expected even by them. Then we see him in person as a Lutheran who toward the end of life, as Lutheranism is stagnating against the background of the Enlightenment, plays a last card: the "catholic" card, that is, a supraconfessional mass with a credo in the center.

Bach's Lutheranism subsumes Pietism. It is fruitless to argue whether the emotional Jesus-focused piety, which speaks from his sacred music and specifically from his passions and dialogic cantatas, is in the old tradition of Lutheran mysticism or is a contemporary result of direct Pietist experience.[7] But clearly all through his vocal music Bach makes use of arias with Pietist connotations: catchy four-beat or dancelike three-beat meters. When this is coupled with frequent modulations and sublimations, it is a simple matter for the listener to hear the appropriate context.[8]

It is no scandal for a Lutheran like Bach to glean some positive aspects from the views of Philipp Jacob Spener and Francke. In terms of intellectual and spiritual history there is no reason to avoid the term *Pietism* with regard to Bach. Even Friedrich Nietzsche has expressed the view that with Bach, modern, soulful music first came to light in Protestantism—under the sign of Pietism: "Without that deeply religious change of heart, without the fading sound of a most inwardly agitated soul, music would have remained learned or operatic."[9]

Lutheranism and Pietism both acted as a foil for Bach's staunch faith in Christ. This faith can be heard throughout his work, but it is expressly confirmed in an album entry from the year 1747. As mentioned in the chapter on Cöthen cycles, Bach inscribes the riddle canon BWV 1077 in the family album of Johann Gottfried Fulde, a theology student and member of the Leipzig Concert Society. He adds this *symbolum* to it: Christus Coronabit Crucigeros. "Christ will crown the cross bearers."

It is possible that Fulde chose this motto and Bach agreed to write it. But looking at the canon itself, it seems quite certain that Bach had already been actively working out the theme before dedicating it to Fulde—particularly the *symbolum,* which in this formulation appeared nowhere else. So until more is known, it should be considered Bach's own. Similar mottos are known to exist. Heinrich Müller, a forerunner of Pietism whom Bach admired, included a portrait of himself in one of his publications that shows him pointing at the motto: "Crux Christi nostra Gloria"—"Christ's cross is our glory."[10]

The word *symbolum* and the notes fit together. The ascending chromatic fourth in canon 2 and the descending chromatic fourth in canon 1 were traditionally used in seventeenth-century music, and often by Bach himself, to symbolize suffering and the cross. More important, the characteristic sharps ("sharp" in German is *Kreuz*) for this passus duriusculus—A# and G# in canon 1, C# and D# in canon 2—disappear in the resolution, and from the inversion come the imitating voices needed: Christ absolves the cross bearers of their crosses.[11] The first closed sixteenth-note figure of the canon voices can be read as the crown placed on the cross bearer's head by Christ.

The B-A-C-H motive is at work here too[12]—for example, in the closing notes of the second highest voice in the canon resolution:

Unfortunately this canon—preserved by sheer luck—is the only direct testimony we have of Bach's faith in Christ. It should not be overvalued as evidence but taken more as a symbolic signature under the entire oeuvre, in which the Lutheran theology of the cross occupies a privileged place, not just textually but musically as well. Whoever has grown up with this theology hears in Bach's music the "anxious expectation of all creation" mentioned in Romans 8—a chapter that served as the textual basis for two of Bach's motets. One also hears another verse of this chapter in this music: "Who is he that condemneth? It is Christ that died, yea rather, that is risen again, who is even at the right hand of God, who also maketh intercession for us."

Let us try to approach Bach's theology of music through the three articles of faith. The first article speaks of God's creation.

Whoever discovers and portrays the beauty of its design is praising the divine power of Creation. In this sense, the astronomer Johannes Kepler understood his science as a work of praise.[13] Bach doubtless saw his work in the same way: his art too was one great hymn of praise to God, by showing as artfully and beautifully as he could the possibilities that exist in that work of God's creation called music.

To explain Bach's theology of music, though, requires the second, Christological article of faith, which mentions all Creation (*Kreatur*). The Nicene Creed, as the basis of the B-Minor Mass, says of God the Father that he is Father Almighty, maker of heaven and earth and of all things visible and invisible—no less and no more. *One* movement was enough for Bach to set this. The story of Jesus Christ is told by the creed in all its sweeping breadth: Bach uses one number each to present the divinity, the incarnation, the passion and death, the resurrection, ascension, and the second coming to judge the world.

In the second article of faith, the history of salvation is put into words and images of a human scale. Christians can declare their faith not just generally in God as the Creator but individually by participating in the suffering and glorification of his Son, who was also the Son of Man. Bach identified not with the heroic stories of opera figures but with the history of salvation through Jesus Christ. That was what allowed emotion into his music, to compose not as a wise man but as a feeling human being—"to weep with every other human soul," as Hans Werner Henze put it.[14] The modernity of his music, its realistic transmission of human experience, is grounded and legitimated in his faith in Christ.

Bach speaks of human suffering and the cross because they lead to God. That He can be found only *per passiones et crucem,* that is, through the suffering and the cross of Jesus Christ and his followers,[15] is an insight coming from Luther and one that Bach passed down in a great many different ways in the texts of his cantatas and passions, but most of all in his music itself. With no other composer of Bach's time do figures and emotions showing the suffering and cross of Christ play such an important role. Only through intense suffering does one know the joy of Christ's victory, is *crux* transformed to *gloria*. The notes of suffering even in Bach's instrumental music seem imbued with this idea.

With theonomy and Christocentrism there is a third article of faith, the Holy Ghost. Bach's music has mimetic powers, moving outside the polarities of order and expression, of number and affect—in accord with the statement from the Gospel of St. John about the Holy Ghost: "The wind blows where it will." We find such sounds and linguistic forms as well in the joyful motet "Singet dem Herrn ein neues Lied" and in the concentrated reverence of an English Suite. This music is not specifically Christian but spiritual, that is, connecting us to worlds we do not know but perhaps can sense. "Eye hath not seen, ear hath not heard such Joy" is the *unio mystica* behind Bach's music, which unveils its essential truth without regard to confession or religion. This is the miracle of the Holy Ghost: everyone speaking in his own language yet being understood.

No one need understand Bach's music in this way. But everyone should heed when they hear it. "No one has yet heard Mozart, Beethoven, or Bach as they really are, and what they really have to say; this will happen only in the distant future," says Ernst Bloch in *The Principle of Hope*.[16] Faith cannot be proven, and certainly not by examining a work of art. There remains a difference between conjecture about Bach's Christian faith and the universal experience that his music makes possible; it is the contingency or productive incompleteness of aesthetic discourse.

RHETORIC AND SYMBOLISM

Since the age of humanism there has been a tendency to see music as artful discourse; the elements used for this comparison are rhetorical structure and rhetorical ornamentation. That the structure of a work of music can be compared to that of a speech has become a commonplace. The *Little Sacred Concertos* of Heinrich Schütz are composed speech par excellence. Bach scholars have looked into whether Bach based his works on popular rhetorical patterns. The possibility has been mentioned several times in this book—for example, with the *Musical Offering*. But one doubts that he needed the relatively simple models of school rhetoric to give order and form to his musical ideas. While concrete proof of such correspondence would be welcome, it would not advance much the understanding of Bach's art. It was shown above, in the aria "Widerstehe doch der Sünde," how his music gains rhetorical interest at those moments when it goes against our expectations. In this way, it also gains autonomy.

We are on firmer ground when we discuss the relevance of musical rhetorical figures for Bach's music. Late medieval music theory faced the dilemma that a setting with little or no dissonance conformed to the rules but was boring. The term *figure* was borrowed from the world of rhetoric to justify license, that is, dissonance, the use of which was restricted to certain words. From the seventeenth century on, dissonance was increasingly used in instrumental music.

One of these figures, as mentioned before, was the passus duriusculus, the chromatic fourth passage frequently used in the music of the age of the continuo. Because it used notes that were foreign to the mode, it symbolized error and suffering. Clearly one could compare a musical rhetorical figure with a baroque emblem or symbol. Such emblems consisted of a picture and a motto; often this included an illustrative epigram. As stated in Zedler's *Universal-Lexicon* of 1743, an emblem should aid in meditation and instruction; in this process, the picture was considered the "body," the text the "soul" of the emblem.[1]

In the passus duriusculus the music would be the body, both in its written and tonal form, and its text would be the soul. The following excerpt from the first part (1636) of Schütz's *Little Sacred Concertos* is an example: the continuo makes the "hard passage" of the human being who has fallen away from faith come alive to the senses in a way that may have been frightening to listeners of the time; the words convey the relevant ideas:[2]

The music of the seventeenth and early eighteenth centuries uses a number of such figures. But there is no systematic theory of them, even if the term crops up repeatedly in contemporary music scholarship. In his very useful *Handbook of Musical Figure Theory*,[3] Dietrich Bartel has assembled a great many figures from all kinds of music-theoretical writings of the time, but he cannot deny that there was no theory to guide the composer. Less than ten percent of the two hundred extant works of musical theory of the sixteenth to eighteenth centuries contain a catalogue of figures. These works differ greatly from one another and occasionally contain terms that are the coinage of a single author.[4] The passus duriusculus, which almost no modern Bach analysis can do without, appears just once in the theoretical writings—namely, in the preserved manuscript composition theory work of Schütz's pupil Christoph Bernhard.

The musicologists dealing with musical figures lagged behind accepted compositional practice and saw their task primarily as giving it their approval ex post facto. The more obvious the replacement of old contrapuntal thinking by modern harmonic ideas became, the more superfluous it was to cite the old licenses. The rhetorical figures listed by Bach's contemporary Johann Adolph Scheibe were no longer relevant in a composition theory. When listing such figures as *exclamatio, dubitatio,* ellipsis (omission), *graduatio* (intensification), and *interrogatio,* he is only asking composers to keep the rhetorical sense of the text in mind when setting it to music.[5]

This is a critical point: Bach was able to compose his works without the need to enlist any theory. He may have been familiar with many figures from the instruction and compositions of his predecessors—the passus duriusculus is one—but only as part of the practice of composition. He may have taken many from the collective unconscious; composers such as Beethoven and Schubert worked in this fashion.

It makes sense to point out the musical rhetorical figures in Bach's work and thereby emphasize that Bach approached his texts with care, that in the tradition of Lutheran humanism he wanted to beautify and interpret them with his music. But it would be wrong to put a special aura around the practice: the use of a passus duriusculus in itself is no more sensational than a diminished seventh or a Neapolitan chord. We approach the thinking styles of Bach's age by resorting to the admittedly vague terminology of musical rhetoric, but it brings us no closer to his music. We admire that music, after all, not because it is applied art but because it is original art. An example from the *St. John Passion:* after the setting of the words of the Evangelist "Then Pilate took Jesus and scourged him," comes an arioso and then the tenor aria:

Erwäge, wie sein blutgefärbter Rücken

in allen Stücken dem Himmel gleiche geht.

Daran, nachdem die Wasserwogen

von unsrer Sündflut sich verzogen,

der allerschönste Regenbogen

als Gottes Gnadenzeichen steht.

Consider how his back so stained with bleeding

In every portion doth heaven imitate,

On which, when once the waves and waters

From our own Flood of sin have settled,

The world's most lovely rainbow, arching,

As God's own sign of blessing stands![6]

This is religious high baroque par excellence. The terse statements of the Passion account encourage the writer of the text to sweeping theological and poetic ruminations. The Savior's flayed back resembles a rainbow, in color and form; the rainbow is in turn the visible symbol of the promise that God gave to Noah, his loyal servant, at the end of the flood he had unleashed on humanity: "I do set my bow in the cloud, and it shall be for a token of a covenant between me and the earth,...and the waters shall no more become a flood to destroy all flesh" (Genesis 9.13–15). Christ's martyrdom, in the aria poet's interpretation, is the visible sign that our sins too can forever be blessed with forgiveness through God's grace.

This is an idea as artful as it is direct: it would be lost in a musical setting that was textually neutral but is fully realized here, thanks to Bach's attention to detail. Right at the start, the gesture of weighing, of considering, is brought to the fore:

Er-wä - ge, er-wä - ge, er-wä - - ge, er - wä - - ge,

One can imagine a scale, oscillating first to one side, then the other, but after a while coming to a temporary balance. One could also speak of the dynamic of thought: first it goes in one direction, then the other, all the while growing more focused. Bach paints the rainbow vividly:

al - ler - schön-ste Re - gen - bo - - - - - - - - - - - - gen

—but not as vividly as his contemporary Johann Mattheson, whose rainbow, written for the Brockes-Passion of 1718, shows much finer symmetry:

But this is precisely Bach: he wants not to make musical history with the most beautiful rainbow but to set an aria in such a way that it has both sensual impact and spiritual depth yet remains subordinate to a musical idea and renders the message of a demanding text completely. His music never merely imitates or depicts; it is continually crossing over into meaning.

If we look for similar effects in other arts, we will find them less in rhetoric than in symbolism. In Jacob Bosch's 1702 *Symbolographia* there is an emblem with the motto "Cum libra temperat orbem" ("with a scale he rules the world").[7]

The illustration shows the zodiac sign of Libra, which the sun enters at the autumnal equinox.

According to his explanation, this is a *principium mundi*, a basic principle of the world, and also *pernecessarium*, completely necessary. The earth thus stands in the sign of God's righteousness. In the aria text, this idea is given an additional Christological cast: through His son, God grants grace to every single human being.

Here and elsewhere Bach composed in the symbolic spirit. He had grown up with emblems, as he had encountered them in hymnals, pedagogical and theological literature, and most of all in the artworks of his time. His vocal writing, from the beginning, is heavily influenced by a symbolic style. He seldom devises a recitative whose musical setting is concerned merely with the semantic sense of the words; he seldom writes an aria that has a songlike or dance-like feeling and nothing else.

Hans Heinrich Eggebrecht finds not just an aesthetic meaning but also a symbolic meaning in Bach's music.[8] It is all the more important to recognize this element, since it is given short shrift by Spitta and trivialized by Schweitzer. In the "Crucify!" choruses of Bach's passions, according to one idea, the sign of the cross is revealed when lines are drawn linking the outer and inner note heads of a characteristic segment of the melody. Spitta thought this idea gimmickry at best, comparing it to fish images on medieval church buildings. Such devices do no harm, he argued, but only "because they are supported by a significant musical idea."[9] When Schweitzer emphasized Bach's "pictorial, sculptural, characteristic qualities," he was thinking more in terms of the nineteenth century than of the baroque age, and so in his way also he fails to see Bach correctly.

One can hardly blame Spitta and Schweitzer, considering how much the current Bach scene is dominated by speculations about Bach's "symbolic meaning." It may be good now and again to turn to Goethe, who was no great fan of allegory:

> There is a great difference whether the poet is looking for the particular that goes with the general or sees the general in the particular. The first gives rise to allegory, where the particular counts only as an example, an illustration of the general; but the latter in fact constitutes the nature of poetry, expressing something particular without any thought of the general and without indicating it. Now whoever has this living grasp of the particular is at the same time in possession of the general along with it.[10]

What Weimar classicism meant by allegory was still a faint reflection of what the baroque era saw in the emblem. Nonetheless, we can make use of Goethe's skepticism to approach Bach's art, which is never merely the application of rhetorical or symbolic devices—it always expresses something particular in the medium of music. It is not that Bach composes symbolically but *how* he does so that constitutes his greatness. To continue with Eggebrecht's antithetical train of thought: Bach's music can still speak aesthetically to someone for whom its symbolism is alien; but pronouncements about its symbolic meaning do little to help approach its aesthetic meaning.

The symbolic perspective certainly helps us understand the Riddle Canon. It also gives us an insight into Bach as a baroque thinker, a Christian, and an artist. But it is not useful for a look at the specifics of the music. One might consider some expressly symbolic musical compositions of the baroque era—for example, the *Airs de Cour* from the age of Richelieu[11] or Michael Maier's emblem book *Atlanta fugiens* of 1617—where the epigraphs within are provided with melodies: the distance of these works from Bach could hardly be greater.

In his recent extensive study, Günter Hartmann has explored Bach's work from the perspective of what he calls "BAxCH-emblematic," which may yield further results. The x between BA and CH could stand for the cross but also for *chi*, the first letter of Christ's name in Greek. Here Bach's entire oeuvre, with Canon BWV 1077 as the vanishing point, is seen as "the *subscriptio* of an emblematic confession of faith in Christ." Hartmann sees this BACH emblem realized musically in the "Karg device," a pattern of voice leading that he has named after the composer and musicologist Sigfrid Karg-Elert:

It is hard to go along with the view that this model of voice leading represents "*the* inventive power of Bach's composing."[12] But an observer of goodwill can still be impressed by the quantity of evidence in support of the thesis that Bach as composer and Christian adopted this emblem as his through all his work. Much points to a personal constant in Bach's creative work, and this track might prove to be a more fruitful one than the continual search for figures, symbols, and the use of symbolic numbers.

Trying to find the commonality among all the ideas of this section, we return to the concept, articulated repeatedly in this book, that Bach composed in figures. This does not mean musical rhetorical figures (at least not exclusively) but a general kind of thematic invention: figures that have inherent, stand-alone aesthetic quality but also point to things beyond their sound. A figure has two aspects: meaning and sound. An excellent example is the title aria of the cantata "Ich will den Kreuzstab gerne tragen," BWV 56.

The eleven bars of the opening bass phrase present an essentially closed melody. This melody can stand without text: indeed, it is used as a purely instrumental device at the top of the aria. Still, the device is shaped in such a way that, together with the set text, it conveys more than its melody. Bach fuses two brief figures into a whole. The first has a sturdy feel; it stands both for the upright staff of the cross and for the singer's declaration of willingness to bear it. The descending, seemingly endless series of sighs in the second signify the ongoing, oppressive burden of the cross. The device produces more than a general feeling of suffering, which the music alone conveys: it is an acoustically arresting expression of the willingness to suffer and, at the same time, the experience of suffering.

Bach meticulously fills the figural with meaning. Musically the device is so carefully calculated that its motivic material is sufficient for the whole movement. But his view of the underlying statements of the text is just as accurately detailed. Our calling this style of writing mimetic, symbolic, or emblematic might suggest that the music is primarily a copy of an image, therefore a means to an end. Such a statement might apply to a little sacred concerto of Schütz, which begins with the words "Ich liege und schlafe und erwache" ("I lie and sleep and awake"), where the vocal part depicts the state of sleep with a slow descent and the act of awakening with a "jumping up." Bach's figures have meaning but also point beyond themselves. Words and music are equally effective; neither yields in any way to the other. This is what is unique about Bach's art—the combination of word-driven music with independently invented music. It may be found in Mozart arias and Schubert songs—but rarely, not routinely. Certainly vocal music is the main occasion for such writing. But it also enters instrumental music through the word-oriented organ chorale, in which Bach works constantly with figures as well—one need only think, for instance, of the F-Minor Sinfonia.

PROPORTION AND NUMERICAL RELATIONS
IN BACH'S MUSIC

The biblical wisdom of Solomon says that God ordered all things by "measure, number, and weight": this has long been the theologian's justification for creating or uncovering numerical systems in music. A musically significant theory of Pythagoras holds that all things are derived from number, including music, which was long considered to be a mathematical art. Composers before Bach did not write their works to be works of their own personal architecture, and surely not as an emotional outlet; they were contributing to a preordained, higher order. Quite apart from this theological and philosophical dimension, it was useful to musicians to develop their compositions along patterns based on defined methods of bar arrangement and lengths of measure.

The old Netherlandish motets surely count as "measured" art. They were not dashed-off, occasional music but made a great show of their refined, esoteric qualities. The complex polyphony of these works is best realized when accompanied by clear proportionality in laying out the measures. This connection finds an unusual echo in the works of Anton Bruckner: while his symphonies are often thought of as the epitome of a boundless, subjectively driven style, they reveal the composer's attempt, sometimes almost obsessive, to show his composition's objective "correctness" through the use of regular periodic structure.

More than anyone else in the field of Bach scholarship, Ulrich Siegele has tried to prove that Bach's conception of form was in large measure shaped by ideas of proportionality. In his analysis of the F-Major Duet, BWV 803, from part 3 of the *Clavier-Übung*, he points up the mirror symmetry of the measure arrangement. Its five parts are, respectively, 37 + 31 + 13 + 31 + 37 measures: outer frame, inner frame, middle, inner frame, outer frame. Siegele orders the 37 bars of the outer frame in the sequence: 4 + 5 + 7 + 5 + 7 + 5 + 4; further calculations follow.[1] While in 1978 he saw this *ars combinatoria* as a technique primarily of the mature Bach, he later gradually extended this view to earlier works such as the *Brandenburg Concertos*.

The writer Ruth Mary Tatlow, a skeptic in matters of numeric symbolism, recently proposed the theory that the *St. Matthew Passion* is arranged by a system of measures. She does not see this as the result of theological considerations—as Siegele does with the duet BWV 803—but points, among other things, to a recommendation made by the Mizler Society in 1754, which said that church music in winter should consist of about 350 bars and last approximately twenty-five minutes, while in summer one could augment this by fifty measures, which would come to eight to ten minutes more.[2]

Siegele and Tatlow basically start out from the same place. In genres where the elements of artifice and polish are particularly important, Bach could have set great store on exact proportionality; for more ordinary occasions, he may have simply arranged things by eye but still ended up hitting certain standard proportions quite nicely. Dividing a work according to the proportions of the golden section, since this was a matter of course with most fine artists, was probably automatic with Bach as well. In the manuscript of the B-Minor Mass, at the end of the "Patrem omnipotentem" section, he noted down its measure total: eighty-four. This is unusual, though, and hard to interpret in a symbolic way.

Those who want to know more about this aspect of Bach, who need to come up with round sums or interesting symbolic numbers, often have to go to great lengths to come up with a theory that actually is convincing on paper. The same is true for the use of symbolic numbers in relation to sectional divisions, number of parts, entries, notes, and so on.[3] The more esoteric, artificial, and compact the composition, the surer one is of being on the right path in looking for symbolic numbers. That Bach himself always looked for threes as the symbol of the Holy Trinity need hardly be mentioned. Still, it should be pointed out that in the 1987 publication *Lexikon der mittelarterlichen Zahlenbedeutungen* (Lexicon of Medieval Numerical Meanings), only four numbers between 1 and 50 had no entries in the lexicon: 29, 39, 41, and 43.

Bach owned a book by Caspar Heunisch, in which the numbers mentioned in the *Book of the Apocalypse* are explained.[4] Like his contemporaries, he probably had a sense for symbolic numbers. He put into his music more or less whatever he happened upon—this is shown, for instance, by the ten trumpet entries quoting the chorale "Dies sind die heilgen zehn Gebot" in the cantata "Du sollst Gott, deinen Herren lieben," BWV 77. The question of whether there are any other esoteric numerological speculations in his work, the results of which only God can judge, for now must remain a matter of faith.

Did Bach compose with the use of a numerical alphabet? It can be assumed that as a member of the educated class he knew the concept, but the idea that there was just one such alphabet available to him—namely, where a = 1, b = 2, c= 3, d = 4, and so on—needs revision.[5] It is true that his Leipzig predecessor Johann Kuhnau, in his 1700 novel *Der musicalische Quack-Salber,* did in fact refer to this numerical alphabet. But an instrumental composition—extremely simple too—with which Johann Christoph Faber paid homage to Duke Ludwig Rudolf von Braunschweig-Lüneburg in 1729 uses another one, in which k = 20, m = 30, n = 40, and so on. Moreover, the composer provides the key with which he encoded the name LUDOVICUS in notes, just to be on the safe side.[6]

Skeptics in the ranks of Bach scholarship continue to doubt even the discoveries of Friedrich Smend. In 1950, in a paper that was then much noted, Smend showed the numbers 14 and 41 as Bach numbers: 14 = B + A + C + H, 41 = J + S + B + A + C + H.[7] It has been often said before and is true here as well: in esoteric works such as the Riddle Canon, BWV 1076, cited by Smend, these numbers may in fact play the role that he suspects. But it remains to be seen whether looking for numerical symbols in all Bach's work is productive. What sense is there in counting up the number of notes, bar lines, articulation symbols, ligatures, and letters (first converted to numbers) in the *Musical Offering*, to obtain a "*summa summarum* of the dedicatory copy*" of 68,921, a number that, along with other variants and partial sums, can be interpreted in any number of ways?[8] What do we gain by converting the twenty-three ascending and descending notes of a phrase from the violin solos into numerical values, for a sum of 712, and then by declaring that in the numerical alphabet this number stands for these words from the Nicene creed: "Et expecto Resurrectionem mortuorum et vitam venturi saeculi— Amen" ("and I look for the resurrection of the dead and the life of the world to come")?[9]

Whoever deals professionally with Bach manuscripts sees slips of the pen, unclear notations, slurred notes, unsystematically placed double bars, inconsistent articulation symbols, and—on top of this— many changes. Arriving at a musically definitive, graphically correct version is generally a long process and often ends in a question mark. In the history of any work, it is hard to decide where Bach might have used numerical symbolism—especially when dealing with additions and multiplications going into the thousands. Walter Kolneder has ridiculed some of these speculations, holding them up against Bach's own labored efforts to add together ten numbers from his everyday life.[10] Many numerological scholars might be a little quieter if they had to work with facsimiles of Bach's autographs instead of the beautifully engraved or typeset complete editions at their disposal.

One could object that a great many things come into Bach somewhat unconsciously and that this could include features of structure. But either way we love Bach's music not for its structure, which one could also find in the composition of a crystal, the grain of a piece of wood, or anywhere, but for its beauty.

Others have come up with countercalculations of ironic intent. Glenn Gould once announced to his listeners "with delight" that the sums of his first and last names were 52 and 59, "of which, as everyone can see, the sum of the digits are respectively 7 and 14."[11] In

Hofstadter's *Gödel, Escher, Bach,* readers are at first fascinated by the information that 1742, the presumed year of publication of the *Goldberg Variations,* is the result of two prime numbers, 1723 and 19. But then they are disillusioned by the fact that all even numbers greater than 6, thus infinitely many of them, can be represented as the sum of two prime numbers.[12] In closing, we should bear in mind that this kind of humor does not do justice to the problem.

THEOLOGICAL BACH RESEARCH: BETWEEN SCHOLARSHIP AND FAITH-INSPIRED LEARNING

In theology in general and in theological Bach research in particular, one can distinguish between scholarship and faith-inspired learning: this does not mean to imply a value judgment but rather to emphasize different aspects. It is the task of theological Bach scholarship to work on issues of ecclesiastical, devotional, and liturgical history as well as historical attitudes in the church that affect Bach's life and work. It goes without saying that this context is often just as important as the text, that context and text are indeed inseparable. Anyone who does not dogmatically insist that music is a thing unto itself will see it as a discourse that, in Bach's case, theology can do much to illuminate.

If the theological branch of scholarship starts with the question, "What does the age say to Bach?," the branch of faith-inspired scholarship might ask, "What does Bach say to me?," by creating links between theological thinking and musical experience. As long as the statement, "This is how I see it," is not confused with the statement, "This is how it is!," this kind of thinking can have great significance. There is, after all, not just the theological discourse that took place "back then," that we can approach only through careful research, but also the theological discourse of those who came later. This begins with the praise of the *St. Matthew Passion* as the "greatest and most sacred work of the greatest composer"[1] on the occasion of its reperformance by Felix Mendelssohn Bartholdy in 1829 and continues via the apostrophizing of this work as a "fifth Gospel" by the Swedish archbishop Nathan Söderblom in 1920. It goes on up to the present day.[2]

Söderblom could point to Martin Luther: the music of Josquin Desprez prompted Luther to say that God also preached His Gospel through Josquin's music.[3] In our day, calling Bach's vocal works a "musical language of faith"[4] can be justified in the same way, especially since the experience of many Christians can be included under this heading. Sermons on the cantata texts that Bach set, which also deal with the music itself, can expand the horizon of our understanding. Whether this is also true for wild numerological speculation is anyone's guess; those who indulge in it are certainly entitled to meditate and speculate about the world in their own way. Anthroposophic interpretations of Bach also have their place.

But for now, this is enough thinking about horizons. Bach's music refuses categorical assertions; no flashy conclusion, no one-sentence summation, no matter how brilliant, will capture it. May this book, then, end simply with Bach's signature:

ACKNOWLEDGMENTS

This book could not have been written without the contributions and insights furnished by a great many Bach scholars. I wish to acknowledge my indebtedness to them, but especially to those colleagues who read the manuscript in whole or in part: Klaus Hofmann (Göttingen), Yoshitake Kobyashi (Tokyo), Jean-Claude Zehnder (Basel), Peter Schleuning (Bremen), and Pieter Dirksen (Wadenoijen). I am also grateful to my collaborator, Ares Wolf.

Sincere thanks to Ms. Shoko Komiyama of Seijo University, Tokyo, doctoral student of Prof. Yoshitake Kobayashi, for the musical examples.

NOTES

These abbreviations are used in the notes and bibliography:

AfMw   Archiv für Musikwissenschaft
BJ   *Bach-Jahrbuch*
BzBF   *Beiträge zu Bach-Forschung*
Dok 1, 2, 3   *Bach-Dokumente.* Bach-Archiv Leipzig. Vols. 1–3.
              1963–72.
Mf   *Die Musikforschung*
MGG   *Die Musik in Geschichte und Gegenwart*
MuK   *Musik und Kirche*
Schweitzer   Albert Schweitzer, *Johann Sebastian Bach,*
              Leipzig o. J., 64.–66. Tausend
Spitta 1, 2   Philipp Spitta, *Johann Sebastian Bach.* 2
              vols. 6th ed. Wiesbaden, 1964.

————————————————————————————————— PREFACE
APPROACHING BACH

What Do We Know about Bach?

1	Dok 2: 474		7	Dok 2: 348
2	217		8	Dok 3: 288
3	325		9	Dok 3: 83ff
4	119ff		10	Breig 1998
5	Hindemith 1950, 5		11	Dok 2: 434ff
6	Wohlfarth 1971, 52			

The Grand Old Men of Bach Biography: Forkel, Spitta, Schweitzer

1   Suchalla 1994, 485
2   Forkel 1802, 69, 58, 24
3   viii, v, 68
4   Blume 1949, Sp. 1867
5   Schilling 1994, 178
6   Qtd. in Gülke 1989, 51ff
7   Schilling 1994, 268
8   Spitta 2: 543
9   Spitta 1: 740
10   Letter to Zelter from Munich,
     22 June 1830, in Mendelssohn
     1882, 17
11   Dilthey 1957, 213
12   Spitta 1: 456
13   Spitta 1882, 17–19
14   Spitta 1894, 387, 401
15   Spitta 1: 487
16   Spitta 1: xxviii
17   Schilling 1994, 190
18   Blume 1963
19   Cf. the following Hanheide 1990
20   Hanheide 1990, 10
21   Schweitzer, v
22   Schweitzer 1932, 53ff
23   Schilling 1994, 188
24   Hanheide 1990, 75ff
25   Lecture at the Dortmund Bach
     Festival, 20 March 1909, cited in
     Hanheide 1990, 76ff
26   Schweitzer, 540ff
27   Düsseldorf Bach lecture 1928,
     cited in Hanheide 1990, 24, 78
28   Langhans 1887, 2

Transmission of the Works

1   Cf. this excerpt with Kobayashi
     1992 and Wollny 1997a, here
     especially 27ff
2   Virneisel 1962, Sp. 1366
3   Wollny 1997a, 36
4   Wollny 1997a, 48
5   Marx, 1865, 85
6   BG 1863, xvii
7   Herz 1984, 152
8   Moser 1959, 93

--- PART ONE

THE STATIONS OF BACH'S LIFE

From Matins Singer to Hofkapellmeister

1   Grimm 1854, col. 1057
2   Dok 1: 255
3   63
4   Rollberg 1927, 141
5   Kaiser 1994
6   Mund 1997, 130
7   Kaiser 1994, 178
8   Dok 2: 3ff
9   Forkel 1802, 45. Similarly Dok 2:
     303
10   Dok 3:81ff. C. P. E. Bach's quote
     is on 288.
11   Zehnder 1999
12   Küster 1996b, 82–109. Cf.
     Schulze 1997 for another view.
13   Dok 3: 82

14 Facsimile in Küster 1996b, 93
15 Dok 3: 82
16 423
17 Wolff 1985b, 103
18 109
19 Dok 3: 82
20 82
21 Wolff 1985b, 110ff
22 Fock 1950, 43
23 Petzoldt 1985
24 Dok 3: 288
25 Mund 1997, 134ff
26 Register names are given as in the source; other terms are simplified as in Petzoldt 1992, 22.
27 Glöckner 1996, 62
28 Dok 2: 14
29 Dok 3: 82
30 Mattheson 1740, 94
31 Dok 3: 82
32 Dok 2: 11
33 Oefner 1975, 20ff
34 Dok 2: 21
35 16, 15
36 21
37 Dok 3: 288
38 Geiringer 1958, 99
39 Claus, 1995
40 Williams 1996, 274ff
41 Cf. esp. Schulze 1984, 30ff; Hill 1991.
42 Schulze 1984, 40
43 Marshall 1988
44 Cf. discussion of Christoph Wolff in Heller and Schulze 1995, 347.
45 Wolff 1996d
46 Gerber 1812, col. 208ff
47 Cf. esp. Zehnder i. V., 1999, 1995, 1988, 1991, and 1997.
48 Gadamer 1946, 3
49 Dok 2: 50
50 Dok 2: 25

51 Walther 1987, 219ff
52 Dok II, 23
53 Adlung 1768, 260ff. Register names are given as in the original, other terms are simplified.
54 Petzoldt 1992, 148ff
55 Chrysander 1855, 680
56 Rifkin 1982a
57 Dok 2: 28; Dok 1: 258
58 Wolff 1997b, 155ff
59 Dok 2: 405
60 Dok 1: 1
61 Dok 1: 19
62 Küster 1996b, 167ff
63 Dok 1: 63ff; see *New Bach Reader* 145–51.
64 Dok 1: 67; see *New Bach Reader* 151.
65 Küster 1996b, 164
66 Petzoldt 1992, 132
67 Dok 2: 50; see also *New Bach Reader* 67.
68 Spitta 1: 355ff. For a different evaluation, cf. Petzoldt 1992, 133ff
69 Paumgartner 1950, 274
70 Petzoldt 1992, 133
71 Küster 1996b, 186ff
72 Dok 2: 35ff
73 Köhler 1730, 18
74 Herrmann 1915, 228
75 Köhler 1730, 24
76 Bojanowski 1903, 18
77 Dok 3: 285
78 Beaulieau Marconnay 1872, 144, 243
79 Stauffer 1996, 90
80 Dok 1: 22ff
81 Dok 3: 289
82 Dok 3: 289; 1: 107
83 Dok 3: 474–81; Wolff 1966c, 162; Dok 3: 480

84 Städler 1970, 165ff; Dok 3: 649

85 Dok 2: 65

86 David 1951, 88

87 Seiffert 1904, 595ff

88 Wollny 1984a, 32; Dok 2: 49

89 Dok 2: 51

90 Dok 1: 23

91 Dok 2: 53

92 Steude 1984, vii

93 Wolff 1968, 163ff; Beisswenger 1992

94 Dürr 1951; Hofmann 1993b

95 Chrysander 1858, 22

96 For another view, cf. Petzoldt 1993a and Wollny 1994a

97 Wolff 1996a

98 Hofmann 1993b, 27ff

99 Beisswenger 1992, 62ff

100 Schulze 1983b

101 Dirksen 1992b; cf. Rampe and Zapf 1997; cf. also the responses in Dirksen 1998b and Rampe 1998

102 DDT 1958, xiii

103 Dok 2: 67

104 Dok 2: 65

105 Glöckner 1988a, 141

106 Dok 3: 468

107 Dok 2: 81, 85

108 Zimpel and Hoppe 1994

109 Stauffer 1988, 258

110 Dok 2: 82, 71; the reference is to a "Mar. Magd. Wilken."

111 Dok 2: 83

112 78

113 186ff

114 Stein 1955, col. 1840

115 Dok 3: 84; 1: 67

116 Hoppe 1994 and 1998; 1994, 98

117 Rampe and Zapf 1997, 32

118 Hoppe 1983, 24ff; Rampe and Zapf 1997, 32

119 Hoppe 1997, 70

120 Rampe and Zapf 1997, 34

121 Schleuning 1989, 14

122 Dok 2: 68

123 70

124 93

125 Rampe and Zapf 1997, 33

126 Dok 1: 216ff

127 Wolff 1985a

128 Rifkin 1999

129 Krey 1961; Hofmann 1997b; Kobayashi 1991; Dirksen 1992b; Rolf 1997

130 Blum 1998, 126ff

131 Hoppe 1994, 106–11

132 Zimpel 1979

133 Dok 1: 67ff

134 Hoppe 1998, 35

Cantor at St. Thomas and City Music Director in Leipzig

1 Schering 1926, 53

2 Müller-Blattau 1963, 42ff

3 Schütz 1955

4 Dok 1: 37

5 248, 37

6 Schering 1926, 56

7 131ff

8 Stadtarchiv Leipzig, document collection 97.1, kindly conveyed by Dr. Andreas Glöckner

9 Scheibel 1721, 30

10 Glöckner 1990, 82

11 Schering 1926, 46

12 "Written statement of Lord (Duke) Ernst August of Saxony, as presented at the general visitation, Erfurt 1640. Synodal decision ratified after the General Visitation of the Church

and the State of Saxony," acc. to
Holl 1928.

13 Geck 1961, 179,174ff
14 Cf. Siegele 1983, 1984, and 1986
15 Siegele 1998
16 Dok 1: 60
17 Becker 1956, 39
18 Sittard 1890, 1
19 Dok 1: 38; Petzoldt 1982, 46
20 Dok 2: 88
21 91, 92. See *Bach Reader* 101
22 Schulze 1990b, 18
23 See *Bach Reader* 102.
24 Dok 2: 94
25 96
26 94
27 Bitter 1881, 107
28 Dok 2: 95
29 See *Bach Reader* 101.
30 Dok 2: 98ff
31 Dok 1: 177ff
32 Petzoldt 1998a, 27
33 Dok 2: 99, 630
34 104, 105 and 104
35 See *Bach Reader* 106–08.
36 Dok 2: 205
37 Schulze 1987, 13ff
38 Kaemmel 1909, 236
39 Marpurg 1754, 439
40 (appendix) 7
41 Petzoldt 1983
42 See *Bach Reader* 151–52.
43 Dok 1: 63. See also *Bach Reader* 149–50.
44 Fröde 1984, 53
45 Dok 2: 480
46 Zedler 1737, 1800ff
47 Jens 1996, 724; Gottsched 1732, 662
48 Christoph Ernst Sicul, *Neo-Annalium Lipsiensium Continuatio* II, 570, qtd. in Schering 1918, xli

49 Rochlitz 1868, 4: 280
50 Dürr 1977, 166
51 Hobohm 1973, 14
52 Geck 1965, 63ff
53 Wolff 1982
54 Cf. Wolff 1998, 24ff
55 Petzoldt 1993b, 16, 743, 744
56 Blume 1963, 470–72
57 Geck 1961a, 264
58 Dok 1: 249
59 250
60 Illgen 1836, 22
61 Telemann 1972, 41ff
62 This comparison is in Schneiderheinze 1988, 81.
63 Zedler 1740, 1738
64 Schulze 1998b, 118
65 123
66 Kreutzer 1991, 21
67 Hobohm 1973, 31
68 Dok 2: 146
69 See *Bach Reader* 118.
70 Dok 1: 31
71 Geck 1967, 138
72 Dok 1: 57
73 Dürr 1957, 95; Rifkin 1975
74 Dürr 1969, 11
75 See *Bach Reader* 135–36.
76 Dok 2: 174
77 175, 176
78 Dehio 1924, 217
79 Cf. *Bach Compendium* under G14.
80 Häfner 1977a
81 Schulze 1984, 98
82 Dok 2: 183
83 Dok 3: 290
84 Dok 2: 179
85 185
86 182
87 Dok 1: 55
88 Dok 2: 196ff
89 202
90 204ff

91 205
92 206
93 335
94 The citations are from the "Short but Most Necessary Draft" in Dok 1: 60–64
95 Schering 1936, 30
96 Schering 1936, 31
97 Scheibel 1721, 54
98 Glöckner 1990, 85f.
99 Schulze 1998a, also: Koopman 1998
100 Dok 1: 67f. For complete text of the letter, See *Bach Reader* 151–2
101 Kessler 1979, col. 355
102 Dok 2: 252
103 Dok 2: 141
104 Dok 2: 339. See *Bach Reader* 204
105 Spitta 2, 175
106 This view ultimately in Häfner 1982
107 Glöckner 1988b
108 Dok 3: 418
109 Dok 2: 214
110 Schulze 1990a, 87
111 Dok 1: 74
112 Dok 2: 278
113 Cf. Kobayashi 1990
114 Dok 2: 271f.
115 Dok 1: 99

Director of the Collegium Musicum and Composer of Secular Music

1 Spitta 2, 492
2 Zedler 1739, col. 1488
3 Mattheson 1731, 173f.
4 Glöckner 1997, 294
5 Mattheson 1740, 117f.
6 Hiller 1784, 184ff
7 Glöckner 1997, 298
8 Rifkin 1997
9 Dok 1: 57
10 Dok 2: 192
11 Glöckner 1990, 89
12 Siegele 1986, 47
13 Criticism of this view in Boresch 1993, 22f.
14 Dok 2: 250
15 Dok 2: 251
16 Dok 1: 198
17 Dok 2: 278
18 Dok 1: 139
19 Wollny 1997c, 289
20 Witkowski 1909, 355
21 Dörffel 1884, 4
22 Schering 1941, 265
23 Scheibe 1745, 3
24 Scheibe 1745, 52–54
25 Dok 2: 286f.
26 Dok 2: 307
27 Dok 2: 317
28 Dok 2: 318
29 Gottsched 1732, 662
30 Dok 2: 373
31 Herz 1978, 149
32 Dok 2: 336
33 Dok 2: 352
34 Dok 2: 322
35 Dok 2: 337f.
36 Dok 2: 305
37 Beisswenger 1992, 303f.
38 Dok 3: 289
39 Dok 2: 323
40 Dok 2: 303
41 Kossmaly 1844, col. 20
42 Dok 2: 332f.
43 Mattheson 1739, 71
44 Dok 2: 301
45 Adorno 1993, 72
46 Adorno 1958, 498
47 Dok 2: 461

48 Hoffmann 1922, 359f.
49 Dok 2: 160f.
50 Mattheson 1717, title page
51 Dok 2: 223
52 Dok 2: 231
53 Beisswenger 1995
54 Schweitzer, 3
55 Mattheson 1739, 133
56 Dok 2: 305
57 Dok 2: 370
58 Selection as in Ahrens 1986, 70f.
59 Dok 2: 335
60 Butler 1990, 21f.
61 Schäfertöns 1996, 143
62 Dok 2: 653
63 Wolff 1984b, 17—Butler 1990, 13
64 Mattheson 1739, 441
65 Butler 1983a, 304
66 Wolff 1981, 30
67 Dok 2: 117
68 Dirksen 1992a 137f.
69 Schenk 1953, 51
70 Forkel 1802, 52
71 Wolff 1984b
72 Edler 1997, 301
73 Wolff 1981, 29
74 Mizler 1742a
75 Spitta 2, 605
76 Mizler 1742, 119f.
77 Dok 2: 302
78 Wolff 1983a, 360
79 Dok 3: 87
80 Dirksen 1992a, 83
81 Kämper 1989, 116
82 Dok 2: 413
83 Dirksen 1992a, 90ff, 136ff
84 Dok 2: 434f.
85 Forkel 1802, 9f.
86 Dok 2: 436
87 Sackmann and Rampe 1997, 84
88 Wöhlke 1941, 115
89 Schering 1941, 195
90 Dok 3: 89

91 Mizler 1739, 74
92 Schulze 1981, 38f.
93 Dok 3: 3
94 Fröde 1984, 57f.
95 Dok 2: 457
96 Dok 1: 122
97 Dok 1: 124
98 Wiemer 1977, esp. 50
99 Kobayashi 1995, 241
100 Wolff 1991
101 Husmann 1938, 21
102 Leonhardt 1952, Leonhardt 1969
103 Siegele 1988, 223
104 Wilhelmi 1992, 102
105 Breig 1982, 111
106 Kohneder 1977a, 258
107 Dok 3: 495
108 Winterfeld 1847, 422
109 Smend 1955, VIII f., XII
110 Schleuning 1993, 89
111 Forkel 1802, 56
112 Kobayashi 1987
113 Dok 2: 470
114 Dok 3: 13
115 Schulze 1981, 40
116 Kobayashi 1973, 109, 270
117 Forkel 1802, 53
118 Wolff 1974
119 Dok 2: 468
120 Dok 3: 85. See *Bach Reader* 303
121 Kranemann 1990
122 Dok 2: 474
123 Dok 3: 104
124 Dok 2: 513
125 Dok 3: 6f. See *Bach Reader*
     331–314
126 Richter 1906, 68
127 The following paragraphs are
     essentially as in Dadelsen 1998.
128 Heuss, 1913, 129
129 Witkowski 1909, 308
130 Dok 2: 325. See *Bach Reader* 199
131 Pottgiesser 1912, 9

132 Dok 2: 384. See *Bach Reader* 208–209

133 Dok 2: 391f.

134 Dok 2: 366. See *Bach Reader* 213

135 Dok 2: 124. See *Bach Reader* 204

136 Dok 2: 483

137 Dok 3: 153. See *Bach Reader* 248

138 Schleuning 1993, 93

139 Dok 1: 72f.

140 Bitter 1881, 166

141 Dok 1: 107

142 Spitta 2, 754. See *Bach Reader* 200–201

143 Engelke 1927, 433

144 Dok 1: 267

145 Borges 1999

The Early and Weimar Cantatas

1   Skepticism as to this attribution in Küster 1996a, 85f.

2   Cf. esp. Krummacher 1969—Krummacher 1991b—Wollny 1996

3   Kobayashi 1998

4   Küster 1996b, 154

5   Oechsle 1995, 127

6   Bartel 1997, 223ff

7   Cf. Mainka 1977, 157

8   Dok 2: 349

9   Krummacher 1995b

10 Wolff 1983b, 28

11 Spitta 1, 346

12 Schweitzer, 481

13 Vetter 1709, last page of preface

14 Dok 3: 288

15 Stauffer 1996, 100

16 Steiger, 1989

17 Alciatus 1542, 246

18 Geck and Rolf 2000

19 Hiller 1876, 107

20 Hauptmann 1871, v. 1, 86

21 Hensel 1882, 307

22 Mendelssohn Bartholdy 1863, 90

23 Lämmerhirt 1925, 119

24 Wiora 1962

25 Chafe 1991, 90–123

26 Krummacher 1991c, 180

27 Petzoldt 1996, 144

28 Dok 2: 153

29 Petzoldt 1993a, 31

30 Schering 1934, iv

31 Schulze 1996, afterword

32 Wolff 1996a

33 Wollny 1996, 39

34 Hofmann 1993b

35 Rochlitz 1868, v. 3, 235 and 240

36 Dürr 1985, 394

37 Smend 1966, notebook 1, 24ff

38 Dürr 1985, 121

39 BG 1863, VII

40 Schweitzer, 592ff

41 Schering 1950, 191ff

42 Mattheson 1739, 236–39

43 Mattheson 1739, 235

44 Kalbeck 1903, 37

45 Schweitzer, 592

46 Besseler 1950, 118ff

47 Kunze 1996, 100

48 Marx 1988, 154

49 Besseler 1950, 117 and 119

50 Schulze 1991, 200

The Leipzig Cantatas

1 For further discussion of "signs," cf. Geck 2000e.

2 Blankenburg 1979, col. 425

3 Schriftgemäßes Gesangbuch, Nordhausen 1687. Cf. Fornaçon 1963, 168

4 Wetzel 1721, 395f.

5 Blankenburg 1957, 110

6 Geck 2000c

7 Schulze 1998b, 110

8 Schulze 1998b, 111

9 Petzoldt 1998b, 133

10 Petzoldt 1991, 80

11 Oechsle 1995, 595

12 Spitta 2, 261 and 263

13 Schering 1925, 56f.

14 Schweitzer, 418 and 545

15 Herz 1985, 214

16 Dadelsen 1983, 192

17 Krummacher 1985b, 212 and 216

18 Rienäcker 1991, 128

19 Henze 1983

20 On definition of "discourse," cf. Link 1997, 50

21 Schering 1950, 127

22 Gojowy 1975—cf. Bischoff and Siebert 1991

23 Hofmann 1998b

24 Cf. Crist 1985, 220f.—cf. also "The Genesis of Homophonic Aria Ritornelli" in Marshall 1968, 424

25 Wolff 1998, 19

26 Schering 1926, 233

27 Koldewy 1893, 702f.

28 Schulze 1998b, 116

29 Mattheson 1739, 7

30 Krummacher 1969, 47

31 Binding and Nussbaum 1978, 221 and Table 29

32 Oechsle 1995, 303

33 Hammerstein 1956

34 Geck 1998

35 Adorno 1968, 220

36 Adorno 1970, 316

37 Cf. Kobayashi 2001

38 Vetter 1713, penultimate page of preface

39 Dürr 1985, 157

40 Oechsle 1995, 357f.

41 Hofmann 1983—Kube 1992

42 Cf. Platen 1959, 64f. and 108f.— Smend 1966, Heft VI, 41–44— Rienäcker 1983—Dürr 1985, 285–88—Steiger 1992, 77ff— Krummacher 1995a, 133–45

43 Gerlach 1973, 63

44 Krummacher 1981, 126

45 Cf. Kimura 1999

46 Cf. Schneiderheinze 1991

The Passions

1 Telemann 1972, 17

2 Telemann 1972, 20. Cited there as "Lebenslauf III"

3 Axmacher 1984

4 Cf. orchestration lists, esp. of the Hamburger Oper of 1738, in Becker 1962, Table after col. 192

5 Grout 1965

6 Scheibel 1721, 34ff

7 Bunge 1970, 27

8 Mattheson 1725, Teil 15, 13ff

9 Schleuning 1985

10 Müller 1705, 1585

11 Geck 1995a

12 Hofmann 1998

13 Hoffmann-Axthelm 1989

14 Chafe 1989; Marissen 1998
15 Breig 1988
16 Hofmann 1991b, 81. Hofmann
    mentions earlier thoughts on this
    idea.
17 Smend 1926
18 Moser 1932
19 Cf. Breig 1985, 65–96 and Dürr
    1988, 116ff
20 Chafe 1981; Chafe 1989; Chafe
    1991
21 Geck 1991, 102
22 Axmacher 1978. Text synopsis

    from: Petzoldt o. J., 42
23 Gottsched 1751, 728
24 Geck 1967, 137
25 Finke-Hecklinger 1970, 82—cf.
    also Schleuning 1998, 47
26 Petzoldt 1990, 62
27 Mattheson 1739, 208
28 Finke-Hecklinger 1970, 60
29 Platen 1997, 185
30 Braun 1981, 215
31 Neumann 1967, 6
32 Mosewius 1852, 56
33 Wolff 1984a, 240

Secular Cantatas and The *Christmas Oratorio*

1   Boresch 1993, 106
2   Wolff 1997a, 13
3   Rienäcker 1999
4   Wollny 1997b, 35
5   Mattheson 1722, 143ff
6   Bach 1753, 122
7   Schleuning 1998, 37
8   Blankenburg 1985, 56
9   Schweitzer, 637
10 Dürr 1967, 39
11 Schleuning 1998, 66

12 Dilthey 1957, 237
13 Boresch 1993, 17
14 Finscher 1969, 105
15 Häfner 1977b; Siegele 1995
16 Krummacher 1991a, 78
17 Paul 1974, 127
18 Grüss 1991, 75
19 Schleuning 1998, 106
20 Geck 1993, 65f.
21 Spitta 2, 472
22 Witkowski 1909, 276

The Magnificat and The Masses

1   Dok 2: 484
2   Terry 1929, 17ff
3   Marshall 1989, 13
4   Schleuning 1978
5   Marshall 1989, 14ff
6   Rifkin 1982b and Rifkin 1988
7   Wolff 1967
8   Marshall 1976, 339
9   Häfner 1987, 240ff
10 Dürr 1992, 124
11 Marshall 1980, 232
12 Krummacher 1991a, 80
13 Spitta 2, 513
14 Wolff 1968, 149ff

15 Wollny 1994b
16 Osthoff 1987, 121
17 Häfner 1987, 328ff
18 Häfner 1987, 329ff
19 Rifkin 1982b
20 Kobayashi 1999
21 Schulze 1991, 203
22 Schulze 1988, 25
23 Kobayashi 1998
24 Schulze 1991, 203
25 Gruss 1991, 78
26 Jauss 1973, 26
27 Nies 1968
28 Scheibe 1745, 756

29 Zachariä 1763, 189. Cited here in Grimm 1958, col. 1008

30 Reichardt 1782, 196f.

31 Weber 1828, 68

32 AMZ 1818, col. 531

33 Cf. Wolff 1968, 133—

34 Georgiades 1954, 79ff

35 Dilthey 1957, 243

36 Dilthey 1957, 239

The Motets

1 Dok 3: 558

2 Geck 1969b, 129 (on: "Lieblingsmotette")—Wagner (no year given), 108

3 Wiora 1951, col. 362

4 Dok 3: 636

5 Müller 1934

6 Geck 1969b, 129

7 Siegele 1962, 38

8 Krummacher 1983, 211f.

9 Danckwardt 1987, 202

10 Dok 3: 100

11 Cf. Steude 1995, 212

12 Schulze 1986, 11

13 Krummacher 1974, 18

14 Weiss 1729, 86ff

15 Melamed 1989, 198ff—Melamed 1991

16 Oechsle 1995, 544—Hoffmann 1993a considers the section original

17 Melamed 1991, 282 considers Part II an adaptation, and Part III original

18 Häfner 1987, 195ff

19 Schweitzer, 628

20 BG 1892, Foreword

21 Melamed 1991, 283

22 Neumann 1953, 85

PART THREE
THE INSTRUMENTAL WORKS

The Art of the Toccata

1 Edler 1997, 426

2 Zehnder i. V.—Breig i. V.

3 Keller 1948, 62

4 Cf. Schmidt 1990, 109

5 Edler 1995, 106

6 Spitta 1, 404

7 Williams 1996, 85

8 Breig 1993

9 Edler 1995, 108

10 Mendelssohn Bartholdy 1863b, 282

11 Sackmann 1988, 357

12 Zehnder 1991, 90ff

13 Birk, 1970

14 In conversation with Jean-Claude Zehnder

15 Schleuning 1998, 49ff

16 Gwinner 1968

17 Spitta 1, 416

18 Mahnkopf 1992, 175

19 Breig 1995

20 Keller 1948, 91

21 Zehnder 1997, 118

22 Breig 1986a, 33

23 Breig 1986b

24 Wiemer 1988, 166f.

25 Cf. Dirksen 1998a, col. 606

26 Edler 1997, 435

27 Seidel 1970, 439

28 Forkel 1802, 17

29 Schulenberg 1992

30 Märker 1999

31 Goldschmidt 1977, 60

32 Kirkendale 1966, 214

33 Zenck 1986, 199ff

34 Geck 2000e

35 Dammann 1967, 379ff

36 Schleuning 1969—Schleuning
1992

37 Geck 1995b

38 Nietzsche 1969, 41

39 Dok 3:32f.

40 Schulenberg 1992, 120

41 Forkel 1802, 56

42 Siegele 1981 (et alii)

43 Cf. Schmidt 1986

44 Keller 1948, 121

45 Adlung 1758, 360

46 Discussion by Michael Talbot
and Arnfried Edler in: Heller
and Schulze 1955, 350—Wollny
1997c

The Organic Chorales

1 Emans 1997

2 For a different view, cf. Williams
1998, 318

3 Breig 1998b, 9

4 Wolff 1998b

5 Sachs 1980, 143

6 Acc. to Sachs 1980, 146

7 Besseler 1955a, 210

8 Schweitzer, 247

9 Besseler 1951, 124

10 Schumann 1904, 177

11 Williams 1998, 118

12 Budday 1977

13 Dok 3: 84

14 Mendelssohn Bartholdy 1870, 215

15 Schumann 1871, v. 1, 128. For
another interpretation of
Mendelssohn's statement, cf.
Schumann 1948, 39

16 Schumann 1948, 174

17 Spitta 1, 607

18 Schweitzer 1995, 250

19 Breig 1987, 104

20 Deutsch 1964, 235

21 Williams 1998, 220

22 Wolff 1969, 152

23 Wolff 1969, 144

24 Krieger 1930, 83

25 Ehrmann 1933, 81

26 Trautmann 1984

27 Dok 2: 423

28 Brückner 1973, 6ff

29 Boulez 1979, 74

30 Cf. Jacob 1997, 195

31 Cf. e.g. Keller 1948, 205ff

32 Bäumlin 1990

33 Edler 1997, 101

34 Dessau 1974, 124

35 Boulez 1979, 75

36 Zacher 1981

37 Williams 1998, 144

38 Dok 3: 313 and 441

39 Wolff 1977

The Cöthen Demonstration Cycles: *Inventions and Sinfonias, The Well-Tempered Clavier,* Six Solos for Violin

1   Webern 1960, 36
2   Dok 3: 288
3   Wolff 1983a, 358
4   Dok 3: 87
5   Dok 2: 302
6   Dok 2: 349
7   Vassar 1972
8   Dok 3: 476
9   Bach 1753, Part I, Chapter I, §7
10 Siedentopf 1967, 121
11 Dok 2: 334
12 Niedt 1700
13 Constantini 1969
14 Cf. Krummacher 1985a, 123
15 Mattheson 1739, 88
16 Jöde 1926, 12
17 Ratz 1973, 8f
18 David 1957, 36
19 Keller 1950, 121
20 Hindermann 1985, 23
21 Fischer 1950, 155ff
22 Dok 3: 226
23 Spitta 1, 676
24 Hindemith 1940, 245
25 Borris 1955, 299
26 Breig 1972, 24—Dahlhaus 1988a, 137
27 Keller 1950, 121 – Besseler 1955a, 206
28 Hindermann 1985, 26
29 Hartmann 1996, v. 1, 544ff and 474ff—cf. also Chafe 1991, 39ff
30 Siegele 1981, 144
31 Friedländer 1953, 295—Toduta and Türk 1977, 190ff
32 Edler 1997, 427 and 435
33 Werckmeister 1707, 116
34 Dok 3: 666
35 Cf. Finscher and Laubenthal 1990, 358
36 Edler 1997, 419—Seidel 1970, 439ff
37 Cf. Dürr 1998, 92ff—For further interpretations cf. Werker 1922
38 Wagner 1976, v. 1, 356
39 Keller 1950, 236
40 Riemann 1890b, 114
41 Bergner 1986, 106
42 Thorau 1999, 178
43 Kunze 1969, 86
44 Dahlhaus 1988b, 446
45 Edler 1997, 437ff
46 Wagner 1976, v. 2, 264
47 Wagner 1976, v. 2, 264
48 Riemann 1890a, vi
49 Cf. Bergner 1986
50 Mattheson 1725, 267ff. Cf. Butler 1977, 69
51 Zacher 1993a
52 Kunze 1988, 94
53 Joël 1928, 392
54 Joël 1928, 393
55 Leibniz 1968, 101—Leibniz 1960, 53
56 Joël 1928, 569
57 Deleuze 1995, 214
58 Deleuze 1995, 218
59 Leibniz 1960, 63
60 Feder 1969, 180—Johannes Brahms to Clara Schumann, 1877
61 Thoene 1994
62 Lucktenberg 1983
63 Goebel 1988, 85
64 Eller 1969, 133
65 Huber 1970, esp. 22

The Concertos

1　Gurlitt 1936, 54
2　Mattheson 1713, 265
3　Talbot 1999, 282ff
4　Lasocki 1992
5　Marissen 1995a, 35ff
6　Schleuning 1997, 216 and 211
7　Rolf 1998
8　Pickett 1994
9　Böhmer 1995, esp. 16
10　Defant 1985, 115
11　Cf. Fischer 1915
12　Pfister 1987, 302
13　Kunze 1987, 159
14　Talbot 1999, 261
15　Geck 1970, 143
16　Walther 1732, 244
17　Dok 2: 332
18　Budde 1997, 75
19　Mattheson 1739, 236
20　Gerber 1965, 27
21　Florand 1950, 145ff
22　Vetter 1950, 223
23　Platen 1969
24　Siegele 1997, 168
25　Braun 1971
26　Mattheson 1725, 169ff
27　Boer 1980, 27
28　Schleuning 1990, 228
29　Harnoncourt 1987, 211
30　Zehnder 1997, 110
31　Defant 1985
32　Geck 1997b, 179
33　Hofmann 1997b
34　Rienäcker 1997, 197
35　Rienäcker 1997, 194

36　Kurth 1922, 238
37　Heller 1975, 17
38　Besseler 1970, 15
39　Eppstein 1966, 25
40　Preussner 1949, 67
41　DDT 1958, xiii
42　Besseler 1956
43　Dirksen 1992b, 176
44　Rampe and Zapf 1997. Cf. the responses in Dirksen 1998b and Rampe 1998
45　Dirksen 1992b, 178ff
46　Marissen 1992
47　Boyd 1993, 60ff
48　Rolf 1997
49　Forkel 1802, 49
50　Kunze 1988, 95
51　Menuhin 1976, 49
52　Schweitzer, 365
53　Wagner 1976, v. 2, 229
54　Lenz 1869, 219
55　Wiesend 1987, 28
56　Schweitzer, 365
57　Steglich 1935, 102
58　Moser 1935, 161
59　Besseler 1955b, 118
60　Dok 2: 260
61　Emery and Wolff 1981
62　Beisswenger 1995, 18
63　Mattheson 1739, 168
64　Jacob 1997, 167ff
65　Hirschmann 1988, 161ff
66　Halm 1919, 18
67　Breig 1991, 297
68　Krebs 1994

The Sonatas and Suites

1　Wollny 1997b
2　Smend 1954, 214
3　Siegele 1981, 140ff
4　Dreyfus 1985, Afterword 56

5　Eppstein 1966, 75–90
6　Hofmann 1998a, 49
7　Beurmann 1952m 40—Asmus 1986, 161

8   Gerstenberg 1963, 158

9   Spitta 1, 720

10 Vogt 1981, 201

11 Scheibe 1745, 675

12 Swack 1993

13 Dreyfus 1985, Afterword 56—
    Wolff 1985a, 234

14 Hsu 1984

15 Spitta 1, 727

16 Dreyfus 1987

17 Spitta 1, 727

18 Kunze 1987, 342

19 Zenck 1986, 188

20 Kunze 1987, 50

21 Kurth 1922, 204

22 Paul 1974, 132

23 Kilian 1969, 12

24 Forkel 1802, 60

25 Williams 1996, 22

26 Dok 3: 441

27 Tilmouth 1980

28 Blum 1998, 121ff

29 Hofmann 1991a

30 Siegele 1960, 167

31 Jaccottet 1986

32 Cf. Blum 1998, 126

33 Edler 1997, 244

34 Zehnder 1993, 162

35 Schulze 1983a

36 Dadelsen 1991, 75

37 Dok 3: 469

38 Gülke 1976, 49ff

39 Abraham and Dahlhaus 1972, 174

40 Mattheson 1731, 174

41 Telemann 1972, 176ff

42 Dok 3: 649ff

43 Rifkin 1999, 327ff, esp. note 1,
    341

44 Rifkin, unpub. lecture

45 Wolff 1985a, 237

46 Scheibe 1745, 670 and 672

The Late Cycles

1   Kunze 1988, 91

2   Butler 1983b

3   Hoffmann 1922, 188ff

4   Dammann 1986, 76

5   Geiringer 1950, 367

6   Flotzinger 1967

7   Hartmann 1997, 58

8   Nettl 1921—Nettl 1922

9   Wolff 1976a

10 Facsimile in: Kaussler 1985, 224

11 Schumann 1871, v. 2, 368

12 Niemöller 1985, 9

13 Breig 1975

14 Dammann 1986, 213

15 Zenck 1985, 79ff

16 Türcke 1985

17 Forkel 1802, 3

18 Dok 3: 87

19 Baensch 1934, 322ff

20 Müller-Blattau 1959, 218

21 Marshall 1976, 343ff

22 Neumann 1985

23 Elster 1988

24 Zehnder 1993, 162

25 Duse 1981, 108

26 Zacher 1993b

27 Cf. Schleuning 1993, 243

28 Eggebrecht 1984a, 91ff

29 Mattheson 1739, 75

30 Dok 3: 144ff

31 Schleuning 1993, 112ff, 116

32 Tovey 1944, 84ff

33 Schwebsch 1931, 278f

34 Bergel 1985, 86f

35 Eggebrecht 1984a, 86

36 Mattheson 1739, 422

37 Besseler and Grüss 1967, 121ff

38 Spitta 2, 685

39 Schleuning 1993, 216

40 Wöhlke 1941, 43ff

41	Schleuning 1993, 182
42	Graeser 1924
43	Kolneder 1977b, Part 5, 659ff
44	Kolneder 1977b, Part 4, 567
45	Schäfer 1935, 35
46	Program note in author's possession; Kolneder 1977b, Part 5, 694ff
47	Busoni 1922, 197
48	Spitta 2, 676
49	Kirkendale 1997
50	Mattheson 1739, 235

51	Forchert 1987, 171
52	Cf. Critique of Wolff 1996b, 421ff and of Walker 1995, 175
53	Wolff 1971
54	Dok 3: 276
55	Dok 3: 656
56	Wolff 1976b, 105
57	Lowinsky 1956—Elders 1968, 169ff
58	Benjamin 1996, 66
59	Marissen 1995b

Bach's Art

1	Dok 2: 349
2	Dok 3: 358
3	Dok 3: 408
4	Dok 3: 586
5	Geck 1967, 46ff
6	Dok 3: 409
7	Wagner 1976, v. 2, 446
8	Dok 3: 305. (Engl. tr. *New Bach Reader*, rev. 1998, p. 347.)
9	Siegele 1999, 220

10	Wolff 1987, 162ff
11	Webern 1960, 36
12	Dahlhaus 1969, 277
13	Elders 1988
14	Kant 1908, 229
15	Hegel (no year given), v. 2, 271
16	Adorno 1993, S. 72
17	Picht 1980, 272
18	Geck 2000b
19	Schumann 1885, 187

Bach as a Christian

1	Dok 2: 494–96
2	Leaver 1983, 18
3	Preuss 1928, 107
4	Leaver 1983, 42
5	Trautmann 1969, 3
6	Trautmann 1969, 12ff
7	Blankenburg 1987
8	Geck 2000c
9	Nietzsche 1980, 576ff (tr. Helen Zimmern, pub. 1909–1913 (website: publicappeal.org))

10	Illustration in Leaver 1983, 110.
11	An observation of Wolfgang Osthoff mentioned in Hoffmann-Erbrecht 1983, 122
12	Bergel 1985, 195—Chafe 1991, 40
13	Hübner 1982, 65–78
14	Henze 1983
15	Loewenich 1982, 20ff
16	Bloch 1959, 1227

Rhetoric and Symbolism

1   Zedler 1743, col. 1690
2   Eggebrecht 1984b, 86
3   Bartel 1997
4   Klassen 1997
5   Forchert 1987, 171
6   *Bach-Cantatas.com.* 2006 Bach Cantatas Web site. <http://www.bach-cantatas.com>
7   Boschius 1702, Classis III, Tabula XXVII
8   Eggebrecht 1992, 136
9   Spitta 2, 379
10 Goethe 1907, 146. Eng. tr. Penguin Edition, Goethe: *Maxims and Reflections,* trans. Elisabeth Stopp and Peter Hutchinson, Penguin Books, 1998, London
11 Stoll 1983
12 Hartmann 1996. Quotes in this excerpt from the book jacket text.

Proportion and Numerical Relations in Bach's Music

1   Siegele 1978, 12ff
2   Tatlow 1999
3   Cf. Gravenhorst 1995
4   Leaver 1983, 135
5   Tatlow 1991
6   Dehnhard 1987, 450ff
7   Smend 1950
8   Böss 1991
9   Thoene 1994, 67
10 Kolneder 1991, 348
11 Gould 1988, 57
12 Hofstadter 1979, 422

Theological Bach Research: Between Scholarship and Faith-Inspired Learning

1   Geck 1967, 25
2   Petzoldt (no year given), 50
3   Luther 1913, 11ff
4   Walter 1994

BIBLIOGRAPHY

Abraham, Lars Ulrich und Carl Dahlhaus. Melodielehre, Köln 1972

Adlung, Jacob. Anleitung zu der musikalischen Gelahrtheit, Erfurt 1758

———. Musica Mechanica Organoedi, Bd. 1, Berlin 1768, fotomechanischer Nachdruck, 2. Aufl. Kassel 1961

Adorno Theodor W. [in der Diskussion mit Eugen Kogon], Offenbarung oder autonome Vernunft, in: Frankfurter Hefte 13, 1958, S. 392–402, 484–498

———. Einleitung in die Musiksoziologie, Reinbek 1968

———. Ästhetische Theorie, Frankfurt a. M. 1970

———. Beethoven. Philosophie der Musik. Fragmente und Texte, hrsg. v. Rolf Tiedemann, Frankfurt a. M. 1993

Ahrens, Christian. Joh. Seb. Back und der «neue Gusto» in der Musik um 1740, in: BJ 1986, S. 69–79

Alciati, Andreas. Emblematum Libellus, fotomechanischer Nachdruck der Ausgabe von 1542, Darmstadt 1987

AMZ. An., «Notizen», in: Allgemeine Musikalische Zeitung, Bd. 20, 1818, Sp. 531 f.

Asmus, Jürgen. Zur thematischen Arbeit und Formbildung in Bachschen langsamen Sonatensätzen, in: Bach-Studien, Bd. 9, Leipzig 1986, S. 151–162

Axmacher, Elke. Ein Quellenfund zum Text der Matthäuspassion, in: BJ 1978, S. 181–191

———. «Aus Liebe will mein Heyland sterben». Untersuchungen zum Wandel des Passionsverständnisses im frühen 18. Jahrhundert, Neuhausen-Stuttgart 1984

Bach, Carl Philipp Emanuel. Versuch über die wahre Art, das Clavier zu spielen, Bd. 1, Berlin 1753, Faksimile hrsg. v. Lothar Hoffmann-Erbrecht, Leipzig 1978

Baensch, Otto. Nochmals das Quodlibet der Goldbergvariationen, in: Zeitschrift für Musikwissenschaft, 101, 1934, S. 322 f.

Bartel, Dietrich. Handbuch der musikalischen Figurenlehre, 3. Auflage, Laaber 1997

Bäumlin, Klaus. «Mit unaussprechlichem Seufzen». J. S. Bachs großes Vater-Unser-Vorspiel (BWV 682), in: MuK 60, 1990, S. 310–320

Beaulieu Marconnay, Carl Freiherr von. Ernst August, Herzog von Sachsen-Weimar-Eisenach, Leipzig 1872

Becker, Heinz. Die frühe Hamburgische Tagespresse als musikgeschichtliche Quelle, in: Heinrich Husmann (Hrsg.), Beiträge zur Hamburgischen Musikgeschichte, Hamburg 1956, S. 22–45

Becker, Heinz. Artikel «Orchester. B», in: MGG^{I}, Bd. 10, 1962, Sp. 172–194

Beißwenger, Kirsten. Johann Sebastian Bachs Notenbibliothek, Kassel 1992

————. An early version of the first movement of the Italian Concerto BWV 971 from the Scholz collection?, in: Daniel R. Melamed, Bach Studies 2, Cambridge 1995, S. 1–19.

Benjamin, Walter. Ursprung des deutschen Trauerspiels, 7. Aufl. Frankfurt a. M. 1996

Bergel, Erich. Bachs letzte Fuge. Die «Kunst der Fuge»—ein zyklisches Werk. Enstehungsgeschichte—Erstausgabe—Ordnungsprinzipen, o. O. 1985

Bergner, Christoph. Studien zur Form der Präludien des Wohltemperierten Klaviers von Johann Sebastian Bach, Neuhausen-Stuttgart 1986

Berke, Dietrich und Dorothee Hanemann. Alte Musik als ästhetische Gegenwart, Kongreßbericht Stuttgart 1985, 2 Bde., Kassel usw. 1987

Besseler, Heinrich. Die Meisterzeit Bachs in Weimar, in: Johann Sebastian Bach in Thüringen. Festgabe zum Gedenkjahr 1950, Weimar 1950, S. 106–119

————. Bach und das Mittelalter, in: Bericht über die Wissenschaftliche Bachtagung, Leipzig 1950, Leipzig 1951, S. 108–130

————. Bach als Wegbereiter (1955), in: Walter Blankenburg (Hrsg.), Johann Sebastian Bach. Wege der Forschung, Darmstadt 1970, S. 196–246

————. Zur Chronologie der Konzerte Joh. Seb. Bachs, in: Festschrift Max Schneider zum achtzigsten Geburtstage, Leipzig 1955, S. 115–128

————. Kritischer Bericht zu NBA VII/2: Sechs Brandenburgische Konzerte, Kassel und Basel 1956

————. Johann Sebastian Bach, in: Walter Blankenburg (Hrsg.), Johann Sebastian Bach. Wege der Forschung, Darmstadt 1970, S. 1–22

Besseler, Heinrich und Hans Grüss. Kritischer Bericht zu NBA VII/1: Vier Ouvertüren, Kassel usw. 1967

Beurmann, Erich. Die Klaviersonaten Carl Philipp Emanuel Bachs, Phil. Diss. Göttingen 1952

Bach-Gesamtausgabe. Bd. 6, Leipzig 1860

————. Wilhelm Rust im Vorwort zur Bach-Gesamtausgabe, Bd. 12, 2, Leipzig 1862

————. Bd. 39, Leipzig 1892

Binding, Günther und Norbert Nussbaum. Der mittelalterliche Baubetrieb nördlich der Alpen in zeitgenössischen Darstellungen, Darmstadt 1978

Birk, Reinhold. Bachs Toccata in F und Beethovens Eroica, Satz I, in: MuK 40, 1970, S. 261–276

Bischoff, Bodo und Ulrich Siebert. Zum Rezitativ Nr. 2 aus der Kantate «Ihr Menschen, rühmet Gottes Liebe» BWV 167 von J. S. Bach. Versuch einer Analyse, in: Bach-Studien, Bd. 10, Wiesbaden und Leipzig 1991, S. 137–154

Bitter, Carl Heinrich. Johann Sebastian Bach, 4 Bde., 2. Auflage Berlin 1881

Blankenburg, Walter. Geschichte der Melodien des evangelischen Kirchengesangbuchs, in: Handbuch zum Evangelischen Kirchengesangbuch, Bd. 11, 2, Göttingen 1957

————. Einführung in Bachs h-moll-Messe BWV 232, 3. Auflage Kassel 1974

————. Artikel «Gastorius, Severus», in: MGG¹, Bd. 16, 1979, Sp. 425

————. Das Weihnachts-Oratorium von Johann Sebastian Bach, 2. Aufl. München und Kassel 1985

————. Mystik in der Musik J. S. Bachs, in: ders. und Renate Steiger (Hrsg.), Theologische Bach-Studien I, Neuhausen-Stuttgart 1987, S. 47–66

Bloch, Ernst. Das Prinzip Hoffnung, Bd. 3, Frankfurt a. M. 1959

Blum, Gerhard. «Kompositorische Entwicklung». Formale und chronologische Aspekte in den Suitenwerken Telemanns und Bachs, in: Arolser Beiträge zur Musikforschung, Bd. 6, 1998, S. 115–140

Blume, Friedrich. Artikel Karl Heinrich Bitter, MGG¹, Bd. 1, 1949–1951, Sp. 1866–1868

————. Umrisse eines neuen Bach=Bildes, in: Syntagma musicologicum. Gesammelte Reden und Schriften, Kassel usw. 1963, S. 466 ff

Boer, Bertil H. van. Observations on Bach's use of the Horn, Teil 1, in: Bach. The Quarterly Journal of the Riemenschneider Bach Institute, Bd. 11, 1980, S. 21–28

Böhmer, Karl. Bachs mythologisches Geheimnis. Philip Pickett, Reinhard Goebel und das verborgene Programm der Brandenburgischen Konzerte, in: Concerto, 12, 1995/96, H. 6, S. 15–17

Bojanowski, Paul von. Das Weimar Johann Sebastian Bachs, Weimar 1903

Boresch, Hans-Werner. Besetzung und Instrumentation, Studien zur kompositorischen Praxis Bachs, Kassel usw. 1993 (= Bochumer Arbeiten zur Musikwissenschaft, Bd. 1)

Borges, Jorge Luis. Der Geschmack eines Apfels. Gedichte, ausgewählt von Raoul Schrott, München 1999

Borris, Siegfried. Hindemiths harmonische Analysen, in: Festschrift Max Schneider zum achtzigsten Geburtstage, Leipzig 1955, S. 295–301

Boschius, Jacobus. Symbolographia, Augsburg und Dillingen 1702

Böß, Reinhard. Die Kunst des Rätselkanons im Musikalischen Opfer, Wilhelmshaven 1991

Boulez, Pierre. Anhaltspunkte. Essays, Kassel und München 1979

Boyd, Malcolm. Bach: The Brandenburg Concertos, Cambridge 1993

Braun, Werner. Entwurf für eine Typologie der «Hautboisten», in: Walter Salmen (Hrsg.), Der Sozialstatus des Berufsmusikers vom 17. bis 19. Jahrhundert, Kassel usw. 1971, S. 43–63

———. Die Musik des 17. Jahrhunderts, Wiesbaden und Laaber 1981 (= Neues Handbuch der Musikwissenschaft Bd. 4)

Breig, Werner. Zur Harmonik von Bachs f-moll-Sinfonia, in: Lars Ulrich Abraham (Hrsg.), Festschrift Erich Doflein, Mainz 1972, S. 17–26

———. Bachs Goldberg-Variationen als zyklisches Werk, in: AfMw 32, 1975, S. 243–265

———. Bachs «Kunst der Fuge»: Zur instrumentalen Bestimmung und zum Zyklus-Charakter, in: BJ 1982, S. 103–123

———. Bemerkungen zur zyklischen Symmetrie in Bachs Leipziger Vokalmusik, in: MuK; 53, 1983, S. 173–179

———. Zu den Turba-Chören der Johannes-Passion, in: Hamburger Jahrbuch für Musikwissenschaft 8, Laaber 1985, S. 65–96

———. Bachs freie Orgelmusik unter dem Einfluß der italienischen Konzertform, in: Bach-Studien 9, Leipzig 1986, S. 29–43

———. J. S. Bachs Orgeltoccata BWV 538 und ihre Entstehungsgeschichte, in: Festschrift Martin Ruhnke zum 65. Geburtstag, Neuhausen-Stuttgart 1986, S. 56–67

———. Bachs Orgelchoral und die italienische Instrumentalmusik, in: Wiesend 1987, S. 91–108

———. Grundzüge einer Geschichte von Bachs vierstimmigem Choralsatz, in: AfMw Jg. 45, 1988, S. 165–185 und 300–319

———. Zum geschichtlichen Hintergrund und zur Kompositionsgeschichte von Bachs ‹Orgel-Büchlein›, in: Bachs ‹Orgel-Büchlein› in nieuw perspectiv, Utrecht 1988, S. 7–20

———. Das Ostinatoprinzip in Johann Sebastian Bachs langsamen Konzertsätzen, in: Frank Heidlberger u.a. (Hrsg.), Festschrift Martin Just, Kassel 1991, S. 287–300

———. Form Problems in Bach's Early Organ Fugues, in: Paul Brainard and Ray Robinson, A Bach Tribute. Essays in Honor of William H. Scheide, Kassel usw. 1993, S. 45–56

———. Versuch einer Theorie der Bachschen Orgelfuge, in: Mf 48, 1995, S. 33–52

———. Bach und Marchand in Dresden. Eine überlieferungskritische Studie, in: BJ 1998, S. 7–18

———. Bachs Umarbeitungen seiner Orgelwerke als Ausdruck personalstilistischer Wandlungen, in: «Die Zeit, die Tag und Jahre macht.» Zur Chronologie des Schaffens bei Johann Sebastian Bach. Internationales wissenschaftliches Colloquium aus Anlaß des 80. Geburtstags von Dr. DMus. h. c. Alfred Dürr, Göttingen, 13.–15. März 1998, Druck in Vorbereitung

Brinkmann, Reinhold. (Hrsg.), Bachforshung und Bach-interpretation heute. Bericht über das Bachfest-Symposium 1978, Leipzig 1981

Brückner, Christian. J. S. Bachs «Dritter Theil der Clavier Übung», Separatdruck aus der Zeitschrift Musik und Gottesdienst, Heft 3 und 4, 1973

Budday, Wolfgang. Musikalische Figuren als satztechnische Freiheiten in Bachs Orgelchoral «Durch Adams Fall ist ganz verderbt», in: BJ 1977, S. 139 ff

Budde, Elmar. Musikalische Form und rhetorische dispositio. Zum ersten Satz des dritten Brandenburgischen Konzerts, in: Hartmut Krones (Hrsg.), Alte Musik und Musikpäd-agogik, Wien, Köln und Weimar 1997, S. 69–83

Bunge, Hans. Fragen Sie mehr über Brecht. Hanns Eisler im Gespräch, München 1970

Busoni, Ferruccio. Von der Einheit der Musik, Berlin 1922

Butler, Gregory G. Fugue and Rhetoric, in: Journal of Music Theory 21, 1977, S. 49–109

————. Der vollkommene Capellmeister as a stimulus to J. S. Bach's late fugal writing, in: George J. Buelow und Hans Joachim Marx (Hrsg.), New Mattheson Studies, Cam-bridge usw. 1983, S. 293–305

————. Ordering Problems in J. S. Bach's Art of Fugue Resolved, in: The Musical Quar-terly 69, 1983, S. 44–61

————. Bach's Clavier-Übung III. The making of a print, Durham and London 1990

Chafe, Eric. Key Structure and Tonal Allegory in the Passions of J. S. Bach: An introduc-tion, in: Current Musicology, Nr. 31, 1981, S. 39–54

————. The St. John Passion: Theology and musical structure, in: Bach Studies 1, Don O. Franklin, Cambridge 1989, S. 75–112

————. Tonal Allegory in the Vocal Music of J. S. Bach, Berkeley, Los Angeles, Oxford 1991

Chrysander, Friedrich. Neue Beiträge zur mecklenburgischen Musikgeschichte, in: Archiv für Landeskunde in den Großherzogthümern Mecklenburg, 6, 1855, S. 12

————. G. F. Händel, Bd. 1, Leipzig 1858

Claus, Rolf Dietrich. Zur Echtheit von Toccata und Fuge d-moll BWV 565, Köln-Rheinkassel 1995

Constantini, Franz-Peter. Zur Typusgeschichte von J. S. Bachs Wohltemperiertem Klavier, in: BJ 1969, S. 31–45

Crist, Stephen A. Bach's début at Leipzig. Observations on the genesis of Cantatas 75 and 76, in: Early Music 13, 1985, S. 212–226

Dadelsen, Georg von. Bachs Kantate 77, wieder abgedruckt in: ders., Über Bach und an-deres. Aufsätze und Vorträge 1957–1982, Laaber 1983, S. 185–193

————. (Hrsg.), Klavierbüchlein für Anna Magdalena 1725, Faksimile der Originalhand-schrift mit einem Nachwort, Kassel 1988

————. Bach, der Violinist. Anmerkungen zu den Soli für Violine und für Violoncello, in: BzBF 9/10, Leipzig 1991, S. 70–76

Dahlhaus, Carl. Plädoyer für eine romantische Kategorie, in: Neue Zeitschrift für Musik, 130, 1969, wieder abgedruckt in: Schönberg und andere. Gesammelte Aufsätze, Mainz 1978, S. 270–278

————. Bach und der Zerfall der musikalischen Figurenlehre, in: Musica, 42, 1988, S. 137–140

————. Klassische und romantische Musikästhetik, Laaber 1988

Dammann, Rolf. Der Musikbegriff im deutschen Barock, Köln 1967

————. Johann Sebastian Bachs «Goldberg-Variationen», Mainz usw. 1986

Danckwardt, Marianne. Zur Aria aus J. S. Bachs Motette «Komm, Jesu, komm!» in: AfMw 44, 1987, S. 195–202

David, Werner. Johann Sebastian Bach's Orgeln, Berlin 1951

David, Johann Nepomuk. Die zweistimmigen Inventionen von Johann Sebastian Bach, Göttingen 1957

Denkmäler Deutscher Tonkunst, 1. Folge, Bd. 28, 2. Auflage Wiesbaden und Graz 1958

Defant, Christine. Kammermusik und Stylus phantasticus. Studien zu Dietrich Buxtehudes Triosonaten, Frankfurt a. M. 1985

Dehio, Georg. Handbuch der Deutschen Kunstdenkmäler, Bd. 1: Mitteldeutschland, 3. Aufl. Berlin 1924

Dehnhard, Walther. Kritik der Zahlensymbolischen Deutung im Werk Johann Sebastian Bachs, in: Berke und Hanemann 1987, S. 450–452

Deleuze, Gilles. Die Falte. Leibniz und der Barock, übersetzt von Ulrich Johannes Schneider, Frankfurt a. M. 1995

Dessau, Paul. Analyse eines Bach-Werkes: «Einige kanonische Veränderungen über das Weihnachtslied ‹Vom Himmel hoch, da komm ich her›», in: Notizen zu Noten, Leipzig 1974, S. 109–124

Deutsch, Otto Erich. Schubert. Die Dokumente seines Lebens, hrsg. von Otto Erich Deutsch, Leipzig 1964

Dilthey, Wilhelm. Von deutscher Dichtung und Musik. Aus den Studien zur Geschichte des deutschen Geistes, 2. Aufl. Stuttgart und Göttingen 1957

Dirksen, Pieter. Studien zur Kunst der Fuge von Johann Sebastian Bach. Untersuchungen zur Entstehungsgeschichte, Struktur und Aufführungspraxis, Wilhelmshaven 1992

———. The Background to Bach's Fifth Brandenburg Concerto, in: ders. (Hrsg.), The Harpsichord and Its Repertoire. Proceedings of the International Harpsichord Symposion Utrecht 1990, Utrecht 1992, S. 157–185

———. Artikel «Toccata» in MGG², Bd. 2, 1998, Sp. 599–611

———. Replik auf Rampe und Zapf 1997, in: Concerto 15, 1998, H. 137, S. 15 ff

Dörffel, Alfred. Die Gewandhauskonzerte zu Leipzig, 1781–1881, Leipzig 1884, Repr. Leipzig 1980

Dreyfus, Laurence. Ausgabe der Gambensonaten von J. S. Bach, Leipzig und Dresden 1985

———. J. S. Bach and the Status of Genre: Problems of Style in the G-Minor Sonata BWV 1029, in: Journal of Musicology, 5, 1987, S. 55–78

Dürr, Alfred. Studien über die frühen Kantaten J. S. Bachs, Leipzig 1951

———. Zur Chronologie der Leipziger Vokalwerke J. S. Bachs, in: BJ 1957, S. 6–162

———. Johann Sebastian Bach. Weihnachts-Oratorium BWV 248 (Meisterwerke der Musik), München 1967

———. Zur Entstehungsgeschichte des Bachschen Choralkantaten-Jahrgangs, in: Geck 1969a, S. 7–11

———. Bemerkungen zu Bachs Leipziger Kantatenaufführungen, in: Bericht über die Wissenschaftliche Konferenz zum III. Internationalen Bach-Fest der DDR 1975, Leipzig 1977, S. 165–172

———. Die Kantaten von Johann Sebastian Bach, 2 Bde., 5. Aufl. München, Kassel usw. 1985

———. Die Johannes-Passion von Johann Sebastian Bach, München und Kassel 1988

———. Zur Parodiefrage in Bachs h-moll-Messe, in: Mf 45, 1992, S. 117–138

———. Johann Sebastian Bach. Das Wohltemperierte Klavier, Kassel usw. 1998

Duse, Ugo. Musik und Schweigen in der Kunst der Fuge, in: Musik-Konzepte 17/18, München 1981, S. 83–113

Edler, Arnfried. Thematik und Figuration in der Tastenmusik des jungen Bach, in: Heller und Schulze 1995, S. 87–115

———. Gattungen der Musik für Tasteninstrumente, Teil I: Von den Anfängen bis 1750, Laaber 1997 (Handbuch der musikalischen Gattungen, Bd. 7)

Eggebrecht, Hans Heinrich. Bachs Kunst der Fuge, Erscheinung und Deutung, München 1984

———. Heinrich Schütz. Musicus poeticus, 2. Aufl. Wilhelmshaven 1984

———. Bach—wer ist das? Zum Verständnis der Musik Johann Sebastian Bachs, München und Mainz 1992

Ehmann, Wilhelm. J. S. Bachs «Dritter Theil der Clavier Übung» in seiner gottesdien-
stlichen Bedeutung und Verwendung, in: MuK 5, 1933, S. 77–87

Elders, Willem. Studien zur Symbolik in der Musik der alten Niederländer, Bilthoven 1968
————. Kompositionsverfahren in der Musik der alten Niederländer und die Kunst J. S.
Bachs, in: BzBF 6, Leipzig 1988, S. 110–135

Eller, Rudolf. Serie und Zyklus in Bachs Instrumentalsammlungen, in: Geck 1969a,
S. 126–143

Elster, Peter. Anmerkungen zur Aria der sogenannten Goldberg-variationen BWV 988.
Bachs Bearbeitung eines französischen Menuetts, in: Hoffmann und Schneiderheinze
1988, S. 259–267

Emans, Reinmar. (Hrsg.), Johann Sebastian Bach. Orgelchoräle zweifelhafter Echtheit.
Thematischer Katalog, Göttingen 1997

Emery, Walter, und Christoph Wolff, Kritischer Bericht zu NBA V/2: Zweiter und vierter
Teil der Klavierübung, Vierzehn Kanons BWV 1087, Kassel usw. 1981

Engelke, Bernhard. Gerstenberg und die Musik seiner Zeit, in: Zeitschrift der Gesellschaft
für Schleswig-Holsteinische Geschichte, Bd. 56, 1927, S. 417–448

Eppstein, Hans. Studien über J. S. Bachs Sonaten für ein Melodieinstrument und obligates
Cembalo, Uppsala 1966

Feder, Georg. Geschichte der Bearbeitungen von Bachs Chaconne, in: Geck 1969a,
S. 168–189

Finke-Hecklinger, Doris. Tanzcharaktere in Johann Sebastian Bachs Vokalmusik, 2. Aufl.
Trossingen 1970

Finscher, Ludwig. Zum Parodieproblem bei Bach, in: Geck 1969a, S. 94–105

Finscher, Ludwig, und Annegrit Laubenthal, «Cantiones quae vulgo motectae vocantur».
Arten der Motette im 15. und 16. Jahrhundert, in: Handbuch der Musikwissenschaft,
Bd. 3,2, Laaber 1990, S. 227–370

Fischer, Wilhelm. Zur Entwicklungsgeschichte des Wiener klassischen Stils, Leipzig 1915
(= Studien zur Musikwissenschaft H. 3)

Fischer, Kurt von. Zum Formproblem bei Bach. Studien an den Inventionen, Sinfonien
und Duetten, in: Karl Matthaei (Hrsg.), Bach-Gedenkschrift 1950, Zürich 1950,
S. 150–162

Florand, François. Johann Sebastian Bach. Das Orgelwerk, deutsch Lindau 1950

Flotzinger, Rudolf. Die Gagliarda Italjana. Zur Frage der barocken Thementypologie, in:
Acta Musicologica 39, 1967, S. 92–100

Fock, Gustav. Der junge Bach in Lüneburg, Hamburg 1950

Forchert, Arno. Bach und die Tradition der Rhetorik, in: Berke und Hanemann 1987, Bd.
1, S. 169–178

Forkel, Johann Nikolaus. Ueber Johann Sebastian Bachs Leben, Kunst und Kunstwerke.
Für patriotische Verehrer echter musikalischer Kunst, Leipzig 1802, Faksimile-
Nachdruck Frankfurt a. M. 1950

Fornaçon, Siegfried. Werke von Severus Gastorius, in: Jahrbuch für Hymnologie und
Liturgik, Bd. 8, 1963, S. 165–170

Friedländer, Walther. Die formbildenden Kräfte und ihre Entfaltung in Bachs f-moll-
Invention, in: Schweizer Musikzeitung 1953, S. 295–297

Fröde, Christine. Zu einer Kritik des Thomanerchores von 1749, in: BJ 1984, S. 53–58

Fujiwara, Kazuhiro. Die Grundlagen der Temperaturtheorie Andreas Werckmeisters, in:
Renate Steiger (Hrsg.), Die Quellen Johann Sebastian Bachs. Bachs Musik im Gottes-
dienst. Bericht über das Symposium Stuttgart, 4.–8. Oktober 1995, Heidelberg 1998,
S. 153–161

Gadamer, Hans-Georg. Bach und Weimar, Weimar 1946

Geck, Martin. J. S. Bachs Weihnachts-Magnificat und sein Traditionszusammenhang, in:
MuK 31, 1961, S. 257–266

————. Ph. J. Spener und die Kirchenmusik, in: MuK 31, 1961, S. 97–106 und 172–184
————. Die Vokalmusik Dietrich Buxtehudes und der frühe Pietismus, Kassel usw. 1965
————. Die Wiederentdeckung der Matthäuspassion im 19. Jahrhundert. Die zeitgenössischen Dokumente und ihre ideengeschichtliche Deutung, Regensburg 1967
————. (Hrsg.), Bach-Interpretationen, Göttingen 1969
————. Richard Wagner und die ältere Musik, in: Walter Wiora (Hrsg.), Die Ausbreitung des Historismus über die Musik, Regensburg 1969, S. 123–146
————. Gattungstraditionen und Altersschichten in den Brandenburgischen Konzerten, in: Mf 23, 1970, S. 139–152
————. J. S. Bachs Johannespassion, München 1991
————. Von Beethoven bis Mahler. Die Musik des deutschen Idealismus, Stuttgart und Weimar 1993
————. «Charivari», in: MGG², Bd. 2, 1995, Sp. 642 f.
————. Humor und Melancholie als kategoriale Bestimmungen der «absoluten» Musik, in: Studien zur Musikgeschichte. Eine Festschrift für Ludwig Finscher, Kassel usw. 1995, S. 309–316
————. (Hrsg.), Bachs Orchesterwerke, Bericht über das 1. Dortmunder Bach-Symposion 1996, Witten 1997 (Dortmunder Bach-Forschungen, Bd. 1)
————. Faßlich und künstlich, Betrachtungen zu Bachs Schreibart anläßlich des zweiten Brandenburgischen Konzerts, in: Geck 1997a, S. 173–184
————. Via Beethoven & Schönberg. Theodor W. Adornos Bach-Verständnis, in: Richard Klein und Claus-Steffen Mahnkopf (Hrsg.), Mit den Ohren denken. Adornos Philosophie der Musik, Frankfurt a. M. 1998, S. 229–239
————. (Hrsg.), Bach und die Stile. Bericht über das 2. Dortmunder Bach-Symposion 1998, Dortmund 1999 (Dortmunder Bach-Forschungen, Bd. 2)
————. «Denn alles findet bei Bach statt.» Erforschtes und Erfahrenes, Stuttgart und Weimar 2000
————. Bach als Genre-Komponist. Akustische Umwelt in seiner Musik, in: Geck 2000a, S. 56–74
————. Bach und der Pietismus, in: Geck 2000a, S. 88–108
————. Gottes Zeichen. Welt, Wort, Musik bei Luther und Bach, in: Geck 2000a, S. 75–87
————. Trauerarbeit. Beethovens Klaviersonate op. 110 in der Tradition von Bachs *Chromatischer Phantasie und Fuge*, in: Geck 2000a, S. 141–146
Geck, Martin, und Ares Rolf (Hrsg.), Bachs Actus tragicus in den Bearbeitungen durch Mortiz Hauptmann und Robert Franz, Dortmund (in preparation)
Geiringer, Karl. Artistic Interrelations of the Bachs, in: The Musical Quarterly 36, 1950, S. 363–374
————. Die Musikerfamilie Bach. Leben und Wirken in drei Jahrhunderten, München 1958
Georgiades, Thrasybulos. Musik und Sprache. Das Werden der abendländischen Musik dargestellt an der Vertonung der Messe, Berlin usw. 1954
Gerber, Johann Ludwig. Neues historisch-biographisches Lexikon der Tonkünstler, Teil 1, Leipzig 1812
Gerber, Rudolf. Bachs Brandenburgische Konzerte. Eine Einführung in ihre formale und geistige Wesensart, 2. Aufl. Kassel 1965
Gerlach, Reinhard. Besetzung und Instrumentation der Kirchenkantaten J. S. Bachs und ihre Bedingungen, in: BJ 1973, S. 53–71
Gerstenberg, Walter. Andante, in: Kongreßbericht Kassel 1962, Kassel 1963, S. 156–158
Glöckner, Andreas. Gründe für Johann Sebastian Bachs Weggang von Weimar, in: Hoffmann und Schneiderheinze 1988, S. 137–143
————. Überlegungen zu J. S. Bachs Kantatenschaffen nach 1730, in: BzBF 6, Leipzig 1988, S. 54–64

————. Die Musikpflege an der Leipziger Neukirche zur Zeit Johann Sebastian Bachs, Leipzig 1990 (BzBF 8)

————. Lebens- und Wirkungsstationen Bachs, in: Wolff und Koopman 1996, S. 59–85

————. Zur Vorgeschichte des «Bachischen» Collegium musicum, in: Geck 1997a, S. 293–303

Goebel, Reinhard. Fragen der instrumentalen Solo- und Ensemblepraxis Bachs, in: Wolff 1988a, S. 84–94

Goethe, Johann Wolfgang von. Maximen und Reflexionen, in: Sophien-Ausgabe, Bd. 42,2, Weimar 1907

Gojowy, Detlef. Ein Zwölftonfeld bei Johann Sebastian Bach? Beobachtungen am Rezitativ BWV 167, Satz 2, Takte 13–19, in: Bach-Studien, Bd. 5, Leipzig 1975, S. 43–48

Goldschmidt, Harry. Um die Unsterbliche Geliebte, Leipzig 1977

Gottsched, Johann Christoph. Beyträge zur Critischen Historie der deutschen Sprache, Poesie und Beredsamkeit, Reprogr. Nachdruck der Ausgabe Leipzig 1732–44, Hildesheim 1970

————. Versuch einer Critischen Dichtkunst, 4. Aufl. Leipzig 1751

Gould, Glenn. Von Bach bis Boulez, 4. Aufl. München 1988

Graeser, Wolfgang. Bachs «Kunst der Fuge». in: BJ 1924, S. 1–104

Gravenhorst, Tobias. Proportion und Allegorie in der Musik des Hochbarock: Untersuchungen zur Zahlenmystik des 17. Jahrhunderts, Frankfurt a. M. 1995

Gregor-Dellin, Martin, und Dietrich Mack (Hrsg.), Cosima Wagner. Die Tagebücher, Bd. 2, München und Zürich 1977

Grimm, Jacob und Wilhelm. Artikel «Bach», in: Dies. (Hrsg.), Deutsches Wörterbuch, Bd. 1, Leipzig 1854, Sp. 1057–1060

————. Artikel «Gotisch» in: Dies. (Hrsg.), Deutsches Wörterbuch, Bd. 4, 1.5., Leipzig 1958, Sp. 1000–1016

Grout, Donald J. Historical approach: No. 12, «Ich folge dir gleichfalls» from Bach Passion according to St. John, in: College Music-Symposium, Bd. 5, Boulder, Colorado 1965, S. 68–76

Grüss, Hans. Über Wertkriterien Bachscher Musik, in: Bach-Studien 10, Wiesbaden und Leipzig 1991, S. 74–79

Gülke, Peter. Über das Verhältnis zu Stil- und Gattungstraditionen bei Bach und Händel, in: Bericht über das wissenschaftliche Kolloquium der 24. Händelfestspiele 1975, Halle 1976, S. 47–52

————. Brahms–Bruckner, Kassel und Basel 1989

Gurlitt, Wilibald. Johann Sebastian Bach. Der Meister und sein Werk, Berlin 1936

Gwinner, Volker. Bachs Tokkata in C-dur als «Orgelprobe», in: MuK 38, 1968, S. 115–117

Häfner, Klaus. Über die Herkunft von zwei Sätzen der h-Moll-Messe, in: BJ 1977, S. 55–74

————. Zum Problem der Entstehungsgeschichte von BWV 248a, in: Mf 30, 1977, S. 304–308

————. Picander, der Textdichter von Bachs viertem Kantatenjahrgang. Ein neuer Hinweis, in: Mf 35, 1982, S. 156–162

————. Aspekte des Parodieverfahrens bei Johann Sebastian Bach, Laaber 1987

Halm, August. Über J. S. Bachs Konzertform, in: BJ 1919, S. 1–44

Hammerstein, Reinhold. Der Gesang der geharnischten Männer. Eine Studie zu Mozarts Bachbild, in: AfMw 13, 1956, S. 1–24

Hanheide, Stefan. Johann Sebastian Bach im Verständnis Albert Schweitzers, München und Salzburg 1990 (= Musikwissenschaftliche Schriften, Bd. 25)

Harnoncourt, Nikolaus. Der musikalische Dialog. Gedanken zu Monteverdi, Bach und Mozart, München und Kassel 1987

Hartmann, Günter. Die Tonfolge B-A-C-H. Zur Emblematik des Kreuzes im Werk Joh. Seb. Bachs, 2 Bde., Bonn 1996

————. BWV 988: Bergamasca-Variationen? oder Das aus dem Rahmen fallende Quodlibet, Lahnstein 1997

Hauptmann, Moritz. Briefe an Franz Hauser, hrsg. v. Alfred Schöne, Leipzig 1871

Hegel, o. J. Georg Friedrich Wilhelm Hegel, Vorlesungen über Ästhetik, hrsg. von F. Bassenge, Frankfurt a. M. o. J.

Heller, Karl. Thematische Arbeit bei J. S. Bach. Über einen Teilaspekt der «Modernität» Bachscher Musik, in: Beiträge zur Musikwissenschaft 17, 1975, S. 15–27

Heller, Karl, und Hans-Joachim Schulze (Hrsg.), Das Frühwerk Johann Sebastian Bachs, Kolloquium Rostock 1990, Köln 1995

Hensel, Sebastian. Die Familie Mendelssohn. 1729–1847. Nach Briefen und Tagebüchern, hrsg. v. Sebastian Hensel, Bd. 1, 3. Aufl. Berlin 1882

Henze, Hans Werner. Johann Sebastian Bach und die Musik unserer Zeit, in: Die Zeit, 28. 10. 1983, hier zitiert nach: ders., Musik und Politik. Schriften und Gespräche 1955–1984, erweiterte Neuausgabe, München 1984, S. 361–368

Herrmann, Rudolf. Die Bedeutung des Herzogs Wilhelm Ernst von Sachsen-Weimar (1683–1728) für die Weimarische evangelische Kirche, in: Zeitschrift des Vereins für Thüringische Geschichte und Altertumskunde, Neue Folge, Bd. 22, Heft 2, Jena 1915, S. 225–278

Herz, Gerhard. Der lombardische Rhythmus in Bachs Vokalschaffen, in: BJ 1978, S. 148–180

————. Bach-Quellen in Amerika. Bach Sources in America, Kassel usw. 1984

————. Thoughts on the First Movement of Johann Sebastian Bach's Cantata No. 77, in: ders., Essays on J. S. Bach, Ann Arbor 1985, S. 205–217

Heuß, Alfred. J. S. Bachs Aria «Erbauliche Gedanken eines Tabakrauchers», in: BJ 1913, S. 128–144

Hill, Robert. Introduction to Keyboard Music from the Andreas Bach Book and the Möller Manuscript, Cambridge/MA and London 1991

Hiller, Johann Adam. Lebensbeschreibungen berühmter Musikgelehrten und Tonkünstler, neuerer Zeit, Leipzig 1784

Hiller, Ferdinand. Briefe von Moritz Hauptmann an Louis Spohr und Andere, hrsg. v. Ferdinand Hiller, Leipzig 1876

Hindemith, Paul. Unterweisung im Tonsatz, Bd. 1, 2. Aufl. Mainz 1940

————. Johann Sebastian Bach. Ein verpflichtendes Erbe, Mainz 1950

Hindermann, Walter F. «…ein wahres…Vexierspiel» (P. Hindemith). Zu den Gestaltungsdimensionen von Bachs Sinfonia f-Moll, BWV 795, in: Schweizer musikpädagogische Blätter 1985, S. 21–28

Hirschmann, Wolfgang. Zur konzertanten Struktur der Ecksätze von Johann Sebastian Bachs Concerto BWV 971, in: AfMw 45, 1988, S. 148–162

Hobohm, Wolf. Neue «Texte zur Leipziger Kirchen-Music», in: BJ 1973, S. 5–32

Hoffmann, E. T. A. Musikalische Dichtungen und Aufsätze, Stuttgart 1922

Hoffmann, Winfried, und Armin Schneiderheinze (Hrsg.), Bericht über die Wissenschaftliche Konferenz zum V. Internationalen Bachfest der DDR, Leipzig 1985, Leipzig 1988

Hoffmann-Axthelm, Dagmar. Bach und die Perfidia iudaica. Zur Symmetrie der Juden-Turbae in der Johannes-Passion, in: Basler Jahrbuch für historische Musikpraxis 13, 1989, S. 31–54

Hoffmann-Erbrecht, Lothar. Von der Urentsprechung zum Symbol. Versuch einer Systematisierung musikalischer Sinnbilder, in: Rehm 1983, S. 116–125

Hofmann, Klaus. BWV 78 «Jesu, der du meine Seele», in: Sommerakademie J. S. Bach: Bach und Brahms, Stuttgart 1983, S. 44–49

————. Zu Bachs zweiteiligen Klavierpräludien, in: Bach-Studien, Bd. 10, Leipzig 1991, S. 162–171

————. Zur Tonartenordnung der Johannes-Passion von Johann Sebastian Bach, in: MuK 61, 1991, S. 78–86

————. «Denn er vertritt...» Gedanken zu einer Bachschen Motettenfuge, in: Musica Bd. 47, 1993, S. 268–271

————. Neue Überlegungen zu Bachs Weimarer Kantaten-Kalender, in: BJ 1993, S. 9–29

————. Kritischer Bericht zu NBA VIII/2.1, Kassel usw. 1996

————. Perfidia und Fanfare. Zur Echtheit der Bach-Kantate «Lobe den Herrn, meine Seele» BWV 143, in: Barbara Mohn und Hans Ryschawy (Hrsg.), Cari amici. Festschrift 25 Jahre Carus-Verlag, Stuttgart 1997, S. 34–43

————. Zur Fassungsgeschichte des zweiten Brandenburgischen Konzerts, in: Geck 1997a, S. 185–192

————. Auf der Suche nach der verlorenen Urfassung. Diskurs zur Vorgeschichte der Sonate in h-Moll für Querflöte und obligates Cembalo von J. S. Bach, in: BJ 1998, S. 31–59

————. Perfidia-Techniken und -Figuren bei Bach, in: Renate Steiger (Hrsg.), Die Quellen Johann Sebastian Bachs. Bachs Musik im Gottesdienst. Bericht über das Symposium Stuttgart, 4.–8. Oktober 1995, Heidelberg 1998, S. 281–299

Hofstadter, Douglas R. Gödel, Escher, Bach, ein endloses geflochtenes Band (1979), 11. Aufl., Stuttgart 1988

Holl, Karl. Die Bedeutung der großen Kriege für das religiöse und kirchliche Leben innerhalb des deutschen Protestantismus, in: Gesammelte Aufsätze zur Kirchengeschichte, Bd. 3, Tübingen 1928, S. 302–384

Hoppe, Günther. Die [Köthener] Hofkapelle nach ihrer personellen Entwicklung und sozialen Stellung, in: Cöthener Bach-Hefte 2, Köthen 1983, S. 22–25

————. Leopold von Anhalt-Köthen und die «Rathische Partei». Vom harmvollen Regiment eines «Music lebenden als kennenden Serenissimi», in: Cöthener Bach-Hefte 6, Köthen 1994, S. 95–125

————. Musikalisches Leben am Köthener Hof: in: Wolff und Koopman 1997, S. 65–79

————. Zu musikalisch-kulturellen Befindlichkeiten des anhalt-köthnischen Hofes zwischen 1710 und 1730, in: Köthener Bach-Hefte 8, Köthen 1998, S. 9–51

Hsu, John, and Johann Sebastian Bach, Concerto in D Minor, New York 1984

Huber, Nicolaus A. Die Kompositionstechnik Bachs in seinen Sonaten und Partiten für Violine solo und ihre Anwendung in Weberns op. 27, II, in: Zeitschrift für Musiktheorie 1, 1970, Heft 2, S. 22–31

Hübner, Jürgen. «Johannes Kepler», in: Martin Greschat (Hrsg.), Gestalten der Kirchengeschichte, Bd. 7, Stuttgart usw. 1982, S. 65–78

Husmann, Heinrich. Die «Kunst der Fuge» als Klavierwerk. Besetzung und Anordnung, in: BJ 1938, S. 1–61

Illgen, Ch. F. Historiae Collegii Philobiblici Lipsiensis Pars I, o. O. 1836

Jaccottet, Christiane. L'influence de la musique française pour clavecin dans les Suites Anglaises de Johann Sebastian Bach, et, plus spécialement, la première en La Majeur BWV 806, in: Werner Birtel und Christoph-Hellmut Mahling (Hrsg.), Aufklärung. Studien zur deutsch-französischen Musikgeschichte, Bd. 2, Heidelberg 1986, S. 195–199

Jacob, Andreas. Studien zu Kompositionsart und Kompositionsbegriff in Bachs Klavierübungen, Stuttgart 1997

Jauss, Hans Robert. Ästhetische Normen und geschichtliche Reflexion in der ‹Querelle des Anciens et des Modernes›, München 1973 (= Sonderdruck der Einleitung zur Neuausgabe von Perraults ‹Parallèle des Anciens et des Modernes›)

Jens, Walter. (Hrsg.), Kindlers neues Literatur-Lexikon, Bd. 6, München 1996

Jöde, Fritz. Die Kunst Bachs. Dargestellt an seinen Inventionen, Wolfenbüttel 1926

Joël, Karl. Wandlungen der Weltanschauungen. Eine Philosophiegeschichte als Geschichtsphilosophie, Tübingen 1928

Kaemmel, Otto. Geschichte des Leipziger Schulwesens, Leipzig und Berlin 1909

Kaiser, Rainer. Johann Sebastian Bach als Schüler einer «deutschen Schule» in Eisenach? in: BJ 1994, S. 177–184

Kalbeck, Max. Johannes Brahms. Sein Lebensgang vom Jahre 1833–1862, Wien und Leipzig o. J. (1903)

Kämper, Dietrich. Vincenzo Ruffos Capricci und die Vorgeschichte des Musikalischen Kunstbuchs, in: Klaus Hortschansky (Hrsg.), Zeichen und Struktur in der Musik der Renaissance, Kassel usw. 1989, S. 107–120

Kant, Immanuel. Kritik der Urteilskraft, Bd. 5, Berlin 1908

Kaußler, Ingrid und Helmut. Die Goldberg-Variationen von J. S. Bach, Stuttgart 1985

Keller, Hermann. Die Orgelwerke Bachs, Leipzig 1948

——. Die Klavierwerke Bachs, Leipzig 1950

Kellner, Herbert Anton. Stimmungssysteme im 17. und 18. Jahrhundert, in: Hartmut Krones (Hrsg.), Alte Musik und Musikpädagogik, Wien, Köln und Weimar 1997, S. 247–250

Keßler, Franz. Artikel «Freißlich», in: MGG¹, Bd. 16, Kassel 1979, Sp. 355–358

Kilian, Dietrich. Dreisätzige Fassungen Bachscher Orgelwerke, in: Geck 1969a, S. 12–21

Kimura, Sachiko. Die Choraltextkantaten J. S. Bachs, Phil. Diss. Bochum 1999, mashinenschriftlich

Kirkendale, Warren. Fuge und Fugato in der Kammermusik des Rokoko und der Klassik, Tutzing 1966

——. On the Theoretical Interpretation of the Ricercar and J. S. Bach's Musical Offering, in: Studi Musicali 26, 1997, S. 331–376

Klassen, Janina. «Nur als zukker und gewürze zu brauchen». Musikalisch-rhetorische Figuren im Kontext von Musikschriften des 16. bis 18. Jahrhunderts, ungedruckte Habilitationsschrift, Berlin 1997

Kobayashi, Yoshitake. Franz Hauser und seine Bach-Handschriftensammlung, Phil. Diss. Göttingen 1973

——. Die Universalität Bachs in der h-moll-Messe. Ein Beitrag zum Bach-Bild der letzten Lebensjahre, in: MuK 57, 1987, S. 9–24

——. Bachs Spätwerke. Versuch einer Korrektur, in: Johann Sebastian Bach. Messe h-Moll, Stuttgart und Kassel 1990 (= Schriftenreihe der Internationalen Bachakademie Stuttgart, Bd. 3), S. 132–148

——. Some methodological reflections on the dating of Johann Sebastian Bach's early works, in: Tradition and its future in music. Kongreßbericht Osaka 1990, Tokyo and Osaka 1991, S. 109–116

——. Zur Teilung des Bachschen Erbes, in: Acht kleine Präludien und Studien über BACH, Georg von Dadelsen zum 70. Geburtstag, Wiesbaden, Leipzig, Paris 1992, S. 67–75

——. Bach—Densho no nazo wo ou, Tokyo 1995

——. Zitate in Bachs Musik, unveröffentlichter Vortrag zur Eröffnung der Bachtage der Universität Dortmund im Januar 1998

——. Bach und der Pergolesi-Stil—ein weiteres Beispiel der Entlehnung?, in: Geck 1999, S. 147–159

——. in: «Die Zeit, die Tag und Jahre macht.» Zur Chronologie des Schaffens bei Johann Sebastian Bach. Internationales wissenschaftliches Colloquium aus Anlaß des 80. Geburtstags von Dr. DMus. h. c. Alfred Dürr, Göttingen, 13.–15. März 1998, Druck in Vorbereitung

Köhler, Johann David. Historischer Münz-Belustigung Anderer Theil, Nürnberg 1730

Koldewey, F. Andreas Stübel, in: Allgemeine Deutsche Biographie, Bd. 36, Leipzig 1893, S. 702–704

Kolneder, Walter. (Neue) Forschungsergebnisse zur Kunst der Fuge, in: Bericht über die Wissenschaftliche Konferenz zum III. Internationalen Bach-Fest der DDR in Leipzig 1975, Leipzig 1977, S. 253–259

————. Die Kunst der Fuge. Mythen des 20. Jahrhunderts, 5 Tle. in 4 Bden., Wilhelmshaven 1977

————. J. S. Bach (1685–1750). Leben, Werk und Nachwirken in zeitgenössischen Dokumenten, Wilhelmshaven 1991

Koopman, Ton. Bachs Chor und Orchester, in: Wolff und Koopman 1998, S. 233–249

Kossmaly, Carl. Ueber Robert Schumann's Clavierkompositionen, in: Allgemeine Musikalische Zeitung, Leipzig 1844, Sp. 1–5, 17–21 und 33–37

Kranemann, Detlev. Johann Sebastian Bachs Krankheit und Todesursache—Versuch einer Deutung, in: BJ 1990, S. 53–64

Krebs, Johann Ludwig. Vier Piècen für Klavier, hrsg. von Felix Friedrich, Locarno 1994

Kreutzer, Hans-Joachim. Bach und das literarische Leipzig der Aufklärung, in: BJ 1991, S. 7–31

Krey, Johannes. Zur Entstehungsgeschichte des ersten Brandenburgischen Konzerts, in: Festschrift Heinrich Besseler zum sechzigsten Geburtstag, hrsg. vom Institut für Musikwissenschaft der Karl-Marx-Universität, Leipzig 1961, S. 337–342

Krieger, Erhard. Die Spätwerke J. S. Bachs, in: Zeitschrift für evangelische Kirchenmusik, 9, 1930

Krummacher, Friedhelm. Die Tradition in Bachs vokalen Choralbearbeitungen, in: Geck 1969a, S. 29–56

————. Textauslegung und Satzstruktur in Bachs Motetten, in: BJ 1974, S. 5–43

————. Bachs Vokalmusik als Problem der Analyse, in: Brinkmann 1981, S. 97–126

————. Werkstruktur und Textexegese in Bachs Motette Fürchte dich nicht, ich bin bei dir (BWV 228), in: Heinrich Poos (Hrsg.), Chormusik und Analyse, Bd. 1, Mainz usw. 1983, S. 195–212

————. Bach und die norddeutsche Orgeltoccata, in: BJ 1985, S. 119–134

————. Explikation als Struktur: Zum Kopfsatz der Kantate BWV 77, in: Hoffmann und Schneiderheinze 1988, S. 207–217

————. Bach als Zeitgenosse. Zum historischen und aktuellen Verständnis von Bachs Musik, in: AfMw 48, 1991, S. 64–83

————. Bachs frühe Kantaten im Kontext der Tradition, in: Mf 44, 1991, S. 9–32

————. Bachs frühe Kantaten im Kontext der Tradition, in: Bach-Studien 10, Leipzig 1991, S. 172–201

————. Bachs Zyklus der Choralkantaten. Aufgaben und Lösungen, Göttingen 1995

————. Traditionen der Choraltropierung in Bachs frühem Vokalwerk, in: Heller und Schulze 1995, S. 217–243

Kube, Michael. Bachs «tour de force». Analytischer Versuch über den Eingangschor der Kantate «Jesu, der du meine Seele» BWV 78, in: Mf 45, 1992, S. 138–152

Kuhnau, Johann. Der Musicalische Quack-Salber, Leipzig 1700, Neuausgabe Berlin 1900

Kunze, Stefan. Gattungen der Fuge in Bachs Wohltemperiertem Klavier, in: Geck 1969a, S. 74–93

————. Bachs instrumentale Sprache, in: Bachtage Berlin 1988, S. 91–96

————. (Hrsg.), Ludwig van Beethoven, Die Werke im Spiegel seiner Zeit. Gesammelte Konzertberichte und Rezensionen bis 1830, Laaber 1987

Kurth, Ernst. Grundlagen des Linearen Kontrapunkts. Bachs melodische Polyphonie, 3. Aufl. Berlin 1922

Küster, Konrad. «Der Herr denket an uns» BWV 196, in: MuK 66, 1996, S. 84–96

————. Der junge Bach, Stuttgart 1996

Lämmerhirt, Hugo. Bachs Mutter und ihre Sippe, in: BJ 1925, S. 101–137

Langhans, Wilhelm. Die Geschichte der Musik des 17., 18. und 19. Jahrhunderts in chronologischem Anschlusse an die Musikgeschichte von A. W. Ambros, Bd. 2, Leipzig 1887

Lasocki, David. Paisible's Echo Flute, Bononcini's «Flauti Eco», and Bach's «Fiauti d'Echo», in: The Galpin Society Journal 45, 1992, S. 59–66

Leaver, Robin A. Bachs Theologische Bibliothek, Neuhausen-Stuttgart 1983

Leibniz, Gottfried Wilhelm. Vernunftprinzipien der Natur und Gnade. Monadologie, Hamburg 1960

———. Die Theodizee, übersetzt von Artur Buchenau, 2. Aufl. Hamburg 1968

Lenz, Wilhelm v. Beethoven. Eine Kunst-Studie, Bd. 5, Hamburg 1860

Leonhardt, Gustav M. The Art of Fugue. Bach's Last Harpsichord Work, Den Haag 1952

———. J. S. Bach, Die Kunst der Fuge, Beiheft zur Schallplattenaufnahme Deutsche Harmonia Mundi 1969

Link, Jürgen. Versuch über den Normalismus, Opladen 1977 (Reihe: Historische Diskursanalyse der Literatur)

Loewenich, Walther von. Luthers Theologia crucis, 6. Auflage Bielefeld 1982

Lowinsky, Edward E. Matthaeus Greiter's ‹Fortuna›: An experiment in Chromaticism and in musical iconography, in: The Musical Quarterly 42/43, 1956/57, S. 500–519 und S. 68–85

Lucktenberg, Jerrie Cadek. Unaccompanied Violin Music of the 17th and 18th Centuries: Precursors of Bach's Works for Violin Solo, Diss. University of South Carolina 1983

Luther, Martin. Weimarer Ausgabe der Tischreden, Bd. 2, Weimar 1913

Mahnkopf, Claus-Steffen. J. S. Bach und das Rhetorische—Zu Toccata, Adagio und Fuge C-Dur BWV 564, in: Ars Organi 40, 1992, S. 171–176

Mainka, Jürgen. Zum Naturbegriff bei Bach. Aspekte des Scheibe-Birnbaum-Disputs, in: Bericht über die Wissenschaftliche Konferenz zum III. Internationalen Bach-Fest der DDR, 1975, Leipzig 1977, S. 155–163

Marissen, Michael. On linking Bach's F-Major Sinfonia and His Hunt Cantata, in: Bach 23/2, 1992, S. 31–46

———. The Social and Religious Designs of J. S. Bach's Brandenburg Concertos, Princeton 1995

———. The theological character of J. S. Bach's Musical Offering, in: Bach Studies 2, Cambridge 1995, S. 85–106

———. Lutheranism, Anti-Judaism, and Bach's St. John Passion, Oxford u.a. 1998

Märker, Michael. Johann Sebastian Bach und der rezitativische Stil, in: Geck 1999, S. 51–60

Marpurg, Friedrich Wilhelm. Historisch-Kritische Beyträge zur Aufnahme der Musik, Bd. 1, 5. Stück, Berlin 1754/55

Marshall, Robert L. Musical Sketches in J. S. Bach's Cantata Autographs, in: Harold S. Powers (Hrsg.), Studies in Music History. Essays for Oliver Strunk, Princeton 1968, S. 405–427

———. Bach the Progressive: Observations on His Later Works, in: The Musical Quarterly 62, 1976, S. 313–357

———. Beobachtungen am Autograph der h-Moll-Messe, in: MuK 50, 1980, S. 230–239

———. Orgel oder «Klavier»? Instrumentenangaben in den frühen Quellen der Bach-schen Tastenmusik, in: Hoffmann und Schneiderheinze 1988, S. 303–314

———. On the origin of Bach's Magnificat: a Lutheran composer's challenge, in: Bach Studies, Bd. 1, hrsg. von Don O. Franklin, Cambridge 1989, S. 3–17

Marx, Adolf Bernhard. Erinnerungen aus meinem Leben, Bd. 2, Berlin 1865

Marx, Hans Joachim. Bach und der «theatralische Stil», in: Wolff 1988a, S. 148–154

Mattheson, Johann. Das Neu=Eröffnete Orchestre, Hamburg 1713

———. Critica Musica, Bd. 1, Hamburg 1722

———. Critica Musica, Bd. 2, Hamburg 1725

———. Grosse General=Baß=Schule, Hamburg 1731

———. Der Vollkommene Capellmeister, Hamburg 1739

———. Grundlage einer Ehren-Pforte, Hamburg 1740

Melamed, Daniel R. The Authorship of the Motet Ich lasse dich nicht (BWV Anh. 159), in: Journal of the American Musicological Society 46, 1988, S. 491–526

————. J. S. Bach and the German motet, Phil. Diss. Harvard 1989
————. Probleme zu Chronologie, Stil und Zweck der Motetten Johann Sebastian Bachs, in: BzBF 9/10, Leipzig 1991, 277–284
Mellers, Wilfrid. Bach and the Dance of God, London and Boston 1980
Mendelssohn Bartholdy, Felix. Briefe aus den Jahren 1833 bis 1847, hrsg. v. Paul und Carl Mendelssohn Bartholdy, Bd. 2, Leipzig 1863
————. Reisebriefe aus den Jahren 1830 bis 1832, 5. Auflage Leipzig 1863
————. Briefe aus den Jahren 1830 bis 1847, hrsg. v. Paul und Carl Mendelssohn Bartholdy, Leipzig 1870
————. Reisebriefe aus den Jahren 1830–1832 von Felix Mendelssohn Bartholdy, hrsg. v. Paul Mendelssohn, 9. Aufl. Leipzig 1882
Menuhin, Yehudi. Unvollendete Reise. Lebenserinnerungen, München 1976
Mizler, Lorenz Christoph. Neu eröffnete Musikalische Bibliothek, Bd. 1, 4. Teil, Leipzig 1739
————. Gradus ad Parnassum…ins Teutsche übersetzt, Leipzig 1742, Faksimilenachdruck Hildesheim 1984
————. Neu eröffnete Musikalische Bibliothek, Bd. 2, Teil 4, 1742, Reprint Hilversum 1966
Moser, Hans Joachim. Zum Bau von Bachs Johannespassion, in: BJ 1932, S. 155–157
————. Joh. Seb. Bach, Berlin 1935
————. Besuch bei einem Bach-Autograph, in: MuK 29, 1959, S. 93 f.
Mosewius, Johann Theodor. Johann Sebastian Bach's Matthäus=Passion, musikalisch-aesthetisch dargestellt, Berlin 1852
Müller, Heinrich. Evangelischer Herzens=Spiegel…Nebst beygefügten Passions=Predigten, Stade 1705
Müller, Christa. Das Lob Gottes bei Luther, vornehmlich nach seinen Auslegungen des Psalters, München 1934
Müller-Blattau, Joseph. Bachs Goldberg-Variationen, in: AfMw 16, 1959, S. 207–219
————. (Hrsg.), Die Kompositionslehre Heinrich Schützens in der Fassung seines Schülers Christoph Bernhard, 2. Auflage Kassel usw. 1963
Mund, Frank. Lebenskrisen als Raum der Freiheit. Johann Sebastian Bach in seinen Briefen, Kassel usw. 1997
Nettl, Paul. Die Wiener Tanzkomposition in der zweiten Hälfte des 17. Jahrhunderts, in: Studien zur Musikwissenschaft 8, 1921, S. 45–175
————. Die Bergamasca, in: Zeitschrift für Musikwissenschaft 5, 1922/23, S. 291–295
Neumann, Werner. J. S. Bachs Chorfuge, 3. Aufl. Leipzig 1953
————. Handbuch der Kantaten Johann Sebastian Bachs, 3. Auflage Leipzig 1967
Neumann, Frederick. Bach: Progressive or Conservative and the Authorship of the Goldberg Aria, in: The Musical Quarterly 71, 1985, S. 281–294
Niedt, Friedrich Erhard. Musicalische Handleitung, Teil 1, Hamburg 1700. Published as The Musical Guide, trans. Pamela L. Poulin, Oxford, Clarendon, 1989
Niemöller, Heinz Hermann. Polonaise und Quodlibet. Der innere Kosmos der Goldberg-Variationen, in: Musik-Konzepte, Bd. 42, München 1985, S. 3–28
Nies, Fritz. Die semantische Aufwertung von fr. gothique vor Châteaubriand, in: Zeitschrift für Romanische Philologie, Bd. 84, 1968, S. 67–88
Nietzsche, Friedrich. Der Fall Wagner, in: Werke, hrsg. v. Giorgio Colli und Mazzino Montinari, Bd. VI, 3, Berlin 1969
————. Menschliches, Allzumenschliches, § 219: Aus der Seele der Künstler und Schriftsteller, in: Werke in sechs Bänden, hrsg. von Karl Schlechta, Bd. 2, München 1980
Oechsle, Siegfried. Bachs Arbeit am strengen Satz. Studien zum Kantatenwerk, Habilitationsschrift Kiel 1995, maschinenschriftl.
————. Johann Sebastian Bachs Rezeption des stile antico. Zwischen Traditionalismus und Geschichtsbewußtsein, in: Geck 1999, S. 103–122

Oefner, Claus. Das Musikleben in Eisenach 1650–1750, Phil. Diss. Halle 1975, maschinenschriftlich

———. Neues zur Biographie von Johann Christoph Bach (geb. 1776), in: Deutsches Jahrbuch der Musikbibliothek Peters 14, 1996

Osthoff, Wolfgang. Das «Credo» der h-moll-Messe: italienische Vorbilder und Anregungen, in: Wolfgang Osthoff und Reinhard Wiesend (Hrsg.), Bach und die italienische Musik, Venedig 1987, S. 109–140

Paul, Jean. Vorschule der Ästhetik, hrsg. v. Norbert Miller, 2. Auflage München 1974

Paumgartner, Bernhard. Johann Sebastian Bach. Leben und Werk, Bd. 1, Zürich 1950

Petzoldt, Martin. Überlegungen zur theologischen und geistigen Integration Bachs in Leipzig 1723, in: Beiträge zur Bachforschung, Bd. 1, Leipzig 1982, S. 46–53

———. Zur Frage nach den Funktionen des Kantors Johann Sebastian Bach in Leipzig, in: MuK 53, 1983, S. 167–173

———. «Ut probus & doctus reddar». Zum Anteil der Theologie bei der Schulausbildung J. S. Bachs, in: BJ 1985, S. 7–42

———. Zur Theologie der Matthäus-Passion in zeitgenössischer Perspektive, in: Johann Sebastian Bach. Matthäus-Passion, BWV 244. Vorträge der Sommerakademie Johann Sebastian Bach, Kassel 1990, S. 50–75

———. Zur Differenz zwischen Vorlage und komponiertem Text in Kantaten Johann Sebastian Bachs am Beispiel von BWV 25, in: Bach-Studien, Bd. 10, Wiesbaden und Leipzig 1991, S. 80–107

———. Bach-Stätten aufsuchen, Leipzig 1992

———. «Die kräfftige Erquickung unter der schweren Angst=Last». Möglicherweise Neues zur Entstehung der Kantate BWV 21, in: BJ 1993, S. 31–46

———. «Texte zur Leipziger Kirchen=Music». Zum Verständnis der Kantatentexte Johann Sebastian Bachs, Wiesbaden usw. 1993

———. Bibel, Gesangbuch und Gottesdienst, in: Wolff und Koopman 1996, S. 144–155

———. Bachs Prüfung vor dem Kurfürstlichen Konsistorium zu Leipzig, in: BJ 1998, S. 19–30

———. Theologische Aspekte der Leipziger Kantaten Bachs, in: Wolff und Koopman 1998, S. 127–141

———. Bach und die Bibel. Katalog zur gleichnamigen Austellung, Leipzig o. J.

Pfister, Werner. Briefwechsel Goethe-Zelter, ausgewählt und hrsg. v. Werner Pfister, Zürich und München 1987

Picht, Georg. Die Dimension der Universalität von Johann Sebastian Bach, in: ders., Hier und Jetzt. Philosophieren nach Auschwitz und Hiroshima, Bd. 1, Stuttgart 1980, S. 260–272

Pickett, Philip. Johann Sebastian Bach. Brandenburgische Konzerte. Ein neuer Interpretationsansatz, in: Begleitheft zu der 1994 erschienenen Einspielung der Brandenburgischen Konzerte innerhalb der «Editions de L'Oiseau-Lyre», S. 28–37

Platen, Emil. Untersuchungen zur Struktur der chorischen Choralbearbeitung Johann Sebastian Bachs, Phil. Diss. Bonn 1959

———. Zum Problem des Mittelsatzes im dritten Brandenburgischen Konzert Bachs, in: Manfred Kluge (Hrsg.), Chorerziehung und Neue Musik, Wiesbaden 1969, S. 67–70

———. Johann Sebastian Bach, Die Matthäus-Passion. Entstehung, Werkbeschreibung, Rezeption, 2. Aufl. Kassel 1997

Pottgießer, Karl. Die Briefentwürfe des Johann Elias Bach, in: Die Musik 12/2, 1912/13, H. 7, S. 3–19

Preuß, Hans. Bachs Bibliothek, in: Festgabe für Theodor Zahn, Leipzig 1928, S. 105–129

Preußner, Eberhard. Die musikalischen Reisen des Herrn von Uffenbach, Kassel 1949

Rampe, Siegbert. Antwort auf Pieter Dirksen, in: Concerto 15, 1998, Nr. 137, S. 15–17

Rampe, Siegbert, und Michael Zapf. Neues zu Besetzung und Instrumentarium in Joh. Seb. Bachs Brandenburgischen Konzerten Nr. 4 und 5, in: Concerto 14, 1997/98, Nr. 129, S. 30–38 und 15, 1998, Nr. 130, S. 19–22

Ratz, Erwin. Einführung in die musikalische Formenlehre, 3. Aufl. Wien 1973

Rehm, Wolfgang. (Hrsg.), Bachiana et alia musicologica. Festschrift Alfred Dürr zum 65. Geburtstag, Kassel usw. 1983

Reichardt, Johann Friedrich. Musikalisches Kunstmagazin, Bd. I, Berlin 1782

Richter, Bernhard Friedrich. Über die Schicksale der Thomasschule zu Leipzig angehörenden Kantaten Joh. Seb. Bachs, in: BJ 1906, S. 43–73

Riemann, Hugo. Handbuch der Fugenkomposition, Teil 1 (1890), 5. Auflage Berlin o. J., S. VI

———. Handbuch der Fugenkomposition, Teil 2 (1890), 5. Aufl. Berlin o. J.

Rienäcker, Gerd. Beobachtungen zum Eingangschor der Kantate BWV 127, in: BzBF 2, Leipzig 1983, S. 5–15

———. Beobachtungen zum Eingangschor BWV 25, in: Bach-Studien, Bd. 10, Wiesbaden und Leipzig 1991, S. 108–130

———. Kurven, Widerspiele—Zum ersten Satz des vierten Brandenburgischen Konzerts, in: Geck 1997a, S. 193–202

———. Nachdenken über sinnvolles Musizieren?—Marginalien zu J. S. Bachs «Der Streit zwischen Phöbus und Pan», in: Geck 1999b, S. 161–168

Rifkin, Joshua. The Chronology of Bach's Saint Matthew Passion, in: Musical Quarterly 61, 1975, S. 360–387

———. Bach's Chorus. A Preliminary Report, in: The Musical Times 123, 1982, S. 747–754

———. Beiheft zu seiner Schallplattenaufnahme Johann Sebastian Bach, Mass in B minor, Nonesuch 79036, 1982

———. Rezension von Faksimile-Ausgaben der h-Moll-Messe, in: Notes 44, 1988, S. 787–798

———. Verlorene Quellen, verlorene Werke. Miszellen zu Bachs Instrumentalkomposition, in: Geck 1997a, S. 59–61

———. Klangpracht und Stilauffassung. Zu den Trompeten der Ouvertüre BWV 1069, in: Geck 1999, S. 327–345

Rilling, Helmuth. Johann Sebastian Bachs H-moll-Messe, Neuhausen-Stuttgart 1979

Rochlitz, Friedrich. Für Freunde der Tonkunst, 4 Bde., 3. Aufl. Leipzig 1868

Rolf, Ares. Der Mittelsatz des sechsten Brandenburgischen Konzerts. Gedanken zu seiner Entstehungsgeschichte, in: Geck 1997a, S. 223–233

———. Die Besetzung des sechsten Brandenburgischen Konzerts, in: BJ 1998, S. 171–181

Rollberg, Fritz. Johann Ambrosius Bach, in: BJ 1927, S. 133–152

Sachs, Klaus-Jürgen. Die «Anleitung..., auff allerhand Arth einen Choral durchzuführen» als Paradigma der Lehre und der Satzkunst Johann Sebastian Bachs, in: AfMw 37, 1980, S. 135–154

Sackmann, Dominik. Toccata F-Dur (BWV 540)—eine analytische Studie, in: Hoffmann und Schneiderheinze 1988, S. 351–360

———, und Siegbert Rampe, Bach, Berlin, Quantz und die Flötensonate Es-Dur BWV 1031, in: BJ 1997, S. 51–85

Schäfer, Wilhelm. Johann Sebastian Bach. Eine Rede, München 1935

Schäfertöns, Reinhard. Die Organistenprobe—ein Beitrag zur Geschichte der Orgelmusik im 17. und 18. Jahrhundert, in: Mf 49, 1996, S. 142–152

Scheibe, Johann Adolph. Critischer Musicus, 2. Aufl. Leipzig 1745

Scheibel, Gottfried Ephraim. Zufällige Gedancken von der Kirchen-Music, Wie sie heutigen Tages beschaffen ist, Frankfurt und Leipzig 1721

Schenk, Erich. Das «Musikalische Opfer» von Johann Sebastian Bach, in: Anzeiger der phil.-hist. Klasse der Österreichischen Akademie der Wissenschaften, Bd. 90, Wien 1953, S. 51–66

Schering, Arnold. (Hrsg.), Denkmäler Deutscher Tonkunst 1. Folge, Bd. 58/59, Leipzig 1918

———. Bach und das Symbol, in: BJ 1925, S. 40–63

———. Musikgeschichte Leipzigs, Bd. 2, Leipzig 1926

————. Johann Sebastian Bach, Ich hatte viel Bekümmernis, Studienpartitur, hrsg. v. Arnold Schering, London usw. 1934

————. Johann Sebastian Bachs Leipziger Kirchenmusik. Studien und Wege zu ihrer Erkenntnis, Leipzig 1936

————. Johann Sebastian Bach und das Musikleben Leipzigs im 18. Jahrhundert (Musikgeschichte Leipzigs, Bd. 3), Leipzig 1941

————. Über Kantaten Johann Sebastian Bachs, 2. Aufl. Leipzig 1950

Schilling, Ulrike. Philipp Spitta. Leben und Wirken im Spiegel seiner Briefwechsel, Kassel usw. 1994

Schleuning, Peter. «Diese Fantasie ist einzig...» Das Recitativ in Bachs Chromatischer Fantasie und seine Bedeutung für die Ausbildung der Freien Fantasie, in: Geck 1969a, S. 57–73

————. Deponite potentes de sede! Stoßt die Mächtigen vom Stuhl! Ein Bach-Zitat in Hanns Eislers Musik zur «Mutter», in: ders. (Hrsg.), Warum wir von Beethoven erschüttert werden und andere Aufsätze über Musik, Frankfurt a. M. 1978, S. 75–93

————. «...auf daß zur heilgen Liebe werder unser Haß». Auf der Suche nach dem schwarzen Diamanten: Haß in der Musik, in: Renate Kahle u. a. (Hrsg.), Haß. Die Macht eines unerwünschten Gefühls, Reinbek 1985, S. 137–143

————. Der Kapellmeister Bach, in: Programmbuch Bachfest Berlin 1989, S. 11–22

————. «Alle Kreatur sehnt sich mit uns und ängstigt sich noch immerdar» (Römer 8, 22). Fragen des ersten «Brandenburgischen Konzerts» an uns, in: Hans Werner Henze (Hrsg.), Die Chiffren. Musik und Sprache. Neue Aspekte der musikalischen Ästhetik IV, Frankfurt a. M. 1990, S. 219–262

————. The Chromatic Fantasia of Johann Sebastian Bach and the Genesis of «Sturm und Drang», in: Pieter Dirksen (Hrsg.), The Harpsichord and Its Repertoire. Proceedings of the International Harpsichord Symposion Utrecht 1990, Utrecht 1992, S. 217–229

————. Johann Sebastian Bachs ‹Kunst der Fuge›. Ideologien—Entstehung—Analyse, Kassel 1993

————. Bachs sechstes Brandenburgisches Konzert—eine Pastorale, in: Geck 1997a, S. 203–221

————. Die Sprache der Natur. Natur in der Musik des 18. Jahrhunderts, Stuttgart und Weimar 1998

Schmidt, Christian Martin. Zu Entwicklung der Form im emphatischen Sinne. Bachs Orgelpräludium h-Moll BWV 544, in: Musiktheorie 1, 1986 S. 195–204

————. Analyse und Geschichtsauffassung. Bachs Präludium und Fuge für Orgel BWV 552, in: Josef Kukkertz u. a. (Hrsg.), Neue Musik und Tradition, Festschrift Rudolf Stephan, Laaber 1990, S. 99–111

Schneiderheinze, Armin. Hierarchie und Individualität—Aspekte zu Bach, in: Hoffmann und Schneiderheinze 1988, S. 77–84

————. Zwischen Selbst- und Fremdbestimmung. Überlegungen um Kantate 174, in: BzBF 9/10, Leipzig 1991, S. 205–213

Schütz, Heinrich. Neue Ausgabe Sämtlicher Werke, Bd. 1, Kassel usw. 1955

Schulenberg, David. The Keyboard Music of J. S. Bach, New York usw. 1992

Schulze, Hans-Joachim. Über die «unvermeidlichen Lücken» in Bachs Lebensbeschreibung, in: Brinkmann 1981, S. 32–42

————. «Monsieur Schouster»—ein vergessener Zeitgenosse Johann Sebastian Bachs, in: Rehm 1983, S. 243–250

————. Telemann—Pisendel—Bach. Zu einem unbekannten Bach-Autograph, in: Die Bedeutung Georg Philipp Telemanns für die Entwicklung der europäischen Musikkultur im 18. Jahrhundert. Bericht über die Internationale Wissenschaftliche Konferenz anläßlich der Georg-Philipp-Telemann-Ehrung der DDR, Magdeburg, 12.–18. März 1981, Teil 2, Magdeburg 1983, S. 73–77

———. Studien zur Bach-Überlieferung im 18. Jahrhundert, Leipzig und Dresden 1984

———. Bachs Leipziger Wirken und die «Ehemalige Arth von Music», in: Bach-Studien 9, Leipzig 1986, S. 9–18

———. Ordnung der Schule zu S. Thomae, Leipzig 1723, Faksimilenachdruck, hrsg. von Hans-Joachim Schulze, Leipzig 1987

———. «Wer der alte Bach geweßen, weiß ich wol». Anmerkungen zum Thema Kunstwerk und Biographie, in: Wolff 1988a, S. 23–31

———. J. S. Bachs Missa h-Moll BWV 232^I. Die Dresdner Widmungsstimmen von 1733. Entstehung und Überlieferung, in: Johann Sebastian Bach. Messe h-Moll, Stuttgart und Kassel 1990, Schriftenreihe der Internationalen Bachakademie Stuttgart, Bd. 3, S. 84–102

———. Von der Schwierigkeit, einen Nachfolger zu finden. Die Vakanz im Leipziger Thomaskantorat 1722–1723, in: Bachtage, Berlin, 2.–8. Juli 1990, S. 11–21

———. Florilegium—Pasticcio—Parodie—Vermächtnis. Beobachtungen an ausgewählten Vokalwerken Johann Sebastian Bachs, in: BzBF 9/10, Leipzig 1991, S. 199–204

———. Johann Sebastian Bach, Präludium und Fuge in G-Dur BWV 541, im Faksimiledruck hrsg. v. Hans-Joachim Schulze, Leipzig 1996

———. Rezension von Konrad Küster, Der junge Bach, Stuttgart 1996, in: BJ 1997, S. 203–205

———. Bachs Aufführungsapparat—Zusammensetzung und Organisation, in: Wolff und Koopman 1998, S. 143–155

———. Texte und Textdichter, in: Wolff und Koopman 1998, S. 109–125

Schumann, Robert. Gesammelte Schriften über Musik und Musiker, 2 Bde., 2. Aufl. Leipzig 1871

———. Jugendbriefe, nach den Originalen mitgeteilt von Clara Schumann, Leipzig 1885

———. Robert Schumanns Briefe. Neue Folge, hrsg. v. F. Gustav Jansen, 2. Aufl. Leipzig 1904

———. Erinnerungen an Felix Mendelssohn Bartholdy. Nachgelassene Aufzeichnungen von Robert Schumann, hrsg. v. Georg Eismann, Zwickau 1948

Schwebsch, Erich. Joh. Seb. Bach und die Kunst der Fuge, Stuttgart usw. 1931

Schweitzer, Albert. Aus meinem Leben und Denken, Leipzig 1932

———. Die Orgelwerke Johann Sebastian Bachs. Vorworte zu den «Sämtlichen Orgelwerken», Hildesheim usw. 1995

Seidel, Elmar. Ein chromatisches Harmonisierungsmodell in Schuberts «Winterreise», in: Kongreßbericht Leipzig 1966, Leipzig und Kassel 1970, S. 437–451

Seiffert, Max. Joh. Seb. Bach 1716 in Halle, in: Sammelbände der Internationalen Musikgesellschaft, Bd. 6, 1904/05, S. 595 f.

Siedentopf, Henning. Beobachtungen zur Spieltechnik in der Klaviermusik Johann Sebastian Bachs, Diss. Tübingen 1967

Siegele, Ulrich. Die musiktheoretische Lehre einer Bachschen Gigue, in: AfMw 17, 1960, S. 152–167

———. Bemerkungen zu Bachs Motetten, in: BJ 1962, S. 33–57

———. Bachs theologischer Formbegriff und das Duett F-Dur, Neuhausen-Stuttgart 1978

———. Erfahrungen bei der Analyse Bachscher Musik, in: Brinkmann 1981, S. 137–145

———. Bachs Stellung in der Leipziger Kulturpolitik seiner Zeit (I), in: BJ 1983, S. 7–50

———. Bachs Stellung in der Leipziger Kulturpolitik seiner Zeit (II), in: BJ 1984, S. 7–43

———. Bachs Stellung in der Leipziger Kulturpolitik seiner Zeit (III), in: BJ 1986, S. 33–67

———. Wie unvollständig ist Bachs «Kunst der Fuge»? in: Hoffmann und Schneiderheinze 1988, S. 219–225

———. Das Parodieverfahren des Weihnachtsoratoriums von J. S. Bach als dispositionelles Problem, in: Annegrit Laubenthal und Kara Kusan-Windweh (Hrsg.), Studien zur Musikgeschichte: Eine Festschrift für Ludwig Finscher, Kassel usw. 1995, S. 257–266

————. Proportionierung als kompositorisches Arbeitsinstrument in Konzerten J. S. Bachs, in: Geck 1997a, S. 159–171

————. Kursächsischer Absolutismus und deutsche Frühaufklärung. Jakob Heinrich von Flemming, Gottfried Lange und Johann Sebastian Bach, Vortrag auf dem Internationalen Kongreß der Gesellschaft für Musikforschung, Halle (Saale) 1998

————. Die wundersame Karriere des Johann Sebastian Bach, in: MuK 69, 1999, S. 216–220

Sittard, Josef. Geschichte des Musik- und Concertwesens in Hamburg, Altona und Leipzig 1890

Smend, Friedrich. Die Johannes-Passion von Bach. Auf ihren Bau untersucht, in: BJ 1926, S. 105–128

————. Johann Sebastian Bach bei seinem Namen gerufen. Eine Noteninschrift und ihre Deutung (1950), in: ders., Bach-Studien. Gesammelte Reden und Aufsätze, hrsg. von Christoph Wolff, Kassel usw. 1969, S. 176–194

————. Goethes Verhältnis zu Bach (1954), in: ders., Bach-Studien. Gesammelte Reden und Aufsätze, hrsg. von Christoph Wolff, Kassel 1969, S. 212–236

————. Vorwort zur Studienausgabe von NBA II, 1, Leipzig 1955

————. J. S. Bach. Kirchenkantaten, VI Hefte, Berlin 1966

Spitta, Philipp. Ein Lebensbild Robert Schumann's, in: Paul Graf Waldersee (Hrsg.), Sammlung Musikalischer Vorträge, Vierte Reihe, Nr. 37/38, Leipzig 1882

————. Ueber Robert Schumanns Schriften, in: Musikgeschichtliche Aufsätze, Berlin 1894

Städler, F. Ein Augsburger als Schüler bei Joh. Seb. Bach, in: Gottesdienst und Kirchenmusik 1970, S. 165–167

Stauffer, George B. «Diese Fantasie... hat nie ihre Gleichen gehabt». Zur Rätselhaftigkeit und zur Chronologie der Bachschen Chromatischen Fantasie und Fuge BWV 903, in: Hoffmann und Schneiderheinze 1988, S. 253–258

————. Bach, der Organist, in: Wolff und Koopman 1996, S. 87–101

Steglich, Rudolf. Einführung in die Werke des Reichs-Bach-Festes und des 22. Deutschen Bach-Festes, in: Bach-Festbuch, Leipzig 1935, S. 92–105

Steiger, Renate. Actus tragicus und ars moriendi. Bachs Textvorlage für die Kantate «Gottes Zeit ist die allerbeste Zeit» (BWV 106) in: MuK 59, 1989, S. 11–23

Steiger, Lothar und Renate. Sehet! Wir gehen hinauf nach Jerusalem. J. S. Bachs Kantaten für Estomihi, Göttingen 1992

Stein, Fritz. Artikel «Gerstenbüttel», in: MGG¹ Bd. 4, 1955, Sp. 1840–1842

Schütz, Heinrich. Der Schwanengesang, Neue Ausgabe sämtlicher Werke, Bd. 39, hrsg. v. Wolfram Steude, Kassel 1984

Steude, Wolfram. Der galante Motettenstil seit dem ausgehenden 17. Jahrhundert und Johann Sebastian Bach, in: Heller und Schulze 1995, S. 203–216

Stoll, Albrecht D. Figur und Affekt. Zur höfischen Musik und zur bürgerlichen Musiktheorie der Epoche Richelius, 3. Aufl. Tutzing 1983

Suchalla, Ernst. Carl Philipp Emanuel Bach, Briefe und Dokumente, 2 Bde., hrsg. v. Ernst Suchalla, Göttingen 1994

Swack, Jeanne R. On the origins of the Sonate auf Concertenart, in: Journal of the American Musicological Society 46, 1993, S. 369–414

Talbot, Michael. Purpose and Peculiarities of the Brandenburg Concertos, in: Geck 1999b, S. 255–290

Tatlow, Ruth Mary. Bach and the Riddle of Number Alphabet, Cambridge 1991

————. Towards a Theory of Bach's Pre-compositional Style, in: Geck 1999b, S. 19–36

Telemann, G. Ph. Briefwechsel, hrsg. v. H. Große und H. R. Jung, Leipzig 1972

Terry, Charles Sanford. Bach. The Magnificat, Lutheran Masses and Motets, London 1929

Thoene, Helga. Johann Sebastian Bach. Ciaccona. Tanz oder Tombeau. Verborgene Sprache eines berühmten Werkes, in: Cöthener Bach-Hefte 6, Köthen 1994, S. 15–81

Thorau, Christian. Richard Wagners Bach, in: Michael Heinemann u. Hans-Joachim Hinrichsen (Hrsg.), Bach und die Nachwelt, Bd. 2, Laaber 1999, S. 163–199

Tilmouth, Michael. Art. «Binary form», in: The New Grove, Bd. 2, 1980, S. 707–709

Toduta, Sigismund, und Hans Peter Türk. Bachs Inventionen und Sinfonien—Ästhetisch-stilistische Beiträge, in: Bericht über die Wissenschaftliche Konferenz zum III. Internationalen Bach-Fest 1975, Leipzig 1977, S. 189–204

Tovey, Donald Francis. Essays in Musical Analysis, Chamber Music (1944), 9. Aufl. Oxford u. New York 1989

Trautmann, Christoph. «Calovii Schrifften. 3. Bände» aus Johann Sebastian Bachs Nachlaß und ihre Bedeutung für das Bild des lutherischen Kantors Bach, Sonderdruck aus MuK 39, 1969

———. Ein Beitrag der Bachforschung zum Lutherjahr: Die ideelle Grundlage von Bachs drittem Teil der Klavierübung, in: MuK 54, 1984, S. 127–133

Türcke, Bertold. Das unendliche Rezitativ, in: Musik-Konzepte, Bd. 42, München 1985, S. 93–103

Vassar, James B. The Bach Two-Part Inventions: A Question of Authorship, in: The Music Review 33, 1972, S. 14–21

Vetter, Daniel. Musicalische Kirch= und Hauß=Ergötzlichkeit, 1. Teil, Leipzig 1709

———. Musicalische Kirch= und Haus=Ergötzlichkeit, 2. Teil, Leipzig 1713

Vetter, Walther. Der Kapellmeister Bach, Potsdam 1950

Virneisel, Wilhelm. Artikel «Poelchau», in: MGG^I, Bd. 10, 1962, S. 1365 f.

Vogt, Hans. Johann Sebastian Bachs Kammermusik. Voraussetzungen, Analysen, Einzelwerke, Stuttgart 1981

Wagner, Cosima. Die Tagebücher, hrsg. v. Martin Gregor-Dellin und Dietrich Mack, 2 Bde., München und Zürich 1976

Wagner, Richard. Sämtliche Schriften und Dichtungen, Bd. 7, 5. Aufl. Leipzig o. J.

Walker, Paul. Rhetoric, the Ricercar, and J. S. Bach's «Musical Offering», in: Bach Studies 2, Cambridge 1995, S. 175–191

Walter, Meinrad. Musik-Sprache des Glaubens. Zum geistlichen Vokalwerk Johann Sebastian Bachs, Frankfurt a. M. 1994

Walther, Johann Gottfried. Musicalisches Lexicon oder musicalische Bibliothec, Leipzig 1732, Faks. Kassel und Basel 1953

———. Briefe, hrsg. v. Klaus Beckmann und Hans-Joachim Schulze, Leipzig 1987

Weber, Carl Maria von. Hinterlassene Schriften, Bd. 3, Dresden und Leipzig 1828

Webern, Anton. Der Weg zur Neuen Musik, hrsg. von Willi Reich, Wien 1960

Weiß, Christian. [Leichenpredigt] auf Johann Heinrich Ernesti, Leipzig 1729

Werckmeister, Andreas. Musicalische Paradoxal-Discourse, Quedlinburg 1707

Werker, Wilhelm. Studien über die Symmetrie im Bau der Fugen und die motivische Zusammengehörigkeit der Präludien und Fugen des «Wohltemperierten Klaviers» von Johann Sebastian Bach, Leipzig 1922

Wetzel, Johann Caspar. Historische Lebens=Beschreibung Der berühmtesten Lieder= Dichter, Anderer Theil, Hernstadt 1721

Wiemer, Wolfgang. Die wiederhergestellte Ordnung in Johann Sebastian Bachs Kunst der Fuge. Untersuchungen am Originaldruck, Wiesbaden 1977

———. Carl Philipp Emanuel Bachs Fantasie C-moll—ein Lamento auf den Tod des Vaters? in: BJ 1988, S. 163–177

Wiesend, Reinhard. «Erbarme dich», alla Siciliana, in: Wolfgang Osthoff u. ders. (Hrsg.), Bach und die italienische Musik, Venedig 1987, S. 19–41

Wilhelmi, Thomas. Carl Philipp Emanuel Bachs «Avertissement» über den Druck der Kunst der Fuge, in: BJ 1992, S. 101–105

Williams, Peter. Johann Sebastian Bachs Orgelwerke, Bd. 1, Mainz usw. 1996

———. Johann Sebastian Bachs Orgelwerke, Bd. 2, Mainz usw. 1998

Winterfeld, Carl von. Der evangelische Kirchengesang und sein Verhältnis zur Kunst des Tonsatzes, 3. Teil, Leipzig 1847

Wiora, Walter. Artikel «Alpenmusik», in: MGG^{I}, Bd. 1, 1951, Sp. 359–370

———. Jubilare sine verbis, in: In Memoriam Jacques Handschin, Straßburg 1962, S. 39–65

Witkowski, Georg. Geschichte des literarischen Lebens in Leipzig, Leipzig und Berlin 1909

Wohlfarth, Hannsdieter. Johann Christoph Friedrich Bach. Ein Komponist im Vorfeld der Klassik, Bern und München 1971

Wöhlke, Franz. Lorenz Christoph Mizler. Ein Beitrag zur musikalischen Gelehrtengeschichte des 18. Jh. Diss. Berlin 1941

Wolff, Christoph. Zur musikalischen Vorgeschichte des Kyrie aus Johann Sebastian Bachs Messe in h-moll, in: Festschrift Bruno Stäblein zum 70. Geburtstag, Kassel 1967, S. 316–326

———. Der stile antico in der Musik Johann Sebastian Bachs. Studien zu Bachs Spätwerk, Wiesbaden 1968

———. Ordnungsprinzipien in den Originaldrucken Bachscher Werke, in: Geck 1969a, S. 144–167

———. New Research on the Musical Offering (1971), with Postscript in: Wolff 1996b, S. 239–258

———. Johann Sebastian Bachs «Sterbechoral»: Kritische Fragen zu einem Mythos, in: Robert L. Marshall (Hrsg.), Studies in Renaissance and Baroque Music in Honor of Arthur Mendel, Kassel 1974, S. 283–297

———. Bach's Handexemplar of the Goldberg Variations, in: Journal of the American Musicological Society 29, 1976, S. 224–241

———. Kritischer Bericht zu NBA VIII, 1, Kassel usw. 1976

———. Bachs Handexemplar der Schübler-Choräle, in: BJ 1977, S. 120–129

———. Probleme und Neuansätze der Bach-Biographik, in: Brinkmann 1981, S. 21–31

———. Wo blieb Bachs fünfter Kantatenjahrgang? in: BJ 1982, S. 151 f.

———. «Die sonderbaren Vollkommenheiten des Herrn Hofcompositeurs». Versuch über die Eigenart der Bachschen Musik, in: Rehm 1983, S. 356–362

———. Textbeilage zu Kassette 9 der Gesamteinspielung der Bach-Kantaten durch Helmuth Rilling im Hänssler Verlag, Stuttgart 1983

———. «O ew'ge Nacht! wann wirst du schwinden?» Zum Verständnis der Sprecherszene im ersten Finale von Mozarts «Zauberflöte», in: Werner Breig u. a. (Hrsg.), Analysen. Festschrift für Hans-Heinrich Eggebrecht, Stuttgart 1984, S. 234–247

———. Johann Sebastian Bachs Klavierübung. Kommentar zur Faksimile-Ausgabe, Leipzig und Dresden 1984

———. Bach's Leipzig Chamber Music, in: Wolff 1996b, S. 223–238; zuerst veröffentlicht in: Early Music 13, 1985, S. 165–175

———. Johann Adam Reinken und Johann Sebastian Bach. Zum Kontext des Bachschen Frühwerks, in: BJ 1985, S. 99–118

———. Zur Rezeptionsgeschichte Bachs im 18. Jahrhundert, in: Berke und Hanemann 1987, Bd. 1, S. 162–164

———. (Hrsg.), Johann Sebastian Bachs Spätwerk und dessen Umfeld. Bericht über das wissenschaftliche Symposion anläßlich des 61. Bachfestes der Neuen Bachgesellschaft Duisburg 1986, Kassel usw. 1988

———. Zur Problematik der Chronologie und der Stilentwicklung des Bachschen Frühwerkes, insbesondere zur musikalischen Vorgeschichte des Orgelbüchleins, in: Hoffmann und Schneiderheinze 1988, S. 449–455

———. Bach's Last Fugue: Unfinished? (1991) in: Wolff 1996b, S. 259–264

———. «Die betrübte und wieder getröstete Seele»: Zum Dialog-Charakter der Kantate «Ich hatte viel Bekümmernis» BWV 21, in: BJ 1996, S. 139–145

―――. Bach. Essays on his life and his music, 3. Aufl. Cambridge, Mass. usw. 1996

―――. Chor und Instrumentarium, in: Wolff und Koopman 1996, S. 157–167

―――. The Neumeister Collection of Chorale Preludes from the Bach Circle, in: Wolff 1996b, S. 107–127

―――. Bachs weltliche Kantaten: Repertoire und Kontext, in: Wolff und Koopman 1997, S. 13–31

―――. Zum Quellenwert der Neumeister-Sammlung: Bachs Orgelchoral «Der Tag der ist so freudenreich» BWV 719, in: BJ 1997, S. 155–167

―――. Bachs Leipziger Kirchenkantaten: Repertoire und Kontext, in: Wolff und Koopman 1998, S. 13–35

Wolff, Christoph, und Ton Koopman. (Hrsg.), Die Welt der Bach Kantaten, Bd. 1, Stuttgart, Weimar und Kassel 1996

―――. (Hrsg.), Die Welt der Bach Kantaten, Bd. 2, Stuttgart, Weimar und Kassel 1997

―――. (Hrsg.), Die Welt der Bach Kantaten, Bd. 3, Stuttgart, Weimar und Kassel 1998

Wollny, Peter. Bachs Bewerbung um die Organistenstelle an der Marienkirche zu Halle und ihr Kontext, in: BJ 1994, S. 25–39

―――. Ein Quellenfund zur Entstehungsgeschichte der h-Moll-Messe, in: BJ 1994, S. 163–169

―――. Gattungen und Stil der Kirchenmusik um 1700, in: Wolff und Koopman 1996, S. 29–43

―――. Abschriften und Autographe, Sammler und Kopisten, in: Michael Heinemann u. Hans-Joachim Hinrichsen (Hrsg.), Bach und die Nachwelt, Bd. 1, Laaber 1997, S. 27–62

―――. Neue Bach-Funde, in: BJ 1997, S. 7–50

―――. Überlegungen zum Tripelkonzert a-Moll BWV 1044, in: Geck 1997a, S. 283–291

Zachariä, Friedrich Wilhelm. Poetische Schriften Bd. 2, Braunschweig 1763

Zacher, Gerd. Canonische Veränderungen. BWV 769 und 769a, in: Johann Sebastian Bach, Das spekulative Spätwerk, Musik-Konzepte, Bd. 17/18, München 1981, S. 3–19

―――. Mißglückt? Die Form des Praeludiums Es-Dur aus dem Wohltemperierten Clavier, in: Musik-Konzepte, Bd. 79/80, München 1993, S. 31–49

―――. Zum Tonalitätsverständnis bei Bach, in: Musik-Konzepte, Bd. 79/80, München 1993, S. 55–73

Zedler. Artikel «Leipzig», in: Zedler, Grosses vollständiges Universal Lexicon, Bd. 16, Halle und Leipzig 1737, Sp. 1652–1811

―――. Artikel «Musicum Collegium», in: ebda., Bd. 22, 1739, Sp. 1488

―――. Artikel «Oratorium», in: ebda., Bd. 25, 1740, Sp. 1738 f.

―――. Artikel «Sinnbild», in: ebda., Bd. 29, 1743, Sp. 1690 f.

Zehnder, Jean-Claude. Georg Böhm und Johann Sebastian Bach. Zur Chronologie der Bachschen Stilentwicklung, in: BJ 1988, S. 73–110

―――. Giuseppe Torelli und Johann Sebastian Bach. Zu Bachs Weimarer Konzertform, in: BJ 1991, S. 33–95

―――. Rezension des Buches von Peter Schleuning über die Kunst der Fuge, in: L'Organo, 28, 1993/94, S. 155–163

―――. Zu Bachs Stilentwicklung in der Mühlhäuser und Weimarer Zeit, in: Heller und Schulze 1995, S. 311–338

―――. Zum späten Weimarer Stil Johann Sebastian Bachs, in: Geck 1997a, S. 89–124

―――. «Des seeligen Unterricht in Ohrdruf mag wohl einen Organisten zum Vorwurf gehabt haben…». Zum musikalischen Umfeld Bachs in Ohrdruf, insbesondere auf dem Gebiet des Orgelchorals, in: Geck 1999, S. 169–195

―――. Auf der Suche nach chronologischen Argumenten in Bachs Frühwerk (vor etwa 1707), in: «Die Zeit, die Tag und Jahre macht.» Zur Chronologie des Schaffens bei Johann Sebastian Bach. Internationales wissenschaftliches Colloquium aus Anlaß des 80.

Geburtstags von Dr. DMus. h. c. Alfred Dürr, Göttingen, 13.–15. März 1998, Druck in Vorbereitung

Zenck, Martin. «Bach, der Progressive». Die Goldberg-Variationen in der Perspektive von Beethovens Diabelli-Variationen, in: Musik-Konzepte, Bd. 42, München 1985, S. 29–92

———. Die Bach-Rezeption des späten Beethoven. Zum Verhältnis von Musikhistoriographie und Rezeptionsgeschichts-schreibung der «Klassik», Stuttgart 1986

Zimpel, Herbert. Der Streit zwischen Reformierten und Lutheranern in Köthen während Bachs Amtszeit, in: BJ 1979, S. 97–106

———, und Günther Hoppe. Stiftsstraße 11—eines der Köthener Bachhäuser? in: Cöthener Bach-Hefte 6, Köthen 1994, S. 83–88

INDEX

Abel, Christian Ferdinand, 98, 102, 103
Abhandlung von der Fuge (Marpurg), 491
Adler, Guido, 12
Adlung, Jacob, 65, 495
Adorno, Theodor W., 216, 372, 491, 500, 650–51
Advent cantatas, 144
Aeolus Propitiated, 417–18
Agricola, Johann Friedrich, 6, 258, 436
Ahle, Johann Georg, 63
Albinoni, Tomaso, 80, 94, 437, 482
Altnickol, Johann Christoph (son-in-law), 4, 27, 179, 183, 231–32, 244, 254–55, 267, 307
Amalia, Anna, 30, 546
Ambrose, Z. Philip, 328, 329, 424
Andreas Bach Book, 40, 57–58, 481, 489
Anhalt-Cöthen, Leopold von, 78, 95, 101–2, 103, 106, 112–13, 128–29, 166, 413–14, 569, 582
archcantor, 146
aria variata, 230
Aria with Diverse Variations for Clavicembalo with Two Manuals, written for the Delight of Lovers of the Instrument, 228
Ariadne Musica, 533, 534, 543
arioso, 361, 362, 391, 410
Arndt, Johan, 653
Arnstadt, 44, 47–62
Art of Fugue, The, 17, 22, 24, 220, 228, 232–35, 236, 244, 247, 248–51, 253, 254, 255, 268, 349, 435, 440, 451, 463, 608, 609–10, 620–33

Art of Strict Musical Composition, The (Kirnberger), 518, 531
Attempts in Fixed Forms (von Ziegler), 152
August, Ernst, 78, 79, 95, 96

B-A-C-H sequence/theme, 531–32, 629, 639, 652, 657, 667, 672
B-Minor Mass, 23, 24, 25, 28, 157, 163, 185, 197, 212, 222, 227, 247, 251–54, 308, 312, 375, 421, 438, 440, 441–52, 608, 609, 617
Baal, Johann Marianus, 85, 90
Bach and the Dance of God (Mellers), 450
"Bach and the Symbol" (Schering), 352
Bach, Anna Magdalena (second wife), 104, 263, 264–66, 619; Bach's death, 3, 267–68; Bach's manuscripts, 23, 27, 30, 248; children, 4, 156, 166; as copyist, 159, 181, 219, 229, 231, 260–61, 262; musical compositions written for, 109, 164, 261–62, 598
Bach Archives, 4
Bach, Carl Philipp Emanuel (son), 175, 200, 239, 243, 266, 267, 268, 269, 271, 289, 421, 595; childhood, 79, 97, 99, 156, 164–65; as copyist, 181; father's cantata cycles, 525, 527, 630; father's manuscripts, 27, 28–29, 250, 251; father's obituary, 6, 7, 258; Forkel and, 9, 46, 54, 77–78, 212; musical performances/compositions, 23, 28, 262, 448, 598–99, 601
Bach, Catharina Dorothea (daughter), 69–70, 79, 96, 99, 267

Christian, Friedrich, 195
Christliche Betschule (Olearius), 291
Christmas cantatas, 85, 88–89, 147–48, 172, 183, 383
Christmas chorales, 499–500
Christmas Oratorio, 18, 25, 26, 28, 142, 184–85, 204, 209, 310, 422–31, 449
"Chronology of the Leipzig Vocal Works of J. S. Bach" (Dürr), 157
Chrysander, Friedrich, 11, 12, 87
church music: appropriateness of artistic, 167; Bach "choir," 69, 172, 174; Bach's dissatisfaction with vocal, 71–75; Bach's organist positions, 44, 46, 47–75; Bach's "quintessential cantor" image, 3, 17; hymns conflict, 165–66; Latin, 179–80, 183, 184; modern music controversy, 155–56; ode of mourning, 160–61; passion performances, 176–78; "Scattered Thoughts on Church Music" (Scheibel), 173–74; "Short but Most Necessary Draft for a Well-Appointed Church Music" (Bach), 136–37, 139, 169–71, 172; *St. John Passion* controversy, 139, 146, 148–51; "well-regulated," 70–72, 83, 114, 141, 145–46
Cicero, 45, 634
circular canons, 229
Clauder, Johann Christoph, 196
clavier symphonies, 591
clavier toccatas, 59
Clavier-Übung, 23, 24, 164, 217, 225, 226, 228, 232, 233, 253, 495, 496, 517; part one of, 261, 598, 600; part two of, 219; part three of, 220, 223, 224, 244, 484, 499, 512, 514, 515, 516, 518, 521, 522, 671; part four of, 229, 230, 231, 617, 619
Clementi, Muzio, 231
Collegium Academicum, 42
Collegium Musicum, Bach's directorship of, 107, 171, 173, 188, 189–219
Colloquia scholastica (Corderius), 133
Comenius, Johann Amos, 38
Compendium locorum theologicorum (Hutter), 45
Compenius, Ludwig, 82
Compleat Kapellmeister (Mattheson), 215, 224, 368
concerto style compositions: Bach's, 92–94; Bach's heading "concerto,"

348–49; Italian concerto style, 79, 309–10, 481–82; sonata in concerto style, 588–89; Vivaldi-style concerto, 93, 483, 556, 570
concertos, 550–78
concordia discors, principle of, 645
Conti, Francesco Bartolomeo, 89, 90
copyists, Bach's, 80, 159, 181, 199, 247–48, 260–61, 262–63
Corderius, Maturinus, 133
Corresponding Society of the Musical Sciences, 242, 243–44
Cöthen, 72, 76, 91, 94, 95, 96–114, 167; Bach as kapellmeister of, 102–14; Cöthen demonstration cycles, 525–49
Couperin, François, 261
Craft of Musical Composition (Hindemith), 531
Credo, 279
Critica Musica (Mattheson), 300, 541
Crüger, Johann, 464
cultural unity, concept of, 9
Currende music, 38, 40, 372, 374

Dadelson, George von, 352–53
Dahlhaus, Carl, 538, 648
Dammann, Rolf, 490, 616
d'Angelbert, Jean-Henri, 229
David, Hans Theodor, 631
David, Johann Nepomuk, 529
David League, 15
de Grigny, Nicolas, 91, 212
De vita musica (Biedermann), 246–47
"Death Fugue" (Celan), 632
Dedekind, Constantin Christian, 85
Defense of Bach against Scheibe's Attacks (Birnbaum), 210–11
Dehio, Georg, 162
Deiter, Hermann, 11
Deleuze, Gilles, 544
Der critische Musicus an der Spree (Marpurg), 217
Der critische Musicus (Scheibe), 205, 211, 215
Der musikalische Patriot (Mattheson), 99, 165
Der musikalische Quack-Salber (Kuhnau), 356, 672
Der vollkommene Capellmeister (Mattheson), 316

oratorio, defined, 150
oratorium, 422, 423
ordinary music, 117
organ: Bach's organist positions, 44, 46,
    47–96; and keyboard works, 59–61;
    organ inspections, 82–83, 236; organ
    rebuilding, 48, 65–66
organ chorales, 498–524; *Andreas Bach
    Book,* 57–59; Bach's, 18–19, 41–42, 44,
    51, 56, 60, 63, 64, 80; concerto style
    compositions, 92–94; Little Organ
    Book, 91–92, 507; *Möller Manuscript,*
    57–59; *Plauen Organ Book,* 57, 59
Orgelbüchlein, 18, 22, 24, 56, 60, 80, 91, 92,
    227, 255, 486, 499, 500, 501, 502–8, 510,
    513, 514, 521
orthodoxy. *See* Pietism
Osthoff, Wolfgang, 442
Otto, Valentin, 115
"Outline of a New Picture of Bach"
    (lecture, Blume), 146

Pachelbel, Johann, 40, 41, 57, 280, 281,
    557, 613
parodies, use of, 342
passion oratorio, 120–21
Passions, the, 385–414
Patriotism, concept of, 18
Paul, Jean, 431–32
Pauline church, 155
Penzel, Christian Friedrich, 254
Peranda, Marco Giuseppe, 85
Perfect Kapellmeister, The (Mattheson),
    609, 624, 628
perfidia, 365–66, 398–99
Pergolesi, Giovanni Battista, 443, 447
permutation fugues, 290, 351
Perti, Giacomo Antonio, 436
Petzold, Christian, 261
Pez, Johann Christoph, 85
Pfleger, Augustin, 68–69
Phrygian modal key, 517, 518–19, 561
Picander (Christian Friedrich Henrici),
    141, 152–54, 156–57, 162, 163, 166, 176,
    179, 194, 202, 203, 342, 388, 402–3,
    404, 412, 434
Picht, Georg, 651
Pickett, Philip, 553–54
Pietism, 149, 185, 278, 298, 307, 322,
    334–35, 457; artistic church music and,
    123–24, 125; orthodoxy and, 74, 75, 77,
    87, 331, 464, 653–59

Piranesi, Giambattista, 630
Pirro, André, 18
Pisendel, Johann Georg, 94, 190, 258
Platen, Emil, 561
Plauen Organ Book, 57, 59
Plaz, Abraham Christoph, 124, 125, 128,
    129, 149
Poelchau, Georg, 29
poetry, German, 152, 153, 156–57
Pohl, Ferdinand, 11
Pohle, David, 557
polyphonic music, 85, 86
Porpora, Nicola Antonio, 199
Potsdam, 236–40
Praecepta der musicalischen Composition,
    90
prefatory, 296–97
Premier livre d'orgue, 91
"principal music," 117, 141
Principle of Hope, The (Bloch), 659
*Principles of Form in the Inventions and
    Fugues of J. S. Bach and their
    Significance in the Compositions of
    Beethoven* (Ratz), 529
Privilegierte Zeitung, 236
Protestantism, 16, 17, 18, 303, 655
Prussian Fugue, 226–27
Prussianism, concept of, 18
Psalter and Harp, 11
puzzle canon, 90, 224–25, 244

Quantz, Johann Joachim, 180, 242
Quintilian, 214, 633–34

Rambach, Johann Jacob, 340–41
Rameau, Jean Philippe, 535, 622
Rampe, Siegbert, 569
Ranke, Leopold von, 13
Rathgeber, Valentin, 617
Ratz, Erwin, 529
Reformation chorale, 335
Reger, Max, 51
Reichardt, Adam Andreas, 96
Reichardt, Johann Friedrich, 217, 447, 643
Reiche, Johann Gottfried, 138, 197, 351,
    552–53
Reichle, Leonhard, 654
Reinken, Johann Adam, 44, 45, 91, 227,
    473, 475, 509
Reyher, Andreas, 45, 516
ricercars, 240–41, 635, 637
Riemann, Hugo, 536, 541